VOLUME 5

PRACTICAL

LIFE-CHANGING

WESLEY
BIBLE LESSON COMMENTARY

For Teachers and Students

wesleyan
publishing
house

Indianapolis, Indiana

www.WesleyBible.com

Contributors: Jim Dyet, Diane Gardner, Julie-Allyson Ieron, Doug Schmidt, Tami Stevenson, Annie Wamberg, Steve Wamberg, Jim Watkins, and Heather Gemmen Wilson

Editors/Designers: Craig Bubeck, Mary McNeil, Lyn Rayn, Kevin Scott, and Rachael Stevenson

CONTENTS

ACCESSIBLE AND APPLICABLE

*W*esley Bible Lesson Commentary Volume 5 is a powerful resource designed to support anyone who desires to be a thoughtful student of God's Word—the kind of holy practitioner in God's kingdom who "correctly handles the word of truth" (2 Tim. 2:15). To that end, we've designed this lesson commentary with particular features to make it as broadly accessible and applicable as possible.

UNDATED

One key feature is that there are no date references throughout the commentary and lessons. While the contents of each lesson correlate with and support the dated studies in the Wesley Adult Curriculum, the contents within this commentary itself are identified by units (instead of seasonal quarters) and lesson or week numbers (without specific dates). This allows other audiences to use the studies in *Wesley Bible Lesson Commentary Volume 5* in subsequent years without the confusion of the curriculum's dates and seasons.

YEAR AT A GLANCE

This popular feature, while no longer published in this book, is posted for easy access on the Wesley Bible website (www.WesleyBible.com) along with previous "Year at a Glance" charts from other commentaries in this series. These unique calendars are great sources of knowledge of what happened on particular dates in church history.

COMMENTARY SERIES

The entire "Wesley Bible Lesson Commentary Series" is located at the back of this book, identifying all the Bible studies that will be available in this seven-volume series. You can choose the study that corresponds to your curriculum, or whatever Bible book or topic best suits your small group Bible study needs.

EASY REFERENCE TO ADULT CURRICULUM SCHEDULE

The "Wesley Adult Bible Studies Scope and Sequence" is located in the back of the book. It connects each unit and lesson in this book to the dated adult curriculum lessons. It is a quick reference for any Wesley Adult Curriculum student who might otherwise find the undated unit and lesson numbering confusing.

CONVENIENTLY DESIGNED APPEARANCE

The lesson layout is familiar territory especially for Wesley Adult Curriculum users, but it also is conveniently designed for new users of the commentary. *Wesley Bible Lesson Commentary* users have readily embraced our updates and even are joining us in making this powerful resource available to those who desire to know God more deeply, beyond the parameters of how curriculum users have traditionally used it in the past. We are seeing the fruits of our labors borne out; God's Word does not return void.

God's richest blessings to you in your ministry,

Craig Bubeck
Editorial Director

*PS: I'd love to hear how your studies have been going. Visit me online at **www.WesleyBible.com** or send me a note at **editor@WesleyBible.com**.*

HOW TO USE THIS BOOK

Whether you're a teacher, small group leader, or student of the Bible, *Wesley Bible Lesson Commentary Volume 5* will help you get more from your study time.

More for Teachers

- *More Confidence* for teaching from in-depth Bible commentary!
- *More Creativity* in your teaching from Interactive Learning Ideas.
- *More Variety* in your lesson plans from helpful sidebars, maps, and charts.
- *More Discussion* by students from small group guides and "What Do You Think?" sidebars.
- *More Activity* in your class from tear-out activities, puzzles, and games.

More for Students

- *More Knowledge* from in-depth commentary on each Bible lesson.
- *More Insight* from Interactive Learning Ideas you can explore.
- *More Clarity* from impactful sidebar statements.
- *More Support* for your Bible study from guided readings and background Scriptures.
- *More Discovery* through puzzles, games, and activities that reinforce learning.

HERE'S WHAT YOU GET

Unit Preview

This helpful summary of the unit highlights the *key ideas* you will discover. Use it to prepare for your study of the lessons.

A map, chart, or other graphic for each unit brings focus to important facts and information.

Tip: Tear out the graphics to use as handouts for your class!

Bible Commentary

The heart of each lesson's entry is a brief commentary on the study text. This insightful writing provides the background information that will bring each Scripture passage to life!

Read this article first in your lesson preparation.

Sidebars

Informative sidebars are loaded with interesting facts and discussion starters!

Use these nuggets of information to enliven your teaching and start class discussion.

Maps, Charts, Graphics

Helpful maps, charts, and other graphics bring clarity to teaching points.

Use the larger items as handouts for your class!

Interactive Learning Ideas

Each lesson includes four interactive, activity-based options for exploring the content of the lesson. These optional activities can be used as alternative lesson plans, in-class activities, or exercises for students to pursue on their own.

The four types of activities are—

- *Class* — Try this group activity with your Sunday school or small group.
- *Individual* — Do this activity at home on your own.
- *Outside* — Engage your group in an activity *outside* the church or home.
- *Family* — Learn together with children or grandchildren, using these interactive ideas geared for kids.

Small Group Guide

Use this handy tear-out sheet to start a Bible study group at work or in your home, or use the thought-provoking questions to boost the discussion in your existing class.

Tip: You can use this page as an alternative method of teaching your class!

Reproducible Activity Pages

Puzzles, maps, charts, fun! Each lesson has one activity you can do by yourself or with your group. (Permission is granted to reproduce these pages for use in your local church.)

Tips for Using This Resource

Here are some tips for making the most of this valuable Bible study resource.

Through the Week

If you're a teacher, group leader, or simply enjoy reading the Bible, here's how to make the most of this resource:

- *Follow* the Daily Bible Readings throughout the week to get you primed for the study.
- *Read* the Study Passage (always listed as Saturday's reading).
- *Dig* in, using the Bible Commentary and sidebars.
- *Choose* an Interactive Learning Idea for yourself or your family.
- *Enjoy* the Reproducible Activity Page that accompanies each lesson.

Preparing for Sunday

If you're a Bible study leader or Sunday school teacher, this resource will double the effectiveness of your preparation time.

- *Prepare* for teaching, using the Bible Commentary.

- *Consider* an Interactive Learning Idea for your class or group.
- *Pepper* your teaching with questions and Aha! moments from the sidebars.
- *Direct* discussion, using the Small Group Guide.
- *Distribute* the Reproducible Activity Page (permission granted for use in your local church).
- *Challenge* your group to use *Wesley Bible Lesson Commentary Volume 5* for their own study and spiritual growth.

Have a Great Idea?

We'd love to hear your ideas for making this resource even better! Visit **www.WesleyBible.com** or e-mail your comments to **feedback@WesleyBible.com**.

Unit 1
Christ Alone
The Supremacy of the Gospel

Lesson 1
Lesson 2
Lesson 3
Lesson 4
Lesson 5
Lesson 6
Lesson 7
Lesson 8
Lesson 9
Lesson 10
Lesson 11
Lesson 12
Lesson 13

LIFE IS BETTER NOW

Unit 1 Preview

It wasn't long ago that computers, cell phones, iPads, air conditioning, and microwave ovens didn't exist. Life was low-tech or almost no-tech (from our perspective) in the old days. People often lined up at telephone booths to place a call, labored at manual typewriters, searched libraries for information, perspired at home and in their cars on hot days, and cooked meals the old-fashioned way—patiently on stovetop burners or in regular ovens. Today, however, we can establish communication immediately, get information instantly, enjoy cool comfort at home or as we drive, and prepare microwavable food within minutes or sometimes seconds. These are only a few of the ways life is better than it used to be.

Life is far better, too, for post-Calvary believers than it was for those who lived in Old Testament times. This is what the writer of Hebrews communicated in that lofty but practical book.

We Have a Better Priest

The first section of Hebrews appealed to readers who were drifting away from the Christian faith because they preferred the visible forms and functions of Judaism. The writer of Hebrews urged them not to drift away, but by faith to perceive Jesus as better than the Old Testament prophets, the angels, and even Moses. Jesus, he explained, is God's risen Son, our Lord, and our High Priest. He provides eternal rest and intercedes for us at the Father's right hand. Through Him, we can approach the throne of grace at any time and lay any request or burden there.

We Have a Better Sacrifice

In Old Testament times, priests offered multiple sacrifices for sin, and annually, on the Day of Atonement, Israel's high priest carried the blood of a bull and a goat into the Most Holy Place for a covering for his sins and for the people's sins. But by offering His own blood on the cross as a once-for-all, perfect sacrifice, Jesus, our High Priest, removed our sins forever. Hebrews 10:11–12 declares: "Day after day every priest stands and performs his religious duties; again and again he offers the same sacrifices, which can never take away sins. But when this priest [Jesus] had offered for all time one sacrifice for sins, he sat down at the right hand of God."

We Have a Better Covenant

The old covenant that God delivered through Moses to the Israelites in the wilderness showed them God is holy and requires holiness of His people, but it could never make them holy. The covenant of law revealed sin but was powerless to remove it. Its purpose was to show the people how desperately they needed the Redeemer, the Messiah. By contrast, Christ is the mediator of a new covenant (Heb. 9:15), and all who have believed in Him have the new covenant written on their hearts.

As we study Hebrews, we will marvel at the privileges we enjoy as God's redeemed children. Life is better for us than it was for those who lived under the old covenant, but with privilege comes responsibility. As God's responsible children, let us pursue holiness, engage in fervent prayer, live by faith, love our heavenly Father and one another, cling to the promises, and loyally follow Jesus all the way home! ◆

JESUS IS GREATER

Jesus Is Greater than Angels
"So he became as much superior to the angels as the name he has inherited is superior to theirs" (Heb. 1:4).

Jesus Is Greater than Moses
"Jesus has been found worthy of greater honor than Moses, just as the builder of a house has greater honor than the house itself" (Heb. 3:3).

Jesus Is Greater than Joshua
"For if Joshua had given them rest, God would not have spoken later about another day. There remains, then, a Sabbath-rest for the people of God; for anyone who enters God's rest also rests from his own work, just as God did from his" (Heb. 4:8–10).

Jesus Is Greater than Every Other High Priest
"Therefore, since we have a great high priest who has gone through the heavens, Jesus the Son of God, let us hold firmly to the faith we profess. For we do not have a high priest who is unable to sympathize with our weaknesses, but we have one who has been tempted in every way, just as we are—yet was without sin" (Heb. 4:14–15).

Jesus Mediates a Better Covenant
"Because of this oath, Jesus has become the guarantee of a better covenant" (Heb. 7:22).

Jesus Offers a Superior Ministry
"But the ministry Jesus has received is as superior to theirs as the covenant of which he is mediator is superior to the old one, and it is founded on better promises" (Heb. 8:6).

Jesus Serves in a Greater Temple
"When Christ came as a high priest of the good things that are already here, he went through the greater and more perfect tabernacle that is man-made, that is to say, not a part of this creation" (Heb. 9:11).

Jesus Offered a Better Sacrifice
"By one sacrifice he has made perfect forever those who are being made holy" (Heb. 10:14).

Jesus alone is the source of redeeming grace.

LESSON 1

THE FINALITY OF GOD'S SALVATION

Hebrews 1:1–14

KEY VERSE

The Son is the radiance of God's glory and the exact representation of his being, sustaining all things by his powerful word. After he had provided purification for sins, he sat down at the right hand of the Majesty in heaven.

—Hebrews 1:3

BACKGROUND SCRIPTURES

John 1:1–14

God the Son, Jesus, "the Word" incarnate: creator of the universe, who is simultaneously "with" God and likewise is himself God—the second person of the Trinity, and fully the glory of God

Philippians 2:5–11

Christ Jesus, in His very nature God, humbled himself by becoming fully human and then dying as a servant upon the cross. So God exalted Him, restoring Him to glory at His "right hand."

DAILY BIBLE READINGS

Monday:	Romans 1:1–17
Tuesday:	2 Thessalonians 2:13–17
Wednesday:	Ephesians 3:14–20
Thursday:	Hebrews 10:19–25
Friday:	Philippians 3:12—4:1
Saturday:	Hebrews 1:1–14
Sunday:	Psalm 13:1–6

WHY THIS MATTERS

A list of the world's most admired people might include powerful political leaders, record-holding athletes, outstanding musicians, philanthropists, gifted authors, successful educators, well-known scientists, and dedicated preachers. But not even the most admired person deserves the kind of esteem that we should ascribe to Jesus. As the writer to the Hebrews pointed out, He is even higher than the angels, because He is God's glorious Son. He embodies God's message, sustains the universe, and owns the right to receive worship and to reign forever.

This lesson will inspire you to bow humbly before Jesus and to serve Him lovingly and faithfully. You will see that no human being, regardless of his or her credentials or accomplishments, can compare with Jesus.

BIBLE COMMENTARY

By Kevin Scott

Perhaps no letter in the New Testament is more mysterious to modern Christian audiences than the epistle to the Hebrews. There are at least three reasons for this: (1) We can't say with any certainty who the author was; (2) we can't say with any certainty who the original recipients of the letter were; and (3) we find it hard to account for the unusual emphasis on seemingly esoteric subjects like the angels, the Old Testament sacrificial system, and the obscure priest Melchizedek. More than any other New Testament book (with the possible exception of Revelation), the epistle to the Hebrews feels like it's coming to us from another world.

Yet, there is much we can say with confidence about this letter and much to be gained by a careful reading of it. The author was almost certainly a converted Christian Jew, and he had a passionate and pastoral heart for the people to whom the letter was addressed. The intended recipients of the letter were also Jewish Christians. They had already experienced persecution as a result of their faith in Jesus (Heb. 10:32–34), and it seems that they were trying to strengthen their resolve for an expected second round of persecution, this time more severe (12:3–4). Some of them, however, were probably tempted by the thought of returning to their Judaism (10:35–36), since it was a protected religion in the Empire. This letter, written in the form of a sermon, was intended to strengthen their faith and steel their resolve to follow Jesus whatever may come.

Jesus, the Image of God (Heb. 1:1–7)

The theme of Hebrews might best be summarized by a single verse near the end of the letter: "Let us fix our eyes on Jesus, the author and perfecter of our faith, who for the joy set before him endured the cross, scorning its shame, and sat down at the right hand of the throne of God" (12:2). It is clear that the author had his eyes fixed on Jesus from the first sentence: **In the past God spoke to our forefathers through the prophets at many times and in various ways, but in these last days he has spoken to us by his Son, whom he appointed heir of all things, and through whom he made the universe** (1:1–2).

With that power-packed opening sentence, the author focused his readers' eyes on Jesus and established a theme and pattern that would carry through the entire letter: The Old Testament, or old covenant, was great, but it was always intended to point the way forward to something better. **God spoke to our forefathers through the prophets** (v. 1), who would have included not only the "writing prophets" like Isaiah and Jeremiah, but also men and women like Moses, Deborah, Samuel, and David. Such were the heroes of the Jewish faith, and the author of Hebrews did not diminish their importance. Yet, one had come who was greater than all the prophets who had gone before: **his Son** (v. 2).

The Emperor Trajan holding a scepter. "Your throne, O God, will last for ever and ever, and righteousness will be the scepter of your kingdom" (Heb. 1:8).

In a flurry of phrases designed to put the superiority of Jesus beyond dispute, the author of Hebrews forcefully demonstrated how Jesus surpassed the greatest of the great men and women of the faith. In the process, the author introduced many of the themes to which he would later return. Jesus was **appointed heir of all things** and it was through him God **made the universe**. He was **the radiance of God's glory and the exact representation of his being**. He **provided purification for sins** and then **sat down at the right hand of the Majesty in heaven** (vv. 2–3). While the Old Testament prophets, from Moses to Malachi, had given a true and accurate representation of God's Word, Jesus *became* God's Word to His creation, in three dimensions and high-definition.

WHAT DO YOU THINK?
How does the world attempt to diminish Christ's image? How should Christians respond when they encounter a misrepresentation about Jesus?

Many students of Scripture have puzzled over why the author of Hebrews felt it necessary to assert Jesus' superiority over the angels. There was a well-established Jewish tradition that taught that God had delivered His law to Moses by angels. In a sense, then, the angels seemed to hold an even higher place as messengers of God than the great prophets did. So the author wanted there to be no mistake; not only was Jesus superior to the prophets, but he was **superior to the angels** as well (v. 4). Jesus had a special relationship with God as His **Father** that the angels were not privileged to enjoy. He was God's **Son**, the Messiah, Israel's true king (vv. 5–6; quoting from Ps. 2:7 and 2 Sam. 7:14). The angels, on the other hand, were instructed to **worship him** (perhaps quoting Ps. 97:7), because they were **his servants** (quoting Ps. 104:4); only Jesus was **the exact representation of his being** (Heb. 1:3).

AHA!
Jesus is God!

Jesus, the Just Judge (Heb. 1:8–9)

After a one-verse description of the angels' role as servants (v. 7), the author spent the rest of this first chapter focusing on the contrasting role of Jesus as Lord. First, he quoted Psalm 45:6–7, which described the coming Messiah as a just judge. The psalm as a whole was a wedding song written about the king of Israel (45:1); it described him (and his bride) in glowing, almost godlike terms. In fact, the most straightforward translation of verse 6 reads as if the

DID YOU KNOW?
Hebrews is the only New Testament book that describes Jesus as our High Priest.

WHAT DO YOU THINK?
What roles do guardian angels play in the lives of Christians? How would your life be different if the angels did not complete their appointed tasks on your behalf?

psalmist was addressing the king as "God." Uncomfortable with this, many have tried to find an alternate translation or interpretation. But the author of Hebrews had no trouble with it; he interpreted it as referring to Jesus.

Earlier, the author said that Jesus, after dealing with our sins, "sat down at the right hand of the Majesty in heaven" (Heb. 1:3). This is a way of saying that Jesus had assumed the position of power and authority over the universe. The verses quoted here, from Psalm 45, returned to this theme, equating the godlike king of the Psalm with Jesus: **Your throne, O God, will last for ever and ever** (Heb. 1:8). When Jesus returned to heaven, God made Him king; and the throne will belong to Him for eternity. While the angels are merely servants, Jesus has the power and authority to administer the kingdom forever.

Throughout the Old Testament, the kings of Israel and other nations were judged according to their desire and capacity to administer justice and righteousness within their kingdoms. Too often, even the kings of Judah and Israel allowed injustice and wickedness to go unchecked on their watch. By contrast, Jesus' reign will be char-

The Premise of Hebrews: Christ Jesus Is Fully God	
Christ is the crowning Word of God.	Hebrews 1:1–2
Christ is the precise representation of God.	Hebrews 1:2–3
Christ embodies the highest authority of God.	Hebrews 1:4–13

acterized by justice: **and righteousness will be the scepter of** His **kingdom** (v. 9). While we tend to think of justice in terms of someone getting the punishment they deserve, the biblical concept of justice is broader than that. It includes the idea of making right what was wrong. Part of God's vision for His kingdom is that there will no longer be a place for sin or wickedness.

According to the psalm, this was Jesus' primary qualification for becoming king: **You have loved righteousness and hated wickedness; therefore God, your God, has set you above your companions by anointing you with the oil of joy** (v. 9). While, at one level, we can say, "Of course, Jesus would be king. He's God's Son," at another level, we should remember that He earned the role of king by demonstrating a passion for justice and righteousness by His journey to the cross.

AHA!
Angels watch over us!

Jesus, Creator and Re-Creator (Heb. 1:10–12)

Jesus' superiority over the angels is also demonstrated by His role in creation. We have already seen a quick hit on this theme in verse 2, where the author of Hebrews said that Jesus was superior to the prophets because He is God's "Son . . . through whom he made the universe." Here, the author returned to that theme in relation to the angels, quoting from Psalm 102: **In the beginning, O Lord, you laid the foundations of the earth, and the heavens are the work of your hands** (Heb. 1:10). There is nothing to suggest that these verses in Psalm 102 were ever understood to be a reference to the Messiah, so it is somewhat surprising that the author of Hebrews applied them to Jesus at this point. However, since he had already taken the step of equating Jesus with God, it was not a stretch to say Jesus performed this act that had always been attributed to God.

DID YOU KNOW?
Hebrews was intended for a specific group of Jewish Christians.

A significant part of the Jewish hope was the belief that one day God, through the Messiah, would create new heavens and a new earth, where justice, righteousness, and peace would endure forever (see, for example, Isa. 65:17–25). Just as Jesus was presumably involved in the creation of the heavens and earth, the author of Hebrews suggested that He would be the one to oversee the transition to the new heavens and earth: **They will perish, but you remain; they will all wear out like a garment. You will roll them up like a robe; like a garment they will be changed. But you remain the same, and your years will never end** (Heb. 1:11–12). The angels will also make the transition to the next age, just as all the saints in Christ will; but it will not be the saints, prophets, or angels who will remove the "robe" of the current universe and roll it up; none of them will give the heavens and earth a new change of clothes. That task is reserved for the Lord, the king, Jesus. Just as He created the heavens and earth that have been our home in the past and present, He will create the new heavens and earth that will serve as our eternal home.

WHAT ABOUT YOU?
How has your view of Christ grown over the years?

Jesus, the True King (Heb. 1:13–14)

Finally, the author of Hebrews described the role of the Messiah, Jesus, as the true king. This quote comes from Psalm 110: **Sit at my right hand until I make your enemies a footstool for your feet** (Heb. 1:13). The quotation is the first verse of the most quoted psalm in the New Testament. Peter, Paul, the author of Hebrews, and even Jesus himself (according to Matthew, Mark, and Luke) referred to this psalm in their efforts to interpret and explain what it means that Jesus is Messiah. In fact, the author of Hebrews would come back to it again later. The psalm described the enthronement of the Messiah as king at God's right hand and the inevitable defeat of every enemy of God. Again, the writer of Hebrews argued that such an honor was never given to an angel. They are ministers; not kings. They don't administer justice, righteousness, redemption, or salvation; their role is to **serve those who will inherit salvation** (v. 14). The fact that Jesus is the Messiah, the eternal king seated at God's right hand, demonstrates His superiority over the prophets and angels.

PRAYER
Heavenly Father, thank You for giving me Your Son, who is the exact representation of Your being. To see Jesus is to see You.

While it is difficult for modern readers to jump into the first chapter of Hebrews and grasp the flow of its argument, the original recipients of the letter would have had no problem getting the point. Some of them were considering returning to their original Judaism; all of them would be faced with the choice of being faithful to Christ or being obedient to Caesar. But the author of Hebrews, the passionate pastor, argued that now that the people knew Jesus, there could be no turning back to the prophets who spoke God's word or the angels who (according to tradition) delivered God's law. Both the prophets and angels were simply messengers who pointed forward to Jesus—the one true Lord, Redeemer, and King. ◆

INTERACTIVE LEARNING IDEAS

GET THE CLASS INVOLVED
Comparison

The writer of Hebrews went to great lengths to contrast Jesus (as the Son of God) with the created angels. There were probably false teachers during this time who were beginning to insinuate that Jesus was a created being, like the angels. So the writer of Hebrews wanted to be sure his readers knew the difference.

Have the students pair off. Make sure each pair has a blank sheet of paper and something with which to write. Have one of the students draw a line down the middle and label the left column "Jesus" and the right column "Angels."

Instruct the pairs to identify as many contrasts between Jesus and the angels that come to mind. For example: Jesus is divine; angels are created beings; Jesus (as God) is self-existent; angels have a definitive beginning; Jesus is fully human; angels are not.

When they are done, draw two columns on a white board with the same headings. Ask the pairs to give you their answers, and write them down in the appropriate column.

When you are done, review the many differences between Jesus and the angels.

TRY THIS ON YOUR OWN
Heresy Research

The book of Hebrews is the source of most theological information on orthodox Christology, which as its core states that Jesus is fully God and fully human. Most scholars believe Hebrews was written to counteract most of the incipient heresies that were attempting to weave their way into church beliefs.

Do an Internet search on the common Christological heresies, and how they clearly contradict the biblical evidence. The names of some of these heresies include: Adoptionism, Modalism, Arianism, Polytheism (namely that the Trinity represents three different gods), Nestorianism, Manichaeanism, Monophysitism, Pelagiansim, and Gnosticism.

In this study, note how these heresies have crept into the theologies of many modern-day cults, thus setting these fringe groups apart from orthodox Christianity.

TAKING IT TO THE STREET
Talking to Cultists

Many modern-day "Christian" cults twist what is said about Jesus in biblical letters like the one to the Hebrews. They are imposing their theology on to the text. In some cases, they are forced to "retranslate" the Hebrew and Greek to make the text fit their unorthodox doctrines.

Prepare the people in your class to have a meaningful dialogue with people from various cults, should those people come knocking on the door. There are many helpful resources out there to begin and guide such discussions.

Warn your students to be careful about their own vulnerabilities when talking with a cultist. They're trained to appeal the deepest insecurities and weaknesses, gaps of which we might not even be aware.

WITH YOUR FAMILY
The *Jesus* Film

The book of Hebrews focuses on the true deity and humanity of Jesus. It's crucial for your family's spiritual development to understand these essentials of orthodox Christology.

Set aside an evening to watch the *Jesus* film with your family. This film is the most-watched movie ever made. Since it is shown all over the world in a variety of languages, no movie has ever received so much exposure. There is a kids' version of the movie that tones down the portrayal of the crucifixion without losing any of its impact.

After the movie, ask each other these questions: What did Jesus do to show us He was human? What did Jesus do to show us He was God? How did Jesus interact with His disciples? Why does it seem like it took them so long to fully understand Jesus' mission? ◆

HEBREWS 1:1–14

1 In the past God spoke to our forefathers through the prophets at many times and in various ways,

2 but in these last days he has spoken to us by his Son, whom he appointed heir of all things, and through whom he made the universe.

3 The Son is the radiance of God's glory and the exact representation of his being, sustaining all things by his powerful word. After he had provided purification for sins, he sat down at the right hand of the Majesty in heaven.

4 So he became as much superior to the angels as the name he has inherited is superior to theirs.

5 For to which of the angels did God ever say, "You are my Son; today I have become your Father"? Or again, "I will be his Father, and he will be my Son"?

6 And again, when God brings his firstborn into the world, he says, "Let all God's angels worship him."

7 In speaking of the angels he says, "He makes his angels winds, his servants flames of fire."

8 But about the Son he says, "Your throne, O God, will last for ever and ever, and righteousness will be the scepter of your kingdom.

9 You have loved righteousness and hated wickedness; therefore God, your God, has set you above your companions by anointing you with the oil of joy."

10 He also says, "In the beginning, O Lord, you laid the foundations of the earth, and the heavens are the work of your hands.

11 They will perish, but you remain; they will all wear out like a garment.

12 You will roll them up like a robe; like a garment they will be changed. But you remain the same, and your years will never end."

13 To which of the angels did God ever say, "Sit at my right hand until I make your enemies a footstool for your feet"?

14 Are not all angels ministering spirits sent to serve those who will inherit salvation?

> "Your throne, O God, will last
> for ever and ever."
> —*Psalm 45:6*

The Finality of God's Salvation

Jesus alone is the source of redeeming grace.

INTO THE SUBJECT

Many people would agree that Jesus once lived upon the earth as a great teacher, but what more do they need to know about Him?

INTO THE WORD

1. How would you use Hebrews 1:1–2 to refute the claim that God has never been involved in history?

2. What works and ministries does the writer to the Hebrews ascribe to Jesus in verses 2–3?

3. If a cultist told you Jesus was a high-ranking angel, how would you answer him or her (vv. 4–9)?

4. What significance do you find in the fact that Jesus sat down at God's right hand "after he had provided purification for sins" (v. 3)?

5. How does the fact that Jesus occupies an everlasting throne (v. 8) help you face troubled times?

6. What evidence of Jesus' almighty power do you find in verses 10–13?

7. How will your worship of Jesus be more meaningful because of the portrayal of Him in Hebrews 1:1–14?

8. How does this passage motivate you to tell others about Jesus?

INTO THE WORLD

Tell at least one person this week how Jesus gives you peace and confidence in the midst of troublesome world conditions.

Christ Is God

This lesson focuses on three main ideas: Christ is the crowning word of God, Christ is the precise representation of God, and Christ embodies the highest authority of God.

Christ is the crowning word of God.

What were some of the ways God spoke to our forefathers?

_____

_____

How does He speak to us now?

_____

_____

Christ is the precise representation of God.

Jesus will reign for eternity at the right hand of God. Write a prayer of thanks to God for His work and provision in Jesus.

_____

_____

Christ embodies the highest authority of God.

Write two things you've discovered in this lesson that you either didn't know before or were reminded of as a result of this lesson.

_____

_____

How can what you've learned impact your relationship with God?

_____

_____

TREASURE YOUR GREATEST TREASURE

Hebrews 2:1–18

WHY THIS MATTERS

Two boaters in their mid-twenties will never forget June 2, 2011. That was the day their craft lost power on the river above Niagara Falls and drifted within seven hundred feet of Horseshoe Falls on the Canadian side of the river. Using a cell phone, they issued an urgent plea for help and received it in the nick of time. The Erie County Sheriff's Marine Unit arrived within minutes and used a rope to tow the boaters to safety.

Drifting toward Niagara Falls is certainly perilous, but drifting away from biblical truth is even more so because it endangers the soul. This lesson offers strong incentives to stay firmly anchored to the truth and committed to Jesus Christ.

BIBLE COMMENTARY

By Kevin Scott

For at least five hundred years, the Christian church has been embroiled in a debate over the theological doctrines of perseverance and apostasy. The question has been debated endlessly—especially between Calvinists and Arminians—whether a person who is a true believer can later reject the faith. Those who argue for perseverance say that a true believer will persevere to the end and be saved; God guarantees it, they say. Those who argue for the possibility of apostasy say that a person's genuine faith today offers no guarantee that he or she will continue in faith to the end, because faith is a matter of the human will. Those who argue for perseverance say that a person who commits apostasy (abandons their faith) was never a genuine Christian at any time. The person who argues for the possibility of apostasy says that while God is always faithful, humans sometimes break faith.

The debate over the theology of perseverance and apostasy often mires down in technical, theoretical, and philosophical wrangling. When the arguments turn to Scripture, however, much of the biblical focus in this theological debate rests on the letter to the Hebrews. The Hebrew Christians, who had already experienced one round of persecution were facing the possibility of another round. Many were afraid and tempted to abandon their Christian faith and return to the safer confines of Judaism. In response, the author of Hebrews included several strongly worded warnings in his letter to them. The first of these is in the first part of today's passage (2:1–4). For the author and his readers, however, this was no theological debate. They were not attempting to discover a definitive answer to a theoretical, philosophical question. They were in the midst of real life, facing genuine danger, and they needed practical guidance and wisdom. Thus, the author of Hebrews warned them, in no certain terms, to cling to and avoid falling away from their faith in Jesus Christ.

KEY VERSE

How shall we escape if we ignore such a great salvation?
—Hebrews 2:3

BACKGROUND SCRIPTURES

Genesis 1:26–27; 2:7
God created humans in His own likeness. So when God breathed the breath of life into man, man became a living "being"—a spiritual person with a soul.

Romans 5:12–20
By one man, Adam, death came into the world; and by one man, Christ Jesus, do we receive God's grace.

1 Corinthians 15:45–49
The first Adam became a living being; the last Adam was the life-giving Spirit.

DAILY BIBLE READINGS

Monday: 2 Samuel 22:31–37
Tuesday: 2 Corinthians 5:14–21
Wednesday: Luke 18:18–29
Thursday: Matthew 28:16–20; Mark 16:19–20
Friday: Acts 17:24–31
Saturday: Hebrews 2:1–18
Sunday: Psalm 15

Jesus—Don't Neglect Him (Heb. 2:1–4)

WHAT DO YOU THINK?
How do we keep ourselves from taking our faith for granted? What can believers do to regularly renew their faith?

After a majestic first chapter, in which the author of Hebrews helped his readers focus their eyes on Jesus, the one who is superior to the Old Testament prophets and the angels who (in Jewish tradition) delivered the law to Moses, he paused his argumentation long enough to make a direct application of this truth to his readers: **We must pay more careful attention** (v. 1). It is interesting that the author did not simply tell his readers to "stay the course" or to keep doing what they were doing in spite of the threat of persecution. Instead, he essentially said, "If you're tempted to turn back, you need to go deeper. There's more to Jesus than you know." The danger the author had in mind was clear; he was concerned that they would **drift away** (v. 1) from their faith in Jesus.

When you're in a boat, drifting is not usually the result of a conscious decision but because of distraction. So in faith, people do not usually intend to drift away. Instead, they become distracted, lose their focus, and even stop caring, until they suddenly find themselves in waters that are too dangerous for them to handle. So the author urged his readers to **pay more careful attention . . . to what** they had **heard** (v. 1).

"The message spoken by angels was binding" (Heb. 2:2).

The readers of this letter were distracted by the threat of persecution and in danger of losing their focus on and interest in Jesus. They were attracted to the relative safety and comfort they felt under the Jewish Law. So the author of Hebrews reminded his readers about the importance with which God treated the law: **the message spoken by angels was binding, and every violation and disobedience received its just punishment** (v. 2). If God's administration of the old covenant delivered by the angels was so strict and severe, He would certainly not be lax in administering the new covenant delivered by His own Son. **How shall we escape if ignore such a great salvation** (v. 3)? The old and new covenants are the same in the sense that there are covenant stipulations or requirements and then blessings that come to those who keep the covenants and curses on those who break them. God had proven himself faithful in keeping the old covenant, both in the blessings and curses. We should not think that He will be any looser in administering the blessings and curses of the new covenant.

AHA!
Jesus is fully human!

Then the author reminded his readers of what they already knew about this new covenant but to which they needed to pay more careful attention. **This salvation . . . was first announced by the Lord** (v. 3). This time God did not send His message via His messengers, the angels. This time the King showed up to deliver the message in person. What do you expect would happen if you ignored or neglected a message that was so important the King delivered it in person? **This salvation** also **was confirmed to us by those who heard him** (v. 3). This phrase strongly suggests that the author of Hebrews was not an original disciple or the apostle Paul, one of those who had personally received the message of salvation from Jesus. The message was confirmed by eyewitnesses who faithfully passed it on to the author of Hebrews and his readers. Even more than that, **God also testified to it by signs, wonders and various**

DID YOU KNOW?
There are many credible opinions about who wrote Hebrews.

miracles, and gifts of the Holy Spirit distributed according to his will (v. 4). The Spirit testifies directly to our hearts the truth of the message of salvation, as we find that God is transforming our hearts, giving us the ability to become the people He has called us to be.

Jesus, the True Man (Heb. 2:5–9)

After his stern warning about paying more careful attention to what they had heard about Jesus, the author of Hebrews returned to the argument he had put forth in the first chapter, picking up some of its threads and expanding on them. In chapter 1, he had spoken about the superiority of Jesus over the angels (vv. 4–7, 14) and about the transition from creation to new creation, from the present age to the age to come (vv. 10–12). Here, he returned to both themes as he reflected on the authority structure of the new world: **It is not to angels that he has subjected the world to come, about which we are speaking** (2:5). The angels will presumably survive the transition, but they will still have a subordinate role in the new heavens and earth.

The quotation in verses 6–7 is from Psalm 8:4–6. The word translated "man" is the Hebrew word for "human." The phrase "son of man" is a Hebrew idiom that meant something like "average Joe." However, the prophet Daniel invested this common Hebrew idiom with a deeper level of meaning, when he used the phrase to refer to the coming Messiah: "In my vision at night I looked, and there was one like a son of man, coming with the clouds of heaven. He approached the Ancient of Days and was led into his presence. He was given authority, glory and sovereign power; all peoples, nations and men of every language worship him. His dominion is an everlasting dominion that will not pass away, and his kingdom is one that will never be destroyed" (Dan. 7:13–14). Jesus often referred to himself as the "Son of Man" in this Daniel 7 sense. Psalm 8 teaches that God's plan was to give humanity His glory and the authority to rule over His creation; however, humanity fell short of the calling to reflect God's glory. Daniel 7 prophesied that there would be another human who would not fail in this vocation. The author of Hebrews said that man was Jesus: **In putting everything under him, God left nothing that is not subject to him** (Heb. 2:8).

The only problem, according to the author of Hebrews, is that **at present we do not see everything subject to him** (v. 8). And we may echo a hearty "amen." As we look at the world around us, we see so much poverty, injustice, and unrighteousness. In some ways, it appears that humanity is doing no better at administering God's creation than we ever have since the beginning of time. The difference is, however, **we see Jesus**. We see the true and faithful human being. He was **made** like us **a little lower than the angels**. He **suffered death** like all humanity has or will. But He is **now crowned with glory and honor** (v. 9). He has pioneered the way for us, demonstrating what it means to reflect God's glory and effectively administer His creation. In suffering a sacrificial death, He became our representative—standing in our place, doing what we could never do—so that we can be transformed and take our place alongside Him as part of the new, redeemed humanity.

WHAT DO YOU THINK?
How do we see the sovereignty of God at work in the lives of those who refuse to acknowledge Him? To what degree is the church in submission to the will of God?

We are meant to be in this together.	
Safety of the Fellowship	Hebrews 2:1–4
Shepherd of the Fellowship	Hebrews 2:5–18

AHA!
Jesus knows our every weakness!

DID YOU KNOW?
The early church fathers thought Paul wrote the book of Hebrews.

WHAT ABOUT YOU?
What has kept your faith
alive and vibrant in the
past? To what degree is
your life in submission to
the will of God?

PRAYER
Lord, help me to pay close
attention to my faith, and
to take nothing You have
given me for granted. Help
me to endure and overcome
temptation, as Jesus did.

Jesus, the Older Brother (Heb. 2:10–18)

Jesus once (or perhaps many times) told a parable about a young man who cashed in his inheritance, wasted it on hedonistic pleasures, and then returned home to an unexpected welcome by his father. Perhaps the greatest villain of the story is the older brother, who was jealous and refused to welcome the younger brother home. As the author of Hebrews continued to focus his readers' eyes on Jesus, he presented Him as the older brother; but he is not *that* kind of older brother. Instead, Jesus is the older brother that provides true leadership and takes genuine responsibility for His siblings: **Both the one who makes men holy and those who are made holy are of the same family. So Jesus is not ashamed to call them brothers** (v. 11).

It was hinted in the previous section about how part of Jesus' vocation was in **bringing many sons to glory** to help us find our way again to the place where we are reflecting God's glory. The pathway the older brother had to take to make this happen was one of suffering: **it was fitting that God . . . should make the author of their salvation perfect through suffering** (v. 10). The quotation in verse 12 might not be familiar, but the passage from which it comes is well-known. Psalm 22 is the classic prophecy of Jesus' crucifixion, and the verse quoted begins the conclusion of the psalmist's account of the Messiah's suffering. The two quotations in Hebrews 2:13—from Isaiah 8:17 and 18—emphasizes that Jesus claims us as part of His family. He is the kind of older brother who will suffer the worst so that we can have the opportunity for the best. Again, we might ask, "How shall we escape if we ignore such a great salvation?" (Heb. 2:3).

Jesus was the true man—the older brother of the new, transformed humanity—and because He was willing to suffer on our behalf, He is bringing many to glory. This points to another reason for the superiority of Jesus: through His sacrificial death, He became the true high priest and destroyed forever the power of sin and death. He could not do this without taking His place among His younger brothers and sisters. He could not remain aloof. **Since the children have flesh and blood, he too shared in their humanity so that by his death he might destroy him who holds the power of death. . . . For this reason he had to be made like his brothers in every way** (vv. 14, 17). It is only because Jesus was willing to be made "a little lower than the angels" (v. 7) and be made **perfect through suffering** (v. 10) that He could **become a merciful and faithful high priest in service to God** (v. 17). For all of these reasons, Jesus is perfectly suited **to help those who are being tempted** (v. 18), which is exactly the situation in which the Hebrew Christians were finding themselves. Thus the author's exhortation to "pay more careful attention . . . to what we have heard, so that we do not drift away" (v. 1). ✦

HEBREWS 2:1–18

1 We must pay more careful attention, therefore, to what we have heard, so that we do not drift away.

2 For if the message spoken by angels was binding, and every violation and disobedience received its just punishment,

3 how shall we escape if we ignore such a great salvation? This salvation, which was first announced by the Lord, was confirmed to us by those who heard him.

4 God also testified to it by signs, wonders and various miracles, and gifts of the Holy Spirit distributed according to his will.

5 It is not to angels that he has subjected the world to come, about which we are speaking.

6 But there is a place where someone has testified: "What is man that you are mindful of him, the son of man that you care for him?

7 You made him a little lower than the angels; you crowned him with glory and honor

8 and put everything under his feet." In putting everything under him, God left nothing that is not subject to him. Yet at present we do not see everything subject to him.

9 But we see Jesus, who was made a little lower than the angels, now crowned with glory and honor because he suffered death, so that by the grace of God he might taste death for everyone.

10 In bringing many sons to glory, it was fitting that God, for whom and through whom everything exists, should make the author of their salvation perfect through suffering.

11 Both the one who makes men holy and those who are made holy are of the same family. So Jesus is not ashamed to call them brothers.

12 He says, "I will declare your name to my brothers; in the presence of the congregation I will sing your praises."

13 And again, "I will put my trust in him." And again he says, "Here am I, and the children God has given me."

14 Since the children have flesh and blood, he too shared in their humanity so that by his death he might destroy him who holds the power of death—that is, the devil—

15 and free those who all their lives were held in slavery by their fear of death.

16 For surely it is not angels he helps, but Abraham's descendants.

17 For this reason he had to be made like his brothers in every way, in order that he might become a merciful and faithful high priest in service to God, and that he might make atonement for the sins of the people.

18 Because he himself suffered when he was tempted, he is able to help those who are being tempted.

Treasure Your Greatest Treasure

Stay firmly anchored to the truth revealed in Jesus Christ.

INTO THE SUBJECT

Having come to a knowledge of the truth, is it possible to drift away from it? How can we stay anchored in the faith?

INTO THE WORD

1. What do you think the writer was referring to by "what we have heard" (Heb. 2:1)?

2. What do you think causes someone to drift away?

3. Why do you agree or disagree that even a "seasoned" believer may drift away?

4. Why do you agree or disagree that a believer may ignore salvation?

5. According to verse 4, what was the purpose of apostolic "signs, wonders and various miracles"?

6. According to verses 9–15, what did Jesus accomplish by His death?

7. How has Jesus, your "merciful and faithful high priest" (v. 17), helped you in the past week?

8. Why is Jesus able to help you when you are tempted (v. 18)?

9. How has a truth in Hebrews 2:1–18 anchored your faith more firmly?

INTO THE WORLD

Offer to pray for a coworker, friend, or relative who tells you he or she is experiencing a hard trial. Share the good news that Jesus cares and helps those who trust in Him.

THE WORD IN FLESH

As the lesson states, Christ came not only to communicate the word of God, but to be the Word housed in skin. He did this so He could say He felt and endured things just as those around Him had.

Memorize Hebrews 2:17–18: "For this reason he had to be made like his brothers in every way, in order that he might become a merciful and faithful high priest in service to God, and that he might make atonement for the sins of the people. Because he himself suffered when he was tempted, he is able to help those who are being tempted."

There are many methods for memorization. Here are several to try:

 Write the verse on index cards, two to three words per card. Mix up the cards and time yourself putting them into order. Each time you should be able to put them in order faster than the time before.

 Type the verse over and over.

 Draw the verse. You might draw a picture of a group of brothers and a person serving God for verse 17 and a picture of someone being tempted for verse 18.

 Memorize the verse in sections, at natural breaking points. Add a section each time you master the one before it.

INTERACTIVE LEARNING IDEAS

GET THE CLASS INVOLVED
Pay Close Attention

The writer of Hebrews told us to pay close attention to our faith, and how we are living it out, so we do not drift away.

Let's play an old game that requires people to pay very close attention to what's going on. This is a version of "telephone," where a message is whispered from person to person to see how much the message changes, if at all, during its transmission.

Here are the rules: Each person can speak as slowly as he or she wishes, but the messenger can only say the message once; no repeating or starting over.

Have everyone sit in a circle so it's easy to lean over and whisper in each other's ears.

Here is the message; whisper it once into the ear of the first person in line: "The elderly Mrs. Salnowiki had three cats named Zipper, Buttons, and Slide Rule. Every Saturday at 8:33 a.m., she would take the neighbor's ferret, Stiches, for a walk to the deli to pick up some cream, steamed liver, and rain gear."

When everyone has had a chance to pass the message along, have last person say out loud what he or she heard. After a few laughs, point out the importance of paying close attention to matters of faith.

TRY THIS ON YOUR OWN
Signs and Wonders

God testified to His salvation by means of signs, wonders, miracles, and various manifestations by the Holy Spirit (Heb. 2:4).

Beginning in Genesis, scan the Bible for all the miracles you can find. Many of the Old Testament prophets performed miracles and had visions (like Elijah and Elisha), while some did not (like Jeremiah). In the New Testament, note the miracles of Jesus, and those of the apostles in the book of Acts.

As you're reading these accounts, ask yourself these questions: Why was the miracle being performed? How did the miracle add authenticity and credibility to the integrity of God's truth? How did people respond to the miracle? How did some people try to explain the miracle away? What are the dangers of having a faith that is dependent upon the consistent manifestation of miracles?

TAKING IT TO THE STREET
Freedom of Religion

The writer of Hebrews stated that while God is sovereign over all, not all those in authority are subject to Him (at least they do not acknowledge Him). Of course, one day this will all change when Jesus returns, but it's not the state we find ourselves in today.

Go visit someone in elected office, and ask their opinion about freedom of religion. Is there a difference between freedom of worship and freedom of religion?

If the person is willing to answer, ask about their own religious views, and how that affects their professional decision (if at all). Of course, at all times be polite and respectful of personal boundaries. This can be a sensitive topic, especially for politicians!

WITH YOUR FAMILY
Spiritual Growth Assessment

We are told in Hebrews that Jesus brought many sons and daughters to glory (Heb. 2:10). What this means, in part, is that Jesus is intimately involved in the spiritual development and growth of every person who follows Him, young and old.

Around the dinner table, talk about each person's spiritual growth, and how he or she is becoming more like Christ. The adults should begin, setting a good example of being honest about strengths and weaknesses and needed areas of growth.

It might also be helpful for the adults to talk about "what they know now" in regard to spiritual growth that they didn't know as children. Then the younger people should speak, and talk about what God has been teaching them lately. ◆

> "Complacency is a deadly foe of all spiritual growth. Acute desire must be present or there will be no manifestation of Christ to His people."
>
> —A. W. Tozer

Keep your focus on Jesus so that sin will not draw you away.

LESSON 3

FIX YOUR EYES ON JESUS

Hebrews 3:1–19

KEY VERSE

Therefore, holy brothers, who share in the heavenly calling, fix your thoughts on Jesus, the apostle and high priest whom we confess.

—Hebrews 3:1

WHY THIS MATTERS

A physical examination is incomplete if it does not include the heart. A healthy heart pumps blood effectively to every part of the body and helps us lead a strong, energetic, and vigorous life. Physicians and nutritionists encourage us to eat properly and exercise regularly. However, temptations to neglect the heart assail us. Junk food is readily available, and the couch or recliner may seem more inviting than a treadmill or an elliptical. Nevertheless, junk food and a sedentary lifestyle can clog our arteries and contribute to heart disease.

This lesson emphasizes the need to guard our hearts from unbelief and sin's deceitfulness and thereby avoid hardening of the "hearteries."

BIBLE COMMENTARY

By Jim Moretz

The letter to the Hebrews is what we would call a systematic theology. That is, it begins with a basic premise—that Jesus is "the radiance of God's glory and the exact representation of his being" (1:3). The rest of the work is a system of "therefores," building a logical framework of beliefs and ethics based on the basic premise. Therefore, we must study Hebrews from the beginning and keep in mind everything we learn as we go along.

Another premise of the letter is the validity of the old covenant as revealed by God in the Old Testament. The author repeatedly acknowledged the worth and usefulness of the old covenant. However, he made the case that Jesus fulfilled the old covenant and introduced a new covenant. The author challenged his readers to wrestle with the concept of a *new* covenant. There is something qualitatively different about the covenant we have in Christ as compared to the covenant the Hebrews had in Moses and the prophets. The new covenant is not the old covenant only better. It is a new way of understanding the relationship between God and His creation; it includes old covenant concepts and introduces new revelation that the old covenant was unable to sustain.

Throughout the letter, the author warned the Hebrews not to fall into the temptation of relying on the old covenant. This would have been easy because that is what they knew and what was familiar. The old covenant was restrictive and prescriptive. The new covenant is universal and descriptive. The analogy the author used is that of food. When we are young, we live on milk because we have no choice. Our bodies cannot digest solid foods. As we grow, we eat solid foods, and we choose those foods that we will eat. It is a move from sustenance to nutrition, from survival to living.

The author was careful to make clear that he was writing for "we who have believed" (4:3). His immediate audience was Jews who believed Jesus is the Christ. He relied heavily on their knowledge of Scripture and tradition. His

BACKGROUND SCRIPTURES

Exodus 17:1–7
   The Israelites questioned God.
Numbers 14
   God declared that generation would not enter His rest.
Numbers 20
   Moses distrusted God.
Deuteronomy 32:48–52
   God only let Moses see the Promised Land.
Psalm 95
   The psalmist recounted Exodus 17.

DAILY BIBLE READINGS

Monday: 1 John 5:1–13
Tuesday: 1 Peter 5:6–12
Wednesday: Philippians 3:7–15
Thursday: Hebrews 11:1–6
Friday: Hebrews 12:1–3
Saturday: Hebrews 3:1–9
Sunday: Psalm 16:5–11

concern was that believers did not come to depend on their faith as a system of religion which contains a formula for faith, but that "faith is being sure of what we hope for and certain of what we do not see" (11:1).

Modern Christians need to study Hebrews in a similar fashion. After we have been in the church for a while, we are tempted to rely on our goodness and good deeds as merits for our salvation. We can come to believe the way we worship is the best way, the way we run our church is the way everyone should run their church. The passage we are studying today is exactly on that point. We must be diligent to remain in a constant state of faith so the things we see around us do not become more important to us than Jesus, whom we cannot see.

Jesus Is the Center of Our Faith (Heb. 3:1–6)

Verse 1 of chapter 3 is a summary of everything written in the first two chapters. It is a transition statement from the detailed description of Jesus (chap. 1) and the relationship between Jesus, God, and humanity (chap. 2) into a description of the implications of our faithfulness (chap. 3). The letter focuses our thoughts on relationships, and this passage emphasizes the relationship between believers and Jesus and between believers and sin.

Verse 1 shows us the importance of understanding these relationships in this order. Jesus is described as **the apostle and high priest whom we confess**. The apostle was the one sent with the good news of salvation. The high priest was the one who made atonement for the sin of the people. Our relationship with Jesus is the basis for dealing with sin. If the former relationship is not right, then the latter relationship is hopeless. Our relationship with Jesus is based on Him, not us.

Dietrich Bonhoeffer said that anyone who would take up Christianity must discard as irrelevant two questions: "How am I to be good?" and "How am I to do good?" Instead, he said, the Christian must ask the utterly different question, "What is the will of God?" Hebrews tells us that to know Jesus is to know the will of God. God's will is not ethereal, but personal and tangible as incarnated in Christ. We can only understand ourselves as the center of God's affection if we make Jesus the center of our affection, as a person, not a concept or religious structure.

Verses 2–5 acknowledge the benefits of religious concepts and structure. Many people object to what they call "institutionalized religion," but institutionalization is as necessary to human function as shelter is necessary for human survival. We need organization. We need set boundaries so we can determine right and wrong beliefs, right and wrong actions. However, we must always remember that houses are made for people to live in, and organizations are made to help people grow. The author wrote, **the builder of a house has greater honor than the house itself** (v. 3). He encouraged us to remember that the church is for the people. If the church becomes more important than the people, we have slipped into idolatry and the new covenant is of no use to us.

The author emphasized this point in verse 6 when he wrote that **we are his house, if we hold on to our courage and the hope of which we boast.** So what is this courage and hope? We must fix our thoughts on Jesus to know. He hung on the cross and said, "Father, forgive them, for they do not know what

WHAT DO YOU THINK?
In what ways do we share our heavenly calling with our brothers and sisters in Christ? What prevents "lone ranger" Christians from growing spiritually?

AHA!
Jesus is greater than Moses!

DID YOU KNOW?
The Old Testament quotations in Hebrews are always quoted from the Septuagint.

WHAT DO YOU THINK?
What are the signs of a
gradually hardening heart?
How do we effectively
confront those symptoms
in ourselves and others?

AHA!
Encouragement softens
hearts!

DID YOU KNOW?
The author of Hebrews
quoted the most from the
Pentateuch and the Psalms.

they are doing" (Luke 23:34). He said to pray for our enemies and bless those who persecute us. He said to give forgiveness every time it is requested. He showed us that relationships—people—are worth dying for. If we try to save our lives, we will lose them. If we lose them for His sake, we will find eternal life.

Christianity Is a Relationship with God (Heb. 3:7–11)

Because Christianity is based on relationships, it is a way of living, a way of being marked by revelation and action. Sometimes we focus so much on our sin and our need of a Savior that we treat our faith as only an end to sinning rather than the beginning of an intimate relationship with a holy God, one that will result in holy behavior. This allows us to objectify our faith and neglect the God of our faith. That is, we develop mental checklists to judge ourselves, independent of direct communication with God. As a result, we do not hear His voice daily and we end up "having a form of godliness but denying its power" (2 Tim. 3:5).

The result is that people end up coming to and serving in the church, but that is the extent of their faith. It is all in what they do, and what they do is a neat and organized part of their lives. It is a compartmentalized faith, a controlled faith. Anyone who approaches a friendship or marriage like this is doomed to disaster. We cannot control other people. We must learn to relate to them and allow the relationship to be dynamic and constantly developing. New things constantly arise in healthy relationships. It is a distinctive of relationships.

If we know God personally, if we hear His voice, then we have no need for signs, wonders, or checklists of goodness. We can move at His prompting; talk to our neighbors about Jesus; give away material items we don't need; reject ambition for money, fame, and power. God calls us to go into the highways and hedges, to welcome the outcasts of society, and to befriend the oppressed. The rich young ruler turned away from Jesus because he valued his wealth more than discovering how to live in communion with God and others. God calls us to be selfless, to be self-sacrificial. Many times we decide in our own minds what that means for us, and usually it is quite comfortable. When God speaks, He may well call us into a desert or ask us to do something that seems gigantic to us. After departing Egypt, the Hebrews were afraid to enter the Promised Land because the people living there were physically imposing. They hardened their hearts by trusting in what they could see rather than being confident in what they could not see. They traded the rest and peace of God for forty years of wandering in the desert. Unless we seek God's voice and act upon what we hear, regardless of what we see, we too will trade His rest for a lifetime of stress.

Read the background Scriptures in Exodus, Numbers, and Deuteronomy, and then read how the psalmist commented on them in Psalm 95. Then reread this passage and note how the author of Hebrews used Psalm 95 in his situation. Commenting on Scripture is essentially appropriating it to our current situation. This is what we mean by Scripture being "living and active." It can always be appropriated to us in order that we may know God and "therefore" enter His rest.

People Who Heard God's Voice with Open Hearts		
Person Called	**Scripture Reference**	**Key Verse**
Abraham	Genesis 12:1–9	So Abram left, as the LORD had told him.
Isaiah	Isaiah 6:1–8	Here am I. Send me!
Jeremiah	Jeremiah 1:4–10	You must go to everyone I send you to and say whatever I command you. Do not be afraid.
Samuel	1 Samuel 3:1–10	Speak, for your servant is listening.
Disciples	Matthew 4:18–22; Mark 1:14–20; Luke 5:1–11	At once they left their nets and followed him.

WHAT ABOUT YOU?
How soft or hard is your heart these days?

Christianity Is a Relationship with Others (Heb. 3:12–19)

John Wesley said there is no such holiness as solitary holiness. In other words, we cannot be Christians by ourselves. Sin is too powerful. We will be overcome. We have a responsibility to watch over the lives of one another. We cannot assume that anyone among us is immune to **sin's deceitfulness** (v. 13). Verse 16 reminds us that those who rebelled were the very ones who witnessed God part the Red Sea and save them from Pharaoh's army. We do no one any favors by placing them upon a spiritual pedestal. In fact, we may put them at risk. Remember the saying, "familiarity breeds contempt." We must be careful that our familiarity with God and the church does not lull us into a false sense of security in which we begin to rationalize our wishes and desires as the will of God. This means we need to pray for the saints of the church just as diligently as we pray for the salvation of those outside the church, for an unbelieving heart is a self-centered heart, and self-centeredness is a constant threat.

What was **their unbelief** as the author described those who were unable to enter God's rest in verse 19? It was their refusal to act upon the promise of God. Under the old covenant the promise entailed an inheritance of land with physical, geographical boundaries. This implied that God would supply all their needs, water being essential to a desert people. Over and over, the Israelites failed to act on God's promise to supply their basic needs and, instead, they tried to be self-sufficient and complained against God for His apparent lack of faithfulness.

PRAYER
Lord, keep my heart soft, so that I might not drift away as those who did so in the wilderness. Remind me to constantly look for opportunities to encourage others in the faith.

The new covenant promise is an inheritance of an eternal land where there is no death and disease, no crying or pain. The old covenant required battle with greater forces. The new covenant requires loving where there is no love given in return. Both are based on God's promise that faithfulness to the covenant will bring rest and peace. Neither is evident to the human eye. Both assail the self-centeredness of sinful humanity. Both require a collective effort of all those who believe.

Selfless love requires us to believe that God will supply our basic needs. This frees us from the worries of life that we may live for others. This is faith. This is God's rest. This is how we live for and in today. May God bless the study of His promise. Today if you hear His voice, may you act and not harden your heart. ◆

INTERACTIVE LEARNING IDEAS

GET THE CLASS INVOLVED
Greater Honor

The writer of Hebrews wrote that Jesus has even more honor than Moses, that the builder of the house of faith is even greater than the house itself.

It's important, every once in a while, to honor those who do significant work in the church. As a class, spend some time identifying fruitful and productive people in your church, especially those who work behind the scenes, and then think of some ways to creatively honor them.

These are the people who quietly make things happen, never drawing attention to themselves, simply doing the work of ministry. Spend a few minutes talking about each person and the unique things they do for God and His kingdom in your church. How would your church be different if this person did not consistently exercise his or her particular gifts?

Have someone act as a secretary, writing down these ideas. Ask if someone in the class would be willing to take this information home and create a simple thank-you certificate, highlighting the things you discussed in class.

Then next week, quietly present each person with his or her certificate, reminding that person that their quiet work for Jesus does not go unnoticed.

TRY THIS ON YOUR OWN
Encouragement Texts

Hebrews 3:13 tells us to encourage one another daily. If we do this, said the writer of Hebrews, we can prevent the root of bitterness from gaining a hold in our hearts and in the souls of our brothers and sisters in Christ.

Consider sending one encouraging text every day to someone who might need lifting up. Some people become bitter because they feel like their work, or even they themselves, are simply taken for granted. Being noticed could make all the difference for them.

Be specific about the positive traits and actions that have consistently caught your attention. Tell that person about how you have benefited from his or her faithful acts of service. Be sure to express your gratitude for the impact he or she has made in your life.

TAKING IT TO THE STREET
Worldview Walk

The people of Israel, those who wandered in the wilderness, were not allowed to enter into the Promised Land because of their unbelief (Heb. 3:19). Even after all God had done for them, they were not able to connect what they witnessed with faith.

Go on a "worldview walk" with your class in the nearest urban center to you. Take a look around at the billboards, postings, headlines, and so forth. From these, try to determine the type of worldview these things represent. It's unlikely that any of these things will express any type of security in God. Rather, they will be encouraging people to put their security in things, what they wear, the cars they drive, or the trendy places where they will be seen.

In other words, these things will represent a culture of unbelief.

WITH YOUR FAMILY
Family Impact

Jesus had even greater honor that Moses in God's house, even as faithful as Moses proved to be (Heb. 3:3–4).

As a family, spend some time talking about relatives (who are still alive), and the positive impact they have had on your family. Each family member should tell whatever stories they remember about each of these individuals. What spiritual impact did the family members have on the generations that followed?

After the discussion, spend some time writing notes to these people, thanking and honoring them for all the good they have done for your family. Perhaps you can get a card that has enough room for everyone to write something encouraging. Put that relative's name and address on the envelope, put a stamp on it, and go to the mailbox together to send it off. After dropping it in the box, hold hands together and offer a short prayer for the person who will receive the note. ◆

HEBREWS 3:1–19

1 Therefore, holy brothers, who share in the heavenly calling, fix your thoughts on Jesus, the apostle and high priest whom we confess.

2 He was faithful to the one who appointed him, just as Moses was faithful in all God's house.

3 Jesus has been found worthy of greater honor than Moses, just as the builder of a house has greater honor than the house itself.

4 For every house is built by someone, but God is the builder of everything.

5 Moses was faithful as a servant in all God's house, testifying to what would be said in the future.

6 But Christ is faithful as a son over God's house. And we are his house, if we hold on to our courage and the hope of which we boast.

7 So, as the Holy Spirit says: "Today, if you hear his voice,

8 do not harden your hearts as you did in the rebellion, during the time of testing in the desert,

9 where your fathers tested and tried me and for forty years saw what I did.

10 That is why I was angry with that generation, and I said, 'Their hearts are always going astray, and they have not known my ways.'

11 So I declared on oath in my anger, 'They shall never enter my rest.'"

12 See to it, brothers, that none of you has a sinful, unbelieving heart that turns away from the living God.

13 But encourage one another daily, as long as it is called Today, so that none of you may be hardened by sin's deceitfulness.

14 We have come to share in Christ if we hold firmly till the end the confidence we had at first.

15 As has just been said: "Today, if you hear his voice, do not harden your hearts as you did in the rebellion."

16 Who were they who heard and rebelled? Were they not all those Moses led out of Egypt?

17 And with whom was he angry for forty years? Was it not with those who sinned, whose bodies fell in the desert?

18 And to whom did God swear that they would never enter his rest if not to those who disobeyed?

19 So we see that they were not able to enter, because of their unbelief.

> "He is our God and we are the
> people of his pasture."
> —*Psalm 95:7*

Fix Your Eyes on Jesus

*Keep your focus on Jesus so that
sin will not draw you away.*

INTO THE SUBJECT

It is common to hear religious people called "people of faith." But is Christianity a matter of placing one's faith in a list of doctrines, or is it primarily a matter of anchoring one's faith in Jesus?

INTO THE WORD

1. What do you think it means to fix your thoughts on Jesus (Heb. 3:1)?

2. Why is Jesus worthy of greater honor than Moses (v. 2)?

3. How do you define "God's house"?

4. How does a person enter into a saving relationship with God?

5. What help do you find in verses 12–15 for strengthening your relationship with God?

6. What, if anything, might be threatening your relationship with God? What will you do to remove that threat?

7. What is the best thing you can do to help a fellow believer fix his or her eyes on Jesus?

8. How does the hope of heaven help you stay close to Jesus?

INTO THE WORLD

Share with an unbeliever this week the difference between having faith in a creed and faith in Christ.

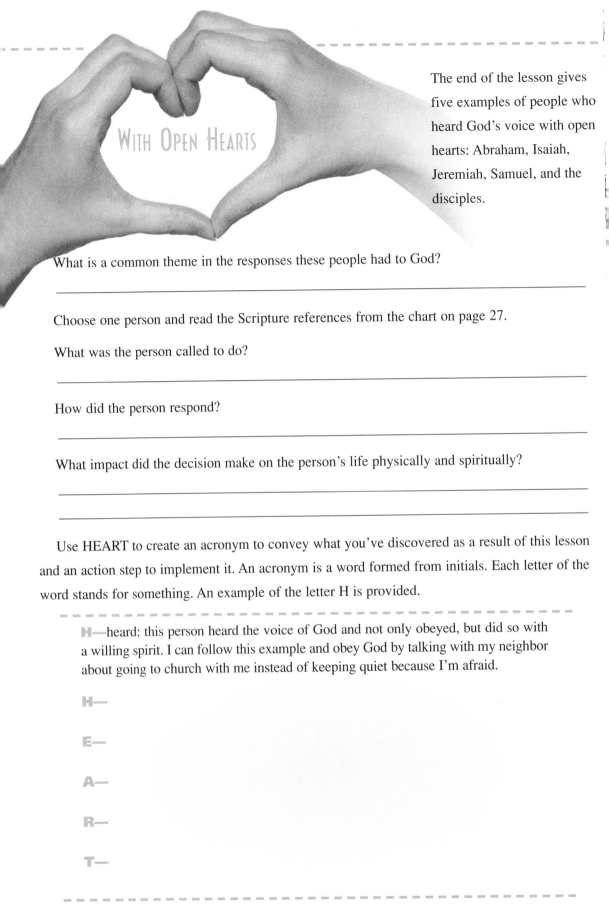

WITH OPEN HEARTS

The end of the lesson gives five examples of people who heard God's voice with open hearts: Abraham, Isaiah, Jeremiah, Samuel, and the disciples.

What is a common theme in the responses these people had to God?

_____

Choose one person and read the Scripture references from the chart on page 27.

What was the person called to do?

_____

How did the person respond?

_____

What impact did the decision make on the person's life physically and spiritually?

_____

_____

Use HEART to create an acronym to convey what you've discovered as a result of this lesson and an action step to implement it. An acronym is a word formed from initials. Each letter of the word stands for something. An example of the letter H is provided.

H—heard: this person heard the voice of God and not only obeyed, but did so with a willing spirit. I can follow this example and obey God by talking with my neighbor about going to church with me instead of keeping quiet because I'm afraid.

H—

E—

A—

R—

T—

Make every effort to enter God's rest through faith in Jesus Christ.

FAITH—THE KEY TO ENTERING GOD'S REST

Hebrews 4:1–16

WHY THIS MATTERS

Consistent, adequate sleep may be as important to good health as proper diet and exercise. It allows the body to rebuild, relax, and refresh. Stress and anxiety do not trouble the heart and mind during sound, restful sleep. Further, a good sleep pattern may help to prolong life for cancer patients. The Cancer Prevention Study II of the American Cancer Society followed more than a million participants for six years. The best survival rate was found among those who slept about seven hours a night, the worst among those who slept less than four and a half hours.

This lesson inspires us to enjoy the spiritual rest God offers His people. This rest lets us cast aside our anxieties and approach the throne of grace confidently.

BIBLE COMMENTARY

By Stephen B. Smith

The book of Hebrews is a beautifully crafted sermon that is masterfully designed to teach and encourage the Christians to whom it was sent. We do not know for sure who the author of the book was or the exact date of its composition. However, the rich biblical exposition and soul-stirring challenges of this writer are as relevant for us today as they were nearly two thousand years ago. Most likely this sermon was written in the latter half of the first century and sent as a letter to a house church made up of Christians from a Jewish background, possibly living in the area of Rome. It seems they had grown discouraged and were tempted to turn back from following Christ to the comfort and familiarity of Judaism. Since Judaism was an approved religion in the Roman Empire, they could avoid the Roman persecution that had or was soon to plague the Christian community. They could also evade the shame and ridicule heaped upon them by friends and family who did not understand why they would follow this new way of Christianity.

The passionate, pastoral heart of the author came through clearly as he did his best to motivate and encourage his audience to persevere in following Christ and "hold firmly to the faith we profess" (4:14). His sermon is a combination of alternating sections that explain passages from the Old Testament and sections that strongly exhort them to continue on the pilgrimage they had begun toward the heavenly city. The central purpose of this sermon was to cause the listeners to understand the superiority of Jesus Christ and the sufficient provision He has made that enabled them to enjoy fellowship with God and lead faithful lives, ultimately joining Him and all the heroes of the faith in the heavenly homeland forever.

Chapter 4 comes at the conclusion of the opening section (1:1—4:13) of this book, which demonstrates the superiority of the Son's message over the

KEY VERSE

Let us then approach the throne of grace with confidence, so that we may receive mercy and find grace to help us in our time of need.

—Hebrews 4:16

BACKGROUND SCRIPTURES

Numbers 13–14
   The wilderness generation disobeyed God.

Psalm 139
   We can never escape from the presence of God.

James 1:22–25
   We must be hearers *and* doers of the Word.

Matthew 11:28–30
   Jesus offers rest to all who will come to Him.

DAILY BIBLE READINGS

Monday: Isaiah 30:15–18
Tuesday: Ephesians 3:14–21
Wednesday: John 10:1–10
Thursday: Matthew 11:25–30
Friday: John 14:25–31
Saturday: Hebrews 4:1–16
Sunday: Psalm 18:1–3, 16–19

WHAT DO YOU THINK?
What happens when a
person unites the truth of
God's Word with faith?
What happens when God's
truth is not united with faith?

former revelation that came through the prophets and the angels, as well as His supremacy over the great leader of God's people, Moses the lawgiver. Verses 14–16 are a bridge leading us into the central section of this book (4:14–10:31), which describes this great high priest, Jesus Christ, and the perfect sacrifice He has made on our behalf. This chapter progresses from the warning and encouragement not to fail to enter God's rest (vv. 1–11) to the reality of our complete exposure before the living Word (vv. 12–13) and concludes with the wonderful hope of our great High Priest (vv. 14–16). He has provided all the resources we need to enter God's rest and successfully pass examination before the penetrating Word of God.

The Danger of Failing to Enter God's Rest (Heb. 4:1–5)

In the preceding section (3:7–19), the writer used Psalm 95:7–11 to show his listeners the danger of failing to believe and obey God. The psalmist referred to the events of Numbers 13–14 in which the children of Israel failed to enter the Promised Land of Canaan. Instead, they doubted God's ability to lead them victoriously against the land's inhabitants and rebelled against the leadership of Moses and Aaron. They are often referred to as the "wilderness generation" because their disobedience resulted in their deaths in the wilderness instead of entering the land of security and rest. The recipients of the letter to the Hebrews would have known Psalm 95 from worship, so the writer used it to set up a sharp contrast between those who obey and enter God's rest and those who do not.

The promise of entering his rest still stands (Heb. 4:1), but they must **be careful** not to end up like the wilderness generation. They should not give in to the same disobedience and failure. The NASB captures the importance of the first phrase of this verse by following it with "let us fear" (rather than the NIV's

AHA!
Rest is God's reward!

The Disobedient Example of the Wilderness Generation versus the Proper Response	
They did not combine the message they heard with faith (v. 2).	We are to believe and enter God's rest (v. 3).
They could not enter God's rest because of their disobedience (v. 6).	We must hear God's voice today and not harden our hearts against Him (v.7).
They left behind an example of failure because they insisted on doing things their own way (v. 11).	We are to rest from our own works and enter the rest based on God's example (v. 10).

"let us be careful). The danger was that, after hearing the gospel, they would be like **those who heard** that message, but **did not combine it with faith** (v. 2). The result of this failure was God's pronouncement from Psalm 95:11: "**So I declared on oath in my anger, 'They shall never enter my rest'**" (Heb. 4:3). It is not enough to just hear the Word; hearers must receive it in obedient faith and become doers of the Word (compare James 1:22–25).

DID YOU KNOW?
Hebrews attributes two
quotes from the Old
Testament to Christ
(2:11–12; 10:5).

This is the first time *faith* appears in the book of Hebrews, and it will reappear numerous times, especially in chapter 11. In this context, obedience is faith in action, as God's people are called to live as if God's power is real in the present and His promises for the future are certain. This life of active faith is the opposite of the wilderness generation's tragic example and ends in a completely different result, for **we who have believed enter that rest** (4:3).

In verse 4, the writer returned to the Old Testament to prove his point. Since Psalm 95 revealed that this rest is God's rest, he took his listeners to the natural place in the Old Testament where an explanation was offered of what God's rest looks like. Here he interpreted the Scriptures using a rabbinic technique known as "verbal analogy." Since the noun *rest* in Psalm 95:11 is from the same word family as the verb *rested* in Genesis 2:2, he associated these two passages to demonstrate that God's **work has been finished since the creation of the world** (Heb. 4:3). Consequently, this rest is patterned after the rest God himself entered into after finishing His work of creation. In the next section, the author stressed the importance for his hearers to properly respond to this rest.

The Command to Enter God's Rest Today (Heb. 4:6–11)

The rest that the Israelites forfeited **because of their disobedience** is still offered to those who respond in faith, and **it still remains that some will enter that rest** (v. 6). The writer again quoted from Psalm 95, this time directing his audience to focus on the word *today* (Ps. 95:7–8). **Today, if you hear his voice, do not harden your hearts** (Heb. 4:7). Anticipating the response that this promise referred to Canaan and was fulfilled when the next generation finally entered the land, he countered that **if Joshua had given them rest, God would not have spoken later about another day** (v. 8). In other words, the rest promised by God through David could not have been the rest Joshua had already given Israel. Thus, this important message of warning and encouragement was urged upon the Hebrews as a present-tense reality.

The writer concluded: **There remains, then, a Sabbath-rest for the people of God; for anyone who enters God's rest also rests from his own work, just as God did from his** (vv. 9–10). In combination with the earlier reference to God's rest after completing creation (v. 4), we can see that this rest the Hebrews are to enter into is based on the pattern of God's own rest and characterized by ceasing to seek after our own way and designs. Instead, the writer urged his audience to turn to God's plan for them with faithful and obedient hearts that are submissive to His will.

Ironically, they must **make every effort to enter** this resting, yielded fellowship with God (v. 11). Rather than **following their example of disobedience**, the Hebrews (and we) are to demonstrate the faith that the wilderness generation should have modeled, and must diligently strive to be both hearers and faithful doers of the Word of God.

Finally, the writer was concerned in verses 1–11 that all members of the community enter this rest and do their best to help those around them do the same. The Greek phrases in verse 1 ("that none of you be found to have fallen short") and verse 11 (**that no one will fall**) alert us to the fact that every individual is important. We must be concerned with the spiritual conditions of our Christian brothers and sisters and do our best to encourage them to faithfully and obediently persevere in following Christ and entering God's promised rest.

The Penetrating Word of God (Heb. 4:12–13)

These verses are an appropriate closing to the first major division of the book, which began with the announcement of God's speaking in these last days by His Son (1:1–2). The same Greek word is used for this **word of God** (v. 12)

"For the word of God is living and active. Sharper than any double-edged sword, it penetrates even to dividing soul and spirit, joints and marrow" (Heb. 4:12).

WHAT DO YOU THINK?
What is the difference between temptation and sin? How could Jesus be tempted and yet not sin?

AHA!
Jesus empathizes with me!

DID YOU KNOW?
Hebrews never names the human author of any Old Testament quote.

WHAT ABOUT YOU?
What affects your confidence when you approach the Lord?

as was used for the message the wilderness generation rejected in verse 2. However, this word of God is still **living and active** today, penetrating to the very depths of our being. It exposes even the motives behind our actions as **it judges the thoughts and attitudes of the heart** (v. 12). No one is exempt from this examination, since **nothing in all creation is hidden from God's sight** (v. 13; compare Ps. 139). This fact of God's completely accurate, all-encompassing, inescapable knowledge of our actions and intentions is either the best or worst news we could ever hear. For those who respond to the Word with faith and obediently enter into God's rest, there is the assurance that God sees and knows the hearts that are turned toward Him. But for those who foolishly follow the example of the wilderness generation, there is the assurance that nothing can be hidden from God, and He will ultimately call them to **give account** (v. 13) for their response to His Word.

Our Great High Priest (Heb. 4:14–16)

These final verses introduce the section of Hebrews (4:14—10:31) that describes our great High Priest, Jesus Christ, and His ministry. The power of His effective sacrifice provides the resources we need to do our part and enter into God's rest. These verses are also a bridge leading us from the discussion of God's word spoken through His Son (1:1—4:13) to the next part of the book, which describes the content of that revelation.

The writer stressed the fact that **we have a great high priest** (v. 14); as we will see in chapter 5, this High Priest is unlike any other high priest who ever served in the temple. He **has gone through the heavens** into the very presence of God. Because of this reality, we are to **hold firmly to the faith we profess** (v. 14).

Following this exhortation, the writer provided a further description of this great High Priest. He is not **unable to sympathize with our weaknesses**; instead, he **has been tempted in every way, just as we are** (v. 15). When Jesus Christ lived among us, He experienced the temptations, pains, and trials that are part of what it means to be a human being in a fallen world. He knows what we are going through in our day-to-day struggles. However, the writer added a vitally important qualification: Jesus **was without sin** (v. 15). This fact sets this great High Priest apart from all other high priests.

Because of this, the writer urged his listeners to **approach the throne of grace with confidence** (v. 16). This chapter that began with an exhortation to enter God's rest ends with the reason why we can do so: we have a great High Priest who knows what it is like to be human, has lived a sinless life, and has provided all of the resources we need to hear and obey God's voice. Because of Him, **we may receive mercy and find grace to help us in our time of need** (v. 16). This summary of the writer's message about our great High Priest presented in verses 14–16 captures the heart of his entire sermon. ✦

PRAYER
Lord, thank You for the Bible, which is able to pierce through any pretense. Thank You for a Savior who can empathize with any trial I may be experiencing.

HEBREWS 4:1–16

1 Therefore, since the promise of entering his rest still stands, let us be careful that none of you be found to have fallen short of it.

2 For we also have had the gospel preached to us, just as they did; but the message they heard was of no value to them, because those who heard did not combine it with faith.

3 Now we who have believed enter that rest, just as God has said, "So I declared on oath in my anger, 'They shall never enter my rest.'" And yet his work has been finished since the creation of the world.

4 For somewhere he has spoken about the seventh day in these words: "And on the seventh day God rested from all his work."

5 And again in the passage above he says, "They shall never enter my rest."

6 It still remains that some will enter that rest, and those who formerly had the gospel preached to them did not go in, because of their disobedience.

7 Therefore God again set a certain day, calling it Today, when a long time later he spoke through David, as was said before: "Today, if you hear his voice, do not harden your hearts."

8 For if Joshua had given them rest, God would not have spoken later about another day.

9 There remains, then, a Sabbath-rest for the people of God;

10 for anyone who enters God's rest also rests from his own work, just as God did from his.

11 Let us, therefore, make every effort to enter that rest, so that no one will fall by following their example of disobedience.

12 For the word of God is living and active. Sharper than any double-edged sword, it penetrates even to dividing soul and spirit, joints and marrow; it judges the thoughts and attitudes of the heart.

13 Nothing in all creation is hidden from God's sight. Everything is uncovered and laid bare before the eyes of him to whom we must give account.

14 Therefore, since we have a great high priest who has gone through the heavens, Jesus the Son of God, let us hold firmly to the faith we profess.

15 For we do not have a high priest who is unable to sympathize with our weaknesses, but we have one who has been tempted in every way, just as we are—yet was without sin.

16 Let us then approach the throne of grace with confidence, so that we may receive mercy and find grace to help us in our time of need.

Faith—The Key to Entering God's Rest

Make every effort to enter God's rest through faith in Jesus Christ.

INTO THE SUBJECT

Nearly everyone values rest, whether it is nighttime rest or a well-earned vacation. But entering God's rest deserves our greatest attention. How do we enter His rest?

INTO THE WORD

1. Why didn't the Israelites in the wilderness enter into God's rest (Heb. 4:2, 6)?

2. How do you know life in Canaan was not the ultimate rest God had promised?

3. How do you know we cannot enter God's rest by performing good works (v. 10)?

4. How does verse 12 complement the truth that God looks at the heart?

5. Why are pure motives and attitudes so important in what we say and do?

6. Why is it futile to pretend to be God's follower (v. 13)?

7. Find in verses 14–15 several facts about our great High Priest Jesus that distinguish Him from all the other high priests in Israel's history.

8. When you pray, how confident are you that your deepest needs will be met? What truths in verses 14–15 boost your confidence?

INTO THE WORLD

Possessing spiritual rest does not exempt the believer from trials and crises, but roll your cares onto Jesus' shoulders and demonstrate true rest before those who are examining your testimony daily.

Rest and Persevere

The author of Hebrews urged the listeners to enter God's rest and persevere in their faith. Allow the words hidden in this word search to be reminders of our need to enter God's rest and seek after Him. Words can be up, down, left to right, right to left, or diagonal.

```
P  V  Z  U  I  Z  N  E  M  R  C  Y  T  E  X  K  A  Z  O  Q
C  O  N  F  I  D  E  N  C  E  E  H  Q  C  F  I  T  E  B  C
H  C  A  O  R  P  P  A  D  P  O  C  D  N  F  X  T  T  P  F
S  P  T  S  E  I  D  L  A  U  E  N  E  E  B  Q  I  Q  O  H
O  W  A  C  W  W  O  O  G  J  A  R  K  I  N  C  T  N  Y  E
X  C  E  G  P  H  O  H  L  M  L  T  S  D  V  D  U  V  C  A
M  G  A  R  M  B  T  U  M  T  P  L  W  E  M  E  D  L  E  R
K  R  S  C  B  S  R  O  G  R  G  L  W  B  V  Q  E  X  Z  T
V  F  V  M  U  E  C  G  I  N  W  G  T  O  E  E  S  R  X  S
S  A  B  B  A  T  H  E  I  P  B  O  W  S  S  D  R  S  N  M
Q  I  J  B  X  Y  S  T  T  L  K  T  R  I  I  H  R  E  X  K
W  O  R  K  W  T  A  G  O  O  A  Z  A  D  M  G  T  C  T  F
Q  H  K  Q  K  R  R  E  T  N  E  J  I  P  O  N  D  I  R  Z
L  F  B  D  T  H  C  Q  Y  K  C  J  G  G  R  J  E  W  A  L
X  E  G  E  N  I  I  Z  A  Z  A  H  Q  N  P  E  X  H  G  F
H  Z  N  B  A  Y  I  G  H  V  R  V  L  Q  G  I  Z  J  K  A
Q  E  K  Q  S  Q  J  A  Z  V  G  B  F  S  D  D  M  V  F  U
P  C  L  L  E  V  X  N  W  N  G  A  W  F  I  O  G  O  I  W
T  A  H  A  I  N  C  X  G  G  V  H  I  L  C  X  N  A  Z  S
X  T  P  T  M  F  T  V  U  U  Y  W  G  X  M  D  E  L  B  W
```

APPROACH	ENTER	HOLD	RECEIVE
ATTITUDES	FAITH	PENETRATING	SABBATH
COMMAND	GRACE	PERSEVERE	THOUGHTS
CONFIDENCE	HEARTS	PRIEST	WORD
DISOBEDIENCE	HEBREWS	PROMISE	WORK

What is one way you can persevere for your faith? Write it on an index card and put the card on your fridge as a reminder of how to persevere.

INTERACTIVE LEARNING IDEAS

GET THE CLASS INVOLVED
Valuing God's Truth

The writer of Hebrews wrote that some people do not value the good news of Christ's work on their behalf because they do not receive the message in faith. However, for those who believe, the message has infinite value. To be fruitful and to never take God for granted, we must keep reminding ourselves of these things.

To highlight this value, play a word-association game with the class. You will call out certain words that are associated with the good news of the gospel. Then, the students, in response, should offer a two-to-three-word phrase that illustrates the eternal value of the word you offered.

For example, you might say, "Salvation." In return, the students might respond with, "Reconciled with God," "Forgiveness," "Peace on earth," or "Heaven awaits."

Repeat this exercise using the following words: To warm up: *vocation*, *vacation*, *evaluation*. Then offer these salvation-related words: *atonement*, *the cross*, *resurrection*, *reconciliation*, *purpose*, *kingdom*.

When everyone has finished, discuss further the "value-added" phrases of every aspect of our salvation. In doing so, we heed the warning in today's text to not take the salvation of God lightly, but instead, to connect the content of God's truth with saving faith.

TRY THIS ON YOUR OWN
Time to Reflect

Hebrews 4 focuses on how God rested in His work, and how we should imitate Him in this regard. We look forward to entering His rest when our journey is over, but we also need to get reenergized along the way.

What kinds of restful activities "recharge" your batteries? Introverts tend to gain energy when they're by themselves, and extroverts generally gain energy when they're around others.

Either way, set aside some time each week to reflect on what has happened over the past week, and what you think is going to happen over the coming week. Devote these things to prayer. Ask God what He's trying to teach you through these events. Don't burn out in your faith because you're not getting enough rest.

TAKING IT TO THE STREET
Tempted in Every Way

Jesus was tempted in every way that we are, and yet He did not sin, ever, in response to those temptations. Giving in to temptations is what relieves their "pressure." Jesus never gave in, and so bore the full weight of His temptations.

Take a walk through an indoor mall, and point out (to each other) all the things that might be tempting. For example, to overeat at the food court; to steal something you cannot afford; or to spend money on an extravagance that your family had set aside for something else.

Talk about the respective weights that go with these temptations. What ways of escape has God provided for each of these? What would be the consequences of giving in to these temptations? What are the spiritual benefits of "riding out" the temptations without giving in to them?

WITH YOUR FAMILY
Rest Day

The writer of Hebrews wrote that a Sabbath rest awaits the people of God. They will rest as God rested from His work of creation (Heb. 4:9).

Spend the entire day as a family doing something that is restful and fun for everyone. Be sure each person's interests are represented in the day's events. You could go camping by a lake, spending the day fishing, hiking, and perhaps just sitting around a campfire. You might want to go visit some relatives and spend a quiet day in their home catching up on things.

At the end of the day, have dinner together and talk about the day's events. Discuss how taking time to rest gives our bodies a chance to slow down and gives us some time to think and reflect about all God is trying to accomplish through us. ◆

Jesus is uniquely qualified to be our high priest.

LESSON 5

JESUS MEETS THE QUALIFICATIONS
Hebrews 5:1–14

KEY VERSE

And, once made perfect, he became the source of eternal salvation for all who obey him.

—Hebrews 5:9

BACKGROUND SCRIPTURES

Psalm 2:7
    The divine sonship of Jesus
Psalm 110:4
    The eternal High Priesthood of Jesus
Luke 22:42
    The obedient submission of Jesus in the garden of Gethsemane
Numbers 15:22–31
    Sins of ignorance contrasted with presumptuous sins
Ephesians 4:11–16
    How to progress in spiritual maturity

DAILY BIBLE READINGS

Monday: Hebrews 10:1–9
Tuesday: Philippians 2:5–11
Wednesday: Hebrews 10:19–25
Thursday: John 10:11–18
Friday: 1 Peter 1:3–9
Saturday: Hebrews 5:1–14
Sunday: Psalm 18:28–36

WHY THIS MATTERS

Unless an adult's digestive system can handle only baby food, adults choose to eat food they can sink their teeth into, chew, and mash. After a hard day of work, who wants to pop a tiny jar of strained veggies prepared for babies and spoon it into his or her mouth glob by glob? Steak and potatoes might seem much more tantalizing and appetizing.

Believers who choose to stay with a diet of elementary truths long after their conversion are like adults stuck on baby food. They need to progress from milk and soft food to solid food. They will not become mature believers until they sink their teeth into the meat of the Word.

This lesson motivates us to become mature believers.

BIBLE COMMENTARY

By Stephen B. Smith

The author of the book of Hebrews continued in chapter 5 with a mix of exposition of Old Testament Scriptures and exhortation to warn and encourage the people to whom he was writing. He moved from discussing God's Word spoken through His Son in 1:1—4:13 to the heart of the book of Hebrews, which describes the ministry of Jesus Christ in 4:14—10:31. The bridge into this section occurs in 4:14–16, where he discussed the resources provided for his audience by their great High Priest, Jesus the Son of God. He began to explain the high priesthood of Jesus, starting in 5:1–10 with a comparison and contrast between His ministry and the ministry of the high priests who were descendents of Aaron.

The Structure of the Comparison (*Chiasmus*) in Hebrews 5:1–10		
Aaron		**Jesus Christ**
v. 1	The high priesthoods of Aaron and Christ	v. 10
v. 2	High priestly ministry	v. 9
v. 2	Humanity of the high priest	v. 8
v. 3	Sacrifice of the high priest	v. 7
v. 4	Appointment of the high priest	vv. 5–6

In the development of verses 1–10, the writer used a carefully constructed literary device called a *chiasmus* to describe the two high priesthoods he was comparing and contrasting. Thus, his first and last points correspond, his second and second to last points are related, and so on (see chart above). This organized his discussion and made it easier for his audience to remember. It also focused their attention on the center section (vv. 4–6). The five elements of correspondence in this chiasmus are (1) the high priesthood of Aaron and the high priesthood of the Son (vv. 1, 10), (2) their high priestly ministries (vv. 2, 9), (3) their humanity (vv. 2, 8), (4) their sacrifices (vv. 3, 7), and (5) their appointments as high priests (vv. 4, 5–6).

The remainder of the chapter (vv. 11–14) is the beginning of an exhortation concerning the problem of spiritual immaturity.

A Mortal, Sinful High Priest (Heb. 5:1–4)

We must not let the chapter divisions in our English Bibles cause us to forget the relationship between 4:14–16 and 5:1–10. The writer introduced the great High Priest, Jesus, to his audience, and then contrasted this great High Priest with the mortal high priests who descended from the line of Aaron, the first high priest of Israel.

In verse 1, we find that **every high priest** must be **selected from among men** and **appointed to represent them in matters related to God**. Thus, he must be chosen as a representative of his fellow human beings; it is the job of the high priest to stand before God on their behalf. On the Day of Atonement (Lev. 16), he would enter the Most Holy Place and offer a sacrifice to make atonement for the people. There were also other times during the year in which he would **offer gifts and sacrifices for sins** (v. 1).

This Aaronic high priest was **able to deal gently** and compassionately with those he represented because **he himself** was **subject to weakness** (v. 2) in the same way they were. On the Day of Atonement, the high priest was required to make atonement for himself before he could represent the people. Because he also was **subject to weaknesses** (v. 2), **he** had **to offer sacrifices for his own sins, as well as for the sins of the people** (v. 3).

It should be pointed out that verse 2 describes the people he was making atonement for as **those who are ignorant and are going astray**. Under the Old Testament's sacrificial system, the priests were required to offer sacrifices for sins committed unintentionally or those that were not explicitly premeditated. The high priests were held to a high standard of holiness before God with even stricter regulations than those laid upon ordinary priests. They could not live in defiant rebellion against God; however, these men were still fallible human beings and needed atonement.

Finally, like their ancestor Aaron, these priests had to **be called by God** (v. 4). The priesthood was an important position, and **no one** took **this honor upon himself**. It was only bestowed upon a man who was appointed by God in accordance with the conditions God himself had established.

Next the writer turned to a comparison and contrast of this mortal, sinful high priest with the eternal, obedient High Priest, who was the focus of his entire sermon.

An Eternal, Obedient High Priest (Heb. 5:5–10)

In the structure of the chiasmus the preacher was using, his audience's attention was drawn in this central comparison (vv. 4–6) to the position of authority given to those high priests who were appointed by God. Even the Christ **did not take upon himself the glory of becoming a high priest** (v. 5). Instead, the author of Hebrews

Let us offer up our own prayers and petitions to the Lord. He hears us.

WHAT DO YOU THINK?
How spiritually mature are you? How do you know when you have grown in Christ?

AHA!
We can be in a constant state of spiritual growth!

DID YOU KNOW?
Since there is no mention of the temple's destruction, Hebrews was probably written before A.D. 70.

again returned to the Old Testament to demonstrate that He was appointed to this role of high priest by His Father. In verse 5, the preacher quoted Psalm 2:7, which he used at the beginning of his sermon to establish the divine Sonship of Jesus (Heb. 1:5). Also quoted is Psalm 110:4, where God instituted Christ as High Priest with the words, "**You are a priest forever, in the order of Melchizedek**" (Heb. 5:6). (The relationship between Jesus and Melchizedek will be further explored in Hebrews 7.) The preacher uses these two Old Testament quotations to tie together the Sonship and the priesthood of Jesus Christ. These two aspects have already been discussed independently (1:1–14; 2:16–18), but now we understand that they are inseparably linked and His high priesthood is effective because He is the Son of God. Building upon the superiority of the Son, which was seen in the first part of the book, we now find an incomparably superior High Priest who has been appointed to a position of unequaled authority.

The preacher then turned his focus to the ministry of the Son during His **life on earth** (v. 7). Perhaps referring to Jesus' prayer to His Father in the garden of Gethsemane, he said **he offered up prayers and petitions with loud cries and tears to the one who could save him from death, and he was heard because of his reverent submission** (v. 7). We see that although the Son willingly submitted to death on the cross in order to carry out His high priestly ministry, through His subsequent resurrection and exaltation to the right hand of the Father, He was indeed rescued from the power of death and now He triumphantly holds the keys of death and the grave (Rev. 1:18)!

Just as the Aaronic high priest could identify with the people he represented, Jesus, **although he was a son, . . . learned obedience from what he suffered** (Heb. 5:8). Even though this High Priest was exalted to the highest level of authority and prominence as the Son, He subjected himself to suffering during His life on earth, and lived out a pattern of obedient submission to the will of His Father, climaxing with His death on the cross. He learned obedience by being the paramount example of a life completely surrendered to doing the will of God. Unlike the Aaronic high priests, He never sinned (compare 4:15) or disobeyed His Father in any way; thus His ministry was infinitely more effective than theirs.

Because of this life of complete obedience, Jesus was **made perfect** and **became the source of eternal salvation for all who obey him** (v. 9). Here we see the strongest discontinuity between the effects of the Aaronic high priesthood and Jesus'. While they could only "deal gently" with sinners because they themselves were also "subject to weakness" (5:2), Jesus is able to provide **eternal salvation for all who obey him**. Any power that the Aaronic priesthood's often-repeated sacrifices had to atone for sin was provided through the once and for all sacrifice of the Son's obedient life and death. Jesus was made perfect, or complete, in the sense that He lived an obedient life and made an effective sacrifice that provides complete atonement for sin. The present active tense of the verb *obey* in verse 9 indicates that this eternal salvation is only available to those who continuously and consistently live a life modeled after the Son's complete submission to the will of His Father.

This section closes with a reaffirmation of God's appointment of the Son to a superior position of authority as a **high priest in the order of Melchizedek** (v. 10). This order was an eternal priesthood that vastly surpassed the limited ministries of the mortal, Aaronic high priests (compare 7:1–28).

The writer more fully explained the high priesthood of Jesus Christ throughout the rest of his sermon. However, he first turned his attention to a matter that could have prevented his listeners from understanding what he wanted to say. He addressed the problem of their spiritual immaturity and called them to a higher level.

The Problem of Spiritual Immaturity (Heb. 5:11–14)

Verses 11–14 begin an exhortation concerning the negative effects of spiritual immaturity; this section continues until 6:8. The author had **much to say about this** great High Priest and His ministry, but it was **hard to explain** because his audience was **slow to learn** (v. 11). This last phrase can literally be translated "dull of hearing" (KJV, NASB). Just as a person with a physical hearing handicap might struggle to hear the speech of others and even mishear or fail to understand important portions of conversations, the writer was impeded in his explanation because of the "spiritually hard-of-hearing" condition of his listeners. The fact that they were berated for this hearing problem shows there was something they could do about it. They fell into this condition because of their neglect to quickly and obediently act on what they had heard.

Although they **ought to be teachers** themselves, instead it was necessary for **someone** else **to teach** them **the elementary truths of God's word all over again** (v. 12). They were compared to infants who **need milk, not solid food** (vv. 12–13). This solid food is the **teaching about righteousness** (v. 13), which includes the instruction about Jesus' high priestly ministry and the benefits it entails for obedient believers. This teaching comes from the Word of God as it has been revealed through the Son.

In verse 14, the preacher revealed to his audience how this condition of spiritual immaturity might be avoided or remedied. The **solid food** that was vitally needed for them to grow and develop as they should **is for the mature, who by constant use have trained themselves to distinguish good from evil** (v. 14). The spiritual discernment of the believer concerning what is good or evil must be exercised faithfully for the person to make choices that please God. As Christians regularly give their spiritual discernment a workout, they participate in a "circle of maturity." That is, faithfully listening to God's Word and obeying Him leads to further spiritual development and deeper understanding of God's Word. This deepened understanding then allows one to hear more clearly God's voice and live a life of submissive obedience. This process of growth and development enables the believer to live in a way that increasingly resembles the example of our eternal, obedient High Priest, who lived a life of "reverent submission" to His Father's will (5:7) and is now "the source of eternal salvation for all who obey him" (v. 9). ◆

WHAT ABOUT YOU?
What's the next level in whatever stage of spiritual maturity you find yourself? How will you get there?

PRAYER
Lord, teach me to learn obedience through suffering, just as Jesus did. Increase my confidence that You use everything in my life, even my trials and tribulations; You waste nothing.

INTERACTIVE LEARNING IDEAS

GET THE CLASS INVOLVED
Spiritual Maturity

The writer of Hebrews chided his original readers for not being more mature in the faith. At the time, they should have been able to be teachers. Instead, they were still trying to grapple with the rudimentary teachings of the faith. They should have been able to handle "meat" like adults, not merely "milk" as spiritual infants.

To better understand this concept, choose five people in your class to play the role of toddler, child, adolescent, young adult, and mature adult. Give them an everyday scenario, and ask them to interpret the meaning of what has happened, according to their role-played age level.

End the activity with a brief discussion about varying levels of spiritual maturity.

TRY THIS ON YOUR OWN
Lessons in Suffering

Jesus learned obedience through suffering (Heb. 5:8). What has God taught you through the trials of life?

Get out a piece of paper and lay it as landscape. Draw a line at the bottom of the paper. On this line, draw marks for the number of years you've been alive.

Now, draw a simple up and down line graph of your life, noting the peaks (when things were going well), with the valleys (during difficult circumstances). Label the peaks and valleys according to what happening during those times.

How did your perspective changes during the peaks and valleys? Is it easier to see what God was doing in hindsight than during the trials? If so, why? Did you feel closer to God during the peak periods or during the valleys? Explain. What was He teaching you during those times?

TAKING IT TO THE STREET
Food Metaphors

The original readers of Hebrews were rebuked for not advancing along in their spiritual maturity as they ought. They were like babies longing for milk, instead of mature adults living on solid food (Heb. 5:13–14).

Take a trip together to a grocery store and extend this spiritual nutrition and growth analogy. Go down each aisle and talk about what each food group might represent.

Meat might be the solid truth of God's Word. Bread reminds of Jesus as the bread of life. Water is the living water of God's Spirit. Vitamin-rich produce might represent the healthy exercise of spiritual gifts and peaceful relationships within the body of Christ. Without these things, we would perish (spiritually speaking).

The candy aisle might represent sugary gossip. The diet foods aisle might represent the consequences of spiritual gluttony. The baby food aisle might represent those who are stuck in the spiritual growth process.

WITH YOUR FAMILY
Age Levels

Spiritual growth and maturity can be likened to different age levels (Heb. 5:13–14). New Christians are like babies, who can then go through stages of growth parallel to childhood, adolescence, young adulthood, and then mature adulthood.

Identify the stage of life for each member of the family. Talk about what is unique about each person at his or her particular stage of life. Perhaps some of the older people can reflect (out loud) on what life was like for them at various ages.

Conclude the discussion by talking about the "next step" for each person, spiritually speaking. Should that person focus on Bible study, or any of the spiritual disciplines? Should that person find new ways to exercise his or her spiritual gifts? Are there any unresolved conflicts that need to be addressed? Help each person determine his or her best "next step." ◆

> "Solid food is for the mature, who by constant use have trained themselves to distinguish good from evil."
>
> —*Hebrews 5:14*

HEBREWS 5:1–14

1 Every high priest is selected from among men and is appointed to represent them in matters related to God, to offer gifts and sacrifices for sins.
2 He is able to deal gently with those who are ignorant and are going astray, since he himself is subject to weakness.
3 This is why he has to offer sacrifices for his own sins, as well as for the sins of the people.
4 No one takes this honor upon himself; he must be called by God, just as Aaron was.
5 So Christ also did not take upon himself the glory of becoming a high priest. But God said to him, "You are my Son; today I have become your Father."
6 And he says in another place, "You are a priest forever, in the order of Melchizedek."
7 During the days of Jesus' life on earth, he offered up prayers and petitions with loud cries and tears to the one who could save him from death, and he was heard because of his reverent submission.
8 Although he was a son, he learned obedience from what he suffered
9 and, once made perfect, he became the source of eternal salvation for all who obey him
10 and was designated by God to be high priest in the order of Melchizedek.
11 We have much to say about this, but it is hard to explain because you are slow to learn.
12 In fact, though by this time you ought to be teachers, you need someone to teach you the elementary truths of God's word all over again. You need milk, not solid food!
13 Anyone who lives on milk, being still an infant, is not acquainted with the teaching about righteousness.
14 But solid food is for the mature, who by constant use have trained themselves to distinguish good from evil.

"[Jesus] offered up prayers and petitions with loud cries."
—*Hebrews 5:7*

Jesus Meets the Qualifications

Jesus is uniquely qualified to be our high priest.

INTO THE SUBJECT

Likely you have interviewed for a job and been asked about your qualifications. How was Jesus qualified for the position and ministry of high priest?

INTO THE WORD

1. According to Hebrews 5:1, what were the responsibilities of every high priest?

2. What proof do you find in verses 2–3 that each of Israel's high priests was imperfect?

3. Verses 4–5 cite both similarities and differences between Israel's high priests and Jesus, our High Priest. What similarities do you find? What differences do you find?

4. Reflecting on the life and ministry of Jesus, what suffering did He experience?

5. On what occasions did Jesus pray?

6. What specific event do you think verse 7 refers to?

7. What indications that Jesus was truly human as well as truly God do you find in verses 7–9?

8. How does verse 9 show that salvation is based on Christ and not on works?

9. How does God's Word help you grow stronger every day?

INTO THE WORLD

Let others know this week that Jesus is distinctly qualified to be their Savior and High Priest.

Avoid or Remedy?

Fill in the blanks. Try to do as much as you can without looking at the lesson.

1. The two themes that emerge from this passage are: the identity and _____ between the high priests and the people they _____.

2. Under the Old Testament's sacrificial system, priests were required to offer _____ for sins both unintentional and premeditated.

3. Jesus learned obedience by being an example of a life that was _____ _____ to doing the will of God.

4. Christians must give their spiritual discipline a _____ to grow in spiritual _____.

The author of Hebrews says that spiritual immaturity can be avoided or remedied. What spiritual muscles have you allowed to atrophy?

_____

_____

_____

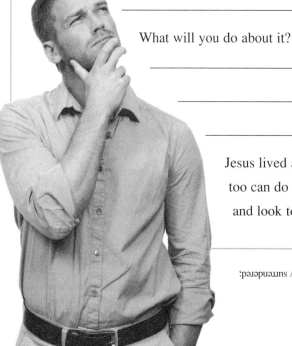

What will you do about it?

_____

_____

_____

Jesus lived a life of reverent submission to God. We too can do so when we acknowledge our weaknesses and look to God for help.

Christian perfection is a lifelong pursuit in full cooperation with God.

PURSUING PERFECTION
Hebrews 6:1–20

WHY THIS MATTERS

Ron, a retired high school history teacher, maintains a website that promotes atheism. But he hasn't always been an atheist. As a matter of fact, he used to profess to be a believer. He grew up espousing biblical truth, and in his youth, he graduated from a Bible college. His classmates admired his devotion to Christ and his ability to teach Sunday school children successfully. His friends say Ron's departure from the faith occurred after Bible college, when he studied education at a secular university.

One thing is clear: Ron chose to fall away.

This lesson inspires us to choose *not* to fall away, but to go on to maturity in Christ.

BIBLE COMMENTARY

By Lee M. Haines

The author of Hebrews wrote to show that "Christ is better." In 1:1–4, he declared Christ to be better than the prophets. In chapters 1–7, he showed Christ to be better than other mediators: better than angels (1:5—2:18), better than Moses (3:1—4:13), and better than Aaron (4:14—7:28). In this latter section, he declared Christ to be a sympathetic High Priest (4:14–16) and a perfect High Priest (5:1–10). In Hebrews 5:6, the author quoted from Psalm 110:4, saying our Lord is "a priest forever, in the order of Melchizedek." And then in 5:10, he declared that Christ "was designated by God to be high priest in the order of Melchizedek." But then he stepped aside from that discussion and did not return to it again until 6:20 and 7:1.

The material between 5:10 and 7:1 is one of several digressions or interludes from the main discussion, which is more theological in nature. These interludes are given to practical exhortations. (For the other interludes, see 2:1–4; 3:7–19; 4:11–16; 10:19–39; 12:25–29; 13:9–16.) In 5:11—6:20, the author expressed a deep pastoral concern for the Hebrew Christians to whom he was writing. He was fearful that their slowness to grow and mature in Christ may have hindered them in understanding what he would say about Christ as a high priest in the order of Melchizedek. And beginning with Hebrews 6, he exhorted them to "go on to maturity." He warned them of possible irrevocable loss if they did not. He assured them that this did not have to happen. And he exhorted them to pursue a "maturity" (NIV), "perfection" (KJV), or completeness anchored in the love of Jesus.

The Need to Go On (Heb. 6:1–3)

The author had called his readers to task for their spiritual immaturity; they had been Christians long enough that they should have been teaching others

KEY VERSE

Therefore let us leave the elementary teachings about Christ and go on to maturity, not laying again the foundation of repentance from acts that lead to death, and of faith in God.
—Hebrews 6:1

BACKGROUND SCRIPTURES

Genesis 22:16
    God's oath to Abraham
Psalm 110:4
    A priest in the order
    of Melchizedek
Acts 6:3–6; 8:17; 9:17–18;
13:2–3; 18:24–26; 19:1–6;
28:8
    Laying on of hands
Philippians 1:6
    God will continue the
    work He began.
2 Timothy 1:6
    Gifts conferred by the
    laying on of hands

DAILY BIBLE READINGS

Monday: Hebrews
             13:18–21
Tuesday: 1 Thessalonians
             3:6–13
Wednesday: Philippians
             3:12–21
Thursday: Philippians
             2:12–18
Friday: Matthew
             5:43–48
Saturday: Hebrews 6:1–20
Sunday: Psalm 19:7–14

WHAT DO YOU THINK?
What causes some believers to get stuck, spiritually speaking? What is the remedy?

AHA!
God will never forget what we've done for Him!

DID YOU KNOW?
It was common to lay hands on someone during a commissioning for service in the first century.

(Heb. 5:11–14). Then he told them what they were to leave and what they were to go on to. They were to **leave the elementary teachings about Christ** (v. 1). Three pairs of elementary teachings are listed. Some scholars have thought the elementary teachings were familiar elements from Judaism, which foreshadowed or pointed forward to the Christian gospel. These needed to be left behind for the Hebrews to really become Christians. Other scholars have thought the elementary teachings were matters taught to new converts at the beginning of their Christian experience in a kind of catechism. These introductory truths needed to left behind to go on to the deeper truths of the gospel. The fact that the elementary teachings were about Christ tends to establish the second interpretation. The writer to the Hebrews spoke of these as the foundation that does not need to be, nor should it be, laid **again**. It was time to grow up, to **go on to maturity** or "perfection" (KJV). The words used for "perfect" and "perfection" in the New Testament refer to wholeness, completeness—everything in that should be in, and nothing that shouldn't. John spoke repeatedly of love made perfect or complete (1 John 4:12, 17–18).

The first pair of elementary teachings is **repentance from acts that lead to death** and **faith in God**. Repentance is not just being sorry for being "caught," nor even just a genuine sorrow because of sins committed. The word signifies a complete change of mind and a reversal of direction. Repentance is a significant emphasis in the Old Testament as God sought to transform His people. John the Baptist, Jesus, and the apostles repeatedly called for repentance in announcing the good news of salvation. It has always been the first response required of humans when turning to God. But it must be paired with faith in God. For the Jews, the Old Testament had virtually equated believing God with obeying God. For the Christian, this is a call to faith in His love and invitation, faith in His Son, whom the Father provided as our sacrifice.

The second pair of elementary teachings includes **instruction about baptisms** and **the laying on of hands** (v. 2). "Baptisms" could also be translated "washings." The Hebrews would be well acquainted with the ceremonial washings of the Old Testament for cleansing from ceremonial uncleanness. And they performed a kind of baptism on Gentiles who converted to Judaism. For the Christians, baptism in water was the initiating ritual for those being added to the church. The plural form, "baptisms," is unusual. However, John the Baptist talked about two baptisms—one in water and one in the Holy Spirit. Priscilla and Aquila in Acts 18:24–26, and Paul in Acts 19:1–6, taught about the differences between the two. Perhaps, in the catechism classes, converts were taught the differences. The "laying on of hands" was familiar from the Old Testament in the conferring of a blessing (Gen. 48:10–20), the offering of a sacrifice to God (Ex. 29:10), and in setting a person apart for an office or ministry (Num. 27:18–22; Deut. 34:9). In the New Testament church, the laying on of hands was used to impart the gift of the Holy Spirit (Acts 8:17; 9:17–18), commission persons to service (6:3–6; 13:2–3), bring healing (28:8), and confer a blessing or spiritual gift (2 Tim. 1:6).

The third pair of elementary teachings spoke about matters yet to come: **the resurrection of the dead** and **eternal judgment** (v. 2)—the one very promising, the other potentially very threatening. These were mostly just hinted at in the Old Testament, but resurrection and the final judgment were more fully developed in Judaism in the centuries between the Old Testament and the New Testament. In the teachings of Jesus and the apostles, they were strong emphases. They dealt with eternal destiny.

The Danger of Falling Away (Heb. 6:4–8)

In this passage, the writer to the Hebrews wrote some of the most solemn words in the New Testament. He spoke of persons thoroughly converted to Christ as indicated by five evidences: they had **once been enlightened,** they had **tasted the heavenly gift** (salvation), they had **shared in the Holy Spirit**, they had **tasted the goodness of the word of God** (both written and spoken) **and the powers of the coming age** (experiencing or performing miracles or mighty acts in the service of God) (vv. 4–5). This is not a description of persons with a shallow or superficial acquaintance with the gospel. The word *tasted* used here repeatedly also can be translated "partake of" or "enjoy." It was also used by this same writer with reference to Jesus' death on the cross, speaking in Hebrews 2:9 of His "tasting" (KJV) death. The persons referred to had been truly and fully converted.

If such persons fall away, **it is impossible for** them **to be brought back to repentance.** This is **because . . . they are crucifying the Son of God all over again** (vv. 4, 6). The falling away is not just a matter of spiritually slipping and falling. Forgiveness for that is readily available (1 John 2:1–2). It is not a mere stumbling or temporary backsliding. Falling away is an intentional, willful rejection of Christ after having known Him intimately. In effect, they are crucifying the Son of God all over again. The writer to the Hebrews said it is possible for believers, advanced in the faith, to willfully rebel, to fall away, and be lost. If such is true of the mature, how much greater is the danger of those who cling to spiritual babyhood and fail to go on to maturity in Christ?

Does the writer mean to say there is no hope for truly and fully converted persons who fall away? The word translated "because" in verse 6 can also be translated "while." Thus it would mean that such persons could not be brought back to repentance *while* they were crucifying Christ again. If such persons would turn from their rebellion, repentance would still be possible. But the awful truth remains that willful and sustained rejection of the Savior after having a relationship with Him *can* lead to total and final lostness. The writer then illustrated the results from agriculture, as land producing good crops is blessed and land producing bad crops is cursed. This is not intended to teach that persons who serve the Lord well will be saved and those who serve Him poorly will be lost. Salvation is a matter of relationship rather than a matter of performance. But while the keeping is done by the Lord, the repentance and faith that first led the believer to salvation is to be continued as obedience and faith throughout this life.

Need for Faith and Patience (Heb. 6:9–12)

The writer hastened to say that he did not believe that his readers had fallen away so as to be without hope. **We are confident of better things in your**

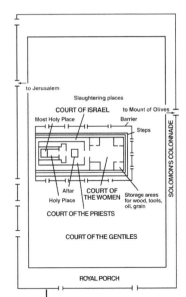

THE TEMPLE IN JESUS' DAY
Illustration of the temple, showing the inner sanctuary behind the curtain

WHAT DO YOU THINK?
How do you know when someone is telling you the truth? What factors affect your ability to trust someone?

AHA!
God never lies!

DID YOU KNOW?
The Greek word for "falling away" is found only in Hebrews.

case—**things that accompany salvation** (v. 9). They had **shown** their **love** to **God** by helping and continuing to help **his people**. God would not forget their **love** or their **work** (v. 10). But instead of tarrying in immaturity, they were **to show . . . diligence to the very end** (v. 11). They were not to **become lazy**. Rather, they were to **imitate** others who **through faith and patience** had inherited **what has been promised** (v. 12), making their **hope sure** (v. 11) or certain—faith in God who will always do His part, and for their part patience, persistence, steadfastness, endurance, pursuing the perfection or completeness available in Christ. The apostle Paul said on one occasion that he was "confident of this, that he who began a good work in you will carry it on to completion until the day of Christ Jesus" (Phil. 1:6). This is what the writer to the Hebrews was saying also.

WHAT ABOUT YOU?
What will keep you spiritually diligent to the end of your race?

PRAYER
Lord, teach me to desire growth; may I never become complacent in my faith. Spur me on to become more and more like Jesus every day.

Our Anchor in Jesus (Heb. 6:13–20)

The writer to the Hebrews wanted to emphasize strongly the certainty of his readers' hope in Christ. So he turned to the Old Testament and cited their founding father, Abraham. He reminded his readers of God's promise to childless Abraham that he would have innumerable descendants, beginning with a son through Sarah (Gen. 12:1–3, 7; 13:14–17; 15:1–19; 17:1–22; 18:10–15; 22:15–18). And God had not stopped, even with seven promises. At the time of the last promise, God added to His **promise** (v. 13, which was guarantee enough) an **oath** (v. 16) to make it doubly sure. He said, "I swear by myself" (Gen. 22:16). The writer to the Hebrews pointed out that **men swear by someone greater than themselves, and the oath confirms what is said and puts an end to all argument** (v. 16). There was no one greater than God for God to swear by, so He swore by himself. Thus there should be no question about the certainty of the promise.

Seven Practical Exhortations in Hebrews	
Hebrews 2:1–4	Beware of drifting
Hebrews 3:7–19	Beware of doubting
Hebrews 4:11–16	Beware of delaying
Hebrews 5:11—6:12	Beware of spiritual deadness
Hebrews 10:19–39	Beware of denying Christ
Hebrews 12:25–29	Beware of denying God's mercy
Hebrews 13:9–16	Beware of departing from God

adapted from Charles W. Carter, *The Wesleyan Bible Commentary* (Eerdmans, 1966)

The writer to the Hebrews picked up on this. It was **because God wanted to make the unchanging nature of his purpose very clear** (v. 17). This was **so that, by two unchangeable things** (promise and oath) **in which it is impossible for God to lie, we who have fled to take hold of the hope offered to us may be greatly encouraged** (v. 18). This hope is **an anchor for the soul**. Like an anchor, it is **firm and secure** (v. 19). But it is a most unusual anchor. Other anchors reach down through the watery depths to grasp something and hold tight. This one reaches up into heaven where the real temple is. **It enters the inner sanctuary**, the Most Holy Place, **behind the curtain** or veil, fastening itself in the place that most fully represents the reality and presence of God. Our hope can do so because Jesus, our High Priest, **has entered** there **on our behalf** (v. 20). He did so through His death; our hope, our certainty, and our anchor were purchased by His love. ✦

HEBREWS 6:1–20

1 Therefore let us leave the elementary teachings about Christ and go on to maturity, not laying again the foundation of repentance from acts that lead to death, and of faith in God,

2 instruction about baptisms, the laying on of hands, the resurrection of the dead, and eternal judgment.

3 And God permitting, we will do so.

4 It is impossible for those who have once been enlightened, who have tasted the heavenly gift, who have shared in the Holy Spirit,

5 who have tasted the goodness of the word of God and the powers of the coming age,

6 if they fall away, to be brought back to repentance, because to their loss they are crucifying the Son of God all over again and subjecting him to public disgrace.

7 Land that drinks in the rain often falling on it and that produces a crop useful to those for whom it is farmed receives the blessing of God.

8 But land that produces thorns and thistles is worthless and is in danger of being cursed. In the end it will be burned.

9 Even though we speak like this, dear friends, we are confident of better things in your case—things that accompany salvation.

10 God is not unjust; he will not forget your work and the love you have shown him as you have helped his people and continue to help them.

11 We want each of you to show this same diligence to the very end, in order to make your hope sure.

12 We do not want you to become lazy, but to imitate those who through faith and patience inherit what has been promised.

13 When God made his promise to Abraham, since there was no one greater for him to swear by, he swore by himself,

14 saying, "I will surely bless you and give you many descendants."

15 And so after waiting patiently, Abraham received what was promised.

16 Men swear by someone greater than themselves, and the oath confirms what is said and puts an end to all argument.

17 Because God wanted to make the unchanging nature of his purpose very clear to the heirs of what was promised, he confirmed it with an oath.

18 God did this so that, by two unchangeable things in which it is impossible for God to lie, we who have fled to take hold of the hope offered to us may be greatly encouraged.

Pursuing Perfection

Christian perfection is a lifelong pursuit in full cooperation with God.

INTO THE SUBJECT

It would be tragic if an adult with average intelligence knew only after his ABCs and numbers from one to ten. Isn't it even more tragic if a Christian fails to progress beyond the elementary teachings about Christ?

INTO THE WORD

1. What elementary teachings do you find in Hebrews 6:1–3?

2. The writer to the Hebrews urged his readers to "go on to maturity" (v. 1). How would you define spiritual maturity?

3. Why do you agree or disagree that the persons referred to as falling away (v. 6) had been truly converted?

4. How would you define the falling away referred to in verse 6?

5. What evidence of genuine faith did the writer of Hebrews see in his readers' lives (vv. 9–10)?

6. How will you imitate those who demonstrated faith and patience (v. 12)?

7. What personal comfort and encouragement do you derive from the fact that God cannot lie (v. 18)?

8. On a scale of one to ten, how firm and secure do you believe your anchor of hope is today? How may you apply the truths given in Hebrews 6 to strengthen your hope?

INTO THE WORLD

Write a note to someone facing a difficult trial. Make it uplifting by pointing out that Jesus offers firm and secure hope.

19 We have this hope as an anchor for the soul, firm and secure. It enters the inner sanctuary behind the curtain,

20 where Jesus, who went before us, has entered on our behalf. He has become a high priest forever, in the order of Melchizedek.

LEAVE AND MOVE ON

The author of Hebrews told his readers they were to leave the elementary teachings about Christ. Fill in the blanks accordingly. Try to do as much as you can without looking at the lesson.

Elementary Teachings They Were to Leave		
First Pair	Repentance from acts that lead to _____.	Faith in God.
Second Pair	Instruction about _____.	The laying on of _____.
Third Pair	The resurrection of the dead.	Eternal _____.

The readers of Hebrews were to leave the elementary teachings and move on to _____ or _____.

Hebrews provides five evidences by which people could be known as converted to Christ.

Five Evidences of Persons Thoroughly Converted to Christ
They had once been _____.
They had tasted the _____ gift.
They had shared in the _____ _____.
They had tasted the goodness of the _____ of God.
They had tasted the _____ of the coming age.

Can these still be used as evidence today? Explain why each one can or cannot be.

INTERACTIVE LEARNING IDEAS

GET THE CLASS INVOLVED
Never Forgotten

The writer of Hebrews reminded his readers that God was not unjust and would never forget the works they did on His behalf, for His kingdom, out of love for His people.

Give the people in your class a few minutes to think of an older believer who has made a significant impact in their lives. Have your students reflect on how they are different today because of this person's faithfulness or dedication to the work of God. Some of your students might find it helpful to take some notes as they reflect on this person.

Perhaps it was a Sunday school teacher who faithfully conveyed the stories of the Bible to a young kid who fidgeted in his chair. Perhaps it was an older gentleman whose kids had grown, but he still took a troubled youth under his wing, coaching him through a painful time in the teen's life.

Spend a few minutes, then, sharing these stories with one another. It will be helpful for the students to hear each other's stories—some might one day be this type of inspiration to a younger believer. You might be surprised at the stories you hear. Be sure to have one of your own ready.

TRY THIS ON YOUR OWN
Elementary Teachings

The writer of Hebrews wanted his readers to move on from the elementary teachings of the faith toward maturity. What are these elementary teachings? What are the essentials of the faith? In what areas can Christians have legitimate differences without violating the elementary teachings of Christianity?

Take a piece of paper, and draw a line down the middle. On the top of the left column, write the word *essentials*. On the top of the right column, write the word *nonessentials*.

In the left column, write the essentials of the faith in regard to Christ, the Trinity, the Bible, and salvation. In the right column, list the areas in which you believe Christians can exercise flexibility without compromising any biblical standards. (For example, some Christians might include the types of instruments than can be used in worship.)

TAKING IT TO THE STREET
Tasting Tests

Those who have once tasted of the heavenly gift and shared in the Holy Spirit, and then have fallen away, cannot be brought back to repentance (Heb. 6:4–6). This "tasting" was enough to understand the real thing, and it was still rejected.

Go with your class to a warehouse-type of store where you know they will be giving out free taste samples of various foods. Be sure to make the full circuit with your group. Listen politely to the sales pitch most sample clerks share along with their tasty samples. Some of the people in your group may choose to go ahead and pick up entire packages of something they've tasted.

Discuss how having just a taste of something can affect our desire for more of the real thing. Then draw the appropriate spiritual parallels.

WITH YOUR FAMILY
Getting Unstuck

The writer of Hebrews implies that people can get stuck at various stages of their spiritual growth (Heb. 6:1–3). Usually it takes help from other believers to see the actual "rut," and then help them get unstuck.

Have each family member try to get into smaller and smaller containers of some kind. Or, perhaps you can use a small closet or storage room for this exercise.

At some point, somebody is going to have a hard time getting out of his or her box. Perhaps the best way to help them out is to carefully rip the box to give the person room to escape.

How is this exercise like helping people to get "unstuck," spiritually speaking? What specific things can we do to help each other move forward through the stages of spiritual growth? ◆

Jesus is the mediator of a new covenant.

LESSON 7

DO WE NEED A HIGH PRIEST?

Hebrews 7:11–17, 25; 8:1–7

KEY VERSE

This is the covenant I will make with the house of Israel after that time, declares the Lord. I will put my laws in their minds, and write them on their hearts. I will be their God, and they will be my people.

—Hebrews 8:10

BACKGROUND SCRIPTURES

Genesis 14:18–20
    Story of Melchizedek
Genesis 15 and 17
    God's covenants with
    Abraham
Exodus 19–24
    God's covenant with
    Israel
Numbers 25:10–13
    God's covenant with
    Phinehas as high priest
2 Samuel 7:5–16
    God's covenant with
    David as king
Psalm 110:1–4
    The Messiah as King
    and Priest
Jeremiah 31:31–34
    The promise of a new
    covenant

DAILY BIBLE READINGS

Monday: Deuteronomy
           7:7–11
Tuesday: 1 Timothy 2:1–7
Wednesday: 2 Corinthians
           3:7–18
Thursday: Philippians
           2:1–11
Friday: Colossians
           3:1–11
Saturday: Hebrews
           7:11–17, 25;
           8:1–7
Sunday: Psalm 20

WHY THIS MATTERS

Technology keeps advancing, and as it does, life changes—usually for the better. Cataract surgery used to require a hospital stay of several days, but technology has made it possible to recover on an outpatient basis. Typists used to cover errors with white-out. Today, the delete key performs the same function with less mess. Messages that once took days or weeks to arrive at their destination are now delivered within seconds of hitting the send button. It's hard to imagine reverting to a time before such technological advances.

The recipients of the letter to the Hebrews needed to understand that the new covenant and Jesus' priesthood were far superior to the old covenant and the former priesthood. This lesson inspires in us a deeper appreciation of what we have under the new covenant.

BIBLE COMMENTARY

By Lee M. Haines

This study concludes the part of Hebrews that argues "Christ is better than other mediators" (chaps. 1–7), and it brings to a climax the section showing that He is better than Aaron (4:14—7:28). It then begins the next part of Hebrews, which argues that "Christ provides a better covenant" (8:1—10:39). Chapter 8 shows that it is a better covenant because it is spiritual and inward.

The writer to the Hebrews first mentioned Melchizedek in 5:5. There he cited Psalm 110:4 and went on in verse 10 to declare that that prophecy had been fulfilled in that Jesus "was designated by God to be high priest in the order of Melchizedek." But then he interrupted his theological discussion because he was fearful the Hebrews were lingering in spiritual babyhood and would find it difficult to understand (5:11–14). So he proceeded to exhort them to make their "hope sure" (6:11) and "to imitate those who through faith and patience inherit what has been promised" (6:12). He closed chapter 6 by saying again that Jesus "has become a high priest forever, in the order of Melchizedek" (6:20). He was then ready to resume his theological discussion.

In 7:1–10, the writer to the Hebrews summarized what little was known about Melchizedek from the Old Testament. He cited the story from Genesis 14 about a war between two alliances of kings, which led to the capture and removal of Abraham's nephew Lot and his family and possessions. Abraham and a band of his friends and servants defeated the kingly alliance that was responsible and rescued their captives. As Abraham was returning from this victory, Melchizedek came out to meet him (Gen. 14:18–20). He was referred to as "king of Salem" and as "priest of God Most High." His name means "king of righteousness." *Salem* may be a shortened form of Jerusalem, but it also means "peace." So this mysterious person who appeared so abruptly on the

pages of sacred writing and quickly vanished again was both the "king of righteousness" and the "king of peace." While he apparently lived in the midst of
the wicked and idolatrous Canaanites, he was the "priest of God Most High."
In Genesis 14:22, Abraham referred to his own God as God Most High, indicating that Melchizedek served the true God. Contrary to the usual introduction of persons in Genesis, nothing is said about Melchizedek's ancestry or
parents, his birth or his death. But his greatness is shown by the fact that
Abraham yielded to his blessing and paid tithes to him. The writer to the
Hebrews pointed out that the lesser person is blessed by the greater person, so
Melchizedek was greater than Abraham. And since the Levites, Israel's
appointed tithe collectors, were descendants of Abraham, they paid tithes to
Melchizedek through Abraham, and Melchizedek was greater than the Levites
and the priesthood derived from them.

WHAT DO YOU THINK?
Why is Jesus the perfect
High Priest? How does
Jesus fulfill this role for
believers today?

Need for a Different Priestly Order (Heb. 7:11–17)

The writer to the Hebrews then used Melchizedek as a type or foreshadowing of Jesus. He quoted before from Psalm 110:4 and he did so again in 7:17.
Psalm 110 is a Messianic psalm. Verses 1–3 of that psalm spoke of the Messiah
as a king established by the Lord (Yahweh). Jesus quoted from Psalm 110:1
and applied it to himself in one of His conversations with the Jewish religious
leaders (Matt. 22:44). And Peter also quoted it at Pentecost, identifying Jesus
with the second Lord (Adonai) spoken of there (Acts 2:34–36). The writer to
the Hebrews cited Psalm 110:4 as predicting that the Messiah would also be **a
priest forever in the order of Melchizedek** (Heb. 7:17).

AHA!
Jesus is absolutely without
sin!

The writer to the Hebrews then began to point out the deficiencies of the old
priesthood and the superiority of the new. He declared that **if perfection could
have been attained through the Levitical priesthood,** there would have been
no **need for another priest to come** (v. 11). The **change of the priesthood**
would also require **a change of the law** (v. 12). The old code of regulations was
to be replaced with what James 2:8 calls the "royal law" of love (compare Matt.
5:43–45; John 13:34–35; 1 John 2:3–11). He called attention to the fact that
Jesus was not from the tribe of Levi, but **from Judah** (v. 14), which had no relationship to the old priesthood. The old priesthood staked its claim on **ancestry,**
but Jesus' claim was based on **the power of an indestructible life** (v. 16). The
appearance of Melchizedek in Genesis without reference to a beginning or an
ending made him a type of Jesus, who really did not have a beginning or an
ending, but is eternal. While the writer did not develop the thought any further,
Melchizedek's identity as "king of righteousness" and "king of peace" also
looked forward to Jesus as the Messiah. He was the true king of righteousness
and peace (compare Isa. 9:6–7).

DID YOU KNOW?
"King of Salem" may mean
"King of Jerusalem."

In Hebrews 7:18–24, the writer became more specific: The old way "was
weak and useless" (7:18); "the law made nothing perfect" (7:19). Both in 7:11
and 7:19, the writer implied that a priesthood was needed that could "perfectly"
or "completely" serve as the "go-between" or mediator between God and
humans. He said that with the new priesthood, "a better hope is introduced, by
which we draw near to God" (7:19). And he pointed out that in Psalm 110:4,
God had declared with an oath that the Messiah would be a priest forever. The

The Jerusalem temple

WHAT DO YOU THINK?
What are some obsolete traditions in the church that need to be set aside? What God-honoring traditions will take their place?

AHA!
Jesus saves completely!

DID YOU KNOW?
The priests were dependent upon the tithes of God's people to live.

old priesthood involved no oath; the new one is better because God doubly guaranteed it (compare Heb. 6:13–18). "Because of this oath, Jesus has become the guarantee of a better covenant" (7:22).

In 7:23–24, the writer pointed out that there has been a constantly recurring turnover in the old priesthood, because those priests were mortal and "death prevented them from continuing in office." But "Jesus lives forever," and therefore "he has a permanent priesthood."

Provision of a More Effective Priest (Heb. 7:25)

The writer then declared that Jesus **is able to save completely those who come to God through him, because he always lives to intercede for them.** The word translated *completely* (NIV) is "to the uttermost" in the KJV. Some translators key it to the time element and say that He is able to save forever. Probably both elements are intended. There is no aspect of sin Jesus cannot deal with and redeem us from, and He can do it forever. The Lord Jesus Christ can forgive past sins and He can cleanse us from the tendency to sin. He can break sinful habits and make sin distasteful to the transformed heart. And His ministry lasts, "because he always lives to intercede for" us (compare Rom. 8:26–27, 34).

It is important to note that this complete, full, whole, lasting salvation is for those who come to God through Jesus. It is not for those who try to come by some other way. Jesus himself said, "I am the way and the truth and the life. No one comes to the Father except through me" (John 14:6). If we want to have a saving, joyful, intimate, lasting relationship with God, it comes through Jesus.

In Hebrews 7:26–28, the writer continued to compare the inadequate old priesthood with the perfect priesthood of Christ. While the former priests were "men who" were "weak" (7:28) and in need of daily sacrifice for their "own sins" (7:27), Jesus "is holy, blameless, pure, set apart from sinners, exalted above the heavens" (7:26). He is the "high priest" who "meets our need," or "the fitting one," "the suitable one" for us (7:26). While the former priests had "to offer sacrifices day after day . . . He sacrificed . . . once for all when he offered himself" (7:27). The law appointed the former priests, but God's oath appointed Jesus (7:28). Not only was Jesus a better priest, but His offering of himself provided a sacrifice far superior to the animals and products of the soil offered on Israel's altars.

Provision of a More Effective Covenant (Heb. 8:1–7)

In these verses, the writer to the Hebrews asserted that the real **sanctuary** or place of worship, **the true tabernacle**, is in heaven, **set up by the Lord, not by man** (v. 2). It had been **shown** as **the pattern** to Moses **on the mountain**. So the tabernacle Moses built in the wilderness was just **a copy and shadow of what is in heaven** (v. 5). Jesus, our **high priest . . . sat down at the right hand of the throne of the Majesty in heaven** (v. 1), and He serves as the High Priest in the heavenly sanctuary. It is here that He intercedes for us (compare Rom. 8:34; Heb. 7:25).

The writer went on to say that not only is Jesus' ministry superior to that of the former priesthood, but God has made a new and better covenant with His people. The old agreement between God and Israel was inadequate. If it had not been, **no place would have been sought for another** (8:7). It was common in biblical times for rulers to enter into covenants or agreements with their people. God had entered into covenants in the Old Testament beginning with Noah and continuing with individuals and with His people as a whole. Some covenants were determined entirely by the superior party; some required certain things of both the superior and inferior parties. God's covenant with Israel had stipulated certain things both were to do. That covenant was being replaced. It had failed because the people failed (Heb. 8:9). The new covenant was to be based solely on the grace of God. Not only will He do what He has promised to do, but He will *enable* His people to live in obedience to Him.

WHAT ABOUT YOU?
How would you like Jesus to intercede for you today?

The Two Covenants in Hebrews 8	
Old Covenant	**New Covenant**
Failed because people failed; 8:9	Depends on God's grace; 8:10, 12
External, materialistic	Internal, spiritual; 8:10
Recorded on stone tablets, scrolls	Written in minds, on hearts; 8:10
People needed to remind each other to know the Lord; 8:11	Direct, intimate, personal knowledge of and relationship with the Lord; 8:11
Obsolete and aging; 8:13	New and ongoing

In 8:8–13, the writer cited Jeremiah 31:31–34, in which the Lord had promised there would be a new covenant. The old one had failed because the people had not been "faithful" (8:9). The new covenant was not to be external and materialistic but inward and spiritual. God's law was no longer to be only on stone tablets or scrolls, but "I will put my laws in their minds, and write them on their hearts" (8:10). There was now to be a personal relationship between God and each person, and no longer would a "neighbor" or "brother" be needed to remind them to "Know the Lord" because each one would know Him, "from the least of them to the greatest" (8:11). This "new" covenant rendered "the first one obsolete; and what is obsolete and aging will soon disappear" (8:13). This new covenant of an inner, spiritual knowledge of and personal relationship with God is what we have in Christ. ◆

PRAYER
Lord, thank You for the new covenant, purchased by the atoning work of Your Son and my Savior, Jesus. Save me completely, O God, and give me what I need to persevere to the end of my race.

INTERACTIVE LEARNING IDEAS

GET THE CLASS INVOLVED
Mediation

The writer of Hebrews describes Jesus as our High Priest, the supreme mediator between God and man.

As believers, we can mediate disputes between one another. In fact, the Bible makes it clear that God has called us to a ministry of reconciliation. In our roles as mediators, we can have a hand in reconciling disputing Christians so there can be peace in the church. Without mediation, quite often sides are taken, and rifts grow wider in congregations.

Ask a few students to role-play a mediation between two Christians who are arguing about giving the pastor a raise when giving has been steadily going down over the past few months. Have one person play the role of mediator, one person who thinks the pastor should get a raise, and the other who thinks the church should cut the salary of the pastor.

Have each person give his or her perspective on the issue. Have the opposing person paraphrase the other person's position without necessarily agreeing with it. And then let the other person articulate his view, while the other paraphrases.

When each person feels like he or she has been heard and understood by the other, have the mediator coach them through possible solutions where each side's interests are represented.

After the role-play, talk about real-life disputes where this kind of dialogue might be helpful.

TRY THIS ON YOUR OWN
Perfect Version

Hebrews tells us that perfection could never be attained through the Levitical priesthood, but only through the High Priesthood of Jesus Christ.

What would a perfect version of you look like? How would you think? How would you act?

Make a list of all of your current weaknesses that would disappear in a perfect version of yourself. What tendencies toward specific sins would go away? What would you have the capacity to do? What possible dangers would perfection hold for you?

How much of this is attainable in this life? What kinds of things might be holding you back? How could you get rid of those obstacles?

Write down your answers in a journal, and check back on your entries in six months or so. Note what has changed in the interim.

TAKING IT TO THE STREET
Obsolete Laws

When the atoning work of Jesus completed the new covenant, the old regulations were set aside. They were now obsolete, no longer holding any power over people (Heb. 7:18).

Prior to class, do an Internet search on laws that are still on the books that have long since become obsolete. Be sure to verify that they're still in effect. For example, in Alabama, there's a law that says a person can take only five minutes to cast a vote. In Illinois, it's illegal to allow any kind of pet to smoke a cigar.

After you've found some of these laws for your particular area, spend some time with the class writing letters to the appropriate representatives about why these laws are still in effect. Are any of them still enforced? What would it take to rescind these silly laws?

WITH YOUR FAMILY
Family Covenant

Jesus has established a new covenant with the people of God, one characterized by grace and mercy (Heb. 8:6). This new covenant has replaced the old, which had become ineffective and obsolete.

Spend some time together creating a family covenant. Covenants articulate promises family members make to one another. When expectations are clearly spelled out in a family covenant, everybody can have more fun with one another.

These are the questions your covenant should address: What is your family's purpose? Why did God bring you together as a family? What are your expectations of each other? What role does each person play in the family? Are chores divvied up fairly? Would anyone like to trade responsibilities?

When everyone has had a chance to contribute, have one person put it all in a document. When everyone is happy with the final form, have each family member sign it. Then go put it into practice! ♦

HEBREWS 7:11–17, 25; 8:1–7

7:11 If perfection could have been attained through the Levitical priesthood (for on the basis of it the law was given to the people), why was there still need for another priest to come—one in the order of Melchizedek, not in the order of Aaron?

12 For when there is a change of the priesthood, there must also be a change of the law.

13 He of whom these things are said belonged to a different tribe, and no one from that tribe has ever served at the altar.

14 For it is clear that our Lord descended from Judah, and in regard to that tribe Moses said nothing about priests.

15 And what we have said is even more clear if another priest like Melchizedek appears,

16 one who has become a priest not on the basis of a regulation as to his ancestry but on the basis of the power of an indestructible life.

17 For it is declared: "You are a priest forever, in the order of Melchizedek."

25 Therefore he is able to save completely those who come to God through him, because he always lives to intercede for them.

8:1 The point of what we are saying is this: We do have such a high priest, who sat down at the right hand of the throne of the Majesty in heaven,

2 and who serves in the sanctuary, the true tabernacle set up by the Lord, not by man.

3 Every high priest is appointed to offer both gifts and sacrifices, and so it was necessary for this one also to have something to offer.

4 If he were on earth, he would not be a priest, for there are already men who offer the gifts prescribed by the law.

5 They serve at a sanctuary that is a copy and shadow of what is in heaven. This is why Moses was warned when he was about to build the tabernacle: "See to it that you make everything according to the pattern shown you on the mountain."

6 But the ministry Jesus has received is as superior to theirs as the covenant of which he is mediator is superior to the old one, and it is founded on better promises.

7 For if there had been nothing wrong with that first covenant, no place would have been sought for another.

Do We Need a High Priest?

Jesus is the mediator of a new covenant.

INTO THE SUBJECT

Better is a key marketing word. Who doesn't appreciate a better computer, a better cell phone, or a better car? Israel had a good priesthood, but a better priesthood arrived. What was it?

INTO THE WORD

1. Which tribe supplied Israel's priesthood under the law of Moses?

2. Since Jesus belonged to the tribe of Judah, how did He qualify as a high priest?

3. What do you learn about Jesus' priesthood from Hebrews 7:15–17?

4. Compare Hebrews 7:1–3 and Isaiah 9:6–7. How did the priesthood of Melchizedek foreshadow Jesus' priesthood?

5. What does it mean to you personally that Jesus is your High Priest?

6. Why was the old covenant powerless to make anything perfect?

7. What significance do you attach to the fact that our High Priest "sat down at the right hand of the throne of the Majesty in heaven" (Heb. 8:1)?

8. Compare Hebrews 8:6–7 and Jeremiah 31:31–34. How is the new covenant better than the old covenant?

9. What are a few ways your life shows that God has written His laws in your heart?

INTO THE WORLD

Share the good news with someone this week that Jesus, the great High Priest, is alive forever.

The Old and the New Covenant

Complete the crossword puzzle.

Across

2. The story of Melchizedek is found in this book of the Bible.
5. Psalm 110 is this type of psalm.
6. The old covenant was this way.
7. The new covenant is new and
   _____.
9. He quoted Psalm 110:1 at Pentecost.
11. The old priesthood staked its claim on this.
14. The KJV translates it "to the uttermost" and the NIV translates it this way.
15. The change of the priesthood also required a change of this.
16. Chapter 110, verse 4 of this book is referenced in Hebrews 5:5.
17. Former priests were _____.

Down

1. The true tabernacle is here.
3. With the new priesthood, a better _____ was introduced.
4. Means peace.
5. Used as a foreshadowing of Jesus.
8. The new covenant depends on it.
10. The old covenant failed because the _____ failed.
12. Melchizedek was known as "king of _____."
13. He is the more effective priest.

Jesus' death on the cross was the perfect sacrifice.

THE PRECIOUS BLOOD OF CHRIST

Hebrews 9:11–28

WHY THIS MATTERS

"It is finished!" Jesus spoke these triumphant words from the cross to signify His work of redemption was complete and perfect. Nothing needed to be added to it. The Greek word *tetelestai* means literally, "It stands finished." The word was written on sales transactions to indicate, "paid in full." An artist might step back from his canvas, inspect his painting, and exclaim, "Tetelestai," meaning nothing further needed to be done to the work.

This lesson focuses attention on the perfect sacrifice Jesus offered on the cross. Looking by faith to the cross, we can say with conviction, "Tetelestai!"

BIBLE COMMENTARY

By Gareth Lee Cockerill

Why was Jesus' death so important? To answer this question, the writer of Hebrews presented Jesus as our High Priest and His incarnation and death as the ultimate atoning sacrifice for sin. Through this sacrifice God's people can be truly cleansed of sin and have access to God, both now and forever. It was urgent that his readers grasp this reality so they would persevere in faith until the end. He exhorted and urged them with deep pastoral concern, and so it is fitting to refer to the writer of this book as the "pastor."

The pastor demonstrated the full sufficiency of Christ's atoning sacrifice in 8:1—10:18. The theme of sacrifice is by far the greatest, for it is by His sacrifice that the incarnate Son of God opened the way into heaven, the "sanctuary" of God's presence. It is also by this sacrifice that He initiated a new covenant or arrangement of approaching God. Under this covenant there is real forgiveness and true heart cleansing for obedience (10:16–18).

The author stated this theme in relationship to one another. Since Jesus is at God's right hand in the heavenly sanctuary (8:1–2, compare Ps. 110:1), He must have offered a greater sacrifice than those who served in the earthly sanctuary (8:3–5). The covenant He established is also superior, as indicated by the prophecy of Jeremiah 31:31–34, quoted in Hebrews 8:8–12. The fact that Jeremiah spoke of a new covenant indicated the old was inadequate (8:6–14).

Later, the pastor played this theme in richer harmony by looking back at the Mosaic sanctuary (9:1–10) and covenant (9:16–22). According to 9:1–10, the description of that sanctuary showed that it was woefully inadequate, only a rough draft of what the Son of God would accomplish.

Perfect Sacrifice (Heb. 9:11–15)

There had been no adequate access to God, but **when Christ came as high priest of the good things that are already here** (v. 11), everything changed. The "good things" are forgiveness, heart cleansing, and access to the Father.

KEY VERSE

How much more, then, will the blood of Christ, who through the eternal Spirit offered himself unblemished to God, cleanse our consciences from acts that lead to death, so that we may serve the living God!
—Hebrews 9:14

BACKGROUND SCRIPTURES

Leviticus 16:1–28
A description of the Day of Atonement sacrifice, which Christ fulfills according to Hebrews 9:11–14

Hebrews 10:5–10
Christ's sacrifice was acceptable because He is the eternal Son of God who lived a completely obedient human life.

1 Corinthians 15:3–4
Christ died for our sins in fulfillment of the Scriptures.

1 Corinthians 5:21
Christ took our sin on himself.

DAILY BIBLE READINGS

Monday: Galatians 3:21–29
Tuesday: 2 Corinthians 4:7–15
Wednesday: 1 John 1:9—2:6
Thursday: Ephesians 2:4–10
Friday: Colossians 2:6–15
Saturday: Hebrews 9:11–28
Sunday: Psalm 21:1–7

WHAT DO YOU THINK?
How is the earthly Christian walk a "copy and a shadow" of our redeemed life in heaven? What can you do now to affect what your life will be like in the age to come?

AHA!
Jesus mediates between us and God!

What did Christ do that was different? He ministered not in a **man-made** tabernacle or temple that was part of **the creation**. He passed through **the greater and more perfect tabernacle** into that heavenly sanctuary of God's presence.

The pastor calls this heavenly sanctuary **the Most Holy Place** (v. 12) by analogy with the inner sanctum of the Mosaic sanctuary, which the high priest could enter only on the Day of Atonement (Lev. 16). Jesus entered the heavenly sanctuary not once every year but **once for all** and forever. On what basis did He enter? Not on the basis of **the blood of goats and calves** like those offered on the Day of Atonement. His was not some animal sacrifice. It was **his own** precious **blood**. He offered himself and **obtained eternal** and effective **redemption** for His people from the guilt and power of sin.

Hebrews 9:13–14 contrasts the **blood of goats and bulls** with **the blood of Christ**. In verse 13, the pastor affirmed that the Old Testament sacrifices provided outward or ritual purification. The blood of goats and bulls was sprinkled on the outside and could cleanse only the outside, those who were **ceremonially unclean**. The pastor emphasized the fact that those sacrifices bought outward purity by referring to the ritual use of the **ashes** of the red **heifer**. This ritual was only for ceremonial cleansing (Num. 19:1–22).

Since those sacrifices, which did not bring true cleansing and access to God, did bring ceremonial or ritual cleansing, then certainly the **blood of Christ** (Heb. 9:14) must bring much more. First, He offered himself **through the eternal Spirit**. He was the eternal Son of God (1:1–14; 5:5–6) who became a high priest "by the power of an indestructible life" (7:15). Second, He **offered himself unblemished** (9:14). He

Two Sacrifices Compared Hebrews 9:11–28		
	The Aaronic High Priest	**The Son of God**
The Time of the Sacrifice	Once every year (vv. 7, 25)	Once for all (vv. 12, 26)
The Nature of the Sacrifice	The lives of bulls and goats without physical defect (v. 13)	His own life lived in complete obedience to the Father (vv. 14, 26).
The Effects of the Sacrifice	1. Outward ceremonial purification (v. 13) 2. Annual access to the earthly Most Holy Place (v. 7)	1. Inward heart purification (v. 14) 2. Permanent access to the heavenly Most Holy Place (vv. 27–28)

lived His entire human life in obedience to the Father and thus His self-offering was acceptable. Hebrews 10:5–10 makes the nature of this obedience clear. Since He is the eternal Son of God who lived a completely obedient human life, His self-offering has the power to **cleanse our consciences from acts that lead to death** (9:14). This cleansing takes away the guilt, corruption, and power of sin. The conscience is used here as the equivalent of the heart. By Christ's sacrifice the "evil heart of unbelief" (3:12) becomes a "true" heart (10:22). The NIV's "acts that lead to death" is an accurate interpretation of the King James' more literal "dead works." Nevertheless, "dead works" is a very expressive phrase. These works encumber the heart and weigh it down drawing the person to eternal death. The heart is cleansed from being a heart that is attracted to and controlled by the doing of such works. Freedom from this bondage enables the faithful believer to **serve the living God**. Thus this cleansing leads to a life of holiness, to a life in which God's laws are written on the heart (see Heb. 10:16–18).

DID YOU KNOW?
The tabernacle was a portable place of worship for the Jews during their time in the wilderness.

If Christ's sacrifice makes true atonement for sin and cleanses the believer's heart from its guilt and bondage, then He **is the mediator of a new covenant** (9:15). A new way of approaching God is in effect. This new covenant is the means by which God's people can enter the **promised eternal inheritance**. Only the eternal Son of God through His obedient human life and atoning death could provide this access. It is through His **death** that they have been redeemed from those sins they committed under the **first covenant**, for which that covenant had no adequate remedy.

Jesus' Sacrifice Removes Sin (Heb. 9:16–22)

The Old Testament covenant sacrifices represented the deaths of those who entered into the covenant. Those entering the covenant symbolically pledged their lives if they broke faith.

The word here translated **will** (vv. 16–17) is the same word translated "covenant" in verse 15 and in verses 18–22. It is probably most accurate to translate this word "covenant" in verses 16–17 as well. Also, the word translated "to prove" in verse 16 does not have that meaning elsewhere, but it can mean "bear" or "bring." Finally, the Greek behind the phrase in verse 17, **when someone has died**, is "on the basis of deaths." Thus the verses might be better translated: "In the case of a covenant it is necessary for the death of the one who made it to be offered, because a covenant is in force only on the basis of sacrifices (or deaths). It does not take effect until the maker's death has been symbolically enacted on the basis of sacrifices."

Thus the **first** covenant was **put into effect** on the basis of **blood** sacrifices (v. 18). By those sacrifices the Israelites pledged their own deaths for violation of the covenant.

Verse 19 reflects Moses' establishment of the Sinai Covenant in Exodus 24:3–8. First, Moses declared **every commandment of the law** to the people so they would adequately understand the covenant before accepting it. Then Moses took the **blood** of the sacrifice and **sprinkled** both **the scroll**, representing God, and **the people**. Exodus actually says that Moses sprinkled the altar and the people. Perhaps the scroll was on the altar. By using the scroll to represent God, the pastor emphasized the necessity of keeping the stipulations of the covenant. Exodus 24 doesn't actually say Moses used **water, scarlet wool and branches of hyssop**, but these were commonly used for purification (Lev. 14:4–9; Num. 19:6–10; Ps. 51:7; John 19:29).

Hebrews 9:20 paraphrases the final words Moses used to establish the covenant in Exodus 24:8: **This is the blood of the covenant, which God has commanded you to keep.** This statement emphasizes the significance of the blood sacrifice and the necessity of keeping what God has commanded. Violation of the covenant invoked one's own death. By the blood of the Old Testament covenant, the people pledged their own deaths for violation. By His sacrifice, however, Christ took that covenant curse on himself and ransomed them from "the sins committed under the first covenant." Our sin stands under the judgment of that covenant law until cleansed by Christ.

The importance of this blood is emphasized by the assertion that Moses sprinkled not only the scroll of the law but also the **tabernacle and everything**

WHAT DO YOU THINK?
What gift did Jesus offer to be our High Priest? How has this gift impacted you?

AHA!
God has given us a new covenant!

DID YOU KNOW?
The people who lived in Qumran (during Jesus' day) were looking for a "new covenant" with God.

used in its ceremonies (v. 21). The sprinkling of blood was pervasive both in establishing the old covenant and in maintaining it. When one lived under the old covenant, almost everything was **cleansed with blood** (v. 22), though a few things were not. Under the old covenant, **without the shedding of blood there is no forgiveness**. The word *remission* in some translations better represents the pastor's thought. More than forgiveness is at stake; it is the remission or the removal of sin. Without blood, there was and is no removal, remission, redemption, or cleansing, and no access to God.

Christ Died Once for All (Heb. 9:23–28)

The high priest purified the Most Holy Place on the Day of Atonement, and these were only **copies** of the **heavenly** (v. 23) dwelling place of God. If animals were needed to purify the copies, then the original had to be purified with infinitely **better sacrifices**. The sacrifice of Christ brought such purification.

Then the pastor said plainly that the sanctuary Christ entered was not **man-made** (v. 24); it was not the earthly **copy**. **He entered heaven itself**, the eternal dwelling place of God. He had been with God prior to His incarnation, but this time He entered as our high priest, appearing **for us in God's presence** (v. 24). Thus we are able to draw near to God through Him "in order to find mercy and grace to help in time of need" (4:16).

In verses 25–28, the pastor wrote more on the sacrificial death of Jesus. The Aaronic high priest went into the Most Holy Place **every year** (v. 25). He entered on the basis of **blood . . . not his own**. Christ, however, did not enter the heavenly sanctuary repeatedly. No, **he has appeared once for all** (v. 26). According to Psalm 110:1 (see Heb. 1:14), He sat down once for all at God's right hand **at the end of the ages** (9:26), the great turning point of history. He did so to **do away with sin** once and for all. All this could be accomplished only **by the sacrifice of himself**.

By emphasizing that Christ has come once for all and done away with sin, the pastor did not want to deny the second coming and our consequent responsibility before Him at that coming. Every human being must **die once** and **face the judgment** (v. 27) at Christ's return (see 12:25–29). Thus Christ has been **sacrificed once** to take care of **the sins of many** and will come a second time **to bring** full and final **salvation** (v. 28) to those who are anticipating His coming with faith and obedience. "Many" emphasizes the all-inclusiveness of Christ's work. He died only once but it was totally adequate for the sins of many. He experienced death for "all" (2:9). Thus the pastor brought this section to a close on this note of assured hope. ◆

WHAT ABOUT YOU?
How do you know that the "law of God" has been written in your heart?

PRAYER
Lord, thank You for making forgiveness even possible through the shedding of Jesus' blood on the cross. Give me the patience, endurance, and wisdom to forgive others as You have forgiven me.

HEBREWS 9:11–28

11 When Christ came as high priest of the good things that are already here, he went through the greater and more perfect tabernacle that is not man-made, that is to say, not a part of this creation.
12 He did not enter by means of the blood of goats and calves; but he entered the Most Holy Place once for all by his own blood, having obtained eternal redemption.
13 The blood of goats and bulls and the ashes of a heifer sprinkled on those who are ceremonially unclean sanctify them so that they are outwardly clean.
14 How much more, then, will the blood of Christ, who through the eternal Spirit offered himself unblemished to God, cleanse our consciences from acts that lead to death, so that we may serve the living God!
15 For this reason Christ is the mediator of a new covenant, that those who are called may receive the promised eternal inheritance—now that he has died as a ransom to set them free from the sins committed under the first covenant.
16 In the case of a will, it is necessary to prove the death of the one who made it,
17 because a will is in force only when somebody has died; it never takes effect while the one who made it is living.
18 This is why even the first covenant was not put into effect without blood.
19 When Moses had proclaimed every commandment of the law to all the people, he took the blood of calves, together with water, scarlet wool and branches of hyssop, and sprinkled the scroll and all the people.
20 He said, "This is the blood of the covenant, which God has commanded you to keep."
21 In the same way, he sprinkled with the blood both the tabernacle and everything used in its ceremonies.
22 In fact, the law requires that nearly everything be cleansed with blood, and without the shedding of blood there is no forgiveness.
23 It was necessary, then, for the copies of the heavenly things to be purified with these sacrifices, but the heavenly things themselves with better sacrifices than these.
24 For Christ did not enter a man-made sanctuary that was only a copy of the true one; he entered heaven itself, now to appear for us in God's presence.
25 Nor did he enter heaven to offer himself again and again, the way the high priest enters the Most Holy Place every year with blood that is not his own.
26 Then Christ would have had to suffer many times since the creation of the world. But now he has appeared once for all at the end of the ages to do away with sin by the sacrifice of himself.

The Precious Blood of Christ

Jesus' death on the cross was the perfect sacrifice.

INTO THE SUBJECT

In Old Testament times, worshipers offered blood sacrifices. What purpose did they serve? Why was this practice discontinued?

INTO THE WORD

1. How did Israel's high priests enter the Most Holy Place?

2. What evidence do you find in Hebrews 9:11–14 that Jesus' priestly ministry was superior to that of the Old Testament?

3. What evidence do you find in verses 11–14 that Jesus was a superior high priest?

4. How would you answer someone who insists salvation depends on good works, not on Jesus' blood?

5. Based on verse 26, what kind of life did Jesus lead?

6. Why do you agree or disagree that Jesus had to be sinless in order to die for sinners?

7. How did Jesus' once-for-all sacrifice for sin accomplish what the many Old Testament sacrifices could not accomplish?

8. In what sense will Jesus' second coming bring salvation (v. 28)?

9. What will you do for Jesus while you wait for His return?

INTO THE WORLD

An old chorus says, "I'm so happy. Here's the reason why—Jesus took my burdens all away." Show happiness and joy this week, and when someone asks what you have to be so happy about, tell him or her Jesus took your burdens (sins) all away.

27 Just as man is destined to die once, and after that to face judgment,
28 so Christ was sacrificed once to take away the sins of many people; and he will appear a second time, not to bear sin, but to bring salvation to those who are waiting for him.

Expressing Gratitude

Hebrews 9:11–28 paints a picture that contrasts the difference between the Aaronic high priests and Jesus. Look closely at the time, nature, and effects of Jesus' sacrifice and take in the grandness of it. Write a poem expressing your gratitude to God for sending Jesus to be this sacrifice. It can be any style of poetry: free style, haiku (three lines—five syllables, seven syllables, five syllables), quatrain (four lines with varying rhyming schemes), and so forth. The style doesn't matter as much as your heart's expression.

_____

_____

_____

_____

_____

_____

_____

_____

_____

_____

_____

_____

Consider sharing your poem to encourage and move others to a spirit of thankfulness. E-mail it to family and friends, post it on a social website, or share it with people in your class.

INTERACTIVE LEARNING IDEAS

GET THE CLASS INVOLVED
Reading of the Will

The writer of Hebrews reminded us that a will does not go into effect until after a person for whom the will is written has died.

Pretend your class is at the reading of a will. A godly person has passed away and is ready to bequeath great treasures to everyone in the class. In addition to items of worldly wealth, this person is also able to pass along the types of gifts God gives to those who love and honor Him with their lives (like wisdom, good friends, or a deep sense of purpose and significance).

Create a list with everyone's name on it. Be sure you are able to pronounce every name correctly. Tell them you're about to read this will where they will receive an "intangible gift" from a godly person, as is described above.

Have everyone sit in a circle, and try to create the aura of a solemn setting. When everyone is settled, say something like, "To [fill in a student's name], I bequeath . . ." and then have that student fill in the blank with what that person would want from God, if they could have anything in the world.

After everyone has had a chance to answer, lead a brief discussion about the types of gifts we'd like to leave to others.

TRY THIS ON YOUR OWN
Loss Inventory

The writer of Hebrews told us there is no forgiveness without the shedding of blood. Christ's blood needed to be shed, meeting God's requirement of justice, so that the forgiveness of sins would be possible. God willingly accepted an incredible loss so He'd be able to forgive those who would one day want to be reconciled with Him.

Some people find it hard to forgive because they cannot come to terms with what they have lost because of someone's indifference, negligence, or malice. The first step in the forgiveness process is knowing *what* we have to forgive.

Is there anyone in your life you've been trying to forgive, but just can't? Start by making a list of everything you lost because of this situation, even the intangibles. Maybe this person spread a false rumor about you, and you lost your reputation. Maybe someone betrayed you, and you lost your ability to trust.

Go down your list of losses and say something like, "I used to have this thing, but I don't anymore. I leave it in Your hands, Lord, knowing You may or may not choose to restore it to me. Thank You that You know me and Your plans for me." At first that might make you angry, but as you move through the grieving process, you'll find it easier and easier to forgive.

TAKING IT TO THE STREET
Clean Conscience

The sacrifices of bulls and goats might make people outwardly clean, but these sacrifices were not enough to cleanse the consciences of those who had sinned. Only the shed blood of Christ was able to make people clean, inside and out.

Just for fun, do this cleaning activity with your group. Coordinate a car wash with your group, and donate any money you bring it to a ministry in the church. Ask people to bring all their cleaning supplies with them. It's helpful to be near a faucet and hose, so you may have to do this in someone's driveway. Places of business might also allow you to use part of their parking lots (and water supply) for this charitable activity.

Note how most of the people who come want the outside of their cars washed, but not the inside. Quite often, people looking for a quick release from guilt are doing something similar.

WITH YOUR FAMILY
Make Out Your Will

The writer of Hebrews described what a will does, and when it's supposed to go into effect (Heb. 9:16). Sometimes family members don't even know what's in a will before the person dies.

Consider putting a will together for your family, and making it a group discussion. The head of the family could talk about what assets might exist when the will is finally executed. Mention that you're discussing this now to prevent any disputes in the future. Sometimes once-close family members stop talking to one another because of who gets what.

End the discussion about the type of inheritance that will never go away—namely, a godly legacy that can be passed down from generation to generation. ✦

Our walk of faith is strengthened by fellowship with His people.

LESSON 9

WALKING TOGETHER BY FAITH

Hebrews 10:19–39

KEY VERSE

Let us hold unswervingly to the hope we profess, for he who promised is faithful.
—Hebrews 10:23

BACKGROUND SCRIPTURES

Mark 15:38
  A mention of the curtain of the Most Holy Place being ripped in two at Christ's death; Hebrews 10:20 refers to Christ's body being the "new and living way," thereby replacing the curtain.
Habakkuk 2:4
  Old and New Testaments alike emphasize the centrality of faith in the believer's relationship with God. See also Romans 1:17.
Matthew 26:28
  Jesus' discussion of the blood of the covenant; see Hebrews 10:29 and Exodus 24:8.

DAILY BIBLE READINGS

Monday: Ephesians 4:1–7
Tuesday: Romans 1:1–16
Wednesday: Romans 3:21–31
Thursday: 1 John 1:1–10
Friday: Colossians 3:12–17
Saturday: Hebrews 10:19–39
Sunday: Psalm 22:1–5, 19

WHY THIS MATTERS

Riding a bicycle in heavy traffic is not always easy, but it is best to keep pedaling. Big trouble can befall the cyclist who stops when cars and trucks are behind or beside him or her. Similarly, the Christian life demands that we persevere and encourage one another to do so. We place ourselves in jeopardy if we think we can stop learning, growing, and serving. We must stay the course, spur one another to love and good works, and keep on assembling for fellowship and worship. If we fail to persevere, we run the risk of incurring divine judgment, a consequence far worse than that of a cyclist getting struck by a car or truck.

This lesson inspires us to "keep pedaling"!

BIBLE COMMENTARY

By Michael B. Thompson

It is easy to become fixated on elements of the letter to the Hebrews that are unknown to us. We do not know the author of the epistle. We don't exactly know when it was written. And we cannot say with absolute assurance who the specific audience was. These open questions could discourage us from believing it is possible to discern a clear and accurate message. But that perspective is mistaken, because the open questions have reasonable, approximate answers and the thrust of the message of Hebrews rings forcefully true.

First, the author was an intellectual, likely from the Jewish priestly class, who had a firm grasp on the content of the Old Testament and its implications. He was clearly a Christian leader the church revered and trusted. Second, it was written sometime during the second half of the first century A.D. by which time Christianity had spread through the Mediterranean world and had second-generation converts. Third, the probable audience was a group of Jewish Christians who had experienced a measure of persecution from the Roman Empire and were likely to experience more. The author wrote to help them better understand God's redemptive work in history culminating in Christ, and he encouraged them to persevere in their faith in Christ rather than revert to a mind-set and practices mired in the old covenant, which was only a foreshadowing of the hope found in Jesus Christ.

The overarching theme of the book of Hebrews is that Jesus Christ, the Son of God, is the supreme expression of God's redemptive plan in history. The writer said Jesus is the ultimate sacrifice for the sins of human beings and that He is the great High Priest mediating the atoning sacrifice rite on behalf of all humanity. The writer began in chapter 1 by pointing out that in the past God acted decisively in history to make His will known in various ways. He spoke through events, the patriarchs, and the prophets, but the supreme expression of

His saving will and work was manifested in Jesus. The writer went on in chapters 1 and 2 to advance his thesis that Jesus Christ is the ultimate expression of God by saying He is greater than the angels. He continued building his case in chapters 3 and 4 by declaring that Jesus is greater than Moses—the most revered of all past Hebrew luminaries. In chapters 4–7, the writer made it clear that Jesus is also superior to the whole Aaronic priesthood. The ritualistic work of the priests appeased God through the bloody, tedious, and cumbersome sacrificial system, but Christ is the one high priest who supersedes the whole line of Aaronic priests by presiding over the once-and-for-all atonement.

The message of the letter then builds to a climax in chapters 8–10, where the writer declared that Jesus Christ is the one and only sacrifice that was possible and needed for the salvation of all persons. The crescendo of the climax comes in Hebrews 9:14: "How much more, then, will the blood of Christ, who through the eternal Spirit offered himself unblemished to God, cleanse our consciences from acts that lead to death, so that we may serve the living God!"

Once the writer established that Christ is the supreme, efficacious sacrifice to provide salvation, his attention turned to the practical implications of Christ's redemptive work for believers.

Christocentric Implications and Exhortations (Heb. 10:19–25)

Therefore (v. 19) indicates a pivot in the thematic thrust of the author's message. Since Christ's sacrifice made obsolete the old sacrificial system, there are practical implications for believers. The endearing term **brothers** suggests that the author wrote with a familial tenderness and pleading. While Hebrews is a scholarly theological treatise, it was written with warm pastoral sentiment. The writer appealed to his readers to embrace these ideas and let them have full effect in their lives.

We have confidence to enter the Most Holy Place by the blood of Jesus (v. 19). In observance of the old covenant directives, the high priest entered the Most Holy Place of the tabernacle once a year, never more often, and presented the blood of a bull and goat in atonement for the sins of God's people over the previous year (see Lev. 16). The high priest approached this ritual with trepidation and fastidious attention to detail. He did not want to violate any element of the sacrificial regulations for fear of incurring the wrath of God. In contrast to the climate of the old sacrificial rite is the climate of approaching God because of Jesus' sacrifice. A Christian can step into God's presence with authorization, certainty, and assurance. **A new and living way opened for us** (Heb. 10:20). Under the old covenant only the high priest had direct access to God for atonement of sins, but now all barriers created by sin have been destroyed and Christ is the means by which anyone can have direct access to God. The motif of confidence is one that was clearly on the writer's mind throughout the letter (see 3:14; 4:16; 6:9; 10:22; 10:35). To the writer, confidence in approaching God comes from a clear conscience, and a clear conscience is made possible by accepting the provision of forgiveness of sins through Christ's sacrifice. No longer does a person have to be haunted by the guilt of sins committed (see 9:14; 10:22; 13:18). In this notion of confidence we see the author's pastoral impulse—he did not want anyone to miss the relief

WHAT DO YOU THINK?
What is the only thing that can cleanse a conscience? Why is this thing often so difficult to do?

AHA!
Your sins are completely covered by the blood of Christ!

DID YOU KNOW?
The veil of the temple was made up of many layers of cloth and was more than three feet thick. The high priest had to walk through what was essentially a maze to enter the Most Holy Place.

Christians in the coliseum

"Remember those earlier days after you had received the light, when you stood your ground in a great contest in the face of suffering. Sometimes you were publicly exposed to insult and persecution; at other times you stood side by side with those who were so treated" (Heb. 10:32–33).

WHAT DO YOU THINK?

Why is it important to have the right expectations when it comes to faith-related difficulties? Why will we be more effective in our work for the kingdom when our expectations are biblically accurate?

AHA!

Believers can trust the Bible to address every area of their lives!

DID YOU KNOW?

The "ashes of a heifer" were used in a purification ceremony described in Numbers 19.

and exhilaration of a clear conscience and the consequent confidence that comes in approaching God.

Since believers can have confidence through the saving work of Christ, how should they behave? The writer gave a flurry of exhortations to answer that question. First, **let us hold unswervingly to the hope we profess** (v. 23). The writer gave numerous exhortations to persevere and hang on for dear life to our beliefs in Christ. Note these expressions: "Fix your thoughts on Jesus" (3:1); "We have come to share in Christ if we hold firmly till the end" (3:14); "Let us hold firmly to the faith we profess" (4:14); "Let us run with perseverance" (12:1). The intensity and frequency of these "hold on" exhortations suggests that the writer was deeply concerned that these Christians were drifting in their faith and that their defection from the Christian faith was a distinct possibility. Second, **Let us consider how we may spur one another on toward love and good deeds** (v. 24). To be a Christian is to look like Christ in our conduct. Christians must consciously work to enact the ethos of Christ as taught and exemplified in the Gospels. A Christian who has been freed from guilt can rest and relax in God's grace, but he or she must exert great moral effort to be like Christ. We can never *earn* our salvation, but Christians should make every *effort* to live in accordance with their salvation. They should incite and stimulate each other to do good works. Third, **Let us not give up meeting together** (v. 25). A manifestation of the spiritual drift of some of the Christians mentioned in 2:1 was their failure to gather together in worship and fellowship. The tone of this strongly worded exhortation suggests the importance of gathering with other believers. Fourth, **Let us encourage one another—and all the more as you see the Day approaching** (10:25). Believers should remind each other of the fundamentals of Christian faith and practice in anticipation of the day when Christ will come a second time.

When these "Let us" exhortations are taken together, they emphasize that Christians do not exist as isolated spiritual beings practicing an individualized faith. Instead each Christian belongs to every other Christian, and each one has the responsibility to be sensitive and submissive to his or her brothers and sisters, and is also charged with the task of monitoring and caring for the welfare of his or her brothers and sisters.

A Chilling Warning (Heb. 10:26–31)

If we deliberately keep on sinning after we have received the knowledge of the truth, no sacrifice for sins is left, but only a fearful expectation of judgment and of raging fire (vv. 26–27). The writer delivered his message of Christ's sacrifice with pathos, tenderness, and pastoral urging. He pled with readers to take full advantage of God's redemptive bounty made possible by Christ's death on the cross. He reiterated that the opportunities to be experienced through Christ are unprecedented and incomparable. But on a few occasions in the text the writer conveyed a stern warning. This message is the flipside of the coin of the good news. It is the possibility of a tragic outcome. Essentially the writer said that since God's grace expressed in Christ's redemptive work is so grand, to discard it, ignore it, or harden our hearts against it would bring catastrophic consequences. And so the book of Hebrews contains urgings and warnings not to cast away the only means whereby a person can be saved; otherwise a harsh judgment is inevitable. In verse 28, the writer alluded to a law from the book of Deuteronomy. He reminded the reader that just as worshiping other gods in the Hebrew community brought upon one the penalty of death, so anyone rejecting Christ's sacrifice would experience God's wrath (see Deut. 17:2–7). Since Christ is the only means of salvation, to reject Him would be folly. The repeated warnings of the writer to these drifting believers not to "harden your hearts" (3:8; 4:7) and the reminders that if they reject Christ their doom was sealed (6:4–7; 10:26) were designed to help these believers appreciate the gravity of what was at stake.

It would be unwise to take these warning texts and stitch together a doctrine of an unpardonable sin. The writer of Hebrews did not appear to build a case that a certain sin is so egregious that it merits automatic damnation. The only sin that is unpardonable is an unconfessed sin hidden away in a hardened heart (see Matt. 12:32). Any sin can be immediately cleansed away if it is confessed and Christ's sacrifice is embraced for that sin (see 1 John 1:9). Such is the expanse of God's grace expressed in Christ. Still, the writer of Hebrews pointed out the alarming and devastating consequences for rejecting Christ's sacrifice for sin.

A Plea to Persevere (Heb. 10:32–39)

In this section, the writer revisited a frequently mentioned motif—perseverance (Heb. 12:1ff.). He called these Christians to hold on to their confidence in Christ's redemptive work and not to acquiesce to any moments of doubt or to quit because of adversity. With the words **stood side by side** (10:33), the writer emphasized the mutuality and communal nature in their past experience of the Christian faith. He insisted that if Christians are to persevere in their faith it will be in part through the encouragement and loyalty of brothers and sisters in Christ. **You sympathized with those in prison and joyfully accepted the confiscation of your property** (v. 34). The writer harkened back to trials these Christians experienced in the past to prepare them for additional assaults. It is likely that the Roman Empire was starting (or restarting) a campaign of terror against these Christians (perhaps under the reign of Nero ca. A.D. 64 or Domitian ca. A.D. 85). **So do not throw away your confidence; it will be richly rewarded** (v. 35). In verse 35, we start to see the writer's transition to his next theme. The foundation of perseverance is confidence and faith in God. The next chapter will contain an extended presentation on the necessity of faith for the persevering Christian journey. ◆

WHAT ABOUT YOU?
How has Jesus rescued you from trials in the past?

PRAYER
Lord, give me a clean heart and spotless conscience as I confess my sins to You, blaming no one but myself for what I have chosen. Thank You for the full assurance that faith brings.

INTERACTIVE LEARNING IDEAS

GET THE CLASS INVOLVED
Spurring On

The writer of Hebrews encouraged his readers to spur or encourage one another to love and good deeds. We should be all the more motivated to do this because we believe Jesus could return at any time.

Make sure everyone has a half sheet of paper, something to write with, and some tape. On the pieces of paper, have each person write one thing they love doing for God. It could be serving, teaching, counseling, maintenance . . . any number of roles in the church.

After everyone is done, get class members to tape these "signs" on the respective person's back (so the label can be read from behind).

Have each person go to the front, let everyone read the sign on his or her back, and then have a seat in the front. Let each person in the class take turns encouraging and "spurring on" the person up front in his or her area of passion.

Make sure people note past examples where they've seen this person in action, and perhaps suggest new ways they might be able to use their gifts. Perhaps even the person up front might be able to "dream" a little about how to use his or her gifts in new and fruitful ways.

TRY THIS ON YOUR OWN
Guilt Eraser

While the blood of bulls and goats could never cleanse a guilty conscience, the perfect atoning work of Christ enables us to be completely free of the emotional burdens of sin (Heb. 10:22).

The path to doing this is to fully acknowledge our sins and take responsibility for them and the dark motivations behind them.

Guilt in the spirit is like pain in the body—it's an indication that something is wrong and needs to be addressed. (If the guilt you are feeling is vague, undefined, and cannot be traced to a specific action, then it is probably false guilt.)

Make a list of the specific things you have done that are dishonoring to God. Be as honest with this list as if it were coming from someone who hurt you and yet wants to be reconciled with you. Put credit where credit is due—do not blame anyone else for your decisions or actions. When you do this before God, He will forgive you of your sins, and you can finally be free of a guilty conscience.

TAKING IT TO THE STREET
Courtroom

Those who have not been reconciled with God through the blood of Jesus have every reason to fear judgment. If they find themselves in such a state, they will be defenseless.

Take your class to a public courtroom and watch the proceedings. How do the prosecutors present their cases? How do the defense attorneys try to protect the rights of their clients? What kinds of questions do they ask prospective jurors? Who do they retain, and who do they dismiss? Can you guess why in each case?

Afterward, go out for coffee and talk about what everyone observed. How will the final judgment of God be like what they just witnessed? How will it be very different, in that no one will need to speculate about motives?

WITH YOUR FAMILY
Church Ready

The writer of Hebrews warned his readers about the dangers of not regularly getting together as Christians (Heb. 10:25). Of course, for us this means going to church regularly.

Make a plan as a family on how to get to church every weekend, and to make it a fruitful experience every time you go. Be sure that the night before, everybody has what he or she needs for the next day, so time is not wasted looking for things. Agree to hold off on all arguments before heading to church, ready to discuss the issues when you get back.

Set aside some time after the service to talk about the sermon and what each person learned. Talk about what happened in Sunday school, and the biblical principles presented. Make sure each person has a way to exercise his or her spiritual gifts in the church. Everyone in the body of Christ is important, just like every part of the physical body has a role to play. ◆

HEBREWS 10:19–39

19 Therefore, brothers, since we have confidence to enter the Most Holy Place by the blood of Jesus,

20 by a new and living way opened for us through the curtain, that is, his body,

21 and since we have a great priest over the house of God,

22 let us draw near to God with a sincere heart in full assurance of faith, having our hearts sprinkled to cleanse us from a guilty conscience and having our bodies washed with pure water.

23 Let us hold unswervingly to the hope we profess, for he who promised is faithful.

24 And let us consider how we may spur one another on toward love and good deeds.

25 Let us not give up meeting together, as some are in the habit of doing, but let us encourage one another—and all the more as you see the Day approaching.

26 If we deliberately keep on sinning after we have received the knowledge of the truth, no sacrifice for sins is left,

27 but only a fearful expectation of judgment and of raging fire that will consume the enemies of God.

28 Anyone who rejected the law of Moses died without mercy on the testimony of two or three witnesses.

29 How much more severely do you think a man deserves to be punished who has trampled the Son of God under foot, who has treated as an unholy thing the blood of the covenant that sanctified him, and who has insulted the Spirit of grace?

30 For we know him who said, "It is mine to avenge; I will repay," and again, "The Lord will judge his people."

31 It is a dreadful thing to fall into the hands of the living God.

32 Remember those earlier days after you had received the light, when you stood your ground in a great contest in the face of suffering.

33 Sometimes you were publicly exposed to insult and persecution; at other times you stood side by side with those who were so treated.

34 You sympathized with those in prison and joyfully accepted the confiscation of your property, because you knew that you yourselves had better and lasting possessions.

35 So do not throw away your confidence; it will be richly rewarded.

36 You need to persevere so that when you have done the will of God, you will receive what he has promised.

37 For in just a very little while, "He who is coming will come and will not delay.

Walking Together by Faith

Our walk of faith is strengthened by fellowship with His people.

INTO THE SUBJECT

Have you started on a long walk or hike and at some point wanted to turn back? Nevertheless you persevered. How did you feel when that perseverance carried you to your destination?

INTO THE WORD

1. What personal privileges do you find in Hebrews 10:19–20?

2. What personal obligations do you find in verses 22–25?

3. How has a fellow Christian encouraged you recently? How have you encouraged a fellow Christian recently?

4. How would you describe the consequences of rejecting Christ's sacrifice (vv. 26–31)?

5. Why do you agree or disagree that God's justice and wrath are seldom taught in books and sermons?

6. What do see as the greatest threats to faith?

7. How had the Hebrews demonstrated persevering faith in the past (vv. 32–34)?

8. What are a few past experiences that have bolstered your present confidence in the Lord?

9. Does the hope of being rewarded for doing God's will help you persevere? If so, how?

INTO THE WORLD

Jesus promised that in the world we will have tribulation, but we can be of good cheer because He has overcome the world. Triumph over every trial this week through faith in our living Lord!

38 But my righteous one will live by faith. And if he shrinks back, I will not be pleased with him."

39 But we are not of those who shrink back and are destroyed, but of those who believe and are saved.

Perseverance

A theme in this lesson is perseverance. The readers of Hebrews were encouraged to persevere and maintain confidence during moments of doubt or because of adversity.

As it was for the readers of Hebrews, this journey looks to be long. It's easy to see how one might be discouraged. There's a lot of ground covered and yet there is still so far to go. And what lies ahead can be uncertain.

The readers of Hebrews experienced many trials before and most likely after the writing of this letter. Journal about a time you faced uncertainty in your walk with God. Did someone say something that caused you to doubt God? Maybe something happened to you or a loved one that caused you to question God's love. What was it, and now that you can look back down the path, what do you see that you wouldn't have known or understood had you not had this experience? How has it strengthened your confidence in God?

_____

_____

_____

_____

_____

_____

Run the race of faith with perseverance.

FAITH THAT MOVES GOD

Hebrews 11:1–16

WHY THIS MATTERS

The United States is home to several sports halls of fame. For example, Canton, Ohio, is the site of the Pro Football Hall of Fame. Cooperstown, New York, hosts the National Baseball Hall of Fame, and Springfield, Massachusetts, is home to the Basketball Hall of Fame. Sports fans readily recognize most of the names inscribed in those halls.

Hebrews 11 has been called the Hall of Faith chapter of the Bible. Most of the names that appear there are readily recognized, but many other people are unnamed. It is an impressive roster of men and women of faith who are worthy of our emulation.

This lesson stimulates us to have faith in God as we seek to honor and serve Him.

BIBLE COMMENTARY

By Lee M. Haines

Hebrews 10 ends with a strong emphasis on faith. Verse 38 quotes from Habakkuk 2:3–4, one of the greatest Old Testament statements on faith: "my righteous one will live by faith." And 10:39 declares, "We are not of those who shrink back and are destroyed, but of those who believe and are saved." These verses provide the perfect springboard from which to launch the writer's discourse on faith in chapter 11.

Chapter 11 is the great "faith chapter" of the Bible. The writer had been encouraging his readers in many ways throughout the epistle, not to doubt but to believe. In 11:1–3, he explained the significance of faith. Beginning in verse 4, he called the roll of those in faith's hall of fame—painting word portraits of them in a gallery of the heroes of faith.

The Significance of Faith (Heb. 11:1–3)

The writer to the Hebrews began his treatise of faith by helping his readers understand the importance of faith—its practical effect in the life of the believer. **Faith is being sure of what we hope for** (v. 1). The original word for "being sure of" had three possible meanings, all of which have some application here: (1) "Substance" or the reality that underlies what we see, or in this case, what we hope for; (2) "foundation" or that which "stands under," that which gives a basis to hopes that would otherwise be little more than wistful desires; and (3) "assurance," a word that was commonly used in business documents as the basis or guarantee of transactions. This final interpretation is suggested by one translation: "Faith is the title-deed of things hoped for" (Moulton and Milligan). The writer went on to say, **Faith is being . . . certain of what we do not see**. The word for "certain" here is a strong word that means "proof" or

KEY VERSE

And without faith it is impossible to please God, because anyone who comes to him must believe that he exists and that he rewards those who earnestly seek him.
—Hebrews 11:6

BACKGROUND SCRIPTURES

Habakkuk 2:4;
Matthew 17:20; 21:21
  Faith
Genesis 4:1–12;
Hebrews 12:24
  Abel
Genesis 5:21–24
  Enoch
Genesis 6:8—9:29
  Noah
Genesis 11:27—18:33;
20:1—25:11;
Romans 4:1–25
  Abraham
Genesis 18:1–15; 21:1–7
  Sarah
1 Corinthians 9:24–27;
Philippians 3:13–14;
2 Timothy 4:7–8
  Athletic contests
  illustrating spiritual
  truths

DAILY BIBLE READINGS

Monday: Isaiah 60:1–5
Tuesday: Psalm 37:3–9
Wednesday: 1 Thessalonians
            5:16–24
Thursday: Psalm 23
Friday: James 1:2–12
Saturday: Hebrews
            11:1–16; 12:1–3
Sunday: Jude 17–22

"conviction." It was frequently used of putting something to a test, demonstrating or proving that it is so. It is being convinced of the truth of that which is not seen. So faith is not some flight of fancy, being lost in imagination. It brings with it both a guarantee and a conviction.

This is what the ancients were commended for (v. 2) "Ancients" refers to the ancestors of the Jewish nation, whose stories were told in the Old Testament. The writer to the Hebrews had built a powerful argument to demonstrate that Christ is superior to all other religious leaders, and His new covenant is superior to the old. Then he turned to the practical application of all he had said and called for his readers to be "of those who believe and are saved" (10:39), and he prepared to show it was by faith that the ancients had pleased God. Faith is not some new substitute for the old covenant and the law. Rather, it was the basis on which those were initiated. He bound the Jewish Christians of the New Testament era with their past, and also bound us with all who have gone before. He went on to show in the rest of the chapter the significance of faith in the history of God's dealing with His people, setting it forth in the individual and cumulative stories of those who made a difference by believing God.

The writer began at the beginning. He cited belief about the origin of our universe as one of the practical ways in which faith's significance is demonstrated. **By faith we understand that the universe was formed at God's command, so that what is seen was not made out of what was visible** (11:3). This is a clear reference to the story of Genesis 1. No human was on hand to observe the early stages of creation. We cannot know about it on the basis of physical sense or human reason. So the only way we can know about it is by divine revelation. God told us about it in His Word, and by faith we can be as sure and certain of it as any of the things we know through sight or touch.

The Witnesses to Faith (Heb. 11:4–16)

Our study features five heroes of faith described in Hebrews 11:4–16.

The story in Genesis 4 about Cain and Abel does not speak of faith as a factor in Abel's successful worship. That account has led some to suppose Abel's sacrifice was preferable because it involved the shedding of the sacrificial animal's blood. Cain brought of the fruits of the soil. However, the Old Testament sacrificial system included not only animal sacrifices, but sacrifices of grain, wine, olive oil, and incense as well (see Ex. 29:40; Num. 7:13–14). So both Cain and Abel had brought what they had to offer. It was not the *offering* that made the difference, but the *offerer*. **By faith Abel offered God a better sacrifice than Cain did** (Heb. 11:4). Faith made the difference. We are not told what prompted Abel's faith. Perhaps he had heard of God's promise of a future deliverer made to Eve in Genesis 3:15. Or perhaps it was God's sacrifice of animals to make skin garments for Adam and Eve in 3:21. Cain apparently offered as a mere formality. Faith is essential for worship.

Enoch was one who **by faith . . . was taken from this life, so that he did not experience death** (Heb. 11:5). Like Moses, whose body God hid, Enoch **could not be found**, but for him it was **because God had taken him away** (compare Gen. 5:24; Deut. 34:1–8). **Before he was taken, he was commended as one who pleased God.** "Commended" is the same word in

WHAT DO YOU THINK?
Why is hope crucial to faith? Is faith blind because it is the "conviction of things not seen"? Explain.

AHA!
We must always be ready to handle any task God assigns to us!

DID YOU KNOW?
Abraham is mentioned ten times in Hebrews; Moses is mentioned eleven times.

Hebrews 11:2, and **commended** and **spoke well of** in 11:4. It was faith that enabled Enoch to please God. He lived such a holy life that God took him heavenward about five hundred years before others in his age were dying.

In 11:6, the writer followed up on the reference to Enoch's pleasing God by saying that **without faith it is impossible to please God**. Two acts of faith are required: **believe that** God **exists**, and **that he rewards those who earnestly seek him**. No one could come **to him** if they did not believe in His existence. But more is required. The one coming to God must believe that God relates to humans, to the point of giving rewards. To believe God exists and made all things falls short if we think of God as someone detached from His creation, unavailable to us. Faith is the key to a better understanding and a real relationship.

Noah (v. 7) is next on the roll of faith's heroes. His **faith** caused him to take it seriously when he was **warned about things not yet seen**. Others no doubt scoffed at him for building an ark on dry land. But **in holy fear** he was enabled **to save his family. By his faith he condemned the world and became heir of the righteousness that comes by faith.**

Abraham (v. 8) appears next on the Hebrews list in faith's hall of fame. In Romans 4:11, Paul called him "the father of all who believe," not only of the Jews, but also of the Christians. So he is our spiritual father as well. Three demonstrations of his outstanding faith are mentioned in Hebrews 11, two in this study (vv. 8–10, 11–12), plus another later in the chapter (vv. 17–19). The first one had to do with his response to God's call to leave the cultured city life he had always known in Mesopotamia. He was **to go to a place he would later receive as his inheritance. He obeyed and went, even though he did not know where he was going.** There, **he**, his son, and his grandson **lived** not inside city walls, but **in tents** (v. 9). This was because **he was looking forward**, beyond the physical Promised Land, **to the city with foundations, whose architect and builder is God** (v. 10).

In the second demonstration of faith, **Abraham** shares attention with **Sarah** (v. 11). **He was past age** and she **was barren**. But they had a son **by faith**. It was because Abraham **considered him faithful who had made the promise**. Even though he was **as good as dead** (v. 12), he had **descendants as numerous as the stars in the sky and as countless as the sand on the seashore**.

Benefits of Faith		
Abel	Hebrews 11:4	Worship accepted
Enoch	Hebrews 11:5	Taken to heaven
Noah	Hebrews 11:7	Saved his family
Abraham	Hebrews 11:8–12	Received inheritance and multitude of descendants
Sarah	Hebrews 11:11	Child in old age

Then the writer paused in his storytelling to state something of a summary about the persons thus far. They all **were still living by faith when they died. They did not receive the things promised; they only saw them and welcomed them from a distance** (v. 13). They were **aliens and strangers on** this **earth. They** were **looking for a country of their own . . . a better country— a heavenly one. For God . . . has prepared a city for them** (vv. 14–16). Only tents while here, but a city yet to come. The book of Revelation had probably not yet been written, but our thoughts go immediately to the new Jerusalem of Revelation 21:1–7.

The writer to the Hebrews renewed the calling of the roll in 11:17 with the story about Abraham's near offering of Isaac as a burnt offering to the Lord. He

WHAT DO YOU THINK?
How is the "great cloud of witnesses" a source of comfort and encouragement to Christians today?

AHA!
God rewards faithful service!

DID YOU KNOW?
Tradition tells us Isaiah was martyred by being sawn in two.

WHAT ABOUT YOU?
How would your faith
be described if you were
included in the Hebrews 11
"Hall of Faith"?

PRAYER
Lord, spur me on by the
examples of faith of the
saints of old, and the faithful
ones today. Thank You for
saving faith, which spurs me
on to acts of service and
righteousness.

then proceeded through the Old Testament and possibly the intertestamental period, when the Maccabees and others lived by faith. And he said in 11:39–40, that none of these heroes "received what had been promised," because "God had planned something better for us so that only together with us would they be made perfect" or complete. All of us together will inherit the promises God began to give so long ago. ◆

HEBREWS 11:1–16

11:1 Now faith is being sure of what we hope for and certain of what we do not see.

2 This is what the ancients were commended for.

3 By faith we understand that the universe was formed at God's command, so that what is seen was not made out of what was visible.

4 By faith Abel offered God a better sacrifice than Cain did. By faith he was commended as a righteous man, when God spoke well of his offerings. And by faith he still speaks, even though he is dead.

5 By faith Enoch was taken from this life, so that he did not experience death; he could not be found, because God had taken him away. For before he was taken, he was commended as one who pleased God.

6 And without faith it is impossible to please God, because anyone who comes to him must believe that he exists and that he rewards those who earnestly seek him.

7 By faith Noah, when warned about things not yet seen, in holy fear built an ark to save his family. By his faith he condemned the world and became heir of the righteousness that comes by faith.

8 By faith Abraham, when called to go to a place he would later receive as his inheritance, obeyed and went, even though he did not know where he was going.

9 By faith he made his home in the promised land like a stranger in a foreign country; he lived in tents, as did Isaac and Jacob, who were heirs with him of the same promise.

10 For he was looking forward to the city with foundations, whose architect and builder is God.

11 By faith Abraham, even though he was past age—and Sarah herself was barren—was enabled to become a father because he considered him faithful who had made the promise.

12 And so from this one man, and he as good as dead, came descendants as numerous as the stars in the sky and as countless as the sand on the seashore.

13 All these people were still living by faith when they died. They did not receive the things promised; they only saw them and welcomed them from a distance. And they admitted that they were aliens and strangers on earth.

14 People who say such things show that they are looking for a country of their own.

15 If they had been thinking of the country they had left, they would have had opportunity to return.

16 Instead, they were longing for a better country—a heavenly one. Therefore God is not ashamed to be called their God, for he has prepared a city for them.

Faith That Moves God

Run the race of faith with perseverance.

INTO THE SUBJECT

We exercise faith every day, although we may not think about it. We exercise faith in our doctors, the prescriptions they write, in the safety of the food we eat and the water we drink. The list could go on, but is our faith in God what it ought to be?

INTO THE WORD

1. Read Hebrews 11:1, and then define faith in your own words. How accurate in your definition in light of this verse?

2. Why do you agree or disagree that it takes a belief that is not so different from faith to accept a scientific theory such as evolution?

3. Read Hebrews 11:4–10. Which example of faith do you consider most astonishing? Why?

4. Enoch "was commended as one who pleased God" (v. 5). How would you describe the life of faith that pleases God?

5. How might having faith make you feel like an alien and stranger on the earth?

6. Read Hebrews 12:1. Do you think departed believers watch us? Why or why not?

7. What may distract you from running the Christian race with perseverance and with your eyes fixed on Jesus? How will you avoid those distractions?

INTO THE WORD

Demonstrate your faith in Jesus this week by being positive and confident about His plans for you.

WHO DID WHAT?

Match the people on the left side with their actions of faith on the right side.

1. Jacob	A. Was obedient to God and built an ark
2. People of Israel	B. Did not experience death
3. Abraham	C. Blessed each of Joseph's sons
4. Enoch	D. Welcomed the spies and was spared
5. Moses	E. Kept the Passover and saved the firstborn of Israel
6. Noah	F. Was commended as righteous because of his offering
7. Abel	G. Blessed Jacob and Esau
8. Isaac	H. Offered Isaac as a sacrifice
9. Rahab	I. Passed through the Red Sea to escape Pharaoh

INTERACTIVE LEARNING IDEAS

GET THE CLASS INVOLVED
Hall of Faith

Hebrews 11 is often called the "Hall of Faith" because it highlights the works and attitudes of God's champions. But we have champions of the faith among us too, don't we? These are people, in many cases, on whose shoulders we stand.

Create a "Wall of Faith" in your classroom. Pass out a piece of paper to each person. Have each person identify someone who is a champion of the faith for them. It could be someone in your church, someone from the past, or even a well-known Christian who has had a significant impact on a large number of people.

Just for fun, have each person sketch a mini-portrait of the person they have in mind. Depending on the artistic abilities of the people in your class, these might not turn out to have the highest artistic quality. That's OK; it will all be part of the fun.

Underneath each portrait, have each student highlight some of the great things this person did for God. They could be missionaries, pastors, teachers, authors, or even stay-at-home-moms who taught their kids to love Jesus, or humble workers in the church kitchen making sure everyone has had enough to eat.

When the portraits are done, have each person bring his or hers up to the white board or wall to hang.

End the activity by thanking God for these "champions of the faith."

TRY THIS ON YOUR OWN
By Faith

The Hall of Faith in Hebrews 11 lists the faith-driven actions of the saints in biblical history. They did what they did out of a deeply abiding trust in God.

If you were listed in the Hall of Faith, what acts of yours would be highlighted?

Start some journal entries that begin with the words "By faith, [insert name]," and then complete the entry. This is not boasting as much as it is simply an expression how you express your faith—both during the spectacular events of life and the humdrum mundane of daily living.

How would you like this list to read in five years? Fill in the blanks as if those things had already happened (as the Lord wills).

TAKING IT TO THE STREET
In the Race

The writer of Hebrews encouraged his readers to complete the race they found themselves in, to persevere to the very end. We are to fix our eyes on Jesus, who is also in the race with us (see Heb. 12:1–2).

Take your class to a local high school track, and start walking around it. (Make sure everyone has the appropriate medical clearance to take a long walk.) Most tracks are a quarter-mile long, so four laps will equal a complete mile.

As you walk around the track, talk about the different components of a race: the starting blocks; the gun that begins the race; the pacing of the runners, especially in a long race; how some runners get disqualified; and how some runners find a "second wind" when it seems like they've run out of gas.

Of course, as you are leading this discussion about literal races, be sure to draw the appropriate spiritual parallels.

WITH YOUR FAMILY
Moving Plans

A few people in the Hall of Faith, like Moses and Abraham, had to move to another place where God wanted them to be (Heb. 11:8). God still does that today.

Make a moving plan as a family. That way, if something comes up—usually job related—that requires a move, you will be ready as a family. Your plan should address things like the following: What will we take with us? What will we give away or throw out? How will we get our place of residence ready? How will we pack?

What will we tell our friends? Will it be hard to leave them? How can we help each other through the tough things we'll have to give up because of the move?

What would we like to be different in our new home? What's the best way to go about making new friends?

How shall we look for a new church home?

Appoint someone to be a secretary to write all these answers down. And then you'll be ready to go, if that turns out to be part of God's plan for your family. ✦

"By faith Abraham . . . obeyed and went, even though he did not know where he was going."

—Hebrews 11:8

God has promised new life that requires us to live it.

LESSON 11

NEW LIFE CHANGES EVERYTHING

Hebrews 12:14–29

KEY VERSE

Make every effort to live in peace with all men and to be holy; without holiness no one will see the Lord.
—Hebrews 12:14

BACKGROUND SCRIPTURES

Leviticus 26:6;
Genesis 15:15; Job 22:21;
Psalms 34:14; 119:165;
Romans 5:1; Mark 9:5
   Compare the Old Testament concepts of peace with those found in the New Testament.
1 Corinthians 1:2 (compare 3:30); John 17:17, 19;
1 Thessalonians 5:23
   Note the way *sanctify* is used in the passages. Compare to Hebrews 12:14.
Genesis 25:30–34; 27:1–39
   Esau sold his birthright.
Exodus 19:12–22
   Moses on the mountain

DAILY BIBLE READINGS

Monday: Zechariah 4:1–8
Tuesday: 1 John 5:1–5
Wednesday: Revelation 2:1–11
Thursday: 2 Peter 1:3–11
Friday: John 17:20—18:1
Saturday: Hebrews 12:14–29
Sunday: Psalm 24:7–10

WHY THIS MATTERS

A mother asked her five-year-old son what he was drawing. "I'm drawing a picture of God," he replied.

"But no one knows what God looks like," Mom said.

The boy glanced at his mother. "They will when I finish this picture."

Many adults, too, draw their own pictures of God, depicting Him to be what they want Him to be. However, their representations of Him often contrast with the biblical portrayal of God as not only loving, merciful, and forgiving, but also holy, righteous, and just. Furthermore, He has summoned His children to live righteously and pursue holiness.

This lesson spurs us to walk daily in true holiness.

BIBLE COMMENTARY

By John H. Connor

A quick review of Hebrews' thematic content will help us understand our present study passage in chapter 12.

The book can easily be broken down into thematic patterns with appropriate asides and additional arguments from Jewish cultural logic and Scripture. God spoke through His Son (1:1); this is altogether better than through angels (1:4) or even through Moses (3:3). Jesus is a better high priest (4:14), even better than Melchizedek (6:20). Jesus provides a better rest (3:11), better promises (4:1), a better covenant (7:22), a better priesthood (7:26), a better tabernacle (9:11), and a better sacrifice (9:23). Consequently this brings a better, more complete salvation (2:3; 5:9; 10:2). Therefore (note the logical progression that "therefore" indicates throughout the book: 1:9; 2:1; 3:1; 4:1, 7, 11, 14; 6:1; 7:25; 10:5, 19; 11:16; 12:1, 12, 28; 13:15), we who participate in this astounding salvation should be better people (10:19), not backsliders (10:26), full of faith (11:1), full of endurance (12:1), and full of steadfast love (13:1).

Chapter 11 of Hebrews is the faith chapter. It gives a listing of men and women of faith and in some instances the cost of their faith to their personal well-being. Part of the emphasis is that the "payoff" for faith is not necessarily always physical or imminent. The last two verses of chapter 11 spell that out specifically. The theme of spiritual recompense occurs again at the end of chapter 12.

Chapter 12 begins with a "therefore," indicating progression of the argument. There are two concepts here. One is that expressed above, that recompense is not always physical and imminent. The second is that sometimes physical recompense is for another generation. This applies to us: "They did that for our benefit, therefore . . ." what kind of people should we be? And it also applies by implication to generations that will follow us. We stand on both sides of this equation. So the evangelist writer moved to the bottom line and hit the ground running: "Let us throw off everything that hinders . . . let us run with perseverance . . . Let us fix our eyes on Jesus . . . not grow weary and lose heart" (12:1–3). This is the picture of a runner who has left robe, sash, turban, and sandals scattered all along the track as he runs down the track in absolute concentration on the finish line.

WHAT DO YOU THINK?
As far as it depends on you, how can you live at peace with people? What should you do if they reject your overtures of reconciliation?

While "discipline" can mean punishment, and punishment is indicated in 12:6, the major emphasis in 12:4–11 is the kind of discipline that the motivated runner would put himself under in order to run the race. The discipline of a loving father is not done to inflict misery, but to ingrain protective and positive boundaries so that goals might be reached. The illustration has direct implications in that "God disciplines us for our good, that we may share in his holiness" (12:10). These concepts all lead to the section we want to study with another "therefore" (12:12). Here is a loose paraphrase of verses 12–13: "Since all of the above is true, tuck in your shirttail, pull up your socks, stand up, and get started." Following are some specifics of the discipline regimen.

Holy People Try Harder (Heb. 12:14–17)

In 12:14–28, the writer focused on living a better life. He began with the simple command to **make every effort to live in peace with all men** (v. 14). The Christian life cannot be lived on cruise control. The concept of making every effort is a cognitive, persistent pursuit. It's a "put your back into it" kind of pursuit. A mistaken idea of peace in the Old Testament (*shalom*) was that it was something God would do without our help. This led, for instance, to the lifestyle pictured in Judges 17:6: "Everyone did as he saw fit." The presence of the carnal nature makes living in peace with others a difficult task indeed. However, the Christlike person has the Holy Spirit's help in pursuing peace.

AHA!
Christians must not tolerate false teachings in the church!

The statement **without holiness no one will see the Lord** (Heb. 12:14) is sometimes quoted out of context. Holiness can be both progressive and a finished work of heart purity. The passage here is a part of the "make every effort" concept. It is progressive. Verse 14 in the KJV appears to be closer in some ways to the Greek text than the NIV. It says, "Follow peace with all men and holiness, with out which no man shall see the Lord." The thing that will keep us from seeing the Lord is failing to follow after holiness.

Entire sanctification is not static. There is growth after the first moment (crisis) of entire sanctification. Holiness, whether before entire sanctification or following the cleansing of the sinful nature, is never static. Some have used the logic that if a person has not been entirely sanctified, then he or she can legitimately be impure with immunity, that sin is unimportant in God's eyes at certain stages of the Christian life. Not true. This passage means that from the very first spiritual breath of new birth, God expects us to be pursuers of holiness. A part of that holiness requires making every effort and includes progression. Immaturity is not an excuse for being unholy; God requires the pursuit of holiness, or we will never see Him. The whole concept is based in this better salvation provided by Christ.

DID YOU KNOW?
Jewish legends attribute a variety of sins to Esau; apparently there were very few that he missed.

A pastor who was arguing against the logic of holiness of heart and life said to me, "This type of life is impossible unless God does something for us." And then the light went on, because we had been talking about entire sanctification. There are two foundational keys that relate to entire sanctification in this passage. The first is the holiness that begins at salvation, or, as John Wesley called it, "initial sanctification." The second is the grace of God mentioned in verse 15: **See to it that no one misses the grace of God.**

The definition of grace as being the "unmerited favor of God" is a truth that is often quoted. But the "make every effort" portion of grace is sometimes overlooked or misrepresented. In this passage, it is expressed by, "See to it that no one misses." Grace is unmerited favor, but God doesn't shove it down our throats. He offers it to us. The implication is that grace can be missed.

The Bible in story, explicit command, and implication shows us that God likes to work cooperatively with us. God is sovereign, and, if He wants, He can send a flood to wipe out the world, harden Pharaoh's heart, or in the end destroy the world. If He wants to, He can. But God is so big that He can also offer unmerited favor to you and actually allow you to make a choice without altering Him or His ultimate plan no matter how you choose. Your response to His grace will have an effect on you. Actually, your response to God's grace may affect others as well. If the **bitter root grows up**, it will **cause trouble and defile many** (v. 15). How many sad stories can we recount in that category?

A pastor asked John Wesley how often he should preach on entire sanctification and Wesley's response was "scarcely at all." His whole approach was to teach about God's grace and responding always positively to God's grace. The natural result would lead to the experience of holiness of heart. He said, "Teach free grace not free will." He taught that sin is "a willful transgression against the known law of God." The exact opposite of that would be faith: willful acceptance and obedience to the known law of God. The space between sin and faith is grace, the unmerited favor of God.

WHAT DO YOU THINK?
What are some ways to express our gratitude for our salvation? What makes our worship "acceptable" to God?

"But you have come to Mount Zion, to the heavenly Jerusalem, the city of the living God" (Heb. 12:22).

AHA!
Godly actions confirm the integrity of a person's faith!

DID YOU KNOW?
The first 12 chapters of Hebrews are written as a single unit; chapter 13 is like an appendix.

God's Unmerited Favor

We don't deserve it, but we must respond to it one way or the other and everyone does. The point the Hebrews writer was making is that God's grace is overwhelming. Now what are you going to do? The sin aspect mentioned in verses 16–17 is not a little glitch; he mentioned **sexual immorality** and being **godless.** Those things would fit Wesley's sin definition, and the consequence is a loss of inheritance. "See to it that no one misses the grace of God." Missing the grace misses the mark; it misses the narrow path and misses the inheritance. Responding to grace positively is faith. Responding to grace negatively is sin. Persistent positive response to grace is the path of holiness. That is why without the pursuit of holiness we will never see the Lord.

Who Is the God You Serve? (Heb. 12:18–24)

In the Old Testament, God is often portrayed as a transcendent Being of power and wrath. This is depicted in verses 18–21. He is the God on the mountain **burning with fire . . . darkness, gloom and storm** and **trumpet blast** (vv. 18–19). And the whole thing was so overwhelming and terrifying that even poor old **Moses said, "I am trembling with fear"** (v. 21). Verse 22 begins with the word **but**, which indicates a contrast. If it was set to music, verses 18–21 could be the "March of the Charioteers" from *Ben Hur* with kettle drums and cymbals. The contrast in 22–24 might be music taken from the *Sound of Music* with lightness and joy on the mountaintop to the accompaniment of stringed instruments. One depicts transcendence; the other depicts immanence. One is the God away and aloof, powerful and fearful. The other depicts the God with us—Immanuel, near us, who knows us by name and gives to us **a better word** (v. 24).

Remember that this was being offered to a Jewish audience. In these two sections (vv. 18–21 as contrasted to vv. 22–23), the writer of Hebrews pulled in the picture of everything he'd previously written in the book and, as a true evangelist, demanded a cognitive response to grace.

Cooperating with God (Heb. 12:25–29)

As a true evangelist, the writer also felt compelled to give a warning, just as he did in chapter 10. **See to it that you do not refuse him who speaks** (v. 25). The theological term for cooperating with God is *synergism*. The work of salvation was God's work alone, but He offers it to us. We, by an act of faith, must reach out and take hold of this great salvation. That is synergism. God, in His infinite goodness, speaks to us, offers His grace to us, but we must listen. We must respond. That is synergism. "See to it that no one misses the grace of God" (12:15); **See to it the you do not refuse him who speaks** (v. 25). What a concept! The sovereign God who created the universe by a word, this God of transcendent might, can offer us His grace and can speak His word to us and we can miss the grace and refuse Him. We can **turn away from him** (v. 25). Indeed, "how shall we escape if we ignore such a great salvation?" (2:2).

The writer's purpose was not to scare the socks off his readers; his purpose was to bring them to the logical conclusion. The logic of verses 26–27 might seem a little shaky in our culture, but the point is solidly clear. There is a metaphysical and physical world. One is shaky ground; the other cannot be shaken. Our greatest concern should be the metaphysical—the spiritual world; it alone is the real deal. **Therefore, since we are receiving a kingdom that cannot be shaken, let us be thankful, and so worship God acceptably with reverence and awe, for our "God is a consuming fire"** (vv. 28–29). ✦

INTERACTIVE LEARNING IDEAS

GET THE CLASS INVOLVED
Holy Living

The writer of Hebrews said that without holiness, no one will see the Lord.

Have your students break up into small groups of three to four, and talk about the nuts and bolts of holy living.

What does it mean to be holy in marriage? In parenting? In our vocations? In our homes? In church? In our respective ministries? In our leisure time?

Is there such a thing as artificial or manufactured holiness? Explain. How can you tell the real thing from that which is just being faked?

What motivates the godly believer toward holiness? What are some less than acceptable motivations toward holiness? Is holiness something than can be affirmed or disconfirmed by other believers? Explain.

What is the difference between Spirit-driven holiness and the type that is merely spurred on by human strength?

What type of actions or attitudes threaten holiness? What types of things can derail a person's faith? Are those sorts of things usually sudden or gradual downward turns? How can you prevent such a thing from happening?

When the groups are done discussing these questions, bring the large group back to together. Ask one person from each group summarize their answers. Close the activity in prayer, asking the Lord to give each person the ability to pursue holiness in ways that are honoring to God.

TRY THIS ON YOUR OWN
Seek the Blessing

Esau lost the blessing of the older son because he treated it with contempt. Even though later he sought after it with tears, he was denied that blessing (Heb. 12:16–17).

Many people today long for the blessing of their fathers, but for one reason or another have not obtained it. But not because they've treated with contempt. Sometimes those fathers have passed on, or it's simply inappropriate to ask.

You can still seek out the blessing of an older saint. Prayerfully consider what kind of blessing you'd like an older man or woman to pronounce over you. Consider talking with an elderly saint about doing this very thing. Get their input and perspective on what you're asking. Then, if you come to an agreement, you too can receive a blessing for which you've longed perhaps for many years.

TAKING IT TO THE STREET
Around the Campfire

The writer of Hebrew described God as a consuming fire. He is so holy that any kind of evil cannot survive in His presence (Heb. 12:29).

Take your class to a place where you can safely build a campfire. You might want to make this a social event and bring food like hot dogs and s'mores.

Make sure everyone has a piece of paper. As everyone is looking at the campfire, talk about how God is a consuming fire. To those who are reconciled with God, this is a comfort. It means He will burn away the dross in our lives, so that all that's left is the "real thing."

Ask your students to take their piece of paper and write down any particular sins they recently committed. Have them spend a few minutes silently acknowledging their responsibility in the matter. Then have them throw their papers into the fire. This is a symbol of how God removes sin from their hearts—as far as the east is from the west.

WITH YOUR FAMILY
Living in Peace

Hebrews 12:14 tells us to make every effort to be at peace with everyone. This can be especially hard with family members, with whom you need to rub shoulders every day.

Have the family sit in a circle. Make sure each family member has several sheets of paper and something with which to write. Have them complete the following sentence: "It seems to me that [insert a perceived problem]." When everyone has had a chance to write two to three things, put them into a bowl, and then pull out one at a time.

Discuss each issue as it comes up. Make sure each person has a chance to express his or her view. Come up with possible solutions to each perceived problem in such a way that everybody's concerns are addressed. ◆

HEBREWS 12:14–29

14 Make every effort to live in peace with all men and to be holy; without holiness no one will see the Lord.

15 See to it that no one misses the grace of God and that no bitter root grows up to cause trouble and defile many.

16 See that no one is sexually immoral, or is godless like Esau, who for a single meal sold his inheritance rights as the oldest son.

17 Afterward, as you know, when he wanted to inherit this blessing, he was rejected. He could bring about no change of mind, though he sought the blessing with tears.

18 You have not come to a mountain that can be touched and that is burning with fire; to darkness, gloom and storm;

19 to a trumpet blast or to such a voice speaking words that those who heard it begged that no further word be spoken to them,

20 because they could not bear what was commanded: "If even an animal touches the mountain, it must be stoned."

21 The sight was so terrifying that Moses said, "I am trembling with fear."

22 But you have come to Mount Zion, to the heavenly Jerusalem, the city of the living God. You have come to thousands upon thousands of angels in joyful assembly,

23 to the church of the firstborn, whose names are written in heaven. You have come to God, the judge of all men, to the spirits of righteous men made perfect,

24 to Jesus the mediator of a new covenant, and to the sprinkled blood that speaks a better word than the blood of Abel.

25 See to it that you do not refuse him who speaks. If they did not escape when they refused him who warned them on earth, how much less will we, if we turn away from him who warns us from heaven?

26 At that time his voice shook the earth, but now he has promised, "Once more I will shake not only the earth but also the heavens."

27 The words "once more" indicate the removing of what can be shaken—that is, created things—so that what cannot be shaken may remain.

28 Therefore, since we are receiving a kingdom that cannot be shaken, let us be thankful, and so worship God acceptably with reverence and awe,

29 for our "God is a consuming fire."

New Life Changes Everything

*God has promised new life that
requires us to live it.*

INTO THE SUBJECT

Life is full of choices. Every day we choose what we will wear, what we will eat, how hard we will work, and what we will do in our leisure time. Our relationship with God also depends on what we choose to make of it. Will we avail ourselves of His grace and grow or reject it and suffer the consequences?

INTO THE WORD

1. Why is it often hard to live in peace with others, as instructed in Hebrews 12:14?

2. Why do you agree or disagree that it takes effort to lead a holy life?

3. Why do you agree or disagree that sexual immorality among believers is increasing? What factors do you think contribute to sexual immorality?

4. Why is bitterness such a destructive quality?

5. Esau is called "godless" in verse 16. What was his sin, and how can a believer today avoid committing this sin?

6. What indications of God's holiness do you see in verses 18–21?

7. Read verses 22–28. What characteristics of the spiritual kingdom make it far superior to the present world?

8. What thoughts and emotions are awakened in you as you contemplate the fact that "God is a consuming fire" (v. 29)?

INTO THE WORLD

Refuse to let down your spiritual guard and be satisfied with your current stage of holiness. Keep on keeping on!

SCRAMBLER

Unscramble each of the clue words. Take the letters that appear in ◯ boxes and unscramble them for the final message.

REFFOT

CEPAE

HEISOLSN

GACRE

TIHFA

TECOAPOER

REESV

SEHBERW

To love God and others is the true sacrifice God desires.

THANKFULNESS—THE LOVING SACRIFICE

Hebrews 13:15–16; Acts 2:42–47

WHY THIS MATTERS

What tastes better and refreshes instantly like a cup of mountain spring water? Some businesses contract with mountain spring water companies to keep their water coolers supplied with that wonderful H_2O, not only for their employees, but also for customers.

Believers are constant beneficiaries of wonderful blessings that God generously pours upon them. The blessings refresh our lives and instill a spirit of thankfulness in us. But we should not hoard what God bestows on us. This lesson motivates us to offer a sacrifice of praise to God for all His benefits and to share those benefits with others.

BIBLE COMMENTARY

By Kevin Scott

What would you say to a group of dear friends who were facing the likelihood of severe persecution, perhaps even the loss of limb or life? What if you knew that they could easily avoid all of that fear, anxiety, and potential pain and loss by making one simple decision? And what if that one simple decision was to reject their commitment to Christ, to return to their previous way of life, and to blend in again with their neighbors?

That was the precise situation facing the unknown author of Hebrews. While we know little for certain about the recipients of the book of Hebrews, there are several things we can discern from the text. The recipients of the letter were likely converts from Judaism to Christianity. This would explain why the author assumed a detailed knowledge of the Old Testament and argued vigorously for the superiority of Christ over the Jewish sacrificial system. We know that this group of Jewish believers had endured a round of persecution several years before and that many of them had experienced loss associated with that persecution (10:32–34). It seems they were preparing themselves for another, potentially more severe, threat of persecution and that this time their lives might be threatened (12:3–4). Because of all of this, some of them were probably tempted to renounce their allegiance to Christ (10:35–36), perhaps to return to their Jewish faith, since it was a protected religion in the Roman Empire.

The book of Hebrews was written to address head-on the temptation these believers were experiencing in the face of persecution. Written in the form of a sermon, the book was intended to be read aloud to the Hebrew Christians, and perhaps passed from house church to house church. The purpose of the book was to strengthen their resolve and to urge them to remain faithful to Christ in the face of persecution. The author accomplished this by focusing relentlessly—and helping the recipients to focus—on Jesus Messiah. As the sermon reached its conclusion, the author offered a clear, concise picture of the

KEY VERSE

Through Jesus, therefore, let us continually offer to God a sacrifice of praise— the fruit of lips that confess his name.
—Hebrews 13:15

BACKGROUND SCRIPTURES

Proverbs 3:9–10
 Honor God for His providence.
1 Thessalonians 5:16–18
 The conclusion of Paul's epistle challenges believers to always be giving praise and thanksgiving.
Ephesians 5:20
 Always be thankful to God for the fellowship of believers.
Philippians 4:6–7
 All prayer should be characterized by thankfulness.

DAILY BIBLE READINGS

Monday: Exodus
                  15:20–21
Tuesday: Proverbs 3:9–10
Wednesday: Philippians 4:6
Thursday: 1 Thessalonians
                  5:16–18
Friday: Ephesians
                  5:18–21
Saturday: Hebrews
                  13:15–16
Sunday: Psalm 105:1–5

mature Christian life lived in the unique fellowship of genuine Christian love and community. In the author's words, we can hear the echo of Jesus' reply to the inquiry about the Greatest Commandment of the law: "'Love the Lord your God with all your heart and with all your soul and with all your mind.' This is the first and greatest commandment. And the second is like it: 'Love your neighbor as yourself.' All the Law and the Prophets hang on these two commandments" (Matt. 22:37–40). And it begins with a heart of gratitude, which is the true sacrifice God requires from His people.

Love God (Heb. 13:15)

The sacrifice offered by Jesus Messiah was superior in every way to the Levitical sacrificial system. This is the central argument of the book of Hebrews. By giving His life as a sacrifice on the cross, Jesus fulfilled and exceeded the demands of the Old Testament law. As a result, there is no further need for those who follow Jesus to atone for their sins through burnt offerings. Yet there are still sacrifices that God requires.

First, Christians are to express our love **to God** the Father. The author of Hebrews calls this **a sacrifice of praise** (v. 15). True worship arises not from a sense of obligation or duty but from a deep sense of gratitude for all God has done for the Christian. God was in no way obligated to fix the situation humanity created. He could have opted for judgment without mercy. He could have chosen destruction without the possibility of redemption. But while we were disobedient and rebellious, He was faithful. While we were sinners, He was not only righteous and holy, but merciful and loving. When He saw that we had marred his image in us, rather than casting us away, He chose to redeem and restore us. For all of this and more, we owe Him our undying thankfulness. Such informed gratitude is the heart of genuine worship.

The author of Hebrews described the content of this sacrifice of praise as **the fruit of lips that confess his name** (v. 15). Before Christ, God required blood on the altar for the forgiveness of sins; but Christ's sacrifice made the blood offering obsolete. The worshiper's sins have been atoned for once and for all, paid in full. The only sacrifice left to bring is the sacrifice of praise, the fruit of a heart that has been redeemed.

The phrase "fruit of lips" was apparently borrowed from the prophet Hosea, who urged Israel to repent and say to God: "Forgive all our sins and receive us graciously, that we may offer the fruit of our lips" (Hos. 14:2). The organic metaphor of fruit points to the genuine nature of the praise we are to offer God. These are not words that someone places in our mouths. No one can merely feed us our lines in worship. The sacrifice of praise grows internally and proceeds naturally from our hearts through our mouths.

The word *continually* should clue us in to the fact that the author of Hebrews is talking about something that goes beyond a one-hour worship service on Sunday. The sacrifice of praise required by God is a way of life. As the apostle Paul said, we are to offer our lives as sacrifices—and this is the only reasonable act of worship—in light of what God has done for us (Rom. 12:1–2). In other words, the sacrifice of praise is not an activity; it is a lifestyle of worship. By every word and deed our lives should proclaim that Jesus is our Lord and Redeemer.

WHAT DO YOU THINK?
Why would God consider good works and sharing a type of sacrifice? Why do these types of offerings give Him pleasure?

AHA!
God expects mature Christians to mentor young believers!

DID YOU KNOW?
There were many traveling preachers in the first century who always needed lodging.

By this point in the book of Hebrews it should be no surprise that this every-moment worship lifestyle God expects is only possible **through Jesus** (Heb. 13:15). Through His life, death, and resurrection, He has become the mediator between God and humanity. And it is only through Him that we can offer a sacrifice of praise that is acceptable to the Father.

The mature Christian life, then, is a life of gratitude—for God's decision to reclaim us rather than cast us away and for Jesus' willingness to lay down His life so we can have life. This gratitude is reflected in our love for God and a lifestyle of unending worship.

"Through Jesus, therefore, let us continually offer to God a sacrifice of praise— the fruit of lips that confess his name" (Heb. 13:15).

Love Your Neighbor (Heb. 13:16)

The second sacrifice God requires is to love your neighbor. The author of Hebrews expresses this requirement in two ways. First, we are to **not forget to do good** (v. 16). To do good is not a solitary act; you can only do good if you take the time to be involved in other peoples' lives. Doing good is about how we relate to others. We are to treat one another with kindness and compassion, look out for others' needs as much as ours, and seek peace and justice. Doing good involves turning away from a self-centered lifestyle to becoming actively involved in the lives of others. And as Jesus illustrated in the parable of the good Samaritan, it means not picking and choosing who we consider our neighbor.

Doing good is part of the lifestyle of gratitude. At times, our hearts are so full of God's love for us that it overflows into the lives of others. At other times, when it doesn't flow so easily, we are to remember to do good anyway. In other words, we must be intentional about doing good at all times. This is part of what makes it a sacrifice; we make it a point to do good when we feel like it and when we don't.

The second part of loving our neighbor that the author of Hebrews highlighted is to remember **to share with others** (v. 16). This is a lifestyle of generosity. It is the positive side of the exhortation earlier in the chapter to "Keep your lives free from the love of money and be content with what you have, because God has said, 'Never will I leave you; never will I forsake you'" (v. 5). The assurance we have that God will always be there to meet our needs frees us from any potential bondage to money. The positive, practical side of that is that we should be willing to share with those in need. These two exhortations—to do good and share with others—are intended as a quick summary of the multifaceted ways Christians are to learn to love one another. These, too, are sacrifices that come from a heart filled with gratitude for all God has done for us.

We should remember that these sacrifices are different than those required by the Jewish Law. They do not provide for our atonement or redemption; that has already been accomplished. But they are the fruit of our redemption. And the author of Hebrews said that **with such sacrifices God is pleased** (v. 16). In Ephesians, the apostle Paul said that "we are God's workmanship" (Eph. 2:10); or as some scholars have translated it, "God's artwork." Like an artist admiring a new creation, God takes pleasure in seeing the fruit of heart that is redeemed.

WHAT DO YOU THINK?
What consistent practices in your church correspond to those listed Acts 2:42–47? Are there any missing?

AHA!
Living a consistent and godly life will silence slander!

DID YOU KNOW?
Christian sacrifice does not include bulls and goats, but praise, good deeds, and works of service.

Live in Community (Acts 2:42–47)

The context in which a believer grows into maturity as a Christian—into genuinely loving God and others—is always the context of a Christian faith community, a church. Sure, there might be isolated exceptions where a person flourishes in their relationship with Christ apart from the fellowship of other Christians; but these are exceptions and never meant to be the norm. The gospel of Jesus Christ creates and nurtures Christian community.

Many scholars and teachers have suggested that Acts 2:42 contains the four marks of the true church: **They devoted themselves to** (1) **the apostles' teaching**, (2) **the fellowship** of believers, (3) **the breaking of bread** together, and (4) **prayer** offered to the one true God. The rest of the passage demonstrates the remarkable thing that occurs when God's Spirit sanctifies the church: they become a new family, an extended family.

All the believers were together and had everything in common (v. 44). In other words, they stopped viewing their possessions as belonging to them, to be used only for their benefit. Instead, they chose to share their possessions with their new family. No longer was it "your house" or "their house"; it was "our house." No longer was it "your money" or "their money"; it was "our money." **Selling their possessions and goods, they gave to anyone as he had need** (v. 45). In other words, they lived and behaved as if they were part of a single family.

This kind of community does not occur naturally. It does not just happen automatically. You will not find people accidentally living this way. This kind of loving, caring community—where everyone's needs are provided for and no one has to face life alone—can only occur where Jesus is proclaimed as Lord and Redeemer, and where the Holy Spirit is given free rein to sanctify and reorder our lives and community of faith. As a result, when this kind of community occurs—and when it is genuinely a manifestation of the Holy Spirit—it is exceptionally attractive, even to those who do not believe. And Luke said that when this group of early believers began to experience this kind of loving fellowship and community, they were **enjoying the favor of all the people** (v. 47).

That is not to say that living in community is always convenient or easy; in fact, it is hard work. Even in the power of the Holy Spirit, it requires intentionality and constant effort. And sometimes it draws the wrong kind of attention, as the recipients of the book of Hebrews found out. But when this kind of community happens, no one can dispute the presence of God in the church. And it is precisely this kind of community that will sustain us during difficult days—whether the direct pressures of persecution or the more normal stresses and anxieties of everyday life in a fallen world. ✦

WHAT ABOUT YOU?
Do you have everything you need? How can you help other believers get what they need?

PRAYER
Lord, thank You for providing so much that I might share with others. Give me a generous heart for those who are in need.

HEBREWS 13:15–16; ACTS 2:42–47

Hebrews 13:15 Through Jesus, therefore, let us continually offer to God a sacrifice of praise—the fruit of lips that confess his name.

16 And do not forget to do good and to share with others, for with such sacrifices God is pleased.

Acts 2:42 They devoted themselves to the apostles' teaching and to the fellowship, to the breaking of bread and to prayer.

43 Everyone was filled with awe, and many wonders and miraculous signs were done by the apostles.

44 All the believers were together and had everything in common.

45 Selling their possessions and goods, they gave to anyone as he had need.

46 Every day they continued to meet together in the temple courts. They broke bread in their homes and ate together with glad and sincere hearts,

47 praising God and enjoying the favor of all the people. And the Lord added to their number daily those who were being saved.

"For flowers that bloom about our feet;
For tender grass, so fresh, so sweet;
For song of bird, and hum of bee;
For all things fair we hear or see,
Father in heaven, we thank Thee!"

—*Ralph Waldo Emerson*

Thankfulness—The Loving Sacrifice

*To love God and others is the
true sacrifice God desires.*

INTO THE SUBJECT

At Thanksgiving, our tables bear undeniable testimony to God's bountiful care of us, but do we offer Him heartfelt thanks every day of every year?

INTO THE WORD

1. What indication is there in Hebrews 13:15 that our thanks to God must flow through the proper "channel"?

2. How often should we offer thanks to God?

3. Why do you agree or disagree that praise may be simply the utterance of hollow words?

4. How might parents instill a spirit of thanksgiving in their children?

5. According to verse 16, what are two ways to please God? How well do you think you are pleasing God in these two matters?

6. Read Acts 2:42–47. What evidence of thankfulness and praise did the church at Jerusalem show?

7. How did the church at Jerusalem demonstrate a willingness to share?

8. Read Acts 2:47. How might the people of your community respond if they saw similar sharing among believers?

9. Why should praise be from the heart, and why should sharing be voluntary?

INTO THE WORLD

Spend more time in daily praise, and seek opportunities to share freely with a needy person.

Memorize and Symbolize

Memorize Hebrews 13:15–16: "Through Jesus, therefore, let us continually offer to God a sacrifice of praise—the fruit of lips that confess his name. And do not forget to do good and to share with others, for with such sacrifices God is pleased."

To reinforce the meaning of this passage and to help you remember its focus, draw two pictures that represent the verses. The first picture might be hands lifted high or someone singing. The second picture could show someone serving another.

INTERACTIVE LEARNING IDEAS

GET THE CLASS INVOLVED
Time to Sing

The writer of Hebrews encouraged Christians to offer up a sacrifice of praise to God. For most believers, this often involves some sort of singing.

Obtain some hymnals and spend some time singing praises to God together. This is not a time to worry about how well or poorly a person sings. What matters is what comes from the heart.

You may want to first read the lyrics out loud and discuss some of the deep theology behind them.

Perhaps you might want to start with this great hymn by John Wesley . . .

> Holy, holy, holy Lord,
> God the Father, and the Word,
> God the Comforter, receive
> Blessings more than we can give!
> Mixed with those beyond the sky,
> Chanters to the Lord Most High,
> We our hearts and voices raise,
> Echoing Thy eternal praise.
>
> One, inexplicably Three,
> Three, in simplest Unity,
> God, incline Thy gracious ear,
> Us, Thy lisping creatures, hear!
> Thee while man, the earth-born, sings,
> Angels shrink within their wings;
> Prostrate seraphim above
> Breathe unutterable love.

End the activity in prayer, praising God for the gifts of songs He has provided for those who would worship Him.

TRY THIS ON YOUR OWN
Give It Away

Christians in the early church freely gave of their possessions so there wouldn't be anyone in need (Heb. 13:15–16; Acts 2:42–45).

Set aside a day to get rid of everything in your home that you haven't looked at or used in the last year. If you haven't even touched the item in a year, it's unlikely you need it at all.

If something is worn out and you'd be embarrassed to pass it along to one of your friends, throw it out. If it's still in good shape, consider giving it to a thrift store so someone who is low on funds can enjoy what you no longer use. In fact, if you already know someone who would benefit from your no-longer-used items, simply give those items to them directly.

You might be amazed how good it feels to just get rid of things you'll never use.

TAKING IT TO THE STREET
To Those in Need

The writer of Hebrews told us to share with those in need, much like the early church did for those who found themselves in need (Heb. 13:15–16; Acts 2:42–45). The reason for their poverty made no difference. Christians are to serve them anyway.

Take your class to a local homeless shelter or food bank and offer yourselves as volunteers. Talk with the people who arrive and listen to their stories. Remember, you are there to serve them, not necessarily to offer opinions on how to change their situations (unless, of course, they ask for that type of advice).

Later, talk about the Christian's obligation to help the poor, both in regard to short-term survival and long-term self-sustaining activities.

WITH YOUR FAMILY
Share with Others

The writer of Hebrews reminded us of the importance of sharing with others, much like the early church did for those who were in need.

Go to a store that also has a grocery section with your family to pick up things you can put into small care packages. These care packages can go to homeless people or the people who stand on street corners with cardboard signs, asking for some change.

Ask yourselves, "If we were struggling, what kinds of things in a care package might be helpful?" Foods that are nonperishable in easy-to-open packages might be good. A new pair of socks might be helpful. Maybe you could include a gift card for a local store or restaurant. You might also want to include an encouraging note and small Bible.

During a time when you can all get together, go out and distribute your care packages. Look for the people on the corners or where homeless people can usually be found. Or course, always be safe. And always be kind and respectful to those you are serving. ◆

We are expected and equipped by the Spirit to live holy lives.

LESSON 13

HOLY ACTIONS FOLLOW HOLY MOTIVES
Hebrews 13:1–21

KEY VERSE

May the God of peace . . . equip you with everything good for doing his will, and may he work in us what is pleasing to him, through Jesus Christ.
                 —Hebrews 13:20–21

BACKGROUND SCRIPTURES

Isaiah 54:5; 62:5;
Jeremiah 3:14;
Hosea 2:19–20;
Matthew 9:15;
2 Corinthians 11:2;
Revelation 19:7; 21:2
    Marriage figurative of
    God and Israel and
    Christ and the church
Galatians 5:13–15;
1 Thessalonians 4:9–10;
1 Peter 4:8; 1 John 2:10; 4:21
    Loving fellow
    Christians
1 Timothy 3; Titus 1
    Qualifications for
    spiritual leadership

DAILY BIBLE READINGS

Monday: 1 Corinthians
             2:6–10
Tuesday: Romans 8:18–25
Wednesday: 1 Thessalonians
             3:6–13
Thursday: 2 Peter 3:8–18
Friday: Luke 21:29–36
Saturday: Hebrews
             13:1–21
Sunday: Psalm 25:1–10

WHY THIS MATTERS

Someone quipped, "I can't believe the things that go on in my kid's school: drugs, sex, shootings, stabbings, stealing. At least we have managed to keep prayer out of the classroom." Modern culture is drowning in sin while refusing to call on God for help.

Certainly the culture at its worst needs the church at its best. As Hebrews 13 points out, Christians ought to maintain high standards of love, purity, and holiness in every area of life. Our hearts and minds ought to be pure; our homes ought to be hospitable; and our churches ought to be peaceful.

This lesson inspires us to let our light shine in many directions.

BIBLE COMMENTARY
By John H. Connor

While the style of chapter 13 is different from the rest of the book, there is still progression of thought. The word *therefore* in 12:28 ties in chapter 13 to the earlier chapters. This transition could be loosely translated: "If it has been proven in the previous chapters that Jesus brings us a better, more complete way of salvation and holiness, a better understanding of the kingdom of God, and a better understanding of who God is, what are some specifics of practical Christian life and faith?" The answer is chapter 13.

Brotherly Love (Heb. 13:1)

The first practical aspect of Christian life is **keep on loving each other as brothers** (v. 1). This was an admonition Jesus gave His disciples in John 13:34–35: "A new command I give you: Love one another. As I have loved you, so you must love one another. By this all men will know that you are my disciples, if you love one another" (compare also 1 Pet. 1:22).

The great majority of people in the world outside the church have no interest in our theological debates or religious arguments. The razor-sharp arguments that the Hebrew writer so aptly laid out in the rest of the book leave the majority of the unsaved world of his day, and ours, cold, bored, and uninterested. There is only one argument the church has that attracts the world, and that is love. When a church body falls apart because of infighting and carnal recrimination, the church not only loses its vision, but also its mission. All that precedes and all that follows in the book of Hebrews rests on this point.

Compassion (Heb. 13:2–3)

Among the BaTonga people of Zambia, there is a proverb that says, "The stranger's seat is for sitting and his mouth is for eating." Hebrews says to **entertain strangers** (v. 2). As missionaries, my wife and I travel to many different churches around the country. One thing we have discovered is that if there is a community meal with a line in which "the missionariers go first," we end up sitting at a table alone. Entertaining strangers includes compassion for those we don't know, who live far away, but surely it also means those who are near at hand.

In the churches I grew up in, strangers who came to services on Sunday morning always went home with someone for lunch. Perhaps it was because we didn't expect folks to eat out, or most stores were closed and strangers wouldn't find food in our towns. Whatever the reason, entertaining strangers seems to have gone out of style. When was the last time we entertained a stranger?

A second aspect of entertaining strangers is for those strangers who are far away. Compassion for tsunami victims whom we don't know and have never met is a part of Christian compassion. Jo Anne Lyon, founder of World Hope International, tells of going to view the devastation of Sierra Leone following the civil war there. By God's providence, a journalist from one of the major US newspapers traveled along with her. The journalist kept asking, "What are you going to do about this?" Jo Anne's reaction was defensive; what could she do? She was a social worker and a pastor's wife in the States. She had no money, no foundations, no means. Surely this wasn't her responsibility—or was it?

While love must start at home, it must go beyond home if it is true. Christian compassion reaches out to **those in prison** and to **those who are mistreated** and **suffering** (v. 3) whether across the street, state, nation, or world.

WHAT DO YOU THINK?
How is hospitality a type of spiritual gift? How can you be content and still desire to grow?

Sexual Purity (Heb. 13:4)

Married Sex Is Good. In verse 4, the writer gave three aspects of sexual purity that are Christian standards. The first is a positive statement about sex within the marriage relationship: **Marriage should be honored by all, and the marriage bed kept pure.** Throughout church history there have been elements of the Christian community who have rejected all sex, even in marriage. Most notable was the Shaker community in nineteenth and early twentieth centuries. Their misunderstanding of Scripture made biological growth of the community impossible and conversion to the community unattractive, so they died out. Some have felt uncomfortable with Song of Solomon because of its sexual implications. In the Old Testament, the intimacy of the marriage relationship is often used as an illustration of God and Israel. The whole book of Hosea is based around that theme. In the New Testament, the church is described as the bride of Christ. Revelation 19:7 says, "For the wedding of the Lamb has come, and his bride has made herself ready." Paul summed it up succinctly in Ephesians 5:31–32: "'For this reason a man will leave his father and mother and be united to his wife, and the two will become one flesh.' This is a profound mystery—but I am talking about Christ and the church."

Just in case there is some doubt about the meaning of "one flesh" being a sexual relationship, in 1 Corinthians 6:16, he spelled it out: "Do you not know that he who unites himself with a prostitute is one with her in body? For it is said, 'The two will become one flesh.'"

Adultery Is Sin. The next statement in Hebrews 13:4 that relates to sex is a negative statement: **God will judge the adulterer.** *Adulterer* is a specific Greek term, and the meaning is a married person who has a sexual relationship with

AHA!
God has saved us from so much!

DID YOU KNOW?
The concluding chapter of Hebrews is made up of practical commands not connected by any theme.

another person to whom he or she is not married. This was one of the Ten Commandments: "You shall not commit adultery" (Deut. 5:18). The punishment was death by stoning (Deut. 22:22). Israel's relationship to God was often depicted under this illustration of the adulterous wife (see Hos. 4:14–18).

Sex Trade Is Perverse. The third element that deals with sex in Hebrews 13:4 is **all the sexually immoral**. The Greek term here is *pornos*. The word is related to sex, but the base meaning is "to sell." A whole family of terms relating to the selling of sex evolved out of this root word, including pornography (the selling of sex-related graphics). The KJV translates this word as "whoremongers." In other places, it is translated as "fornicators," but the NIV's translation is all-inclusive. While **all sexually immoral** might include prostitution, it also includes pornography, whether Internet or hard copy. *Pornos* would encompass sex clubs, books, magazines, videos, DVDs, movies, TV programs, and anything else where there is profit from the sale of sex. **God will judge . . . all the sexually immoral**.

WHAT DO YOU THINK?
Whose faith would you not hesitate to imitate? Explain.

Reference	Under the Old Covenant	Under the New Covenant
Hebrews 13:9	Ceremonial food—no spiritual value	Heart strengthened by grace
13:10	Priestly functions limited to a small group who can serve	Priestly functions not limited to a small group, but there are higher standards for service
13:11–13	Sin offering by the blood of animals	Sin offering by the blood of Christ
13:14	Seeking a physical kingdom	Seeking a spiritual kingdom
13:15–16	Sacrifices were daily, physical offerings to God	Perpetual praise, good works, and sharing with others are offerings that please God

Freedom from Avarice (Heb. 13:5–6)

AHA!
God wants us to live godly and productive lives!

It is not necessary to possess money to be possessed by money. It is **the love of money** from which the writer enjoins readers to **keep your lives free** (v. 5). First Timothy 6:10 is sometimes quoted out of context but emphasizes the same point: "For the love of money is a root of all kinds of evil. Some people, eager for money, have wandered from the faith and pierced themselves with many griefs."

The basic flaw with avarice, as the Hebrews writer saw it, is that it transfers a trust that belongs to God to material things. God's efficacy is in doubt when we have that type of infatuation with money. If contentment is not found without money as the primary ingredient, it will not be found with money as the main ingredient. Contentment is not a material physical entity and therefore cannot be bought.

Spiritual Authority (Heb. 13:7, 17–21)

DID YOU KNOW?
The "strange teachings" mentioned in Hebrews were connected to Gnosticism, which denied Jesus' true humanity.

There are three specific things to note in these passages about spiritual authority. The first is the element of tradition. The second is the spiritual leader's responsibility, and the third is the Christian's response to spiritual authority.

Tradition Is a Guide. **Remember your leaders, who spoke the word of God to you** (v. 7). John Wesley studied and often quoted from the early church fathers. If we forget where we came from, we will forget where we're going. North American culture puts so much emphasis on the isolated individual that it discounts history and community. The emphasis in this verse is not to idealize the past, but rather not to forget it. If you take note of the wounds of others, you can avoid the same wounds yourself. But beyond this, if you learn from the spiritual successes of others you can take thoughtful consideration **of their way of life and imitate their faith** (v. 7).

Leaders with Spiritual Authority Have Responsibility. There are specific things spiritual leaders do as outlined in Hebrews 13. They are to speak **the word of God** (v. 7). This indicates truth spoken with authority.

Next, their way of life must be as authentic as their manner of speaking. They don't preach one thing and live another. Their faith and life are inseparable, so others can imitate their faith. There is an African proverb that says, "When the elephants fight, the grass gets hurt." The proverb has all kinds of implications, but one is that when the "big people" fail, the fallout is immeasurable suffering for "little people."

Spiritual leaders have a responsibility to speak with authority. Others under authority are to **obey your leaders** (v. 17). In Western society, we don't talk about this much. Culturally, we like to view ourselves as all being on a horizontal plane. But unless **submit to their authority** can be understood as something besides leaders taking authority and giving instructions, it must be assumed they are giving instructions that need obedient responses. There is a check to this authority: they **must give an account**. A part of what will come into account is motives (v. 18). So leaders with spiritual authority have a responsibility to use their authority overtly with the conscious understanding that they will one day give account to the perfect Judge who even knows motives.

Those Being Led Have Responsibility. There are five specific things that those under authority are to do: (1) Remember what spiritual leaders have said and done (v. 7); (2) imitate their lives (v. 7); (3) obey your leaders (v. 17); (4) submit to their authority (v. 17); and (5) pray for them (vv. 18–19).

Discerners of Truth (Heb. 13:8–16)

Do not be carried away by all kinds of strange teachings (v. 9). Before we can follow this instruction, we have to know truth. When truth is taught, strange teachings are easy to identify.

The next few verses (10–14) are a recap summary of the truth the writer has been teaching in the chapters that preceded chapter 13. The writer gave us some functional substitutes for some specific Old Testament teachings and rituals. ✦

WHAT ABOUT YOU?
How has identifying with Christ cost you, either personally or professionally?

PRAYER
Lord, keep me family-focused, hospitable, and ready to open my home as You have need of it. Keep me focused on sound teaching, and help me imitate the faithful leaders You have provided.

INTERACTIVE LEARNING IDEAS

GET THE CLASS INVOLVED
Family Trees

The writer of Hebrews exhorted us to love one another like brothers and sisters. By using the language of our biological families, we can better understand what it means to be part of a spiritual family.

Ask the people in your class to take a piece of paper and start mapping out their family trees, going as far back as they possibly can (or for time, a couple generations). Have them start with their own families and work their way backward. Be sure they identify all the connections between aunts and uncles, cousins, grandparents, and so forth.

Once all the connections are made, have the students label each relationship in the family tree as either positive or negative, free-flowing or characterized by tension. Perhaps they have some relatives who have not spoken to one another for decades. Some of them might not even remember why they're not speaking to one another. Some of them might remember all too vividly.

End the activity by drawing parallels between our spiritual family and our biological families. How are they similar? How are they different? How can we prevent some of the problems we've seen in our biological families from happening in our spiritual families? What are the reasons we often see the same problems in both?

TRY THIS ON YOUR OWN
Imitation

Hebrews 13:7 tells us to look at those who set a good example in the faith and make them our spiritual role models—believers worth imitating.

Who are your role models in the faith? Whose faith would you imitate without a moment's notice?

If possible, invite that person out for coffee and tell him or her what you admire about the consistency of their faith. If geographical distance is an issue, send that person a letter or an e-mail. Ask people you'd be willing to "copy" how they've handled difficult situations in their lives. Pick their brains about challenges you may be facing.

What have been the outcomes of their work and effort on God's behalf? What could you expect if you were to imitate that kind of faith?

TAKING IT TO THE STREET
Go to Jail

We are to remember those in prison as if we were in prison along with them (Heb. 13:3). We are to judge the reasons why they are there, but only to serve them.

Look around for a local prison ministry and join them the next time they visit a jail. Follow their instructions and respect all the rules of the prison. Listen to the prisoners' stories; that's probably their biggest need—just to have someone hear about their lives. Be careful about committing anything to them, especially on their release. Those who have done prison ministry for a while might have some good tips for you in this regard.

Share your experience with your class the next time you meet. Encourage them to keep these prisoners in their prayers.

WITH YOUR FAMILY
Marriage Priority

The writer of Hebrews reminded us that marriages should be protected and honored, not just by the couple, but also by those in their circle of influence, especially their families.

As soon as you can, attend a wedding together as a family. Have everyone listen carefully to the vows and what the husband- and wife-to-be are promising each other. Notice that they're exchanging vows in front of people, who will act as their witnesses.

Go home and talk about the marriage that is a part of the family. Talk about the vows that were exchanged and how they were similar or different from what everyone heard during the wedding. Talk about the importance of protecting the marriage and giving the couple whatever time they need to be together to keep things going strong. In the end, the whole family is strengthened when the marriages that are at the core of those families get the attention they need. ◆

HEBREWS 13:1–21

1 Keep on loving each other as brothers.

2 Do not forget to entertain strangers, for by so doing some people have entertained angels without knowing it.

3 Remember those in prison as if you were their fellow prisoners, and those who are mistreated as if you yourselves were suffering.

4 Marriage should be honored by all, and the marriage bed kept pure, for God will judge the adulterer and all the sexually immoral.

5 Keep your lives free from the love of money and be content with what you have, because God has said, "Never will I leave you; never will I forsake you."

6 So we say with confidence, "The Lord is my helper; I will not be afraid. What can man do to me?"

7 Remember your leaders, who spoke the word of God to you. Consider the outcome of their way of life and imitate their faith.

8 Jesus Christ is the same yesterday and today and forever.

9 Do not be carried away by all kinds of strange teachings. It is good for our hearts to be strengthened by grace, not by ceremonial foods, which are of no value to those who eat them.

10 We have an altar from which those who minister at the tabernacle have no right to eat.

11 The high priest carries the blood of animals into the Most Holy Place as a sin offering, but the bodies are burned outside the camp.

12 And so Jesus also suffered outside the city gate to make the people holy through his own blood.

13 Let us, then, go to him outside the camp, bearing the disgrace he bore.

14 For here we do not have an enduring city, but we are looking for the city that is to come.

15 Through Jesus, therefore, let us continually offer to God a sacrifice of praise—the fruit of lips that confess his name.

16 And do not forget to do good and to share with others, for with such sacrifices God is pleased.

17 Obey your leaders and submit to their authority. They keep watch over you as men who must give an account. Obey them so that their work will be a joy, not a burden, for that would be of no advantage to you.

18 Pray for us. We are sure that we have a clear conscience and desire to live honorably in every way.

19 I particularly urge you to pray so that I may be restored to you soon.

Holy Actions Follow Holy Motives

*We are expected and equipped by
the Spirit to live holy lives.*

INTO THE SUBJECT

Unbelievers may have high expectations for the way believers conduct themselves inside the local church and in the community. What kind of people should we be?

INTO THE WORD

1. Of all the exhortations found in Hebrews 13:1–10, which one do you think needs the greatest emphasis today? Why?

2. In what practical ways might a local church practice brotherly love?

3. If you wanted to promote hospitality among your Christian friends, what first steps would you take?

4. How might you "remember those who are in prison" (v. 3)?

5. What situations do you think pose the greatest danger to marital fidelity? To sexual purity?

6. How can a believer not be covetous in a materialistic world?

7. What elements of effective spiritual leadership do you see in verse 7?

8. What reasons to love Jesus do you find in verses 8–21?

INTO THE WORLD

Invite a few neighbors to your home for coffee and conversation this week, and then tactfully share your testimony as opportunity presents itself.

20 May the God of peace, who through the blood of the eternal covenant brought back from the dead our Lord Jesus, that great Shepherd of the sheep,

21 equip you with everything good for doing his will, and may he work in us what is pleasing to him, through Jesus Christ, to whom be glory for ever and ever. Amen.

Practical Steps

There are six practical aspects listed in this lesson: brotherly love, compassion, sexual purity, freedom from avarice, spiritual authority, and being discerners of truth.

Look at each more closely and prayerfully consider what you can do in each of these aspects today, tomorrow, next week, and so on. These truths won't mean much unless they are acted upon in daily life.

Here's an example: Brotherly Love—Next time my neighbor yells at me about parking too close to his property line, I will respond in love and will not yell in return.

Brotherly Love— _____

_____

_____

Compassion— _____

_____

_____

Sexual Purity— _____

_____

_____

Freedom from Avarice— _____

_____

_____

Spiritual Authority— _____

_____

_____

Being a Discerner of the Truth— _____

_____

_____

Lesson
1

Lesson
2

Lesson
3

Lesson
4

Lesson
5

Lesson
6

Lesson
7

Lesson
8

Lesson
9

Lesson
10

Lesson
11

Lesson
12

Lesson
13

Unit 2
Deliver Us
God Redeems His People

LET FREEDOM RING!

Unit 2 Preview

Visitors to Independence Hall in Philadelphia can view the Liberty Bell and reflect on the freedom it represents. On July 8, 1776, when the Declaration of Independence was read, bells rang throughout the American colonies, and historians believe the Liberty Bell was one of them. Famous for its inscription, "Proclaim LIBERTY throughout all the land unto all the inhabitants thereof," the bell was dubbed the Liberty Bell by abolitionist groups in the 1830s.

Freedom from Slavery

The book of Exodus begins with a gloomy scene. The Egyptian pharaoh subjected the Hebrews, Joseph's descendants, to harsh slavery because he felt threatened by their increasing population. But God's people cried out to Him, and He heard them. He appointed Moses to deliver them. Through a series of intense plagues on Egypt, God sent a strong message to Pharaoh: "Let my people go!" The tenth and final plague struck down all the firstborn of Egypt, except the firstborn in homes displaying the blood of the Passover lamb. Soon, God miraculously made a way through the Red Sea for His redeemed people, but the same waters engulfed and drowned the pursuing Egyptian cavalry.

As you study the first fifteen chapters of Exodus, rejoice that the blood of Jesus, God's spotless Lamb, has redeemed you from sin.

Freedom to Be God's Holy People

Exodus teaches us that God is holy. From the burning bush to the Ten Commandments to the glory that filled the tabernacle, we see that God is holy. But we also see that His people should be holy. He promised Israel would be "a kingdom of priests and a holy nation," if she would keep His covenant (Ex. 19:5–6). Similarly, He has redeemed us to be a holy priesthood (1 Pet. 2:5).

Freedom to Worship God Exclusively

At Sinai, God gave the Ten Commandments. The first four commandments instructed Israel to worship Him exclusively and reverently. However, soon the people resorted to the idolatrous worship they had witnessed in Egypt. As we read about that treasonous act, we ought to set a guard at our hearts. We may be tempted to worship false gods: money, popularity, pleasure, or ease. Remember, God freed us to worship Him alone.

Freedom to Do Things God's Way

In the closing chapters of Exodus, we discover that God commanded Moses to build the tabernacle and to follow every detail God prescribed for its design, furnishings, and ministry. Nothing was left to human devising. Further, He gifted the workers who would carry out His plans.

God freed us from the slave market of sin to be His devoted servants (Rom. 6:19–22). Our chief goal in life, therefore, should be to fulfill every detail of His will. He has gifted us to serve Him skillfully, and He has charged us to be faithful (1 Cor. 4:2).

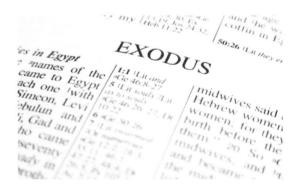

The book of Exodus begins with a gloomy scene, but it ends with a glorious scene as the glory of the Lord filled the tabernacle. As you study Exodus, may you catch a glimpse of the glory of our holy God, and may you be inspired and equipped to reflect that glory wherever you go. ◆

The mountain traditionally identified as Mount Sinai.

"On the morning of the third day there was thunder and lightning, with a thick cloud
over the mountain, and a very loud trumpet blast. Everyone in the camp trembled.
Then Moses led the people out of the camp to meet with God, and they stood at the
foot of the mountain. Mount Sinai was covered with smoke, because the LORD descended
on it in fire. The smoke billowed up from it like smoke from a furnace, the whole
mountain trembled violently, and the sound of the trumpet grew louder and louder.
Then Moses spoke and the voice of God answered him."
—Exodus 19:16–19

God's work through His people is nonstop and unstoppable.

GOD, UNSTOPPING AND UNSTOPPABLE
Exodus 1:6–22

KEY VERSE
Then a new king, who did not know about Joseph, came to power in Egypt.
—Exodus 1:8

BACKGROUND SCRIPTURES
Mark 10:42–45
Christians are called to be slaves to each other.
John 8:34
Sinners are enslaved by sin.
Acts 7:2–44
Stephen gave a summary of Genesis and Exodus.
Romans 6
Christians are set free from slavery to sin to be slaves to righteousness.
Galatians 4:1–7
God has made us His children, not slaves.

DAILY BIBLE READINGS
Monday: Romans 12:1–8
Tuesday: Matthew 12:16–50
Wednesday: Psalm 143:7–10
Thursday: 2 Corinthians 1:18–22
Friday: Philippians 2:12–16
Saturday: Exodus 1:6–22
Sunday: Psalm 17:14–15

WHY THIS MATTERS

Soon there may be a prosperity-gospel-preacher doll on the market. Pull its string, and it will tell the owner what she wants to hear. Who can deny the fact that some congregations are told only what they want to hear? They are told God wants them to be healthy, happy, and wealthy—all the time. Instead, the Bible predicts suffering and persecution for all who truly follow Jesus. But it also tells us we can triumph over trials by embracing God's promises and understanding how trials strengthen our faith and fulfill God's will for our lives.

This lesson helps us grip God's promises firmly with hearts full of faith and hope.

BIBLE COMMENTARY

By Mark Haines

If at first glance it appears our study text begins in the middle of a story, that's because it does. The author presupposed that his readers knew about Joseph and his brothers and why a king should have known about Joseph. So let's take a moment to review the beginning of the story from the book of Genesis.

"In the beginning God created the heavens and the earth" (Gen. 1:1). He placed the first man and the first woman in the garden of Eden, but they believed a serpent's lies. The snake told them God had lied to them—that they could be just like God—and all they needed to do was eat the forbidden fruit. Their distrust and disobedience destroyed their relationship with God. They were condemned to hard labor and death—driven out of the garden and God's presence. And so, Genesis 3 ends with an implied question: "What will God do now that His creation has rebelled?"

The answer came quickly. God revealed the truth about himself to individuals such as Abel, Enoch, and Noah. These men trusted God and did what He asked of them. In Genesis 12, God revealed himself to Abram, commanding him to move to an undisclosed country. "Abram believed the LORD, and he credited it to him as righteousness" (Gen. 15:6).

Abram became Abraham and fathered Isaac. Isaac became the father of Jacob. Jacob had twelve sons—Joseph and all his brothers. Joseph's brothers sold him into slavery in a fit of jealous rage. But the Lord was with him, and Joseph became something like the prime minister of Egypt. Because of his God-given wisdom, he saved the people of Egypt and his own family from a terrible famine. In all this time, God's promises to Abraham were still unfulfilled, but his descendants remembered and kept on trusting.

The book of Exodus takes up the story of God's people in Egypt hundreds of years later. A new problem had arisen. The Israelites were slaves and God seemed distant (Ex. 2:23–25). A whole new generation of Abraham's descendants needed a fresh revelation from God so they could trust and obey Him.

So God came "down to rescue them from the hand of the Egyptians and to bring them up out of that land into a good and spacious land, a land flowing with milk and honey" (Ex. 3:8). God had promised this land to Abraham, Isaac, and Jacob. He chose Moses, an Israelite raised in Pharaoh's own palace, to lead the people out.

God delivered the people from slavery in Egypt through a series of plagues. These plagues revealed the truth about God to the Israelites and Egyptians "so that [they would] know there is no one like the LORD" (Ex. 8:10).

God's people weren't released from bondage to simply do whatever pleased them. They received the Ten Commandments and the plans for a Tent of Meeting at Mount Sinai. Exodus ends with an entirely new situation. "Moses [and the people] finished the work [of building the Tent of Meeting]. Then the cloud [symbolizing God's presence] covered the Tent of Meeting, and the glory of the LORD filled the tabernacle. Moses could not enter the Tent of Meeting because the cloud had settled upon it, and the glory of the LORD filled the tabernacle. In all the travels of the Israelites, whenever the cloud lifted from above the tabernacle, they would set out; but if the cloud did not lift, they did not set out—until the day it lifted. So the cloud of the LORD was over the tabernacle by day, and fire was in the cloud by night, in the sight of all the house of Israel during all their travels" (Ex. 40:33–38). The Israelites were free and God was living in the middle of their camp!

This is the big picture of Genesis and Exodus. Humans destroyed their relationship to God with distrust and disobedience. However, God revealed the truth about himself, and a few chose to trust and obey. God promised to bless all nations through Abraham, Isaac, Jacob, and their descendants, the Israelites. To keep His promise, God needed to deliver the Israelites from slavery. By setting them free and moving into their camp, God revealed himself to them and called them to trust and obey.

A New Situation (Ex. 1:6–10)

Time marches on even for God's people. When Jacob joined Joseph in Egypt, Jacob was 130 years old (Gen. 47:9). Seventeen years later (Gen. 47:28), he called his sons together to bless them before he died. He made them promise to bury him in the family tomb. Abraham had purchased it from Ephron the Hittite. Abraham and Sarah, Isaac and Rebekah were buried there, along with Jacob's first wife, Leah (Gen. 49:29–32). Joseph lived to see his great-grandchildren, but eventually **Joseph and all his brothers and all that generation died** (Ex. 1:6).

As the years passed, the population of Abraham's descendants exploded. The author used four phrases piled on each other to describe the growth of Israel. First, **the Israelites were fruitful** (v. 7). Second, they **multiplied greatly**. Third, they **became exceedingly numerous**. Fourth, **the land was**

Israelite slaves were used to build Egyptian monuments.

WHAT DO YOU THINK?
How has God kept His promises to preserve the Israeli people in modern history?

filled with them. This description indicates that their growth was more than a natural occurrence. God was blessing Israel just as He had promised their forefathers.

Then a new king, who did not know about Joseph, came to power in Egypt (v. 8). This king was probably the beginning of a new dynasty. There was a time when another people, the Hyksos, ruled Egypt. The Hyksos were Semitic shepherds like the Israelites. The Egyptians rebelled and kicked them out. Perhaps this new king was the first Egyptian to take the throne after the Hyksos were removed. That might even explain his distrust of the Israelites—**if war breaks out,** they **will join our enemies,** [and] **fight against us** (v. 10). That's why the new king decided to **deal shrewdly with** the people of Israel, so they would not **become** even more **numerous** (v. 9).

Harsh Conditions (Ex. 1:11–14)

The king's plan was to enslave the Israelites and to reduce their population through attrition. Those who survived the conditions of slavery would be too exhausted to reproduce. **They put slave masters over them to oppress them with forced labor, and they built Pithom and Rameses as store cities** (v. 11). These two cities were located in the northeastern part of the Nile River delta near Goshen—the land Pharaoh gave to Joseph's family (Gen. 47:6). They were probably used to store weapons and supplies for the Egyptian army protecting the northeastern border. The slave masters must have viewed the Israelites as a disposable workforce. Exodus 1:14 tells us **they made their lives bitter with hard labor in brick and mortar and with all kinds of work in the fields; in all their hard labor the Egyptians used them ruthlessly**.

But the more they were oppressed, the more they multiplied and spread (v. 12). God continued to bless the Israelites. The affliction intended to beat them down brought more growth, not less. **So the Egyptians came to dread the Israelites**. The Egyptians started out afraid that the Israelites might join forces with their enemies. Then their fear increased because they couldn't control the Israelites' growth.

AHA!
God's promises are forever!

Attempted Genocide (Ex. 1:15–22)

The king came up with a new plan. If the Israelites couldn't be worked to death, then he would kill off the male babies and keep them from reproducing. He told **the Hebrew midwives . . . "When you help the Hebrew women in childbirth and observe them on the delivery stool, if it is a boy, kill him; but if it is a girl, let her live"** (vv. 15–16). The girls could be absorbed into the Egyptian population through marriage. Without males to carry on the ethnic heritage, God's people would die off.

This plan to kill off the males at birth in order to control the Israelites failed too. There were two reasons. First, **the midwives . . . feared God and did not do what the king of Egypt had told them to do; they let the boys live** (v. 17). The second reason might not have been completely true, but it must have had enough truth in it to be believable. When the king asked the midwives, **"Why have you let the boys live?"** They said, **"Hebrew women are not like**

DID YOU KNOW?
Egypt's Tempest Stele, a stone carving from 1550 B.C., notes a time when "a thick darkness, without the least light, spread itself over the Egyptians. Hail was sent down from heaven, and such hail it was, as the climate of Egypt had never suffered before."

Egyptian women; they are vigorous and give birth before the midwives arrive" (vv. 18–19).

How did God respond to the midwives' rebellion and possible deception? **God was kind to the midwives** (v. 20) protecting them from the king. But He went further **and because the midwives feared God, he gave them families of their own** (v. 21).

The king had tried to work the Israelites to death, and they **multiplied and spread** (v. 12). He asked the midwives to kill the baby boys, and yet **the people increased and became even more numerous** (v. 20). In a final act of desperation, **Pharaoh gave this order to all his people: "Every boy that is born you must throw into the Nile, but let every girl live"** (v. 22). It is not clear how long this genocide lasted. There is no indication that the Egyptians complied with the command. However, we do know that this drastic measure also failed. God's people were not destroyed by any of the king's edicts.

What Kind of God Is Revealed?

Genesis reveals that God made promises. He promised to give Abraham a son, and Isaac was born years later. God promised to give Abraham the land he traveled through as a migrating shepherd. God also promised to bless all the nations of the world through Abraham. When Abraham died, the only land he owned was a cave for his family tomb, and the world's blessing had not come. Isaac inherited these promises and passed them on to Jacob when he died. Jacob passed the promises on to his sons, but they all died in Egypt.

More than four centuries passed as the Israelites lived in Egypt (Ex. 12:40). In all those years, the promises God made to Abraham, Isaac, and Jacob remained unfulfilled. This first chapter of Exodus even found the existence of the Israelites in jeopardy. If God did not act to deliver His people, it could mean only one of two things: Either God could not keep His promises because He was weak, or God would not keep His promises because He used them to deceive humans. No matter what, if God did not intervene to deliver His people, no one would be able to trust Him.

But God did act! God kept His promise to Abraham's descendants. He rescued them from slavery and from Pharaoh's attempts at ethnic cleansing. Therefore, we too can trust God. God is strong enough to keep His promises and He does not lie. ◆

WHAT ABOUT YOU?
What promise are you holding on to despite obstacles?

PRAYER
Father, may I trust in the dark what You have promised in the light.

INTERACTIVE LEARNING IDEAS

GET THE CLASS INVOLVED
Remember When?

The new pharaoh's failure to remember Joseph—or rather to remember the miraculous way Joseph's God used the young man to sustain the nation of Egypt during a season of tremendous famine—ultimately cost the ruler his eldest son and his own life.

We may look at his life and frown. Yet, isn't it just as easy for us, in a time of success or season of plenty, to forget how we got to that place? Isn't it human nature to jump to the conclusion that our own ingenuity, power, or quick thinking brought us success? In Pharaoh's life, that self-centered worldview tempted him to tread upon others and eventually led to his destruction.

Divide into pairs. Direct each person to consider one instance when God's guiding or guarding hand was expressly evident in their lives. Take turns within the pairs sharing that story, crediting God's role in it all.

Invite two pairs to share a story with the entire group.

Spend the rest of your time discussing the practical difference between rightfully crediting God for working on our behalf and stealing credit for ourselves.

TRY THIS ON YOUR OWN
Babies in the Way

The population control attempts of the paranoid pharaoh focused around newborns. They might have been a threat to him when they grew up, so he attempted to do away with them before they could fight for themselves.

Using Internet sources, educate yourself about population control attempts through history up to today. Where is it happening today? Who is perpetrating it? What are their reasons? (Be careful not to stop at what tyrants are doing in other countries; look at your culture's actions, too.) What do you suppose God thinks about this?

As you encounter each instance, pray specifically about it—and continue to pray each day during your quiet time. Ask God to intervene. Invite Him to use you to educate others or to make a difference in their lives. Then, be ready and willing to act on the challenges He places on your heart.

TAKING IT TO THE STREET
Spiff Up a Tent of Meeting

The lesson makes a point of taking the story beyond the obvious circumstance of God's people needing release from bondage. It leads us to consider the people's more subtle need for a place of consistent fellowship with God. Today, in addition to the Spirit of God living within the hearts of believers (John 17:26), we meet with God in our symbolic tents of meeting—local churches.

Take the initiative to contact the pastor or office staff of a church in your area that lacks financial resources. Ask about service projects to enhance or help restore their building.

Ask members of your study to join you in volunteering for whatever cleaning, construction, or repair project is most needed. Pick a day and time that works for you all, and work toward completing the project.

WITH YOUR FAMILY
What Culture Sees in a Bible Story

One story that is key to understanding Exodus occurs in Genesis—namely, how the nation of Israel landed in Egypt. The plot of Joseph and his brothers has fascinated storytellers and charmed listeners for generations. In fact, it captivated Andrew Lloyd Webber enough for him to use it as a starting point for his blockbuster musical *Joseph and the Amazing Technicolor Dreamcoat*.

Check with your public library or your favorite movie rental site to see whether the DVD or soundtrack of the Webber production is available. (Alternately, check the Internet for plot synopsis and sample tracks.)

After you view (or listen to) the production as a family, read the account of Joseph from a contemporary translation (key moments include Gen. 37:2–28; 39:1–23; 41:14–41; 45:1–11).

Have each member of the family (starting with the youngest) identify one big lesson from Joseph's life as described in the Scriptures. Talk about the way the musical was similar to Scripture and the way it differed. How consistent or inconsistent is the theme of the musical with the themes you noticed in the Scripture account? How is the real account of Joseph's life relevant to your daily life? ◆

EXODUS 1:6–22

6 Now Joseph and all his brothers and all that generation died,

7 but the Israelites were fruitful and multiplied greatly and became exceedingly numerous, so that the land was filled with them.

8 Then a new king, who did not know about Joseph, came to power in Egypt.

9 "Look," he said to his people, "the Israelites have become much too numerous for us.

10 Come, we must deal shrewdly with them or they will become even more numerous and, if war breaks out, will join our enemies, fight against us and leave the country."

11 So they put slave masters over them to oppress them with forced labor, and they built Pithom and Rameses as store cities for Pharaoh.

12 But the more they were oppressed, the more they multiplied and spread; so the Egyptians came to dread the Israelites

13 and worked them ruthlessly.

14 They made their lives bitter with hard labor in brick and mortar and with all kinds of work in the fields; in all their hard labor the Egyptians used them ruthlessly.

15 The king of Egypt said to the Hebrew midwives, whose names were Shiphrah and Puah,

16 "When you help the Hebrew women in childbirth and observe them on the delivery stool, if it is a boy, kill him; but if it is a girl, let her live."

17 The midwives, however, feared God and did not do what the king of Egypt had told them to do; they let the boys live.

18 Then the king of Egypt summoned the midwives and asked them, "Why have you done this? Why have you let the boys live?"

19 The midwives answered Pharaoh, "Hebrew women are not like Egyptian women; they are vigorous and give birth before the midwives arrive."

20 So God was kind to the midwives and the people increased and became even more numerous.

21 And because the midwives feared God, he gave them families of their own.

22 Then Pharaoh gave this order to all his people: "Every boy that is born you must throw into the Nile, but let every girl live."

God, Unstopping and Unstoppable

God's work through His people is nonstop and unstoppable.

INTO THE SUBJECT

Situations change. A new boss may change the policy handbook and make the workplace stressful and harsh. But what would life be like if a harsh, pagan government replaced one that was kind and considerate of believers?

INTO THE WORD

1. What worried the new pharaoh about the Israelites?

2. How did Pharaoh try to solve what he perceived to be a problem?

3. Read Genesis 12:1–3. Why have so many attempts in history to subdue or eradicate the people of Israel failed?

4. What second plan did Pharaoh put into action? Why did this plan also fail?

5. Why do you agree or disagree that sometimes God-fearing people should practice civil disobedience?

6. How have you seen God overturn a plan or an action that was meant to harm you?

7. What characteristics of God do you find in Exodus 1:6–22?

INTO THE WORLD

Triumph over difficult circumstances this week with resolute confidence in God!

THERE'S NO STOPPING GOD

Scripture says that "the Israelites were exceedingly fruitful; they multiplied greatly, increased in numbers and became so numerous that the land was filled with them" (Ex. 1:7).

Name the ways the Egyptians tried to stop God from enlarging His people.

Verse 11:

_____

Verse 13:

_____

Verse 16:

_____

Verse 22:

_____

How effective were their efforts?

_____

Verse 12:

_____

Verses 17, 21:

_____

What are some ways you have experienced resistance to your work for the Lord?

_____

_____

Based on this story, how effective do you think that resistance will be?

_____

_____

God uses small events to bring about the deliverance of His people.

LESSON 2

THE DELIVERANCE OF A DELIVERER

Exodus 2:1–15

WHY THIS MATTERS

Frederick Douglass was born into slavery in Easton, Maryland, and at age seven he was sent to Baltimore to serve the Auld family as a slave. Mrs. Auld began to teach Frederick how to read and write, but her husband put a stop to the lessons. Ultimately, Frederick taught himself to read and write and then taught other black people. In later years, he gained freedom and became a famous abolitionist and the first African-American to buy a home in the Old Anacostia neighborhood of Washington, D.C.

Little baby Moses was born into slavery in Egypt more than three thousand years before Frederick Douglass was born. This lesson helps us see that God never abandons His people, even when their circumstances appear extremely bleak.

BIBLE COMMENTARY

By Mark Haines

At the beginning of Genesis, Adam and Eve destroyed their relationship to God by believing the serpent's lies about God, which led them to distrust and disobey. Throughout Genesis, God revealed the truth about himself, and a few persons chose to believe, which led them to trust and obey. God promised to bless all nations through Abraham, Isaac, Jacob, and their descendants, the Israelites.

At the end of Genesis, Abraham's descendants were living in Egypt, far from the land God promised to give to them. As the years passed, their population exploded: "The Israelites were fruitful and multiplied greatly and became exceedingly numerous, so that the land was filled with them" (Ex. 1:7). Their growth was supernatural.

Then a new king came to power in Egypt. He did not trust the Israelites, thinking they might join forces with some future invading army. The king decided to enslave the Israelites and to reduce their population through attrition. Those who survived the conditions of slavery would be too exhausted to reproduce. But that plan failed because "the more they were oppressed, the more they multiplied and spread" (Ex. 1:12).

The king's next plan called for the Hebrew midwives to kill every male baby as it was being born. This plan also failed. "The midwives, however, feared God and did not do what the king of Egypt had told them to do; they let the boys live" (Ex. 1:17). Finally in an act of desperation, "Pharaoh gave this order to all his people: 'Every boy that is born you must throw into the Nile, but let every girl live'" (Ex. 1:22).

But every attempt to control the growth of the Israelites failed. No matter what the king decided to do to them, his plans were thwarted. Oppressive slavery made

KEY VERSE

By faith Moses' parents hid him for three months after he was born, because they saw he was no ordinary child, and they were not afraid of the king's edict.
—Hebrews 11:23

BACKGROUND SCRIPTURES

Numbers 32:23;
Luke 12:1–3
    Our secret sins will be exposed.
Book of Esther
    God is not named in the entire book, but He is obviously at work behind the scenes just as He is here in Exodus 1–2.
Acts 7:17–44
    Stephen gave a summary of Moses' birth and life.
Hebrews 11:23
    The faith of Moses' parents is described.
Hebrews 11:24–26
    Moses' faith was honored.

DAILY BIBLE READINGS

Monday: Genesis 45:4–7
Tuesday: Ruth 2:11–12;
                 4:13–17
Wednesday: 1 Samuel
                 16:4–13
Thursday: Jeremiah 23:5–8
Friday: Luke 1:26–33
Saturday: Exodus 2:1–15
Sunday: Psalm 18:1–15

them more numerous. The Hebrew midwives refused to kill the baby boys. Jochebed and Miriam hid Moses. The king's own daughter adopted one of the Hebrew boys and brought him into Pharaoh's house as her son. This king was powerless against the God who was protecting the Israelites.

A Son Is Born (Ex. 2:1–4)

In this atmosphere of hatred, violence, fear, and oppression **a man of the house of Levi married a Levite woman** (v. 1). According to Exodus 6:20, the husband's name was Amram and the wife was Jochebed. **She became pregnant and gave birth to a son** (v. 2), but he was not their first child. They had an older son, Aaron, who became the first priest for Israel (Ex. 28:1). Apparently Aaron was born before the king's command to throw all the male babies into the Nile River. Amram and Jochebed also had an older daughter, Miriam, who became a prophetess (Ex. 15:20).

When her second son was born, Jochebed **saw that he was a fine child** and **hid him for three months** (v. 2). But as he grew and his cries became stronger **she could hide him no longer**, so **she got a papyrus basket for him and coated it with tar and pitch** (v. 3). The basket was literally an "ark." Noah's family and Moses are the only ones in the Old Testament to be saved in an ark. **Then she placed the child in** [the ark] **and put it among the reeds along the bank of the Nile**. To keep the baby as safe as possible, **his sister stood at a distance** (v. 4) to watch over him.

A Son Is Pulled Out (Ex. 2:5–10)

Throughout the first two chapters of Exodus, God remained behind the scenes. In chapter 1, He is mentioned only in reference to the midwives who defied Pharaoh and were rewarded. God is not mentioned until the end of chapter 2, where the author said, "The Israelites groaned in their slavery and cried out, and their cry for help because of their slavery went up to God. God heard their groaning and he remembered his covenant with Abraham, with Isaac and with Jacob. So God looked on the Israelites and was concerned about them" (Ex. 2:23–25). It appears that God was often content to be active anonymously. The next event was a prime example of it.

Then Pharaoh's daughter went down to the Nile to bathe, and her attendants were walking along the river bank. She saw the basket among the reeds and sent her slave girl to get it (v. 5). Whether Jochebed had observed the princess bathing at this place in the river or God simply guided her to the right place, we don't know. The baby, however, was discovered by one of the most powerful women in the land. When the ark was in her possession, the princess **opened it and saw the baby. He was crying, and she felt sorry for him**. She immediately recognized that he was **one of the Hebrew babies** (v. 6). There were three possible ways for the princess to identify the baby as a Hebrew: Perhaps it was because he was circumcised, or it could have been his clothing or skin color. No matter how she did it, Pharaoh's daughter defied her father's decree and had pity on the baby.

Miriam displayed a lot of courage when she stepped forward and addressed the king's daughter. She **asked Pharaoh's daughter, "Shall I go and get one**

WHAT DO YOU THINK?
Do you see any correlations between the view of human life the Egyptians held and the view of life held by other countries around the world today?

AHA!
The more God's people are "oppressed, the more they multipl[y] and spread" (Ex. 1:12)!

DID YOU KNOW?
Despite the constant campaigning of the "pro-choice" movement, there are now more "pro-life" crisis pregnancy centers than abortion clinics, and the number of abortions has dropped 9 percent in five years in the United States.

of the Hebrew women to nurse the baby for you?" (v. 7). The immediate answer **"Yes, go,"** (v. 8) indicates that the princess had already decided to save this Hebrew baby. In an ironic twist of events, **the girl went and got the baby's mother. Pharaoh's daughter said to her, "Take this baby and nurse him for me, and I will pay you." So the woman took the baby and nursed him** (vv. 8–9). In other words, God rewarded Jochebed's faith by arranging for the king's family to pay her for raising her own son.

When the child grew older, she took him to Pharaoh's daughter and he became her son. She named him Moses, saying, "I drew him out of the water" (v. 10). In Egyptian, *Moses* is related to words meaning "to produce" or "to draw out" or "child." It was associated with the birth process and was often a part of a king's name. In Hebrew, *Moses* sounds like the word meaning "to draw out." This play on words was obvious in both languages. The baby was literally drawn out of the water, but beyond that, he became the man God used to draw His people out of Egypt through the Red Sea.

Murder and Exile (Ex. 2:11–15)

According to Acts 7:23, Moses was forty years old when **he went out to where his own people were and watched them at their hard labor** (Ex. 2:11). While he watched his people at work, **he saw an Egyptian beating a Hebrew, one of his own people**. There is no indication as to why Moses went out to see the Israelites, but the repeated phrase "his own people" may indicate that he had begun to identify with them. Moses' response to the injustice he saw was calculated and violent. After **glancing this way and that and seeing no one, he killed the Egyptian and hid him in the sand** (v. 12). Apparently the Egyptian was beating the Israelite murderously, because the same Hebrew word that is translated "beating" in verse 11 is translated "killed" in verse 12. Moses hid the body in the sand of the desert and went home thinking he would never be caught.

However, he found out that "there is nothing concealed that will not be disclosed, or hidden that will not be made known" (Luke 12:2). **The next day he went out and saw two Hebrews fighting. He asked the one in the wrong, "Why are you hitting your fellow Hebrew?" The man said, "Who made you ruler and judge over us? Are you thinking of killing me as you killed the Egyptian?" Then Moses was afraid and thought, "What I did must have become known"** (Ex. 2:13–14). I'm sure this experience put conviction in his voice years later when he told the people of Israel, "You may be sure that your sin will find you out" (Num. 32:23).

God's Often Unseen Hand (Ex. 1–2)	
God's Anonymous Work	**Works Credited to God**
The Israelites' population growth	
Their continued growth in slavery	
	The midwives who spared the male babies
A couple was married and had children	
A unique son was born	
His parents hid him for three months	
His mother put him in an ark	
A princess adopted the boy	
He was raised in the palace of Egypt	
He fled to Midian and married a priest's daughter	
The Israelites cried out	
	God heard their groaning
	God remembered His covenant
	God saw the Israelites' situation
	God was concerned about them

WHAT ABOUT YOU?
How has God worked in
your distant past to fulfill
His plan for your future?
How have your grandparents
and parents, children and
grandchildren, carried on
God's plan?

In Acts 7:25, Stephen said, "Moses thought that his own people would real-ize that God was using him to rescue them, but they did not." That's obvious from the man's question: "Who made you ruler and judge over us?" The lead-ers in the book of Judges were both "rulers" and "deliverers." The man wanted to know who had given Moses the authority to act as the Israelites' liberator. Since Moses had simply appointed himself, he was afraid.

When Pharaoh heard of this, he tried to kill Moses, but Moses fled from Pharaoh (Ex. 2:15). There was no escape from the king's wrath—even for the adopted son of his daughter. Moses had no choice aside from leaving the country, and so he **went to live in Midian** (v. 15). Midian was located on the eastern side of the eastern arm of the Red Sea, south of the Promised Land, in modern Saudi Arabia. The people of Midian were descendants of Abraham like the Israelites (Gen. 25:1–6).

When Moses arrived in Midian, **he sat down by a well** (Ex. 2:15). It was at this well that Moses met the seven daughters of Reuel (also called Jethro in Ex. 3:1). He was the priest of Midian. Perhaps, Abraham's faith in God had been passed on through this branch of his family too. Later, when Moses returned to the desert with the Israelites, Jethro offered sacrifices to God for all He had done for His people.

In Midian, Moses married Jethro's daughter Zipporah. Moses named their first son Gershom, which sounds like the Hebrew for "an alien or sojourner." He chose this name because he had "become an alien in a foreign land" (Ex. 2:21–22). He named their second son Eliezer, which means "God helps," because "God was my helper; he saved me from the sword of Pharaoh" (Ex. 18:4).

Meanwhile, back in Egypt, the stage was being set for Moses to return as God's appointed judge and ruler over the Israelites. "The king of Egypt died" and "the Israelites groaned in their slavery and cried out, and their cry for help because of their slavery went up to God" (Ex. 2:23). The man who wanted to kill Moses was removed from the scene, and God's people began to pray in earnest.

Take special note of Exodus 2:24–25. These two verses expose the reason behind God's coming deliverance: "God heard their groaning and he remem-bered his covenant with Abraham, with Isaac and with Jacob. So God looked on the Israelites and was concerned about them." God remembered His prom-ises and knew it was time to act in order to keep those vows. ✦

PRAYER
Father, "may all who come
behind us find us faithful."

EXODUS 2:1–15

1 Now a man of the house of Levi married a Levite woman,

2 and she became pregnant and gave birth to a son. When she saw that he was a fine child, she hid him for three months.

3 But when she could hide him no longer, she got a papyrus basket for him and coated it with tar and pitch. Then she placed the child in it and put it among the reeds along the bank of the Nile.

4 His sister stood at a distance to see what would happen to him.

5 Then Pharaoh's daughter went down to the Nile to bathe, and her attendants were walking along the river bank. She saw the basket among the reeds and sent her slave girl to get it.

6 She opened it and saw the baby. He was crying, and she felt sorry for him. "This is one of the Hebrew babies," she said.

7 Then his sister asked Pharaoh's daughter, "Shall I go and get one of the Hebrew women to nurse the baby for you?"

8 "Yes, go," she answered. And the girl went and got the baby's mother.

9 Pharaoh's daughter said to her, "Take this baby and nurse him for me, and I will pay you." So the woman took the baby and nursed him.

10 When the child grew older, she took him to Pharaoh's daughter and he became her son. She named him Moses, saying, "I drew him out of the water."

11 One day, after Moses had grown up, he went out to where his own people were and watched them at their hard labor. He saw an Egyptian beating a Hebrew, one of his own people.

12 Glancing this way and that and seeing no one, he killed the Egyptian and hid him in the sand.

13 The next day he went out and saw two Hebrews fighting. He asked the one in the wrong, "Why are you hitting your fellow Hebrew?"

14 The man said, "Who made you ruler and judge over us? Are you thinking of killing me as you killed the Egyptian?" Then Moses was afraid and thought, "What I did must have become known."

15 When Pharaoh heard of this, he tried to kill Moses, but Moses fled from Pharaoh and went to live in Midian, where he sat down by a well.

The Deliverance of a Deliverer

God uses small events to bring about the deliverance of His people.

INTO THE SUBJECT

Parents celebrate the birth of a baby and perhaps dream about what he or she will become as an adult. Moses was born into slavery in Egypt, and Pharaoh ordered that he be killed. What would this baby's parents do? What would God do?

INTO THE WORD

1. What evidence of a mother's love do you find in Exodus 2:1–3?

2. Why would it be hard to keep baby Moses hidden longer than three months?

3. What evidence of divine intervention in baby Moses' life do you find in verses 4–9?

4. What evidence of divine intervention have you seen in your life?

5. How was this rescued baby eventually related to Egypt's royal family?

6. Although Moses was destined to deliver the Hebrews from Egypt, he failed to wait for God's perfect timing. What blunder did he make, and what were the consequences?

7. Is it hard to wait for God's timing in your life? Why or why not?

8. Read verses 13–14 and Numbers 32:23. How do these passages relate to each other?

9. What cover-up have you seen exposed?

INTO THE WORLD

Live each day with the realization that God may have appointed you to deliver someone from some kind of bondage. But get involved when it is God's time for you to do so.

THE RIVER NILE

Moses' mother placed him in a basket in the Nile River and left his sister to watch what would happen. Do you think they expected a miracle? If so, it wasn't because they believed in the river.

1. It was huge: The Nile is the longest river in the world—6,670 kilometers.
   - What might have happened to Moses?
   - What characteristic of God might have given his mother hope?

   _____

   _____

2. It was busy: Most Egyptians lived near the Nile because it provided water, food, transportation, and excellent soil for growing food.
   - What might have happened to Moses?
   - What characteristic of God might have given his mother hope?

   _____

   _____

3. It was feared: The Egyptians believed a false god named Hapi had power over the river.
   - What might have happened to Moses?
   - What characteristic of God might have given his mother hope?

   _____

   _____

4. It was dark: The ancient Egyptians called the river Ar, which means black, because of its color.
   - What might have happened to Moses?
   - What characteristic of God might have given his mother hope?

   _____

   _____

5. It was inhabited: Crocodiles and other creatures lived in the river.
   - What might have happened to Moses?
   - What characteristic of God might have given his mother hope?

   _____

   _____

What did happen to Moses?

   _____

   _____

Answers: 1. God is more powerful than the river (Jer. 32:17). 2. God is also at the river; he is omnipresent (Jer. 23:23–24). 3. God is the one true God (John 17:3). 4. God is light (1 John 1:5). 5. God is not afraid of the creatures of the water; he created the leviathan (Job 41:1–34).

INTERACTIVE LEARNING IDEAS

GET THE CLASS INVOLVED
Grumble Board

Put yourself in the place of the Israelites in Exodus 2:23. They had every right to groan about the way the Egyptians treated them—and they were on the right path when they entrusted those complaints to Almighty God.

On a whiteboard or flipchart write every complaint group members imagine they would be groaning about if they had been Hebrew slaves.

Together reread Exodus 2:25, which the English Standard Version translates as "God saw the people of Israel—and God knew."

Returning to your board, list all the things "God saw" and "God knew" about His people's enslavement. Include both physical concerns and the spiritual picture only God could see. Share observations about how the people might have felt if they'd seen physical evidence that "God saw" and "God knew."

Then invite volunteers to describe one item that would appear on their personal whiteboard list of complaints. Carry their complaints before God and invite Him to reveal the greater picture He knows and sees.

TRY THIS ON YOUR OWN
Whispers and Shouts

Moses felt the weight of the fact that his little secret wasn't so secret after all. With that in mind, choose a quiet place where you can listen for God's quiet prompting. Open your Bible to the cross-reference text Luke 12:1–3, where Jesus promised that secrets will not remain hidden and whispers will be announced from housetops. Consider that whispers may be secret sins or godly thoughts, words, and actions unnoticed on earth.

As you read, take note of your feelings. Are you feeling threatened or heartened? Uneasy or comforted?

In a heartfelt prayer lay out before God what His Spirit is showing you about the hidden things (good or bad) in your life. Silently wait for His prompting. Act on what He reveals to you—whether it is affirmation, forgiveness, direction to act, comfort, or challenge. Pray for courage to live a life that will leave you unashamed as it is unwrapped in His presence one day.

TAKING IT TO THE STREET
Desert Life

When Moses feared for his life after he had killed the Egyptian oppressor, he fled to the desert of Midian. What he gave up was pampered life in the lush, bountiful palace of the most prosperous country of his day. What he gained was the hard work of a shepherd in the arid, gritty desert of Arabia. Desert life wasn't easy, but it was a place where he learned lessons unknown to a posh royal court.

With a friend from your study group, plan a field trip to a veteran's hospital where you can visit with servicemen and women who are recovering from injuries sustained in the war on terror in the dusty sands near where Moses spent his exile.

Go with no agenda but to listen. Be available to hold a hand or look an injured warrior in the eye. Listen for their grief over what they lost, for the sacrifices they made in serving, for the deeper needs of their hearts.

If you are able, visit again on your own—and ask for God's guidance as you begin to build a friendship with at least one of the injured warriors you meet.

WITH YOUR FAMILY
Make a Basket

Go to your local craft store and purchase supplies to create an inexpensive woven basket. You might want to weave it out of rope or wicker (similar to the papyrus reeds Jochebed used), but paper strips will do in a pinch. Consult a website such as http://www.ehow.com to print instructions on how to weave a basket.

With your children, set out the supplies, read the instructions, and weave a basket—large enough to hold a small doll or animal. Talk about what it would take to make the basket watertight. Ask each family member how it might feel to have a favorite doll or pet set sail in that makeshift ark.

Transition to how Moses' mother must have felt placing the child she loved in a basket like this one—and how she must have trusted God for courage.

Keep the basket visible in your home for the week (perhaps as a napkin holder in the kitchen or a mail holder in your entrance hall), where it can remind you all of how trustworthy God is. ◆

God seeks humble, available servants.

LESSON 3

SAY YES TO GOD'S CALL

Exodus 3:1–15

KEY VERSE
So now, go. I am sending you to Pharaoh to bring my people the Israelites out of Egypt.

—Exodus 3:10

BACKGROUND SCRIPTURES
Genesis 18
    The angel of the Lord stopped Abraham and keeps him from sacrificing Isaac.
Exodus 33:12–23
    Moses sought God's presence and the privilege of seeing His glory.
Judges 13:1–23
    The angel of the Lord appeared to the parents of Samson.
1 Kings 19:1–10
    The angel of the Lord encouraged and fed Elijah.
John 8:58–59
    Jesus used the name God gave Moses at the burning bush to describe himself and is nearly killed.

DAILY BIBLE READINGS
Monday: Judges 6:11–16
Tuesday: Jonah 1:9–17
Wednesday: Isaiah 30:19–21
Thursday: 1 Corinthians
                 1:26–31
Friday: Ephesians
                 1:15–21
Saturday: Exodus 3:1–15
Sunday: Psalm 18:16–24

WHY THIS MATTERS

A wise old preacher used to observe that a highly educated professor's PhD might stand for "phenomenal dud" if his thinking excludes God. After all, wisdom begins with the fear of God; and God often confounds the worldly wise by choosing common people in common walks of life to fulfill His noblest purposes. He delights to fill and use empty vessels.

He chose Moses to lead His people from slavery when Moses was a humble shepherd in the Negev, not when he was a prince in an Egyptian palace. Moses' availability and God's ability would accomplish the impossible.

This lesson inspires us to offer ourselves to God as His humble, available servants.

BIBLE COMMENTARY

By Mark Haines

Exodus began with a new king coming to power in Egypt. He did not trust the Israelites. Their population was increasing faster than was natural. Thinking they might join forces with some future invading army, he decided to enslave the descendants of Abraham. His goal was to reduce their population through attrition. Those who survived the conditions of slavery would be too exhausted to have children. But his plan failed. "The more [the Israelites] were oppressed, the more they multiplied and spread" (Ex. 1:12).

The king's next strategy was to command the Hebrew midwives to kill every male Israelite baby as he was being born. This plan also fell short. "The midwives . . . feared God and did not do what the king of Egypt had told them to do; they let the boys live" (Ex. 1:17). At the end of Exodus 1, "Pharaoh gave this order to all his people: 'Every boy that is born you must throw into the Nile, but let every girl live'" (Ex. 1:22).

Every effort to reduce the number of the Israelites fizzled out. No matter what the king tried to do to them, his plans were defeated. Oppressive slavery made the Israelites more numerous. The Hebrew midwives refused to kill the baby boys. The pharaoh was impotent against the Israelites' continuing expansion.

In this atmosphere of hatred, violence, fear, and oppression, a man named Amram married a woman called Jochebed. She became pregnant and gave birth to a son who was adopted by the king's daughter. She gave him the name Moses.

Moses was raised in the palace of Egypt. Nevertheless, "when he had grown up, [Moses] refused to be known as the son of Pharaoh's daughter. He chose to be mistreated along with the people of God rather than to enjoy the pleasures of sin for a short time" (Heb. 11:24–25).

According to Acts 7:23, Moses was forty years old when he went out to where his own people were and watched them at their hard labor. He saw an Egyptian beating a Hebrew, one of his own people (Ex. 2:11). Moses' response to the injustice he saw was calculated and violent. After "glancing this way and that and seeing no one, he killed the Egyptian and hid him in the sand" (Ex. 2:12).

He thought the murder had been committed without witnesses, but the next day he discovered he was wrong. When Moses tried to break up a fight between two Israelites, one of the men asked, "Who made you ruler and judge over us? Are you thinking of killing me as you killed the Egyptian?" (Ex. 2:14).

Pharaoh wanted to kill Moses, so he fled to Midian, a land east of the Red Sea. While he lived in exile there, he married Zipporah, one of the seven daughters of Jethro, a priest in Midian. Moses had two sons in the forty years he lived in Midian (Acts 7:30).

"The angel of the LORD appeared to [Moses] in flames of fire from within a bush" (Ex. 3:2; see also Acts 7:30).

A Bush Is Burning (Ex. 3:1–4)

Now Moses was tending the flock of Jethro his father-in-law, the priest of Midian, and he led the flock to the far side of the desert and came to Horeb, the mountain of God (v. 1). Just as surely as his life in the palace of Egypt prepared Moses to represent God to Pharaoh, his life as a shepherd in the desert prepared him to guide the Israelites when God delivered them. The exact locations of Horeb and Mount Sinai are not certain. Although the names seem to be used interchangeably at times, they could be two mountains in the same general area. Traditionally, this area is identified as the southeastern region of the Sinai Peninsula.

There the angel of the LORD appeared to him in flames of fire from within a bush (v. 2). The angel of the Lord appeared to several other persons throughout the Old Testament: Hagar, Abraham, Balaam, Gideon, the parents of Samson, and Elijah. In most of these situations the angel of the Lord seems to have been a manifestation of God himself. That's what we find here in the burning bush as well. Verse 4 says, **When the LORD saw that he had gone over to look, God called to him from within the bush**.

A Voice Is Speaking (Ex. 3:5–6)

"Do not come any closer," God said. "Take off your sandals, for the place where you are standing is holy ground" (v. 5). Removing one's sandals in a sacred place is still a common custom in that part of the world. **Then he said, "I am the God of your father, the God of Abraham, the God of Isaac and the God of Jacob." At this, Moses hid his face, because he was afraid to look at God** (v. 6). Note that the first thing God did was to identify himself by His relationships with significant people in Moses' life—his father and his forefathers.

Note too that Moses had no trouble believing it was God speaking to him. His fear of looking at God was well founded. Sin cannot exist in the presence

WHAT DO YOU THINK?
Have you ever "cried out to God" when it seemed He had forgotten you?

AHA!
God never forgets His promises!

DID YOU KNOW?
The Hebrew word used in Exodus 2:24 for remembrance, *zakar*, can mean to remember or recall, but it can also be translated to *keep remembering*. God doesn't say, "Oh, now I remember those people." Rather, we are in His thoughts every second of every day.

WHAT DO YOU THINK?
How does Moses doubt God's plans and promises? How do we doubt God's plans and promises?

of God's holy fire. Later in Exodus, Moses felt comfortable asking to see God's glory but God said, "You cannot see my face, for no one may see me and live" (see Ex. 33:12–23).

God Has Come Down (Ex. 3:7–10)

In Exodus 2:23, God appeared to be distant and removed from His people: "The Israelites groaned in their slavery and cried out, and their cry for help because of their slavery *went up to God*" (emphasis added). The next two verses indicate that "God heard their groaning and he remembered his covenant with Abraham, with Isaac and with Jacob. So God looked on the Israelites and was concerned about them" (2:24–25).

God's concern for His people and His desire to keep His covenant with Abraham caused Him to act. He told Moses, **I have come down to rescue them from the hand of the Egyptians and to bring them up out of that land into a good and spacious land, a land flowing with milk and honey—the home of the Canaanites, Hittites, Amorites, Perizzites, Hivites and Jebusites** (3:8). Before He declared His plan to rescue the Israelites, God listed three things that moved Him to action. First, **I have indeed seen the misery of my people in Egypt.** Second, **I have heard them crying out because of their slave drivers.** Third, **I am concerned about their suffering** (v. 7). God was moved to action by His compassion for the

Moses' Questions and Objections	God's Answers	The Implications
Who am I to go to Egypt?	I will be with you.	It's not about us. The real issue is God's presence.
What is your name?	"I AM WHO I AM."	God is free to be whatever He chooses to be in order to keep His promises.
What if no one believes me?	What is in your hand?	God can use the resources we have on hand to accomplish His will.
I'm not eloquent.	Who made your mouth?	Our infirmities or handicaps do not limit God. He created us, and His "power is made perfect in weakness" (2 Cor. 12:9).
Please send someone else.	Go, with your brother!	God will insist on obedience from His people. We cannot sidestep His call to serve.

AHA!
God never forgets His plans!

people that He had chosen to be His own possession.

God's monologue took an interesting twist in the following sentences. Perhaps Moses was wondering why God had come down in the desert of Sinai when the problem was in the delta of Egypt. But God summarized His reasons for acting: **And now the cry of the Israelites has reached me, and I have seen the way the Egyptians are oppressing them** (v. 9). Then He commissioned Moses to do the work: **"So now, go. I am sending you to Pharaoh to bring my people the Israelites out of Egypt"** (v. 10). God often answers our questions about why He doesn't do something about hurting people by asking us to do something in His name.

Who Am I? (Ex. 3:11–12)

DID YOU KNOW?
God is "I AM," the eternal God of all time. He is in the past (Abraham, Isaac, Jacob), the present (Moses), and the future (you and me)—currently, right now, all at once.

Moses immediately started objecting to God's choice: **Who am I, that I should go to Pharaoh and bring the Israelites out of Egypt?** (v. 11). Moses must have been thinking about being rejected by the Israelites years before.

"They didn't want me to deliver them when I was a prince of Egypt; why would they accept me as a shepherd from the desert?"

And God said, "I will be with you. And this will be the sign to you that it is I who have sent you: When you have brought the people out of Egypt, you will worship God on this mountain" (v. 12). God's quick response pointed Moses to the real issue: the God of Abraham, Isaac, and Jacob would be present with him. His success this time was inevitable. Moses would return to worship God with all the Israelites. Later, Moses would refuse to go anywhere without God's presence (Ex. 33:12–23).

What Is Your Name? (Ex. 3:13–15)

Moses was still unconvinced. He **said to God, "Suppose I go to the Israelites and say to them, 'The God of your fathers has sent me to you,' and they ask me, 'What is his name?' Then what shall I tell them?"** (v. 13). Biblical names were much more than a label to distinguish individuals from each other. Names were used to describe a person's character or life. For example: Abram (exalted father) became Abraham (father of many), because God promised to give him many descendants (Gen. 17:5). Moses was essentially asking God what His character was like: "What kind of God are You?"

God said to Moses, "I AM WHO I AM. This is what you are to say to the Israelites: 'I AM has sent me to you'" (Ex. 3:13). What does this name tell us about God? He exists and lives in contrast to the idols of Egypt. He is free to choose what He will be, unlike humans who are controlled so much by genetics and environment. He is independent and self-caused. He is victorious and able to do whatever He has determined to do.

But God did not stop with "I AM." He went on to tell Moses to say, **The God of your fathers—the God of Abraham, the God of Isaac and the God of Jacob—has sent me to you** (v. 15). He is the God of relationships with individuals. He is not the "unmoved mover" of philosophy. He is the Lord who hears, sees, and cares about His people. He is the God of the covenant who always keeps His word, and that's the way He wants to be remembered. **"This is my name forever, the name by which I am to be remembered from generation to generation.**

The Rest of the Story

Moses continued to raise questions, and God patiently answered them in Exodus 3:16—4:12. However, when Moses flatly refused to go to Egypt, "the LORD's anger burned against Moses and he said, 'What about your brother, Aaron the Levite? I know he can speak well. . . . He will speak to the people for you, and it will be as if he were your mouth and as if you were God to him. But take this staff in your hand so you can perform miraculous signs with it'" (4:14–17). Finally, Moses obeyed the Lord and went to Egypt. ◆

WHAT ABOUT YOU?
Are you believing in I AM and His plans and promises for your life?

PRAYER
Father, thank You for remembering me from generation to generation.

INTERACTIVE LEARNING IDEAS

GET THE CLASS INVOLVED
Christ's Title: *I AM*

Divide into up to seven teams, and give each a sheet of flipchart or poster paper and a marker. Assign each group at least one of the following Scripture passages, so every passage is assigned:

- John 6:30–35, 41, 48–51
- John 8:12, 28, 58; 9:4–5
- John 10:1–10
- John 10:11–18
- John 11:25–27
- John 14:6–7
- John 15:1–8

In your teams, read the assigned passage where Jesus attributed to himself the Greek word *eimi*, meaning, I exist, I am. Its similarity in meaning with the Hebrew name God chose in Exodus 3 (*hayah*, meaning I AM), was enough to infuriate the Pharisees. They recognized exactly who Jesus was claiming to be.

Discuss within your team why Jesus used this "I am" analogy; then draw a simple sketch that pictures what Jesus called himself.

Invite each team to show its picture of who Jesus said He is. Discuss the significance of each statement—and what it means to you here and now. Post the pictures on a bulletin board in your classroom, where you'll be able to see them as you continue through Exodus. Several of the images will become critical to the nation's survival in its wilderness sojourn—demonstrating the unchanging nature of God.

TRY THIS ON YOUR OWN
Tough Choice

One passage referenced in this week's commentary was Hebrews 11, where Moses receives commendation for his faith both as a young man eschewing the rights of Pharaoh's household and as an older man leading God's people out of bondage.

Open to Hebrews 11:23–27, which covers the faith Moses demonstrated to the point in the story we've reached together. Consider:

- What did Moses give up to honor and obey the God of his fathers?
- Look at the phrase "the pleasures of sin." What do you suppose that means? (For hints, search an online Bible library such as www.biblegateway.com.)
- What did Moses gain for making the tough choices?

Now, ask God to show you a picture of your life choices thus far, from His perspective. Journal your answers to the following:

- What have you given up to follow Christ?
- What have you gained, or what do you expect to gain at some future time?
- When it seems the journey has exacted too high a cost, what has kept you moving on God's path?

TAKING IT TO THE STREET
God's Name Today

Go to a public location where you'll see a wide cross section of people—a train station, sporting event, shopping mall, airport, or a public services building. Take a pad and paper and at least one other member of your group with you. Sit silently, listening for every mention of God's name or the name of another god.

You may hear mention in conversations, in a worker's frustration, in an announcement via a public address system, and so forth. You may even see a mention on a billboard, ad, or multimedia screen.

After a while, make a point of talking to each other, in the hearing of people around. Talk about church or about something God is doing in your lives. Pay attention to the responses of others.

Keep a log of what you observe. Afterward, share your observations.

WITH YOUR FAMILY
Write an Allegory

As God's journey for Moses included stays in Pharaoh's household and the desert of Midian to prepare him for leading Israel, so He often calls us on journeys to places we might not have chosen. The way is seldom easy. Yet, God proves himself faithful—giving grace, forgiveness, strength, and courage as we need them.

Many have learned this by reading John Bunyan's allegory *The Pilgrim's Progress.* Others read about it in contemporary allegories such as Hannah Hurnard's *Hinds' Feet on High Places.*

Convene a family meeting at a relaxed time. After explaining these classics, work together to create your own allegorical hero (like Christian in *Pilgrim* or Much Afraid in *Hinds' Feet*). Put your protagonist on a journey toward heaven, and together write a story. Be creative—inserting energy, emotion, and exclamation as the journey unfolds. Invite questions as each participant comes to terms with what it means to follow Christ on a challenging journey. ◆

EXODUS 3:1–15

1 Now Moses was tending the flock of Jethro his father-in-law, the priest of Midian, and he led the flock to the far side of the desert and came to Horeb, the mountain of God.
2 There the angel of the LORD appeared to him in flames of fire from within a bush. Moses saw that though the bush was on fire it did not burn up.
3 So Moses thought, "I will go over and see this strange sight—why the bush does not burn up."
4 When the LORD saw that he had gone over to look, God called to him from within the bush, "Moses! Moses!" And Moses said, "Here I am."
5 "Do not come any closer," God said. "Take off your sandals, for the place where you are standing is holy ground."
6 Then he said, "I am the God of your father, the God of Abraham, the God of Isaac and the God of Jacob." At this, Moses hid his face, because he was afraid to look at God.
7 The LORD said, "I have indeed seen the misery of my people in Egypt. I have heard them crying out because of their slave drivers, and I am concerned about their suffering.
8 So I have come down to rescue them from the hand of the Egyptians and to bring them up out of that land into a good and spacious land, a land flowing with milk and honey—the home of the Canaanites, Hittites, Amorites, Perizzites, Hivites and Jebusites.
9 And now the cry of the Israelites has reached me, and I have seen the way the Egyptians are oppressing them.
10 So now, go. I am sending you to Pharaoh to bring my people the Israelites out of Egypt."
11 But Moses said to God, "Who am I, that I should go to Pharaoh and bring the Israelites out of Egypt?"
12 And God said, "I will be with you. And this will be the sign to you that it is I who have sent you: When you have brought the people out of Egypt, you will worship God on this mountain."
13 Moses said to God, "Suppose I go to the Israelites and say to them, 'The God of your fathers has sent me to you,' and they ask me, 'What is his name?' Then what shall I tell them?"
14 God said to Moses, "I AM WHO I AM. This is what you are to say to the Israelites: 'I AM has sent me to you.'"
15 God also said to Moses, "Say to the Israelites, 'The LORD, the God of your fathers—the God of Abraham, the God of Isaac and the God of Jacob—

Say Yes to God's Call

God seeks humble, available servants.

INTO THE SUBJECT

The beauty of a blossoming bush may capture your attention, but would you expect to see a bush burn without being consumed? And would you expect to hear a powerful voice emanate from a bush?

INTO THE WORD

1. How different were Moses' circumstances in Midian from those he had been accustomed to in Egypt?

2. What do you learn about God's character in Exodus 3:2–8?

3. Compare Exodus 3:4 and John 10:3. How does it make you feel to realize the Lord knows your name?

4. God told Moses to maintain a distance from Him and to remove his sandals. Why do you agree or disagree that many believers fail to recognize God's holiness?

5. According to Exodus 7–10, what did God plan to rescue His people from? What did He have in store for them?

6. What has God rescued you from? Ultimately, what does He have in store for you?

7. How did God answer Moses' reluctance to represent Him before Pharaoh?

8. What does it mean to you personally that God identifies himself as "I AM" (v. 14)?

INTO THE WORLD

As an ambassador of the Lord, represent Him faithfully and fearlessly this week.

has sent me to you.' This is my name forever, the name by which I am to be remembered from generation to generation.

GOD'S NAMES

God called himself "I AM WHO I AM" to Moses (Ex. 3:14). Learn some of His other names by matching the verse with the name.

1. Genesis 1:1; Psalm 19:1 ____

2. Genesis 2:4 ____

3. Genesis 22:13–14 ____

4. Judges 6:24 ____

5. Romans 8:15 ____

6. Isaiah 9:6 ____

7. Isaiah 7:14 ____

8. Isaiah 6:1–3 ____

9. Matthew 1:2 ____

10. Revelation 15:3 ____

11. John 15:26 ____

12. Malachi 1:6 ____

13. Genesis 16:13 ____

14. 1 Peter 4:19 ____

15. Hebrews 4:14 ____

A. LORD God (or Yahweh, a reference to His divine salvation)

B. The Lord Is Peace (or Jehovah Shalom)

C. God (or Elohim, a reference to His power and might)

D. Advocate, Spirit of Truth

E. Abba (meaning, "Father")

F. Lord Almighty (or Jehovah Sabbaoth)

G. Wonderful Counselor, Mighty God, Everlasting Father, Prince of Peace

H. Immanuel (meaning, "God with us")

I. Creator

J. Jesus (or Joshua, meaning, "the Lord saves")

K. High Priest

L. Lord God Almighty, King of the Nations

M. The Lord Who Provides (or Jehovah Jireh)

N. The One Who Sees (or El-Roi)

O. Lord of Lords (or Adonai)

In Jesus, God entered the world as deliverer.

A Savior Is Born

Luke 2:1–20

WHY THIS MATTERS

Christmas celebrates the Savior's birth, but it is easy to get distracted from this important fact. Families may drive through neighborhoods to look at brightly lit Christmas lights and fail to wonder at the Light that entered the world so long ago. Friends and loved ones may exchange Christmas gifts, yet take little or no time to thank God for the gift of His Son. People may mail Christmas greetings to acquaintances but fail to share the good news with more than a few.

After the shepherds visited baby Jesus, they spread the word about the Savior who had been born. This lesson will inspire us to follow the shepherds' example—at Christmas and every day.

BIBLE COMMENTARY

By Clarence (Bud) Bence

We interrupt our study of the book of Exodus for an obvious reason—the celebration of the birth of our Lord Jesus Christ. This holy day in the yearly calendar requires us to change our time frame, geographical location, and personalities from the last lesson. Chronologically, we move ahead more than one thousand years from the age of the pharaohs to the golden era of the empire of Rome. In location, we shift from the land of Egypt northward to the Promised Land, the modern-day land of Israel. In New Testament times, it was known as Palestine, a puppet state the Romans had only recently conquered from the Greeks, who had previously occupied the land for several centuries. And, of course, we ask our leading actor, Moses, to step into the shadows for a brief moment while we give our attention to the King of Kings.

But for all these changes in time and space, the passage we study in this lesson still deals with the same grand theme: God's sovereign control over history and His eternal plan to deliver His people from bondage. The book of Exodus describes how God delivered the Israelites from their political oppression at the hands of the Egyptians. To free His people from their bondage, God called out a great leader, Moses, and empowered him to stand against the forces of evil that enslaved the children of Israel.

Then, "when the time had fully come" (Gal. 4:4), God confronted an even greater enemy who had enslaved the entire human race in the bondage of sin. Since this enemy was a spiritual, rather than a political, power, God's plan for deliverance included a supernatural Liberator rather than a mere mortal. The Son of God himself came to earth "in appearance as a man" (Phil. 2:8) to defeat the power of Satan and bring salvation to all humanity.

In this lesson, God entered into the human realm. But it was in the most simple and humble way imaginable—a sleeping infant in the hay of a feeding

KEY VERSE
Today in the town of David a Savior has been born to you; he is Christ the Lord.
—Luke 2:11

BACKGROUND SCRIPTURES
Matthew 1:18—2:12
    The account of
    Joseph's dream and the
    visit of the wise men
Luke 1:5–80
    The angel's visit to
    Mary and the birth of
    John the Baptist
John 1:1–14
    John's prologue where
    he identified Christ
    with the eternal Word
    of God
Galatians 4:3–7
    Paul's one reference to
    Christ's birth

DAILY BIBLE READINGS
Monday: Micah 5:1–5
Tuesday: Luke 1:11–17
Wednesday: Luke 1:39–45
Thursday: Luke 1:46–55
Friday: Luke 1:76–80
Saturday: Luke 2:1–20
Sunday: Psalm 18:25–29

WHAT DO YOU THINK?
How are the divine appearances to Moses from a burning bush and the announcement of angels to shepherds from the sky similar?

AHA!
God always provides a deliverer to His people: Israelites under physical oppression, the world under spiritual oppression.

DID YOU KNOW?
There is no "innkeeper" mentioned in Scripture. Jesus was not necessarily born in a stable, but possibly a cave. The angels did not sing, contrary to "Hark! The Herald Angels Sing." And there were not necessarily three magi. The number is derived from the three gifts.

trough. Even with such a quiet arrival, the appropriate response was the same. Like Moses, the shepherds turned aside from their flocks to enter the presence of God. Like Moses, their natural response was to worship.

The Grand Event (Luke 2:1–7)

Luke's account of the birth of Jesus is the most personal of the various narratives in the New Testament. In the opening verses of John's gospel, the advent of Christ is described from the divine perspective. He told of the eternal Word, the Light of the world, who became flesh so we might see the glory of God (John 1:14). Matthew gave us a few details of the family, but focused on the legal and political forces that threatened the well-being of the infant Jesus. The wise men and Herod received top billing, with the birth in Bethlehem getting only passing mention. Mark passed over the birth story altogether. It was Luke who filled in the details surrounding the parents of Jesus and the actual birth day itself.

Joseph, living about seventy-five miles north of Bethlehem in the hill country of Galilee, was ordered by Caesar Augustus to register in the town of his origin. A census like this occurred periodically in the Roman Empire. Unlike our modern ten-year census, these empire-wide registrations were thinly veiled excuses for conscripting men into the Roman army or collecting taxes from the conquered nations. Mary would not have been required to accompany Joseph; women were treated as nonpersons in Roman culture. Furthermore, at the time of Joseph's departure from Nazareth, he and Mary were only betrothed, not married. But her pregnancy would have been a growing embarrassment, and perhaps she sought to avoid the shame of bearing a child out of wedlock in the town of Nazareth by traveling south with her fiancée, despite the hardships of such a journey.

The Scripture passage gives no evidence of a hurried late-term journey to Bethlehem; we only assume that as a way of explaining the lack of a proper birthing place for the Christ child. However, we must remember that Mary had relatives living in "the hill country of Judea" (Luke 1:39), the region just south of Jerusalem and in close proximity to Bethlehem. Furthermore, the fact that Joseph paid his taxes in Bethlehem suggests that he (or his parents) might have lived in that city before moving north to Galilee. If this was the case, Joseph likely would have had relatives living in the area near Bethlehem. For this reason, some scholars suggest that the couple could have traveled to the vicinity of Bethlehem some weeks or even months before Mary's due date, and the journey to the city of Bethlehem might have been a brief excursion during which **the time came for the baby to be born** (2:6).

What is clear from the text is that the Christ child was born in a rather unusual setting. Circumstances were such in Bethlehem that **there was no**

New Testament Passages Pertaining to Christ's Birth		
Author	Scripture Passage	Focus
Matthew	1:18–25 2:1–12	Joseph's dream and decision to wed Mary The wise men's visit and Herod's plot
Mark		(No reference to Jesus' birth)
Luke	1:5–25 1:26–38 1:57–80 2:1–7 2:8–29 2:30–40	Zechariah learns of John the Baptist's birth The angel tells Mary of Jesus' birth John the Baptist's birth The birth in Bethlehem The angels' visit to the shepherds Jesus dedicated to God in the temple
John	1:1–14	The eternal Word who became flesh
Paul	Galatians 4:3–7	Jesus born of a woman in the fullness of time

room for them in the inn (v. 7). The Greek word Luke used for "inn" is the same word he used later in the gospel when referring to the "guest room" (22:11) where Jesus ate the Last Supper with His disciples. Whether Luke was here referring to a public inn or the private guest room in the house of a friend or relative, there was insufficient room for the birth of a child in that place, so Mary and Joseph settled for another place (no mention of barn or stable) that had feeding troughs for animals close at hand. These mangers might have been located in caves near the dwelling (which is what the most ancient traditions indicate) or even in rooms adjacent to the living quarters. It is not uncommon in the Middle East even today for animals to be kept in rooms constructed as part of the house. Here, in a place of privacy away from the crowds in the city, God's ultimate gift was delivered to the world. And like any loving mother in simple peasant surroundings would have, Mary wrapped Jesus in long strips of cloth for warmth and security before placing Him in the safe and soft manger for a bed.

The Spectacular Announcement (Luke 2:8–15)

Because of its close proximity to the temple in Jerusalem, Bethlehem was well suited for raising sheep. Thousands of animals were offered on altars each year, and one could expect a reasonable livelihood from producing sheep both for wool and sacrifice in the hill country surrounding Bethlehem. The fact that **there were shepherds living out in the fields nearby, keeping watch over their flocks at night** (v. 8) gives some support to the argument that Christ was born in late March or April. For most of the year, shepherds brought their sheep into folds near their houses and spent the nights sleeping in their own beds. However, during the lambing season each spring, the pregnant ewes were too fragile to move back and forth from pasture to sheepfold. Therefore, the shepherds would stay in the fields at night to assist with the birthing of the young sheep and to protect the ewes and lambs from wild animals. (The celebration of Christmas in December originated several centuries after the close of the New Testament, probably in association with the Roman festival of Saturn. Since this was the only day in the year slaves were free from their servant duties, it was natural for them to celebrate the birth of their King on this holiday. Hence, the "mass of Christ" or Christmas. By this late date, centuries after the time of Christ, with very few written records, there would have been no way to establish the precise day of His birth.)

The shepherd's quiet evening was interrupted first by light . . . and then by sound. The angel (literally "messenger") of God appeared to them, startling them by the radiance that is often mentioned when describing these heralds of the heavenly King. Calming their natural fears, the angel announced "good news" to these lowly citizens. A Savior had been born in David's city. Linking the term *savior* with the historical King David would certainly have prompted the shepherds to think that this was news of a political deliverer who would reestablish the glory of Israel by gaining independence from the tyranny of Rome. They would have had little idea of the greater deliverance from sin that had been prophesied to Joseph nine months earlier (Matt. 1:21).

The sign promised by the angel should not be understood as some clue in a Christmas scavenger hunt. Babies wrapped in swaddling clothes were an everyday

---

WHAT DO YOU THINK?
Why do you think the announcement of Christ's birth was made to shepherds, who were low on the social ladder?

AHA!
God has a special place in His heart for the poor and "least of these"!

DID YOU KNOW?
Everyone has his or her own style of worship. We see this in the stories of Christ's birth. The shepherds rejoice and race to spread the news, the magi bow with gifts, Mary meditates, Simeon prophesies.

occurrence in biblical times. Even a baby lying in a feeding trough would not have been unusual. The shepherds could easily have found the baby by asking the whereabouts of a newborn baby in a town as small as Bethlehem (only several hundred occupants). The sign spoken of by the angel was linked more to the social status of the baby and God's condescending nature. Although a descendant of David, the newborn Savior would be found in humble settings; He would be one with the poor in spirit and choose to identify with the meek of the earth.

WHAT ABOUT YOU?
How do you respond to the birth of the Deliverer?

While individual angels usually functioned as God's messengers, hosts of angels suggested a moment of high worship. Suddenly the individual angel was joined by **a great company of the heavenly host** (v. 13), praising not the baby in the manger, but the God who reigns on high. This almighty God, in the Christmas birth, had brought peace to the earth and demonstrated that, despite the fall and the corruption of evil, His favor and mercy was still directed toward the sons and daughters of Adam.

The Worshipful Response (Luke 2:16–20)

Like Moses, who had been intrigued by the supernatural interruption of a burning bush, the curiosity of the shepherds prompted them to leave their sheep in the fields and hurry to Bethlehem to "see this thing that has happened" (v. 15). Moses' search led him to an encounter with God, complete with a divine mandate. The shepherds found only a baby, "asleep on the hay." The wise men, who arrived in Bethlehem some time later, "bowed down and worshiped him . . . and presented him with gifts" (Matt. 2:11). No doubt, these wealthy men recognized the royal nature of the newborn "King of the Jews" in a way that was alien to the shepherds' understanding. Instead of bowing down, the shepherds demonstrated their worship by joyous proclamation to others. Instead of private devotion to the child, **they spread the word** (v. 17) while **glorifying and praising God** (v. 20).

PRAYER
Father, thank You for sending Your Son.

Tucked into the closing sentences of the Christmas story is yet another mode of worship—the silent meditation of the mother of Jesus. One can describe the virtues of worship in terms of adoration (the wise men) or public testimony and praise to God (the shepherds). But worship finds its most meaningful purpose when it reaches the level of the heart. **But Mary treasured up all these things** (v. 19). Among those treasured thoughts would be the announcement of the angel Gabriel nine months earlier; the sensitive compassion of Joseph, who valued God's call more than his own reasoned-out plans; the wearisome journey from Nazareth to Bethlehem; the astounding report of the shepherds; and, above all, a mother's joy at birthing her first child. There would be much to ponder too. How would this virgin-born Child save the world? How would His life and teachings reveal God in new ways to humans? ✦

LUKE 2:1–20

1 In those days Caesar Augustus issued a decree that a census should be taken of the entire Roman world.

2 (This was the first census that took place while Quirinius was governor of Syria.)

3 And everyone went to his own town to register.

4 So Joseph also went up from the town of Nazareth in Galilee to Judea, to Bethlehem the town of David, because he belonged to the house and line of David.

5 He went there to register with Mary, who was pledged to be married to him and was expecting a child.

6 While they were there, the time came for the baby to be born,

7 and she gave birth to her firstborn, a son. She wrapped him in cloths and placed him in a manger, because there was no room for them in the inn.

8 And there were shepherds living out in the fields nearby, keeping watch over their flocks at night.

9 An angel of the Lord appeared to them, and the glory of the Lord shone around them, and they were terrified.

10 But the angel said to them, "Do not be afraid. I bring you good news of great joy that will be for all the people.

11 Today in the town of David a Savior has been born to you; he is Christ the Lord.

12 This will be a sign to you: You will find a baby wrapped in cloths and lying in a manger."

13 Suddenly a great company of the heavenly host appeared with the angel, praising God and saying,

14 "Glory to God in the highest, and on earth peace to men on whom his favor rests."

15 When the angels had left them and gone into heaven, the shepherds said to one another, "Let's go to Bethlehem and see this thing that has happened, which the Lord has told us about."

16 So they hurried off and found Mary and Joseph, and the baby, who was lying in the manger.

17 When they had seen him, they spread the word concerning what had been told them about this child,

18 and all who heard it were amazed at what the shepherds said to them.

19 But Mary treasured up all these things and pondered them in her heart.

20 The shepherds returned, glorifying and praising God for all the things they had heard and seen, which were just as they had been told.

A Savior Is Born

In Jesus, God entered the world as deliverer.

INTO THE SUBJECT

Census taking happens periodically at the government's direction, but has your participation in a census changed the course of history?

INTO THE WORD

1. What elements of Luke 2:1–5 establish the historical setting of Jesus' birth?

2. Read Micah 5:2 and Luke 2:1–4. God used the mighty Roman Empire to fulfill Jesus' prophesied birth. How does this fact encourage you in today's tumultuous times?

3. What does it mean to you personally that Jesus was born in humble circumstances (Luke 2:5–7)?

4. What key elements of good news do you find in verses 8–11?

5. How would you show from verses 11–12 that Jesus is both God and man?

6. Why do you agree or disagree it was appropriate that shepherds received the good news about Jesus' birth?

7. What aspects of the shepherds' response to the "birth announcement" in verses 15–20 can you incorporate into your life?

INTO THE WORLD

Much of the world has never heard about Jesus' birth, and many people have yet to hear why He came to earth. Share the good news with others this week.

Nativity Poem

Immensity cloistered in thy dear womb,
Now leaves His well-belov'd imprisonment,
There He hath made Himself to His intent
Weak enough, now into the world to come;
But O, for thee, for Him, hath the inn no room?
Yet lay Him in this stall, and from the Orient,
Stars and wise men will travel to prevent
The effect of Herod's jealous general doom.
Seest thou, my soul, with thy faith's eyes, how He
Which fills all place, yet none holds Him, doth lie?
Was not His pity towards thee wondrous high,
That would have need to be pitied by thee?
Kiss Him, and with Him into Egypt go,
With His kind mother, who partakes thy woe.

—John Dunn

INTERACTIVE LEARNING IDEAS

GET THE CLASS INVOLVED
It's Dramatic

Before the class meets, copy and print the following Scripture passages in sequence, enough copies for everyone. (Each is a prophecy related to the coming of Christ or a fulfillment in the events of His incarnation.) Assign parts to people.

- Jeremiah 23:5–6 (speaker: voice of the Lord)
- Acts 13:23–25 (speaker: Paul)
- Isaiah 7:14 (speaker: voice of the Lord)
- Matthew 1:18–25 (speakers: narrator chorus and angel)
- Micah 5:2 (speaker: prophet)
- Luke 2:4–7 (speakers: narrator chorus)
- Deuteronomy 18:18 (speaker: voice of the Lord)
- Acts 3:20–22 (speakers: Peter and Moses)
- Galatians 4:4–5 (speaker: Paul)

When each speaker's turn comes, stand and read with flare and enthusiasm. Anyone not assigned a named part should stand and read together as the narrator chorus.

After the production, talk about the magnificent way the messianic prophecies *all* were fulfilled in Jesus. Offer to have your group reprise this drama as part of your church's Christmas Eve service.

TRY THIS ON YOUR OWN
The Rest of the Story

The commentary for this lesson corrects modern-day misinformation about the culture surrounding Christ's birth. For example, Luke says nothing about a stable and that instructions given to the shepherds were not a "Christmas treasure hunt."

During a quiet time this week, reread Matthew 1–2 and Luke 2 carefully. Then go online to download a copy of the nineteenth-century book *The Life and Times of Jesus the Messiah* by Alfred Edersheim (it's available as an ebook for around a dollar or free with some Bible software). Or visit a library that has a print copy in its collection.

Read the sections "What Messiah Did the Jews Expect?" and "The Nativity of Jesus the Messiah." Note all the cultural details Edersheim explains that first-century readers would have understood intuitively. Consider how knowing these facts allows you a greater appreciation of the way your Lord chose to enter human history.

TAKING IT TO THE STREET
Liberated!

To most modern Westerners, the concept of liberation is foreign. Most of us haven't been held captive. But a generation or two ago, liberation was uppermost in the minds of the planet.

Bring together two or three members of your study group. Find a World War II veteran living nearby. You might begin by calling a VFW hall or a local nursing home. (If you can't find someone, search online for stories written by vets of that era.)

Make plans to meet the vet. If he's in a care facility, wheel him to the day room and find out whether he can have treats (like Christmas cookies or coffee). Otherwise, take him out for coffee or a snack.

Invite him to talk about how he and his fellow servicemen liberated Europe from Nazi oppression. Let him describe what liberation meant to the people who were in prison camps.

Pray God's blessings of Christmas for him (and his family). Sing a Christmas carol. If God opens the door, share with him how Christ liberated you from sin. Express your thanks to him and the men of his generation for their self-sacrifice.

Back at home, consider the parallels of the liberation brought by freedom's army with the liberation brought by God's only Son.

WITH YOUR FAMILY
You—A Good News Messenger!

The messengers God sent in the Christmas story—awestruck angels and worshiping shepherd—were excited not just to see the Christ child, but also to tell others the amazing news.

As part of your role as a good-news messenger, get together with your family to write a yearend newsletter. Have each person contribute. Be sure it includes a clear, simple description of the good news as God's messenger explained it on the first Christmas night.

Decorate it together. Use pictures of your family taken during the year. Cut out and scan graphics appropriate for the season. Eat your favorite junk-food snack as you create—and make it a fun time for everyone to recall good things that happened during the year.

Finally, upload it to send by email and post on everyone's social media pages to be seen by schoolmates, colleagues, extended family, and friends. Mail copies to those who might not see it online. ◆

God demonstrates that He is in control.

GOD WORKS THROUGH OBEDIENT PEOPLE

Exodus 6:28—7:6, 14–24

KEY VERSE

And the Egyptians will know that I am the LORD when I stretch out my hand against Egypt and bring the Israelites out of it.
—Exodus 7:5

BACKGROUND SCRIPTURES

Exodus 4:21; 7:3; 9:12;
10:1, 20, 27; 11:10; 14:4, 8
    God said He would
    harden Pharaoh's heart.
Acts 7:20–43
    Stephen's narration of
    Moses' story

DAILY BIBLE READINGS

Monday: John 1:11–14
Tuesday: Isaiah 11:1–6
Wednesday: 2 Chronicles
                   20:4–12
Thursday: 2 Chronicles
                   20:13–18
Friday: 2 Chronicles
                   20:21–24
Saturday: Exodus
                   6:28—7:6,
                   14–24
Sunday: Psalm 18:30–36

WHY THIS MATTERS

Bedbugs are taking a bite out of a good night's sleep for a growing number of travelers and stay-at-home families. They have found their way into a number of hotels, motels, dormitories, private residences, and even cruise ships. They are ugly, pesky, nasty, and hard to get rid of. Exterminators may use extremely hot steam to kill the critters. However, when God urged Pharaoh to let the Hebrews leave Egypt, He used plagues—some infestations—to persuade Pharaoh. And by doing so, He turned up the heat, so to speak, on Pharaoh.

This lesson shows that God is greater than even the most powerful ruler. No one can thwart His purposes.

BIBLE COMMENTARY

By Kathy Bence

"I am the LORD" (Ex. 6:28) is the key not only to this passage but the entire Old Testament. The Pentateuch is about a God who wanted to reveal himself to His people, and they didn't get it. Repeatedly, God offered himself, His love, and His power for their benefit.

In the garden of Eden, God prepared the perfect environment to know Him. Then He revealed himself fully to Adam and Eve and offered them relationship. They could hear His voice and converse with Him. They had only to continue in this relationship and keep one command: not to eat of the tree that would destroy this relationship with God. They chose knowledge over a perfect friendship with God and things have never been the same again. From then on, God chose to reveal himself through chosen leaders whose hearts were open to hearing God's voice: Abraham, Isaac, Jacob, and Moses.

God offered not only relationship but land, security, and prosperity to this stubborn people He had chosen if they would obey His guidelines as to how to be His people. This same theme is with us still. God offers friendship and security and (spiritual) prosperity in the context of a covenant relationship—if we can only understand how to relate to a holy God.

The covenant of God was "I will be your God and you will be My people." It's the "being His people" part we haven't managed well. We haven't understood that to be God's people means to live *His way*. The commandments of God are crafted with our well-being in mind. Life simply works better if we obey God's guidelines for getting along with Him and others.

So since we haven't understood, God has used varied methods of getting His message across to His chosen people. In effecting the exodus of the people from slavery, the primary method God used was miracles—in the form of plagues. But He repeatedly said that the miracles were to accomplish the purpose of people knowing that "I am the LORD"—both the Israelites and the Egyptians

("and the Egyptians will know that I am the LORD; 7:5).
God uses many means to reveal himself to us so we can live
together in this covenant relationship of mutual love. God
meant for His people to love Him by worship and obedience as He revealed himself and His power on their behalf.
But the people saw only limitations—those of slavery and
covenant obedience. So they continually missed the love of
God enfolded in the message, and thus they rebelled. This
story has continued from then till now as God uses one
method after another to reach us.

In this passage, we find the first miracle (plague) God used
to show Pharaoh that *he* was not God, and that he should bow
to Yahweh. But Pharaoh, who wanted the worship for himself,
stubbornly refused and ultimately lost all. Pharaoh became the supreme lesson
that anyone who thinks he or she will compete with God and win is a fool.

Egyptian magicians are
terrified over God's true
power.

Setting the Stage for All to Know "I Am the LORD" (Ex. 6:28—7:6)

Moses was to **tell Pharaoh** (v. 29) everything God said. Pharaoh would not
be able to say he didn't know he was contesting God or that God had not
warned him. God offered Pharaoh ample opportunity to change. First of all, he
was to know that God said, **I am the LORD** (v. 29). The intent of this phrase
was not so much to reveal God's name but His character. He was and is a different kind of Lord than Pharaoh was. His character is love and holiness, not
just love of power, as in Pharaoh's case.

God acknowledged Pharaoh as **king of Egypt** (v. 29)—but his kingdom
consisted only of that one country. Pharaoh was to understand that while Egypt
may have been powerful at the time, he did not rule the earth, only part of it.

Egypt, in fact, ruled most of the known world at that time. In ancient times,
one power often ruled an enormous number of countries. Babylon, Persia,
Greece, and Rome followed Egypt as world powers in biblical history. Ironically,
when Moses complained to God that he would not be eloquent enough to debate
with Pharaoh, God said He would make Moses "as God" to Pharaoh. Note the
contrast here: Pharaoh thought he was God, and Yahweh promised to make
Moses appear as God to Pharaoh. In other words, Moses would appear as God in
the flesh to Pharaoh—equals in the contest as men. But Moses would have
Almighty God backing him, thus he was not to fear. God instructed Moses
specifically: **You are to say everything I command you** (7:2). Moses' role was
simply to obey God and then sit back and watch God work.

I will harden Pharaoh's heart (7:3). Nine times the Bible says God hardened
Pharaoh's heart (4:21; 7:3; 9:12; 10:1, 20, 27; 11:10; 14:4, 8). Another nine times
Pharaoh hardened his own heart, including during all of the first five plagues
(7:13–14, 22; 8:15, 19, 32; 9:7, 34–35). Not until the sixth plague did God actually do what He had threatened and harden Pharaoh's heart. Pharaoh had five
chances to repent of his self-worship and claim to be God. But God knew his heart
and that Pharaoh was set on being God rather than worshiping Yahweh.

The Hebrew word for harden actually means obstinate or unmovable.
Pharaoh had decided to resist God obstinately and demand worship for himself

instead. God used the plagues to teach the Egyptians who He is. But if their leader would not bow down to Yahweh, the people had little freedom to do so. God used harsh means of miraculous signs to bend the heart of Pharaoh into submission. They lost their water supply (Nile turned into blood), were overrun with frogs, gnats, and flies that ate all the vegetation, and finally lost their livestock (food supply). But nearly starving his people to death was not adequate to break Pharaoh's stubborn insistence on playing God. He obviously cared little for his people, who innocently endured the plagues because of him.

Notice why the Israelites were asking for a three-day holiday into the wilderness: to worship God. It seemed such a small thing to ask—a three-day religious weekend off. But Pharaoh evidently feared he would lose control of the Israelites if he agreed to any favors. Or perhaps he couldn't bear the thought that the people wanted to worship another god besides him.

The First Disaster (Ex. 7:14–24)

So the thing Moses feared did indeed happen. Pharaoh refused, and Moses and Aaron had to go out to the Nile River, hold up the staff, and watch God turn their only source of water into blood. Realize that some of the plagues had to be endured by the Israelites as well as the Egyptians. This loss of a water source, for instance, affected everyone living for many miles around. Egypt was one of the most arid and waterless countries on earth. The Nile, which annually flooded the plains in the spring, was the only source of irrigation they had to grow their crops. After it slowly receded from the spring floods, they knew they must wait a year for enough rain to water anything. For this, their only water source, to be transformed into blood was an unthinkable disaster. Not only was the Nile affected, but verse 19 says all the water in the **streams**, **canals**, **ponds**, and **reservoirs** (v. 19) was affected as well. So thorough was God that even water already in **buckets** and **stone jars** was instantly changed into blood. Some think the inclusion of blood in wooden buckets and clay jars was due to the Egyptians' belief in gods inhabiting wood, clay, and stone. God was making the statement that their gods were powerless.

Plague	Reference	Egyptian God Mocked
Nile turned into blood	Exodus 7:20	Osiris
Frogs	Exodus 8:6	Heqt
Lice	Exodus 8:17	Seb
Flies	Exodus 8:24	Hatkok
Cattle die	Exodus 9:6	Apis
Boils	Exodus 9:10	Typhon
Hail	Exodus 9:24	Shu
Locusts	Exodus 10:13	Serapia
Darkness	Exodus 10:22	Ra
Death of firstborn	Exodus 12:29	All gods

Remember that Egypt was also a desert country of sun and high temperatures. It wouldn't have been an hour till the blood stank unbearably. All **the fish in the Nile died** (v. 21) immediately, and the people had to dig for water along the Nile boundaries to get any water to drink (v. 24). By filtering the water through sand, it became pure enough for drinking.

In addition, the Nile was an object of worship itself. The Egyptians worshiped the Nile River, which they named the god Hopi. They wrote hymns to praise Hopi and the Nile as the "source of life," which it literally was because it supplied water for them to live. Interestingly, the other plagues also attacked

---

WHAT DO YOU THINK?
How does God show that He alone is all powerful in our world today?

AHA!
God refuses to be second to any power on earth!

DID YOU KNOW?
Not only did Jehovah God establish His absolute power over the supposed Egyptian gods, but He took on the pharaoh's magicians. The Egyptians believed magic could "ward off the blows of fate." The Hebrew word for plague is *blows*!

their beliefs in the gods of nature. For instance, the plague of frogs degraded their worship of Heqt, the frog goddess, believed to assist women in childbirth. God carefully chose to render their own gods powerless in their eyes so they could see Yahweh's almighty power.

Pharaoh had a choice set before him: let the people go or suffer a plague. He chose to pit himself against God rather than let them worship. Worse yet, several times Pharaoh promised to let them go as soon as the plague was removed—then he changed his mind and refused again. He seemed determined to "win" with God. Each reprieve gave him fresh hope that he could outwit this foreign God. To be fair, Pharaoh was not used to dealing with real gods with real power. The Egyptians worshiped the gods of the Nile, the sun, thunderstorms, and most features of nature. The gods were revered, but, never having live interaction with them, Pharaoh truly had no idea that Yahweh was a living God who revealed himself and communicated with His people. So he kept up this game of attempting to outwit or best this God.

WHAT ABOUT YOU?
What gods vie for your attention and adoration?

Pharaoh even used his court magicians to compete with God's miracles. They thought that winning was simply a matter of a better magician. No wonder God repeatedly said He did everything that they may **know that I am the LORD** (v. 17). The magicians seemed to keep up for the first few miracles, and then even they realized they were up against something more than the average god. According to tradition, the magicians were named Jannes and Jambres (see 2 Tim. 3:8). They performed their magic either by sleight of hand or by demonic power.

How did Pharaoh respond? Exodus 7:22 says Pharaoh's **heart became hard**, he wouldn't listen to Moses and Aaron and turned and went into his palace. End of conversation. He clearly believed that if he remained stoic long enough, Moses would give up. We see more clearly the God with whom he was dealing, and we realize how foolish Pharaoh was. Then eight days passed before the next plague hit (frogs). We have no word of what went on during that week. Evidently Moses and Pharaoh had no more contact until the next plague. We can safely assume the people were scrambling, trying to find enough water to live. It could have been days or months until the river cleared. The word *plague* in Hebrew means "blow" or "stroke." Surely Pharaoh felt it as a blow, but he hardened himself to it and determined to tough it out.

PRAYER
Father, keep me from the subtle—but sinister—idols of the world, the flesh, and the devil.

So we see the plagues as a series of "blows" to the pride of the Egyptians, who, although they worshiped a multitude of gods, refused to worship Yahweh. God literally hammered on their hard hearts to convince them He is the Lord. They did not listen.

At the same time, God was preaching the same message to His own people, the Israelites, who often forgot or failed to understand who their great God was. So the plagues acted with dual authority as God's messages of self-revelation and love or, by contrast, to those who refused Him, as the God of power and even destruction. ✦

INTERACTIVE LEARNING IDEAS

GET THE CLASS INVOLVED
Egyptian Plague Jeopardy

Divide into three teams except for one person who will be the "host." Give each team a bell or whistle. Then play this quiz game—looking up each Scripture verse as its related answer is revealed.

- **Plagues:** Classified in the order of *Anura*, the creatures of this plague showed God's power over the Egyptian false god Heqt. (See Ex. 8:6.)
- **Plagues:** This plague involved creatures of the family *Muscidae*, who carry one hundred or more diseases. (See Ex. 8:24.)
- **Plagues:** Animals of the family *Bovinae* died in large numbers in this plague. (See Ex. 9:6.)
- **Plagues:** In the family *Acrididae*, these creatures travel hundreds of miles in a swarm and consume vegetation. (See Ex. 10:13.)
- **Pharaoh:** Pharaoh invited these individuals to imitate the miracles of Moses and Aaron. (See Ex. 7:22.)
- **Pharaoh:** What Pharaoh did after Aaron's rod turned Egypt's water into blood. (See Ex. 7:23.)
- **Pharaoh:** What Pharaoh said and did after the frog plague. (See Ex. 8:8.)
- **Pharaoh:** What God said to Pharaoh to explain why the plagues were necessary. (See Ex. 9:17.)
- **Egyptian Life:** This plant, affected by a plague, was cultivated to make linen in ancient times. (See Ex. 9:31.)
- **Egyptian Life:** This crop could be used to feed people and animals and was ruined in a plague. (See Ex. 9:31.)
- **Egyptian Life:** This was the initiator of the plague of boils. (See Ex. 9:3.)
- **Egyptian Life:** These, affected by the final plague, held special significance in Egyptian families. (See Ex. 11:5.)

TRY THIS ON YOUR OWN
God and You: A Love Story

Psalm 78 is Asaph's retelling of the Exodus story, from the perspective of hundreds of years later. He explains his purpose in verses 1–8; It's all about passing on God's story to future generations. With that in mind, write a concise, focused retelling of how God lovingly led you to salvation and assurance that He is the Lord. Read your story to your family (or your church family)—and tell them where to find it, so you and they will never forget.

TAKING IT TO THE STREET
Dear Editor . . .

Plan to meet with at least one other member of your group. Bring a laptop or writing implements.

Use current events to identify three ways people in our culture act as if they are God. Chat about why this is a pervasive temptation passed down from the first generation of human history.

Together write a letter to the editor of your local newspaper that uses a positive message about the one true God to respond to one of the current events you identified. Be sure to keep your letter constructive (not accusatory), short, and clear. Have each participant sign it, and send it to the editor by e-mail or postal mail.

WITH YOUR FAMILY
Get the Message?

Throughout the Old and New Testaments, God's message "I am the LORD," has many suffixes (and I love you . . . and I demand holiness . . . and I fight on your behalf . . . and I will not tolerate sin . . .), but His unparalleled authority remains at the heart of it all. Although He made it clear in many different ways, it seems humans still aren't getting the point.

To begin getting your mind around the crisis of being misunderstood, try this with your family.

Have one of the children make a statement like "You know I love you, Mom (or Dad)." But instead of responding in kind, you say, "There's no way you could love me." Have another family member try to convince you with another statement of how the child has shown that he or she loves you. Remain unconvinced. Let everyone try to convince you. Continue to refuse. Fold your arms. Frown a lot. Grumble and use all your body language to show how unconvinced you are.

Then, ask the child how it felt to have you not believe the declaration of love. Ask the others who tried to convince you how they felt.

After assuring the family that you love each one and believe they love you, talk about how God must feel when we ignore His message to us. Read John 3:16–17 aloud, and pray together that you all would respond to His love. ◆

EXODUS 6:28—7:6, 14–24

6:28 Now when the LORD spoke to Moses in Egypt, **29** he said to him, "I am the LORD. Tell Pharaoh king of Egypt everything I tell you."
30 But Moses said to the LORD, "Since I speak with faltering lips, why would Pharaoh listen to me?"

7:1 Then the LORD said to Moses, "See, I have made you like God to Pharaoh, and your brother Aaron will be your prophet.
2 You are to say everything I command you, and your brother Aaron is to tell Pharaoh to let the Israelites go out of his country.
3 But I will harden Pharaoh's heart, and though I multiply my miraculous signs and wonders in Egypt, **4** he will not listen to you. Then I will lay my hand on Egypt and with mighty acts of judgment I will bring out my divisions, my people the Israelites.
5 And the Egyptians will know that I am the LORD when I stretch out my hand against Egypt and bring the Israelites out of it."
6 Moses and Aaron did just as the LORD commanded them.

14 Then the LORD said to Moses, "Pharaoh's heart is unyielding; he refuses to let the people go.
15 Go to Pharaoh in the morning as he goes out to the water. Wait on the bank of the Nile to meet him, and take in your hand the staff that was changed into a snake.
16 Then say to him, 'The LORD, the God of the Hebrews, has sent me to say to you: Let my people go, so that they may worship me in the desert. But until now you have not listened.
17 This is what the LORD says: By this you will know that I am the LORD: With the staff that is in my hand I will strike the water of the Nile, and it will be changed into blood.
18 The fish in the Nile will die, and the river will stink; the Egyptians will not be able to drink its water.'"
19 The LORD said to Moses, "Tell Aaron, 'Take your staff and stretch out your hand over the waters of Egypt—over the streams and canals, over the ponds and all the reservoirs'—and they will turn to blood. Blood will be everywhere in Egypt, even in the wooden buckets and stone jars."
20 Moses and Aaron did just as the LORD had commanded. He raised his staff in the presence of Pharaoh and his officials and struck the water of the Nile, and all the water was changed into blood.

God Works through Obedient People

God demonstrates that He is in control.

INTO THE SUBJECT

God is invincible. Whoever declares war on Him must suffer the consequences of such a foolish decision. Pharaoh learned this truth, but what did it take to teach him?

INTO THE WORD

1. What was the main purpose of the plagues God would bring upon Egypt?
2. How do you know Pharaoh's refusal to release the Israelites would not surprise God?
3. Why do you agree or disagree that nothing surprises God?
4. How does God's foreknowledge encourage you?
5. Aaron provided support for Moses. How has a fellow believer provided much-needed support for you?
6. What trait exhibited by Moses and Aaron will you show (v. 6)? What challenging situation currently summons you to exhibit this trait?
7. According to Exodus 7:14–21, what were two intended purposes of the first plague?
8. Why do you agree or disagree that God orchestrates natural disasters?
9. Do you see evidence of spiritual warfare in what verse 22 reports? Why or why not?
10. What evidences do you see today that counterfeit religion battles truth?

INTO THE WORLD

Moses and Aaron were old men when they confronted Pharaoh. Don't let anything dissuade you from representing the Lord this week.

21 The fish in the Nile died, and the river smelled so bad that the Egyptians could not drink its water. Blood was everywhere in Egypt.
22 But the Egyptian magicians did the same things by their secret arts, and Pharaoh's heart became hard; he would not listen to Moses and Aaron, just as the LORD had said.
23 Instead, he turned and went into his palace, and did not take even this to heart.
24 And all the Egyptians dug along the Nile to get drinking water, because they could not drink the water of the river.

OBEDIENCE BRINGS RESULTS

Across

1. name above all names
3. 1a obeyed and _____ all of humankind
4. a basket case
6. collected animals
8. God told twelve to _____
10. couldn't count the stars
13. God told 1a to_____
17. 1d obeyed and led his people into a land _____
19. God told 6a to build a _____
21. 10a obeyed and became the _____ of a great nation
22. in every nativity set

Down

1. walked seven times around a city
2. God told 10a to_____ his son
5. 22a obeyed and became the human father of the _____
7. 4a obeyed and led his people to _____
9. God told 22a to take a _____ woman as his wife
11. God told 1d to attack _____ enemies
12. had scales on his eyes
14. God told 18d to go with_____
15. 18d obeyed and the gospel spread beyond the _____
16. 12d obeyed and became an _____
18. walked on water
20. 6a obeyed and was saved from the _____

God offers the model for humanity's hope.

GOD'S PROVISION FOR DELIVERANCE

Exodus 12:1–14, 29–30

Unit 2
L6

WHY THIS MATTERS

A horrendous tornado raked Joplin, Missouri, on May 22, 2011. It pummeled a nine-story hospital, flattened about a third of the city, caused millions of dollars in damage, and left 153 people dead. Like all tornadoes, this one caused residents to wonder why some neighborhoods and homes were spared, while others were devastated. No one has been able to furnish an answer.

A disastrous event more far-reaching than a tornado struck Egypt in the time of Moses, but no one had to wonder why Hebrew households were spared, while Egyptian households lost their firstborn. This lesson supplies the answer and inspires gratitude for the blood of God's spotless Lamb that causes His judgment to pass over us.

BIBLE COMMENTARY

By Carey B. Vinzant

Of the Old Testament feasts, Passover is probably the one with which Christians are most familiar. At the same time, it has a richness and depth that we rarely explore. To us, the Passover is about blood-smeared doorposts and dead Egyptians. What we often fail to see, however, is the powerful lesson it teaches about the effects of sin. Passover is also a signpost pointing from Exodus far ahead to the cross; in it God hid a host of prophetic clues about Jesus, the coming Messiah.

God's Deliverance Defines Israel (Ex. 12:1–2)

Verses 1–2 make it clear that what was about to happen would be a defining moment for the children of Israel. From this time forward, the Israelites would begin the year in this month. God told the Israelites to begin the year by remembering His deliverance. He redefined the calendar so every time they counted days, they would remember that as their year began with that time, so their history as God's chosen people began there. It was in the Exodus that Israel began to see fulfillment of God's promises to Abraham. In the Exodus they became a "great nation" (Gen. 12:2), and they began to "bless all peoples on earth" (Gen. 12:3) by their testimony to Yahweh's saving power. The Lord made it clear to Israel that they as a people began with His provision, that they must remember God above all else as the source of their identity.

God's Deliverance Is Inclusive (Ex. 12:3–4)

Verse 3 shows that remembering God's provision was for **the whole community of Israel**; it was not just a job for priests. God intended that the yearly rhythm of life among the children of Israel point to His deliverance, and He instituted this annual feast in order that all of His people would

KEY VERSE

The blood will be a sign for you on the houses where you are; and when I see the blood, I will pass over you. No destructive plague will touch you when I strike Egypt.
　　　　　　—Exodus 12:13

BACKGROUND SCRIPTURES

Leviticus 23:4–8
　　Passover described
Matthew 26:17–30
　　Communion narratives
Mark 14:12–26;
Luke 22:7–23; John 1:29
　　Jesus, the Lamb of God
John 6:25–69
　　Jesus, the Bread of Life
1 Corinthians 5:6–8
　　Jesus, our Passover
　　Lamb
Revelation 5
　　"Worthy is the Lamb!"

DAILY BIBLE READINGS

Monday:　Ecclesiastes
　　　　　　3:9–14
Tuesday:　1 Timothy
　　　　　　6:17–19
Wednesday: Romans
　　　　　　5:16–19
Thursday:　2 Kings 13:1–5
Friday:　　Psalm 34:17–22
Saturday:　Exodus
　　　　　　12:1–14, 29–30
Sunday:　　Psalm 18:37–50

Passover symbols reveal the Savior.

recall annually how He had worked on their behalf. Again, God was not creating an exclusive cult for himself in which only the priests may participate. Rather, He called "the whole community of Israel" to celebrate His deliverance, because that deliverance was for all Israel, not just a small religious elite. In this celebration, all of God's people in coming generations would remember that deliverance came from Him alone.

Verse 4 shows how God made provision for those who might otherwise have been unable to celebrate this feast. The sacrifice to which He called His people was not the spiritual equivalent of a tax they had to pay in order to be His people. It was to be a reminder to those who served Him that He is the God who delivers His people from slavery. To that end, He made allowances for people who might not be financially able to celebrate otherwise. God was not demanding a tribute of one lamb from each household in order that Israel might remember who was in charge. He did not need Israel's tribute. Instead, He was making sure that all of His people could participate in the celebration. He wanted all of His people to share in the feast, to remember His deliverance, so He created a standard that would not prevent anyone from celebrating on financial grounds. His goal was not for everyone to pay the sacrifice; it was for everyone to partake of the sacrificial meal.

God's Deliverance Requires Holiness (Ex. 12:5)

Verse 5 points to what will be a major theme throughout the history of God's people—holiness. Wherever God called for a sacrifice throughout the Old Testament, it was to be a sacrifice **without defect** (see also Lev. 1:3, 10; 2:1; 4:3; Mal. 1:6–14). God was so particular on this point because He intended all of the sacrifices to point forward to the final perfect sacrifice Christ would offer to God. The sacrifices of the Old Testament were not instituted in order to pay tribute to a ravening, destructive pagan deity. They were intended to show God's people the destructiveness of sin and to prepare them for the coming of Christ, God's own costly sin offering. The sin of Egypt had precipitated the coming of the ten plagues, but the Lord used this sacrifice as a way to show His people that they, too, needed deliverance from judgment. Only a costly, holy sacrifice would suffice for this lesson, because the sacrifice of Jesus is the most costly and holy of all. Christ's sacrifice keeps us from destruction in the presence of God, the "consuming fire" (Heb. 12:29).

God's Deliverance Demands Personal Investment (Ex. 12:6)

Verse 6 reminds us that the sacrifices the Israelites were to offer to God were not just anonymous farm animals. These animals were personally cared for by the family from the tenth until the fourteenth day of the month. The sacrifice was not an indulgence the children of Israel paid as a license to sin; it was a powerful demonstration that God's people must be participants in His work of deliverance. It was not an option for any of God's people to simply throw money at a problem—He demanded that His people see the costliness of sin at the sacrifice. He shows us that sin destroys things we value.

God's Deliverance Points to Christ (Ex. 12:7–10)

Verse 7 shows how God was beginning to teach His people about the problem of sin and their need for redemption. The children of Israel had heard by now of Moses' words to Pharaoh about this last and most terrible plague. They knew that death was coming to claim the firstborn throughout all Egypt. Then God revealed a way of deliverance from the coming death. His people would be protected from the coming destruction, but only if they were marked as His people. Yahweh's people were to proclaim Him as their God by a step of faith, by the application of a sacrifice to themselves. Here, God pointed forward to the sacrificial laws He would give to His people, and still further forward to Jesus, the One who would fulfill all of the law by His own perfect sacrifice.

The people of Israel began at this moment to be sensitized to their need of deliverance from death. Here God presented them with two basic truths. First, sin must always end in death. In every instance where people disobey God, death is the result. Second, a sacrificial victim may die in the sinner's place. By commanding that His people smear their houses with blood and eat the sacrificial lamb together, Yahweh reminded His people that someone must die for them. In this first Passover, He began a tradition that would span centuries as His people waited for deliverance to come. The supreme irony in the New Testament, however, is that the people of God did not recognize the Deliverer when He came. They expected the Messiah to strike down their oppressors like God did at the first Passover, but instead He was struck down as the final Passover Lamb.

Verse 8 shows God instituting the *seder*, the Passover meal at which His people ate the sacrificial lamb along with **bitter herbs** and **bread made without yeast**. This meal prepared the people of God for the coming of Christ. The Passover meal every year includes bitter herbs, lamb, and unleavened bread. The bitter herbs in the Passover meal signify the bitterness of the Hebrew slavery, which seems to be the backdrop for Paul's discussion of slavery to sin in Romans 6. The Passover lamb, of course, points forward to the sacrifice of Christ, by which the judgment of God passes over those who are in Him (Rom. 5:9). Yeast (or "leaven") often symbolizes sin in the Bible (Matt. 16:5–12; 1 Cor. 5:6–8). The unleavened bread in the Passover feast calls the celebrants to remember the importance of holiness. God's deliverance from the bitterness of slavery to sin and death does not stop with Christ dying as our Lamb. God intends to make us holy and blameless, like bread without yeast.

In the Gospels, Jesus instituted the service of Holy Communion (Matt. 26:17–30; Mark 14:12–26; Luke 22:7–23). His context for doing so, however, was Passover! It was at the *seder* that He said, "This is my body . . . this is my blood." It was the unleavened bread of the Passover, symbolizing His own holy life, that Jesus broke for the disciples to eat. The cup He gave them, speaking of it as His own blood, evokes thoughts of the Passover lamb whose blood was shed in order that God's judgment might pass over His people in Egypt. The Lord's Supper celebrates the completion of God's deliverance for which He began to provide at the first Passover. In the first celebration of the Eucharist, the plan of salvation was laid out; from the bitterness of slavery to sin and death, God provided deliverance by the sacrificial killing of a perfect Lamb.

WHAT DO YOU THINK?
Why is the meaning of the Passover meal hidden from faithful Jews?

AHA!
Christ is concealed in the Old Testament, revealed in the New!

DID YOU KNOW?
For twelve hundred years, at 3 p.m. on the Friday of Passover, the priest would blow the *shophar* (ram's horn) to announce that the sacrifice was finished. At that exact time, Christ cried out, "It is finished!" and died for the sins of the world!

Verses 9–10 make it clear that God did not merely intend His people to have a pleasant meal together. His explicit directions about the preparation of the food and the way in which the leftovers must be destroyed make it plain that this was more than a potluck supper—it was a sacred event. God took steps to ensure that Passover would not be viewed as commonplace. He wanted this feast to cause His people to anticipate His continuing deliverance, which He would complete in Jesus.

God Prepares His People for His Deliverance (Ex. 12:11)

Verse 11 is God's call for the children of Israel to be ready. They were to eat the Passover **in haste** because God intended to deliver them at any moment. They were to dress for travel because God planned to bring them out of slavery on the very night they ate this feast. His delivering works often demand instant obedience from us, His people. God wants us to enjoy the benefits of His powerful working in our lives, so He calls us to readiness.

God Delivers By Judging Sin (Ex. 12:12–14, 29–30)

Verses 12–13 describe how God intended to deliver Israel: He would **strike down every firstborn** in Egypt. He did not simply free His people and leave the Egyptians alone. When God acts in the world, those acts can be seen from the perspective of faith or that of disobedience. The Passover is the act by which God made His people free to serve Him. That act can be seen as the Israelites saw it, as God freeing them because of His great love for Israel. On the other hand, the Egyptians perceived that same act as a terrible epidemic of death. The difference in how we perceive God's acts often lies in our attitude toward Him. To those who obey God, His acts bring freedom, but those same works bring death to the disobedient.

Verse 14 shows God commanding His people to **remember** what happened at the Passover. They must never forget He is the God who has set them free. He called them to remember how their freedom came. God both delivers the obedient and judges the disobedient by His acts in the world. Israel had to remember that their relationship with Yahweh was one defined by their obedience.

Verses 29–30 show the fulfillment of Moses' prophecy to Pharaoh in chapter 11. Pharaoh had continually defied God and belittled His servant Moses. This disobedience brought ruin upon Egypt, just as Moses said it would. In spite of Pharaoh's skepticism and mockery, God had accomplished what He said He would do. Although people deny God's authority, power, and existence, He always accomplishes His plans—either through deliverance or judgment.

Summary

The Passover is a key event in the history of God's chosen people. In the story of Israel, the Passover clearly and powerfully shows God's commitment to His people. He worked powerfully on their behalf so they could live in the freedom He provided. In addition, the Passover points forward to the coming of Christ. The Passover shows that God's deliverance goes hand in hand with His judgment. God calls His people to be ready and obedient in order that they may be delivered into His freedom. ◆

EXODUS 12:1–14, 29–30

1 The LORD said to Moses and Aaron in Egypt,

2 "This month is to be for you the first month, the first month of your year.

3 Tell the whole community of Israel that on the tenth day of this month each man is to take a lamb for his family, one for each household.

4 If any household is too small for a whole lamb, they must share one with their nearest neighbor, having taken into account the number of people there are. You are to determine the amount of lamb needed in accordance with what each person will eat.

5 The animals you choose must be year-old males without defect, and you may take them from the sheep or the goats.

6 Take care of them until the fourteenth day of the month, when all the people of the community of Israel must slaughter them at twilight.

7 Then they are to take some of the blood and put it on the sides and tops of the doorframes of the houses where they eat the lambs.

8 That same night they are to eat the meat roasted over the fire, along with bitter herbs, and bread made without yeast.

9 Do not eat the meat raw or cooked in water, but roast it over the fire—head, legs and inner parts.

10 Do not leave any of it till morning; if some is left till morning, you must burn it.

11 This is how you are to eat it: with your cloak tucked into your belt, your sandals on your feet and your staff in your hand. Eat it in haste; it is the LORD's Passover.

12 "On that same night I will pass through Egypt and strike down every firstborn—both men and animals—and I will bring judgment on all the gods of Egypt. I am the LORD.

13 The blood will be a sign for you on the houses where you are; and when I see the blood, I will pass over you. No destructive plague will touch you when I strike Egypt.

14 "This is a day you are to commemorate; for the generations to come you shall celebrate it as a festival to the LORD—a lasting ordinance.

29 At midnight the LORD struck down all the firstborn in Egypt, from the firstborn of Pharaoh, who sat on the throne, to the firstborn of the prisoner, who was in the dungeon, and the firstborn of all the livestock as well.

30 Pharaoh and all his officials and all the Egyptians got up during the night, and there was loud wailing in Egypt, for there was not a house without someone dead.

God's Provision for Deliverance

God offers the model for humanity's hope.

INTO THE SUBJECT

Happy New Year! This frequently exchanged greeting comes when people anticipate a new year of new opportunities and blessings. How happy and hopeful do you think the people of Israel were to leave slavery behind and then begin a new year and a life of freedom?

INTO THE WORD

1. How do you know from Exodus 12:3–4 that God wanted everyone in Israel to participate in the Passover? How does this desire relate to 1 John 2:2 and Revelation 22:17?

2. What do you see in Exodus 12:5–8 that reminds you of Jesus, God's sacrificial lamb?

3. What indications do you find that God wanted His people to be ready for His deliverance?

4. What future deliverance should believers be ready for?

5. What happens if a sinner applies the blood of the Lamb to his or her heart? What happens if a sinner dies without having applied the blood of the Lamb to his or her heart?

6. How can believers keep the memory of Jesus' sacrifice fresh in their thinking?

7. According to Exodus 12:29–30, how extensive was God's judgment on Egypt's households?

8. How would you respond to the claim that God is too loving to send anyone to hell?

INTO THE WORLD

"Rescue the Perishing" is more than a song; it is a mandate. Tell others this week about Jesus' love and sacrifice to deliver them from hell and eternal punishment.

The Passover

Before Passover, people remove all the leaven from their homes.
Circle the leavened foods.

1. croissants

2. raw vegetables

3. bread without yeast

4. cookies

5. chicken

6. shrimp

7. pancakes

8. pickles

9. cheese

10. bagels

Answers: 1, 4, 7, and 10 are unleavened.

INTERACTIVE LEARNING IDEAS

GET THE CLASS INVOLVED
Digging In to Holiness

One lesson we gain from understanding God's initiation of the Passover is to recognize that God's deliverance requires holiness—only a holy, unblemished sacrifice can pay our sin debt. The response of true believers will be a desire to become more like Christ in our holy living. Remember, God's instruction: "Be holy, because I am holy" (Lev. 11:44; 1 Pet. 1:16).

Divide into groups of three. Using the following list of New Testament passages that describe and define the holy life, have each group create its own definition of holiness—as it is lived out by servants of God. Use the definition of *holiness* in a dictionary as an example

- Romans 1:1–6
- 1 Corinthians 1:26–31
- 2 Corinthians 6:14—7:1
- Galatians 5:16–23
- Ephesians 4:17–32
- 1 Thessalonians 4:1–8

Have all the groups share their definitions. Together, create a synthesis definition of biblical holiness, have someone write it down, and e-mail it to the group during the week.

As you close, use the instruction of 1 Peter 1:16 as a matter of united prayer.

TRY THIS ON YOUR OWN
Jesus—The Ultimate Passover Lamb

Spend time this week reading Mark's account of Jesus' institution of the Lord's Supper during the final Passover meal He celebrated with His disciples in Jerusalem (Mark 14:12–26). Read it at least once each day.

Each time you read it, spend time meditating on the parallels between the Exodus institution of Passover and Jesus' fulfillment of its traditions as the ultimate Passover Lamb. If it will help, read the passage in a contemporary paraphrase or a different translation than you usually use, so the concepts, actions, and significance come alive to you in fresh ways.

Craft a thoughtful prayer to express your response to this magnificent, agonizing plan initiated by God the Father and carried to completion by God the Son. Make it personal—because Christ's Passover sacrifice of himself was on *your* behalf.

TAKING IT TO THE STREET
Passover and Today's Jewish Community

Locate a Jewish temple nearby. Even better, find a messianic community of believers (who recognize Jesus as the Messiah) that you can visit. Make an appointment to talk with the rabbi or preacher of the congregation. Invite anyone in your group who is available to go with you. Go with the heart of a genuine seeker—to ask and learn about the way Jews remember and celebrate the Passover. Use these questions as starting points for your conversation:

- We've been studying the first Passover, and we are interested in how you celebrate it. Could you describe it to us?
- What do you tell your children about Passover? Why?
- What are the preparations like? Who makes them?
- What's the significance of unleavened bread? What's so bad about yeast at this season?
- Why do you go to all that trouble?
- What do the events of that first Passover have to do with your life every other day of the year?
- What have you learned about your God through hearing the story year after year, and through preparing and serving the Passover?

WITH YOUR FAMILY
Passover Meal

Plan a Passover meal with another family from your study. Do research online about the foods of the celebra-  tion. (Two sites where you might begin are www.30minuteseder.com or www.party411.com.)

Together make at least three of the main foods (lamb, bitter herbs, matzo) that are traditional to the meal. Assign one person to download the readings, in English, that go along with the meal.

Celebrate the Passover together. Invite different guests to read the four questions of Passover and the story from Exodus 12. As you eat the foods you've prepared together, talk about God's provision, how the meal symbolizes what Jesus would one day do, and how we can respond to His gift of salvation. ◆

God creatively delivers His people.

LESSON 7

DELIVERANCE WHEN ALL SEEMS LOST
Exodus 14:10–31

And when the Israelites saw the great power the LORD displayed against the Egyptians, the people feared the LORD and put their trust in him and in Moses his servant.

—Exodus 14:31

Hebrews 11:29
    The faith of Israel
John 6:1
    Jesus: another Moses?
1 Corinthians 10:1–5
    Deliverance: a process

Monday: Joshua 3:9–17
Tuesday: Daniel 6:17–23
Wednesday: Acts 12:1–7, 11
Thursday: 2 Corinthians
            1:8–11
Friday: Psalm 37:35–40
Saturday: Exodus
            14:10–31
Sunday: Psalm 19:1–6

WHY THIS MATTERS

British Prime Minister Winston Churchill dubbed it "The Miracle of Dunkirk." He was referring to the evacuation of 338,000 British troops trapped by German forces at Dunkirk in the spring of 1940. The situation seemed hopeless. The waters at Dunkirk were too shallow for a transport vessel to get near the men, so a flotilla of fishing boats and other small craft launched a rescue effort. The daring operation was aided by the sudden settling of a mysterious dense fog over the water. The little boats were able to transport the soldiers to larger ones that carried them safely to a port in southern Britain.

This lesson inspires faith and confidence in the God of might and miracle.

BIBLE COMMENTARY
By Carey B. Vinzant

This passage makes it clear that God helps His people in times of crisis, but it also shows that God's deliverance does not minimize the importance of personal decisions. There is a continuing interplay between human choices and divine acts in this narrative. The interaction of a God who is in control with people who make real choices—that have real consequences—is a major theme. God does not abolish human responsibility; in fact, He enables it.

The crossing of the Red Sea illustrates how God works cooperatively with His people to effect their deliverance. He goes to great lengths not only to deliver His people from slavery, but to make that deliverance a redemptive testimony, an opportunity for faith in Him. Those who believe can experience His care amid any trial; they can live as delivered people growing in the realization of that deliverance. Those who reject Him face His judgment; in rejecting Yahweh, they reject their Protector and Helper.

God's Deliverance Requires Obedience (Ex. 14:10–12)

Verse 10 must be understood remembering what 13:22 tells us: "Neither the pillar of cloud by day nor the pillar of fire by night left its place in front of the people." In other words, the Egyptian army did not merely attack a disordered rabble; the attack was directed toward a vast train of people following the obvious presence of God. After all Egypt had suffered under the terrible, costly judgment of God's ten plagues, Pharaoh remained unconvinced that Yahweh is the one true God. In fact, these verses show clearly what miraculous signs cannot accomplish. In spite of the glory of God visibly going before the Israelites, Pharaoh carried through his assault. In spite of that same glory, the Israelites reacted fearfully to the appearance of the Egyptian army. Signs only convince those who are willing to be convinced.

Verses 11–12 show the Israelites trying to shift blame as the chariots of Egypt drew closer. The people tried to blame Moses, grasping at straws when it appeared their obedience to God was about to cause them trouble. This lack of trust in Yahweh's provision is, sadly, a recurrent pattern throughout the Old Testament. Although the God of Abraham, Isaac, Jacob, and Joseph had made himself known by His prophet Moses and by the working of great and terrible wonders in Egypt, the Israelites doubted His will and ability to deliver them. That doubt resulted in great pain and difficulty for the God's people, both in the Old Testament and today.

God Uses People to Deliver People (Ex. 14:13–14)

Verses 13–14 show God using Moses' testimony to anchor His people in this crisis. When God's people were so afraid that they viewed renewed slavery as their best option, God's man challenged them to persevere. Moses knew that Israel stood at a watershed and what happened next would have far-reaching consequences in the life of God's people. Seeing this crisis for what it was, Moses testified to the trustworthiness of God's promises.

These verses also show the delicate balance of faith and obedience that is crucial to the Christian life. Although he believed God's promises, Moses had not merely waited for God to easily and painlessly deliver His people. He had continually been an active participant in God's redemptive plan. Moses had "stood firm" in his commitment to God and Israel even to the point of defying the pharaoh, whom Moses would have known as a kinsman and possibly even worshiped as a god earlier in his life. On the other hand, he knew the necessity of God's guidance and power, so he commanded the people to **be still** (v. 14). Standing firm and being still are the two sides of faith that obeys in the face of opposition and yet waits for God to do things His way in His time. God uses those who can both obey and wait to deliver His people today, just as He used Moses.

God's Delivering Work Is Continual (Ex. 14:15–16)

Verses 15–16 show that God's deliverance is a continuing process. It was not enough for the Israelites to have left Egypt; there was more to do before they were truly free. God calls His people to still greater faith at every turn. Although they had walked out of Egypt, they had yet to walk through the sea. Indeed, the story of God's deliverance and the obedience it demands never ends. God's call to the children of Israel to **move on** (v. 15) is characteristic of the continued growth and progress we must pursue in the Christian life.

God's Deliverance Shows His Greatness (Ex. 14:17–18)

Verses 17–18 are God's declaration that what happened next would bring Him **glory**. The very enemies of Israel and Yahweh would be used in spite of themselves to show the saving power of God. In the face of Israel's cowardice and doubt, the Lord showed himself to be a trustworthy defender, one so powerful that He even used those who opposed Him to assure Israel that He was in control. God was declaring to Israel that He intended not only to give them freedom but also a testimony. By this process of deliverance *through* trial

WHAT DO YOU THINK?
If God is sovereign (in control), why am I responsible for my choices and actions?

AHA!
God does not abolish human responsibility; He enables it.

DID YOU KNOW?
Some modern scholars have tried to rationalize the miraculous crossing of the Red Sea by arguing it was better known as *Yam Suph*, the Sea of Reeds: more of a marsh than a sea. But why would trained Egyptian charioteers ride into a quagmire and drown?

WHAT DO YOU THINK?
Has God ever nudged you
with "Stop praying and
move on"?

AHA!
"Your arm's too short to
box with God!"

DID YOU KNOW?
Although the Israelites were
declared as God's "chosen"
people, they were under the
same law—and judgment—
of all other nations. He
declared, "I have seen these
people, and they are a stiff-
necked people. Now leave
me alone so that my anger
may burn against them"
(Ex. 32:9–10).

rather than deliverance *from* trial, God fulfilled His promise to Abraham. Israel was becoming a great nation, not just in numbers but, more importantly, in faith. God also began to fulfill a second promise He made to Abraham that, "through your offspring all nations on earth will be blessed" (Gen. 22:18). Already the testimony of Yahweh's saving power was reaching to other nations—even those who were unwilling to hear it.

God Delivers By Enabling Obedience (Ex. 14:19–22)

Verses 19–22 describe God's method of intervention on behalf of His people. Although He did not simply pick up all the Israelites and instantaneously transport them to the Promised Land, He did not leave them to depend on their own resources either. Apart from God placing himself between His people and the armies of Egypt, they would surely have been destroyed, but He *did* intervene; He *does* protect His own.

Although God intervened, however, He did so for a reason: If God were to stand passively by, His people would have been unable to obey Him. In a situation where Israel stood trapped between two insurmountable difficulties, God stepped in and created opportunity where there would have been none otherwise. God is neither stingy nor gratuitous in His use of power. The Creator does things that to human beings are unforeseeable, even amazing, because He is determined that His people will not be left without what they need. Both in the exodus and today He supplies what is necessary for His people to continue the journey of faith.

God's Judges Those Who Oppose His Deliverance (Ex. 14:23–28)

Verse 23 shows the first stage of God's judgment on those who stood against His redemptive purpose: He gave them over to the madness they had chosen to believe. In the midst of miracle after fearful miracle, the Egyptians refused to see that they were outmatched. Even though they had been stricken by the plagues, been held at bay by the pillar of fire, and were now seeing the very sea opening to grant God's people passage, they refused to accept the truth. They saw only their interests being set aside, their slaves escaping. They would not see the God who had both declared and effected the deliverance of those slaves, His people. Yahweh had tried to convince the Egyptians that He is God over all. They refuse to be convinced, so they faced His judgment.

Verses 24–25 show the next phase of God's judgment on those who will not believe: He prevented them from accomplishing their purpose. As the entire army of an Ancient Near Eastern superpower charged in to attack, that army experienced massive, disabling equipment failure. The Egyptians were completely (and humiliatingly) foiled in their attempt to prevent God's people from following Him.

Verse 25 shows the Egyptians trying to salvage their own lives. They at last recognized that they could not successfully oppose God's deliverance of Israel. Rather than recognizing that Yahweh is God above all, however, they seemed still to think of Him as "that Hebrew god." The Egyptians were not concerned with worshiping the Lord; they wanted only to escape Him. The Egyptians said, **The Lord is fighting for** the Israelites **against Egypt**. Their hope was not to come into right relationship with Yahweh; all they wanted was to get away with their skins intact. Their rebellion had gone too far to allow a graceful withdrawal, however. Pharaoh's people had put themselves in a situation where only God's grace could save them—but they still rejected Him.

God parts the Red Sea.

Verse 26 is God's direction to Moses: **Stretch out your hand over the sea.** The God of Israel used Moses to command the sea, and in so doing He taught Moses yet another lesson. Moses would remember what he saw next, because God used him to accomplish it. He would always know that when he obeyed, God would do what He had promised. God gave Moses an active role, not just in the declaration of His message, but in the demonstration of His power. God continued to give Moses a testimony and continued to show Moses His integrity. Moses knew better than ever that his message was both joyous and fearful. God both delivered His people and judged the disobedient, and Moses had been used to accomplish both of those acts.

Verses 27–28 show the completion of God's judgment on the Egyptians. Finally the insane arrogance of the Egyptians destroyed them. As they tried futilely to flee from the power of Yahweh, **the sea went back to its place** (v. 27), and they were in its path. The military technology in which they had placed their trust disappointed them, and the monarch they worshiped as a god was powerless to save them. Even their own attempts to turn back from destruction came to nothing. Egypt's stubborn unbelief had set events into motion that could not be avoided simply by running away. The judgment of God came to pass.

WHAT ABOUT YOU?
Are you for the Lord?

God Delivers His People from Judgment (Ex. 14:29)

Verse 29 contrasts what happened to Israel with what happened to Egypt. The judgment of God was not unrestrained; rather, God was able to accomplish deliverance and judgment simultaneously and with perfect accuracy. He did not throw His power madly about in random bursts of divine rage. The wrath of God is not like the vindictive anger of human beings—He never loses control. Even as God judges the rebellious, He cares for His people. Although from the Egyptian army "not one of them survived" (14:28), God still brought His own people through **on dry ground** (v. 29). Even in those situations where God is most radically judging sin, He still takes care of His people.

God Delivers His People for Faith (Ex. 14:30–31)

Verses 30–31 explain God's purpose in delivering Israel in the way He did. He repeatedly worked wonders on their behalf in order to bring them to this place—belief in Him. He went to the most extraordinary lengths imaginable to show His love and care for Israel. He delivered Israel from terrible enemies and commanded the very sea to grant them passage, all for one reason: He was wooing them to faith. He validated the patriarchs' trust in Him to their descendants, saying, in effect, "I am also *your* God, and I call *you* also to be My people." ◆

PRAYER
Father, may I serve You faithfully in triumph and in trials.

INTERACTIVE LEARNING IDEAS

GET THE CLASS INVOLVED
Sing! Sing! Sing!

After the glorious deliverance God accomplished at the Red Sea, Israel was overjoyed. Out of the overflow of awe, wonder, and ecstasy, they wrote a song—which the entire company sang with gusto. They even danced in praise. Their song, recorded in Exodus 15:1–21, describes God's victory and brought glory to His name.

Now, it's your turn to write a song of praise.

Decide together on a theme. Is it some exploit the Lord has accomplished on behalf of your body of believers? Some victory you've seen as a nation that has His fingerprints on it?

Next list on a whiteboard or flipchart all the details that ought to appear in the song. Invite everyone in the group to participate. Write a memorable chorus—something like the chorus Miriam led the women in singing in verse 21. Focus on how this brings glory to God's name.

Either set it to a simple tune or make it a victory chant. Clap to the beat. If you can find a tambourine, use it to keep time as you enthusiastically tell the story of God's power.

TRY THIS ON YOUR OWN
Enabling Obedience

The scene on both banks of the Red Sea is replete with opportunities to put God's promises to the test. To trust Him. In short—to obey. Moses had to do it when he stretched his hand across the sea. The people had to do it when they stepped foot onto the ground that just hours before had been flooded with menacing waters. Pharaoh had the opportunity to obey God's demand, "Let my people go, that they might worship me."

You can see in the drowned army the high cost of failing to obey. And you can see the great joy of obedience as the people of God danced to safety under His protection.

What opportunity to obey is God holding out before you today? What is He asking you to do that seems—quite frankly—illogical?

Sit quietly before the Lord at least one hour. Open the Word to Exodus and ask God what He would have you do. As His direction becomes clear, pray that He will equip you with every resource you need. Pray for His protection. Then obey.

TAKING IT TO THE STREET
People Who Need People

Another of the themes in this story is how God often chooses to display His provision through acts performed by His faithful followers.

In our world at any given moment, victims of vast and devastating natural disasters are in need of the basics of life. Earthquake survivors. Tsunami-devastated towns and villages. Hurricane- or flood-ravaged cities. Their great needs offer you an opportunity this week to put feet to what you've learned.

Join with three or four others to identify a group of victims who could use tangible help. Work through a mission or church group to obtain a list of their specific needs. (Do they need blankets? Clothing? Pots and pans? Fresh water? Gift cards? Packaged foods? Baby formula? Toothpaste, deodorant, and shampoo? Tents? Building supplies?) Get together to shop for those items. Then deliver them to the ministry group who will transport them.

Add your prayers, postage, and personal notes.

WITH YOUR FAMILY
I'm Scared

If you'd stood between Pharaoh's thundering army and the flood-stage Red Sea, what dominant emotion would you have felt? Abject panic, right? Fear is something we all face—but, as it did with the people of God, it offers us opportunities to see God's provision at the point of our greatest need.

With your family this week, have a conversation about fear. Ask each one what he or she is most afraid of. Maybe thunderstorms. Or being left all alone. Or of being forced to eat Brussels sprouts. Or of being the last chosen on the playground. Leave it open ended, so all are free to express their fears. Be vulnerable enough to share one of your fears too.

Use this supportive environment to be like Moses in encouraging each family member to trust God. Tell about how God used one of your fears to show how much He cares for you. Read Exodus 14:13–14. Then pray that God would fight for each person and provide safety in frightening times. ✦

EXODUS 14:10–31

10 As Pharaoh approached, the Israelites looked up, and there were the Egyptians, marching after them. They were terrified and cried out to the LORD.

11 They said to Moses, "Was it because there were no graves in Egypt that you brought us to the desert to die? What have you done to us by bringing us out of Egypt?

12 Didn't we say to you in Egypt, 'Leave us alone; let us serve the Egyptians'? It would have been better for us to serve the Egyptians than to die in the desert!"

13 Moses answered the people, "Do not be afraid. Stand firm and you will see the deliverance the LORD will bring you today. The Egyptians you see today you will never see again.

14 The LORD will fight for you; you need only to be still."

15 Then the LORD said to Moses, "Why are you crying out to me? Tell the Israelites to move on.

16 Raise your staff and stretch out your hand over the sea to divide the water so that the Israelites can go through the sea on dry ground.

17 I will harden the hearts of the Egyptians so that they will go in after them. And I will gain glory through Pharaoh and all his army, through his chariots and his horsemen.

18 The Egyptians will know that I am the LORD when I gain glory through Pharaoh, his chariots and his horsemen."

19 Then the angel of God, who had been traveling in front of Israel's army, withdrew and went behind them. The pillar of cloud also moved from in front and stood behind them,

20 coming between the armies of Egypt and Israel. Throughout the night the cloud brought darkness to the one side and light to the other side; so neither went near the other all night long.

21 Then Moses stretched out his hand over the sea, and all that night the LORD drove the sea back with a strong east wind and turned it into dry land. The waters were divided,

22 and the Israelites went through the sea on dry ground, with a wall of water on their right and on their left.

23 The Egyptians pursued them, and all Pharaoh's horses and chariots and horsemen followed them into the sea.

24 During the last watch of the night the LORD looked down from the pillar of fire and cloud at the Egyptian army and threw it into confusion.

25 He made the wheels of their chariots come off so that they had difficulty driving. And the Egyptians said, "Let's get away from the Israelites! The LORD is fighting for them against Egypt."

26 Then the LORD said to Moses, "Stretch out your hand over the sea so that the waters may flow back over the Egyptians and their chariots and horsemen."

Deliverance When All Seems Lost

God creatively delivers His people.

INTO THE SUBJECT

Occasionally, we hear that trapped miners or flood victims were delivered from almost certain death. But what would it take to deliver a nation of slaves trapped at an impassable river with the world's most powerful army closing in on them to kill them?

INTO THE WORD

1. When the Israelites camped at the Red Sea, what was the state of Pharaoh's mind? What was the state of his heart?

2. According to Exodus 14:4, what did God plan to accomplish through Pharaoh and his army?

3. What does it say about the human heart that the Israelites panicked and blamed Moses when they saw the approaching Egyptian cavalry?

4. What have you feared unnecessarily in light of God's power and promises?

5. What marks of a strong spiritual leader did Moses show in response to the Israelites' lack of faith?

6. Why would you rather be in a minority on the Lord's side than in a majority opposed to the Lord?

7. What battles will you trust the Lord to fight for you this week?

INTO THE WORLD

Tell someone that no one can save himself, but the Lord saves all who trust in Him. Share Romans 10:13 and Ephesians 2:8–9 with that person.

27 Moses stretched out his hand over the sea, and at daybreak the sea went back to its place. The Egyptians were fleeing toward it, and the LORD swept them into the sea.

28 The water flowed back and covered the chariots and horsemen—the entire army of Pharaoh that had followed the Israelites into the sea. Not one of them survived.

29 But the Israelites went through the sea on dry ground, with a wall of water on their right and on their left.

30 That day the LORD saved Israel from the hands of the Egyptians, and Israel saw the Egyptians lying dead on the shore.

31 And when the Israelites saw the great power the LORD displayed against the Egyptians, the people feared the LORD and put their trust in him and in Moses his servant.

Many of the Psalms cry out to God for help in times of distress. Consider, for example, Psalms 5, 17, 38, 54, 77, 102, and 130.

Write your own psalm to God, asking Him to deliver you or someone you love from a hopeless situation.

_____

_____

_____

_____

_____

_____

_____

_____

_____

_____

_____

_____

_____

_____

_____

_____

_____

_____

_____

_____

_____

_____

_____

God's covenant with us requires our personal cooperation.

RECEIVING GOD'S COVENANT
Exodus 19:3–25

WHY THIS MATTERS

A wedding is not only a beautiful and joyful event; it is also a solemn event. What could be more solemn than two individuals pledging lifelong love and loyalty to each other in the name of the Father, Son, and Holy Spirit? Unfortunately, many couples do not honor their marriage contract for a lifetime. In some cases the marriage grows stale faster than the leftover wedding cake. Sadly, the current divorce rate in the United States stands at about 50 percent.

At Sinai, God entered into a covenant—a contract—with Israel. He pledged to make Israel His treasured possession, and Israel agreed to obey His commands. This lesson will strengthen your confidence in God as holy and true and inspire you to obey Him.

BIBLE COMMENTARY

By James B. Bross, Sr.

Throughout the earlier chapters of Exodus, God demonstrated His power on behalf of the Israelites time and again. The ten plagues on Egypt finally convinced Pharaoh to allow them to leave Egypt. At the same time and throughout each of the plagues, God was with the Israelites, so they were protected.

After releasing them, Pharaoh once again changed his mind. Leading his army, he pursued Israel, ending up in disaster as the Egyptians also attempted to pass through the Red Sea. Following the miraculous deliverance from Pharaoh and the Egyptian army in chapter 14, there was rejoicing among the Israelites. Recorded in Exodus 15:1–18 is the joyful song of Moses and Miriam. From the Red Sea the cloud and the fire led them into the desert, and there they would soon face further testing. God was preparing them, and He would soon offer to enter a covenant with His chosen people. Therefore, He continually demonstrated His power on their behalf, thus making it clear they could trust Him whatever came their way.

Initially, they traveled three days without finding water. Arriving at Marah they found water, but it was not fit to drink (15:22–25). The circumstances were trying, and the people showed they did not yet trust God to provide for them. Rather, they "grumbled against Moses" (15:24), following a pattern of response that showed up repeatedly in later tests. Nevertheless, in mercy, God revealed to Moses how to make the water sweet, and once again God miraculously met their need.

Almost immediately another crisis developed; they had no food supply in the desert. True to form, the Israelites grumbled again, longing to be back in Egypt where there was plenty to eat. Faithfully, God made provision for them, this time with manna, a provision that was to continue for many years. This time God even threw in some quail for them to eat (16:1–36).

KEY VERSE

Now if you obey me fully and keep my covenant, then out of all nations you will be my treasured possession.
—Exodus 19:5

BACKGROUND SCRIPTURES

Exodus 24:7
  Israel's covenant with God at Sinai, sealed with blood
Joshua 24:24
  Israel's covenant with God under Joshua
2 Kings 11:17;
2 Chronicles 23:16
  Judah's covenant with God under Joash as king and Jehoiada as priest
2 Kings 23:3
  Judah's covenant with God under King Josiah
2 Chronicles 23:3
  Judah's covenant with God under King Asa
Nehemiah 10:29
  Under Nehemiah the Jews who had returned from exile renewed their covenant with God.

DAILY BIBLE READINGS

Monday: Genesis 15:1–6, 17–18
Tuesday: Zechariah 2:10–13
Wednesday: Matthew 25:31–35
Thursday: 1 Corinthians 11:23–26
Friday: Hebrews 10:15–18
Saturday: Exodus 19:3–25
Sunday: Psalm 19:7–14

Lasting marriages are covenants rather than contracts.

A third test occurred after they traveled from the Desert of Sin. They came to "Rephidim, but there was no water for the people to drink" (17:1). And again the people grumbled and complained against Moses. Would they never learn to trust God? But once more God provided for them, telling Moses to strike the rock with his staff. When he did, water came out of the rock to satisfy the people (17:1–7). Then they arrived at Horeb. According to scholars Horeb may have been Sinai itself, but possibly it was another mountain near Sinai.

An attack by the Amalekites was a fourth trial for the Israelites as they were still camped at Rephidim. Joshua led the battle against the enemy, and Israel prevailed whenever Moses held up his hands but fell back whenever Moses lowered his hands. Assisted by Aaron and Hur, Moses kept his hands up until the Amalekites were defeated (17:8–16).

Following the battle, Moses' father-in-law Jethro came to meet him. Moses was facing yet another trial, for he was physically and emotionally exhausted. The demands on him were proving too much as he led the people and served as their judge. Jethro advised Moses to delegate most of the responsibility for judging to other capable men. Moses welcomed Jethro's advice and was soon relieved as others shared his load (18:1–27).

They then entered into the Desert of Sinai "in the third month after the Israelites left Egypt" (19:1). Through difficult circumstances, God had been preparing the recalcitrant Israelites for the next step in their relationship with Him. He had showed again and again that they could trust Him implicitly. Now, as they camped by Sinai, He would offer them a covenant with himself in spite of their complaining and mistrust. God's patience with His people was and is truly amazing! Thank God for amazing grace!

Then Moses Went Up to God (Ex. 19:3–6)

Over and over Moses went up Mount Sinai to speak with God on behalf of the people of Israel. God first told Moses to remind the people how He had delivered them from Egypt and cared for them up to that moment: **You yourselves have seen what I did to Egypt, and how I carried you on eagles' wings and brought you to myself** (v. 4). Now the Lord was ready to offer them a covenant forever: **Now if you obey me fully and keep my covenant, then out of all nations you will be my treasured possession** (v. 5). He reminded them that they were His chosen people out of the whole earth: **Although the whole earth is mine, you will be for me a kingdom of priests and a holy nation** (vv. 5–6). The Lord wanted to set Israel apart for himself and for the special calling He had for them. All this the Lord communicated to Moses, His prophet or spokesman. Moses in turn delivered the message to the people.

The Lord wanted Israel to be an example of His grace and power for all the world to see. As Isaiah later observed, "I will also make you a light for the Gentiles" (Isa. 49:6). When they were faithful to the covenant, they accomplished their task. When they were unfaithful, they failed miserably.

We Will Do Everything the Lord Has Said (Ex. 19:7–9)

Moses faithfully conveyed the Lord's words to the elders of the people, and the people responded, promising obedience to the Lord. Moses, the messenger, then took the message of the people to the Lord. It is interesting that God chose to use Moses as a go-between—that God and the people did not communicate directly with each other, only through Moses.

The Lord then promised Moses to come to him in a thick cloud. The people would hear the Lord's voice, but would not see Him. This way the people would learn to trust Moses (v. 9).

WHAT DO YOU THINK?
Is God's covenant with His people still in effect?

Go to the People and Consecrate Them (Ex. 19:10–15)

The Lord then told Moses that on the third day He would **come down on Mount Sinai** (v. 11) and appear to the people. So for the next two days the people were to consecrate themselves in preparation. The fearfulness and holiness of the Lord were to be strictly revered by the people. First, they were to wash their clothes. Then, they were required to stay outside limits Moses put around the mountain under penalty of death by stoning or arrows. (No hand was to be laid on them if they touched the mountain.) The penalty was to be applied to animals as well as to humans. Last, they were to abstain from sexual relations. Absolute awe was required, as was ritual purity.

Major Covenants between God and His People in the Old Testament	
God's covenant with Noah	Genesis 9:8–17
God's first covenant with Abraham	Genesis 15:9–21
God's second covenant with Abraham	Genesis 17
The covenant at Sinai	Exodus 19–24
The new covenant promised	Jeremiah 31:31–34

This was certainly no buddy-buddy relationship with God. The New Testament writer to the Hebrews referred to the terrifying sight of Mount Sinai in contrast to "Mount Zion" and the "heavenly Jerusalem" now provided by Jesus (Heb. 12:18–24). Yet, as Hebrews warns, we must recall that we serve the same God of awesome power who appeared on Sinai. Thank God that Jesus has provided a way for each of us to now come directly to God. Still, we should do so in deepest reverence.

AHA!
God is faithful no matter the unfaithfulness of His people!

On the Morning of the Third Day (Ex. 19:16–19)

The Lord came with **thunder and lightning, with a thick cloud over the mountain, and a very loud trumpet blast. Everyone in the camp trembled** (v. 16). As the people trembled in fear at these terrifying phenomena, additional wonders occurred. Moses led the people to **the foot of the mountain** (v. 17), and **Mount Sinai was covered with smoke, because the LORD descended on it in fire. The smoke billowed up from it like smoke from a furnace, the whole mountain trembled violently, and the sound of the trumpet grew louder and louder** (vv. 18–19). No wonder the fearful people soon asked Moses to speak with God for them (Ex. 20:19).

This was the God who offered to enter into covenant with them. They were terrified! And no wonder. Furthermore, the people had been sternly warned that they would die if they did not stay back from the mountain. As the people trembled in fear, **Moses spoke and the voice of God answered him** (19:19).

DID YOU KNOW?
The Israelites had been sporadic at best and unfaithful at worst in keeping their part of God's legal covenant. But Jeremiah 31 records an encouraging message from the Lord: "I will put my law in their minds and write it on their hearts."

Time and again God had shown the people His gracious and compassionate nature as they left Egypt and passed through the desert on their way to Sinai. Now God revealed His nature as the holy and awesome Lord of the earth. The cloud, the fire, the smoke, the trembling mountain, and the loud trumpet blast all symbolized the Lord God Almighty, who was calling them into covenant with himself. How wonderful and how awesome! And to think that these people only three months earlier had been delivered from slavery!

The Lord Descended to the Top of Mount Sinai and Called Moses to the Top of the Mountain (Ex. 19:20–25)

WHAT ABOUT YOU?
Is your relationship
with God a contract or
a covenant?

Moses ascended the mountain, and again the Lord told him to warn the people not to venture onto the mountain. If they did they would perish. **Even the priests, who approach the LORD, must consecrate themselves, or the LORD will break out against them** (v. 22). The Lord would enter into covenant with the Israelites, but He would not tolerate carelessness or presumption from anyone who approached Him.

Moses then reminded the Lord that He had already set limits beyond which the people could not pass **because you yourself warned us, "Put limits around the mountain and set it apart as holy"** (v. 23). The conversations between the Lord and Moses show Moses as the unusual man he was. No wonder he has been honored by Jews as well as Christians down through subsequent history.

Moses was then instructed, **Go down and bring Aaron up with you**. But no one else was to **force their way through to come up to the LORD, or he will break out against them"** (v. 24). Moses obeyed, continuing his role as prophet and go-between.

The people had agreed to the covenant—to do all that the Lord required of them. But soon their commitment was shown to be rather shallow—at least for many it proved to be rather shallow. In the months and years to come they vacillated in their commitment. Over and over the prophets called them back to their covenant. But like the unfaithful wife of Hosea, Israel repeatedly broke her marriage covenant with the Lord. As a result they suffered the painful consequences of their unfaithfulness—just as Moses had promised they would. But God is merciful and faithful, and He never vacillated, never forgot His covenant. Gradually, though it took many centuries, He refined a people for himself.

PRAYER
Father, put Your law in
my mind and write it
on my heart.

Normally a covenant is between human beings who are equal parties. However, in this case the parties to the covenant were by no means equal. The Lord offered the covenant, and the Israelites could take it or not. There was no negotiation. Furthermore, the human subscribers to a covenant are fallible and may violate the agreement in a variety of ways. But in this case the Lord, who is infallible, will keep the covenant He has made—forever! Any violation would be on the part of Israel if she failed to live up to the terms. And so it was. Israel vacillated, but the Lord remained constant, faithful. In fact, the prophets accused Israel of turning her back on the covenant, but in spite of her sinfulness the Lord refused to give up on her. Hosea 11:8–11 provides a clear illustration of this paradox. God's covenant fidelity led to discipline, and that discipline in turn caused the necessary changes in His covenant people. ✦

EXODUS 19:3–25

3 Then Moses went up to God, and the LORD called to him from the mountain and said, "This is what you are to say to the house of Jacob and what you are to tell the people of Israel:

4 'You yourselves have seen what I did to Egypt, and how I carried you on eagles' wings and brought you to myself.

5 Now if you obey me fully and keep my covenant, then out of all nations you will be my treasured possession. Although the whole earth is mine,

6 you will be for me a kingdom of priests and a holy nation.' These are the words you are to speak to the Israelites."

7 So Moses went back and summoned the elders of the people and set before them all the words the LORD had commanded him to speak.

8 The people all responded together, "We will do everything the LORD has said." So Moses brought their answer back to the LORD.

9 The LORD said to Moses, "I am going to come to you in a dense cloud, so that the people will hear me speaking with you and will always put their trust in you." Then Moses told the LORD what the people had said.

10 And the LORD said to Moses, "Go to the people and consecrate them today and tomorrow. Have them wash their clothes

11 and be ready by the third day, because on that day the LORD will come down on Mount Sinai in the sight of all the people.

12 Put limits for the people around the mountain and tell them, 'Be careful that you do not go up the mountain or touch the foot of it. Whoever touches the mountain shall surely be put to death.

13 He shall surely be stoned or shot with arrows; not a hand is to be laid on him. Whether man or animal, he shall not be permitted to live.' Only when the ram's horn sounds a long blast may they go up to the mountain."

14 After Moses had gone down the mountain to the people, he consecrated them, and they washed their clothes.

15 Then he said to the people, "Prepare yourselves for the third day. Abstain from sexual relations."

16 On the morning of the third day there was thunder and lightning, with a thick cloud over the mountain, and a very loud trumpet blast. Everyone in the camp trembled.

17 Then Moses led the people out of the camp to meet with God, and they stood at the foot of the mountain.

18 Mount Sinai was covered with smoke, because the LORD descended on it in fire. The smoke billowed up from it like smoke from a furnace, the whole mountain trembled violently,

19 and the sound of the trumpet grew louder and louder. Then Moses spoke and the voice of God answered him.

20 The LORD descended to the top of Mount Sinai and called Moses to the top of the mountain. So Moses went up

Receiving God's Covenant

God's covenant with us requires
our personal cooperation.

INTO THE SUBJECT

Contracts are an important part of life. We sign contracts for everything from buying a car to marrying a spouse. But what would it be like to enter into a contract with God?

INTO THE WORD

1. What did God agree to do if the people of Israel obeyed Him (Ex. 19:5–6)?

2. Did the people of Israel promptly agree to the terms of the contract? From what you know of Israel's post-Sinai history, did the people keep the terms of the contract?

3. How did the Lord honor Moses, the mediator of the covenant?

4. From your reading of Exodus 19:10–22, find indicators of God's holiness.

5. Why do you agree or disagree that believers today need to remember that God is holy?

6. How do you strike a balance between familiarity with God and awe of God?

7. It has been observed that at Mount Sinai God set limits so the people could not approach Him, but at Mount Calvary He removed those limits. Why do you agree or disagree with this observation?

INTO THE WORD

God has commanded His people to be holy, because He is holy. Demonstrate holiness in your words and conduct as you work this week.

21 and the LORD said to him, "Go down and warn the people so they do not force their way through to see the LORD and many of them perish.

22 Even the priests, who approach the LORD, must consecrate themselves, or the LORD will break out against them."

23 Moses said to the LORD, "The people cannot come up Mount Sinai, because you yourself warned us, 'Put limits around the mountain and set it apart as holy.'"

24 The LORD replied, "Go down and bring Aaron up with you. But the priests and the people must not force their way through to come up to the LORD, or he will break out against them."

25 So Moses went down to the people and told them.

THE HOLINESS OF GOD

Look up Exodus 19:5–15, and fill in the blanks.

"Now if you obey me fully and keep my covenant, then _____ _____ _____ _____ you will be my _____ _____ . Although the whole earth is mine, you will be for me a kingdom of priests and a _____ _____.' These are the words you are to speak to the Israelites."

So Moses went back and summoned the elders of the people and set before them all the words the LORD had commanded him to speak. The people all responded together, "We will _____ _____ the _____ has _____." So Moses brought their answer back to the LORD.

The LORD said to Moses, "I am going to come to you in a _____ _____, so that the people will hear me speaking with you and will always put their trust in you." Then Moses told the LORD what the people had said.

And the LORD said to Moses, "Go to the people and _____ them today and tomorrow. Have them _____ their clothes and be ready by the third day, because on that day the LORD will come down on Mount Sinai in the sight of all the people. Put _____ for the people around the mountain and tell them, 'Be careful that you _____ _____ _____ _____ the mountain or _____ the foot of it. Whoever touches the mountain shall surely be put to death. He shall surely be stoned or shot with arrows; not a hand is to be _____ _____ _____. Whether man or animal, he shall not be permitted to live.' Only when the ram's horn sounds a long blast may they go up to the mountain."

After Moses had gone down the mountain to the people, he _____ them, and they _____ their clothes. Then he said to the people, "Prepare yourselves for the third day. _____ from sexual relations."

What do the sections you filled in reveal about God and His people?

_____
_____
_____
_____
_____
_____

INTERACTIVE LEARNING IDEAS

GET THE CLASS INVOLVED
Cementing Our Covenant

In allowing them to see a glimpse of His holiness, God was preparing His people to agree to a demanding covenant that would call them to a high standard but allow them privileges of relationship with Him beyond their imagination. Later, Moses' successor Joshua would remind the people of this covenant and invite them to renew their assent to it.

It's good for us, too, to speak aloud our commitment to God. As a group, read aloud the Israelites' covenant renewal from Joshua 24:13–27. Choose someone to begin reading the passage. When the multitude speaks in verses 16–18, 21, and 24, have everyone read in unison.

After you've read, offer sentence prayers (allowing everyone opportunity to participate), committing yourselves to God's service as individuals and as a worshiping community of believers.

TRY THIS ON YOUR OWN
Treasured

In Exodus 19:5, God made a most loving promise: "Now if you obey me fully and keep my covenant, then out of all nations you will be my treasured possession." God's own treasured possession. What a concept! This isn't the only time He makes that promise. And it isn't limited to those born into Israel's ranks. In the New Testament, God included those who believe in Christ among His treasured possession.

Spend your quiet time one day this week examining the following times this phrase appears in Scripture:
- Exodus 19:5
- Deuteronomy 7:6; 14:2; 26:18
- 1 Chronicles 29:3
- Psalm 135:4
- Ecclesiastes 2:8
- Malachi 3:17
- Titus 2:14
- 1 Peter 2:9

Record your thoughts on the magnificent privilege of being God's treasure.

TAKING IT TO THE STREET
Exhausted in Leadership

One of the passages not thoroughly covered in the study is Moses' father-in-law Jethro's visit to the camp in Exodus 18. Jethro quickly identified the stresses and strains on Moses as he led God's people with integrity. He saw what Moses *couldn't* see and what the people *wouldn't* see—that Moses was exhausted and needed help.

His observations provide a good reminder for us to support those in leadership. It may be a boss, pastor, spouse, or aging relative. Someone in your leadership chain may be exhausted and in need of something you can offer—a listening ear, a shoulder to take a bit of the load, an understanding and praying heart to offer support.

Choose one person to whom you're responsible, take him or her out to a quiet meal, and ask:
- How can I make things a little easier on you?
- How can I support you?
- How can I pray for you?

Listen for his or her heartfelt answers, and do what you promise to do.

WITH YOUR FAMILY
Go Between

Some biblical concepts may be difficult to get our minds around. One of these is Jesus' role as the go-between between us and God. That may be one reason God initiated the special relationship with Moses. He displayed His awesome power at Sinai and spoke in His thundering voice, which all the people could see and hear. But they would be destroyed if they came any closer to Him. Only Moses could do that.

To demonstrate this to the youngest members of your family, set up this game. Choose two older members (both parents, for example) and place them in two different rooms. Have the children act as go-betweens to carry messages between the two rooms. Chase them back and forth with directions to bring this or that item, question, or answer to the other room. But the elder members should not go themselves or yell across to the other room. Continue for several rounds of back and forth. (If they get frustrated, all the better.)

Return to the same room and talk about being a go-between. Ask how it felt. Transition into the story of Moses approaching God when the people couldn't—and finally to Jesus approaching God for us, because our sin doesn't allow us to.

Read aloud 1 Timothy 2:5–6: "For there is one God and one mediator between God and men, the man Christ Jesus, who gave himself as a ransom for all." Memorize it together. ✦

God gives guidelines for the good life.

LESSON 9

GOD'S LIFE-SPARING COMMANDS

Exodus 20:1–20

WHY THIS MATTERS

In 2003 a 2.6-ton Ten Commandments monument was removed from Alabama's state judicial building's rotunda, and Alabama Supreme Court Justice Roy Moore was removed from office because he had refused to comply with an order to remove the monument. US District Judge Myron Thompson ruled the granite carving was an unconstitutional endorsement of religion, and Justice Moore was viewed as willfully and publicly putting himself above the law by refusing to remove the monument.

The Ten Commandments include commandments, not suggestions, for relating properly to God and to our fellow humans. This lesson focuses on those commandments and inspires us to do what is right and pleasing in God's sight.

BIBLE COMMENTARY

By James B. Bross, Sr.

Without hesitation the Israelites agreed to the covenant that the Lord offered through Moses. Perhaps they agreed all too quickly! Had they really considered what they said when they promised to obey everything they were commanded (Ex. 19:8)? Later actions certainly belied their promise.

Again in Exodus 24:3–8, they were presented with an opportunity to confirm their covenant with the Lord, and once again they promised to obey all He commanded. By that time Moses had received and delivered the Decalogue and numerous additional laws, so the people had a better grasp of what they were agreeing to. Additionally, in chapter 24 the covenant was sealed with blood as bulls were sacrificed and blood was sprinkled over the people.

The covenant between the Lord and Israel established a relationship, but the details of the relationship were yet to be spelled out. The details came when the Lord gave the law to Moses on Mount Sinai.

This lesson covers the Ten Commandments, which compose the first, and perhaps most important, installment of the law given to Moses. Clearly, the people understood that their covenant with the Lord required that they obey His commands, for in both 19:8 and 24:3 they promised to obey the words of the Lord that Moses conveyed to them. Always, this covenant between the Lord and Israel required obedience on their part. In the passages following the Decalogue, consequences of disobedience were also spelled out.

The first installment consisted of the Ten Commandments. Eight of those commandments are prohibitions and therefore are stated negatively. The other two commandments are stated positively.

The Ten Commandments appear again with few changes in Deuteronomy 5:6–21. There the fourth commandment is changed as to the reason for observing the Sabbath. Exodus gives the reason as based in creation—God rested on the seventh day. Deuteronomy cites the exodus from Egypt as the reason for observing the seventh day. To the fifth commandment Deuteronomy adds "that it may go well with you" as part of the reward for honoring one's parents. Additionally, in the tenth commandment, which forbids covetousness, the order of the items is switched. Exodus forbids coveting your neighbor's house and then forbids coveting your neighbor's wife. Deuteronomy lists wife first and then house. Deuteronomy also adds "land" to the list of things not to be coveted.

Moses with Ten Commandments center in relief at US Supreme Court building

Note that the first four commandments are different from the last six. In the first four, we have vertical commandments, each related to God. In the final six, we have horizontal commandments, each related to our fellow humans. Jesus summarized the first four commandments when He said the greatest commandment is to love God: "Love the Lord your God with all your heart and with all your soul and with all your mind" (Matt. 22:37). If we love God, then we will keep the first four commandments that specifically honor Him. Jesus went on to say, "Love your neighbor as yourself" (Matt. 22:39). This addition summarizes the second group of six commandments. If we love our neighbor appropriately, we will keep each of the final six commandments.

And God Spoke All These Words (Ex. 20:1–2)

Earlier, the Lord spoke to Moses, and he relayed the message to the people. For the Decalogue the pattern was changed. Here, the words appear to be addressed to Moses as well as the people. A preamble was given before the commandments: **I am the LORD your God, who brought you out of Egypt, out of the land of slavery** (v. 2). This introduction is similar to preambles found in royal treaties of that time in which the king stated his gracious qualities leading up to the terms of the treaty. However, here it was God who, as ruler, stated His name and cited the gracious deliverance of Israel from Egypt and slavery. God was their ruler; they must obey.

In the Jewish understanding of the Decalogue, verse 2 is considered the first commandment. They then form the second commandment by combining verses 3–6, thus joining the commands against other gods and against idols.

You Shall Have No Other Gods before Me (Ex. 20:3)

Most Protestant groups consider this verse as the first commandment. Lutherans and Roman Catholics combine it with verses 4–6 to form the first commandment. Then further along they divide verse 17 into two different commandments against coveting.

In the days when this commandment was first given, it clearly addressed a widespread problem. There were beliefs in many gods among the Egyptians and among other peoples surrounding Palestine. However, does this commandment still have application to us today? Indeed it does, for when any person or thing comes before God in our lives, we are breaking this commandment. God claims absolutely the first place the lives of His children.

WHAT DO YOU THINK?
Old Testament professor Wilbur G. Williams notes that we cannot break the Ten Commandments. They will break us if we disobey. Why do you think that statement is true or false?

AHA!
These are not the Ten Suggestions!

DID YOU KNOW?
The Ten Commandments have had an international impact on civil law for the past thirty-five hundred years. Noah Webster wrote, "The moral principles and precepts contained in the Scriptures ought to form the basis of all our civil constitutions and laws."

You Shall Not Make for Yourselves an Idol (Ex. 20:4–6)

Generally Protestants take this to be the second commandment. Yet, it is understandable why Jews, Roman Catholics, and Lutherans join this commandment with that in verse 3. Certainly in application to our lives today, it is difficult to distinguish any practical difference between the first and second commandments. For most Americans today, idols in the form of graven images are hardly a problem. However, in paganism and in many primitive religions, idolatry remains a live issue. Idolatry in the form of putting other things before God certainly remains a problem for us all.

For Israel at the time of the exodus and in the following centuries, this commandment was very practical. They were repeatedly tempted to copy the people around them by making idols and worshiping them. Even while camped at Mount Sinai, Aaron made a golden calf for them to worship (Ex. 32:1–8). That prevailing sin of idolatry plagued them until the Babylonian exile. Then, finally, they seem to have been cured, for afterward they practiced the worship of images no more.

You Shall Not Misuse the Name of the Lord Your God (Ex. 20:7)

The third commandment forbids using the name of the Lord in a false oath. The King James family of versions translates the Hebrew as "not take the name of the LORD your God in vain." The Hebrew word translated "vain" entails the meaning of "empty." Using God's name in any way that is shallow or less than serious is forbidden. Invoking God's name carelessly or paying only lip service are displeasing to God. Perhaps this commandment can be related to the prophets' rebukes of sacrificial ritual not accompanied by just behavior (Amos 5:21–24; Mic. 6:6–8).

Remember the Sabbath Day By Keeping It Holy (Ex. 20:8–11)

The fourth commandment is the last of the group that focuses on honoring God. They were to do no work on the seventh day, following the pattern God set by resting on the seventh day of creation. Observing the Sabbath provides time for worship and rest. The commandment specifies that the rest is to include all—parents, children, servants, and animals. No matter if we feel driven, the need for rest and restoration remains. Individuals and cultures that ignore the need for a day of rest and worship pay a price.

Honor Your Father and Your Mother, So That You May Live Long in the Land the Lord Your God Is Giving You (Ex. 20:12)

The fifth commandment is the only one to which a promise is attached. **Honor** certainly means more than simply to obey one's parents. The NIV Study Bible lists four meanings for honor: (1) prize highly, (2) care for, (3) show respect for, and (4) obey (note for Ex. 20:12). This is a good summary for life-long honoring of parents. It is significant that we are also expected to **honor** God (Ps. 50:23; Prov. 3:9; Isa. 43:20, 23). Surely this says something about our proper attitude toward our parents.

Many commentators have also interpreted this commandment as requiring us to honor temporal authority. With this interpretation, the commandment would also instruct us to honor and obey rulers and magistrates.

WHAT DO YOU THINK?
Do the Ten Commandments influence civil law today?

AHA!
The Ten Commandments are still in effect!

DID YOU KNOW?
While Jesus' sacrificial death and resurrection fulfilled—and did away with—ceremonial law, He strengthened the Ten Commandments by teaching in the Sermon on the Mount that anger is as sinful as murder, lust as sinful as adultery, and so on.

You Shall Not Murder (Ex. 20:13)

Many commentators believe **murder** is the correct translation of the Hebrew rather than the more general word *kill*. The NIV Study Bible says the word usually refers to a premeditated and malicious act. The commandment hardly offers support some claim for an argument against capital punishment or against acts of war. Such arguments might find more support elsewhere in Scripture. This commandment affirms the fundamental right to life for every human. In the Sermon on the Mount, Jesus extended this commandment to forbid disparaging remarks about others (Matt. 5:21–22).

You Shall Not Commit Adultery (Ex. 20:14)

This commandment affirms the sanctity of marriage as the former one affirms the sanctity of life. Marriage is more than a simple promise between spouses; it is a vow that has divine sanction. If marriage is broken through adultery, the sin is against God as well as against the spouse. Jesus expanded this commandment also, forbidding lust as well as the actual act of adultery (Matt. 5:27–30).

You Shall Not Steal (Ex. 20:15)

The eighth commandment affirms the right to property. We should obtain property only in legitimate ways.

You Shall Not Give False Testimony against Your Neighbor (Ex. 20:16)

In its most basic meaning, the ninth commandment applies to court testimony. But it also applies to other words spoken about our neighbors, forbidding gossip and other conversation that falsely portrays them. Our tongues easily set blazes that we cannot extinguish (James 3:6).

You Shall Not Covet (Ex. 20:17)

The last commandment moves beyond the first nine to the motives behind our evil actions. It deals with our inner thoughts and desires. We must not **covet** our **neighbor's house . . . wife . . . manservant or maidservant, his ox or donkey, or anything that belongs to your neighbor** (v. 17). We are to control our desires and thereby avoid the overt sins listed in the earlier commandments.

Note that guilt for breaking this commandment is known only to God and ourselves unless we share our illicit desire with someone else. Coveting is subtle and may creep in even as we keep the other nine commandments. Paul admitted that this commandment was what first made him realize he had broken the law (Rom. 7:7–8). For us today, coveting may be characterized primarily by the attitude of "keeping up with the Joneses." Even in this day of mass production, if we are to be obedient we must avoid coveting.

Do Not Have God Speak to Us or We Will Die (Ex. 20:18–20)

As the people observed the awesome phenomena on Mount Sinai and heard the voice of God, **they trembled with fear** (v. 18). They begged Moses to speak to God for them lest they die. Moses offered them reassurance that God was simply testing them, teaching them to fear God and to avoid sinning. ✦

WHAT ABOUT YOU?
Are you following the letter of the law, or, as Jesus taught, the spirit of the law?

PRAYER
Father, may I fully fulfill Your law by loving You and loving others.

INTERACTIVE LEARNING IDEAS

GET THE CLASS INVOLVED
Keeping the Biggie

When a New Testament scribe asked Jesus, "Of all the commandments, which is the most important?" (Mark 12:29), Jesus cited a passage from Deuteronomy 6.

Go around your study circle and read the chapter aloud, one verse each. When you've concluded, divide into four smaller groups. Assign group 1 the task of creating a word picture of what it looks like to love the Lord with all your heart. Use all your powers of description to take this from abstract concept to concrete example. Group 2 will do the same with "all your soul"; group 3 gets "all your strength"; group 4 gets the bonus Jesus added in Mark 12:30: "with all your mind." (Have group 4 also posit reasons Jesus added this phrase.)

Return to your larger circle, and invite each group to share its word picture. Discuss how these fit into the law as God handed it down to Moses and how they motivate you to love the Lord more perfectly.

TRY THIS ON YOUR OWN
Your Personal Sabbath

The concept of Sabbath—of scheduling a weekly rest day from our labors—is built into the fabric of our being. It's as old as the first week of creation (Gen. 2:2), and it made God's top ten list. But in our driven, pulsating, twenty-first-century lives, taking a Sabbath seems more like a luxury than a reasonable command.

This Saturday, get up early to carve out at least an hour for quiet study. Use Bible reference tools (dictionary, concordances, books on Bible culture, commentaries, etc.) to learn all you can about the Hebrew word *shabbat*. You'll find it in many passages, including the following: Exodus 31:13–16; Leviticus 16:31; Deuteronomy 5:12–15; Isaiah 56:2–6; 58:13–14; and Jeremiah 17:24–27.

Study these passages, paying special attention to God's explanations about why it's important. Journal your observations—and create a plan to honor a weekly Sabbath and keep it holy.

TAKING IT TO THE STREET
Ready, Set, Record!

Break out your camcorder or smartphone, and get ready to be alerted to a pervasive and invasive temptation that lurks everywhere in your community—the temptation to break the tenth commandment. Where our culture still admits that murders are wrong, not coveting is one of those commands we've let slide a bit.

Team up with a carload of study group members. Drive from your church to a major thoroughfare where there are billboards and consumer shopping opportunities. Let one person drive, while the others record every billboard, banner, ad, window display, or parking lot that entices you to want what belongs to someone else. Really pay attention to what you're seeing—especially messages you pass every day without consciously noticing. Next drive through a high-end neighborhood. Record what you see there that you feel like you can't live without.

Create a video montage of the enticements everyone recorded—flashing on each for just a few seconds before cutting to the next. Talk about how often merchants use our human desire to covet what someone else has. Be vulnerable about where your personal temptations come into play. Pray together that the Lord will help you resist the temptation to covet every time it crosses your path.

WITH YOUR FAMILY
Jesus Expands Commandments Inside

Right in the middle of His Sermon on the Mount, Jesus referred to the commandments in Exodus. But what He did with them is shocking—He expanded them from outward appearances to inward motivations.

To make this come alive, plan a family skit night. Here are the props you'll need:

- Copy of *The Message* paraphrase of Matthew 5:13–24, 43–48
- Salt shaker
- Flashlight
- Bowl or bucket
- Dollar (for the offering)
- Inexpensive medal

Have one person be the narrator and read aloud the whole passage from *The Message*. Instruct everyone else to pantomime the scenes being narrated, using the props where they're mentioned. Have the narrator pause wherever the action is taking place, so the mimes can play their parts fully.

After the drama, talk about how hard it is to live up to Jesus' standard, yet how much you want to be like Him. ◆

EXODUS 20:1–20

1 And God spoke all these words:

2 "I am the LORD your God, who brought you out of Egypt, out of the land of slavery.

3 "You shall have no other gods before me.

4 "You shall not make for yourself an idol in the form of anything in heaven above or on the earth beneath or in the waters below.

5 You shall not bow down to them or worship them; for I, the LORD your God, am a jealous God, punishing the children for the sin of the fathers to the third and fourth generation of those who hate me,

6 but showing love to a thousand generations of those who love me and keep my commandments.

7 "You shall not misuse the name of the LORD your God, for the LORD will not hold anyone guiltless who misuses his name.

8 "Remember the Sabbath day by keeping it holy.

9 Six days you shall labor and do all your work,

10 but the seventh day is a Sabbath to the LORD your God. On it you shall not do any work, neither you, nor your son or daughter, nor your manservant or maidservant, nor your animals, nor the alien within your gates.

11 For in six days the LORD made the heavens and the earth, the sea, and all that is in them, but he rested on the seventh day. Therefore the LORD blessed the Sabbath day and made it holy.

12 "Honor your father and your mother, so that you may live long in the land the LORD your God is giving you.

13 "You shall not murder.

14 "You shall not commit adultery.

15 "You shall not steal.

16 "You shall not give false testimony against your neighbor.

17 "You shall not covet your neighbor's house. You shall not covet your neighbor's wife, or his manservant or maidservant, his ox or donkey, or anything that belongs to your neighbor."

18 When the people saw the thunder and lightning and heard the trumpet and saw the mountain in smoke, they trembled with fear. They stayed at a distance

19 and said to Moses, "Speak to us yourself and we will listen. But do not have God speak to us or we will die."

20 Moses said to the people, "Do not be afraid. God has come to test you, so that the fear of God will be with you to keep you from sinning."

God's Life-Sparing Commands

God gives guidelines for the good life.

INTO THE SUBJECT

Contemporary life is marred by lawlessness, but how much worse would conditions be if our legal system had no roots in the Ten Commandments?

INTO THE WORD

1. How does God's reminder in Exodus 20:1 that He redeemed Israel from Egypt serve as an appropriate introduction to the Ten Commandments?

2. What idols occupy the throne of many hearts today? Which idol seems to have the greatest following?

3. How can you help to stem the tide of profane use of God's name by today's media?

4. Why do you agree or disagree that Christians should not work on Sunday?

5. Do you believe an obedient, reverent relationship with God contributes to a loving, law-abiding relationship with one's fellow human beings? Why or why not?

6. How might the honoring of one's parents contribute to longevity?

7. What purpose do you think the thunder, lightning, and trumpet sound served?

8. How would you respond to the claim that the Ten Commandments do not apply to believers in the age of grace?

INTO THE WORLD

Many children do not learn the Ten Commandments at school or at home, but they can learn them at Sunday school. Why not invite a few children to attend Sunday school, and then volunteer to get them there?

First Commandment:

Second Commandment:

THE TEN COMMANDMENTS

See if you can remember each commandment. Look up your answers if you get stuck, and then memorize the list.

Third Commandment:

Fourth Commandment:

Fifth Commandment:

Sixth Commandment:

Seventh Commandment:

Eighth Commandment:

Ninth Commandment:

Tenth Commandment:

God alone is the focus of all true worship.

GOD EXPECTS EXCLUSIVE WORSHIP

Exodus 32:1–6, 19–24, 30–35

WHY THIS MATTERS

"Our church is under attack!" The pastor told a shocked congregation that several couples in the church were involved in immorality. The shock intensified as the pastor revealed that the scandal involved two other pastors and a worship team member.

A few years ago, the national media turned their attention to the pastor of a mega church who also held a prominent position in an evangelical association. His church dismissed him because he had become involved in homosexuality and drug use.

Obviously, when immorality occurs among professing believers, it shows they have turned their backs on God and His commands. This lesson motivates us to resist the world, the flesh, and the devil, and keep God on the throne of our hearts.

BIBLE COMMENTARY

By Gareth Lee Cockerill

In accord with His promises to Abraham, God delivered His people from slavery in Egypt (Ex. 1–14) and preserved their way in the wilderness (Ex. 15–18) so they could enter into covenant relationship with Him as His people and He could dwell among them. God brought them to Mount Sinai, where He established this relationship with them (Ex. 19–24). While at Sinai, He told Moses how to build the tabernacle as the place where His presence would abide (Ex. 25–31). In Exodus 35:1—40:33, Moses carried out these instructions. God brought His plan to a climax in Exodus 35:1—40:33 when with awesome display of power He descended to dwell in the place prepared for Him.

Exodus 32:1—34:35 comes between God's blueprint for the tabernacle and Moses' execution of God's plan. These chapters are the tragic story of how the people who had just been delivered from Egypt and seen God's glory on Sinai turned from Him in apostasy and forfeited the blessing of His presence. Their sin mirrors our own propensity as those privileged with God's blessings to turn from Him. These chapters are also the story of God's great mercy in restoring His delivered people to His presence. The role God gave to Moses as intercessor for the people reminds us of the mediation accomplished by God in the person of Jesus Christ.

Exodus 32:1–6 gives a detailed account of the people's apostasy at the foot of Mount Sinai. In verses 7–14, we join God and Moses on the mountain and hear God's perspective on the people's sin. Then Moses descended the mountain (vv. 15–17) and brought the wrath of God to bear on the people's disobedience (vv. 19–20, 25–29). Aaron's pitiful excuses in verses 21–24 expose our own rationalizations. In the last major paragraph of the chapter, Moses interceded

KEY VERSE

God is spirit, and his worshipers must worship in spirit and in truth.
—John 4:24

BACKGROUND SCRIPTURES

Numbers 13:1—14:38
   Israel's rebellion at
   Kadesh-Barnea
1 Kings 11:26–40;
12:25–33
   Jereboam's apostasy
   despite God's promise
Acts 5:1–11
   The sin of Ananias
   and Sapphira
1 Samuel 15:17–23
   Samuel exposed
   Saul's rationalization.

DAILY BIBLE READINGS

Monday:	2 Kings 17:35–40
Tuesday:	1 Chronicles 16:25–29
Wednesday:	Matthew 4:1–10
Thursday:	John 4:21–24
Friday:	Romans 11:30–36
Saturday:	Exodus 32:1–6, 19–24, 30–35
Sunday:	Psalm 21

for the people (vv. 30–35) and received a reprieve from God. Nevertheless God himself would still punish them (vv. 34–35).

When we have finished reading this chapter, we do not yet know whether God's presence will go with His people! Have they lost the very purpose for which God liberated them? Chapters 33 and 34 relate the rest of the story. God promised to go with them. God himself reestablished the broken covenant. In our God, mercy triumphs over judgment. The triumph of grace, however, only highlights the heinousness of our disobedience and the casuistry of our excuses. The text reminds us that even those who are forgiven must sometimes bear temporal, if not eternal, consequences for their sin.

Apostasy Despite Privilege (Ex. 32:1–6)

Nearly forty days had passed since God called Moses to ascend Mount Sinai (24:18). For the last seven chapters (25:1—31:18), we have been on Sinai with God and Moses. The people of Israel, however, have been waiting at the foot of the mountain. Despite the wonders God had done through Moses when delivering them from Egypt, despite God's miraculous provision of food and water in the wilderness, despite God's speaking to them amid fire and smoke from the top of Sinai, they turned from God because Moses was delayed (v. 1). They went to Aaron, the one Moses left in charge (24:14). The ensuing dialog between the people and Aaron warns us lest we too become fickle and turn from the God who has blessed us. This passage is also a warning against the compromise of Christian leaders.

The people, who had just heard God himself speak the Ten Commandments from the mountain, violated the first two of those commandments by saying, **make us gods who will go before us** (32:1; see 20:3–6). They repudiated the very basis of their covenant relationship with God and denied that He is the One who brought them "out of Egypt, out of slavery" (20:1). They have also repudiated God's leader and chosen intermediary, Moses: **we don't know what has happened to him**.

In verses 3 and 4, Aaron acquiesced to their demand and thus incurred complicity in their sin. We do not know if Aaron intended to restrain them by his request for their **gold earrings** (v. 2). If so, it was a very timid and ineffectual restraint. The Scripture is emphatic in its assertion that Aaron himself made this idol—Aaron **made it into an idol cast in the shape of a calf, fashioning it with a tool** (v. 4).

Perhaps he was a bit shocked when he heard the people proclaim the work of his hands as **the gods** who had brought them **up out of Egypt** (v. 4). Then, again, their declaration may have been his cue. It was the Lord who had brought them from Egypt. So, he quickly **built an altar in front of the calf and announced, "Tomorrow there will be a festival to the LORD"** (v. 5). By using this language he attempted to disguise their disobedience as genuine worship of the Lord. How often do we, as Christian leaders or professed believers, use Christian language to camouflage actions that are alien to our faith? Aaron's refusal to face the truth led to moral anarchy—the people **got up to indulge in revelry** (v. 6). Has our refusal to stand for the truth contributed to the moral decay within our homes and churches?

WHAT DO YOU THINK?
Do spectacular miracles build faith and faithfulness? Why or why not?

AHA!
God demands true worship!

DID YOU KNOW?
The Israelites would have witnessed calf worship in honor of Osiris. While some scholars want to argue that the Israelites were using the golden calf as an icon of the true God, Jehovah had expressly forbade any idols being created.

Judgment without Excuse (Ex. 32:19–24)

The person who loves God knows there is absolutely no excuse for turning away from God and that judgment is the inevitable consequence. Observe the two models of Christian leadership within this passage—one leader stood for truth; the other tried to make excuse.

Moses stood for truth. He had been on the mountain with God and had God's perspective. God had already told him what the people had done, and he had interceded with God for them (vv. 11–14). Nevertheless, when he actually saw for himself **the calf and the dancing, his anger burned** (v. 19) with zeal for God. He knew the people had broken their relationship with God. Thus **at the foot of the mountain** he shattered those tablets that were the basis of their covenant with God—the very tablets that had been given by God on the top of the mountain. He allowed no pretense that everything was all right between them and God. His action in breaking the tablets contrasts sharply with Aaron's fashioning the idol. Moses destroyed the calf by fire and **ground** the remains **to powder** (v. 20) to show that he would make no compromise with their disobedience. By forcing the Israelites to drink this powder mixed with water, Moses demonstrated that they must bear the consequences of their sin.

But Moses' destruction of the calf did not put an end to their sin. The people were still, according to verse 25, "running wild" in their idolatrous immorality. Thus the loyal Levites joined Moses and went through the camp executing those who were putting the whole people in danger because they refused to stop their immoral behavior. Ultimately God himself sent a plague in judgment (v. 35).

Aaron, on the other hand, was a picture of the compromising leader who makes excuse. It was a mockery for him to say, **Do not be angry, my lord** (v. 22). First, he blamed the **people**, who were **prone . . . to evil.** Then he blamed circumstances: **I threw it into the fire, and out came this calf!** (v. 24). We have already seen that the text of Scripture is clear—Aaron made the calf with his own hands (see v. 4). It was almost as if Aaron was blaming God with this bold-faced lie. Because he refused to stand for the truth, Aaron bore partial responsibility for the people's sin; verse 25 says Aaron had let them "get out of control."

Thus he also shared responsibility for the judgment they suffered. Note verse 35: "The LORD struck the people with a plague because of what they did with the calf Aaron had made." Leaders, beware! Our compromise brings grief to those we lead!

Three Inexcusable Excuses		
Aaron	**Saul**	**The Wicked Servant**
Exodus 32:24	1 Samuel 15:20–21	Matthew 25:24–25
I didn't mean to sin, it just happened—it's the fault of circumstances.	My friends made me do it—it's other people's fault.	I was afraid God would let me down—it's God's fault.

Mercy without Complacency (Ex. 32:30–35)

We have seen Moses the godly leader. It is the leader who rejects compromise who is in a position to lead people back to God. In verses 30–35, however, we focus on Moses the mediator, a type and picture of Christ's mediation on our behalf. The purpose of Moses' mediation was to **make atonement for** their **sin** (v. 30), that is, to remove sin's awful impediment and bring them back into fellowship with God. Notice that successful mediation does not minimize sin. Both when speaking to the people and when speaking to God Moses called what they had done **a great sin** (vv. 30–31).

Before coming down the mountain, Moses had already interceded for the people by reminding God of His reputation with the Egyptians and His promises to the patriarchs (vv. 11–13). Moses had one more thing to offer—himself: If You, God, will not forgive them, **blot me out of the book you have written** (v. 32). God refused Moses' offer, for He will only blot out **whoever has sinned against** Him (v. 33). Even one so great as Moses could not take the place of others. Forgiveness comes only through the mercy of God.

WHAT ABOUT YOU?
What idols tempt you?
How can you defend
against those temptations?

Moses' offer of himself points forward to the form God's mercy would take to effect an adequate atonement for sin. Mercy and judgment find their resolution only in Jesus Christ who gave himself for our sin (2 Cor. 5:21)! In the person of His Son, our merciful God took the judgment for our sin on himself so that we can enjoy a restored relationship with Him. How horrible sin must be in the eyes of God! How great and marvelous is His mercy that opens the way for our reconciliation!

Nor does this passage lose sight of sin's gravity. Since God commanded Moses to **lead the people to the place** He **spoke of** (v. 34), it is obvious that He was not going to destroy them for their unfaithfulness. Nevertheless, it was only God's **angel**, not himself, who would go before them. Chapter 33 will show us that full fellowship with God could not be restored until the people came to a place of genuine repentance. The **plague** (v. 35) they suffered reminds us that sin often has consequences in this life. This plague may also have prepared their hearts for the penitence evidenced in the next chapter.

PRAYER
Father, keep me from
loving anything more
than I love You.

Israel's experience with the golden calf stands as a perpetual and ever contemporary warning to God's people. How easy it is for us who have enjoyed God's blessings to turn away from Him. How easy it is to make excuse for our sin. How devastating are the consequences of rationalized disobedience. How inviting is the mercy of God in Christ that would lead us to the restoration of God's presence through true heart repentance. ✦

EXODUS 32:1–6, 19–24, 30–35

1 When the people saw that Moses was so long in coming down from the mountain, they gathered around Aaron and said, "Come, make us gods who will go before us. As for this fellow Moses who brought us up out of Egypt, we don't know what has happened to him."
2 Aaron answered them, "Take off the gold earrings that your wives, your sons and your daughters are wearing, and bring them to me."
3 So all the people took off their earrings and brought them to Aaron.
4 He took what they handed him and made it into an idol cast in the shape of a calf, fashioning it with a tool. Then they said, "These are your gods, O Israel, who brought you up out of Egypt."
5 When Aaron saw this, he built an altar in front of the calf and announced, "Tomorrow there will be a festival to the LORD."
6 So the next day the people rose early and sacrificed burnt offerings and presented fellowship offerings. Afterward they sat down to eat and drink and got up to indulge in revelry.

19 When Moses approached the camp and saw the calf and the dancing, his anger burned and he threw the tablets out of his hands, breaking them to pieces at the foot of the mountain.
20 And he took the calf they had made and burned it in the fire; then he ground it to powder, scattered it on the water and made the Israelites drink it.
21 He said to Aaron, "What did these people do to you, that you led them into such great sin?"
22 "Do not be angry, my lord," Aaron answered. "You know how prone these people are to evil.
23 They said to me, 'Make us gods who will go before us. As for this fellow Moses who brought us up out of Egypt, we don't know what has happened to him.'
24 So I told them, 'Whoever has any gold jewelry, take it off.' Then they gave me the gold, and I threw it into the fire, and out came this calf!"

30 The next day Moses said to the people, "You have committed a great sin. But now I will go up to the LORD; perhaps I can make atonement for your sin."
31 So Moses went back to the LORD and said, "Oh, what a great sin these people have committed! They have made themselves gods of gold.
32 But now, please forgive their sin—but if not, then blot me out of the book you have written."

God Expects Exclusive Worship

God alone is the focus of all true worship.

INTO THE SUBJECT

Out of sight, out of mind. When Moses was absent from the Israelites for a long time, they put the Ten Commandments out of their minds. What happened next?

INTO THE WORD

1. The worship of a bull was common in Egypt. Does it surprise you that the Israelites wanted to engage in this kind of worship? Why or why not?

2. What investment did the Israelites make in idol worship? How do you explain the willingness of so many today to make sizable donations to false religions?

3. What do you think motivated Aaron to give in to the people's demand for gods?

4. What sign of attempted compromise do you see in verse 5?

5. Which commandments did the calf worshipers break (v. 6)?

6. What contrast between Aaron's and Moses' leadership do you find in verses 2–5, 19–24, and 30–35?

7. Read verses 30–31. What comparison between Moses and Jesus do you draw from these verses?

INTO THE WORLD

Resist every attempt to draw you into behavior that offends God and incurs His judgment. Worship God exclusively and obey His commands.

33 The LORD replied to Moses, "Whoever has sinned against me I will blot out of my book.
34 Now go, lead the people to the place I spoke of, and my angel will go before you. However, when the time comes for me to punish, I will punish them for their sin."
35 And the LORD struck the people with a plague because of what they did with the calf Aaron had made.

WHAT IS YOUR GOLDEN CALF?

The Israelites felt separated from God and wanted something to worship, so they created an idol made from gold. Such behavior may seem ridiculous to us . . . until we look more closely at ourselves. Often, the way we fill our days indicates what is important to us.

Fill out the chart below with approximate estimates of how you spend a typical week.

	Monday	Tuesday	Wednesday	Thursday	Friday	Saturday	Sunday
6:00							
7:00							
8:00							
9:00							
10:00							
11:00							
Noon							
1:00							
2:00							
3:00							
4:00							
5:00							
6:00							
7:00							
8:00							
9:00							
10:00							
11:00							

Highlight in yellow all the time dedicated to God. Shade with a pencil all the time spent on self. Use other colors to highlight hobbies or other activities that consume your time. Now glance over the chart to determine what matters to you the most—and what matters to you the least.

INTERACTIVE LEARNING IDEAS

GET THE CLASS INVOLVED
Blame Game

Divide the room into two groups to prepare for a courtroom debate. Hold one person out for the role of judge. Have the judge set up a table, obtain something to serve as a gavel, and don a choir robe.

Meanwhile, assign one group to play attorneys representing the people—they'll blame Aaron for their sin in the desert. Assign the second group the role of Aaron's attorney, claiming the people are at fault.

Give the groups ten minutes to prepare three-minute statements. Then have each group present its statement before the judge. Have the judge decide the winner of the court case. In a surprising twist, end with the judge declaring everyone guilty and sentencing everyone to punishment. The judge's statement should ask the group as they're grumbling over the consequences, Why does justice require that everyone who sinned suffer God's wrath and the plague?

TRY THIS ON YOUR OWN
Intercessor

Like in the days of Moses, sin's enticements lead people astray today. Godly leaders can direct them to follow God, but when those leaders leave or die, people's hearts stray from serving the one true God. The Bible is replete with examples of this. Judges 2:18–19 points out, "Whenever the LORD raised up a judge for them, he was with the judge and saved them out of the hands of their enemies as long as the judge lived . . . But when the judge died, the people returned to ways even more corrupt than those of their fathers, following other gods and serving and worshiping them."

What sinful people need is someone to stand in the gap and intercede for them before a just God. Certainly, Christ does that for us. But God's people also have a role to play. Take that role seriously, and dedicate a day to pray and fast for your nation's leaders and to confess your nation's sins to God. As a model for your prayer, read Daniel 9:1–19, especially the prophet's confession: "We have sinned and done wrong. We have been wicked and have rebelled; we have turned away from your commands and laws. . . . We do not make requests of you because we are righteous, but because of your great mercy. O Lord, listen! O Lord, forgive! O Lord, hear and act!" (vv. 5, 18–19).

TAKING IT TO THE STREET
Justice Prevails

With one other member of your study group, visit a nearby courthouse. Sit in the visitor's area of a courtroom to listen in on a case where one of God's laws (preferably one of the Ten Commandments) was broken. Pay attention to the prosecution's argument against the accused and to the accused's response. Is the legal team shifting blame, denying culpability, or diverting attention? Note how the judge and/or jury have the right to decide the accused's fate and consequences.

On the way home, talk about the balance of justice and grace, not just in your country's legal system, but in the nature of God.

WITH YOUR FAMILY
Just You Wait . . .

Waiting for their leader's return was the time when the people's temptation to sin reached epic proportions. Similarly, waiting for a promise to be fulfilled can lead us to sin by taking matters into our own hands. But, like the Levites who didn't worship the golden calf, it also can lead us to lean harder on God. To illustrate this, think of some event, like a theme park excursion, tickets to a ballgame, or an overnight at a hotel with a pool. Clandestinely set aside time for this treat—making it at least a week away.

Early in the week, promise everyone a special surprise. Talk about the surprise often. Drop hints about what it is—but don't leak anything about *when* it will be. Make them drool about it—but also make them wait.

At the last moment, spring it on them. While you're driving to the activity, ask them how hard it was to wait. Ask whether anyone sneaked a peek in your planner to see if they could find out when the surprise was coming. Talk about temptation—especially as it relates to waiting—and about how the Israelites failed at waiting in Exodus 32. ◆

LESSON 11

INTIMACY WITH GOD

Exodus 33:7–23

WHY THIS MATTERS

People who live along Colorado's Front Range can predict with almost 100 percent accuracy that late every afternoon in the summer thick, billowy black clouds will roll over the Rocky Mountains and bring a pittance of rain. The clouds look ominous, but they don't stay long. Wind chases them away to the east, and then glorious sunshine bursts over the mountains. The transformation from thick darkness to brilliant sunshine seems to picture how divine forgiveness often banishes sin from our lives.

This lesson emphasizes the inky blackness of Israel's sin and God's glorious forgiveness that followed when Moses interceded for the errant nation. Expect to revel in such a gracious God as you study this lesson.

BIBLE COMMENTARY
By Gareth Lee Cockerill

As we saw in the previous lesson, God delivered His people from Egypt so He could bring them into fellowship with himself. At Sinai He came to them on the mountain and established His covenant with them. He gave Moses instructions on how to make the tabernacle—the place where He would dwell among them and they would worship Him. But before Moses could construct the tabernacle, while he was still on Mount Sinai the people turned away in impatient unbelief and constructed a golden calf. Before, so to speak, the ink had dried on God's covenant, they had broken it through idolatry and immorality. They suffered judgment for this grievous violation of their relationship with God, and yet because of Moses' intercession God did not destroy them. As chapter 33 opens it seems that all has been made right—or has it?

Repentance Based on Genuine Humility (Ex. 33:7–11)

In verses 1–3, it appears that God was going to bless His people as He had originally planned. He told them to go to the land He promised to the descendants of Abraham (Gen. 12:7), Isaac (Gen. 26:1–3), and Jacob (Gen. 28:10). As before, He again promised to drive out the inhabitants of the land so that they could have it (Ex. 3:8). It is the same good land of promise, "the land flowing with milk and honey" (33:3).

Nevertheless, verse 1 strikes an ominous note when God called Israel "the people you [Moses] brought up out of Egypt." Isn't God the one who brought them out of Egypt (see Ex. 19:4)? Did He no longer think of them as His people? Then in verse 3 He said, "I will not go with you." God was at Sinai, but He had commanded them to leave Sinai and told them He would not go with them. God's presence is judgment rather than joy to those who rebel against Him. As long as they were the "stiff-necked people" (v. 3) who broke the covenant by making the calf, God's presence would only destroy them.

The people finally came to their senses. These words were so distressing (v. 4) to them because all of God's promises without Him mean nothing. Fellowship with Him in His covenant is the main thing. He was to be their God, and they were to be His people (Ex. 19:5–6). Thus they mourned for their sin and refused to "put on any ornaments." "Blessed are those who mourn, for they will be comforted" (Matt. 5:4). True sorrow for sin is the first step to restoration.

The people expressed their mourning by refusing to put on the ornaments they usually wore. After all, it was their gold rings they had used to make the calf. Perhaps these ornaments were some of the valuables they had taken from the Egyptians when they left Egypt (Ex. 12:35–36). Did this wealth tempt these former slaves to live in luxury, idolatry, and sensuality? Does our modern affluence, with all its comforts and conveniences, weigh us down and draw us away from God? Does it entice us to self-reliance and self-indulgence? What good is it if we become millionaires but lose our own souls—or the souls of our children? Perhaps true repentance would cause us to put aside many distractions.

God will not settle for cheap repentance. His reaction to their mourning was firm: "You are a stiff-necked people" (Ex. 33:5). He highlighted their stubbornness and again emphasized its consequences—"If I were to go with you even for a moment, I might destroy you." The NIV "might" is too tentative. Note the NRSV: "I would consume you." God's presence is delight for believers, but horror for those who refuse to believe. He then commanded them to take off their ornaments. They stripped their ornaments for the rest of the journey through the wilderness. "I will decide what to do with you"—they needed time to realize the seriousness of sin before they could appreciate the grace of forgiveness.

Verses 7–11 tell us how Moses set up a tent outside the camp of Israel, where he would go to meet with God. God would come in the **pillar of cloud** (v. 9) and talk with Moses. The people would stand in their tent doors when Moses went to this place of meeting with God. When they saw the pillar of cloud come, they **stood and worshiped** (v. 10). This account shows us that, although God had said He would not go with the people when they left Sinai, He had not yet left them. Perhaps it was because of their sin that the place where He met with Moses was outside the Israelite camp. These verses emphasize the unique position of Moses in relation to God and also depict the people's renewed respect for and awe of God. Despite the fact that they totally repudiated God's covenant they were, through His mercy, on their way to restoration.

Intercession Based on Divine Constancy (Ex. 33:12–16)

Verse 12 returns to the people's need of restoration. Moses reviewed the situation before God. God told Him to **lead these people**; in verse 1, God told

Moses pleads with God to go with His people.

WHAT DO YOU THINK?
Is it possible to have God's blessings without God?

AHA!
All of God's promises mean nothing without His presence!

DID YOU KNOW?
Last lesson we discussed how God changed His mind after Moses' pleas for mercy. Here, again, we see an additional example: "And the LORD said to Moses, 'I will do the very thing you have asked, because I am pleased with you and I know you by name'" (Ex. 33:17).

him to take them from Sinai. And yet Moses did not yet know whom God would **send** to empower him for this task and guide him on the way. True, God said He would not go himself (33:3) but would send His angel (33:2). Yet God's statement in verse 5 implies the possibility of reconsideration in light of the people's repentance.

Moses the mediator sought a deeper intimacy with God. He appealed to God on the basis of God's own favor and goodness to him—the God of the universe said He knew Moses **by name** (v. 12). God himself had declared that Moses had **found favor** in His sight. What did Moses want? He wanted God to **teach** him God's **ways** (v. 13) so he could know God even better and continue to find an ever-deepening favor with God. Those who truly know God want, more than all else, to know how to please the One they love so they can be even closer to Him.

This one who is intimate with God interceded for God's people: God had called Israel "the people whom you [Moses] brought up" (33:1). Moses called on God to **remember that this nation is your people** (v. 13). Moses was confident that God would be faithful to His promises. Those who know God know they can rely on Him.

What a relief when God said, **My Presence will go with you, and I will give you rest** (v. 14). God answered! God himself would be with them! He would give them rest in the Promised Land, the rest of fellowship with Him. But there was still concern on Moses' part. The English word *you* can be either singular or plural. In Hebrew, however, both of the "yous" in this sentence are singular—My presence will go with **you** (singular) and I will give **you** (singular) rest! God promised to go with Moses as Moses led the people. But Moses wanted to make sure the people were included: **do not send *us* up** (v. 15, emphasis added) unless Your presence goes with us! Note Moses referred to **me** and **your people** and to God going **with us**. Moses wanted the presence of God to **distinguish** (v. 16) Israel as God's holy people, just as God promised at Sinai (19:5–6).

Restoration Established By the Divine Presence (Ex. 33:17–23)

I will do the very thing you have asked (v. 17). Acting according to His merciful character, God granted His mediator's request. We are reminded of the mediator whom Moses foreshadowed—the eternal Son with whom the Father is "well pleased" (Mark 1:11). Only in Jesus do we see the fullness of the faithful love of God that is pictured here in God's response to Moses. In the mediator Jesus, God took the consequences of our sin upon himself and thus established the new covenant of heart obedience (Luke 22:20; Heb. 9:15; 10:15–18).

God confirmed His continued presence by giving Moses a gracious revelation of himself. Yet He did not accede to Moses' request for a vision of God's **glory** (Ex. 33:18). God's "glory" is His very essence or reality—to see God's glory is to see God's **face** (v. 20). Instead, in verse 19, God promised to manifest himself to Moses in two ways: First, He would cause His **goodness** to **pass in front of** Moses. Second, He would **proclaim** His **name, the LORD**, in Moses' presence. Moses would know that this God who had delivered them from Egypt, cared for them, made covenant with them, and promised to give them a new home, is good. When God proclaims His name, He proclaims who He is. The word LORD (with small capitals) is used in most of our English Old Testaments for the Hebrew word *Yahweh*, "I AM WHO I AM," the name God gave in Exodus 3:14–15. This name reveals God as the eternal God of holy love who can be depended upon to keep His covenant and even go beyond His covenant in showing mercy. We cannot presume upon Him by living in sin because He is holy; but when coming in genuine repentance we can rely on Him as the God who **will have mercy on whom** He **will have mercy** and **compassion on whom** He **will have compassion** (33:19). The God who knew Moses' name also allowed Moses to know His name and character.

The people of Israel had a wonderful mediator. Moses had found favor with God. God had given Moses an intimate revelation of himself and His presence. And yet Moses could not see the essence or glory of God. He could not see God's face. How much more wonderful is our mediator Jesus Christ. The glory of God that Moses could not see actually dwelt in Him (John 1:14). Moses could only see, as it were, the **back** (v. 23) of God. We, however, can see the very glory of God in the face of Jesus Christ. Through His life of obedience, death on the cross, and resurrection He revealed this glory. By taking the consequences of our sin on himself, He showed us the true character of this God of holy love (2 Cor. 5:21). In the face of Jesus Christ, we can see this glorious holy love of God and, what is more, we can be transformed into people who reflect His love and holiness (2 Cor. 3:18)!

The people of Israel did not want God's other promises without God himself. They knew the supreme importance of God's presence. Exodus 34 tells how God reestablished His covenant with them. Exodus 35–40 shows how Moses made the tabernacle as the place for God to dwell among them. Through Jesus God has made the new covenant with us. This covenant has no tabernacle or temple, for under this covenant God himself dwells in the very hearts of His people. We are to be distinguished as the holy, loving people of God because God himself is within us!

This passage announces a warning and extends a hope to the cold, indifferent, and worldly church of the twenty-first century. When Israel so grossly turned from God and became enmeshed in the idolatry and sensuality of the surrounding peoples, she suffered judgment and was on the brink of destruction and the total loss of God's presence. Yet, when she repented, God, because of His own character and through His mediator, forgave Israel's sin and restored the intimacy of His presence. Our greater privileges in Christ expose us to greater peril and greater glory. Persistence in worldliness will lead to an eternal experience of God's presence as judgment. Genuine repentance promises the eternal enjoyment of His glorious presence as blessing—a blessing so wonderful that it shatters the very limitations of our present imagination. ◆

WHAT ABOUT YOU?
How can you pray and work for restoration of our culture?

PRAYER
Father, thank You for Your mercy and Your redemption.

INTERACTIVE LEARNING IDEAS

GET THE CLASS INVOLVED
Confronted!

Exodus 32–33 isn't the only place God's people received rebuke and took that confrontation to heart. Recall the story of David, confronted by the prophet Nathan about the sin of adultery with Bathsheba. We not only know that David repented, but we have recorded in Psalm 51 the content of the king's prayer of contrition.

No matter the degree of our individual sinfulness, we all have sinned and fallen short of God's exacting standard (Rom. 3:23). There is a blessing in a time of corporate prayer of confession. So, turn to Psalm 51. Choose a Bible translation and the most emotive speaker in your group. Ask that person to lead a responsive reading. Let the leader read one verse and the group read the next.

Then go around the room with sentence prayers that relate to what you've seen in David's prayer that applies to your life.

TRY THIS ON YOUR OWN
To the Victor

We may be tempted to assume God's exacting standard for people in Old Testament days is superseded by the New Testament advent of grace. Yet in Revelation 2–3, Christ explicitly called His church to high standards—with a grave cost of failure. What differs for us is that God's Holy Spirit dwells within believers and equips us to meet those standards. Yet, this achievement obviously isn't automatic, or Jesus wouldn't have had to speak these tough messages to His church.

Each day this week, read one of Christ's messages to the churches of Asia and restate it in your own words. As you dig in, use cross-referencing tools, commentaries, dictionaries, Bible atlases, and other resources to help you understand the expectations your Master has for you—and for your local congregation of believers.

Pray about whatever the Spirit reveals to you and ask for His resources to make the changes necessary in your life so you may be labeled an "overcomer," or as the Holman Christian Standard Bible translates it, the "victor."

TAKING IT TO THE STREET
Take a Hike

God invited Moses on a short hike to a rock where He would reveal a glimpse of His majesty. While we don't have a promise that the physical manifestation of God's glory will pass by, a great way to refresh our vision of the creativity of our magnificent God is to step out of our everyday lives and observe His handiwork in creation.

Together with others from your study group, plan a short hike in a forest preserve or national park nearby. Wear weather-appropriate gear and pack a Bible and a snack for the journey. Once you've hiked to a rock outcropping reminiscent of the place where Moses saw God's back, read aloud Psalm 8, which begins, "O LORD, our Lord, how majestic is your name in all the earth!" (v. 1).

Then spread out quietly and worship God from your heart—thanking Him for the beauty before you and for revealing himself in what you see all around.

WITH YOUR FAMILY
What's in a Name?

The Bible makes a big deal about names—God's name, of course, but also the names of believers. To illustrate this to your family, spend an hour on the following project. (You'll need Internet access, colored markers, and a poster board for each person.)

Go online together to search for the meaning of each person's first name. Go to a site like www.biblicalmeaningofnames.net, www.meaning-of-names.com, or www.behindthename.com.

Using calligraphy or your fanciest handwriting, write on a poster each person's name and its meaning. Find a Scripture verse that fits that name or can help that person live up to God's expectations. Then let everyone use colored markers to decorate the boards. While you're having fun decorating, read aloud Exodus 33:17: "And the LORD said to Moses, 'I will do the very thing you have asked, because I am pleased with you and I know you by name.'" Talk about what it means that God knows you "by name." Ask each one to describe how that makes him or her feel.

Then display your posters in bedrooms or a family area of your home as a reminder that God knows you by name. ◆

EXODUS 33:7–23

7 Now Moses used to take a tent and pitch it outside the camp some distance away, calling it the "tent of meeting." Anyone inquiring of the Lord would go to the tent of meeting outside the camp.

8 And whenever Moses went out to the tent, all the people rose and stood at the entrances to their tents, watching Moses until he entered the tent.

9 As Moses went into the tent, the pillar of cloud would come down and stay at the entrance, while the Lord spoke with Moses.

10 Whenever the people saw the pillar of cloud standing at the entrance to the tent, they all stood and worshiped, each at the entrance to his tent.

11 The Lord would speak to Moses face to face, as a man speaks with his friend. Then Moses would return to the camp, but his young aide Joshua son of Nun did not leave the tent.

12 Moses said to the Lord, "You have been telling me, 'Lead these people,' but you have not let me know whom you will send with me. You have said, 'I know you by name and you have found favor with me.'

13 If you are pleased with me, teach me your ways so I may know you and continue to find favor with you. Remember that this nation is your people."

14 The Lord replied, "My Presence will go with you, and I will give you rest."

15 Then Moses said to him, "If your Presence does not go with us, do not send us up from here.

16 How will anyone know that you are pleased with me and with your people unless you go with us? What else will distinguish me and your people from all the other people on the face of the earth?"

17 And the Lord said to Moses, "I will do the very thing you have asked, because I am pleased with you and I know you by name."

18 Then Moses said, "Now show me your glory."

19 And the Lord said, "I will cause all my goodness to pass in front of you, and I will proclaim my name, the Lord, in your presence. I will have mercy on whom I will have mercy, and I will have compassion on whom I will have compassion.

20 But," he said, "you cannot see my face, for no one may see me and live."

21 Then the Lord said, "There is a place near me where you may stand on a rock.

22 When my glory passes by, I will put you in a cleft in the rock and cover you with my hand until I have passed by.

23 Then I will remove my hand and you will see my back; but my face must not be seen."

Intimacy with God

Knowing God personally is the privilege of all believers.

INTO THE SUBJECT

It would be interesting to have a conversation with a president or prime minister, but what would it be like to hold a face-to-face conversation with God?

INTO THE WORD

1. What perceptions do you gain in Exodus 33:7–11 of God? Moses? The people of Israel?

2. What help for your prayer life do you find in Moses' conversation with the Lord (vv. 12–18)?

3. Hypothetically speaking, where would you be very reluctant to go with the Lord's presence? Why there?

4. Why is it impossible to see God and live?

5. What evidence of God's grace do you find in verses 19–23?

6. When have you felt closest to the Lord? What was special about that time?

7. Read Exodus 33:13. What are you doing now or plan to do because you want the Lord to be pleased with you?

INTO THE WORLD

Maintain such intimacy with God that you can talk to Him openly about any concern, opportunity, or challenge you encounter this week.

Knowing God

Moses was closer to God than any other human being, and yet when Moses asked to see God's glory, God would let Moses see only His back, not His face. Apparently, being face-to-face with God is too much for humans to bear.

Until we reach eternity, we cannot know God fully. Which of the qualities of God has He revealed to you? Write a memory about how you came to know this about Him.

HIS LOVE

_____

_____

_____

_____

HIS POWER

_____

_____

_____

_____

HIS JUSTICE

_____

_____

_____

_____

HIS BEAUTY

_____

_____

_____

_____

HIS MERCY

_____

_____

_____

_____

HIS GOODNESS

_____

_____

_____

_____

HIS PROVISION

_____

_____

_____

_____

HIS RESTORATION

_____

_____

_____

_____

God has gifted you for a purpose.

ENABLED TO DO WHAT HE COMMANDS

Exodus 35:30—36:5

WHY THIS MATTERS

God always enables His people to do what He commands. He has endowed every believer with at least one spiritual gift for the edifying of the body, the church. However, we must use our gifts in the power of the Spirit. A coffeemaker is a nice, practical wedding gift, but unless it is plugged in and filled, the aroma of coffee will not waft through the newlyweds' home. Nor will the couple savor their very own home-brewed coffee. Zechariah 4:6 tells us God's work is accomplished "not by might nor by power, but by my [God's] Spirit."

This lesson inspires us to accomplish God's work in His way and in the power of His Spirit.

BIBLE COMMENTARY

By Philip Bence

The book of Exodus nears its conclusion. The book began with the nation in slavery. A new pharaoh arose who made life most difficult for God's people (Ex. 1). They cried out to Him and He heard. The story shifts toward Moses—his birth, rescue from death, adoption by Pharaoh's daughter, and his call (Ex. 2–4). Moses returned to Egypt and spoke to Pharaoh. God sent ten successive plagues on Egypt (Ex. 5–12). Pharaoh evicted the Israelites. God miraculously took them through the Red Sea (Ex. 13–15). The miracles did not end there; God led the people to Mount Sinai via a cloud and fiery pillar. On the journey, He provided food and water. He gave them victory over the first enemy they encountered (Ex. 16–18).

At Sinai, even while God gave the law, the people went into idolatry. God gave thought to destroying them all for their sin, but Moses interceded. Even as God judged them, they repented (Ex. 32–33). God gave them another chance. God again gave the law, and invited them once again to build a tabernacle, a portable house of worship. God did not want the people to set up images of their Divine Leader; that had been their great sin at the base of Mount Sinai. At the same time, God recognized that His people needed some visual aids to their worship. The tabernacle, the tent that would "hold" God's presence, would serve that purpose.

God had given detailed instructions for the tabernacle, its furnishings, and those who would serve God and the people within the tent (Ex. 25–30). God had also hand-picked the foremen and equipped artisans for the major construction project (Ex. 31:1–11).

When Moses returned to the people, he passed on to them all the commandments God had given (Ex. 34:29—35:3). Because Moses had interacted directly with God, his face shone. The people struggled to look at him. Then Moses turned his attention toward the tabernacle. In the middle verses of chapter 35, Moses issued two major invitations to the people.

KEY VERSE

So Bezalel, Oholiab and every skilled person to whom the LORD has given skill and ability to know how to carry out all the work of constructing the sanctuary are to do the work just as the LORD has commanded.

—Exodus 36:1

BACKGROUND SCRIPTURES

Genesis 4:20–22
  The first appearance of people with special abilities to work in agriculture, music, and craftsmanship
1 Chronicles 22:2–16
  The collection of material and provision of workers for the construction of the Jerusalem temple
1 Corinthians 12:4–11
  God's Spirit gives a variety of gifts, all to be used under God's direction for the good of the body.

DAILY BIBLE READINGS

Monday: John 6:23–29
Tuesday: Acts 4:23–30
Wednesday: Luke 1:68–75
Thursday: John 9:1–5
Friday: Colossians 3:23–24
Saturday: Exodus 35:30—36:5
Sunday: Psalm 22:16–24

"The LORD has filled him with the Spirit of God . . . with all kinds of skills."

He invited them, out of their possessions, to bring the fine materials and gems for the construction project. (Remember that God had moved the Egyptians to load the Israelites with gifts as they were leaving Egypt [12:36].) "From what you have, take an offering for the LORD" (35:5). How did the people respond? Exodus 35:20–29 describes the people's overwhelming generosity. They brought everything for which Moses had asked—and more!

Moses, likewise, invited people to donate their time and skills to the community effort: "All who are skilled among you are to come and make everything the LORD has commanded" (35:10).

God Appoints the Skilled Workers (Ex. 35:30–35)

God never asks His people to do anything they cannot do, if they will depend on Him for help they need. With God's instruction and strength, Moses gave overall leadership to the nation. But Moses could not do everything. Even with God's help, he was not Superman. Jethro, Moses' father-in-law, felt that even in just governing the people, Moses had taken on too much. Jethro suggested the wise plan of delegating some of Moses' responsibility and authority.

During the American Civil War, the dome on the national capitol building was erected. Abraham Lincoln had his hands full, leading the country. He did not try to act as foreman on the building project, even though that project involved the single most important building in the country.

Likewise, Moses did not have time or energy to give to the erection and furnishing of the tabernacle. God knew that and appointed two men to guide a group of coworkers through this large project. God not only appointed them, but He also gave them special artistic gifts. Perhaps at this point, the Egyptians again unknowingly contributed to God's plans. Just as they had given material gifts to the Israelites as they left Egypt, perhaps the Egyptian artisans had given training to the two men who became the construction supervisors.

Who were these two men and what do we know about them? On Mount Sinai, God specifically appointed Bezalel and Oholiab (31:1–11). The text literally says that God called them by name. God, of course, knew Moses by name (33:12), but not Moses alone; He also knew these men whom God wanted to serve in an essential, even if less known, task. God would have acted kindly even if He had merely provided gifted workers. He took the next step of naming the two He saw as most gifted as project coordinators. God took care of every detail: the blueprints for the sacred tent, the materials for its construction, and the hands to do the work. Let's see what we know about the two God appointed as building superintendents.

First, **Bezalel** (35:30). His name appropriately means "in the shadow of God." His father's name was **Uri**, son of **Hur**. (For more genealogical background, see 1 Chron. 2:3–5, 18–20.) Going back several generations, Bezalel was a descendent of Judah and his daughter-in-law Tamar. That put him in the same family line as Jesus himself (Matt. 1:3). You may remember that Tamar pretended to be a prostitute in order to seduce her father-in-law to have sex with her. She wanted him to fulfill his promise of giving her descendants (Gen. 38).

Judah had failed to keep his promise. Tamar deceived him. Yet out of their relationship came Bezalel, King David, and Jesus himself.

God had **filled** Bezalel **with the Spirit of God** (Ex. 35:31). When we think of Spirit-fillings, we normally think of great spiritual leaders (Judg. 6:34). But here we are reminded that God needs people of all types who will dedicate themselves to Him. In this situation, God needed Spirit-filled construction workers (**skill, ability and knowledge in all kinds of crafts**) as much as He needed Spirit-filled spokespeople.

God loaded Bezalel with an astounding number of skills. Bezalel could work well with **gold, silver and bronze** (Ex. 35:32). He would need these skills. God's instructions for the tabernacle mention gold thirty-five times, silver nine times, and bronze fourteen times. Bezalel could **cut and set stones** (v. 33). Since the people had to be able to carry all the components of the tabernacle, the weight of its components was a factor limiting the use of some materials. While those working on Solomon's subsequent temple constructed its structure of stone, it is not likely that many heavy stones appeared in the tabernacle. In this verse, the word *stones* likely refers to precious gems (see, for example, 25:7 and 35:9). God also equipped Bezalel as a skilled woodworker. Wood served as the primary material for the frame of the tabernacle (26:15), as well as many of its furnishings (including altars [see 30:1] and, of course, the ark of the covenant [25:10]).

Oholiab (35:34) evidently served as the number two man on the job. The text does not specifically give him a secondary role, yet it appears to give Bezalel first billing. Scripture gives us less information about Oholiab. The meaning behind his name is most appropriate for a tentmaker: "My tent is the Father-God." Oholiab's father's name was **Ahisamach**. This family formed part of the larger **tribe of Dan**. At times in the nation's history, members of various tribes competed with each other. God not only gave Bezalel and Oholiab gifts of working with their hands, but He must also have given them gracious personalities. Otherwise, they could never have worked well together or have directed the scores of men and women who served under their leadership.

God gave these two men (Bezalel and Oholiab) a host of additional skills in working with all the textile components of the tabernacle. He made them (and those they taught) **craftsmen, designers, embroiderers in blue, purple and scarlet yarn and fine linen, and weavers** (v. 35). He gave these abilities in abundance; they both became **master craftsmen**.

In most generations, God includes only a few Michelangelos, Mozarts, or Thomas Edisons. People around them recognize their abilities as God-given. It appears that Bezalel and Oholiab were the artistic geniuses of the wilderness generation. We could all wish that their handwork was still available for us to enjoy.

And then, best of all, He gave these men the special ability of multiplying themselves. Two men could never have done all this work alone. Their having such an amazing range of handyman and artistic gifts was astounding. But not every good worker wants to or can skillfully pass his abilities on to others. God gave Bezalel and Oholiab the gift of **teach**ing **others** (v. 34) the skills God had given them.

WHAT DO YOU THINK?
With which Spirit-filled abilities has God equipped you?

AHA!
We are told to "do the work just as the LORD has commanded" (Ex. 36:1)!

DID YOU KNOW?
Persons sixty-five to seventy-four years of age donated the largest percentage of their income (3.1 percent) and those eighteen to twenty-four the least (0.6 percent) to charity. Increasingly, those with lower incomes gave a higher proportion of their income than higher income individuals.

The Skilled Workers Gather (Ex. 36:1–2)

Moses finished this address to the people with words we might interpret as a warning. As Moses spoke to the nation, including those God had selected for the task of constructing the tabernacle, he reminded them all that God called them **to do the work just as the LORD** had **commanded** (v. 1). They could build the tabernacle, but only God could serve as its architect. (We all know people who use God's gifts in ways that oppose God's plans, or at minimum, do nothing to advance them.)

From the crowd, we can picture Bezalel and Oholiab moving toward the front. Along with them, numbers of volunteers accepted Moses' invitation to join the team (v. 2). Perhaps these people had previously recognized their gifts (or used them in Egypt). They might have wondered when the nation would settle long enough for them to use their skills. How appropriate that their first major project as free men and women was to build a place in which the nation could worship God, the One who had given them their freedom.

The Workers Receive the Gifts for the Work (Ex. 36:3–5)

Moses had previously asked the people to contribute the materials necessary for building the tabernacle (35:4–9). The people had evidently brought their donations to a specified location. Moses took the construction crew to show them the stockpile ready for use (36:3). But the people, hearing that work was ready to begin, started a second wave of gifts. They daily **continued to bring** (v. 3) more.

Finally, enough was enough. The workmen were spending so much time receiving gifts (at least they did not need to worry about receipts for tax deductions) that they could not move ahead on the work itself. As a group, they went to Moses to describe their delightful problem. All twenty-first-century pastors and church treasurers dream of having this problem: people giving too much. "Moses, tell them to stop giving gifts, so that the work can go ahead!" (35:5).

Moses and his helpers had to **restrain** the people, for they had already brought **more than enough** (vv. 6–7). ✦

EXODUS 35:30—36:5

35:30 Then Moses said to the Israelites, "See, the LORD has chosen Bezalel son of Uri, the son of Hur, of the tribe of Judah,

31 and he has filled him with the Spirit of God, with skill, ability and knowledge in all kinds of crafts—

32 to make artistic designs for work in gold, silver and bronze,

33 to cut and set stones, to work in wood and to engage in all kinds of artistic craftsmanship.

34 And he has given both him and Oholiab son of Ahisamach, of the tribe of Dan, the ability to teach others.

35 He has filled them with skill to do all kinds of work as craftsmen, designers, embroiderers in blue, purple and scarlet yarn and fine linen, and weavers—all of them master craftsmen and designers.

36:1 So Bezalel, Oholiab and every skilled person to whom the LORD has given skill and ability to know how to carry out all the work of constructing the sanctuary are to do the work just as the LORD has commanded."

2 Then Moses summoned Bezalel and Oholiab and every skilled person to whom the LORD had given ability and who was willing to come and do the work.

3 They received from Moses all the offerings the Israelites had brought to carry out the work of constructing the sanctuary. And the people continued to bring freewill offerings morning after morning.

4 So all the skilled craftsmen who were doing all the work on the sanctuary left their work

5 and said to Moses, "The people are bringing more than enough for doing the work the LORD commanded to be done."

> "Your spiritual gifts were not given for your own benefit but for the benefit of others, just as other people were given gifts for your benefit."
>
> —*Rick Warren*

Enabled to Do What He Commands
God has gifted you for a purpose.

INTO THE SUBJECT

Some skilled men and women know how to construct attractive, strong, comfortable buildings. Others wouldn't be able to build a birdhouse if their lives depended on it. How were the Israelites able to construct the tabernacle in the wilderness?

INTO THE WORD

1. What qualifications for constructing the tabernacle do you see in Exodus 35:30—36:1 that apply to performing the work of the Lord today?

2. Why do you agree or disagree that an unbeliever who is an excellent communicator should be allowed to teach an adult Sunday school class if he or she wants to do so?

3. According to 1 Corinthians 12:4 and 11, who distributes spiritual gifts to members of the body of Christ?

4. According to Ephesians 4:11–16, what is the purpose of spiritual gifts?

5. What spiritual gift(s) do you believe God has given you? Are you employing it (them)?

6. How would you describe the way the Israelites gave to the work of building the tabernacle?

7. What may be some reasons a church can't cover its expenses?

8. What do you think is the best way for a church to become financially sound?

INTO THE WORLD

You can help your church establish or maintain an influential testimony in the community and a strong missionary outreach by faithfully serving and giving as God enables you. Be a faithful steward!

Spiritual Gifts Assessment

Answer each question with a "3" if the statement is true of you most of the time. Answer with a "2" if the statement is true of you sometimes. Answer with a "1" if it is true rarely. It is important to answer how you truly are, not how you wish you were. After you've completed the survey, follow the instructions to discover where you are most gifted.

1. ___ I really want to help lost people get to know Christ.
2. ___ I like to make people think.
3. ___ I really love to study the Bible.
4. ___ When I complete a task, I love to have a visible end result.
5. ___ I am a people person; people energize me.
6. ___ I am usually pretty soft spoken.
7. ___ I am usually drawn to and involved in activities that help people.
8. ___ I am well organized.
9. ___ I make decisions based strictly on facts and things that are proven.
10. ___ Some people think I witness so much that I seem pushy.
11. ___ When I know people are sinning, I feel like it should be exposed.
12. ___ I am constantly thinking of better ways to communicate with others.
13. ___ I am good at thinking about and finding solutions to problems.
14. ___ I spend a lot of time praying for other people.
15. ___ I have a passion for comforting those who need it.
16. ___ I like to work behind the scenes more than in the spotlight.
17. ___ I am sensitive to the needs of others.
18. ___ I often set goals and seek to meet them.

19. ___ I would rather share the gospel than do anything else.
20. ___ It really bothers me when other people do things that are wrong.
21. ___ I am more task oriented than people oriented.
22. ___ When I read Scripture, I look for practical application.
23. ___ I have a great desire to see others grow and learn.
24. ___ I find that I often put myself "in someone else's shoes."
25. ___ I enjoy working with my hands.
26. ___ If a need exists, I am always ready to meet it.
27. ___ I do things on time.
28. ___ I am socially active and get along with people easily.
29. ___ I would rather speak about something than write it.
30. ___ I feel like I must teach people things so I'm sure they're taught correctly.
31. ___ I don't like deep doctrinal and deep theological studies.
32. ___ I am very protective of my friends and family.
33. ___ I act on my emotions more than on logic or thinking.
34. ___ I feel motivated when encouraged to serve.
35. ___ When I give, I always like to give my best.
36. ___ I am willing to attempt impossible tasks for God.

Now, go back through and add up the totals for the following groups of questions.

Numbers 1, 10, 19, 28 = _____ (Evangelism)
Numbers 2, 11, 20, 29 = _____ (Prophecy)
Numbers 3, 12, 21, 30 = _____ (Teaching)
Numbers 4, 13, 22, 31 = _____ (Encouragement)
Numbers 5, 14, 23, 32 = _____ (Pastoral Care)

Numbers 6, 15, 24, 33 = _____ (Mercy)
Numbers 7, 16, 25, 34 = _____ (Service)
Numbers 8, 17, 26, 35 = _____ (Giving)
Numbers 9, 18, 27, 36 = _____ (Administration)

Now, go back through and circle the two highest and two lowest totals. If there's a tie, list both:

Highest Gift Areas: _____, _____

Lowest Gift Areas: _____, _____

If you have a score of 9–12 in an area, you are highly inclined in that area.

If you have a score of 5–8, you are moderately gifted.

If you have a score of 1–4, you are probably not gifted in that area.

*This assessment is taken from http://www.teensundayschool.com/123/activities/spiritual-gifts-analysis.php.

INTERACTIVE LEARNING IDEAS

GET THE CLASS INVOLVED
You're Gifted

What a privilege Bezalel and Oholiab had to be called out by name from the mouth of God—to be gifted with creative talents from His hand and filled with His Spirit to accomplish their callings. In the Old Testament, this infilling was fairly unique. But in the New Testament, believers don't just have a temporary infilling but the permanent *indwelling* Holy Spirit, who gifts and equips us for service to His household.

Divide into pairs. Take turns listing gifts given by God to each person; they may be spiritual gifts, special talents and abilities, unique interests they've cultivated, and so forth. Don't be shy in recognizing your own gifts. After all, they come from God. Be willing to recognize your pair-partner's gifts.

Together, read 1 Corinthians 12:4–7. Talk about ways God has used your gifts in the past, giving Him the glory for ways they've succeeded. Brainstorm ways He might want to use your gifts for the "common good." Be sure each partner has equal time to list, share, and brainstorm.

TRY THIS ON YOUR OWN
Where or How?

While in Exodus God made a huge deal of the place for worship, Jesus showed us that a greater issue is at stake—one that is not visible through physical eyes nor touchable through physical senses. As He explained to the woman at the well in John 4:19–26, the worship profile God desires is a believer who will bow to Him "in spirit and in truth."

Commentator Adam Clarke explained: "A man worships God in spirit, when, under the influence of the Holy Ghost, he brings all his affections, appetites, and desires to the throne of God; and he worships him in truth, when every purpose and passion of his heart, and when every act of his religious worship, is guided and regulated by the word of God."

This is a meaty definition that has ramifications for every breath we take, every moment we spend. Use your quiet hour this week to meditate on Jesus' conversation with the woman about worship. Journal what the Spirit prompts you about what He desires from your personal worship.

TAKING IT TO THE STREET
Overwhelming Generosity

One stand-out lesson from the congregation in Exodus 35 is their generosity. They gave out of their hearts with such liberality that it overwhelmed the tabernacle workers.

In a day when God's people more often are portrayed in the public square as shrill voices against culture, one way we can stand as positive examples for God is in our generous response to community needs.

Scan your local newspaper for hardships that are testing families in your area. It may be a child's illness or a parent's accident. (If you can't find an individual, use your town's food pantry.)

Work with others in your study group, the local financial community, even the local media to start a fund to contribute toward that need. Start by giving the most generous gift you can afford. Lend your energies to encouraging others to join in. If anyone asks why you're doing it, graciously explain that your study of the Bible showed you giving generously is what God asks of you.

WITH YOUR FAMILY
Junior Teachers

In preparation for family study hour, spend time in prayer—asking that the Lord would show you one thing each member of the family is uniquely talented to do. Maybe it's using the computer or playing a musical instrument or pitching a baseball or organizing their closet.

When you gather the family, read Exodus 35:34 and explain how as God gifts everyone with talents, He equips us to teach that knowledge to others. Starting with the youngest, ask each to teach his or her special gift to the rest of you. It may take some preparation, and it may not be finished in one sitting. If that's the case, make a schedule so by the end of the week, everyone has had an opportunity to teach and learn. As you're learning, be enthusiastic and encouraging so they know you respect their talents.

And who knows? You might just enjoy learning something new. ✦

A holy God dwells in a holy place among holy people.

LESSON 13

GOD DWELLS AMONG HIS PEOPLE

Exodus 40:17–38

KEY VERSE

Then the cloud covered the Tent of Meeting, and the glory of the LORD filled the tabernacle.

—Exodus 40:34

BACKGROUND SCRIPTURES

1 Kings 6–9;
2 Chronicles 5–7
    The temple built by
    Solomon was dedicated.
Ezra 6:13–18
    The temple was
    completed and
    dedicated after the exile.
Ezekiel 43:1–5
    God's glory fills the
    temple.
1 Corinthians 3:16;
2 Corinthians 6:16
    God's people are
    His temple.
Hebrews 9
    Jesus is the perfect
    High Priest.

DAILY BIBLE READINGS

Monday: 2 Kings
             17:14–20
Tuesday: Jeremiah
             5:20–25
Wednesday: Hosea 6:1–3
Thursday: Psalm 42:1–6
Friday: 1 Thessalonians
             3:7–13
Saturday: Exodus
             40:17–38
Sunday: Psalm 22:25–31

WHY THIS MATTERS

Where does God dwell on earth today? Does He live in a tabernacle, cathedral, chapel, or church building? A congregation may refer to its place of worship as "God's house," but is it truly God's house?

Church preferences vary greatly, from red brick colonial to highly contemporary to theater, and their building costs also vary from thousands of dollars to multimillions; but what matters most is to understand that a church building is a place of worship, but believers are God's temple. He dwells in His people (1 Cor. 3:16).

When God's presence filled the tabernacle, His glorious presence accompanied the Israelites as they traveled. This lesson inspires us to reflect His glorious presence wherever we go.

BIBLE COMMENTARY

By Kathy Bence

A number of different words are used for the tabernacle in the Old Testament. Sometimes it is called the tent (nineteen times). Variations on tent include "tent of the LORD," "sacred tent" and the "house of the tent." But "tent of meeting" is a more common usage and carries with the name the idea of revelation—that it is God who is met and revealed in the tent. This phrase occurs more than 125 times. Sometimes, in the Greek New Testament, it reads "tent of testimony" or "tabernacle of the covenant"—all of which emphasize the different usages of this meeting time with God.

A third variation is that the tabernacle is often called the "dwelling" or "tent of dwelling"—the place where the presence of God dwells. And lastly, the tabernacle is often called the "sanctuary" or the "holy place" because the holy God dwells there.

There are four main passages that deal with the tabernacle, including Exodus 40, today's passage. They are Exodus 25–29; Exodus 30–31; Exodus 35–40; and Numbers 3:25–51; 4:4–49; and 7:1–89.

The tabernacle construction was entrusted to no one less capable than Moses. The people provided the resources, but Moses was given the privilege and the responsibility to prepare the tabernacle for the Lord's presence to inhabit. It would seem Moses must have had help to do the heavy lifting and arranging, but this passage mentions only Moses and gives him all the credit for the preparation of the glory of the Lord to be revealed in this first "temple."

Why pay so much attention to the "furniture" in the tabernacle? Its arrangement is given special attention in Scripture to teach us the spiritual lessons of how to worship this God of ours. We need to observe the centrality of the tabernacle amid the people. The custom of churches being located in the center of a city to dominate its essence originated here. The holiness of God was placed in the center of the people so they could not miss it or forget that our lives are to revolve around God.

Some scholars would claim that the tabernacle was only symbolic and not a real, historical building. Their claim asserts that it existed only in the imagination of the priests, who were responsible for helping the people worship God. However, there is no validity in this theory and no reason to assume there was not an actual, historical place for the people of Israel to worship. God was providing a visual and actual meeting place for His people to worship an invisible God.

Since we have no remaining drawings of the tabernacle, it is assumed that the structure was oblong with a flat roof and covered in ornate hangings on the walls. We do know it had an outer court that contained an altar built of bronze, for burnt offerings. It is thought that it was divided into roughly two-thirds for the holy place and one-third for the "Holy of Holies." The people set it up to face east.

Preparation for the King of Glory to Come In (Ex. 40:17–33)

The time—**the first month** of **the second year, on the first day** (v. 17)—is mentioned because it was exactly a year after the exodus from Egypt and slavery. Scripture does not always give us time references to help us understand, but when it does, we need to pay attention. There will always be a connection to some other event or some spiritual significance if we check a biblical resource. It was also nine months after their arrival in Sinai, which tells us that they had worked quickly to build the tabernacle and all its intricate furnishings, considering their primitive means of manufacturing everything by hand. And some of this time Moses had spent on the mountain with God, further reducing the time allowed to build and furnish an entire tabernacle.

Verses 20–33 give a "blow by blow" account of each action of Moses. Some of the actions are mundane and warrant only mention (**he put the bases in place, erected the frames, inserted the crossbars and set up the posts** [v. 18]), while others are laden with spiritual meaning regarding appropriate worship of God.

The materials for the tabernacle were made from the voluntary gifts of the people. Many materials are listed: gold; silver; bronze; richly dyed linen of blue, purple, and scarlet; dyed skins of rams and sheep; acacia wood; oil for lamps; spices to scent the oil; incense; and onyx gems. Truly, it must have been a joy to behold in its appeal to the senses: color, smell, and rich texture. The work involved in the production of the richly dyed fabrics and skins was immense. They dug certain plants that they knew to yield rich color and spent hours boiling the materials in the dyes, perhaps multiple times, to obtain the deepest shades of purple and scarlet. And this was *after* the spinning and weaving of the fabric and probably embroidering it as well. The metals that were not donated had to be dug from the earth and beaten into usable shapes. Both the men and the women donated long hours on these labors of love to adorn the dwelling place of God.

The ark of the covenant in the Holy of Holies

WHAT DO YOU THINK?
Why did God need a physical temple in which to "dwell" during the Old Testament period?

AHA!
God has always desired to dwell among His people!

DID YOU KNOW?
Why were the directions for the construction of the tabernacle so specific? Hebrews 8:5 gives a clue: The priests "serve at a sanctuary that is a copy and shadow of what is in heaven."

WHAT DO YOU THINK?
What clues about God's character can we draw from the tabernacle?

AHA!
We are now God's temple (1 Cor. 6:19)!

DID YOU KNOW?
The earthly temple is similar to the temple in heaven, even to the manifestation of God's presence. In Exodus 40 and Revelation 15, both are filled with smoke from the glory of God and from His power.

How was the tabernacle furnished? What was in it? Each item had enormous symbolic meaning. The first and most important was the **ark of the Testimony** (v. 21). Think of it as a box. Scholars estimate it to have been about 3¾ feet x 2¼ feet x 2¼ feet. It was made of wood and was the only furniture in the Holy of Holies, where the high priest went once a year to make atonement for the peoples' sins (see Ex. 25:10–40; 30:1–10).

The ark of the testimony contained the tablets of stone on which the Ten Commandments were written. These are also sometimes called the covenant in the Old Testament and were the written law of God at this time. Later, other laws were added, but these tablets of stone on which the finger of God had etched the law represented the will or desires of God for His people's behavior. The ark also contained some manna (Ex. 16:33–36) left from the wilderness and Aaron's rod that had budded (Num. 17:10). These were symbols of God's miraculous delivery of His people from slavery and His protection of them on their journey (Ex. 40:20–21).

The ark was covered inside and out with sheets of pure gold as well as golden rings and moldings. On top was a slab of gold called the "mercy seat." And cherubim fashioned of gold sat on the ends of the box. They were crafted so as to face in toward the ark and their wings touched overhead. They represented angelic ministers of the Lord who guarded the ark from pollution or harm. Between the cherubim, God's presence dwelt and met with His people through His representatives, Moses and Aaron. The ark was carried by placing poles through the four rings at the sides of the ark. If a person touched the ark, he or she would die, thus portraying the power and holiness and untouchableness of their holy God.

The people of Israel never set eyes on the Holy of Holies with its beautiful and fearful furnishings. Only the high priest could enter, and even he had to make preparations of ceremonial cleansing (physical washing and confession of his own sins) before he could enter and make intercession on behalf of the people. But, although the people never entered, they knew this was the dwelling place of a holy God and they feared (reverenced) God. (The Holy of Holies and the ark were shielded from view by a curtain—the same curtain that was torn down as Jesus died on the cross.) Once a year on the Day of Atonement, the high priest would enter and pray on their behalf as God had decreed them to worship Him. God's presence there hovered as a cloud, which is called the *shekinah* ("that which dwells") glory.

The Holy Place—or the area just outside the Holy of Holies—we would call the sanctuary. It contained three pieces of furniture: (1) a table of showbread; (2) the golden lamp stand; and (3) the golden altar of incense.

The table was made of acacia wood, covered with gold and a gold molding. It, too, had rings and poles for carrying. Accessories on the table consisted of gold plates for holding the loaves, dishes for frankincense, and golden goblets for wine offerings. On this table were placed two piles of twelve loaves of bread, which were replaced weekly. The reason for having twelve loaves was to represent each of the twelve tribes of Israel. The dishes, spoons, and bowls were all of pure gold. This table correlates to an altar in the front of our churches on which we place the Communion elements.

The lampstand was seven-branched and the most ornate of all the furniture. Made of gold, it had six golden branches, three on either side of a main shaft. All were adorned with almonds and flowers crafted of gold. It also had accessories of gold such as snuffers and oil dishes. It was lit by oil and wicks and was kept illuminated all the time. This light represented the presence of God that was never absent (Ex. 40:24–25).

In front of the veil to the Holy of Holies was an altar for incense. It was small (thought to be about twenty inches long and wide and about forty inches high) and constructed of acacia wood and overlaid with gold. On this table, incense was burned continually. Its fire was taken from the main altar for offerings. Incense represents a sweet aroma rising to God from the burnt offerings, offered in obedience to the law. So the aroma was sweet to God because His people were worshiping Him. The modern corollary is prayer. Our prayers are called a sweet aroma to God in 2 Corinthians 2:14–16. Hebrews 9 also offers another detailed description of the holy places of the tabernacle (Ex. 40:26–27).

WHAT ABOUT YOU?
Are you following God's specific instructions for your temple?

Moses also set up an altar for burnt offerings near the entrance to the tabernacle. The people brought their offerings of grain and animals to be burnt on the altar as symbols of their worshiping God, much as we bring our offerings of money. They had no money, so their gifts needed to come from what they could grow. The burnt offerings were supervised by the priests, and a portion of the "cooked" meat was given to the priests to eat since they had no portion of land on which to grow their own food. God did this so the people would take care of the needs of the priests just as we provide an income for our pastors so they can be free to minister without needing to earn a living elsewhere.

Moses also set up a basin for the people to wash before entering the tabernacle—again a symbol of coming to God clean of heart as well as hands and feet (Ex. 40:30–33).

The Glory of the Lord Fills the Tabernacle (Ex. 40:34–38)

What was all the preparation for? For the presence of God to enter the tabernacle and dwell in the midst of His people. And did He ever! Verses 34–35 tell us that the presence of God was so strongly present that not even Moses could enter the tabernacle.

PRAYER
Father, thank You that we all are welcomed into Your holy of holies through the blood sacrifice of Your Son.

While Yahweh was an invisible God, these people could not doubt His being alive and present with them. We do not know exactly what the cloud of His presence looked like nor how His glory appeared to the people, but verse 35 says God's glory **filled the tabernacle**. Whatever form or essence it possessed, even Moses—who had been frequently in the presence of God on the mountain till his face glowed—could not enter God's glorious presence here. It says that God was pleased with the building of the tabernacle and with His people and longed to live in their midst.

This presence of God remained with the Israelites wherever they went. They dismantled the tabernacle, which was in some form a tent, and took it with them. And God's presence guided their travels. If the cloud lifted, they would move on; if it remained stationary, so did they. This represented the presence of God not only with them but guiding them and protecting them (Ex. 40:36–38). ◆

INTERACTIVE LEARNING IDEAS

GET THE CLASS INVOLVED
Tabernacle to Temple

First Kings 6–8 chronicles the building of the "permanent" place of God's dwelling with His people, the temple in Jerusalem. The writer was careful to tell us it had been 480 years since the people left Egypt's slavery, and that only then was it time to exchange the temporary tabernacle of Exodus for a magnificent temple to be built by Solomon.

Divide into four groups and give each a flipchart or large drawing board.

Assign one function to each:

- Use Exodus 36–40 and 1 Kings 6–8 to chart *similarities* between the physical requirements of the two places of worship.
- Use the same passages to chart *differences* between tabernacle and temple.
- Draw pictures of elements that were created for the worship community and explain their uses. (Use Ex. 37 and 1 Kings 7 as your sources.)
- Compare and contrast Moses' instructions to the people throughout Exodus with Solomon's instructions in 1 Kings 8:22–61. (Pay special attention to 8:54–61.)

Come back together and invite group leaders to explain their charts. Discuss the consistency of Scripture—and of God's promises to meet with His people, including Jesus' promise of Matthew 18:20.

TRY THIS ON YOUR OWN
Worship Planning

All the elaborate preparation in Exodus was centered around worship—creating a setting where God would dwell and His people would encounter His awesome presence. Today, believers are the place where the living God dwells. And our worship takes place in everyday life.

Yet, collaborative, community worship takes place weekly in our churches. It doesn't just happen—it takes planning and preparation on the part of the church ministry team.

Find out who is responsible for the worship service planning in your local congregation. Plan to take that individual or ministry team out to a meal this week.

- Thank them for enhancing your worship experience and focusing your attention on God.
- Ask them about how they work through the week to prepare for weekend worship.
- Encourage them in their efforts.
- Pray for them.

TAKING IT TO THE STREET
Ready for the Game

Get tickets to a professional or semi-pro sporting event at a local arena. Make it an end-of-the-Exodus-study group event. Enjoy the game—rooting for your team and enjoying the camaraderie of the crowd.

But have a second agenda: arrive early, so you can observe the last of the preparations for the game. Sometimes multiple sports (like ice hockey and basketball) call the same venue home. Pay special attention to the equipment that makes the arena usable for the event of that day. How would it be different if it were outfitted for another sport? Or a convention of exhibitors?

What if the arena were to be used for a Christian event—like a concert or crusade? What would be needed then? How would God's Spirit be evident in the place at that event? Finally, consider how the spirit of the place would change for an event sponsored by a religion that worships another god. Talk with your group about what you observe—especially in light of what you've just studied about preparing God's tabernacle.

WITH YOUR FAMILY
Deep Colors

Using fabric dyes, have some fun with family time as you illustrate one of the skills the Israelites used to enhance the tabernacle.

What you'll need:

- a white T-shirt for each person
- at least two fabric dyes (be sure to include purple—the color of royalty)
- rubber bands
- rubber gloves
- two large pots of water

Go to a website such as www.ehow.com to find instructions on tie dyeing. Allow each family member to dye his or her shirt (with help, as needed). Encourage creativity in color choice and style. As you're having fun with the dyes, talk about how the people of God in the wilderness dug plants that yielded rich colors, and then pounded and boiled the plants to produce the dye before coloring the fabrics they wove by hand—all to give their best to the place where God would dwell.

After you wash and dry the shirts, have everyone wear them for family worship hour. ◆

EXODUS 40:17–38

17 So the tabernacle was set up on the first day of the first month in the second year.

18 When Moses set up the tabernacle, he put the bases in place, erected the frames, inserted the crossbars and set up the posts.

19 Then he spread the tent over the tabernacle and put the covering over the tent, as the LORD commanded him.

20 He took the Testimony and placed it in the ark, attached the poles to the ark and put the atonement cover over it.

21 Then he brought the ark into the tabernacle and hung the shielding curtain and shielded the ark of the Testimony, as the LORD commanded him.

22 Moses placed the table in the Tent of Meeting on the north side of the tabernacle outside the curtain

23 and set out the bread on it before the LORD, as the LORD commanded him.

24 He placed the lampstand in the Tent of Meeting opposite the table on the south side of the tabernacle

25 and set up the lamps before the LORD, as the LORD commanded him.

26 Moses placed the gold altar in the Tent of Meeting in front of the curtain

27 and burned fragrant incense on it, as the LORD commanded him.

28 Then he put up the curtain at the entrance to the tabernacle.

29 He set the altar of burnt offering near the entrance to the tabernacle, the Tent of Meeting, and offered on it burnt offerings and grain offerings, as the LORD commanded him.

30 He placed the basin between the Tent of Meeting and the altar and put water in it for washing,

31 and Moses and Aaron and his sons used it to wash their hands and feet.

32 They washed whenever they entered the Tent of Meeting or approached the altar, as the LORD commanded Moses.

33 Then Moses set up the courtyard around the tabernacle and altar and put up the curtain at the entrance to the courtyard. And so Moses finished the work.

34 Then the cloud covered the Tent of Meeting, and the glory of the LORD filled the tabernacle.

35 Moses could not enter the Tent of Meeting because the cloud had settled upon it, and the glory of the LORD filled the tabernacle.

36 In all the travels of the Israelites, whenever the cloud lifted from above the tabernacle, they would set out;

God Dwells among His People

A holy God dwells in a holy place among holy people.

INTO THE SUBJECT

Church structures seem to be more varied than boxes of cereal. Nearly everyone has a favorite style of church architecture, but what should we value most highly where we worship? Isn't it God's presence?

INTO THE WORD

1. What furnishings for the tabernacle are listed in Exodus 40:1–8?

2. What measures did the Lord command for the consecration of the tabernacle and its furnishings (vv. 9–11)?

3. Why was it necessary to consecrate Aaron and his sons?

4. What precautions might a congregation take to safeguard the holiness of its pastoral staff?

5. Why is the date given in verse 17 significant?

6. What recurring phrase do you find in verses 18–32? Why is it significant?

7. What do you learn from the altar of burnt offerings and the basin of water about the proper way to approach God?

8. What principle about following God do you glean from verses 34–36?

INTO THE WORLD

Believers are God's dwelling place. Therefore, we need to recognize the privilege and responsibility of manifesting His presence wherever we go and in whatever we do.

37 but if the cloud did not lift, they did not set out—until the day it lifted.

38 So the cloud of the LORD was over the tabernacle by day, and fire was in the cloud by night, in the sight of all the house of Israel during all their travels.

TABERNACLE TABULATION

Look up the passages indicated and label each part of the tabernacle.
Write a few words of description under each line.

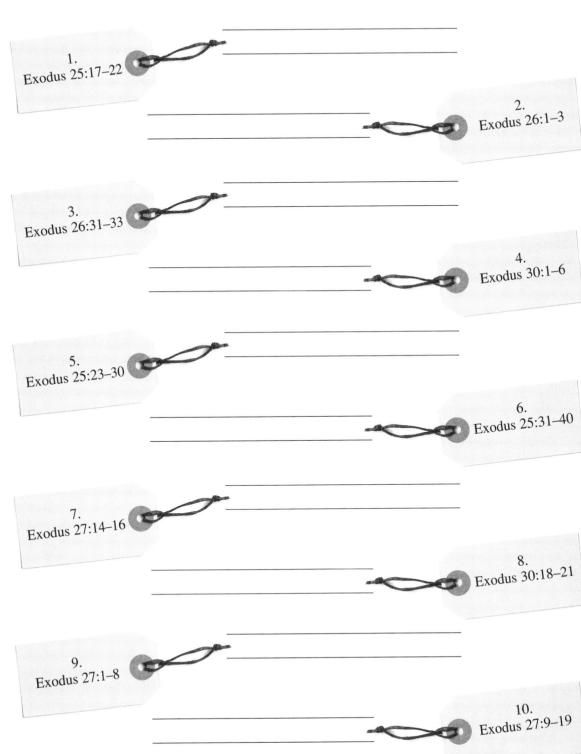

1.
Exodus 25:17–22

2.
Exodus 26:1–3

3.
Exodus 26:31–33

4.
Exodus 30:1–6

5.
Exodus 25:23–30

6.
Exodus 25:31–40

7.
Exodus 27:14–16

8.
Exodus 30:18–21

9.
Exodus 27:1–8

10.
Exodus 27:9–19

UNIT 3
FOLLOW ME
God Is Faithful to His People

Lesson 1
Lesson 2
Lesson 3
Lesson 4
Lesson 5
Lesson 6
Lesson 7
Lesson 8
Lesson 9
Lesson 10
Lesson 11
Lesson 12
Lesson 13

FAITHFULNESS TO ALL GENERATIONS

Unit 3 Preview

According to a 2009 PEW research poll of nearly three thousand people, about two-thirds of the people sixty-five years and older said religion is very important to them. Just over half of those age thirty to forty-nine agreed with the older generation, and only 44 percent of people age eighteen to twenty-nine said religion is very important to them. Apparently, the gap between each generation is not restricted to the younger's uncanny ability to catch on quickly to every advance in technology. Nevertheless, God's patience and mercy span all generations.

From Joshua to the Times of the Judges

When God appointed Joshua to succeed Moses as Israel's leader, He told him to be strong and courageous and to obey His Word. He promised to be with Joshua and deliver the Promised Land into his hand. Joshua lived up to the charge he received from God, and God faithfully granted Joshua the Promised Land. The book of Joshua reports an occasional defeat, but for the most part it spotlights Israel's victories under Joshua's leadership. As you study the book of Joshua, you will be impressed with Joshua's courage and faith and with God's faithfulness to the generation that followed Joshua into the Promised Land. You will also find yourself saying "Amen" often as you read Joshua's farewell address to the nation and his personal testimony: "As for me and my household, we will serve the LORD" (Josh. 24:15). And you will applaud his boldness at commanding the Israelites to "throw away the foreign gods that are among you and yield your hearts to the LORD, the God of Israel" (v. 23)

Yes, that first generation to live in Canaan had held on to foreign gods. Yet God remained faithful to His people—and ever patient with them!

The Times of the Judges

The next generation precipitated a downward spiral away from the Lord. The times of the judges include, but are not limited to, the books of Judges and Ruth. During this period, each generation did what was right in its own eyes (Judg. 17:6; 21:25), which means it did what was wrong in the Lord's eyes.

You will observe an oft-repeated cycle as you study Judges. The Israelites' sin brought divine judgment in the form of an oppressor; the people repented and cried out for deliverance; God appointed a judge to deliver His people; and peace ensued until the people fell into sin again. It is a sorry history, but God's faithfulness throughout that period shines like a diamond against a black background.

"I will sing of the LORD's great love forever; with my mouth I will make your faithfulness known through all generations. I will declare that your love stands firm forever, that you established your faithfulness in heaven itself. You said, 'I have made a covenant with my chosen one, I have sworn to David my servant, I will establish your line forever and make your throne firm through all generations.'"
—*Psalm 89:1–4*

The brief book of Ruth further highlights God's faithfulness and shows how Ruth, a Gentile woman, came to believe in the God of Israel. And even more amazing, she became an ancestress to the Messiah.

The writer of Psalm 89 pledged to sing of the Lord's great love forever and to make His faithfulness known to all generations (v. 1). Let your study inspire you to follow the psalmist's example. ◆

From http://en.wikipedia.org/wiki/File:Jericho8.jpg; public domain.

Tell es-Sultan, the archaeological site of the biblical city of Jericho.

"When the trumpets sounded, the people shouted, and at the sound of the trumpet, when the people gave a loud shout, the wall collapsed; so every man charged straight in and they took the city."
—Joshua 6:20

God chooses to do a great work through a surrendered leader.

LESSON 1

GOD CHOOSES A LEADER

Joshua 1:1–17

KEY VERSE

Have I not commanded you?
Be strong and courageous.
Do not be terrified; do not
be discouraged, for the LORD
your God will be with you
wherever you go.
—Joshua 1:9

BACKGROUND SCRIPTURES

Genesis 12:1–7; 17:1–11
     Promise to Abraham
Deuteronomy 3:12–20
     Moses' instructions
     to the two-and-a-half
     tribes
Deuteronomy 3:21–28;
31:1–23
     Appointing of Joshua
     as Moses' successor
Deuteronomy 17:18
     Instruction for the king
     to copy and read the
     law

DAILY BIBLE READINGS

Monday: Judges 6:7–14
Tuesday: 2 Corinthians
            4:13–18
Wednesday: Deuteronomy
            31:1–8
Thursday: Isaiah 43:1–7
Friday: Isaiah 41:8–10
Saturday: Joshua 1:1–17
Sunday: Psalm 26

WHY THIS MATTERS

God called and equipped Moses, a man of great faith, to lead His people from Egypt to the Promised Land. After Moses died, a new leader was needed. So God appointed Joshua, who had been Moses' assistant. Joshua, too, was a man of faith who would heed God's Word.

This lesson shows us that God appoints godly leaders to guide His people at specific times and for specific purposes. We should thank God for past leaders and cooperate with those He has appointed to lead us now.

BIBLE COMMENTARY

By Kelvin G. Friebel

The book of Joshua divides into three main sections: (1) the entrance into (chapters 1–5) and conquest of (chapters 6–12) the land; (2) the apportioning and division of the land (chapters 13–21), and (3) three different events once the people were in the land (chapters 22–24).

The first chapter of Joshua recounts Joshua's commissioning as leader and establishes the theological paradigm through which the entrance into and conquest of the land are to be understood.

Moses and Joshua

Joshua was first introduced in the Pentateuch. There he was shown to be a military leader in the battle against the Amalekites (Ex. 17:8–14). He was Moses' assistant (that is, leader-in-training; Num. 11:28), present with Moses on Mount Sinai (Ex. 24:12–13; 32:17) and when Moses went into the Tent of Meeting (Ex. 33:11). He was one of the twelve spies sent into the land in Numbers 13–14 (compare Num. 26:65; 32:12).

Near the end of the Pentateuch, Joshua was appointed as Moses' successor (Num. 27:15–23; 34:17; Deut. 1:38; 3:18–22, 28; 31:1–23; 34:9). Given those previous passages in the Pentateuch, Joshua chapter 1 must be seen as a reaffirmation of Joshua's leadership to which he had already been both divinely designated and publicly commissioned, prior to Moses' death.

The repeated mention of Moses in chapter 1 (eleven times) drew a correlation between the two leaders and their tasks so that Joshua's leadership was seen in a comparable light to that of Moses'. The Lord assured Joshua of His presence in the same way He was with Moses (v. 5; compare v. 17). That promise echoed the Lord's declaration to Moses at his calling in Exodus 3:12: "I will be with you." Also, the people reassured Joshua of their obedience based on that given to Moses in verse 17.

First Speech: The Lord's Commissioning of Joshua (Josh. 1:1–9)

The Lord's speech to Joshua was an installation speech, the key component of which is the commissioning of the person to the task the new leadership position entails. The literary form of this type of speech is composed of four common elements:

A Statement of the Task. For Joshua, the task was to lead the people across the Jordan River into the land, to take possession of the land, and to allot it to them as an inheritance (v. 2: **get ready to cross the Jordan River into the land**; v. 6: **you will lead these people to inherit the land**).

An Exhortation of Encouragement. Such exhortations are expressed positively as "be strong, be courageous" or conversely through "do not be afraid." Here that command was repeated three times (v. 6: **Be strong and courageous**; v. 7: **Be strong and very courageous**; v. 9: **Be strong and courageous. Do not be terrified; do not be discouraged**), signifying its centrality in the message. The exhortation was also repeated in the fourth speech in verse 18 as the people exhorted Joshua, "Only be strong and courageous!"

In this speech, the exhortation is tied specifically to all the other elements. In verse 6, it is linked with the statement of the task of leading the people to inherit the land, and in verse 7, it transitions into the command to be obedient to the law (compare also Josh. 23:6). Thus Joshua was to display resoluteness with respect to both his military leadership of the people and his personal devotion to doing God's will, out of which his spiritual leadership would arise.

In verse 9, the exhortation is linked to the promise of the divine presence in such a way that the latter provides the basis as to why Joshua could be strong. In other words, Joshua could be courageous *because* he had the assurance that God was with him, enabling and empowering him. Thus the exhortation must be understood as a call to exercise faith and trust in God's promise rather than being merely a summoning up of one's own inner fortitude, courage, and valor.

An Affirmation of Assurance of the Divine Presence and Help. Such occurs in two ways in this type of speech. The first was through the specific phrasing of "the LORD being with" the person. Twice in this speech the Lord reassured Joshua, **"I will be with you"** (vv. 5, 9). In verse 5, it is further reinforced through **I will never leave you nor forsake you.** This assurance was also expressed in the fourth speech by the people to Joshua in verse 17 ("Only may the LORD your God be with you") as they too acknowledged that a key quality needed by the leader was the divine presence.

That promise of the divine presence did not simply mean the person would in some nebulous way sense God's surrounding presence. Rather, it was a powerful promise of the Lord's abiding with the person specifically to strengthen him or her for the task to which the Lord had called the person (see Jesus' similar promise in Matt. 28:19–20 to us, His followers, as we are commissioned to carry out the task of making disciples throughout the world).

The second affirmation came in declarations that the Lord would fight for them or give them victory. Such assurances of victory are expressed in verses 2–3 (**the land I am about to give to them . . . I will give you every place where you set your foot**) and verse 5 (**No one will be able to stand up against you**).

WHAT DO YOU THINK?
A key quality in a leader is "divine presence." How can God's presence be recognized in a leader? How might it be task specific?

AHA!
No undertaking God calls us to should intimidate us, no matter how impossible it seems. If we are careful to obey His instructions, we know He remains with us, providing all we need for success.

DID YOU KNOW?
The events described in Joshua likely occurred either in the fifteenth century B.C. or the thirteenth century B.C. Science hasn't helped historians settle the date. Archeological evidence can be argued to support both possible time periods.

WHAT DO YOU THINK?
The people of two and a
half tribes already possessed
their land, thus some
security and peace. How
might this make it easier or
more difficult for them to
fight with the other tribes?
Why was their participation
important?

AHA!
As we take on the tasks
God gives, we must help
each other and fully
support our leaders.

DID YOU KNOW?
Those considered "fighting
men" were over twenty
years old, had access to
weapons, and were known
to be brave in battle.

An Exhortation to Keep the Law, which Becomes a Condition for the Successful Fulfilling of the Task. In verses 7–8, the Lord commanded Joshua to be fully observant of the law. The specific designation of the **Book of the Law** (v. 8) probably referred to the portions of the book of Deuteronomy written by Moses as mentioned in Deuteronomy 31:9, 24–26.

This command was emphasized through five repeated phrases, with the similar phrases **Be careful to obey all the law** (v. 7) and **be careful to do everything written in it** (v. 8) beginning and concluding the section. The first two phrases in verse 7 (**Be careful to obey all the law** and **do not turn from it to the right or to the left**) are synonymous and stress complete obedience, without deviating from the law in any way. The first two phrases in verse 8 (**Do not let this Book of the Law depart from your mouth** and **meditate on it day and night**) are probably to be understood in a more contrastive manner. They stress the dual aspect of publicly speaking forth the law to the people and personally taking it in.

The reason for being observant of the law was so that Joshua would have success (v. 7: **that you may be successful wherever you go**; v. 8: **Then you will be prosperous and successful**). The promise of prosperity and success in the context of this type of commissioning speech was not to be understood as a generic, blanket statement that the person would receive manifold material blessings and wealth in the various vicissitudes of life, but was rather tied to the particular task to which God was calling the person. Thus it was a specific promise assuring the success of the specific venture, which in this case was the conquest of the land.

The repeated emphasis on obeying God's law stressed both the spiritual quality necessary for effective leadership (obedience to God) and the source of that spiritual direction (the law of God). Thus, the key to Joshua's carrying out his leadership role and the successful completion of the commissioned task was not his leadership abilities or his military strategies, but rather his unswerving spiritual commitment to obeying the commands of God.

Although delineating the specific task that was to be undertaken, the key persuasive purpose of this type of speech was to give the one commissioned the sense of assurance that the task, regardless of how difficult it was, could nevertheless be carried out because of the divine presence that was there to enable the successful completion. So here, the Lord was trying to encourage Joshua as he assumed the leadership position passed down from Moses, which carried with it the daunting task and responsibility of leading the people to take possession of the land.

Second Speech: Joshua's Commands to the People (Josh. 1:10–11)

In the second (vv. 10–11) and third (vv. 12–15) speeches, Joshua transmitted the divine orders to those to whom they were applicable. In verses 10–11, he gave orders to the **officers of the people** (the tribal leaders who performed military as well as civil and judicial duties). In verse 2, God had told Joshua to "get ready to cross the Jordan River into the land I am about to give to them—to the Israelites." Verses 10–11 suggest the immediate implementation of that divine command, as Joshua communicated almost verbatim the divine command and promise to the people: **Get your supplies ready. Three days from**

now you will cross the Jordan here to go in and take possession of the land the LORD your God is giving you.

The time reference of "three days from now" did not mean "after three days," but rather "the day after tomorrow." The Hebrew idiom included both the current day and the day of the event. The immediacy of Joshua's implementing the divine command was evident, with only enough delay to allow time for the necessary preparations.

Third Speech: Joshua's Commands to the Tribes (Josh. 1:12–15)

In verses 12–15, Joshua reminded the two and a half tribes of the command given to them by Moses (Num. 32:2–32; Deut. 3:18–20). The Lord had given the tribes of Reuben, Gad, and the half-tribe of Manasseh permission to settle and occupy the Transjordan territory captured by the Israelites, with the proviso that they accompany the other tribes across the Jordan to fight with them in taking possession of their land. The conquest of the Promised Land was to be a united effort by *all* the tribes taking possession of *all* the territory.

In verse 14, for the first time in the chapter, the command indicates the military nature of the venture: **all your fighting men, fully armed** (or, in battle array) **must cross over**. Also, the language of verse 15— **taken possession** (also in v. 11)— connotes that such was done by force; it involved the dispossessing of those currently occupying the land. Although they must fight to take the land, the ultimate goal was God giving **rest** (vv. 13, 15). "Rest" in this context meant the cessation of fighting due to the subjugation of the enemies (compare Deut. 12:10; 25:19; Josh. 21:44; 23:1).

WHAT ABOUT YOU?
God sometimes assigns us great tasks. How can you prepare yourself for your call in the following areas: listening to God's instructions better, trusting His promises more fully, sharpening your leadership skills, and developing the support you need?

Key Biblical Events and Miracles at the Jordan River		
Event	Reference	Revelation about God
Lot chose "all the plain of Jordan."	Genesis 13:11	God lets us live with our choices.
Jacob wrestled with his adversary near its banks.	Genesis 32:22–26	God starts something new and transforms our lives.
Israel crossed on dry ground.	Joshua 3:15–17	God keeps His promises.
Elijah crossed on dry ground and was taken by chariot to heaven.	2 Kings 2	God honors His faithful servants.
Naaman was healed of leprosy.	2 Kings 5:13–14	God heals us.
Elisha made an ax head float.	2 Kings 6:1–6	God proves His power.
John preached there and baptized Jesus.	Mark 1:9	God sent salvation.

Fourth Speech: Pledge of Obedience by the People (Josh. 1:16–18)

The main point of the fourth speech was the tribes' pledge of full obedience to Joshua and by implication to God's commands. Although the people pledged complete obedience, one cannot help but read their declaration with a sense of irony. They pledged obedience to Joshua in the same way they were obedient to Moses (v. 17: **Just as we fully obeyed Moses, so we will obey you**). But the Pentateuch repeatedly characterizes the people as not being obedient to Moses! Also, this pledge of loyalty must be read in light of the Lord's and Moses' expectation that this new generation would not be faithful once they were in the land (Deut. 31:14–18, 24–29). Thus the rebellious, stubborn, and obnoxious qualities of the people in relationship to leadership raised the question as to whether the people would completely obey all that Joshua commanded them or be "faithful" to Joshua's commands similar to the way they were "faithful" to those of Moses. ◆

PRAYER
Father, thank You for Your promise to be with me when I faithfully answer Your call. Thank You for those who support me. Help me to obey all You command, completely, and to step forward fearlessly, marching forward toward success.

INTERACTIVE LEARNING IDEAS

GET THE CLASS INVOLVED
To Encourage and Support

Even experienced leaders need support and encouragement. Joshua, after all, stood right by Moses' side through countless miracles. Yet God knew he needed support. Our spiritual leaders today need that too.

Take some time as a group to plan ways to encourage your church leaders. Divide into groups of two to four. Have each group list three practical ways to encourage your leaders. For example, sending notes with encouraging Scripture verses or providing much needed rest by babysitting their children for an evening. Then, have each group write three ways they can support their leaders in their work. Ideas might include purchasing study materials or participating in visitation with them.

After a few minutes, allow time for each group to share ideas. Then commit as a group to at least three of these suggestions. You also might encourage each person to choose one to take on personally as well.

TRY THIS ON YOUR OWN
Brave Examples

Select four biblical stories of valor while following God's will. Several Old Testament books, in addition to Joshua, include rich stories depicting the courage of God's people: Genesis, 1 and 2 Samuel, Daniel, Esther, and more. Or pick four stories of heroes of the faith such as Daniel, Joseph, and Deborah.

As you read the four stories you've chosen, search for any of the following in the main characters:

- Ways God himself supported or encouraged them, directly or indirectly.
- Promises of God they held on to.
- Habits that might have strengthened their courage.
- Character traits worth emulating.
- Ways they stayed true to God's commands, despite obstacles.
- People who encouraged them.

Write these on a sheet of paper. Commit to looking for and cultivating these same qualities in your life.

TAKING IT TO THE STREET
Stretching Feels Good

Plan a service project that requires your study group to work together and to step out in courage a bit more than usual. For example, if your group has never done so, go to an area where the homeless gather and, in small groups, pass out simple sack meals to those in need. (Include food items that don't require refrigeration such as peanut butter sandwiches, chips, and fresh fruit.)

However, if your group regularly does such ministry, choose something different. The idea is to be bold and stretch everyone's comfort zones, at least a little. Some ideas include:

- Helping AIDS patients by providing meals, running errands, or assisting with chores. (Your local social services agency will know of organizations that do this.)
- Taking on a simple community project, such as cleaning a park, in coordination with people of another faith, such as Jehovah's Witness or Unitarian.
- Joining the efforts of an organization in your area that assists refugees or new immigrants as they settle into your community. (Again, check with your local social services agencies.)

Be creative and bold. This can be a one-time event or an ongoing project. Then gather to discuss what you learned and how God showed up to support you in exciting ways!

WITH YOUR FAMILY
Courageous Course

Set up an obstacle course in your backyard or at a nearby park. Create it from simple household items such as chairs, cardboard boxes, blankets, scrap wood, laundry baskets, and more. Make sure no obstacles are likely to hurt anyone. Add in a few silly objects such as balloons or toy hoops for participants to play with in some fun way, like holding the balloon on their nose or spinning the hoop three times.

Give everyone a turn. Take turns blindfolding each other and completing the obstacle course only by listening to everyone else shouting out directions. See who can finish the fastest. (This game can also be played indoors.)

When the game is over, gather together for a simple treat like ice cream or popcorn. Talk about the times when players were a little scared to proceed. Share what courage is and how God calls us to be brave when we follow the plan He has for us. And discuss how important it was to obey the instructions being called out. Success isn't possible without listening closely, just as we must listen and obey all that God tells us to do. ◆

JOSHUA 1:1–17

1 After the death of Moses the servant of the LORD, the LORD said to Joshua son of Nun, Moses' aide:

2 "Moses my servant is dead. Now then, you and all these people, get ready to cross the Jordan River into the land I am about to give to them—to the Israelites.

3 I will give you every place where you set your foot, as I promised Moses.

4 Your territory will extend from the desert to Lebanon, and from the great river, the Euphrates—all the Hittite country—to the Great Sea on the west.

5 No one will be able to stand up against you all the days of your life. As I was with Moses, so I will be with you; I will never leave you nor forsake you.

6 "Be strong and courageous, because you will lead these people to inherit the land I swore to their forefathers to give them.

7 Be strong and very courageous. Be careful to obey all the law my servant Moses gave you; do not turn from it to the right or to the left, that you may be successful wherever you go.

8 Do not let this Book of the Law depart from your mouth; meditate on it day and night, so that you may be careful to do everything written in it. Then you will be prosperous and successful.

9 Have I not commanded you? Be strong and courageous. Do not be terrified; do not be discouraged, for the LORD your God will be with you wherever you go."

10 So Joshua ordered the officers of the people:

11 "Go through the camp and tell the people, 'Get your supplies ready. Three days from now you will cross the Jordan here to go in and take possession of the land the LORD your God is giving you for your own.'"

12 But to the Reubenites, the Gadites and the half-tribe of Manasseh, Joshua said,

13 "Remember the command that Moses the servant of the LORD gave you: 'The LORD your God is giving you rest and has granted you this land.'

14 Your wives, your children and your livestock may stay in the land that Moses gave you east of the Jordan, but all your fighting men, fully armed, must cross over ahead of your brothers. You are to help your brothers

15 until the LORD gives them rest, as he has done for you, and until they too have taken possession of the land that the LORD your God is giving them. After that, you may go back and occupy your own

God Chooses a Leader

God chooses to do a great work through a surrendered leader.

INTO THE SUBJECT

When a company needs a new CEO, it may hire someone from outside the company or it may promote from within. When Moses, Israel's leader for forty years, died, where did his successor come from? Who brought him onboard?

INTO THE WORD

1. Read Exodus 17:13; 24:13; Numbers 14:30, 38; and Deuteronomy 34:9. What do these verses reveal about Joshua's character and credentials?

2. Based on Joshua 1:2–9, what would you say Joshua's job description included?

3. Compare Joshua 1:5 and Hebrews 13:5. How does assurance of the Lord's presence enable you to accept challenges?

4. Why do you think your spiritual leaders need to be strong and courageous?

5. How has the practice of obeying and meditating on God's Word helped you lead a successful life?

6. Read Numbers 32:25–32 and Deuteronomy 3:12–20. What were the Reubenites, the Gadites, and the half-tribe of Manasseh obligated to do before occupying their own land?

7. Why is unity so important to the success of a church?

8. Specifically, what help will you give your Christian brothers and sisters in the ongoing battle against the Devil and his forces?

INTO THE WORLD

Count on the Lord's presence as you stand for Jesus this week, and carry the sword of the Spirit at all times.

land, which Moses the servant of the LORD gave you east of the Jordan toward the sunrise."

16 Then they answered Joshua, "Whatever you have commanded us we will do, and wherever you send us we will go.

17 Just as we fully obeyed Moses, so we will obey you. Only may the LORD your God be with you as he was with Moses.

Four Speeches

The lesson fleshes out the four speeches found in Joshua 1:1–17. Answer the following questions:

1. In the first speech, who commissioned Joshua?

_____

_____

2. The literary type of this speech is composed of four common elements. What are two of these elements?

_____

_____

3. Who does Joshua give commands to in the second speech? Be as specific as possible.

_____

_____

4. What is the ultimate goal of the commands Joshua gives to the two-and-a-half tribes?

_____

_____

5. Why is the people's pledge of obedience to Joshua ironic?

_____

_____

FOR PERSONAL REFLECTION:

When have you pledged obedience to God but have not obeyed?

_____

_____

Faith breaks down the walls between people.

BREAKING DOWN WALLS

Joshua 2:1–14, 17–21

WHY THIS MATTERS

If a poor man wearing unwashed, tattered clothes wandered into the average church service, would he receive a loving welcome? More than a few pastors lament the unwillingness of congregants to accept church visitors whose socioeconomic status is obviously low. But God loves all kinds of people unconditionally and invites "whosoever will" to become a member of His family through faith in Jesus.

And didn't Jesus walk among the poor and reach out to social outcasts: lepers, tax collectors, prostitutes, and drunkards? He received sinners as they were but did not leave them as they were. He changed their lives forever.

This lesson inspires us to relate to everyone as an object of God's love.

BIBLE COMMENTARY

By Jim Moretz

The context of this story is God's continuing faithfulness to Israel amid external dangers and internal faithlessness. Moses was dead, but God appointed Joshua to lead the people into the Promised Land. God said to Joshua, "As I was with Moses, so I will be with you. I will never leave you nor forsake you" (Josh. 1:5). Then God repeated two basic principles to guide Joshua. First, "Do not let this Book of the Law depart from your mouth; meditate on it day and night, so that you may be careful to do everything in it" (1:8; see Deut. 4:1–14 for the similar command given to the people through Moses). Second, God repeated the injunction not to fear (Num. 21:34), for He was working ahead of Joshua to ensure the Israelites' victory. Of course, Israel would violate both of these principles.

Most striking is how the battles against the kings Sihon and Og were branded on the collective conscience of Israel. Because God worked specifically through Israelite history, the Old Testament preserves God's miraculous acts and recounts them as examples of God's faithfulness. We are used to reading recounts of the exodus, even in the New Testament (see background Scriptures). However, these two battles also played an important role, not only in this story, but in its larger context. In fact, these battles were used as historical markers for the giving of the Law in Deuteronomy 1:3–5. They were remembered in the time of Solomon. First Kings 4:19 describes Gilead as "the country of Sihon king of the Amorites and the country of Og king of Bashan." They were also referenced, along with the events in Joshua, when Ezra and Nehemiah reestablished the covenant:

You gave them kingdoms and nations, allotting to them even the remotest frontiers. They took over the country of Sihon king of Heshbon and the

KEY VERSE

By faith the prostitute Rahab, because she welcomed the spies, was not killed with those who were disobedient.
—Hebrews 11:31

BACKGROUND SCRIPTURES

Acts 7; Hebrews 8:9; 11; Jude 5
  Exodus story recounted
Numbers 21:21–35; Deuteronomy 2:24—3:11
  Defeat of Sihon and Og
Matthew 1:5
  Rahab in lineage of Jesus
Ruth 2–4
  Portrait of Boaz

DAILY BIBLE READINGS

Monday: Genesis 26:17–25
Tuesday: John 14:23–31
Wednesday: Galatians 3:26–29
Thursday: Romans 15:5–7
Friday: 1 Corinthians 12:21–27
Saturday: Joshua 2:1–14, 17–21
Sunday: Psalm 28

WHAT DO YOU THINK?
It's a classic moral dilemma: Do you lie to evil, ungodly people to save a life? God commands us not to lie, but what if telling the truth might be abetting murder?

country of Og king of Bashan. You made their sons as numerous as the stars in the sky, and you brought them into the land that you told their fathers to enter and possess. Their sons went in and took possession of the land. You subdued before them the Canaanites, who lived in the land; you handed the Canaanites over to them, along with their kings and the peoples of the land, to deal with them as they pleased. They captured fortified cities and fertile land; they took possession of houses filled with all kinds of good things, wells already dug, vineyards, olive groves and fruit trees in abundance. They ate to the full and were well-nourished; they reveled in your great goodness. (Neh. 9:22–25)

Later we will examine how this came to be, but for now it is important to see the events in this story and in the whole book of Joshua not in isolation, but as a part of a greater whole, the history of the salvation of Israel.

Spying Out Jericho and the Whole Land (Josh. 2:1–7)

By sending spies, Joshua was following the military strategy of Moses. "After Moses had sent spies to Jazer, the Israelites captured its surrounding settlements and drove out the Amorites who were there" (Num. 21:32). Jericho was a fortified city just east of the Jordan River. It was considered the gateway to the west by the Israelites. Much intelligence could be gathered about the land of Canaan from such a city.

AHA!
Jericho's thick wall couldn't protect anyone, but a simple scarlet cord placed with faith in God could.

The NIV notes that the word translated **prostitute** in verse 1 could also be understood as "innkeeper." Either way, Rahab was on the edge of society. Interestingly, verse 15 tells us that her home was a part of the city wall. She was tolerated because her service was needed, but she was effectively a nonperson.

Note **the king of Jericho** (v. 2). During the times of this story, the land was dominated by city-states. That is, each city exerted the maximum independence it could depending upon its size and resources. While periodic dynasties arose that controlled groups of cities, the stronger cities usually reasserted their independence when the controlling king died or when the controlling city weakened or was captured. The fact that the king of Jericho received the report suggests that he, or the city itself, was considered a controlling factor in the area, and they were definitely asserting their independence.

Another characteristic of city-states in this time was that they generally had protective walls and gates. Thus, there is literary irony in the location of Rahab's home. It was the "crack" in the wall. There is also economic irony associated with the walls. Walled cities experienced population growth that often exhausted the food production within the walls. Therefore, the walled cities levied production taxes on unwalled villages and homes in exchange for protection. However, cities could outgrow the production taxes, which led to tax increases, which eventually led to revolts. Thus, the irony was that the wall built to protect the city from the outside actually weakened the city from the inside.

DID YOU KNOW?
After harvest, flax, which often grew to a height of three to four feet, was left on rooftops to dry. Craftspeople then turned the flax into yarn that formed linen cloth.

The gates were closed at or near sunset and not generally reopened until dawn. That is why Rahab's story was convincing to the pursuers. If the spies wanted to see other parts of the land, or if they were wary of being trapped in Jericho for the night, they would have left before the city gate was closed.

There was no other way out. So the spies were safe until morning since the gate was closed after the pursuers left (v. 7).

This part of the story reminds us of the Hebrew midwives who lied to the Egyptians in order to save the Hebrew babies. It also reminds us of Christians who lied to Gestapo soldiers in order to save Jews. These are interesting examples of the descriptive nature of the Bible. All of these people acted within the will of God and yet used deception to do so.

The Story Goes Ahead of the Spies (Josh. 2:8–11)

The stories of the defeat of Sihon and Og are recounted in Numbers 21:21–35 and Deuteronomy 2:24—3:11. That these battles were seared on the collective Israelite memory and the memory of their neighbors is evidenced in verse 10. Similar statements are recorded from the Gibeonites in Joshua 9:9–10: "Your servants have come from a very distant country because of the fame of the LORD your God. For we have heard reports of him: all that he did in Egypt, and all that he did to the two kings of the Amorites east of the Jordan—Sihon king of Heshbon, and Og king of Bashan, who reigned in Ashtaroth."

Ruins of the ancient city of Jericho

The question is how these people heard these stories. One possible answer is through Psalms 135 and 136. Compare verses 8–11 of Joshua 2 with verses 5–12 of Psalm 135. Also note the comparison with Psalm 136:10–22.

If these songs were sung faithfully by the Israelites, it is possible that they were the media through which the stories were spread. Battle songs would be interesting to other people who came in contact with the Israelites, especially ones that recounted the defeat of strong kings. In an age of limited literacy, songs would serve as an effective way to spread stories. Psalm 136 seems more developed than Psalm 135 and is probably dependent upon it for the material. This is further evidence of the lasting effect the defeat of Sihon and Og had on the Israelite community. These events were evidently used as propaganda with positive results against future enemies.

Not only were stories of the battles preserved, they were issued as evidence that the Lord had already given the land to the Israelites "as an inheritance." That is, the Israelites had the right to the land regardless of who was already there. It was not because they claimed it, but because their God—the living God who had created everything and thus had the right to give as He saw fit—had given them the land. Interestingly, ancient documents show that all the civilizations in this area were concerned with property rights within their legal systems. The "inheritance" language would have been quite powerful in their understanding. If human inheritance was guarded by the law, then divine inheritance was unquestionable. Thus, the hearts of those in Jericho failed because of the Israelites. If their God had given them the powerful kings Sihon and Og and delivered them from Egypt, then surely Jericho was theirs to take. Everyone had heard the songs.

The Covenant (Josh. 2:12–14, 17–21)

Rahab wanted assurances that her actions on behalf of the spies would result not only in her salvation, but also in the salvation of her entire family. So

WHAT DO YOU THINK?
"Inheritance rights" determined who claimed, received, and even fought for a given region. Israel's claim that they inherited the land directly from God was especially significant. What, role, if any, does such a perspective play in Middle Eastern conflict today?

AHA!
Sometimes simple stories or songs of God's faithfulness are the most powerful witness of all.

DID YOU KNOW?
Cities like Jericho generally had two walls about twelve to fifteen feet apart. People placed wooden logs across the span between the walls and built houses on top of them. This may be how Rahab's house was designed.

Rahab recognized the truth about Israel's God. The spies saw her faith, not judging her by her culture, background, or past. In what ways do such things impact how you see someone's potential to come to God?

PRAYER

Father, thank You for the "scarlet cord" of Your salvation, pointing ultimately to Your Son. Forgive me for judging others by their past or their background. And grant me wisdom to find Your provision in unexpected places.

she made a pact with them. There are two parallels to this story. Most evident is the parallel between the blood of the lambs placed on the doorposts in the exodus story and the scarlet cord placed in the window. The second parallel is between the covenant between God and Abraham in Genesis 15 and verses 19 and 20 of this story. In Genesis, God passed between the severed offering animals to accept Abraham's blood on His hands if He was not faithful to the covenant. In the same way, the spies, God's representatives, accepted the same toward Rahab. Granted, this is more of an echo than a parallel, but the agreement here was as much between Rahab and the Lord as it was between Rahab and the spies.

Therefore, it illustrates the motif of the "two ways"—the way of obedience that leads to life and the way of disobedience that leads to death. This is one of the themes of the entire Old Testament. It transcends nationalities, gender, and social status. This is the way the national God of the Israelites claimed authority over the world. Whoever was obedient to Him was included in His covenant of life. We see in Matthew 1:5 that Rahab gave birth to Boaz, as also recorded in the book of Ruth. Thus the prostitute was included in the lineage of Jesus, God's Savior of the entire world. So the covenant was complete. Her entire family was brought in. ◆

JOSHUA 2:1–14, 17–21

1 Then Joshua son of Nun secretly sent two spies from Shittim. "Go, look over the land," he said, "especially Jericho." So they went and entered the house of a prostitute named Rahab and stayed there.

2 The king of Jericho was told, "Look! Some of the Israelites have come here tonight to spy out the land."

3 So the king of Jericho sent this message to Rahab: "Bring out the men who came to you and entered your house, because they have come to spy out the whole land."

4 But the woman had taken the two men and hidden them. She said, "Yes, the men came to me, but I did not know where they had come from.

5 At dusk, when it was time to close the city gate, the men left. I don't know which way they went. Go after them quickly. You may catch up with them."

6 (But she had taken them up to the roof and hidden them under the stalks of flax she had laid out on the roof.)

7 So the men set out in pursuit of the spies on the road that leads to the fords of the Jordan, and as soon as the pursuers had gone out, the gate was shut.

8 Before the spies lay down for the night, she went up on the roof

9 and said to them, "I know that the LORD has given this land to you and that a great fear of you has fallen on us, so that all who live in this country are melting in fear because of you.

10 We have heard how the LORD dried up the water of the Red Sea for you when you came out of Egypt, and what you did to Sihon and Og, the two kings of the Amorites east of the Jordan, whom you completely destroyed.

11 When we heard of it, our hearts melted and everyone's courage failed because of you, for the LORD your God is God in heaven above and on the earth below.

12 Now then, please swear to me by the LORD that you will show kindness to my family, because I have shown kindness to you. Give me a sure sign

13 that you will spare the lives of my father and mother, my brothers and sisters, and all who belong to them, and that you will save us from death."

14 "Our lives for your lives!" the men assured her. "If you don't tell what we are doing, we will treat you kindly and faithfully when the LORD gives us the land."

17 The men said to her, "This oath you made us swear will not be binding on us

18 unless, when we enter the land, you have tied this scarlet cord in the window through which you let us down, and unless you have brought your father and mother, your brothers and all your family into your house.

Breaking Down Walls

Faith breaks down the walls between people.

INTO THE SUBJECT

Espionage, intrigue, suspense, and surprise—all these elements run through the story of scouting out Jericho's defenses. Could God break down Jericho's walls?

INTO THE WORD

1. What do you think Joshua wanted to accomplish by sending two spies to Jericho?

2. Read Joshua 2:1–15. Why do you agree or disagree that God directed the spies to Rahab's house? If you agree, what might have been His reasons for leading them there?

3. What indication do you find in verses 8–11 that Israel could have destroyed Jericho at an earlier time?

4. Why do you agree that most of our fears are unfounded?

5. Do you believe it is ethical to use deception to save lives, for example, in time of war?

6. What do you find commendable about Rahab?

7. Do you think the scarlet cord (vv. 18, 21) symbolizes the blood of Christ that saves believing sinners from destruction? Why or why not?

8. Read Matthew 1:5. What divine characteristics do you see in the fact that Rahab became an ancestress of Jesus Christ?

INTO THE WORLD

Be ready to share the gospel without bias. Even the most unlikely person may believe and be saved as you witness this week.

19 If anyone goes outside your house into the street, his blood will be on his own head; we will not be responsible. As for anyone who is in the house with you, his blood will be on our head if a hand is laid on him.

20 But if you tell what we are doing, we will be released from the oath you made us swear."

21 "Agreed," she replied. "Let it be as you say." So she sent them away and they departed. And she tied the scarlet cord in the window.

BATTLE SONG

There are many great battle songs in the Bible as the lesson suggests. Battle songs were sung to tell the story of the war, to make sure the battles were preserved and not forgotten. Write a song about a battle or war that is more recent. Consider focusing on World War II in the 1940s or the Gulf War in the early 1990s. Or write a song about a personal battle you've faced—cancer, a financial crisis, and so forth.

_____

_____

_____

_____

_____

_____

_____

_____

_____

_____

_____

_____

_____

_____

INTERACTIVE LEARNING IDEAS

GET THE CLASS INVOLVED
A Classic Conundrum

Christians sometimes face difficult moral choices. A classic moral puzzle asks what should be done when ungodly or evil people desire to kill God's people and you must either lie to protect them or tell the truth and hand them over. Presenting this question to the group, perhaps giving the example of Christians hiding Jews from the Nazis.

Ask the group to list the moral concerns. It's time to brainstorm, not debate. Is lying still a sin under such circumstances? Is telling the truth abetting murder? What responsibility is there under God's commands to protect the defenseless? What about obeying authorities?

Make a few concordances available and take ten minutes to have small groups look up Scripture verses on the subjects you raised: lying, truth, responsibility toward government, defending the defenseless. Then list on a board the arguments for deception and the arguments for telling the truth. Finally, for fun, make a third list of creative alternatives (tell the truth and fight in defense, evade the question, and more). Discuss how a Christian can best make decisions on challenging questions such as these.

TRY THIS ON YOUR OWN
Peek over Jericho's Walls

Dig into Jericho's history. Starting with a concordance, look up all references to the city and read the stories. Grab a study Bible and check out any notes it includes on the city. Many even include maps that show where the city was located. Then, in a Bible encyclopedia or handbook, read about the city and its history. (If such resources aren't available, hop online and check out some of the great Bible study tools available there or borrow some from your church library.) Search online for information about Jericho in online encyclopedias or other reference sites.

As you work, consider the following: Why was it a key city for the Israelites? What made it a challenging conquest? What were some unique characteristics of the city? If you lived there and heard about the Israelites, would you have been concerned or felt safe and why? If you were an Israelite, how would you have felt about the task of taking that city? What might you have said about Jericho, had you been one of the spies?

TAKING IT TO THE STREET
Wall Hunt

As a group, go on a photo scavenger hunt. You can go as one big group or divide into smaller groups. Each group should have a camera. The goal is to take as many pictures of different types of walls as possible. Provide a list of several specific types. Have people look for walls of different materials such as brick, stone, or stucco. Have them photograph the most unusual wall, the tallest wall, or the shortest wall. Search for fun things, such as walls with a mural, graffiti (nothing offensive), vines, or cracks. Think of challenging things to find or silly things people can do at the walls.

After an hour or two, gather somewhere for coffee, dessert, or a similar treat. Look at each other's pictures. Have a couple small prizes for certain categories: best picture, most found on the list, ugliest wall, etc. If possible, have a laptop available for viewing digital pictures.

As you wrap up, talk about the wall of Jericho and the problem it presented for the Israelites. Discuss the walls we may have in our own lives, things that prevent us from claiming our own "Promised Land." Ask what difficulties these walls present and how we might break them down. Since getting personal might be hard, start by asking about the walls people have in general, then encourage people to share personally.

WITH YOUR FAMILY
Quiet on the Set

Read the story of Rahab and the spies. Together as a family or group of friends, write a script based on the story, everyone taking an acting role. Create costumes and props out of simple household items (a red ribbon for the cord, a cut-up cardboard box for a door, and a sheet for the wall). With a video camera (borrow, if necessary), record everyone acting out the script and create your own fun family film. It'll be a keepsake you'll treasure. Watch it together as a family movie night. Then discuss the story and the role everyone played in God's plan. ◆

LESSON 3

WE WORSHIP AND GOD WORKS

Joshua 3:5–17; 4:4–7

KEY VERSE

Joshua told the people, "Consecrate yourselves, for tomorrow the LORD will do amazing things among you."
—Joshua 3:5

WHY THIS MATTERS

Our impossible circumstances are God's magnificent opportunities. When we face a medical crisis, He gets us through it. When our finances shrink, He stretches our resources and meets our needs. When we are unemployed, He rallies friends and loved ones to help. When we think we can't go on, His everlasting arms uphold us. When we think disappointments will crush us, He shows us they are His appointments to grow us.

This lesson shows how God made a way across the Jordan for His people when the river was at flood stage, not when it was ankle deep. By faith the people stepped into the raging river. This lesson inspires us to trust God and "get our feet wet" when life seems impossible.

BIBLE COMMENTARY

By Patricia J. David

Israel had waited a long time for this day. Some six hundred years ago God had covenanted with Abraham to give them the land of Canaan. They always knew it would be theirs, but the fertile, strategic strip of land seemed always to be just beyond their reach. And now they stood at the doorway to Canaan. But one obstacle remained: the flooded Jordan River. Though normally an easily passable stream, at flood stage the Jordan was formidable. Its waters were swift and treacherous. Once again the Israelites were at the end of their resources. Once again they needed to experience the intervention of the God who had led them there.

And God did not disappoint them.

BACKGROUND SCRIPTURES

Exodus 14:13–22
    The parting of the
    Red Sea
2 Kings 2:8
    Elijah and Elisha
    crossed the Jordan
    River on dry ground.
Psalm 114
    Psalm linking the
    parting of the Red Sea
    and the parting of the
    Jordan River

Consecration: Preparation for the Miracle (Josh. 3:5)

Joshua addressed the people of Israel: **Consecrate yourselves, for tomorrow the LORD will do amazing things among you**. The Hebrew here for "amazing things" means something out of the ordinary, a miracle. God was going to step into history again to accomplish the impossible. In order for the people to be ready for the miracle, they had to prepare. Not just outwardly or militarily— they had to prepare their hearts.

The call to consecration involved washing their clothes (see Ex. 19:10–14), an outward expression of their inward cleansing. It was a call to solemnity, to serious consideration of what lay ahead. It was a call to repentance and complete devotion to God in anticipation of what He was going to do.

DAILY BIBLE READINGS

Monday: Exodus
            14:13–22
Tuesday: Exodus 15:1–7
Wednesday: Philippians
            1:3–11
Thursday: 1 Corinthians
            11:23–26
Friday: Leviticus
            20:7–8
Saturday: Joshua 3:5–17;
            4:4–7
Sunday: Psalm 29

Cooperation: Participation in the Miracle (Josh. 3:6–17)

Normally it was the Kohathites who were charged with carrying the ark of the covenant and the other sacred furnishings of the Tent of Meeting in the

Israelites' travels (see Num. 4:15). But this was no normal occasion. It was a religious procession, and so it was fitting that the **priests** (v. 6) would take the uncovered ark and lead the way with it. The **ark of the covenant** was a visible symbol of God's presence. And now the ark, which was usually in the midst of the camp, was to **pass on ahead of the people**, symbolizing to all Israel that God himself was leading the way.

But they would have to follow. In the desert the Lord had led them by a cloud by day and a pillar of fire by night (Ex. 33:9–10; Num. 14:14). Now this was gone. They had to walk by faith if they wanted to see the miracle.

And the Lord said to Joshua, "Today I will begin to exalt you in the eyes of all Israel, so they may know that I am with you as I was with Moses" (v. 7). The miracle about to take place had more than one purpose. It would be necessary for entering the land, but it would also be a testimony that God had ordained Joshua as Israel's leader. After the miraculous crossing of the Red Sea forty years earlier, Exodus 14:31 tells us, "And when the Israelites saw the great power the Lord displayed against the Egyptians, the people feared the Lord and put their trust in him and in Moses his servant." And the present miracle would have a similar effect: "That day the Lord exalted Joshua in the sight of all Israel; and they revered him all the days of his life, just as they had revered Moses" (Josh. 4:14).

The miracle would also serve as a visible reminder of God's active presence among them and as a guarantee that He would fulfill His promises. **This is how you will know that the living God is among you and that he will certainly drive out before you the Canaanites** (v. 10). In the Hebrew text there is no article ("the") before "living God"; the emphasis is on "living." The miracle would show God as vastly superior to the gods of wood and stone worshiped by the peoples they were about to conquer. The God of Israel was One who could see and hear, who was personal and involved in their lives. He was a God of power, in control over the elements He created and the nations of the earth, vastly superior to any so-called god worshiped in Canaan. As the living God, He had the right to determine who would occupy His land. He would drive out all the inhabitants of Canaan: the Canaanites, who inhabited the lowlands of the seacoast and the Jordan valley, the Hittites to the south, the Hivites in the northern region of Mount Hermon, the Perizzites in the central highlands, the Girgashites near the Sea of Galilee, the Amorites who inhabited the mountainous regions, and the Jebusites occupying the region around Jerusalem. God

Comparison of the Red Sea and Jordan River Crossings	
Similarities	
It was a seemingly insurmountable obstacle of water.	
Both were preceded by acts of consecration (Ex. 13:2; Josh. 3:5).	
God parted the waters, which created a wall or heap.	
The people passed through on dry ground.	
The miracle established the validity of leadership.	
Both revealed God's power over "gods" and nations.	
Differences	
Crossing the Red Sea in Exodus	**Crossing the Jordan River in Joshua**
A strong wind blew all night long.	There was no wind, but a possible earthquake.
The sea parted, then the people entered.	The priests entered and then the waters parted.
They were led by a pillar of cloud.	They were led by the ark of the covenant.
They were fleeing an Egyptian army.	They were pursuing the Promised Land.

The Jordan River. Some areas are lush, while other have less foliage around the bank.

WHAT DO YOU THINK?

God assured Israel they would win their Promised Land, and He even performed miracles to assist along the way. But He didn't just give it to them; they had to fight for it. How does our participation in God's blessings benefit us?

AHA!

Even though we still have to fight, and maybe even slosh through some mud, God still graciously parts the seas in our lives today.

DID YOU KNOW?

The name *Gilgal* means "circle of stones," and since stone circles exist all over Palestine, many towns shared that name.

was greater than all these nations. He was the **LORD of all the earth** (vv. 11, 13).

Joshua foretold what was about to happen: **And as soon as the priests . . . set foot in the Jordan, its waters flowing downstream will be cut off and stand up in a heap** (v. 13). God was about to perform a miracle curiously similar to the crossing of the Red Sea (see Ex. 14:21–22 and Ps. 114, where the two events are linked). It was a new generation that needed a new miracle. But this time, much more faith was required. In the crossing of the Red Sea, a strong wind blew all night long, parting the waters and drying the ground before the Israelites stepped in to cross; this time the priests would have to take a step of faith and set foot in the river before the miracle happened. If they wanted to participate in the miracle, they would have to cooperate with God's plan. They would have to do it His way, walking in faith.

The crossing of the Jordan took place in the month of Nissan (the first month, March–April; see Josh. 4:19) at the time of the barley harvest when the spring rains and the melted snow from Mount Hermon swelled the Jordan River. **Now the Jordan is at flood stage all during harvest** (v. 15). The Hebrew literally says the Jordan was "flowing over all its banks." There was a torrent of water. It was an intimidating sight, but the priests took God at His word and stepped into the water. And **as soon as . . . their feet touched the water's edge, the water from upstream stopped flowing. It piled up in a heap a great distance away, at a town called Adam** (vv. 15–16). The miracle was immediate. And it was just as God had promised through Joshua.

We don't know exactly where this miracle took place, but verse 16 does tell us that **the people crossed over opposite Jericho**. Two million people had to cross. And they had to stay a thousand yards away from the ark (3:4). It is probable that the Israelites were spread out over miles as they crossed the Jordan.

The water piled up at a town called Adam, generally associated with Tell ed-Damiyeh, sixteen miles north of the ford opposite Jericho. On December 8, 1267, the high banks of the Jordan near this tell collapsed, damming the river for ten hours. On July 11, 1927, the same thing occurred, this time damming the Jordan for twenty-one hours. The Jordan River, geologists tell us, follows a fault line, making the region prone to small earthquakes (which may be referenced in Ps. 114:4, 6–7). If God used a natural phenomenon, such as an earthquake, to induce this miracle, it was a miracle nonetheless. His timing was perfect. And the **priests . . . stood firm on dry ground in the middle of the Jordan, while all Israel passed by until the whole nation had completed the crossing on dry ground** (v. 17). Without an all-night wind (as in the Red Sea parting), the ground was made instantly dry and firm. Dry ground— *harabah* in Hebrew—means "not covered with water," not necessarily powder dry. But it was dry enough to make passage safe and effortless.

Crossing the Jordan into Canaan marked a new beginning for Israel. They were leaving their past behind. They were entering into a hostile land. It had been promised to them, but they would have to fight for it. It wouldn't be easy, but if they continued to follow the Lord and obey Him, they would be a part of the miracle of the acquisition of the land.

Commemoration: Preservation of the Miracle (Josh. 4:4–7)

Before the Israelites had crossed the Jordan, Joshua set apart twelve men, one from each of the tribes of Israel, for a special task (4:4; see 3:12). Now he commands them, **Go over before the ark** [not before in time, but "in the presence of" the ark] **. . . into the middle of the Jordan. Each of you is to take up a stone on his shoulder** (v. 5). These men took their stones from the very spot where the priests had stood with the ark of the covenant (4:2), and they set them up (either in a pile or a circle) at Gilgal, where the Israelites set up camp (4:20). The rough memorial was **to serve as a sign among** them (v. 6). It was to be a visual reminder of the miracle that had taken place. In 1 Samuel 11:15 and 2 Samuel 19:15, national gatherings were later held here, probably because of this faith-evoking memorial. It was a reminder to them, but it was also to be a testimony to future generations. **In the future, when your children ask you, "What do these stones mean?" tell them . . . These stones are to be a memorial to the people of Israel forever** (vv. 6–7).

God was always concerned that faith in Him be passed down from one generation to another (see Ps. 145:4). The sacrifices and feasts, the Sabbath celebration, the rituals and traditions—all these were tools for teaching successive generations about the God of Israel (see Deut. 4:9; 6:6–9). They would be reminders of His miracles and His expectations. They would serve as an enduring testimony. The history of God's work among them would be preserved and recounted, invoking faith in each new generation.

Today we rarely use symbols as reminders of God's faithfulness. But we have the written Word of God, the testimony not only of the Israelites, but also of the apostles who bore witness to the greatest miracle of all—the resurrection of Jesus Christ. And we have our own miracle stories of God's work in our individual lives. We have an obligation to preserve these miracles, to find a way to commemorate them, and to celebrate them so our children, and our children's children, hear about the greatness of the living God. ◆

WHAT ABOUT YOU?
God taught His people many ways to memorialize His work in their lives, and to remember important truths: feasts, memorial stones, and rituals, for example. What physical reminder do you use to recall God's hand in your life?

PRAYER
Lord, You are so good to me. Thank You for parting the "Jordan Rivers" in my life. Help me to recognize Your gracious hand and to remember Your work on my behalf.

INTERACTIVE LEARNING IDEAS

GET THE CLASS INVOLVED
Remembering Together

God gave His people ways to remember His miracles and works on their behalf. It's easy for time to fade them from memory. In addition to the memorial stones mentioned in Joshua, God established feasts such as the Passover—and, later the Lord's Supper—and rituals such as the yearly building of booths.

As a group, brainstorm ways your church might create a physical memorial to God's great and miraculous works. The memorial should be tangible and ongoing. It should be placed somewhere public to encourage others. Strive to ensure the "miracles" it memorializes will be specific and known to all. Here are a few suggestions to get you started:

- Invite people to anonymously write answers to their prayers on a wall in the church. Yes, directly on the wall in marker . . . a "praise wall"!
- If God has done something significant in your church recently, have a plaque made in honor of what He has done.
- Place a journal, or several, in a common area of the church and invite people to share praises and miracles in it. Encourage people to visit it when they need a lift.

Once your group has several ideas, choose one from your list and make it happen.

TRY THIS ON YOUR OWN
Everyday a Gift from God

While public remembrances of God's hand in our lives are powerful, sometimes what we most need is a more personal way to remember what God has done in our lives.

If you do not have a journal, purchase one. If you do, allow space for the following activity. At the end of each day, write down one to three ways God was faithful or answered prayer. A sentence or two will do. Many of these will be meaningful, everyday evidences of His loving care. (On difficult days, it might just be that God was with you.)

But sometimes God will do something particularly powerful in your life. A "parting the Jordan" moment. Spend more time writing these out in detail, sharing the specifics of the need and what God did. Enjoy looking back through the notebook every month or year and remembering God's hand in your life.

TAKING IT TO THE STREET
Prayer for the Crossing

Ask the church leadership for the names of people facing their own "Jordan River," who might appreciate some support. This might be someone fighting cancer or a single mom experiencing difficult times. As a group, visit that person for a time of prayer. Bring at least one small but uplifting gift that will remind them you care . . . sermon DVDs for the homebound cancer patient, or a homemade meal for the single mom to heat later.

If possible, find something practical you can do as a group. Perhaps you can do yard work for the cancer patient or take the single mom's kids to the park for an afternoon off. Then commit to pray for that person on a continuing basis.

WITH YOUR FAMILY
Notes of God's Faithfulness

Create your own family memorial to God's miracles. Purchase an inexpensive, large poster frame. They can be found in craft stores and "big box" superstores. Cut a piece of blank paper to fit the inside the frame. If you don't have paper large enough, try the reverse (white) side of wrapping paper. Write across the top, "We Remember God's Faithfulness." Place it inside the glass of the frame. Cut cardboard to fit around the frame, to create a larger frame a few inches thick. Then cover the cardboard by gluing more white paper around it. Finally, glue the covered cardboard to the frame. Allow to dry.

Gather as a family with markers, stickers, paint, and other artistic items. Together, decorate the frame. Let everyone be as creative as they like. While everyone creates, share the story of the Jordan River crossing and the memorial stones. Discuss why remembering God's miracles and everyday work in our lives is important. Using colorful dry-erase markers, have everyone write some wonderful things God has done in their lives directly on the glass. Then hang the poster frame where everyone can see it. Leave the dry-erase markers nearby so everyone can write praises to God anytime they like. From time to time, write the praises somewhere permanent, wipe the glass clean, and start over. ◆

JOSHUA 3:5–17; 4:4–7

3:5 Joshua told the people, "Consecrate yourselves, for tomorrow the LORD will do amazing things among you."

6 Joshua said to the priests, "Take up the ark of the covenant and pass on ahead of the people." So they took it up and went ahead of them.

7 And the LORD said to Joshua, "Today I will begin to exalt you in the eyes of all Israel, so they may know that I am with you as I was with Moses.

8 Tell the priests who carry the ark of the covenant: 'When you reach the edge of the Jordan's waters, go and stand in the river.'"

9 Joshua said to the Israelites, "Come here and listen to the words of the LORD your God.

10 This is how you will know that the living God is among you and that he will certainly drive out before you the Canaanites, Hittites, Hivites, Perizzites, Girgashites, Amorites and Jebusites.

11 See, the ark of the covenant of the Lord of all the earth will go into the Jordan ahead of you.

12 Now then, choose twelve men from the tribes of Israel, one from each tribe.

13 And as soon as the priests who carry the ark of the LORD—the Lord of all the earth—set foot in the Jordan, its waters flowing downstream will be cut off and stand up in a heap."

14 So when the people broke camp to cross the Jordan, the priests carrying the ark of the covenant went ahead of them.

15 Now the Jordan is at flood stage all during harvest. Yet as soon as the priests who carried the ark reached the Jordan and their feet touched the water's edge,

16 the water from upstream stopped flowing. It piled up in a heap a great distance away, at a town called Adam in the vicinity of Zarethan, while the water flowing down to the Sea of the Arabah (the Salt Sea) was completely cut off. So the people crossed over opposite Jericho.

17 The priests who carried the ark of the covenant of the LORD stood firm on dry ground in the middle of the Jordan, while all Israel passed by until the whole nation had completed the crossing on dry ground.

4:4 So Joshua called together the twelve men he had appointed from the Israelites, one from each tribe,

5 and said to them, "Go over before the ark of the LORD your God into the middle of the Jordan. Each of you is to take up a stone on his shoulder, according to the number of the tribes of the Israelites,

We Worship and God Works

Consecrate yourselves, watch what
God is doing, and remember.

INTO THE SUBJECT

Moving is an adventure, especially when it involves entering an area where the locals will oppose you with all their might. Before moving, wouldn't you pray and place yourself in God's strong hands?

INTO THE WORD

1. According to Joshua 3:2–4, what instructions concerning the ark were the Israelites supposed to follow?

2. Why do you think the people were commanded to keep a distance of about a thousand yards between them and the ark?

3. Why is it so important to be consecrated to the Lord before engaging the enemy?

4. Compare verses 7 and 15. Why did it require an act of faith to obey Joshua's instructions?

5. When did you recently meet a challenge by stepping out in faith?

6. What leadership qualities do you admire in Joshua? In the priests?

7. What was the intended purpose of the monument of stones (vv. 4–7)?

8. What are some excellent ways to remind future generations of the Lord's wonderful deeds?

INTO THE WORLD

Begin every day with a prayer of consecration, and during the day look for ways to step out in faith to follow the Lord.

6 to serve as a sign among you. In the future, when your children ask you, 'What do these stones mean?'

7 tell them that the flow of the Jordan was cut off before the ark of the covenant of the LORD. When it crossed the Jordan, the waters of the Jordan were cut off. These stones are to be a memorial to the people of Israel forever."

MIRACLE MEMORIAL

Twelve men took stones from the place where the priests entered the Jordan River. They took these stones to create a memorial that would serve as a visual reminder to their children of the miracle God performed and that He was true to what He said He would do.

Think of a time in your life when God fulfilled a promise to you or performed a miracle. Maybe it's the promise of Joshua 1:5, when God told Joshua He would never leave nor forsake him or the Israelites. Perhaps a financial crisis afflicted you, and God brought the right amount of money at the right time. Draw a picture of the memorial you would build to represent what God did in this particular instance.

Sin is infectious, and its effects are extensive.

SIN INFECTS AND AFFECTS
Joshua 7:2–13, 19–26

WHY THIS MATTERS

Toys were almost a fatal attraction for a three-year-old boy in Sydney, Australia. Lured by the toys he saw in a vending machine at an Australian shopping center and separated from his mother, little Callum must have climbed into the machine through the delivery chute. He reached the toys, but couldn't climb back out. When his mother called his name, he answered from inside the machine. Fortunately rescuers were able to remove the door from the back of the machine and extricate the boy. He had been trapped for about an hour.

This lesson emphasizes the harm covetousness can cause, and it motivates us to make God's will our highest priority.

BIBLE COMMENTARY

By Kelvin G. Friebel

Joshua 7 deals with the Israelites' initial attempts to capture the city of Ai. Ai is located in the hill country about fifteen miles west of Jericho. Joshua 7:2–13, 19–26 is part of the larger literary unit of 7:1—8:29 that has the seven subsections (see chart).

7:1	Narrative report of the sin
7:2–5	Israelites' initial attack and defeat at Ai
7:6–9	Israelites' response and Joshua's prayer
7:10–15	Divine response to the prayer
7:16–26	Israelites' discernment of the sin and its punishment
8:1–2	Divine promise and commands for the battle against Ai
8:3–29	Capture of Ai

Initial Attack and the Subsequent Defeat (Josh. 7:2–5)

Totally unaware that a sin had been committed, Joshua sent out spies to investigate the situation of Ai: **Now Joshua sent men from Jericho to Ai . . . and told them, "Go up and spy out the region." So the men went up and spied out Ai** (v. 2). Earlier, when the spies were sent to check out Jericho, God gave a promise: "I have delivered Jericho into your hands" (6:2) and specific instructions about the battle strategy (6:3–5). Joshua moved against Jericho in complete obedience to the divine instructions. Here in chapter 7, there is no divine assurance of victory or battle plan for Ai. In the absence of such, one would expect Joshua to make an inquiry of God so as to secure them (see Num. 27:20–21). An inquiry of God likely would have revealed to Joshua the divine disfavor (compare 1 Sam. 14:36–43). But Joshua forged ahead without any divine directive, following instead the suggestion of the spies: **Send two or three thousand men to take it. . . . So about three thousand men went up** (Josh. 7:3–4).

KEY VERSE

Go, consecrate the people. Tell them, "Consecrate yourselves in preparation for tomorrow; for this is what the LORD, the God of Israel, says: That which is devoted is among you, O Israel. You cannot stand against your enemies until you remove it."
—Joshua 7:13

BACKGROUND SCRIPTURES

Deuteronomy 7:1–6; 13:12–18; 20:16–18; Joshua 6:18–19
     Commands regarding "devoted things"
Deuteronomy 28:15–68
     Consequences of disobedience
Acts 5:1–11
     God's punishment for sin
1 Corinthians 5:1–13
     Corporate effects of sin

DAILY BIBLE READINGS

Monday: Romans 2:1–6
Tuesday: 1 Corinthians 5:6–13
Wednesday: Ephesians 4:25–32
Thursday: 1 Corinthians 12:12–20
Friday: Titus 3:1–11
Saturday: Joshua 7:2–13, 19–26
Sunday: Psalm 30

WHAT DO YOU THINK?
Joshua, expecting victory,
forged ahead without
consulting God and was
defeated. It's easy to be
over-confident after a
victory. What are some
ways to guard against that?

AHA!
When God's favor doesn't
seem to be on us, our first
response should be to check
whether we've disobeyed
Him in any way.

DID YOU KNOW?
The city of Ai sat fifteen
miles away from Jericho
on top of a ridge. A ravine
separated the two cities.
Its conquest would provide
Israel a foothold in the
central highlands beyond
the Jordan Valley.

Unlike the Jericho narrative, which ended with the people's triumphant victory due to God's fighting the battle for them, the Ai account tersely notes: **but they were routed by the men of Ai, who killed about thirty-six of them. They chased the Israelites from the city gate as far as the stone quarries and struck them down on the slopes** (vv. 4–5). Thirty-six might seem like an insignificant number of losses, but given the lack of casualties against the more daunting city of Jericho, the loss of thirty-six probably seemed excessive.

Besides the military defeat of the Israelites, this was also a psychological defeat, as **the hearts of the people melted and became like water** (v. 5). Whereas before, at Jericho, the Canaanites' hearts were melting in fear before the Israelites (2:11, 24; 5:1), now the situation was completely reversed.

Joshua's Prayer (Josh. 7:6–9)

In response to the defeat, Joshua and the elders of Israel went through typical gestures of mourning: he **tore his clothes**; he **fell face-down to the ground**, and the elders did likewise and also **sprinkled dust on their heads** (v. 6). These acts indicated a person's humbleness in the midst of sadness and contrition. Joshua did these in the presence **of the LORD**, that is, **before the ark**.

In his prayer, Joshua questioned what the Lord was doing, spoke about the tragedy of the event, and speculated about the future ramifications of it (vv. 7–9). Only in verse 9 is there an indirect petition in the form of a question, requesting some kind of divine intervention (**What then will you do . . . ?**). Joshua perceived the defeat as an indication of the Lord's disfavor, but he did not understand the cause. He seemed to view the divine disfavor as a result of a fickleness or capriciousness on the part of God. In verse 7, he attributed negative intents and motives to God (**Why did you ever bring this people across the Jordan to deliver us into the hands of the Amorites to destroy us?**) and desired that the previous condition could prevail (**If only we had been content to stay on the other side of the Jordan!**).

In verses 8–9, Joshua raised two legitimate issues. The first was that, in light of the Israelites being routed, the Canaanites might now have the courage to counterattack (v. 9). God had expressed His intent that the other nations would "fear him," and such had been the nations' response (see 2:9–11, 24; 5:1). But now that psychological and spiritual advantage was in jeopardy, with potentially dire ramifications for the Israelites.

The second issue was the Lord's perceived reputation. If the Israelites were exterminated by God or their enemies, or merely allowed to be shamefully defeated in battle, such would result in derision and contempt for the Israelites' God.

Divine Response (Josh. 7:10–13)

The divine response to Joshua's prayer subdivides into two sections: verses 10–12, the divine indictment for the sin; and verses 13–15, the instructions for restoration. Whereas Joshua's prayer focused on God's role in the situation, the Lord focused completely on the Israelites' role.

God's response indicated that Joshua's prayer was not wholly appropriate (v. 10, **What are you doing down on your face?**). In light of the divine promise of success and defeat of the enemies (1:2–6), Joshua's question (7:7) suggesting that God intended to deliver the Israelites to their enemies was an invalid accusation. And in light of the divine command to cross the Jordan (1:2), Joshua's declaration (7:7) that they should not have done so was an inappropriate regret of doing what God commanded. Finally, since success was to be contingent upon the people's obedience (1:7–9), Joshua needed not to be in a posture of questioning; the lack of success indicated disobedience.

God stressed that the defeat was not His fault, but rather Israel's. In verse 11, the indictment moved from a general expression (**Israel has sinned; they have violated my covenant**) to a delineation of the specific sins committed (**They have taken some of the devoted things; they have stolen, they have lied, they have put them with their own possessions**). Although only Achan had committed the specific action, the whole nation was held culpable.

In verse 12, the consequences were expressed first with reference to the specifics of the occasion: **That is why the Israelites cannot stand against their enemies; they turn their backs and run because they have been made liable to destruction.** Then a more generalized ramification was noted: **I will not be with you anymore.** The latter, as it reflected a future possibility, made it clear that the consequences were more serious than this one defeat.

But at this point, the removal of the divine presence was only a hypothetical possibility. It would only occur if the people did not deal with the sin (v. 12). The opportunity for restoration was offered to the people, and God then detailed the means by which such could take place (vv. 13–15).

The initial instruction in verse 13 was for the people to prepare themselves: **"Go, consecrate the people. Tell them, 'Consecrate yourselves in preparation.'"** The phrase is literally "make holy" in the sense of purifying so as to come into the presence of the Lord. The sacredness of the holy assembly that would occur the next day was emphasized through the necessity of the people's ritual purifying in preparation for it.

Israel's Discernment and Punishment of the Sin (Josh. 7:19–26)

Whereas disobedience had disrupted the covenant relationship with God, the people were particularly careful to be fully observant of what God told them to do, so as to assure restoration.

The Public Confession (vv. 19–21). Although Achan was the one "chosen," the verification occurred first through a public admission of guilt. Achan's confession involved three things: an acknowledgment of sin (v. 20), a description of the specific thing he did (vv. 20–21), and information about where the loot was hidden (v. 21). The fact that Achan concealed the items indicates that he sought to keep his action a secret. His disclosure of where the items were was important because the Lord had commanded that for restoration to take place the people needed to "destroy whatever among you is devoted to destruction" (7:12).

Verification through Producing the Evidence (vv. 22–23). The messengers dispatched by Joshua found the items, just as Achan had said (vv. 21–22). The stolen goods were then "entered into evidence" (v. 23, **brought them to Joshua and all the Israelites and spread them out before the LORD**), so the "devoted things," which belonged to the Lord, were returned to their rightful owner.

WHAT DO YOU THINK?
God's punishment seems harsh, on first glance. In what ways might it actually reflect His mercy and loving concern for His children as a whole?

AHA!
One man's sin had repercussions for all. Sound familiar?

DID YOU KNOW?
The Valley of Achor would later form part of Judah's border. In Isaiah 65:10, God said this "Valley of Trouble" would become "a resting place for herds, for my people who seek me."

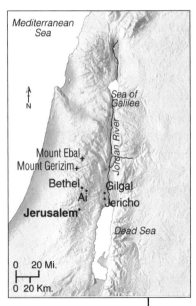

THE BATTLE FOR AI

Joshua 8:1–29

During the night, Joshua sent one detachment of soldiers to the west of Ai to lie in wait. The next morning he led a second group north of Ai. When the army of Ai attacked, the Isralites to the north pretended to scatter, only to turn on the enemy as the men lying in ambush moved in and burned the city.

WHAT ABOUT YOU?

Achan possibly thought his little sin couldn't matter much in the grand scheme of things. What "little sins" do you excuse or justify in your life?

PRAYER

Father, search my heart and reveal to me all my sins, great and small, because they're all evil in Your sight. Keep me from the slightest deviation from Your will. Please forgive me.

Punishment of Achan (vv. 24–26). **Joshua** then **took Achan** (v. 24), along with the stolen devoted items—**the silver, the robe, the gold wedge**—and all that belonged to him (7:15) to the place where they would be executed. The place was called **the Valley of Achor**, "the Valley of Trouble." It was so named because of the play on the term in Joshua's statement in verse 25, which echoed the command in 6:18, where it is declared that if they kept any of the devoted things they would "bring trouble on" ("bring disaster on") Israel.

The punishment is described in verse 25. First Achan was **stoned**, then the other living beings (family and animals) were stoned, and then everything was **burned** (v. 25), after which the ash remains were buried by covering them with **a large pile of rocks** (v. 26).

On the surface, the punishment seems harsh. After all, Achan confessed and "came clean" with respect to what he had done. Yet no mercy was extended in the sense of his being granted forgiveness and his life spared. Achan's punishment must be seen in light of two things. First, the people had made a pledge: "Whoever rebels against your word and does not obey your words . . . will be put to death" (1:18). Thus Achan's punishment adhered to that pledge. Second, the Lord had specifically commanded in this case, "He who is caught with the devoted things shall be destroyed by fire" (7:15).

Another issue related to the severity of the punishment is that Achan's family was killed and all his belongings destroyed. Nothing in the text implicates his family (his sons and daughters) as coconspirators or even their being aware of his actions. Any theory of his family's collaboration still does not explain the inclusion of his cattle, donkeys, and sheep (v. 24). The inclusiveness of the punishment revolves around the nature of the stolen items. Since Ai and all its inhabitants and contents were "liable to destruction," when Achan took some of those devoted things, he aligned himself with Ai and also became "liable to destruction" (v. 12), coming under the command in 6:17–18.

Two "memorials" of this event served as reminders (that is, warnings) to future generations about the consequences of disobedience. One was the visible burial pile of rocks, which remained **to this day** (7:26; that is, the author's day). The other was the name of the place, the Valley of Achor ("Trouble"), by which it had been called **ever since** (literally, "to this [the author's] day"). Those "memorials" provided the catalyst for the continued recapitulation of the story and its spiritual lessons, just like the "memorial" stones set up at the crossing of the Jordan, which were there "to this day" (3:8–9, 20–24).

Once the guilty party had been punished, **Then the LORD turned from his fierce anger** (7:26). The restoration process was complete. The rest of the story is in chapter 8. Once the rectification of the disobedience had been achieved, victory over Ai occurred as the people trusted in God's promises and followed His battle plan. Defeat due to disobedience (chapter 7) gave way to victory because of obedience (chapter 8). ◆

JOSHUA 7:2–13, 19–26

2 Now Joshua sent men from Jericho to Ai, which is near Beth Aven to the east of Bethel, and told them, "Go up and spy out the region." So the men went up and spied out Ai.

3 When they returned to Joshua, they said, "Not all the people will have to go up against Ai. Send two or three thousand men to take it and do not weary all the people, for only a few men are there."

4 So about three thousand men went up; but they were routed by the men of Ai,

5 who killed about thirty-six of them. They chased the Israelites from the city gate as far as the stone quarries and struck them down on the slopes. At this the hearts of the people melted and became like water.

6 Then Joshua tore his clothes and fell facedown to the ground before the ark of the LORD, remaining there till evening. The elders of Israel did the same, and sprinkled dust on their heads.

7 And Joshua said, "Ah, Sovereign LORD, why did you ever bring this people across the Jordan to deliver us into the hands of the Amorites to destroy us? If only we had been content to stay on the other side of the Jordan!

8 O Lord, what can I say, now that Israel has been routed by its enemies?

9 The Canaanites and the other people of the country will hear about this and they will surround us and wipe out our name from the earth. What then will you do for your own great name?"

10 The LORD said to Joshua, "Stand up! What are you doing down on your face?

11 Israel has sinned; they have violated my covenant, which I commanded them to keep. They have taken some of the devoted things; they have stolen, they have lied, they have put them with their own possessions.

12 That is why the Israelites cannot stand against their enemies; they turn their backs and run because they have been made liable to destruction. I will not be with you anymore unless you destroy whatever among you is devoted to destruction.

13 "Go, consecrate the people. Tell them, 'Consecrate yourselves in preparation for tomorrow; for this is what the LORD, the God of Israel, says: That which is devoted is among you, O Israel. You cannot stand against your enemies until you remove it.'"

19 Then Joshua said to Achan, "My son, give glory to the LORD, the God of Israel, and give him the praise. Tell me what you have done; do not hide it from me."

20 Achan replied, "It is true! I have sinned against the LORD, the God of Israel. This is what I have done:

21 When I saw in the plunder a beautiful robe from Babylonia, two hundred shekels of silver and a wedge of gold weighing fifty shekels, I coveted them and took them. They are hidden in the ground inside my tent, with the silver underneath."

22 So Joshua sent messengers, and they ran to the tent, and there it was, hidden in his tent, with the silver underneath.

23 They took the things from the tent, brought them to Joshua and all the Israelites and spread them out before the LORD.

24 Then Joshua, together with all Israel, took Achan son of Zerah, the silver, the robe, the gold wedge, his sons

Sin Infects and Affects

Sin is infectious, and its effects are extensive.

INTO THE SUBJECT

One drop of ink in a glass of water taints the whole glass. Can one sin hurt an entire family—even an entire nation?

INTO THE WORD

1. We do not read that Joshua and the Israelites consulted the Lord before they attacked Ai. Why didn't they do so?

2. Joshua consulted the Lord after Israel's defeat. Have you prayed after a defeat that probably would not have occurred if you had prayed before the incident? What was the occasion?

3. Why did Israel suffer defeat at the hands of the men of Ai (Josh. 7:10–12)?

4. What would it take to regain the Lord's favor and help (vv. 12–13)?

5. Why do you agree or disagree that church discipline is almost archaic?

6. What excuses might a church use for failing to exercise church discipline?

7. What sin led to Achan's deceptive act? Why do you agree or disagree that the sin you identified is prevalent among Christians?

8. Achan and his family were punished by death. How would you respond to the claim that we should love and forgive every offender, because none of us is perfect?

INTO THE WORLD

Covetousness is idolatry. Show those who know you well that eternal treasures are far more important to you than earthly possessions.

and daughters, his cattle, donkeys and sheep, his tent and all that he had, to the Valley of Achor.

25 Joshua said, "Why have you brought this trouble on us? The LORD will bring trouble on you today." Then all Israel stoned him, and after they had stoned the rest, they burned them.

26 Over Achan they heaped up a large pile of rocks, which remains to this day. Then the LORD turned from his fierce anger. Therefore that place has been called the Valley of Achor ever since.

DISOBEDIENCE VS. OBEDIENCE

Fill in the blanks appropriately.
Try to complete as much as you can
without looking at the lesson.

Unaware that _____ had been committed, Joshua sent out spies to investigate the situation of Ai.

Besides physical defeat of the Israelites, there was also their _____ defeat.

Although only Achan had committed the specific action, the whole nation is spoken of as being held _____.

Discernment and punishment of the sin included

- Discernment of the _____ party;
- The public _____;
- _____ through producing the evidence; and
- _____ of Achan.

The related Scriptures for this lesson tell us of the _____ of disobedience, _____ punishment for sin, and the _____ effects of sin.

Here is a simple graphic to remember the basic plot of this account.

Disobedience ➝ **Defeat**

Obedience ➝ **Victory**

INTERACTIVE LEARNING IDEAS

GET THE CLASS INVOLVED
Will the Jury Please Rise

Sometimes God perplexes us. We know He's a God of love and justice. Yet we see Him punishing seemingly innocent people for someone else's sin. Let the class wrestle with this problem through a mock trial—a trial to determine whether Achan's family should receive the death penalty.

Begin by discussing what laws or commands Achan broke. Then talk about how God is a God of both justice and mercy, and a God who will never tolerate sin. You can have verses and Bible stories on these topics ready ahead of time (look in a concordance). Or hand out a few concordances, and let the group find the verses. Don't discuss them yet.

Then, choose a prosecutor. Assign him or her half the group for a "prosecution team." Select someone else as the defense attorney, supported by the rest of the group, the "defense team." Call the trial to order. Allow two minutes for the prosecution to present the case, prosecutor only. Then grant the defense two minutes to present their case, defense attorney only. Open it up for rebuttal, back and forth between sides. Now each side's "team" can assist with "arguments." To close, as judge, discuss generational sin, how in Scripture one man often represents a group, and that God ultimately needed to protect the whole group. If you like, have several explanations from commentaries ready as well. Pronounce the family guilty.

TRY THIS ON YOUR OWN
Humble Time

Sometimes, justification of sin comes easily, especially when we convince ourselves that the sin is little or unimportant. But, as the story of Achan shows, God takes even seemingly insignificant sin very seriously. And we can't hide it from Him.

Set aside some time specifically to come before God in quiet humility. Ask God to search your heart and reveal any unconfessed or hidden sin. Be still before Him for several minutes. If this silence gets difficult, read Psalm 51. Listen for His Spirit to reveal any unresolved sin. Then confess it and repent. Close your prayer time with thanksgiving to God for His full and complete forgiveness through His Son.

TAKING IT TO THE STREET
Cleaning Up

Plan an afternoon in the park. It can be as casual as families meeting to play or as formal as organized games. Consider including a potluck picnic. Ask everyone to come an hour or so before events begin, work gloves and garbage bags in hand. Have everyone work together to clean the park.

After cleaning up, gather in a shady spot. Discuss the story of Achan and his sin. Point out how it impacted everything, just as garbage diminishes the whole park. Talk about how sin "trashes" the community of believers. Ponder what keeps a community "clean and healthy" when it comes to sin. And consider together how you can help keep your own lives pure. Pray for your group and church. Then enjoy an afternoon at the park!

WITH YOUR FAMILY
Turning the Whole Thing Black

Make a pitcher of lemonade for your family at dinner. (A glass or clear pitcher works best.) Have red, blue, and green food coloring nearby. As you reach for the pitcher to pour everyone's drinks, tell them you love red and want some in your lemonade. Put a few drops of red in the pitcher, enough to color the liquid. Then notice the blue and explain that you can't resist blue. Put a few drops in the lemonade. Pause, then say that you've heard green tastes really good, and put a few green drops in. The drink will turn an dark color. Look at it quizzically and say, "Ugh. It looks pretty nasty. A few drops such made a mess. I guess we're all stuck with it now." Pour the dark liquid—it'll taste fine, of course—and wait for everyone's reaction.

Tell the story of Achan's sin. Explain that just as only a few drops of food coloring impacted the entire pitcher of lemonade, so the smallest sin by one person impacted everyone. Talk about the importance of staying right with God. Enjoy the "colorful" lemonade. Or have another "untainted" pitcher available and pass around the food coloring for everyone to create unique colors in their own glasses. ◆

LESSON 5

THE EMPTY TOMB—A GIFT FOR ETERNITY
Mark 16:1–16

WHY THIS MATTERS

Charles Wesley exulted in our Savior's resurrection. He wrote: "Christ, the Lord, is risen today, Alleluia! Sons of men and angels say, Alleluia! Raise your joys and triumphs high, Alleluia! Sing, ye heavens, and earth, reply, Alleluia!"

Christianity doesn't rest on the lid of a casket, but on an open tomb. Jesus rose to verify the fact that His death on the cross was sufficient for our redemption. Also, He rose to give us a living hope. Because He lives, we too shall live. Further, He lives at the Father's right hand to intercede for us.

This lesson will inspire us to sing Charles Wesley's joyful words from the heart: "Christ, the Lord, is risen today, Alleluia!"

BIBLE COMMENTARY

By Jim Moretz

After Mark 16:8, the NIV places a line in the text followed by the parenthetical statement, "The most reliable early manuscripts and other ancient witnesses do not have Mark 16:9–20." The context of these verses is clouded in historical debate. There are some "internal" issues (things within the passage) that may suggest it was added later and maybe not by Mark. First, verse 9 begins as if it were an independent account of the resurrection. The appearance to Mary Magdalene seems out of place since she had already been at the center of the story in the latter part of chapter 15. Second, Jesus' rebuke of the disciples in verse 14 seems impersonal and secondary in contrast to the "Do not be afraid" motif recorded by the other Gospels in their resurrection appearances. Third, the snakes and deadly poison signs are unexpected, with no real scriptural parallel or obvious interpretive value. Finally, verse 19 reads like a developed creedal statement instead of what scholars call a "primitive eyewitness account." Notice the addition of "Lord" to Jesus and the phrase "sat at the right hand of God." This type of developed religious language does not fit within Mark's style.

Most likely early Christians were uncomfortable with Mark's gospel ending so abruptly at verse 8, especially without an account of Jesus appearing to the disciples after the resurrection. So at some point, verses 9–20 were added to fill out the rest of the story. However, if verses 9–20 are an addition, they are probably a very early addition, and they are definitely dependent upon other material found in the other Gospels. This means we can have confidence that a faithful reading of these verses will edify the believer in the faith of Christ.

People Have Limits; God Is Unlimited (Mark 16:1–8)

This passage calls us to wrestle with our limitations and the reality of God's limitless power. The women had been prevented from duly anointing the body of Jesus because of the old covenant Jesus had come to fulfill and replace. We do not know much about exact burial practices of the ancient Israelites, but we do know burial was to honor the body of the deceased and thereby honor the life the body represented. Because of the lack of scriptural protocol, we may assume the oral law provided much of the burial ritual.

Mark mentioned the time of day in order to clue in the reader that something important, and possibly unexpected, was about to happen. In Mark 1:35, Jesus prayed early in the morning before beginning His ministry throughout Galilee (a pivotal and unexpected event). In Mark 15:1, the critical decision by the Sanhedrin to hand Jesus over to Pilate was reached "very early in the morning." So the time of day was critical to the impact of the story by building anticipation in the reader.

Mark 16:3 contains the crucial question of the passage: **Who will roll the stone away from the tomb?** Who will do what we cannot? To whom do we look for help in times of trouble? Here we must pause and feel the women's helplessness. The most common error people make reading the Bible is reading it strictly for data ("what to do") and missing the divine/human drama that is the story of

Key Verses to Memorize for Help "Moving the Stones"	
Scripture Reference	Verse
Nahum 1:7	The LORD is good, a refuge in times of trouble. He cares for those who trust in him.
Psalm 9:9	The LORD is a refuge for the oppressed, a stronghold in times of trouble.
Psalm 86:7	In the day of my trouble I will call to you, for you will answer me.
Psalm 41:1	Blessed is he who has regard for the weak; the LORD delivers him in times of trouble.
John 16:33	I have told you these things, so that in me you may have peace. In this world you will have trouble. But take heart! I have overcome the world.

salvation. Before we can fully appreciate the wonder of the resurrection, we must face the hopelessness of the tomb and the impossible task of moving the stone, which parallels the sin in our lives.

Verses 4–7 give the answer—Jesus, the one who has defeated death. It is interesting that **when they looked up** (v. 4), they saw that the stone had been moved. Not to make too much of what may be a grammatical coincidence, but it adds to the theological point of dying (going down) and rising (going up). Not only do we look "up" to God; we look to Jesus, the one God raised up.

The resurrected Jesus is not a static figure, but an active and living person. **He is going ahead of you into Galilee. There you will see him, just as he told you** (v. 7). The affirmation of Jesus' prior claim to the resurrection is important as it links the ideas of the living God, His living Word, and the Incarnate Christ as the living Word. We believe in Jesus because He is the Word that was given, and everything about Him affirms this claim.

While this is a comfort, it should also be a bit unsettling if we take the implications seriously. The women were afraid. A main truth in their lives, the reality and inevitability of death, had been destroyed. Life as they knew it had fundamentally changed. Mark emphasized the women's fear by mentioning it both before and after the announcement of Jesus' resurrection. He did this to highlight the radical change that Jesus' resurrection brought into the world and into the lives of those who follow Him. In some way, the resurrection of Christ should make us stand mute, awestruck by the limitless power of God.

WHAT DO YOU THINK?
At times, people seem slow to believe in the resurrection of Christ, as the disciples were when the women came to them. What does this passage tell us about our responsibility, and God's responsibility, when that happens?

Slow to Believe (Mark 16:9–14)

These verses contain three accounts of disbelief in the resurrection. First, the testimony of an eyewitness was rejected. Second, Jesus' testimony about himself, though concealed, was rejected. Finally, Jesus appeared plainly and rebuked the disciples for being slow to believe. The point of these three accounts is that rejection of testimony about Jesus (the gospel story) is rejection of Jesus himself.

The other Gospels also spoke of disbelief concerning the resurrection; however, only in Mark is the disbelief not balanced by the belief of others. For example, Matthew 28:16–17 reads, "Then the eleven disciples went to Galilee, to the mountain where Jesus had told them to go. When they saw him, they worshiped him; but some doubted."

Luke 24:11–12 reads, "But they did not believe the women, because their words seemed to them like nonsense. Peter, however, got up and ran to the tomb. Bending over, he saw the strips of linen lying by themselves, and he went away, wondering to himself what had happened."

In Luke 24:25, Jesus said to the men on the road, "How foolish you are, and how slow of heart to believe all that the prophets have spoken!" Then the men urged Jesus to stay and eat with them. Interestingly, Luke says that when Jesus broke the bread and gave it to them, "Then their eyes were opened and they recognized him." Similarly, when Jesus appeared to the disciples in Jerusalem, Luke 24:45 says, "Then he opened their minds so they could understand the Scriptures."

AHA!
Sometimes when we feel discouraged and heartbroken, we simply need to look up! We might see something that bolsters our faith and belief.

For John, the reason to tell the story of Thomas was to show that God will give evidence of His reality to those who ask. It is interesting to note that Thomas did not actually touch Jesus as he said he must. Seeing was enough.

So Mark records the harshest treatment of unbelief. Again, this tends to set this section "against" the other gospel accounts. However, unbelief is something with which humans, even believers, continue to wrestle. Here we must wrestle with the human tendency to rely on our own wisdom and senses to define reality rather than to rely on God's revelation, which will always be beyond our full comprehension, even if He tells us plainly. Let us listen to Mark's rebuke of us when we are slow to believe Jesus' promises. Let us say with the father in Mark 9:24, "I do believe; help me overcome my unbelief!"

Go and Preach (Mark 16:15)

Verses 15 and 16 contain the basic principles upon which the early church was founded. Verse 15 describes the mission, message, and purpose of the church. Verse 16 describes the potential response to the church's message and the implications for the people who hear that message. For study purposes, verse 15 can be examined in three parts: (1) Go into all the world; (2) preach the good news; (3) to all creation.

DID YOU KNOW?
The disciples were traveling to Emmaus, a city name that means "hot baths." Its exact location remains uncertain, although it is known to be approximately seven miles from Jerusalem.

First, **go into all the world** gives the church of Christ a mission with no boundaries or borders. Paul understood the God of Israel as the God of everyone and everything in creation. "There is neither Jew nor Greek, slave nor free, male nor female, for you are all one in Christ Jesus" (Gal. 3:28). Again, in Romans 1:14, Paul wrote, "I am obligated both to Greeks and non-Greeks, both to the wise and the foolish" (that is, the educated and the uneducated). Ultimately, Paul asserted, "Is God the God of Jews only? Is he not the God of Gentiles too? Yes, of Gentiles too" (Rom. 3:29; see also Rom. 3:9).

Second, **preach the good news** gives the church its message. The "good news" (Greek, *euangelion*) was understood in those days to be primarily good news regarding a battle or war. The "good news" of Jesus is that He has decisively won the war against sin and the powers of evil. This message is relevant as long as humanity is under the oppression of temptation and sin. It is also relevant to those who suffer from oppressors like poverty, disease, and a myriad of handicaps. Anything that inhibits a person from being whole has been defeated in the person of Christ Jesus.

Third, the purpose of the church is to "preach" (in other words, to proclaim both in word and deed) this freedom wherever there are ears to hear, **to all creation**. In Romans 8:19–21, Paul wrote, "The creation waits in eager expectation for the sons of God to be revealed. For the creation was subjected to frustration, not by its own choice, but by the will of the one who subjected it, in hope that the creation itself will be liberated from its bondage to decay and brought into the glorious freedom of the children of God."

This is to say the gospel of Jesus has implications for ecology, ethical treatment of animals, and the ethics of technological research and development. Preach and teach within the church we must, but we must also behave within all creation as those who have been set free so that the creation itself will have hope in the children of God!

Believing versus Not Believing (Mark 16:16)

Whoever believes and is baptized will be saved, but whoever does not believe will be condemned. The idea is worship. Baptism is the ritual of initiation into the church, but this verse does not suggest that baptism is all one must do or that baptism is necessary for salvation. Early Christians understood baptism to signify entering into a new way of life. A life characterized by a relationship with God unhindered by sin. Notice the lack of action associated with unbelieving. This underscores the biblical theme of life versus death. In death (unbelieving) there is no movement, so there is nothing to be done. In life (believing) the resultant activity is worship. Matthew stated it more directly in 28:19–20: "Therefore go and make disciples of all nations, baptizing them in the name of the Father and of the Son and of the Holy Spirit, and teaching them to obey everything I have commanded you." Whoever believes is given new life and so is commanded to live. Whoever does not believe cannot receive any such command because the unbeliever lies in death. ◆

WHAT ABOUT YOU?
We are told to go and preach and tell the good news of Christ's resurrection. Who will you tell today?

PRAYER
Father, thank You for Your Son's resurrection and the salvation it brings. Grant me faith to believe that Your miracles can go beyond my expectation. And give me wisdom and courage to tell others of Your Son.

The Great Commission is actually several passages, not just one. Each passage reveals a little more.

The Great Commission				
What	**Where**	**How**	**To What End**	**Empowered By**
"Make disciples" (Matt. 28:16–20)	"All the world" (Mark 16:17)	Miracles (Mark 16:17)	Belief (Mark 16:16)	Holy Spirit (Acts 1:8)
"Teaching them to obey" (Matt. 28:20)	"All nations" (Matt. 28:19)	We will be His witnesses. (Acts 1:8)		Jesus (Matt. 28:20)
	Jerusalem, Judea, Samaria, and the whole earth (Acts 1:8)			

INTERACTIVE LEARNING IDEAS

GET THE CLASS INVOLVED
To Tell the Tale

Mary and the other women ran to tell others what they discovered on that first Easter morning. Likewise, God calls us to share our testimony of what Christ's resurrection means. What better place to practice sharing that than within a safe, loving group.

Provide note paper. Allow five minutes for each person to write down three reasons Easter is significant to them. First, they should simply note their three reasons. One likely may be salvation itself. But encourage the group to think beyond that as well. Once people choose three things, they should detail why they chose what they did. Once the time is up, ask each person to share one of their three answers and the reason. Let this be practice for telling others about the importance of the resurrection on a personal level.

TRY THIS ON YOUR OWN
Creativity in Sharing

God gives each of us creative gifts. But sometimes, we forget to use them to share our hearts regarding what God has done for us. As Easter is celebrated, use your gifts to express in some creative way what Easter means to you.

Your gift may be writing. If so, write a poem that shares what Easter does for your heart. If it is painting, create a work of art depicting the meaning of Easter. If your talent is woodworking, carve a beautiful remembrance of Christ's resurrection. If you feel your gifts aren't as creative, don't worry—this is just between you and God, and He revels in your efforts. Try writing a poem or drawing a picture anyway! And practical talents can work as well for this too. (Mechanics can help a neighbor fix a car to reflect the sacrifice of Christ, for example.)

TAKING IT TO THE STREET
A Neighborly Visit

Take some time as a group to introduce your church neighbors to the truth of Christ's resurrection. In advance, ask someone with a little creative talent and computer savvy to develop some simple invitations to your church. They don't need to be fancy, just something bright and joyful that says, in essence, "You're welcome at our church. We'd love to have you with us!"

As a group, go door to door in your church neighborhood and pass out the invitations. Let this time be casual. No one should feel any pressure to evangelize, although they should let the Spirit lead. Simply let your neighbors know you'd love for them to visit with you. After the invitations are passed out, gather together back at the church. Discuss what the experience was like and talk about the challenges and joys of sharing the good news of the risen Christ. Then pray for the needs of the community.

WITH YOUR FAMILY
Barbecue with a Purpose

As a family, learn to be bold about sharing the good news of Jesus' resurrection. Invite your neighbors over for a neighborhood barbecue. You can make it potluck or provide all the food yourself. Make sure everyone in the family helps prepare for the event. But stop as you get ready and gather as a family. Talk about how important it is for our friends and neighbors to know the Lord. And discuss ways to share His good news. Today, your family will practice one method—a fairly easy one. Everyone old enough should try this task.

At some point as you are enjoying the barbecue, ask the people you are near if they celebrate Easter and how. What did they do, or what do they plan to do for Easter? If they do not know the Lord, let this be an opening to share how much Easter means to you personally and why it is a meaningful time for you. Then ask what they think about Jesus. Simply listen. Don't press the issue, unless you sense the Sprit saying otherwise. This is a time for casual conversation without hard-sell evangelism. Practice as a family the fine art of introducing spiritual conversation comfortably into relationships with nonbelievers. When everyone else has gone home, discuss how it went and discover what you each learned. ◆

MARK 16:1–16

1 When the Sabbath was over, Mary Magdalene, Mary the mother of James, and Salome bought spices so that they might go to anoint Jesus' body.
2 Very early on the first day of the week, just after sunrise, they were on their way to the tomb
3 and they asked each other, "Who will roll the stone away from the entrance of the tomb?"
4 But when they looked up, they saw that the stone, which was very large, had been rolled away.
5 As they entered the tomb, they saw a young man dressed in a white robe sitting on the right side, and they were alarmed.
6 "Don't be alarmed," he said. "You are looking for Jesus the Nazarene, who was crucified. He has risen! He is not here. See the place where they laid him.
7 But go, tell his disciples and Peter, 'He is going ahead of you into Galilee. There you will see him, just as he told you.'"
8 Trembling and bewildered, the women went out and fled from the tomb. They said nothing to anyone, because they were afraid. [The earliest manuscripts and some other ancient witnesses do not have Mark 16:9–20.]
9 When Jesus rose early on the first day of the week, he appeared first to Mary Magdalene, out of whom he had driven seven demons.
10 She went and told those who had been with him and who were mourning and weeping.
11 When they heard that Jesus was alive and that she had seen him, they did not believe it.
12 Afterward Jesus appeared in a different form to two of them while they were walking in the country.
13 These returned and reported it to the rest; but they did not believe them either.
14 Later Jesus appeared to the Eleven as they were eating; he rebuked them for their lack of faith and their stubborn refusal to believe those who had seen him after he had risen.
15 He said to them, "Go into all the world and preach the good news to all creation.
16 Whoever believes and is baptized will be saved, but whoever does not believe will be condemned.

The Empty Tomb—A Gift for Eternity

Jesus is risen . . . believe it!

INTO THE SUBJECT

Darkness covered the face of the earth when Jesus hung on the cross. It was a gloomy, somber day. Furthermore, Jesus' followers thought the future was dark and gloomy. But along came Sunday, resurrection day! What changes did it bring?

INTO THE WORD

1. What seemingly impossible task did the women face when they planned to anoint Jesus' body?

2. What does it say about their devotion to Jesus that they did not scrap their plan?

3. What seemingly impossible situation are you facing that requires God's intervention?

4. Compare Matthew 27:65; Mark 16:4; and Luke 24:1–12. How would you describe the power that was involved in rolling the stone away from the tomb? Why was it rolled away?

5. Some skeptics claim Jesus' followers simply contrived the story of the resurrection because they were in denial about Jesus' death. What do you find in Mark 16:1–11 that refutes that claim?

6. Compare Luke 24:36–43 and Mark 16:14. How strong was the disciples' unbelief? What did it take to change their thinking?

7. Why do you agree or disagree that the church's foremost responsibility is to proclaim the gospel worldwide?

8. How would you answer the claim that baptism is required for salvation?

INTO THE WORLD

Proactively support missions this week by praying for missionaries, giving generously to missions, and sharing the gospel whenever and wherever you can.

God Is Unlimited

Find the words listed below in the word search.
Words can be up, down, left to right, right to left, or diagonal.

```
W H S Y J F R B H N B C M M H E M N T J
M J U H M O E C I J O N G C U C E E A O
V F K Z D L U M Y N I F C F L R A B U L
Y I W Y I L J N D S J V T A D C M E X U
H L W E A O V E L R O B Q L H P Z M R O
C N F F Y W M D F I E J I C U H I L L P
R J H D U N N S O V M H N Q T P H V U V
U S K U E Z H W D A C I O A S N F H Y H
H Q Z D L R I D O S V W T N T O V A Z K
C F E J E S U S G J A F O E M I O F O D
W X E W C Q N I X X U I X P D T O X S I
L O O I M C H R I S T I A N S A H N W S
H P R D L S P N J C O X E W A E R S S C
X E X L D E K L E P S O G M O R U D N I
E W I X D I B R B A P T I S M C W S H P
L B T N Q S R N F U H Q D G I M Z A R L
H C M O U U V K U P K E W R U M V V K E
D Y H O S V M F E R U T P I R C S E T S
Z T I E T P V D S H L N I L H M H D H Y
H K R A M P J A H D O G I Z G W V W S G
```

BAPTISM	DISCIPLES	POWER	TOMB
BELIEF	FOLLOW	PREACH	UNBELIEF
CHILDREN	GOD	RESURRECTION	UNLIMITED
CHRISTIANS	GOSPEL	SAVED	WORLD
CHURCH	JESUS	SCRIPTURE	
CONDEMNED	MARK	SIN	
CREATION	NATIONS	TEACH	

REMEMBER: People have limits; God is unlimited.

Wholehearted devotion to God is the key to finishing well.

THE SECRETS OF WHOLEHEARTED DEVOTION

Joshua 14:5–15

WHY THIS MATTERS

It's called a bucket list—a list of things a person wants to do before he or she "kicks the bucket." A bowler may hope to bowl in every Canadian province before he or she dies. A golfer may choose to play St. Andrews' Old Course. A bucket list may include such feats as climbing Mount Everest, parachuting from an airplane, traveling around the world, skiing in Aspen, or peering into a live volcano. However, it's highly unlikely that a bucket list would include the feat of routing a well-armed enemy from a mountain. But that is precisely what eighty-five-year-old Caleb did by faith.

This lesson will motivate you to wholly follow the Lord and rely on Him all the days of your life.

BIBLE COMMENTARY

By James B. Bross, Sr.

Some forty-five years before the time of our lesson, Joshua and Caleb had gone on a mission along with ten other Israelites. Their task was to explore the land of Canaan that God had promised to Israel. The exploration was preliminary preparation for the people of Israel to possess the Promised Land. The twelve spies set out from Kadesh Barnea, consisting of one representative from each of the tribes of Israel. For forty days they explored the length and breadth of the land God had promised to give them. In Numbers 13–14, we read the account of their mission, including their report to the people after they had returned.

Upon their return to Kadesh Barnea, they presented amazing spoils from the Promised Land. Evidently, all twelve of the spies gave glowing reports about the land and its bounty. However, their reports were not all positive. Only Joshua and Caleb reported that the Israelites should press ahead, trusting God to give them success in their conquest. The other ten men were fearful, and those ten predicted defeat for Israel. They reported that the land was populated with many giants and that the people of the land were far too powerful for the Israelites to succeed. They were sure that if Israel entered the land they would be defeated. On the other hand, Joshua and Caleb were confident that God would provide the power to conquer the land and its people. They urged the Israelites to press forward and enter the land immediately. Unfortunately the majority opinion swayed the multitude, and the Israelites rebelled against the Lord by refusing to enter the land of promise there at Kadesh Barnea.

Their disobedience was followed by tragedy. God's anger raged against the people, and He promised that, because of their disobedience, every adult among the multitude of Israelites would die in the wilderness. There were only two exceptions—Joshua and Caleb. Because of their faithfulness, God promised

KEY VERSE
So Hebron has belonged to Caleb son of Jephunneh the Kenizzite ever since, because he followed the LORD, the God of Israel, wholeheartedly.
—Joshua 14:14

BACKGROUND SCRIPTURES
Numbers 13–14
  The account of the twelve spies and their reports, including the reports of Joshua and Caleb
Deuteronomy 1:19–46
  Another account of the twelve spies and the surrounding circumstances
Joshua 15:13–19
  The account of Caleb's conquest of Hebron and the surrounding area
Judges 3:7–11
  The account of Othniel, son-in-law and relative of Caleb, who became the first judge of Israel

DAILY BIBLE READINGS
Monday: Exodus 19:1–8
Tuesday: 2 Corinthians 4:16–18
Wednesday: Luke 9:18–23
Thursday: Hebrews 12:1–3
Friday: Romans 12:1–2, 11
Saturday: Joshua 14:5–15
Sunday: Psalm 32

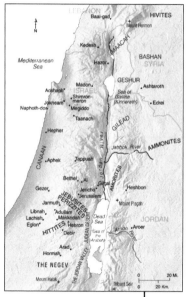

Joshua 11:16—12:24

Joshua displayed brilliant military strategy in the way he went about conquering the land of Canaan. . . . Thirty-one kings and their cities had been defeated. The Israelites had over-powered the Hittites, the Amorites, the Canaanites, the Perizzites, the Hivites, and the Jebusites. Other peoples living in Canaan were yet to be conquered.

WHAT DO YOU THINK?

What gives you strength and patience when waiting for God to fulfill His promises?

AHA!

We never need to fear to stand up and claim God's promises. He always fulfills them.

DID YOU KNOW?

Caleb's name means "dog." It fits a man with such tenacity, obedience, and loyalty to God.

that Joshua and Caleb would be rewarded. Not only would they survive to enter the Promised Land, they would also be given possessions in the land. In this lesson, Caleb was ready to claim that possession that had been promised to him so many years earlier.

Caleb Approaches Joshua about His Inheritance (Josh. 14:5–6)

As the Israelites gathered at Gilgal, most of the land was conquered. It was time to divide the land between the tribes and then to further divide the land between the individual families of each tribe (14:1–5). According to Adam Clarke, they had crossed the Jordan and entered the land perhaps as much as seven years earlier, and ever since then, they had been in a war of conquest. Now, even though there were pockets of resistance remaining, it was time to settle in the land. East of the Jordan, the land had already been assigned to Reuben, Gad, and half of the tribe of Manasseh (13:8–31). Now, **the men of Judah approached Joshua at Gilgal** to receive their allotment (v. 6). Caleb was one of the prominent members of the tribe of Judah; he was the oldest surviving member. He came to Joshua and reminded him of God's special promise made to them: **You know what the LORD said to Moses the man of God at Kadesh Barnea about you and me** (v. 6).

Caleb Reminds Joshua of His Faithfulness (Josh. 14:7–9)

Caleb reminded Joshua that the promise had been made back when Caleb was only **forty years old** (v. 7), and now he was eighty-five years old (14:10). Forty-five years earlier, Caleb had trusted God and His power, giving a report that he believed Israel was able to conquer the land. **"But my brothers who went up with me made the hearts of the people melt with fear. I, however, followed the LORD my God wholeheartedly"** (v. 8). For this faithfulness, God had promised Caleb **The land on which** his **feet** had **walked** (v. 9). Other than in this passage, Hebron was not specified in Scripture as the land promised to Caleb, but here Caleb and Joshua seem to understand that the promise was related to that specific area of the hill country of Judah (v. 12). Caleb continued his request, quoting Deuteronomy 1:36, **"So on that day Moses swore to me, 'The land on which your feet have walked will be your inheritance and that of your children forever, because you have followed the LORD my God wholeheartedly'"** (v. 9). God had blessed Caleb and Joshua with long life, and now they were the only two adults who had survived the wilderness wanderings to enter the land of promise.

Years before, at Kadesh Barnea, Caleb and Joshua had shown great courage as they urged the people to move forward and not to rebel against God. In fact, because they went against majority opinion, "the whole assembly talked about stoning them" (Num. 14:10). When the people rebelled, Moses and Aaron fell on their faces and interceded for them. Because of their intercession, God forgave the Israelites, and He would not destroy them completely. Still God pronounced: "Not one of them will ever see the land I promised on oath to their forefathers. No one who has treated me with contempt will ever see it. But because my servant Caleb has a different spirit and follows me wholeheartedly,

I will bring him into the land he went to, and his descendants will inherit it" (Num. 14:23–24). The passage in Numbers goes on to contrast the consequence of the unfaithfulness of the others with the promise to Joshua and Caleb. The ten men "responsible for spreading the bad report about the land were struck down and died of a plague before the LORD. Of the men who went to explore the land, only Joshua son of Nun and Caleb son of Jephunneh survived" (Num. 14:37–38). Caleb's steadfastness was rewarded then and over the next forty years.

God's Faithfulness to Caleb (Josh. 14:10–11)

For forty years, **Israel moved about in the desert** (v. 10). They finally entered the land, but only after passing through many perils. And those who had rebelled at Kadesh Barnea, had died, one by one, along the way. Now only Joshua and Caleb were left. Not only had Caleb survived to the age of eighty-five, he had survived in splendid health. He told Joshua, **"I am still as strong today as the day Moses sent me out; I'm just as vigorous to go out to battle now as I was then"** (v. 11). God had so blessed Caleb that his statement appears miraculous to us today as it must have appeared there at Gilgal. His vigor at age eighty-five was still as great as it had been at age forty. But Caleb wasn't through yet; now he was ready for his next challenge.

Caleb Claims His Land (Josh. 14:12)

Caleb claimed that Hebron and the area surrounding that city were promised to him. The city of Hebron was in the hill country of Judah, and was the first city visited by the twelve spies (Num. 13:32). The area was occupied by the Anakites, giants according to the report of the ten spies (Num. 13:33). In that report (no doubt exaggerated), the Hebrews "seemed like grasshoppers" beside these giants. Furthermore, **their cities were large and fortified.** This could have been true at that time, or possibly it was a description of earlier times. The account of conquests by Caleb and Othniel (15:13–19) makes it sound like it was a contemporary description. Hebron had already been conquered, according to Joshua 10:36. Perhaps in the meantime Hebron had been reoccupied by the Anakites as the Israelite army moved on to other locations. Another possibility could be that the earlier conquest had not been complete. Whatever the case, Caleb was confident that he would have success: **"The LORD helping me, I will drive them out just as he said."** Giants and fortified cities did not trouble Caleb, for he trusted that God's power would give him what he had been promised those many years earlier. At eighty-five, with the vigor of a forty-year-old, he was ready to tackle the task.

We learn a bit more about Caleb's conquest of Hebron in Joshua 15:13–19. "Caleb drove out the three Anakites—Sheshai, Ahiman and Talmai—descendants of Anak" (15:14). Then Caleb promised his daughter Achsah in marriage to the man who would conquer Debir (also named Kiriath Sepher). His relative Othniel, possibly a cousin or nephew, accepted the challenge and took the city. Thus Othniel was given Achsah in marriage, and Othniel became Caleb's son-in-law. At Achsah's request Caleb also gave them "upper and lower springs" (15:19). In that desert region water was a scarce resource, so this was a very valuable gift.

WHAT DO YOU THINK?
Caleb was eighty-five, and God still had mighty tasks for him to accomplish. How can your church, and you personally, encourage the senior members of your congregation?

AHA!
Some of God's most exciting work happens in the later decades of His children's lives.

DID YOU KNOW?
Hebron, a lush and fertile area, boasted rich soil and an abundance of water. Prime real estate like this would naturally be fought over for centuries by the surrounding peoples— at times held by Amorites, Hittites, Edomites, Babylonians, and more.

WHAT ABOUT YOU?
Sometimes, it's easy to believe we've accomplished all God requires, or that He can't use us for some reason. It's never true. What new task or adventure might He have for you in the next five to ten years?

PRAYER
Father, thank You that You always have an exciting task ahead for me. Thank You for Your promises as I obey You. Help me to hear Your calling each and every day that I might faithfully follow.

Joshua Grants Caleb His Inheritance (Josh. 14:13–15)

Clearly Joshua also understood that Hebron had been promised to Caleb. As an older comrade and as leader of the people, **Joshua blessed Caleb son of Jephunneh and gave him Hebron as his inheritance** (v. 13). The text then brought the record up-to-date as of the time of its writing: **Hebron has belonged to Caleb son of Jephunneh the Kenizzite ever since, because he followed the LORD, the God of Israel, wholeheartedly** (v. 14). Later, Othniel was to become the first judge of Israel (Judg. 3:7–11).

Also, a historical note is given, telling us that **Hebron** was earlier called **Kiriath Arba** (town of Arba) **after Arba, who was the greatest man among the Anakites** (Josh. 14:15).

In a further note the text tells us, **Then the land had rest from war**. The general war of the conquest was over. Future wars were to be more localized as the Israelites continued to root out some of the remaining Canaanites. Unfortunately, not all the enemy was conquered, and the nations remaining continually caused trouble for Israel. In his farewell address several years later Joshua warned the people: "If you turn away and ally yourselves with the survivors of these nations that remain among you and if you intermarry with them and associate with them, then you may be sure that the LORD your God will no longer drive out these nations before you. Instead, they will become snares and traps for you, whips on your backs and thorns in your eyes, until you perish from this good land, which the LORD your God has given you" (23:12–13). Sadly, this prediction came true. Time and again Israel would fall into the snares presented by those remaining nations.

But as for Caleb, he followed God wholeheartedly. For that faithfulness he was blessed with a long life, and he and his descendants after him received Hebron, the land God had promised to give him. ◆

JOSHUA 14:5–15

5 So the Israelites divided the land, just as the LORD had commanded Moses.

6 Now the men of Judah approached Joshua at Gilgal, and Caleb son of Jephunneh the Kenizzite said to him, "You know what the LORD said to Moses the man of God at Kadesh Barnea about you and me.

7 I was forty years old when Moses the servant of the LORD sent me from Kadesh Barnea to explore the land. And I brought him back a report according to my convictions,

8 but my brothers who went up with me made the hearts of the people melt with fear. I, however, followed the LORD my God wholeheartedly.

9 So on that day Moses swore to me, 'The land on which your feet have walked will be your inheritance and that of your children forever, because you have followed the LORD my God wholeheartedly.'

10 "Now then, just as the LORD promised, he has kept me alive for forty-five years since the time he said this to Moses, while Israel moved about in the desert. So here I am today, eighty-five years old!

11 I am still as strong today as the day Moses sent me out; I'm just as vigorous to go out to battle now as I was then.

12 Now give me this hill country that the LORD promised me that day. You yourself heard then that the Anakites were there and their cities were large and fortified, but, the LORD helping me, I will drive them out just as he said."

13 Then Joshua blessed Caleb son of Jephunneh and gave him Hebron as his inheritance.

14 So Hebron has belonged to Caleb son of Jephunneh the Kenizzite ever since, because he followed the LORD, the God of Israel, wholeheartedly.

15 (Hebron used to be called Kiriath Arba after Arba, who was the greatest man among the Anakites.) Then the land had rest from war.

The Secrets of Wholehearted Devotion

*Wholehearted devotion to God is
the key to finishing well.*

INTO THE SUBJECT

The golden years are a period of life in which some adults retire while others refire. While one adult settles into a rocking chair, another straps on a pair of hiking boots. Could the golden years bring new opportunities to stretch one's faith and attempt great things for God?

INTO THE WORD

1. Read Joshua 14:5–12. How old was Caleb when he asked Joshua for his land inheritance?

2. How long had Caleb kept God's promise in his heart?

3. What commendable character traits do you find in Caleb as you read verses 6–12?

4. Choose one of these traits and explain how you will implement it in your life.

5. If the Lord leaves you on earth until you are eighty-five, how do you hope to be serving Him then?

6. How might you show your children or grandchildren how to follow the Lord wholeheartedly?

7. How do you know Caleb was aware of the huge challenges he faced in possessing the land promised to him?

8. Which would you rather have: a cushy life or a challenging life? Why?

INTO THE WORLD

Every time you lead a person to Christ, you claim "territory" for the Lord. By faith, be an active soul winner this week.

Following God Wholeheartedly

These maps show how the land of Canaan looked after the Israelites overtook it and after Joshua divided it up. The land was about eight thousand square miles—just a couple hundred square miles bigger than the state of New Jersey.

THE TRIBES EAST OF THE JORDAN

Joshua 13:8–12

Joshua assigned territory to the tribes of Reuben, Gad, and the half-tribe of Manasseh on the east side of the Jordan where they had chosen to remain because of the wonderful livestock country (Num. 32:1–5).

THE TRIBES WEST OF THE JORDAN

Joshua 18:1–6

Judah, Ephraim, and the other half-tribe of Manasseh were the first tribes to receive land west of the Jordan because of their past acts of faith. The remaining seven tribes—Benjamin, Zebulun, Issachar, Asher, Naphtali, Simeon, and Dan—were slow to conquer and possess the land allotted to them.

Caleb wholeheartedly followed the Lord, which is why Moses promised him Hebron as an inheritance. How did Caleb do this?

_____

_____

_____

What does following the Lord wholeheartedly look like for you today? Is it obedience to a specific action He has called you to do? Is it submission to Him even though you're unsure of what God is doing? It might be offering your tithe with a cheerful attitude. Whatever it is, spend some time journaling about it. Ask God to help you follow Him wholeheartedly even if others around you say it's a mistake or foolish.

_____

_____

_____

INTERACTIVE LEARNING IDEAS

GET THE CLASS INVOLVED
Learn from Experience

Caleb reminded everyone of God's promises, as well as His faithfulness. He also offered lessons in God's blessings as we age. There are people today who can offer similar stories. It's encouraging to hear them.

Invite a small group of four to five senior members of your church to the class time, people who have been mightily used by God. Feel free to include former missionaries or successful businesspersons, of course. But look beyond that, too, to people whose everyday lives speak powerfully of God.

Invite one guest to tell about a time when he or she saw God work powerfully in his or her life. Then ask another to share about a promise of God he or she waited a long time to see fulfilled. Finally, encourage another to talk about what it's like to discover the new tasks God has for him or her at each stage of life. (Does it get harder? Is it more exciting, more freeing? How are tasks different at each stage?) Ask one of these three questions to each visitor. Allow about ten minutes total for these questions. Then provide five to ten minutes for the group to ask follow-up questions.

TRY THIS ON YOUR OWN
Gaining Hope

Caleb received the promise God had given him decades after he first heard it. In the meantime, he had to fight the battles, simply trusting they would lead to fulfillment of all God had said. In our own lives, we often must be patient for God's promises, and we, too, sometimes face battles in the meantime.

Take some time to strengthen your patience and hope. Spend time praying about the promises you wait for Him to fulfill in your life. Openly share your heart and ask God to grant you patience and strength as you wait. Then, read a couple of stories about heroes of the faith who waited. Some ideas include Hannah longing for Samuel; Abraham and Sarah waiting for their son; Joseph in prison; Hebrews 11, which ends honoring many who waited for promises they never saw fulfilled.

TAKING IT TO THE STREET
Used in a Whole New Way

As a group, visit an antique shop. For an hour or so explore the different items on display. Have each person search for an object that can have a fun new use beyond its original purpose. Let everyone be as silly and creative as they want. In a corner of the shop, gather together and view each other's items, sharing the original purpose of the object and the new use you've imagined for it.

Step outside the store to review the story of Caleb. Talk about how important it is to remember that God uses us in every stage of life. Sometimes, He even gives us a whole new purpose and vision. Then pray that each person would be sensitive to obeying God fully today, and in every life-stage to come. If your group is large, leave a brief thank-you note for the shop, expressing appreciation for their store and for letting your group "invade" for a while. And, if possible, have everyone look for an item to encourage an older person in the church. Choose one inexpensive item for your group to purchase to lift someone's spirits.

WITH YOUR FAMILY
Waiting on God's Promises

Early in the week, plan a trip to a playground or the zoo, or some other activity your family will love. Days before the event, leave a note for your children somewhere surprising where they'll find it, and explain that something special is happening over the weekend. But don't say what the activity is. Every day, leave another note that gives a hint. "Animals live there" might be for the zoo. Or "We'll have a swinging time" for the park. Try to do this for at least three days. Let anticipation build.

On the day of the activity, go to do it. But before you begin, talk about how it felt to wait for the day and time to come. Talk about Caleb and how he had to wait for the promises of God. Have everyone share one thing in their lives that was really hard to wait for and one time when they saw God fulfill a promise for them. Then, go enjoy the activity! (Variation, childless couples can plan a secret date night.) ◆

Continually renew your covenant with God.

LESSON 7

RENEWING YOUR COVENANT WITH GOD
Joshua 24:14–27

KEY VERSE

Choose for yourselves this day whom you will serve. . . . But as for me and my household, we will serve the LORD.

—Joshua 24:15

BACKGROUND SCRIPTURES

Leviticus 26
   Blessings for keeping the covenant and punishment for breaking the covenant
Deuteronomy 5
   Moses reminded the Israelites of the stipulations of the covenant.
Joshua 24:1–13
   Joshua reminded the Israelites of their history and of God's recent providence in their behalf.
Joshua 24:28–33
   The deaths of Joshua and of Eleazar son of Aaron; burial of Joseph's bones at Shechem

DAILY BIBLE READINGS

Monday: Luke 24:1–8
Tuesday: John 11:21–27
Wednesday: Hebrews
                 7:24–28
Thursday: Luke 24:36–49
Friday: Revelation
                 1:12–18
Saturday: Joshua
                 24:14–27
Sunday: Psalm 33

WHY THIS MATTERS

After being dismissed from the Korean Conflict by President Truman, General Douglas MacArthur addressed Congress. "Old soldiers never die," he said; "they just fade away." Centuries earlier, another old soldier addressed the nation of Israel, but his remarks were quite different. General Joshua had grown very old and was ready to die, but he would not simply fade away. He rehearsed God's mighty works on behalf of Israel, urged the nation to renew its covenant with the Lord, warned the nation about false gods, challenged everyone to choose whom they would serve, and confessed his and his family's commitment to serve the Lord.

This lesson challenges us to keep on serving the Lord until He calls us home.

BIBLE COMMENTARY
By James B. Bross, Sr.

Joshua was getting older, and the time of his death was coming near. Under Joshua's leadership much had been accomplished: (1) He had led the Israelites into the Promised Land; (2) the land of Canaan had been conquered over a period of several years, and only pockets of the former nations remained in the land; (3) Joshua had divided up the land among the tribes, and eventually the land was further divided among the individual families within the tribes; (4) Levitical cities and cities of refuge had been designated; and (5) Reuben, Gad, and half the tribe of Manasseh had crossed back over the Jordan River, returning to their allotment to the east of the river after helping in the conquest of the land west of the Jordan.

Before he died, Joshua assembled the leaders of Israel to give them final instructions. Also he warned them against marriages with people from the remaining nations and against alliances with those same people (Josh. 23). "Then Joshua assembled all the tribes of Israel at Shechem" (24:1). There Joshua cited the words of the Lord. He sketched a brief history of God's call to Abraham, Isaac, and Jacob and the subsequent deliverance from Egypt under Moses and Aaron. He reminded them of the victories over the Amorites east of the Jordan, and then the victories over Jericho and the various nations through-out the land of Canaan. "I sent the hornet ahead of you, which drove them out before you—also the two Amorite kings. You did not do it with your own sword and bow. So I gave you a land on which you did not toil and cities you did not build; and you live in them and eat from vineyards and olive groves that you did not plant" (24:12–13).

All this was in preparation for Joshua's final charge to the people, calling them to renew their covenant with the Lord. More than anything else he wanted the people he had successfully led for many years to remain faithful to the

Lord. A renewed covenant between Israel and the Lord was a symbol of Joshua's hopes for them. The reminders he cited from their recent history were given to motivate them to reaffirm their allegiance to the Lord. Those victories proved that God had been faithful to keep His promises to them. Thus, as their parents in the previous generation before them had made a covenant under Moses, they agreed to renew the covenant with the Lord. Unfortunately, the future would show that the depth of their commitment was no greater than that of their parents. For their parents had soon broken their covenant with the Lord, disobeyed at Kadesh Barnea, and subsequently died in the wilderness during a forty-year period of wandering.

WHAT DO YOU THINK?
Joshua called the people to abandon their idols. What idols do people in our culture worship today? What idols tempt you?

Now Fear the Lord and Serve Him with All Faithfulness (Josh. 24:14)

The Israelites had a problem being faithful. Idolatry remained a great snare for them throughout their history, at least until the time of the Babylonian exile. Only in that exile was idolatry finally purged from the people. Joshua recognized their weakness in the face of this temptation. He urged them to serve only the Lord (or in Hebrew, Yahweh). He wanted them to break away from the gods their forefathers had served back in Mesopotamia as well as the gods their parents had worshiped in Egypt. The Lord alone was worthy of their worship. The Lord was worthy not only because of who He was but also because of what He had done for them in the miraculous events of the exodus from Egypt and the conquest of Canaan.

AHA!
We can support and encourage our loved ones to be committed to God, but ultimately, the choice remains their own.

The major gods of the conquered peoples of the Promised Land (and Egypt)	
(Their religions usually included many more gods; the Hittites spoke of their "thousand gods.")	
Egyptians	Ra, Isis, Anubis, Osirus, Amun, Geb, Nut
Amorites	Anu, Enki, Enlil, inanna, Utu, Nanna
Canaanites	Baal, El, Yam, Mot, Amat
Hittites	Tarhunt, Illuyanka, Hattic
Jebusites	Zedek
Perizzites, Girgashites, Hivites	Unknown

But as for Me and My Household, We Will Serve the Lord (Josh. 24:15)

The choice was before them, and Joshua insisted that they choose: **"But if serving the LORD seems undesirable to you, then choose for yourselves this day whom you will serve, whether the gods your forefathers served beyond the River, or the gods of the Amorites, in whose land you are living."** As stated above, Joshua had already made his choice to serve the Lord. Now it was their turn, and he was doing all he could to force the issue as well as to influence them to make the right choice. The choice was seen as a group commitment for the people, not as an individual matter. Joshua chose for his family; they must choose for their families. On the other hand, it was also a matter of the heart, which surely is an individual decision.

DID YOU KNOW?
Joshua called the people to abandon the gods their forefathers worshiped. Joshua's own family (through his father) came from Ur and Haran, where the people worshiped the moon god, ironically called Sin (or Nannir).

Abraham had left the gods of his fathers beyond the Euphrates River. Moses had forsaken the gods of Egypt. Always the most important issue was related to the attitude of the heart. Moses had promised, "The LORD your God will circumcise your hearts and the hearts of your descendants, so that you may love him with all your heart and with all your soul, and live" (Deut. 30:6). Joshua wanted the hearts of his people to be devoted to the Lord in the same way his heart was devoted. He could plead with them and push them to serve the Lord, but ultimately in their hearts they had to decide whether to renew their covenant or not.

Then the People Answered, "Far Be It From Us to Forsake the Lord to Serve Other Gods!" (Josh. 24:16–18)

This was a point of high emotion after Joshua had reminded the Israelites of all God had done for them, and the people were ready to reaffirm their covenant with the Lord. It was obvious that God had supplied their needs abundantly and miraculously, delivering them, protecting them, and defeating their enemies time and again. How could they turn Him down after all He had done? They were ready to accept Joshua's challenge and make their choice for the Lord. Now they in turn recited the miraculous ways the Lord had provided for them. The Lord had delivered them from Egypt with miraculous signs, the Lord had protected them on their journey through hostile nations, and the Lord had driven out nations before them. So they affirmed, **"We too will serve the LORD, because he is our God."**

Some Covenants in the Old Testament	
Genesis 9:8–17	God's covenant with Noah and with all living creatures on earth
Genesis 15	God's first covenant with Abraham promising him the land of Canaan
Genesis 17	God's second covenant with Abraham including the sign of circumcision
Exodus 24	God's covenant with Israel presented through Moses at Mount Sinai
Joshua 24	The renewal of the covenant at Shechem under Joshua
2 Samuel 7	God's covenant with David that David's house (dynasty) would never cease
Jeremiah 31:31–34	God's promise to give a new covenant that would be written on people's hearts rather than on tablets of stone

Joshua Said to the People, "You Are Not Able to Serve the Lord" (Josh. 24:19–20)

Joshua recognized that the reply of the people was quite casual, driven by the emotion of the moment. Instead, Joshua wanted a considered and heartfelt response; thus, he questioned their commitment. After all, their parents had been disobedient in the past, and if they continued that pattern of rebellion, the Lord would bring judgment on them. God had been good to them, but goodness could change to punishment. If they served other gods, disaster and destruction would come upon them. Joshua hoped they were more steadfast than their parents had been, but he well knew how fickle people could be.

But the People Said to Joshua, "No! We Will Serve the Lord" (Josh. 24:21–22)

Unfazed by Joshua's challenge, the people strongly affirmed their loyalty to the Lord, and they pledged that they would serve the Lord. Joshua went on to point out that they themselves were witnesses to this promise and they would judge themselves if they failed to serve the Lord. To this all the people replied, **"Yes, we are witnesses"** (v. 22). At that moment they certainly seemed to have neither reservations nor doubts.

"Now Then," Said Joshua, ". . . Yield Your Hearts to the Lord, the God of Israel" (Josh. 24:23–24)

Joshua pressed for more than just words to demonstrate that their promise was genuinely from their hearts. He asked them to take action to rid themselves

WHAT DO YOU THINK?
There is a corporate responsibility to stay committed to God together. How does your church help individuals and families strengthen their commitment to God? What else can it do?

AHA!
Our promises to God mean nothing if they aren't backed by specific and practical action.

DID YOU KNOW?
The Hebrew name *Joshua* has many variations (Oshea, Hosea), and English "translations" of the name vary, too. However, the name's New Testament English equivalent is Jesus.

of the foreign gods that were such a temptation to them. They should get rid of the source of the trouble by throwing those gods away. It was one thing for the Israelites to say they were committed; taking action was the way to show their commitment and demonstrate their resolve. Their commitment to the covenant was a matter of the heart, but actions often reveal better than words what is truly in the heart. Once again the people pledged: **"We will serve the LORD our God and obey him"** (v. 24). We are not told whether any gods actually ended up in the fire that night.

Joshua Made a Covenant for the People (Josh. 24:25–27)

Next Joshua formalized the promises of the people along with God's terms for the covenant by putting them in writing **in the Book of the Law of God** (v. 26). The record of the promises and the terms would be available for guidance and for future reference. If, indeed, the people were to be witnesses against themselves (24:22), then the record was needed for documentation.

Joshua also made a visible and physical expression of their covenant: **Then he took a large stone and set it up there under the oak near the holy place of the LORD. "See!" he said to all the people. "This stone will be a witness against us. It has heard all the words the LORD has said to us. It will be a witness against you if you are untrue to your God"** (vv. 26–27). The use of stones as reminders of important events was common among the Israelites. Several memorials were set up in the conquest of Canaan, and those memorials helped the people remember God's acts on their behalf. This particular stone at Shechem was to be a continual reminder of the covenant Israel had renewed with the Lord under Joshua to encourage their faithfulness. If they failed to keep their covenant, it was to be a continual rebuke to their sins.

After setting up the memorial, Joshua had done all he could to help shape the future course of events for Israel. He had reminded the people of God's miraculous providence in calling the patriarchs and in bringing Israel out of Egypt and into the Promised Land. He had challenged them to make their choice whether or not to serve the Lord. He had warned them of the consequences they would face if they rebelled. He had written down the terms of the covenant. And he had set up a visible reminder for them. The most important part—the inner work on their hearts—was beyond Joshua's reach. The people had to make their choice, and only then could God "circumcise their hearts." ◆

WHAT ABOUT YOU?
How can you strengthen your personal resolve to turn from idols and serve only the Lord? What can you do to lead your family to be solely and wholly committed to God?

PRAYER
Father, I want to serve You and You alone. Show me where there are idols in my life and forgive me for my unfaithfulness to You.

INTERACTIVE LEARNING IDEAS

GET THE CLASS INVOLVED
A Little Idol Trashing

Joshua called his people to throw out and burn all their idols. While we don't worship wooden or metal idols as much in Western cultures today, idols certainly exist. Play a game to help open everyone's eyes to what these may be.

Play the following game for five minutes. Divide the group into two to four teams. Give each a stack of paper and some pencils or pens. Place a trash can about five feet away from each team. When you start the timer, each team must write down one modern-day idol and one way to get rid of it on a piece of paper. They must then throw it in the trash. One idol per paper. The team with the most idols in the trash after five minutes wins! When the game finishes, gather the papers and read them out loud. Take five to ten more minutes discussing the various idols your group came up with and brainstorm more ways to get rid of them.

TRY THIS ON YOUR OWN
A Solemn Commitment

Although Joshua called the corporate group to serve God only and to clear the community of idols, there is also a great sense in which this commitment was made on an individual level. Make a personal, private commitment to God today that you and your family will serve Him and Him alone.

Then create a written document strengthening your commitment to God. First, brainstorm at least five ways you will put God first in your life. For example, "I will spend quality time with Him every morning (or evening)"; "I will put God first in my family by praying for each person's needs, specifically and individually, during dinnertime prayer"; or "I will give up Sunday night football to attend the community Bible study." It can be anything you like; just be sure it's specific and practical. And you might particularly look for idols in your life and commit to eliminate them. Sign the document. Consider buying a picture frame and placing the document in it. The commitment can be updated from time to time.

TAKING IT TO THE STREET
Bowling for Idols

As a group go to a bowling alley for an afternoon or evening of bowling. Before you begin, gather to discuss what kinds of idols might be in our own lives. Talk about how difficult these can be to eliminate and the hold they have on our lives. Have people give examples of idols and ways to destroy them. Then relate the idols to the pins you're about to knock down. Talk about what happens in bowling when pins are left standing (you're further behind in the game) and what happened to the Israelites when idols were left standing (they fell into sin, slipping further and further from the goal—righteousness). And note how much further you get ahead in the game with every pin (idol) knocked down.

For fun, have people list several modern-day idols. (If your group would be open to it, have them list idols in their own lives.) Start bowling. Each "frame" can be one of the idols on each person's list. Encourage fun and silliness as "idols" are knocked down . . . or left standing.

WITH YOUR FAMILY
Establishing the Mold

Joshua had his people set up a stone to remind them of their commitment. Your family can do the same. Go to a craft store, to the craft section of a superstore, or online and purchase an inexpensive plaster of Paris kit. (The kind you might use to save a baby's handprint.) Some allow you to create a decorative stone for the yard. Prepare the plaster of Paris and mold as directed. Talk about Joshua's call to the Israelites and explain that you want your family to do the same. Pray together to make the commitment. Next, at the top in the wet material, write "We will serve the Lord." Then have each family member press their hand into the plaster, lift it out carefully, and then write their name. Set the stone somewhere in your home or in your garden. ◆

JOSHUA 24:14–27

14 "Now fear the LORD and serve him with all faithfulness. Throw away the gods your forefathers worshiped beyond the River and in Egypt, and serve the LORD.

15 But if serving the LORD seems undesirable to you, then choose for yourselves this day whom you will serve, whether the gods your forefathers served beyond the River, or the gods of the Amorites, in whose land you are living. But as for me and my household, we will serve the LORD."

16 Then the people answered, "Far be it from us to forsake the LORD to serve other gods!

17 It was the LORD our God himself who brought us and our fathers up out of Egypt, from that land of slavery, and performed those great signs before our eyes. He protected us on our entire journey and among all the nations through which we traveled.

18 And the LORD drove out before us all the nations, including the Amorites, who lived in the land. We too will serve the LORD, because he is our God."

19 Joshua said to the people, "You are not able to serve the LORD. He is a holy God; he is a jealous God. He will not forgive your rebellion and your sins.

20 If you forsake the LORD and serve foreign gods, he will turn and bring disaster on you and make an end of you, after he has been good to you."

21 But the people said to Joshua, "No! We will serve the LORD."

22 Then Joshua said, "You are witnesses against yourselves that you have chosen to serve the LORD." "Yes, we are witnesses," they replied.

23 "Now then," said Joshua, "throw away the foreign gods that are among you and yield your hearts to the LORD, the God of Israel."

24 And the people said to Joshua, "We will serve the LORD our God and obey him."

25 On that day Joshua made a covenant for the people, and there at Shechem he drew up for them decrees and laws.

26 And Joshua recorded these things in the Book of the Law of God. Then he took a large stone and set it up there under the oak near the holy place of the LORD.

27 "See!" he said to all the people. "This stone will be a witness against us. It has heard all the words the LORD has said to us. It will be a witness against you if you are untrue to your God."

Renewing Your Covenant with God

Continually renew your covenant with God.

INTO THE SUBJECT

Occasionally citizens of the United States recite the Pledge of Allegiance. It is good to do so often and with heartfelt loyalty. Do believers need to renew their "pledge of allegiance" to God occasionally and do so with heartfelt loyalty?

INTO THE WORD

1. What three responsibilities did Joshua give the Israelites in Joshua 24:14?

2. If you were to give the Israelites a report card letter grade for their past faithfulness to the Lord, what would it be? Why?

3. If you were to grade your own past faithfulness to the Lord, what letter would you assign? Why?

4. Why do you agree or disagree that idolatry may occupy a place in the hearts of Christians?

5. What choice did Joshua offer the Israelites? Do believers today have this choice? Why or why not?

6. Joshua assumed spiritual leadership for his household (v. 15). Should the father assume spiritual leadership for his household today? If so, what specific challenges to this leadership might he encounter?

7. In what sense is God "jealous" (v. 19)?

8. How did the Israelites show they would renew their covenant with the Lord?

9. Do you need to throw away any "gods" as you yield your heart to the Lord (v. 23)? If so, what gods will you throw away today?

INTO THE WORLD

Show the world that you have entered into a covenant with the Lord to worship and serve Him exclusively. Refuse to compromise your convictions and Christian lifestyle!

Making a Covenant

Joshua made a covenant for the people of Israel.
They promised to serve the Lord and throw away foreign gods.

What does it mean to throw away foreign gods today?

_____

_____

For the Israelites it was literally throwing away idols. We might not bow down to idols today, but our attention is often caught up in things that we need to do away with. An example might be not watching a certain television show anymore because of its content or the time it takes away from other things you could be doing that have more impact on your spiritual life.

List three idols that take your time and affection away from the Lord.

1.

2.

3.

Now make a covenant between you and the Lord and have a witness sign it.

I, _____,

will throw away the idols that take my affection and attention away

from You, Lord. I will serve You and You alone.

Signed: _____

Witness: _____

Date: _____

Every generation needs to know God and His redemption.

WHAT ABOUT THE NEXT GENERATION?

Judges 2:6–23

WHY THIS MATTERS

How much longer will freedom reign in Western nations? Doesn't it seem that religious liberty is slipping away from both Canada and the United States as each government imposes restrictions on when, where, and how Christian practices may be observed? If we continue on this slippery slope away from God and absolute truth, soon we may resemble the Israelites in the times of the judges. In those days, everyone did what was right in his own eyes, and God responded by allowing Israel's enemies to oppress the nation until she repented. Deliverance came only when Israel repented and turned back to God.

This lesson raises warning flags and summons us to remain loyal to God.

BIBLE COMMENTARY

By Kelvin G. Friebel

The book of Judges has two introductory sections: 1:1—2:5 and 2:6—3:6, and the two are not in chronological sequence. The starting point of 1:1 is "after the death of Joshua," while 2:6 begins during his life. If placed chronologically, 1:1—2:5 would be inserted between 2:6–9 and 2:10 as it recounts events of the generation that outlived Joshua but prior to the period of the judges.

The first introductory section is more historical; it deals with the continued military conquest of the land. The thematic movement is the "lack of conquest" as it recounts the decline of the Israelites' superiority over the Canaanites in the attempts to drive the Canaanites from the land. It concludes with a theological indictment that explains the lack of continued conquest.

The second introductory section is more theological; it provides the framework through which the particular accounts of the judges that follow in 3:7 through chapter 16 are to be understood.

From Joshua to the Judges (Judg. 2:6–10)

Whereas Judges 2:6 begins by referring to the covenant ceremony during the time of Joshua, verse 7 moves ahead to those who outlived Joshua. That generation is characterized as both serving the Lord and as having **seen all the great things the LORD had done for Israel**. Those "great things" involved the divine protection and provision during the years in the wilderness, the defeat of the Transjordan kings, the crossing of the Jordan River, and the conquests under Joshua. Verses 8–9, quoting Joshua 24:29–30, recount the death and burial of Joshua.

The chronological transition continues in 2:10 as it recounts the rise of the subsequent generation. This new generation is contrasted with the preceding one of verse 7. The preceding one had **served the LORD** (v. 7) and seen God's mighty works on their behalf, whereas the new generation **knew neither the LORD nor what he had done for Israel**. From Judges 1:1—2:5 it is evident

Then the LORD raised up judges, who saved them out of the hands of these raiders. Yet they would not listen to their judges but prostituted themselves to other gods and worshiped them.

—Judges 2:16–17

Deuteronomy 28:15–68
    Punishment that will
    result from disobeying
    the covenant
Joshua 24
    Covenant renewal
    ceremony under Joshua
2 Kings 17:7–23
    The Lord forewarns
    before He executes
    judgment.

Monday: Hebrews 6:1–11
Tuesday: 1 Corinthians
             10:12–13
Wednesday: Matthew
             16:23–28
Thursday: 2 Peter 1:3–11
Friday: Jude 1–25
Saturday: Judges 2:6–23
Sunday: Psalm 34

WHAT DO YOU THINK?
The first generation mentioned here followed the Lord. The second "knew neither the Lord nor what he had done for Israel." What can one generation do to ensure the next generation knows the Lord and His works?

AHA!
While we might break our covenant with God, He will never break His covenant with us—even if it means invoking the "consequences clause."

DID YOU KNOW?
Scripture uses the term *Baals* (plural) because many local forms of the god Baal existed. However, worship practices remained the same, often involving sacred prostitution and even child sacrifice.

that the mighty workings of God were declining as the previous generation failed to do what the LORD had intended them to do with respect to driving out the Canaanites, so the chance of this new generation's seeing such things had also diminished. But this new generation was clearly held responsible for not knowing the Lord. So 2:6–10 is a transition from the faithful generation during the time of Joshua, and just subsequent to his death, to the new generation, which lacked commitment to the Lord.

People's Action: Apostasy Provokes the Lord to Anger (Judg. 2:11–13)

The new generation turned away from the Lord and went after other gods. Several passages in Deuteronomy (4:25; 9:18; 31:29) show that the opening phrase (v. 11, **the Israelites did evil in the eyes of the LORD**) plus **they provoked the LORD to anger** (v. 12) were a stereotypical combination. Likewise here, those two phrases form the thesis statement of verses 11–13, with the former being the general accusation and the latter being the evoked result.

The other phrases in verses 11–13 are the specific elaboration of what the evil was. The accusation here in verses 11–13 was not some superficial disobedience about external matters of proper ritual worship or behavior, but was rebellion against the Lord. The forsaking of the Lord and going after other gods was the supreme breach of the covenant relationship because it violated the first commandment of having no other God besides the Lord. And since the Baals and Ashtoreths were idols, the worship of them inevitably led to a violation of the second commandment of not having any carved images.

Divine Response: Sending Enemies Who Oppress the Israelites (Judg. 2:14–16)

The divine response to the people's apostasy was that the anger of the Lord was expressed against them (v. 14, **in his anger against Israel the LORD . . .**) in the form of oppressing them through their enemies. The Lord actively did three things: He **handed them over to raiders . . .** ; **he sold them to their enemies**; and **the hand of the LORD was against them to defeat them** (vv. 14–15). The Israelites came under the afflicting hands of both the Lord and their enemies, which worked in a coordinated way against the Israelites.

Verses 14–15 express three results deriving from the divine action. First, verse 14 gives the result inflicted on the Israelites: the enemies, in sporadic incursions, **plundered them.** Second is the shift to the consequential situations in which the Israelites found themselves: their military powerlessness to stand against the enemies and the chronic condition of being in dire straits both physically and psychologically.

Third is that the judgment the Lord was carrying out was that which He said He would do (**just as he had sworn to them**). Previously, in Joshua 24:20, Joshua had specifically warned the people. "If you forsake the LORD and serve foreign gods, he will turn and bring disaster [that is, 'evil'] on you." That warning is based on the covenant curses for disobedience in Deuteronomy 28:15–68. The fact that the Lord was doing what He had previously sworn to do emphasizes God's faithfulness to the covenant, even when it meant acting in judgment against disobedience.

People's Action: Groaning in Their Affliction Moves the Lord to Change (Judg. 2:18)

Although stressed in the subsequent narratives through the phrase "and the Israelites cried out to the Lord," this aspect of the pattern is only referred to in verse 18: **the LORD had compassion on them as they groaned under those who oppressed and afflicted them**. The language here in verse 18 makes the comparison between the people's current situation and the oppression they experienced in Egypt. Not only is the term *afflicted* used to describe the Egyptian oppression (compare Ex. 3:9), but the term *groaned* is used only three other times, two of which occur in Exodus. There, the people groaned under the slavery, to which the Lord responded by delivering them (Ex. 2:24; 6:5). Just as the Lord responded to their cries for help while in Egypt, so too the Lord responded to their cries of help in the current oppression and sent a deliverer.

The result of the peoples' plea for help was a moving of the Lord to have "compassion on them." The effect of the people's groaning was that the Lord had a "change of mind," which motivated Him to alter what He was doing or causing to happen. Verse 18 affirms that the Lord responded to the people's situation: just as the people's sin provoked the Lord to anger (v. 12), so now the people's cries for help motivated the Lord to alter the course of action He was taking against them so that He delivered them.

Divine Action: Raising Up of Judges Who Deliver the Israelites (Judg. 2:16–19)

The generation that inaugurated the period of the judges was described in verses 10–13. But in verse 17, the negative character of the generations during the judges is amplified even further through the addition of new accusations. First, **they would not listen to their judges** (v. 17). The people's lack of listening to the Lord (v. 20) was mirrored in their lack of listening to the divinely appointed human leaders.

Second, in the description of going after other gods, there is the repetition from verse 12 that they **worshiped them,** but there is the new aspect that they **prostituted themselves to other gods** (v. 17). Prostituting oneself is used metaphorically to liken the people's spiritual infidelity to sexual promiscuity. Its use as a metaphor to describe going after other gods seems apropos given that some of the worship practices related to those pagan fertility deities involved erotic rituals.

The third accusation is made through a contrast with the previous generation, that this generation had **quickly turned from the way . . . of obedience to the LORD's commands**, thus not walking in the way of their ancestors. This generation continued to be as it was described in verses 10–13, in contrast to **their fathers**, whose obedience is described in verse 7. The language here alludes back to the golden calf incident, where occurs the only other use of the expression "quickly turned away" (Ex. 32:8; Deut. 9:12, 16). This generation is like that one who, a mere forty days after having entered into covenant with the Lord, became involved in idolatrous worship.

In verse 19, with respect to the period after each particular judge died, the three sins that are specified (**following other gods and serving and worshiping them**) are all repeated from verses 11–13. Yet what is stressed in verse 19 is an

---

WHAT DO YOU THINK?
God distanced himself from His children by calling them "this nation." How is that similar to angry parents calling their child by his or her full name?

AHA!
Though God will be just, and does discipline His children, He is quick to answer their cries for help when they turn back to Him.

DID YOU KNOW?
God said Israel's people "prostituted" themselves with idols. This term seems doubly appropriate because the Hebrew word for *Baal*, which meant "lord" was the same word women used when referring to their husbands.

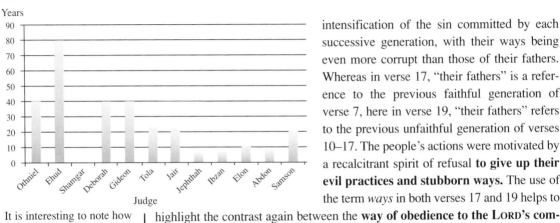

Years

Judge

It is interesting to note how much shorter the judges' service times became as time went on and Israel became less and less willing to listen to them.

WHAT ABOUT YOU?
Problems arose when the baton of faith was not passed from one generation to the next. What are you doing to ensure the next generation knows God and what He has done?

PRAYER
Father, although I cannot make the decision of faith for anyone else, You call me to share about You and Your works to the next generation. Please give me wisdom, creativity, and opportunity to do so.

intensification of the sin committed by each successive generation, with their ways being even more corrupt than those of their fathers. Whereas in verse 17, "their fathers" is a reference to the previous faithful generation of verse 7, here in verse 19, "their fathers" refers to the previous unfaithful generation of verses 10–17. The people's actions were motivated by a recalcitrant spirit of refusal **to give up their evil practices and stubborn ways.** The use of the term *ways* in both verses 17 and 19 helps to highlight the contrast again between the **way of obedience to the LORD's commands** (v. 17) and its opposite, the people's **stubborn ways** (v. 19).

Further Consequence: Nations Left in the Land (Judg. 2:20–23)

Verses 20–22 are a divine declaration in the form of an announcement of judgment, which has three parts: (1) the reason for the judgment is given in verse 20; (2) the declaration of the judgment is given in verses 21–22; and (3) the redemptive purpose of the judgment is stated in verse 22.

As the Lord began His indictment to Israel in verse 20, He called them **this nation**, which gives a sense of the Lord distancing himself from His people. The indictment was expressed in general terms of the people's having **violated the covenant** and **not listened to** the Lord. The indictment was generically that of disobedience, which involved a broad spectrum of transgressions.

The judgment was given in verse 21: the Lord would **no longer drive out before them any of the nations**. Prior to entering the land, in Joshua 1:2–9, God had promised to give His people complete victory in driving out the people of the land. But He had based the success of such on the people's obedience to the covenant law. The judgment here made it clear that the people's lack of obedience had negated the fulfillment of the promise regarding the land. Neither the covenant nor the promises were ultimately voided by the people's disobedience; rather that generation did not realize the fulfillment of the promises.

Whereas in 1:1—2:5, there had been a decline in the "conquest" of the enemies in the land; with this judgment in 2:21, the Lord declared that there would not be any further conquest at all. The fulfillment of this judgment is implicit in the subsequent narratives in which the judges only deal with gaining relief from the enemies' oppression, but are not involved in any way in taking over enemy-held territory allotted to Israel.

In verse 22, however, the Lord declared that even this judgment had a redemptive purpose: **I will use them to test Israel**. The point of this test is to **see whether they will keep the way of the LORD and walk in it** (compare 3:4). Such a test is to be distinguished from any form of tempting to lure someone to do wrong. Whereas a temptation arises out of the desire to have the people fail or fall away, the purpose of a test arises out the desire for the people to prove themselves loyal. In this case, God's desire was that the people would pass the test by remaining faithful to Him and not go after the gods of the nations. ◆

JUDGES 2:6–23

6 After Joshua had dismissed the Israelites, they went to take possession of the land, each to his own inheritance.

7 The people served the LORD throughout the lifetime of Joshua and of the elders who outlived him and who had seen all the great things the LORD had done for Israel.

8 Joshua son of Nun, the servant of the LORD, died at the age of a hundred and ten.

9 And they buried him in the land of his inheritance, at Timnath Heres in the hill country of Ephraim, north of Mount Gaash.

10 After that whole generation had been gathered to their fathers, another generation grew up, who knew neither the LORD nor what he had done for Israel.

11 Then the Israelites did evil in the eyes of the LORD and served the Baals.

12 They forsook the LORD, the God of their fathers, who had brought them out of Egypt. They followed and worshiped various gods of the peoples around them. They provoked the LORD to anger

13 because they forsook him and served Baal and the Ashtoreths.

14 In his anger against Israel the LORD handed them over to raiders who plundered them. He sold them to their enemies all around, whom they were no longer able to resist.

15 Whenever Israel went out to fight, the hand of the LORD was against them to defeat them, just as he had sworn to them. They were in great distress.

16 Then the LORD raised up judges, who saved them out of the hands of these raiders.

17 Yet they would not listen to their judges but prostituted themselves to other gods and worshiped them. Unlike their fathers, they quickly turned from the way in which their fathers had walked, the way of obedience to the LORD's commands.

18 Whenever the LORD raised up a judge for them, he was with the judge and saved them out of the hands of their enemies as long as the judge lived; for the LORD had compassion on them as they groaned under those who oppressed and afflicted them.

19 But when the judge died, the people returned to ways even more corrupt than those of their fathers, following other gods and serving and worshiping them. They refused to give up their evil practices and stubborn ways.

20 Therefore the LORD was very angry with Israel and said, "Because this nation has violated the covenant that I laid down for their forefathers and has not listened to me,

What about the Next Generation?

Every generation needs to know
God and His redemption.

INTO THE SUBJECT

Do you wonder what the next generation "is coming to"? Joshua led the Israelites to renew their covenant with the Lord, but soon after, he died. What became of the next generation?

INTO THE WORD

1. What alarming contrast do you find in Judges 2:6–11?

2. What words come to mind to describe what life would be like if everyone ignored laws and did what was right in his or her own eyes?

3. Why do you agree or disagree that a congregation reaches a critical juncture when a godly pastor retires, passes away, or becomes the pastor of another church?

4. What cycle do you see repeated in verses 10–19?

5. Why do you agree or disagree that any "Christian" nation that declines spiritually puts itself at risk of being subdued by its enemies?

6. What happened in Canaan because the Israelites violated God's covenant (vv. 20–23)?

7. How would you differentiate "freedom of religion" from "freedom from religion"?

8. How would you define "separation of church and state"?

9. Although neither the United States nor Canada is in a covenant relationship with God, what principles for national security can you draw from Joshua 2:6–23?

INTO THE WORLD

Write a letter to the editor this week in which you oppose a political decision that violates God's Word.

21 I will no longer drive out before them any of the nations Joshua left when he died.

22 I will use them to test Israel and see whether they will keep the way of the LORD and walk in it as their forefathers did."

23 The LORD had allowed those nations to remain; he did not drive them out at once by giving them into the hands of Joshua.

WHO'S WHO?

Match the judge on the left with the appropriate information on the right.

1. Abimelech ____

2. Abdon ____

3. Jepthah ____

4. Samson ____

5. Shamgar ____

6. Tola ____

7. Jair ____

8. Ibzan ____

9. Deborah ____

10. Ehud ____

11. Elon ____

12. Gideon ____

13. Othniel ____

14. Barak ____

A. Said that Sisera would be killed by a woman

B. Killed Eglon by stabbing him

C. Asked God for assurance by leaving a wool fleece out

D. Killed six hundred Philistines

E. Caleb's younger brother

F. Took ten thousand men to Mount Tabor and defeated Sisera's army

G. Led Israel for twenty-three years

H. The son of Hillel, led Israel for eight years

I. God had his seventy brothers murdered because of his wickedness

J. Led Israel for twenty-two years and had thirty sons

K. A Zebulunite who led Israel for ten years

L. Defeated the Ammonites but had to sacrifice his daughter because of a vow he made to God

M. Led Israel for seven years and had thirty sons and thirty daughters

N. Killed more people with his death than he did while he lived

INTERACTIVE LEARNING IDEAS

GET THE CLASS INVOLVED
Who's that God?

While the generation of people Joshua worked with ended up following the Lord, the subsequent generations didn't. One of their greatest temptations was to worship the local gods Baal and Ashtoreth. Do some digging together as a group to learn more about Baal and Ashtoreth.

Divide into four groups. Have two Bible dictionaries and two concordances ready. Hand a concordance or dictionary to each group. For five or ten minutes, have them search to see what they can learn about these gods. Then take ten minutes together to share what everyone discovered. Finally discuss how the Israelites might be tempted to worship these gods, and how we are tempted to worship our culture's idols as well.

TRY THIS ON YOUR OWN
A Neighborly Pursuit

In many cases, your neighbors don't worship physical idols (although some may). But they do hold a different religious perspective than you. Perhaps your neighbors are Muslim, Buddhist, Christian Scientist, or Jehovah's Witness. Take some time to understand what they believe and hold it up to the light of Scripture.

Pick the religion of one of your neighbors, or one that simply interests you, and read a book or two about it. Go to the Christian bookstore or to an online Christian bookstore and pick up a book on that subject. Look for books in the comparative religion category, or perhaps evangelism. You'll find books that give you general information on a given faith (or several major faiths) or that teach you how to reach out to folks with a given religious view. As you read, take notes about what that religion teaches. Then consider how the Bible views those same topics. It'll prepare you to not only understand your neighbor, but to respond to any questions or difference of opinion they may have when you discuss spiritual issues.

TAKING IT TO THE STREET
Every Parent's Dream

We all have a responsibility to teach the next generation about God and what He has done. As a group, offer a "parent's night out" for the moms and dads of your church. You'll babysit their children for free. Host it at someone's house. (You may need to have parents sign up in advance if space is limited. Or if your group is large enough, do this in two homes.) During the evening, show a child-friendly movie. Try to find some that have a faith message as well. Some ideas for older children include *Soul Surfer*, *The Blind Side*, or the Narnia series. For young children, try VeggieTales movies, *The Prince of Egypt*, or the Sugar Creek Gang series. Or, in advance, ask parents for titles of movies they recommend that their children love. (That way you know the parents are comfortable with your selection.) You might even be able to borrow a copy. Have healthy snacks available.

Before the movie begins, present a simple gospel message to the children, perhaps using the wordless book or a similar evangelism tool. Pray a simple prayer of salvation as a model. Then invite them to talk to any of the adults if they have any questions. After that, hit play on the movie and enjoy a fun evening with kids.

WITH YOUR FAMILY
Scripture Puzzler

God calls parents to share about Him and His works with their children. Here's a fun family game to help you do that. Grab some blank paper and colored markers. Together as a family, create some Scripture puzzles. Assign each family member an evangelizing verse. Some suggestions include John 3:16; Romans 3:23; Ephesians 2:8–9; and John 1:1. Have each person write out the verse they were assigned on the paper. Include the reference. On the other side, they should draw a picture inspired by their verse. Then, each person should cut the words of the verse apart.

Ask each person to mix up the words of their verse. (Keep each verse separate, of course.) Then pass around the "puzzles" so everyone has a chance to piece all the verses together. After all the verses go around, send them around again, seeing who can put their verse together the fastest. It's a great way to memorize verses together. And you can carefully turn each puzzle over and see the picture on the other side. ✦

God selects and equips people to be His leaders.

LESSON 9

GODLY LEADERSHIP
Judges 4:4–16

BACKGROUND SCRIPTURES

2 Corinthians 5:7
    Living by faith
Hebrews 11
    The hall of faith
    includes Barak.
1 Corinthians 1:27–29
    God uses the weak
    and foolish things
    of the world.
Proverbs 3:5–6
    Where we should
    put our trust
Zechariah 4:6
    Strength is in the
    Spirit of the Lord.

DAILY BIBLE READINGS

Monday: Acts 6:1–7
Tuesday: Exodus 3:4–12
Wednesday: Luke 10:1–11
Thursday: John 21:15–19
Friday: 1 Samuel
            16:10–13
Saturday: Judges 4:4–16
Sunday: Psalm 35

WHY THIS MATTERS

One might wonder how our churches would function without the contribution of godly women. They usually outnumber men as Sunday school teachers, nursery attendants, visitation workers, and choir members. They often give their time and talent unselfishly to the Lord on behalf of others without expecting any praise.

Missionary work, too, often moves forward because dedicated women serve as teachers, nurses, directors of orphanages, and musicians. In many facets of missionary work, they serve where there are no male missionaries. Their commitment and compassion are exemplary.

This lesson spotlights Deborah, a female judge and brave military leader, and it instills gratitude in us for godly women who serve the Lord.

BIBLE COMMENTARY

By Jim Moretz

The book of Judges chronicles the Israelites' struggle to conquer Canaan, both the land and the religion. The story is a cycle of divine deliverance, human disobedience, divine punishment, human repentance, and divine deliverance. The Israelites always seemed outnumbered and seemed to lack the confidence for victory. Repeatedly, the writer of Judges recorded that the Lord went before the military and secured its victory. The men merely needed to do as God commanded. With that sort of confidence, it is an intriguing story to see how quickly the Israelites forgot their God and accepted the foreign teachings of the Canaanite religion.

Also within that cycle is the tragic story of an ever-increasing level of sin within the Israelite people. With each passing judge, the people did more evil in the sight of the Lord than their fathers. Successive judges received less support and more resistance from the people. In the end, Samson, the last judge, was as much a representation of the sinful people as he was a representation of the salvation of God. In fact, the summary of Samson's reign bears no mention of peace in the land while he lived (16:31).

Historically, this story occurred at the end of the Bronze Age and beginning of the Iron Age, roughly 1200 B.C. The iron chariots in verse 3 had iron fittings. They were not made exclusively of iron or they would have been too heavy to move. The Israelites were slow to adapt iron works, so the Canaanite iron chariots were a formidable force to face. This is interesting since the battle happened in the plains, and the Israelites led by Deborah lived in the hill country out of reach of Sisera's chariots. The Israelites intentionally engaged their oppressor.

So another contextual aspect is power. This story explicitly shows the power of God superior to the power of humanity, and the power of faith superior to the power of oppression. Even though power is a constant struggle in the human experience, it was a special concern during this time when power shifted quickly and often between embattled cities and self-proclaimed rulers "of the four corners of the earth." Political intrigue was intense, fueled by extensive intelligence networks and ever-changing alliances. Note that Jabin "reigned in Hazor," but his army commander "lived in Harosheth Haggoyim." This relationship was defined and maintained carefully. It was Sisera's defeat that signaled Jabin's demise (4:23–24). Power was truly precarious.

In one particular way, the story of the Judges is a precursor to the story of Jesus. "Whenever the LORD raised up a judge for them, he was with the judge and saved them out of the hands of their enemies as long as the judge lived; for the LORD has compassion on them as they groaned under those who oppressed and afflicted them" (2:18). That is, the judge was a type of incarnation, though a temporary one. "But when the judge died, the people returned to ways even more corrupt than their fathers" (2:19). As long as there was a living presence of God among them, the Israelites did not deny their God, but without the judge, "everyone did as he saw fit" (21:25).

Deborah and Her Authority (Judg. 4:4–6)

Deborah's authority spanned all aspects of life—religious, civil, and military. The first thing we learn about Deborah is that she was a **prophetess** (v. 4). Despite the modern view of prophecy as foretelling the future, the biblical understanding of prophecy is the utterance of divine words. In the Old Testament, a prophet (or prophetess) was not necessarily a priest. (Later God used prophets to rebuke the priesthood.) So the most important thing the title "prophetess" conveys is that Deborah possessed a personal relationship with God. It was from this relationship that her power was derived. This differs significantly from Israel's neighbors in Canaan. Other peoples considered their leaders not only divinely appointed, but divine themselves. But the task of the prophetess was to mediate the relationship between God and the people as a divine mouthpiece and human exemplar. It is interesting to note that the title "prophet" is not associated with any other judge.

Next, we are introduced to Deborah's husband. We can assume he was an important man simply because he is mentioned in the text. Also telling is the description of Deborah as **the wife of Lappidoth** (v. 4) such that the reader was expected to know that name even if Deborah was somehow unknown.

Third, we see Deborah as the judge of Israel. At this time Israel was governed by tribal clans. There was no king or centralized government. The rest of the region was dominated by city-states with periodic "dynasties" rising to control several cities for relatively short times. However, the biblical precedent, at least since Moses, was for God to appoint a divine speaker to judge civil life according to divine principles. The cases heard by Deborah would be those too difficult for tribal tribunes. She was something like the Supreme Court of Israel.

That **she held court under the Palm of Deborah** (v. 5) may suggest she owned land. It may be that the palm was named after her, that the land was her inheritance, or that the palm had been named after one of her ancestors. The palm usually denotes peace in the Bible. This would be fitting in here due to the association of peace with the lives of the early judges (see 3:11, 30; 5:31).

WHAT DO YOU THINK?
God had secured the victory, but Barak struggled to believe that and needed Deborah to come with him. What do we lean on when we struggle to trust God alone?

AHA!
Wisdom and courage both come from an intimate relationship with God. And that helps to assure us of God's victory.

DID YOU KNOW?
Mount Tabor, a thirteen-hundred-foot-high mountain located northeast of the battle site, is where tradition holds Jesus' transfiguration took place (Mark 9:2), although no concrete evidence supports the claim.

WHAT DO YOU THINK?
Like Barak, we may believe that God is powerful, but still remain uncertain that He'll actually use His strength on our behalf. How can we begin to recognize that God works personally in our lives?

AHA!
We may face the most frightening opponents, with seemingly unbeatable weapons, but God can send them fleeing.

DID YOU KNOW?
The term translated "routed," used to describe how decisively Israel won the victory, is the same word used to describe the overwhelming panic the Egyptians experienced at the Red Sea (Ex. 14:24).

Finally, we see Deborah's authority extended over the military. However, her military authority rested on her role as a prophetess. **"The LORD, the God of Israel, commands you"** (v. 6), she told Barak. We are not told what Barak's military experience was, but we may assume he had some. Israel did not have a standing army at this time. It operated on the militia principle. So any military authority was occasional; that is, the authority existed only as long as the battle or war was fought. Afterward, the fighting men returned to their families, farms, and trades. This system was well fitted for the office of the prophet, which was also occasional in that the prophet did not receive a constant stream of communication from God, but rather received messages that were time sensitive and historically centered. So Deborah did not call Barak on her own authority, but in response to God's word given to Deborah.

All in all, we see in Deborah a person with whom God was intimate. This intimacy manifested itself in authority among her people. Her gender did not seem to be a factor. God did not seem to call her because she was a woman or because no man was fit to lead. We are not told why she was called. We are given a picture of faith, intimacy, and power that transcends human understanding and invites us into the mind of God.

Preparing for Battle (Judg. 4:6–13)

From a militaristic viewpoint, the Israelites had no preparation for this battle. Barak garnered **ten thousand** militia **men** (v. 6) and took a position on the high ground, out of the reach of Sisera's chariots. Then he waited. Before we judge Barak too harshly, we must understand what he understood.

Sisera had extensive military preparation. He had a standing army that included **nine hundred iron chariots** (v. 13). These chariots carried two, possibly three, soldiers each, plus extra weapons. Sisera also had a spy, **Heber the Kenite** (v. 11), who used to have an alliance with Israel. Heber positioned himself between the city of Jabin and the city of Sisera. Since trade was so important, this was probably a primary economic alliance. Probably Harosheth Haggoyim was a valuable trading port, and as such was subject to frequent attacks. Sisera would have defended it before; therefore, he would have had some idea of his battle plan. The story presents Sisera as confidently taking up his position.

The key to preparation for the Israelites was faith. God declared that He would lure Sisera, his chariots, and his army into a vulnerable position, and He would

Key New Testament Verses on Spiritual Battles		
Scripture Reference	**Verse**	**Parallel Concept**
Ephesians 6:12	"For our struggle is not against flesh and blood, but against the rulers, against the authorities, against the powers of this dark world and against the spiritual forces of evil in the heavenly realms."	Barak's battle was against the dark forces of fear. People should not threaten us. They are not our enemies.
1 Timothy 6:12	"Fight the good fight of the faith. Take hold of the eternal life to which you were called when you made your good confession in the presence of many witnesses."	Our decisions have consequences beyond our understanding as did Barak's.
Romans 5:8	"But God demonstrates his own love for us in this: While we were still sinners, Christ died for us."	God has gone ahead of us into the spiritual battle and has secured our victory.

give the Israelites the victory. Barak believed that his God was strong, but he did not understand the personal nature of his God. Barak's mistake was that he treated Deborah like an idol. Armies carried the idols of their gods into battle as talismans. Barak considered Deborah a talisman. He lacked the personal knowledge of God that Deborah had. Barak believed he would win if Deborah were with him because he considered her presence proof of God's presence. Interestingly, Hebrews chapter 11 begins, "Now faith is being sure of what we hope for and certain of what we do not see." However, it is Barak, not Deborah, who is listed in verse 32 as extolling this virtue.

Deborah agreed to go with Barak in a matter-of-fact manner, suggesting she had prior knowledge of Barak's reaction. We need not see the Lord's decision as retribution against Barak as much as it is the logical result of Barak's actions. God promised Barak strength. Barak chose the weaker way, thinking it was the stronger way. So God used what Barak thought was weakness to defeat what Barak thought might be undefeatable.

We must not make the mistake of arguing from the particular to the general so that we see in this story a biblical assertion that women are weaker than men. It is true that men generally posses greater muscular strength than women. It is also true that women were not considered equal to men in most ancient societies. However, this does not constitute a general principle of female subordination. In fact, this story may illustrate the opposite. God uses what society deems weak to defeat what society reveres as strong. Women are not inherently weak. Men are not inherently strong. The issue is faith. While Heber broke his alliance with Israel (an unfaithful act), his wife, Jael, remained faithful. The moral of the story is this: "Trust in the LORD with all thine heart; and lean not unto thine own understanding. In all thy ways acknowledge him, and he shall direct thy paths" (Prov. 3:5–6 KJV).

The Battle (Judg. 4:14–16)

After building the anticipation and setting out the tensions, the battle itself is described simply and briefly. The important points are not how the men were strategically placed or how the chariots became impotent. The vital question is the rhetorical, **"Has not the LORD gone ahead of you?"** (v. 14).

From the resounding yes came two results. First, Sisera abandoned the chariots in which he had placed all his confidence and security. Note the absence of the adjective "iron" in verse 15 that was present in verse 13. The powerful iron chariots were now objects of derision, no longer evoking fear.

Second, Barak continued the pursuit, giving hope that the Israelites might yet conquer the Canaanites. He continued to pursue the enemy back to its source and utterly destroyed it. This is where Israel had failed in the past, refusing to destroy the enemies of God.

Ultimately, the victory came from the recurring biblical motif of "the Day of the LORD." In verse 14, Deborah shouted, **"Go! This is the day the LORD has given Sisera into your hands."** On this day, judgment came to God's enemies and salvation came to His people. That is the essence of "the Day of the LORD." The day the world knows that it lives not by might nor by power, but by the Spirit of the Lord Almighty (Zech. 4:6). ✦

WHAT ABOUT YOU?
When are you like Deborah, trusting with simple faith in God? And when are you like Barak, insecure and struggling to press forward in confidence?

PRAYER
Father, You go before me to defeat my enemies. Teach me to run to the battle with great confidence.

INTERACTIVE LEARNING IDEAS

GET THE CLASS INVOLVED
A Dramatic Victory

The story of Deborah, Barak, and the victory over the Canaanites provides a vivid picture of trusting God for success. It offers a great example for our own lives, as we face battles that seem to overwhelm us. Use a little drama to bring the lesson home.

Divide the group into two. Have one side create a skit based on the Bible story as it reads in Scripture. A few people should play Deborah, Barak, Israelites, and Canaanites. The other half of the group should develop a skit that parallels the story in modern times. There should be a wise advisor (a Deborah) and someone with a battle to fight (a Barak). Be creative with the modern-day battle: an illness, a financial problem, or a moral dilemma at work. Allow five minutes for the groups to create their skits and three minutes each to present them. Bring the group back together for a five-minute discussion of how we can trust God for victory in our own lives.

TRY THIS ON YOUR OWN
Real-Life Victors

God gives His people powerful victories even today. Hearing such stories encourages our hearts and inspires our courage in the midst of battle.

Set up a meeting with someone you admire who you know has faced formidable foes in his or her life: a life-threatening disease, a seemingly insurmountable task, or a deep heartache. Consider getting together for coffee or lunch.

After visiting a while, tell the person you'd like to hear how God accomplished great things in his or her life. Ask how he or she felt when the "battle" was coming. Invite him or her to share how God provided victory. Discuss what made it easy or difficult to trust God. Look for ways He removed obstacles, provided strength, performed miracles, or otherwise showed himself present. Find out if anyone acted as a Deborah, offering encouragement and wisdom. Discover how God works in lives today.

TAKING IT TO THE STREET
Chariot Drag Racing

Deborah and Barak faced a foe with the latest in military technology—iron chariots. But God gave them victory anyway. Enjoy your own "chariot races."

Find large, old blankets (ones you don't mind wrecking) and large pieces of cardboard (big enough to sit on). These are your "chariots." Meet at a park as a group, "chariots" in hand. Divide into teams of at least four. Designate a route with a starting point and a finish line. (It's fun to include a turn or two.) One person from each team should sit on the cardboard (a good task for kids), while the others push and pull them on the blanket to the finish line. Have fun watching the teams race.

During a break in the fun, review the story of Barak and Deborah and how they faced the intimidating military force with advanced weaponry. However, with God on their side, they won anyway. And those chariots that were so state of the art? They became useless.

WITH YOUR FAMILY
A Roller-Coaster Ride

When God calls us into battle, He goes before us, preparing the way. Help your family grasp this truth by creating a handmade marble roller coaster.

First, purchase or gather a few marbles. Then send your family scavenging the house for roller-coaster-making material: toilet paper and wrapping paper tubes, cardboard, heavy paper, funnels, plastic placemats, short pieces of hose, and more. If you'd like a long roller coaster, gather chairs and stacks of books to use as "pillars" to maintain your roller coaster's height and to provide something to attach the other items to. You'll need a small bowl for a landing spot.

Start your roller coaster somewhere high, such as a counter, fireplace mantel, or tabletop. Attach items together with strong tape to create a path for the marble to follow. Keep playing with it  until you form a path that guides a rolling marble down into the bowl. Roll the marble down to see if it works. As you wrap up the activity, talk about how you planned out the course and prepared it so the marble would successfully land exactly where it should. Without your help, the marble would simply fall flat to the ground. Similarly, as seen in the story of Deborah and Barak, God goes before us when we face trials to ensure victory—that we'll land safely and exactly where we should. ◆

JUDGES 4:4–16

4 Deborah, a prophetess, the wife of Lappidoth, was leading Israel at that time.

5 She held court under the Palm of Deborah between Ramah and Bethel in the hill country of Ephraim, and the Israelites came to her to have their disputes decided.

6 She sent for Barak son of Abinoam from Kedesh in Naphtali and said to him, "The LORD, the God of Israel, commands you: 'Go, take with you ten thousand men of Naphtali and Zebulun and lead the way to Mount Tabor.

7 I will lure Sisera, the commander of Jabin's army, with his chariots and his troops to the Kishon River and give him into your hands.'"

8 Barak said to her, "If you go with me, I will go; but if you don't go with me, I won't go."

9 "Very well," Deborah said, "I will go with you. But because of the way you are going about this, the honor will not be yours, for the LORD will hand Sisera over to a woman." So Deborah went with Barak to Kedesh,

10 where he summoned Zebulun and Naphtali. Ten thousand men followed him, and Deborah also went with him.

11 Now Heber the Kenite had left the other Kenites, the descendants of Hobab, Moses' brother-in-law, and pitched his tent by the great tree in Zaanannim near Kedesh.

12 When they told Sisera that Barak son of Abinoam had gone up to Mount Tabor,

13 Sisera gathered together his nine hundred iron chariots and all the men with him, from Harosheth Haggoyim to the Kishon River.

14 Then Deborah said to Barak, "Go! This is the day the LORD has given Sisera into your hands. Has not the LORD gone ahead of you?" So Barak went down Mount Tabor, followed by ten thousand men.

15 At Barak's advance, the LORD routed Sisera and all his chariots and army by the sword, and Sisera abandoned his chariot and fled on foot.

16 But Barak pursued the chariots and army as far as Harosheth Haggoyim. All the troops of Sisera fell by the sword; not a man was left.

> "You gain strength, courage and confidence by every experience in which you really stop to look fear in the face. You must do the thing you think you cannot do."
>
> —*Eleanor Roosevelt*

Godly Leadership

God selects and equips people to be His leaders.

INTO THE SUBJECT

Some nations have assigned the highest office in the land to a woman and then applauded her as a strong, wise, capable leader. What happened centuries ago, when a woman became a leader in Israel when a powerful enemy oppressed the nation?

INTO THE WORD

1. What leadership roles did Deborah fill according to Judges 4:4?

2. How has a Christian woman exerted an outstanding influence in your life?

3. Based on his response to Deborah (see vv. 6–8), what is your first impression of Barak?

4. How did Deborah respond to Barak?

5. How did she encourage him for battle (v. 14)?

6. What admirable qualities do you see in Barak?

7. How does the Lord's victory over Sisera encourage you?

8. In what circumstances has the Lord achieved a great victory for you?

INTO THE WORLD

Christians are a minority and face many adversaries but do not fear. Armed with the knowledge that the Lord fights for you, stand firm in the faith.

Use Scripture to Fight Spiritual Battles

The lesson provides three New Testament Scriptures about spiritual battles.
Memorize all three of these verses.

How could Barak have benefitted from and been encouraged by knowing these verses?

_____

_____

_____

To help you remember them, first write a summary of the verses in your own words.
Then memorize them.

Ephesians 6:12—

_____

_____

_____

_____

1 Timothy 6:12—

The Armor of God

10 Finally, be strong in the Lor
and in the strength of His might.
11 Put on the full armor of God
so that you will be able to stand fir
against the schemes of the devil
12 For our struggle is not agains
Romans 5:8— *and blood, but against the ruler*
against the power
forces of the
spiritual

The power for victory comes from God.

THE BATTLE BELONGS TO THE LORD

Judges 7:1–8, 19–21

WHY THIS MATTERS

A Scottish pastor was criticized by his board because only one soul had accepted Christ during the fiscal year. "That was little Bobby Moffat," one of the board members said despairingly. Little did anyone anticipate at the time that Bobby Moffat would eventually become a missionary to Africa, where he would open mission stations in the interior and translate the Bible into the language of the Bechuanas. But then, God delights to use ordinary people to do extraordinary things. God used Gideon, a peasant farmer, and three hundred poorly armed men to defeat the vast numbers of Midianite invaders.

This lesson inspires confidence in God's unrivaled wisdom and power.

BIBLE COMMENTARY

By Kelvin G. Friebel

The story of Gideon in Judges 6–8 follows the pattern of apostasy to oppression to crying out (groaning) to deliverance established in 2:11–19. The details of the story are filled in more than any of the three preceding accounts. Thus it gives a much more vivid description of the oppression caused by the marauding Midianites, Amalekites, and other eastern peoples. In response to the people's crying out, the Lord sent a prophet to explain the reason for the oppression. The Lord appeared to Gideon, calling and commissioning him to deliver the people. But first, the Lord commanded Gideon to tear down the family and city altar to Baal and cut down the accompanying Asherah pole (6:25–32).

The Setting and Location (Judg. 7:1)

The Midianites were a seminomadic people from that region. The Amalekites were also a nomadic type people. The "eastern peoples" seems to be a generic description of other various nomadic tribes from the Transjordan. Throughout chapter 7, the enemy is simply referred to as "Midian," "the Midianites," "the camp of Midian," which is an inclusive term and does not mean that the Israelites fought only one of these people groups in the battle.

The Midianite camp was located **near the hill of Moreh** (modern Nebi Dahi), lying about four miles north of **the Spring of Harod** (En Harod) at the base of Mount Gilboa, where Gideon's men were. They were encamped some three miles directly east of Gideon's hometown. As the scene began, the Israelite forces were outnumbered at least four to one.

Reduction in the Israelite Forces (Judg. 7:2–8)

Even though Gideon was seriously outnumbered, the Lord told him he had **too many men for me to deliver Midian into their hands** (v. 2). The Lord

KEY VERSE

In order that Israel may not boast against me that her own strength has saved her.
—Judges 7:2

BACKGROUND SCRIPTURES

Deuteronomy 20:1–9
Regulations for those going to battle
1 Samuel 17:1–54
David's defeat of Goliath, because the battle belongs to the Lord
Joshua 6
The Lord's defeat of Jericho through the Israelites' shouting and blowing trumpets
2 Chronicles 20:1–30
The Lord's defeat of the enemies under Jehoshaphat, because the battle belongs to the Lord
Psalm 44:1–8
The Lord gives the victory.
Isaiah 36–37
Hezekiah told to trust in the Lord in light of the invading Assyrians
1 Corinthians 1:26–29
God using the weak

DAILY BIBLE READINGS

Monday: Luke 8:43–48
Tuesday: Titus 2:11–15
Wednesday: Mark 16:1–7
Thursday: 1 Samuel 17:41–47
Friday: Philippians 3:20—4:1
Saturday: Judges 7:1–8, 19–21
Sunday: Psalm 36

WHAT DO YOU THINK?
God's instructions made little military sense at first. Despite that and some fear, Gideon still pressed forward in obedience. Is it possible to have faith and fear at the same time?

AHA!
Sometimes it feels as though God is setting us up for defeat, when He's really preparing a miracle.

DID YOU KNOW?
Harod, the name of the spring where Gideon's men camped, means "trembling." It might refer to how the Israelites felt or to the response of the Midianites when they realized they were under attack.

recognized the potential within the people to take credit for a victory (cf. Deut. 8:11–18). To demonstrate beyond a doubt that it was not the people's achievement, the military force would be pared down to the point that any victory achieved must be considered a miracle granted by the Lord.

The reduction of the army occurred in two stages. The first allowed those who were afraid to leave: **Anyone who trembles with fear may turn back and leave Mount Gilead** (Judg. 7:3). Fear on the part of Israelite soldiers was evidence of a lack of trust in the divine presence and promises. When Gideon's forces were so challenged, almost 70 percent of them left the battle area (**So twenty-two thousand men left, while ten thousand remained** [v. 3]). But the irony is that Gideon was still afraid (vv. 10–11); when those who were afraid were asked to leave, perhaps Gideon should have been among them!

Left with ten thousand men, Gideon must have been further disconcerted when the Lord told him, **"There are still too many men"** (v. 4) and went through a second process of reduction (vv. 4–6). The Lord said: **"I will sift them for you there. If I say, 'This one shall go with you,' he shall go; but if I say, 'This one shall not go with you,' he shall not go."** Since the conditions in verse 5 was revealed only to Gideon (**the LORD told him**), the men were totally unaware of the criterion, and probably even that they were being evaluated.

Once the fighting force had been pared down by another 97 percent, leaving less than 1 percent of the original fighting force, the Lord again gave the promise to Gideon that He would give the victory: **I will save you and give the Midianites into your hands** (v. 7).

To Gideon's credit, he did not question the Lord in this process, but was fully obedient to what the Lord told him to do. When commanded in verse 4, **"Take them down to the water,"** verse 5 tells us, **So Gideon took the men down to the water**. When God told him, with respect to the ninety-seven hundred men, **"Let all the other men go, each to his own place"** (v. 7), **Gideon sent the rest of the Israelites to their tents** (v. 8). Regardless of what Gideon was feeling internally at that point, he was faithful to what the Lord commanded him to do.

The Israelites Executing the Battle Plan (Judg. 7:19–20)

We are not told where Gideon's battle plan came from; there is no reference to it being given directly to him by the Lord. Such stands out in light of the Lord's repeated direct communications with Gideon in verses 2, 4–5, and 7. The silence may indicate that the plan was not explicitly communicated to him, but developed by Gideon through using godly wisdom, which is an equally valid way of following God when there is no explicit new divine directive. It may be that the plan had been preformulated, since in verse 8 the acquiring of the "provisions and trumpets" from the others before they left seems to already anticipate the need of those items in the coming battle. Although "provisions" can refer to supplies and food in a general sense, in this case it is probably more specific, synonymous with "utensils," thus including the jars used in verses 16 and 19–20.

The plan was executed just as Gideon had laid it out (7:16–18). The three hundred men were divided into three companies and stationed at three different locations around the Midianite camp at its very **edge** (v. 19). Each of the three hundred men had a **trumpet**, literally a "ram's horn" (*shofar*) as opposed to a metal trumpet. The different blasts of the ram's horn trumpets were used to direct the troops in battle (see 2 Sam. 18:16; Neh. 4:18–20), and thus normally each soldier would not have one, but only those directing the troop movements. They each also had **torches**, whose flames were concealed in empty pottery **jars** that could be easily broken.

The "attack" took place **at the beginning of the middle** of the night **watch** (Judg. 7:19). Assuming that the night was broken into three watches (8 p.m. to midnight, midnight to 4 a.m., 4 to 8 a.m.), such would be around midnight. It occurred **just after they had changed the guard**, at a point when there would still have been some movement in the camp, which would have made the movements of the Israelites less detectable.

When Gideon's company **blew their trumpets and broke the jars** (v. 19), the other two companies immediately joined in (v. 20). That was followed by the war cry going up: **"A sword for the LORD and for Gideon!"** (v. 20). That cry was synonymous with "The battle [or victory] belongs to the commander, the LORD, and to his human commander, Gideon" (see 1 Sam. 17:47; 2 Chron. 20:15; Prov. 21:31).

The silence of the night was shattered by the repeated blaring of the horns, the unison breaking of the jars, and the repeated shouting of the war cry. The darkness of the night was shattered by the light from the torches. Because it was nighttime—with the majority of the Midianites asleep—in the stupor of their rude awakening, they probably assumed that the multiplicity of horns being blown and the brightness of the many torches meant the Israelites were still at their original level of strength. And the war cry that spoke of the sword suggested that the Israelites had their weapons fully drawn and were attacking the fringes of the camp. But it is clear that the "battle" strategy was intended to create a ruse and a ruckus that would produce panic among the Midianites, and probably stampede their camels, rather than being a strategy of fighting. With the **torches in their left hands and holding in their right hands the trumpets** (Judg. 7:20), they had no free hands with which they could wield any weapons. Also, the Israelites did not invade the Midian camp, rather "each man held his position around the camp" (7:21).

The Result of the Israelites' and the Lord's Actions (Judg. 7:21–22)

In the midst of the Israelites' "nighttime serenade," verse 21 recounts that **the Midianites ran, crying out as they fled**. Because "ran" and "fled" seem redundant, "ran" may have the connotation of "jumping up"—the first reaction they had when the noise disrupted their sleep (see Ps. 18:29; Joel 2:9, where it means "leaping" or "scaling" walls). The Midianites were thrown into a panicked, hysterical flight. But beyond just fleeing from the camp without casualties, verse 22 recounts the other thing that happened. Here the narrator did precisely what the Lord intended in verse 2, in that the result was directly attributed to the Lord. It was the Lord who gave the victory by causing the

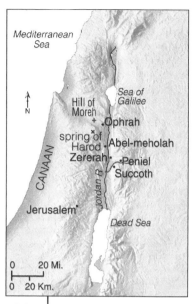

GIDEON'S BATTLE

Judges 6:1—7:22

In spite of Deborah and Barak's victory, the Canaanites still caused trouble in this fertile region. God appeared to Gideon at Ophrah and called him to defeat them. With only 300 fighting men, Gideon routed thousands of Midianites, chasing them to Zererah and Abel-meholah.

WHAT DO YOU THINK?

The soldiers brave enough to fight watched in complete safety as the enemy defeated themselves. How has God surprised you in the way He dealt with a difficult situation on your behalf?

AHA!

When God asks you to do something that seems counterintuitive, obey. Then watch Him work miracles on your behalf.

DID YOU KNOW?

After this battle, the Midianites never again threatened Israel, although they did protect Solomon's foe Hadad (1 Kings 11:18).

WHAT ABOUT YOU?
God asked Gideon and the soldiers to march forward in complete faith in such a way that they could never have claimed victory on their own. What impossible thing is God asking you to trust Him to do?

PRAYER
Father, You work in unexpected ways; Your methods are not mine. Help me to trust You to win the battle when I don't have the resources. And help me to always obey You, with complete confidence in Your ultimate plan.

Midianites to turn on themselves, slaying one another (see 2 Chron. 20:23). Whereas the Israelites had shouted, "The sword of the LORD and of Gideon!" they did not actually wield a sword in the fight. Rather the only swords mentioned were those of the Midianites'—used by the Lord, and turned against themselves.

The casualty statistic for the Midianites is reserved for later in the narrative in 8:10: 120,000 "swordsmen" (note the reference to "sword" again) died in the self-slaughter and the Israelites' initial pursuit of the army—a casualty rate of 89 percent. And more died in the subsequent pursuit by Gideon (8:11–12). An impressive victory indeed, considering the three hundred Israelites did not initially fight, but stood around playing instruments (vv. 21–22)! ✦

JUDGES 7:1–8, 19–21

1 Early in the morning, Jerub-Baal (that is, Gideon) and all his men camped at the spring of Harod. The camp of Midian was north of them in the valley near the hill of Moreh.

2 The LORD said to Gideon, "You have too many men for me to deliver Midian into their hands. In order that Israel may not boast against me that her own strength has saved her,

3 announce now to the people, 'Anyone who trembles with fear may turn back and leave Mount Gilead.'" So twenty-two thousand men left, while ten thousand remained.

4 But the LORD said to Gideon, "There are still too many men. Take them down to the water, and I will sift them for you there. If I say, 'This one shall go with you,' he shall go; but if I say, 'This one shall not go with you,' he shall not go."

5 So Gideon took the men down to the water. There the LORD told him, "Separate those who lap the water with their tongues like a dog from those who kneel down to drink."

6 Three hundred men lapped with their hands to their mouths. All the rest got down on their knees to drink.

7 The LORD said to Gideon, "With the three hundred men that lapped I will save you and give the Midianites into your hands. Let all the other men go, each to his own place."

8 So Gideon sent the rest of the Israelites to their tents but kept the three hundred, who took over the provisions and trumpets of the others. Now the camp of Midian lay below him in the valley.

19 Gideon and the hundred men with him reached the edge of the camp at the beginning of the middle watch, just after they had changed the guard. They blew their trumpets and broke the jars that were in their hands.

20 The three companies blew the trumpets and smashed the jars. Grasping the torches in their left hands and holding in their right hands the trumpets they were to blow, they shouted, "A sword for the LORD and for Gideon!"

21 While each man held his position around the camp, all the Midianites ran, crying out as they fled.

The Battle Belongs to the Lord

The power for victory comes from God.

INTO THE SUBJECT

When the Midianites invaded Israel, they and their allies settled into position as thick as locusts. The Israelites, under the leadership of Gideon, were able to draft thirty-two thousand soldiers, but the Lord dismissed all but three hundred of them. What was the Lord thinking?

INTO THE WORD

1. According to Judges 7:2, what danger was inherent in Gideon's having an army of thirty-two thousand?

2. Of the thirty-two thousand how many were stricken with fear and were sent home?

3. What important military trait did the three hundred who lapped water like a dog possess?

4. Why do you agree or disagree that confidence in numbers may weaken a church?

5. Why do you agree or disagree that a small church may hold back God's power by thinking it is too small to make a difference?

6. Read Judges 7:19–21. How might believers today defeat the enemy by sounding a trumpet and shining their light?

INTO THE WORLD

As you battle evil this week, don't fear the size or strength opposition, but trust in the Lord of Hosts to make you victorious.

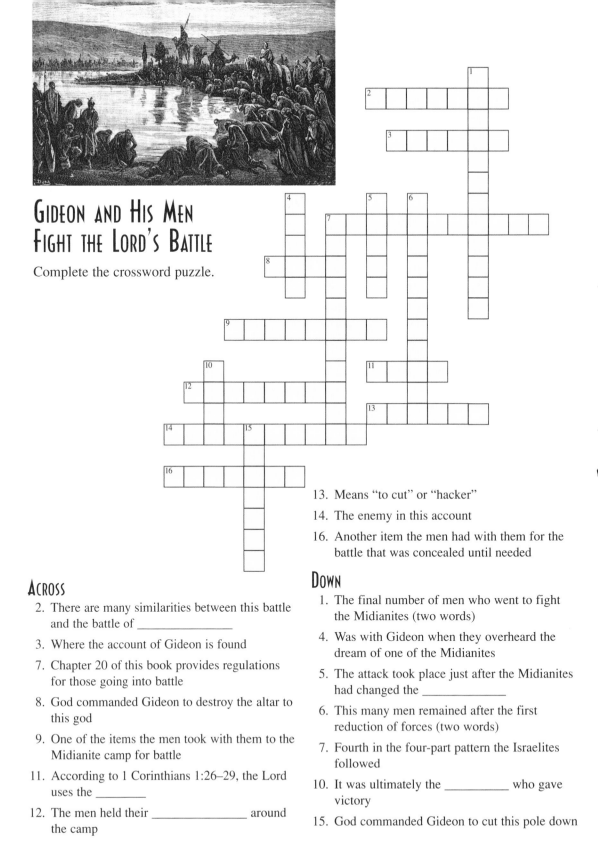

GIDEON AND HIS MEN FIGHT THE LORD'S BATTLE

Complete the crossword puzzle.

13. Means "to cut" or "hacker"

14. The enemy in this account

16. Another item the men had with them for the battle that was concealed until needed

ACROSS

2. There are many similarities between this battle and the battle of _____

3. Where the account of Gideon is found

7. Chapter 20 of this book provides regulations for those going into battle

8. God commanded Gideon to destroy the altar to this god

9. One of the items the men took with them to the Midianite camp for battle

11. According to 1 Corinthians 1:26–29, the Lord uses the _____

12. The men held their _____ around the camp

DOWN

1. The final number of men who went to fight the Midianites (two words)

4. Was with Gideon when they overheard the dream of one of the Midianites

5. The attack took place just after the Midianites had changed the _____

6. This many men remained after the first reduction of forces (two words)

7. Fourth in the four-part pattern the Israelites followed

10. It was ultimately the _____ who gave victory

15. God commanded Gideon to cut this pole down

INTERACTIVE LEARNING IDEAS

GET THE CLASS INVOLVED
Under Attack

God asked Gideon to send home most of his fighting force before they went into battle with the Midianites. Then He either directly gave, or inspired, an unusual battle strategy: torches and horns. Have fun as a group coming up with creative battle strategies.

Provide at least two sets of children's building blocks. (The classic wooden kind, not interlocking blocks.) Then divide the group into two or more teams. Each team should receive a set of blocks with two minutes to build a castle. As they work, they must come up with a way to destroy the other team's castle. They can use anything in the room. But there are a couple of rules. Team members must stay at least five feet away from the other team's castle. And they cannot directly touch the castle. See what battle strategies they come up with and give them a try. Do this at least three times. Teams may not repeat a same battle strategy. For example, if they throw a pencil, they cannot throw anything again.

Gather for a few minutes to discuss how God is infinitely more creative than we are. When we face an enemy, He is able to perform truly unexpected miracles. Talk about how you all have seen this in your own lives.

TRY THIS ON YOUR OWN
Preparing for Battle

Gideon received direction and encouragement from the Lord as he proceeded into war. We too need that support as we face various battles of our own. Spend some time with the Lord, getting direction and encouragement.

First, pray about the situation you face that feels like a battle. Ask the Lord for wisdom and guidance as you proceed. Write a letter to God, perhaps in a journal if you keep one. Write to Him about the situation, how impossible it seems, and how much you need His help. Ask Him for direction, and then quietly listen to His Spirit. Have a Bible handy to hear from His Word. Write what the Spirit is telling you, allowing your thoughts to flow where they may until you feel you have direction. Finish the letter by committing to God to follow His instructions.

TAKING IT TO THE STREET
Seventy-Six Trombones

The sound of the trumpets Gideon's army played frightened and confused the enemy. The sheer number of trumpet calls implied a much greater army than really existed. As a group, discover the various sounds that horns make.

Gather at a music store. Consider calling in advance and see whether any of the employees plays trumpets and horns. If so, inquire whether they might assist with your activity. Otherwise, ask someone in your church who can play horns. Once at the store, have your designated musician play the various horns: trumpet, saxophone, tuba, etc. Talk about the different sounds. Are they high or low, mellow or bright? And discuss which instrument's sound might carry the farthest. If the store has a shofar (the ram's horn trumpet likely used in Gideon's battle), or if you have access to one through a church member, see what that sounds like. Then talk about Gideon's battle, what it must have sounded like, why that might be confusing, and how creative God is in how He wins battles.

WITH YOUR FAMILY
A Mighty Battle

Create your own noisy battle. First, make some "jars" to break. This may need to be done a day or two in advance. Using quick-dry craft clay, have everyone create a few jars. The jars should have thin sides so they will break easily. Allow the jars to dry completely.

On the day of the activity, give everyone a party horn. Have everyone gather outdoors with their jars. Tell the story of Gideon and his battle. Highlight how God won the fight and how creative the strategy was. Then, prepare for battle. The battle could be a water balloon fight, if weather permits. Or, blow up balloons and use them to hit targets. When you yell, "For the Lord and for Gideon," the battle begins. Everyone throws down their jars—hopefully breaking them—blows their horns, and begins the battle game. ♦

God is able to equip and use those whom He calls, even after they fail.

LESSON 11

FAILURE IS NOT FINAL
Judges 13:2–5; 16:23–31

Then Samson prayed to the LORD, "O Sovereign LORD, remember me. O God, please strengthen me just once more."
—Judges 16:28

BACKGROUND SCRIPTURES
1 Samuel 5:1–5
    Another showdown
    between the Lord
    God and Dagon
Psalm 51
    David's repentance
    and petition after his
    moral failure

DAILY BIBLE READINGS
Monday: Psalm 51:7–13
Tuesday: Luke 19:2–9
Wednesday: Philippians
            3:7–11
Thursday: Numbers
            22:26–31
Friday: Galatians
            3:6–14
Saturday: Judges 13:2–5;
            16:23–31
Sunday: Psalm 37

WHY THIS MATTERS

Can you lift a hundred pounds or bend a quarter with your fingers? Strongman Joe Rollino once lifted thirty-two hundred pounds at Coney Island and was still bending quarters with his fingers at age 104. He died that year, when he was struck by a speeding minivan while he was crossing a street in Brooklyn.

The book of Judges reports astounding exploits of strength demonstrated by Samson when the Spirit of the Lord came upon him. Although some misinformed individuals attribute Samson's amazing strength to his long hair, his hair was simply a sign of his separation to God. Sadly, Samson's sinning left him weak, humiliated, and incarcerated.

This lesson emphasizes the need to stay dedicated to God and dependent on His Spirit for spiritual strength.

BIBLE COMMENTARY
By Patricia J. David

The final "judge" (or "deliverer" or "savior") recorded in Judges is a man named Samson. Hebrews 11:32 lists Samson among the heroes of faith, as one "whose weakness was turned to strength" (11:34). But the predominant picture of Samson in Judges 13–16 is of a man whose life was a one-man illustration of the plight of an entire nation.

As the story of Samson's life opens in chapter 13, Israel was again doing "evil in the eyes of the LORD" (13:1). As punishment, God again handed them over to their enemies, this time the Philistines. The Philistines had settled centuries before along the Mediterranean coast between Egypt and Gaza. They didn't much care for the Israelite occupation of Canaan, and they were in continual, though sporadic, conflict with God's people.

Samson's Potential (Judg. 13:2–5)

Samson's father, **Manoah**, was from **Zorah**, (v. 2) located about fourteen miles west of Jerusalem in the foothills of the Shephelah (plains). The town was allotted to the tribe of Judah in Joshua 15:33 but also to the tribe of **Dan** in Joshua 19:40–41. Because 2 Chronicles 11:10 and Nehemiah 11:29 also list Zorah as part of the tribe of Judah, it would be incorrect, as some commentators claim, to hold that ownership was transferred to Dan. It is more probable that both Judah and Dan had claim to the town, lying as it did on the border between the two tribes. The tribe of Dan was small and insignificant compared to the other tribes. It comprised only one clan (Num. 26:42) and was unable to take possession of its allotted land (Josh. 19:47), eventually migrating north to the upper Jordan valley (see Judg. 18) and falling into idolatry.

Manoah's wife was **sterile and remained childless** (v. 2). Since children were considered a gift from God, to be childless was a sign of divine disfavor and disgrace. Like Sarah and Rebekah before her, and Hannah and Elizabeth after her, this desperate woman was visited by an angel of the Lord and comforted with the promise, **you are going to conceive and have a son** (v. 3). Whenever God had a special purpose for a man, there was generally something significant about his birth. This was the case with Isaac, Jacob, Moses, Samuel, Jeremiah, John the Baptist, Jesus . . . and Samson. Like Samuel and John the Baptist after him, Samson

Comparison of Samson and the Nation of Israel	
SAMSON	**ISRAEL**
Chosen by God from birth	Chosen by God from "birth" (Isa. 41:8)
Supernatural potential and strength	God was the source of their victory (Deut. 20:4)
"She's the right one for me" (Judg. 14:3)	"Everyone did as he saw fit" (17:6; 21:25)
Grumbled when thirsty (Judg. 15:18)	Grumbled when thirsty and hungry (Ex. 17:3)
Didn't realize the Lord had left him	Didn't realize God had departed (Ezek. 10:18)
Brought deliverance from the Philistines	Brought deliverance from the enemy of sin through the coming Messiah
Used by God despite moral failures	Used by God to bring forth the Messiah, despite persistent idolatry
Promise of deliverance: his hair began to grow	Promise of deliverance: continued prophecies of coming Messiah, even in exile
Cried out to the Lord to empower him	Israelites cried out to the Lord (Ps. 107:6)

was to be **set apart to God from birth** (v. 5). He would be subject to the Nazirite vow for a lifetime (see 13:7), not for the voluntarily limited time specified in Numbers 6:1–12. As a Nazirite, he was to **drink no wine or other fermented drink** (v. 4), was to avoid eating **anything unclean** (as was the case with all the Israelites), to refrain from shaving his head, and to avoid coming in contact with a dead body. Notice in these verses, though, that his mother was to observe some of these stipulations as well, setting herself apart during her pregnancy, because she would carry no ordinary child. The angel foretold that **he will begin the deliverance of Israel from the hands of the Philistines** (v. 5). He would be God's instrument to save His people.

It is hard to imagine a child with more promise and potential than Samson. He came from humble beginnings but his future was bright. His birth and future success were foretold by an angel. His parents sought wisdom in raising him (13:8). And, "he grew and the LORD blessed him, and the Spirit of the LORD began to stir him" (13:24–25). Throughout Samson's life story, we see his supernatural, God-imparted strength. "The Spirit of the LORD came upon him in power" (14:6, 19; 15:14), enabling him to tear apart a lion with his bare hands (14:6), to strike down thirty Philistines singlehandedly (14:19), and to kill a thousand men with the jawbone of a donkey (15:15). He also caught three hundred foxes and tied their tails together, tore loose the doors of the city gate and carried them away, and freed himself from his enemies' ropes with ease. His strength was well known among the Israelites and among the Philistines whom he tormented. Some commentators believe the mythical stories of Hercules have their foundation in the life story of Samson, so many are the similarities.

In spite of Samson's great promise and potential, he, like the nation he represented, was deeply flawed. He fell in love with a Philistine woman, claiming

WHAT DO YOU THINK?
Samson's mother dedicated him to God, as Hannah did her much-longed-for son. Do you think God gave them special children because they offered their sons to Him or because they themselves would be uniquely God-fearing moms?

AHA!
Sometimes children raised in the Lord go their own way. But God still remains near to them.

DID YOU KNOW?
Angelic birth announcements include those of Ishmael (Gen. 16:11), Isaac (Gen. 18:10), John the Baptist (Luke 1:13), and Jesus (Luke 1:31).

A sculpture of the god
Dagon

"She's the right one for me" (14:3). Later, after his newly acquired wife had been killed by the Philistines, Samson visited a prostitute (16:1), then fell in love with another foreign woman named Delilah, who conspired with the Philistines to set a trap for him (16:4–5). At every turn, Samson treated his heritage and vow with contempt. He married outside his religion, which was strictly forbidden in the law. He touched a dead carcass, eating honey out of the lion's remains. He toyed with Delilah concerning the secret of his strength, eventually allowing her to cut off his hair (16:6–18). He proved himself to be vengeful and ruthless and immature. His whining in 15:18, "Must I now die of thirst?" is reminiscent of the groaning of the Israelites in the desert (Ex. 17:3). Though he possessed great physical strength, Samson was wanting in moral fortitude and wisdom.

Samson finally divulged the secret to his strength: "No razor has ever been used on my head . . . because I have been a Nazirite set apart to God since birth. If my head were shaved, my strength would leave me, and I would become as weak as any other man" (Judg. 16:17). And while he slept Delilah cut off his hair. Sad words are recorded in 16:20: "He awoke from his sleep and thought, 'I'll go out as before and shake myself free.' But he did not know that the LORD had left him." Samson was seized by the Philistines and his eyes were gouged out. He was led out to captivity in bronze shackles. It was a terrible end to a promising beginning.

Samson's Punishment (Judg. 16:23–25)

One of the primary deities of the Philistines was Dagon, some sort of a grain deity (the Hebrew word for "grain" is the same as "Dagon") also worshiped by the Amorites. Some Ugarit texts call Baal "the son of Dagon," and there were temples to this god in Gaza and Ashdod (1 Sam. 5:1–7). Here the Philistines offered sacrifices to Dagon and celebrated because "**Our god has delivered Samson, our enemy, into our hands**" (Judg. 16:23; also in v. 24). They mistakenly equated Samson's capture with the superiority of their god. So, not only did Samson bring his own life to ruin, but he also brought the name of the Lord into disrepute. In reality, Samson was suffering because he had failed to obey the Lord, not because of anything Dagon had done.

While they were in high spirits, they shouted, "Bring out Samson to entertain us." So they called Samson out of the prison, and he performed for them (v. 25). How pitiful. The once-heroic strongman had become an object of scorn and amusement. He performed for them, maybe through dancing to music. It was humiliating. And it was his own fault.

Make no mistake: Sin has disastrous consequences. Though alluring at the moment, it eventually bites us and robs us of our dignity and honor. Sin seeks only to destroy, and its pleasures last but a short time. There is a terrible price to pay for sin. Samson lost everything. And yet, God was still merciful.

The greatest expression of hope in Samson's story is found in 16:22: "But the hair on his head began to grow again after it had been shaved." God wasn't finished with Samson. Although his punishment was great, Samson's hope remained because of the greatness of his God.

Samson's Petition (Judg. 16:26–31)

After performing for his captors, Samson asked the servant leading him to put him where he could **lean against** the **pillars** of the **temple** (v. 26). It is possible that he was truly exhausted from his performance and simply desired to rest, but it is also possible he already had in mind what he planned to do, and he merely pretended to be tired in order to have an excuse to find these support pillars. These were the two primary pillars supporting the weight of the temple. Verse 27 tells us that **the temple was crowded with men and women; all the rulers of the Philistines were there, and on the roof were about three thousand men and women**. The extra weight on the roof would have caused considerable stress to the temple's support structure.

For the first time since Samson's tragic downfall, he called out to the Lord in prayer. He pled with God, **O Sovereign LORD, remember me. O God, please strengthen me just once more** (v. 28). His prayer was one of earnestness and humility. He had finally realized that the secret to his strength was his relationship with the Lord, not the length of his hair (for surely it had not escaped his notice that his hair had grown back). His request to be remembered expressed his desire to have his relationship with God restored. This is a prayer of true repentance and submission to God. Moral failure is tragic, but God is merciful when we return to Him. And so He was merciful to Samson here.

Samson reached toward the two central pillars on which the temple stood . . . Then he pushed with all his might, and down came the temple (vv. 29–30). Samson was willing to die in order to kill these Philistines who had made a mockery of him and of God. Although he asked God to let him **get revenge on the Philistines for** his **two eyes** (v. 28), it's obvious that there was some noble intention to his request. Otherwise God would not have granted it. And so **he killed many more when he died than while he lived** (v. 30). The angel had foretold that he would "begin the deliverance of Israel from the hands of the Philistines" (13:5). And so he did.

Samson's family took his body and buried him **in the tomb of Manoah his father** (16:31), proving his honor had been restored. But it was a sad end to a life that could have been so much more. **He had led Israel twenty years,** which means he was probably only about forty years old when he died. Samson proves that the choices we make can severely limit how God can use us. He is faithful and can still work through us, but we limit our potential by treating our relationship with God too casually. This is a lesson the entire nation of Israel had to learn. And it's one we still need today. ◆

WHAT ABOUT YOU?
Samson's struggles generally came because he didn't take his vows before God seriously. What vows have you made to God, and how seriously do you take them?

PRAYER
Father, help me to live before You as You command. Show me where I fail, that I might not take it lightly. And thank You that You stand ready to forgive and help me when I return to You.

INTERACTIVE LEARNING IDEAS

GET THE CLASS INVOLVED
The God of Second Chances

God forgives and gives second chances when we turn back to Him, as with Sampson. Many key biblical figures can attest to that. Draw your class's attention to them through a little dramatization.

Pick four people to play the following people who received second chances: David, after sinning with Bathsheba (2 Sam. 11–12); Paul, after participating in the stoning of Stephen (Acts 7:54–56; 22:20); Moses, after killing an Egyptian (Ex. 2:11–15); and Jacob, after deceiving his father (Gen. 17:1–37). Have part of the class assist each actor in researching the person's story. Have the groups read the story and, with a concordance, see what else they can learn about the biblical character. They should focus on how the person restored their relationship with God and how God later used them. Give ten minutes for this activity.

Have each "actor" go up to share their character's story, telling it in first person. They should tell what happened, how they repented, the repercussions of their sin, and how God used them in the future. Allow two minutes per person. Then, provide at least five minutes for the group to share insights into what they have learned.

TRY THIS ON YOUR OWN
Lessons in Repentance

When we sin, we suffer the consequences. When we turn back to God and ask for forgiveness, He is faithful to forgive. Sampson is a heartbreaking story of someone whose life choices hurt him, despite incredible gifts from God. Read another kind of story. A story that tells what happens when we turn from sin and come to Christ. Try one of these classic biographies: *The Cross and the Switchblade*, *Lessons from San Quentin*, or *Rebel with a Cause*. As you read, look for the theme of second chances, for the ways people turned back to God, and how God gives new purpose.

TAKING IT TO THE STREET
Golf without the *G?*

Sin sets us back and impacts our lives. However, when we turn back to God, He helps and forgives. As a group, play a game of miniature golf. But add a few silly, although point-making, rules. No one will be allowed to say a word starting with the letter *G*. (This will represent sin.) If anyone says such a word, they get a penalty stroke added to their score. To get rid of a penalty stroke, they must "ask forgiveness" or "repent" by carrying someone else's club for one hole. See how often you can catch each other saying "G" words and enjoy the game.

Afterward, talk about how frustrating it was at first and how it felt to have a chance to "repent" and get rid of the mark. Discuss how frustrating it would be not to have that opportunity to make up for the "sin." Talk about how sin impacts our lives. Do mention that there is one way the golf illustration isn't quite accurate: With God, we just have to ask forgiveness and change our ways; we don't have to *do* anything else.

WITH YOUR FAMILY
Life Lessons on the Board

Play a board game to show your children how sin hinders our progress in life. First, tell Samson's story. Share how he was special to God but didn't take sin as seriously as he should. Give examples of the trouble this caused in his life. Then relate the end of the story, focusing on how God still heard him and answered his prayer once he turned back to God.

Then, play a board game in which progress is occasionally thwarted, even pushed back, by landing on certain squares or drawing a certain card. A good example for young children is Chutes and Ladders. For older children and adults, the game Sorry works well. Play the game. Point out how landing on the wrong square or drawing the wrong card is like sin. As believers, it doesn't take us out of the game, but it does set us back from achieving all we otherwise could for God. Share a time in your life when sin caused trouble or set you back somehow. Then explain how the next turn in the game after a setback is like turning back to God. We can move forward again, although we may have some catching up to do (consequences of sin). ◆

JUDGES 13:2–5; 16:23–31

13:2 A certain man of Zorah, named Manoah, from the clan of the Danites, had a wife who was sterile and remained childless.

3 The angel of the LORD appeared to her and said, "You are sterile and childless, but you are going to conceive and have a son.

4 Now see to it that you drink no wine or other fermented drink and that you do not eat anything unclean,

5 because you will conceive and give birth to a son. No razor may be used on his head, because the boy is to be a Nazirite, set apart to God from birth, and he will begin the deliverance of Israel from the hands of the Philistines."

16:23 Now the rulers of the Philistines assembled to offer a great sacrifice to Dagon their god and to celebrate, saying, "Our god has delivered Samson, our enemy, into our hands."

24 When the people saw him, they praised their god, saying, "Our god has delivered our enemy into our hands, the one who laid waste our land and multiplied our slain."

25 While they were in high spirits, they shouted, "Bring out Samson to entertain us." So they called Samson out of the prison, and he performed for them. When they stood him among the pillars,

26 Samson said to the servant who held his hand, "Put me where I can feel the pillars that support the temple, so that I may lean against them."

27 Now the temple was crowded with men and women; all the rulers of the Philistines were there, and on the roof were about three thousand men and women watching Samson perform.

28 Then Samson prayed to the LORD, "O Sovereign LORD, remember me. O God, please strengthen me just once more, and let me with one blow get revenge on the Philistines for my two eyes."

29 Then Samson reached toward the two central pillars on which the temple stood. Bracing himself against them, his right hand on the one and his left hand on the other,

30 Samson said, "Let me die with the Philistines!" Then he pushed with all his might, and down came the temple on the rulers and all the people in it. Thus he killed many more when he died than while he lived.

31 Then his brothers and his father's whole family went down to get him. They brought him back and buried him between Zorah and Eshtaol in the tomb of Manoah his father. He had led Israel twenty years.

Failure Is Not Final

God is able to equip and use those whom He calls, even after they fail.

INTO THE SUBJECT

A nation may be overly confident in its stockpile of sophisticated weapons and numbers of well-trained, well-equipped military men and women, but doesn't a nation's greatest strength lie in the Lord? What happens when self-reliance replaces confidence in the Lord?

INTO THE WORD

1. Read Judges 13:2–5. How do you think Manoah's barren wife felt upon learning that she would give birth to one God would use to deliver Israel from the Philistines?

2. Israel's deliverer Samson, a Nazarite, became self-reliant after routing the Philistines on several occasions. This led to his capture by the Philistines. According to Judges 13:23, to whom did the Philistines credit this capture?

3. When a believer falls into sin and disgrace, why do unsaved people often rejoice?

4. Why would you agree or disagree that the Philistines intentionally insulted Jehovah by making sport of Samson during a celebration of their god Dagon?

5. Have you known a believer who became an object of derision because he or she fell into sin? How can you guard against a similar fate?

6. According to verse 28, Samson prayed for revenge. Do you think a prayer for revenge is justified today? If so, when?

7. How would you respond to the allegation that Samson used his restored strength to commit suicide?

INTO THE WORLD

Rely on the Lord always. Refuse to become self-confident. Your testimony is worth guarding.

Sin Is Disastrous

Sin has disastrous consequences. Samson's life proves that the choices we make can limit how God can use us.

What do you think about the statement that whenever we sin, we allow people to believe that the god of this world is more powerful than the one true God? Write your thoughts.

_____

_____

_____

_____

When you think about the fact that your sin not only affects you but the people around you, does it make you think differently about your sin? Expound on your thoughts.

_____

_____

_____

_____

Spend time in prayer by yourself. Ask God to show you any of your actions, thoughts, or attitudes that limit how He can use you.

We have a clear choice: God or gods.

FAITHFULNESS REQUIRES COURAGE
Ruth 1:3–18

WHY THIS MATTERS

After withdrawing from the fellowship of a local church, many believers have experienced distress and heartache. A Christian who seeks a better life in the evil world system learns the hard way that he has chosen the wrong environment.

Life was hard at Bethlehem during a famine, but God's people lived there. By choosing to leave Bethlehem and move to pagan Moab, Elimelech jeopardized the faith and well-being of his wife Naomi and their two sons. He and the sons died in Moab, leaving Naomi widowed with two Moabite daughters-in-law.

This lesson shows the importance of making wise choices.

BIBLE COMMENTARY

By Tom Ward

The book of Ruth is one of the most beautiful passages in the Old Testament. It is read annually in synagogues around the world. One fascinating detail about the book is that it is found in the Hebrew Bible immediately after the book of Proverbs. Since the book of Proverbs closes with the discourse on the virtuous woman in chapter 31, the inference might have been that Ruth was an example of what the virtuous woman looks like in real life.

The setting for the book is found in the first verse of the first chapter: "In the days when the judges ruled . . ." The time of the judges was a time of spiritual waywardness for the Israelite people. Sometimes they were on fire for the Lord, and then they would cool off and stray into worshiping foreign deities. They were sometimes spiritually hot, sometimes cold, and generally speaking, inconsistent. As long as they had a strong leader, they seemed to do alright. Whenever there was a change in leadership, they faltered.

The famine mentioned in Ruth 1:1 is generally thought to be judgment from God for their sin. Often the people of the Old Testament viewed natural calamities as punishment from the Almighty. Bethlehem literally means "house of bread." It is interesting that this family left the house of bread and went to Moab in search of provisions. This constituted turning their backs on God.

The family names are Elimelech, Naomi, Mahlon, and Kilion. As you would guess, each of the names has a significant meaning. Elimelech means "to whom God is King." Now we see the situation confounded because the man whose name represents loyalty to the Almighty set his sights on the land of another god. Elimelech proved to be a fair-weather follower of the Lord. When difficult times prevailed, he packed his bags and moved on. There are many people today who live similar spiritual lives. They serve God as long as times are good, but as soon as trouble comes their way they "lose their religion" and do their own thing. Naomi means "pleasant" or "gracious." It depicts her character very well as far as can be discerned from the text. Mahlon means "sickly" or "weak." This most

KEY VERSE

But Ruth replied, "Don't urge me to leave you or to turn back from you. Where you go I will go, and where you stay I will stay. Your people will be my people and your God my God."
—Ruth 1:16

BACKGROUND SCRIPTURES

Matthew 1:5
   Ruth is listed in the genealogy of Christ.
Deuteronomy 7:3
   Israelite law prohibiting marriage with Moabite women
Matthew 22:25–27
   New Testament reference to Levirate marriage
2 Kings 2:2–6
   Elisha refused to leave Elijah.

DAILY BIBLE READINGS

Monday: Esther 4:12–16
Tuesday: 1 Peter 5:6–11
Wednesday: 1 Corinthians 16:13–14
Thursday: John 15:18–25
Friday: Lamentations 3:10–24
Saturday: Ruth 1:3–18
Sunday: Psalm 38

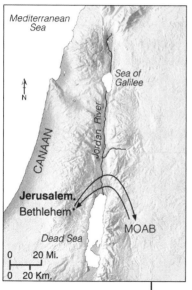

SETTING FOR THE STORY

Ruth 1

Elimelech, Naomi, and their sons traveled from Bethlehem to Moab because of a famine. After her husband and sons died, Naomi returned to Bethlehem with her daughter-in-law Ruth.

WHAT DO YOU THINK?

The Old Testament reveals that God occasionally used famines as a judgment on a people's sins. Do you think He does that today? How might one determine today whether a natural disaster was judgment for sin or just a natural act?

AHA!

Word of God's goodness to His people gets around, calling people to return (or turn) to Him.

DID YOU KNOW?

Much of Moab's terrain was steep. Crops struggled to grow there, but it offered excellent grazing for sheep and goats.

likely describes Mahlon's health even from infancy. It could be that he was somewhat sick and weak physically as a child because he certainly died young. Kilion means "pining." Perhaps Kilion was a conscientious sort of fellow who was, like his brother, of frail constitution. He too died young.

It is interesting that Elimelech chose to take his family to the country of Moab, because Moab was not necessarily a place that the Israelites regarded very highly. Interestingly enough, King David referred to Moab as his "washbasin" (Ps. 60:8) some years later, even though he had once left his parents there for safety when he was running from Saul (1 Sam. 22:3). Ruth was David's great-grandmother, so he probably left his parents there because of their bloodline and connections.

Moab was a land of people descended from Lot's incestuous relationship with his older daughter (Gen. 19:30–38). The Moabite people inhabited Israel during the time of the judges and ruled over them for about eighteen years (Judg. 3:12–14). Additionally, the Moabites mistreated the Israelites during their desert wanderings (Deut. 23:3–6), even calling for Balaam to invoke a curse on them. So, we ask ourselves, "Why in the world would Elimelech move to Moab?" Of all the places where he could move, why would he choose Moab? Perhaps he was so spiritually forlorn that he couldn't think straight. However, we see in the grand scheme of things, God was at work even in Elimelech's waywardness.

Three Widows in Moab (Ruth 1:3–5)

Elimelech died sometime after arriving in Moab. His death is viewed by many as a judgment from God for embracing foreign gods. Mahlon and Kilion, both married Moabite women. Mahlon married Ruth, and Kilion married Orpah. For some reason, after about ten years of living in Moab, both Mahlon and Kilion also died. Hence, there were now three widows.

Planning to Return to Judah (Ruth 1:6–7)

Naomi **heard** that **the LORD had come to the aid of his people** (v. 6) and the famine was over. She felt like the best thing to do was to move back home where, she hoped, some family members would help take care of her in her old age. Naomi gathered her belongings and her two daughters-in-law, and they departed for the journey home to Bethlehem. Naomi felt an obligation to provide for the young widows. It was the custom of the day for childless widows to marry and have children from the deceased husband's brother. This was known as Levirate marriage. It is not practiced in Western cultures today but was very common in Old Testament days when this book was written.

Naomi's Concern for Orpah and Ruth (Ruth 1:8–10)

Naomi then had a change of heart and was moved with compassion for her two widowed daughters-in-law. She encouraged each of them to go back to their mother's home where their families could provide for them. She blessed them with the statement, **"May the LORD show kindness to you, as you have shown to your dead and to me"** (v. 8). She wanted them to **find rest in the home of another husband** (v. 9). They were young and had their whole lives before them;

they should remarry. Naomi gave each of them a parting kiss and together **they wept**. It must have been a moving sight along the dusty road to Judah—three widows weeping and talking and parting company. Both Orpah and Ruth expressed their desire to return to Judah with their mother-in-law. They may have felt some obligation to help care for the woman who had given them their husbands.

Naomi's Feelings (Ruth 1:11–13)

Naomi eased the tension with a speech. She implored them to return home to their families and then addressed the matter of Levirate marriage. Naomi had no other sons, and even if she married that day and became pregnant that night, it would still be many years before the boys were old enough to fulfill the obligation to their deceased brothers by carrying on their family name. **"No,"** she said, **"It is more bitter for me . . . because the LORD's hand has gone out against me!"** (v. 13). Naomi felt that the reason all this calamity had come upon her was because of the Lord's judgment on her life. Sin does indeed have consequences. Naomi felt her life was bitter. She had great reason to feel that way. She was a widow who also had lost both children, and she was living in a foreign land with no relatives to care for her. Her plight was dire indeed.

Orpah and the Gods of Moab (Ruth 1:14–15)

After much weeping, Orpah parted with her mother-in-law and began the journey home to her family where she could mourn her loss and hopefully, remarry and start over. Orpah parted with a kiss goodbye. The Bible says that **Ruth clung to her** mother-in-law (v. 14). She was more acutely attached and perhaps had a closer relationship with Naomi than did Orpah. Whatever the circumstances, Ruth refused to part ways and was determined to move to Judah and take care of her mother-in-law. Naomi again urged Ruth to go home like Orpah to her family and her gods. The prevailing god of Moab was Chemosh. Chemosh was a demanding god who, like Molech, required human sacrifice. The spiritual environment in Moab was dim and dark. Orpah went home, but Ruth had other plans.

Ruth's Poetic and Exemplary Commitment (Ruth 1:16–18)

These are some of the most beautiful and poetic verses in the Old Testament and are great verses to memorize. Ruth refused to leave Naomi and expressed her commitment to her and her God in memorable fashion: **"Where you go I will go, and where you stay I will stay. Your people will be my people and your God my God. Where you die I will die, and there I will be buried. May the LORD deal with me, be it every so severely, if anything but death separates you and me"** (vv. 16–17). Ruth hereby made a public commitment to both Naomi and the Lord. She vowed to be a part of Naomi's future whatever it took and embraced the God of Israel as her own. Her selflessness and religious fervency would be rewarded later, but for now, without knowing what was ahead, Ruth's faith was exemplary. She was casting her lot with the Lord no matter what happened. She was no fair-weather follower of Jehovah like her former father-in-law. She was devoted to seeing matters through regardless of the consequences or circumstances. She walked into the unknown future with

WHAT DO YOU THINK?
Something about Naomi and her relationship with her daughters-in-law was special, especially her friendship with Ruth. What hints does Scripture give us about the character of their relationship and about the women themselves?

AHA!
Sometimes when people hurt, they don't need you to say it'll be okay; they just want you to be with them.

DID YOU KNOW?
Widows have a special place in God's heart. He commands His people to care for them repeatedly in Scripture. See Deuteronomy 10:18; 24:19–21; Jeremiah 7:6; and 1 Timothy 5:3–8 among many others.

WHAT ABOUT YOU?
In-law relationships can be tricky, but, as Ruth and Naomi show, they can be successfully navigated. If you are married, what can you do to encourage a stronger relationship with your in-laws today?

nothing but faith in Jehovah and an aging mother-in-law who would depend on her for survival.

It should be noted that all Ruth had to do to enter the kingdom of God was to embrace His covenant. She did not have to offer a human sacrifice or an animal sacrifice or perform any other type of religious ritual. She simply embraced the God of Israel with a heart of love and was accepted into His domain. Similarly today, in order to become a Christian, all you need to do is put your faith in the death and resurrection of Jesus Christ and repent. You cannot give enough money to the church to get the job done. You cannot get to heaven by doing good works. It is all by faith.

Naomi realized that Ruth was going to accompany her, so she stopped urging her to go home. In a way, this may have been comforting to Naomi. Her lot in life was bitter for sure; however, there was a little glimmer of sunshine found in the hope of better days in Judah and the presence of her daughter-in-law Ruth.

Their Plight

It is good to think for a few moments about the plight of these two widows. First of all, they were women in a male-dominated society. Women did not have the rights and status then as they do today in the West, although many women today still are mistreated simply because they are women. Second, they were widows. Their hearts were overflowing with the pangs of grief. Third, they were not able to work because women in those days typically stayed at home and took care of the household chores. There were few honorable ways for women to support themselves. Fourth, they were probably broke. Most likely, Elimelech sold out when he moved to Moab and whatever was left when he died was used up by Naomi in raising the boys. Fifth, they were childless. They had no descendants upon whom they could depend in their aged years. Society at that time had no Social Security or means for caring for the aged like the West does today.

Hard times were upon these two women and, without the help of their Lord, life would surely add misery to company. It is within this context that the remainder of the book unfolds the plan of God to care for these two women who were so committed to Him. ✦

PRAYER
Father, open my eyes to those around me who need my support, and show me how I can help them. In particular, give me opportunities to bless and assist widows, and so demonstrate Your love.

RUTH 1:3–18

3 Now Elimelech, Naomi's husband, died, and she was left with her two sons.

4 They married Moabite women, one named Orpah and the other Ruth. After they had lived there about ten years,

5 both Mahlon and Kilion also died, and Naomi was left without her two sons and her husband.

6 When she heard in Moab that the LORD had come to the aid of his people by providing food for them, Naomi and her daughters-in-law prepared to return home from there.

7 With her two daughters-in-law she left the place where she had been living and set out on the road that would take them back to the land of Judah.

8 Then Naomi said to her two daughters-in-law, "Go back, each of you, to your mother's home. May the LORD show kindness to you, as you have shown to your dead and to me.

9 May the LORD grant that each of you will find rest in the home of another husband." Then she kissed them and they wept aloud

10 and said to her, "We will go back with you to your people."

11 But Naomi said, "Return home, my daughters. Why would you come with me? Am I going to have any more sons, who could become your husbands?

12 Return home, my daughters; I am too old to have another husband. Even if I thought there was still hope for me—even if I had a husband tonight and then gave birth to sons—

13 would you wait until they grew up? Would you remain unmarried for them? No, my daughters. It is more bitter for me than for you, because the LORD's hand has gone out against me!"

14 At this they wept again. Then Orpah kissed her mother-in-law good-by, but Ruth clung to her.

15 "Look," said Naomi, "your sister-in-law is going back to her people and her gods. Go back with her."

16 But Ruth replied, "Don't urge me to leave you or to turn back from you. Where you go I will go, and where you stay I will stay. Your people will be my people and your God my God.

17 Where you die I will die, and there I will be buried. May the LORD deal with me, be it ever so severely, if anything but death separates you and me."

18 When Naomi realized that Ruth was determined to go with her, she stopped urging her.

Faithfulness Requires Courage

We have a clear choice: God or gods.

INTO THE SUBJECT

It may seem that trouble sometimes comes in bunches. Naomi's husband died, and then her two sons died, leaving her a grieving widow and mother in a foreign land. What was next for her? What would you do in similar circumstances?

INTO THE WORD

1. Do you think Elimelech and Naomi were right or wrong to leave Bethlehem and settle in Moab? Why?

2. How did things go from bad to worse for Naomi in Moab?

3. Naomi's sons married Moabite women. Do you think Christian parents should raise and educate their children where they are unlikely to fall in love with unbelievers? Why or why not?

4. As you read Ruth 1:6–18, what opinion of Naomi do you form?

5. What opinion of Orpah do you form?

6. What opinion of Ruth do you form?

7. What indication in these verses do you find that Naomi maintained a strong faith in the Lord through her trials?

8. How has the Lord brought you or someone you know through a time of deep sorrow?

INTO THE WORLD

Obviously, Naomi's testimony impacted her daughters-in-law. If you meet whatever trials or difficulties come your way this week with faith in the Lord, your testimony may persuade a friend or relative to become a follower of Christ.

NAOMI AND RUTH

Fill in the blanks appropriately. Try to do as much as you can without looking at the lesson.

They were women in a _____ - _____ society.

They were _____.

They were not able to _____ because women in those days typically stayed home.

They were probably _____.

They were _____.

_____ is listed in the genealogy of Christ.

Ruth 1:21: "I went away _____ but the LORD has brought me back _____."

Entering Moab	Returning to Bethlehem
Spiritual _____	Spiritual _____
_____ and children	Widowed and _____
Financially _____	Financially _____
Embrace other _____	Return to the _____

INTERACTIVE LEARNING IDEAS

GET THE CLASS INVOLVED
Love Notes to Widows and Widowers

As a group, reach out to the widows in your church. Together, list the widows and widowers you know in your congregation. Then, as a group, discuss what you know about each one and what their needs might be. Is she a young mother with children to raise? Is he an older man who seems lonely? At this point, simply brainstorm ideas. Then assign one of the widows or widowers to each person in the group. Take a moment for everyone to silently pray for their person.

After prayer, hand out some blank notecards. Ask each person to write a note of encouragement to the person they prayed for. It should be simple, saying, in essence, "Our class was thinking of you today, and we prayed for you. We prayed. . . . Please know we care and if you ever need anything, you can call on us." Add Scripture verses or notes about why that person is special. Then, address and mail the cards. (Ask in advance if your church office will help with this.) Discuss ongoing ways you can follow Ruth's example and gently care for the needs of widows and widowers.

TRY THIS ON YOUR OWN
Planning for the Future

God calls us to care for the needs of widows and widowers. Yet we easily forget those closest to us, even the ones we will leave behind. If you are married, think about your spouse. How have you provided and arranged things for him or her should God call you home first? Pray for wisdom as to how your affairs should be prepared. Then, in the next couple of days, begin to ensure that your spouse will be well cared for. Some ideas include preparing a will or trust, ensuring information your spouse may need is easy to find, purchasing life insurance, or investing in a retirement account your spouse can inherit.

If you are single, plan how you will care for your surviving parent should one of your parents die. Where will they live? How will they finance their needs? What about if they need day-to-day assistance? How can you help with these things?

In either situation, ask God for wisdom. Then thank Him for the opportunity to care for others as Ruth cared for Naomi.

TAKING IT TO THE STREET
Fun and Games

Most folks residing in nursing homes and extended care facilities are widows and widowers. Many don't have a family member, like Ruth, who regularly visits to bring joy and ensure their well-being. Take an evening or afternoon to bring a sense of love and family to people residing in these facilities.

Contact a local nursing home or extended-care facility. Offer to plan a game time. Find out whether an afternoon or evening event is better. Then make sure the word gets out. The facility will probably be glad to advertise the event. Otherwise, print a number of flyers to pass out in advance. Ask what kinds of snacks the residents enjoy and provide a few.

Then, show up on that night or afternoon with snacks and a number of board games the residents might enjoy. Consider chess and checkers as well as family card games such as UNO and board games such as Life. When the game time is over, gather for a few moments to discuss the needs you discovered among the group and to share some of the neat friendships you've made. Consider making this a regular event.

WITH YOUR FAMILY
Extended Family

As a family, adopt a widow or widower in your church. Pray together about who this might be. Then determine how you can include this person in your family. Consider the following:

- Including the person in family holiday events such as Christmas dinner and Fourth of July fireworks
- Inviting the person to children's sports activities and recitals
- Having the person for dinner from time to time
- Asking the person to teach you something, like how to bake that cake they are famous for or build those beautiful birdhouses

Make a commitment together to start doing some of these things. It might be easiest to begin with a simple dinner. Then enjoy getting to know your newest family member! ◆

A God-directed life is its own reward, now and forever.

LESSON 13

DO THE RIGHT THING
Ruth 3:1–11; 4:12–17

KEY VERSE
Trust in the LORD with all
your heart and lean not on
your own understanding; in
all your ways acknowledge
him, and he will make your
paths straight.
　　　　—Proverbs 3:5–6

BACKGROUND SCRIPTURES
Genesis 38
　　The story of Tamar and
　　Judah and an example of
　　a kinsman-redeemer's
　　responsibilities
Leviticus 25:25–34, 47–55;
27:9–33; Numbers 35:9–28;
Deuteronomy 19:1–13;
25:5–10; Joshua 20:2–9
　　Duties and
　　responsibilities of
　　a kinsman-redeemer
Ezekiel 16:8
　　God used the image of
　　putting the corner of
　　His garment over
　　Israel to describe
　　their relationship to
　　each other.
Matthew 1:1–17
　　The genealogy of Jesus

DAILY BIBLE READINGS
Monday:　　1 John 2:15–17
Tuesday:　　Matthew
　　　　　　5:43–48
Wednesday: Luke 22:39–46
Thursday:　Luke 9:57–62
Friday:　　 Revelation
　　　　　　3:11–13
Saturday:　Ruth 3:1–11;
　　　　　　4:12–17
Sunday:　　Psalm 39:1–13

WHY THIS MATTERS

A little boy's sailboat stalled in the middle of a pond when a gentle breeze suddenly subsided. The boy felt he would never retrieve his boat. Then, an older boy picked up stones and threw them near the boat. At first the younger boy thought the older boy would destroy the stranded sailboat, but before long he realized each stone landed just beyond the boat and caused a ripple to form on the water. In turn, each ripple brought the sailboat closer to the shore, and eventually the little boy was reunited with his boat.

This lesson shows how God can use trials to draw us to himself and to work all things for our good and His purposes.

BIBLE COMMENTARY
By Mark Haines

These passages contain the culmination of the story of Naomi and Ruth. All narratives in the Bible need to be studied as stories. In other words, we need to observe the main characters, the plot, and the scenes in order to interpret the book correctly. The story is named after Ruth, the daughter-in-law of Naomi, and in many ways the story is about both of them. This indicates that the plot revolves around these women. The men play supporting roles.

Every story plot has a structure that holds it together. "Pivot" and "chiasm" are especially common literary structures in the Bible. A narrative can change direction or "pivot" on a particular event. For example, the book of Numbers builds a sense of anticipation as the people prepare to enter the Promised Land; but it takes a turn toward despair after the people rebel in chapter 14.

"Chiasm" takes this change of direction further by repeating or matching a series of story components in reverse order after the pivot. The turnaround may involve repetition or paralleling of words, ideas, actions, or characters. For example, Jesus' parable about the lost sons in Luke 15 is built this way.

The plot of Ruth is structured with the same pattern. The book introduces Naomi along with her husband and two sons as a Jewish family living in Moab because of a famine in their home of Bethlehem (Ruth 1:1–2). Then Naomi's husband died and left her with two sons to raise (1:3). Her sons each married women from Moab; this was Ruth's entrance to the story (1:4). About ten years later, Naomi's sons died and left her with two daughters-in-law to support (1:5). Naomi heard from home that the famine was over, so she started to travel back—the pivot in this story's plot (1:6–7).

On the road home, she tried to send her daughters-in-law back to their families, but Ruth refused to go home (1:8–18). So the two main characters returned to Naomi's hometown of Bethlehem, where she told her friends to call her "Bitter" because of the pain she had experienced (1:19–21). Ruth and Naomi arrived in Bethlehem when the barley harvest was ready to be brought in, and Ruth volunteered to gather whatever grain the reapers left behind (1:22—2:2). She ended up gleaning in the fields of a wealthy relative of Naomi's husband. His name was Boaz, and he was also a well-respected man (2:1, 3). Boaz noticed Ruth and asked who she was. When he discovered she was Naomi's daughter-in-law, he arranged for her protection and for extra grain to be left behind for her (2:4–23).

This brings us to an important Old Testament tradition. Naomi thanked God for guiding Ruth into the field of Boaz, whom she called "one of our kinsman-redeemers" (2:20). In a culture without governmental assistance for widows, orphans, and others in poverty, the extended family was expected to care for them. The primary responsibility fell on the nearest male relative. The kinsman-redeemer's two main responsibilities were to retrieve and protect the family property of his near relative when it was offered for sale (Lev. 25:25–34; 27:9–33) and to marry the widow of a dead near relative in order to father children to the name of the dead (Deut. 25:5–10). The "close relative" would also be expected to purchase his kinsman's freedom from voluntary slavery resulting from poverty (Lev. 25:47–55). The "redeemer" might, in fact, avenge the blood of the dead relative if he found the murderer (Num. 35:9–28; Deut. 19:1–13; Josh. 20:2–9).

I Will Do What You Say (Ruth 3:1–6)

Once Ruth and Naomi made connections with Boaz, the restoration of their lives began to accelerate. **One day Naomi** [said to Ruth], **"My daughter, should I not try to find a home for you, where you will be well provided for?"** (v. 1). Naomi wanted to provide security and rest for her loving daughter-in-law. If Ruth found a husband, he would care for both of them.

Naomi reminded Ruth that **Boaz** (v. 2), who had been treating her so kindly, was one of their kinsmen. Then she told Ruth how to ask him to fulfill his responsibilities as the kinsman-redeemer. She said, **"Tonight he will be winnowing barley on the threshing floor."** The threshing floor was a flat piece of land where the husks of the grain were broken so that the seeds could be removed. Winnowing involved gently tossing the seeds and husks into the air to separate them. It usually took place in the late afternoon when there was a breeze. Boaz and his men would stay at the threshing floor all night to guard the harvest from thieves.

Naomi continued, **"Wash and perfume yourself, and put on your best clothes. Then go down to the threshing floor, but don't let him know you are there until he has finished eating and drinking. When he lies down, note the place where he is lying. Then go and uncover his feet and lie down. He will tell you what to do"** (vv. 3–4).

On the surface, this seems a little seductive; however, this was a very appropriate way for a widowed woman to seek help from her kinsman-redeemer. It was in essence a marriage proposal, as we will see.

Ruth's response to Naomi revealed her deep love and respect for her. She replied, **"I will do whatever you say"** (v. 5). And Ruth did it. Her words matched her deeds. Ruth was fully submissive and obedient to Naomi's instructions.

WHAT DO YOU THINK?
Unmarried men and women often wonder what qualities to seek in a spouse. What can we learn from Ruth's character? From Boaz's?

AHA!
It's amazing to step out in faith, with no certainty of the future, and to watch God provide beyond what we could imagine.

DID YOU KNOW?
People in some parts of the Middle East still practice a custom similar to the Levirate marriage.

The Women in Jesus' Genealogy	
Tamar (Matt. 1:3)	Conceived by acting like a prostitute with her father-in-law Judah (Gen. 38)
Rahab (Matt. 1:5)	A prostitute in Jericho who protected the spies sent by Joshua (Josh. 2)
Ruth (Matt. 1:5)	A Gentile widow (Ruth)
Uriah's wife (Matt. 1:6)	Bathsheba committed adultery with King David (2 Sam. 11–12)
Mary (Matt. 1:16)	A woman who became pregnant before she was married (Matt. 1:18)

Wait for Him (Ruth 3:7–11)

Verse 6 told us that she "did everything her mother-in-law told her to do," and these verses give us the details.

In the middle of the night something startled Boaz, so **he turned and discovered a woman lying at his feet** (v. 8). In the dark, he could not recognize who it was, so he asked, **"Who are you?"** (v. 9).

Ruth identified herself and then said, **"Spread the corner of your garment over me, since you are a kinsman-redeemer."** This is the most sensitive point of the account, and the most likely part to be misunderstood. The culture of the ancient Middle East involved the practice of throwing part of a garment over one being claimed for marriage (Ezek. 16:8). It did not imply anything inappropriate.

Boaz was impressed with Ruth once again, and he replied, **"The LORD bless you, my daughter** because **this kindness is greater than that which you showed earlier** (by caring for Naomi). **You have not run after the younger men, whether rich or poor. And now, my daughter, don't be afraid. I will do for you all you ask"** (vv. 10–11). Apparently Boaz had thought about his relationship with Ruth but expected her to seek out a younger man. The fact that the people of Bethlehem knew that Ruth was **a woman of noble character** implies that others had noticed her loving care for Naomi too.

Boaz wanted to marry Ruth, but he knew there was a kinsman-redeemer who was a closer relative to Naomi. That man would have the first opportunity to fulfill the duties and to protect Ruth and Naomi. Boaz told her to stay by him until it was light enough to return to town safely. So the next morning, Ruth reported all that had happened to her mother-in-law. Then Naomi said, "Wait, my daughter, until you find out what happens. For the man will not rest until the matter is settled today" (3:18).

Better Than Seven Sons (Ruth 4:12–17)

At the same time, Boaz went to the town gate (where legal transactions were conducted) and waited there. When the nearer kinsman-redeemer came along, Boaz asked him to sit and talk with him. Then Boaz asked ten of Bethlehem's leading men to join them as witnesses.

Then he told the kinsman-redeemer that Naomi was selling the piece of land that had belonged to her late husband, their relative. Boaz wanted to make sure this man had the opportunity to buy it first. When the closer relative decided he wanted to redeem the land, Boaz added one more concern. Boaz pointed out that as soon as he bought the land from Naomi and Ruth, he would need to marry one of them to keep the land in the name of Naomi's late husband.

At this, the kinsman-redeemer refused to buy the land because he thought it might endanger his own family's inheritance. It seems that the additional expense of providing for a wife, together with the prospect of losing the property

WHAT DO YOU THINK?
Naomi acted as a sort of wise mentor to Ruth, and both benefitted. Such relationships are important. How can we encourage stronger bonds between older and younger members of the church?

AHA!
There are few things ultimately more attractive than a godly character and a reputation for a humble and caring spirit.

DID YOU KNOW?
Ruth really is a "balanced" story, in the tradition of a "chaism." In the original Hebrew, the introduction and the conclusion each contain the same number of words.

if a son would possibly be born to the widow, caused the nearer kinsman to surrender his rights to Boaz. So they made the transfer of responsibility official in the sight of the town elders.

Then the elders and all those at the gate pronounced a blessing on Ruth and Boaz: "May the Lord make the woman who is coming into your home like Rachel and Leah, who together built up the house of Israel. May you have standing . . . and be famous in Bethlehem" (v. 11). Rachel and Leah were the two wives of Jacob who were the mothers, either naturally or through their maids, of the patriarchs of the twelve tribes of Israel.

The elders continued by praying that **through the offspring the Lord gives you by this young woman, may your family be like that of Perez, whom Tamar bore to Judah** (v. 12). Tamar was the widow of Judah's eldest son, and she ended up playing the part of a prostitute with her father-in-law in order to have a son to keep the family name going (Gen. 38). She gave birth to twins. One was named Perez, and he was an ancestor to Boaz (Ruth 4:18–22).

So Boaz took Ruth and she became his wife . . . and the Lord enabled her to conceive, and she gave birth to a son (v. 13). Ruth appears to have been barren while she was married to Naomi's son. When the baby was born, Naomi's friends and neighbors said, **"Praise be to the Lord, who this day has not left you without a kinsman-redeemer. May he** [the baby] **become famous throughout Israel! He will renew your life and sustain you in your old age. For your daughter-in-law, who loves you and who is better to you than seven sons, has given him birth"** (vv. 14–15).

This book introduced Naomi as a widow with no sons to provide for her and living in a foreign land. It ends with God providing her with her loving daughter-in-law Ruth, and a new grandson in her hometown. As far as her friends were concerned, Naomi had a son because she took care of him as if he were her own. They **named him Obed. He was the father of Jesse, the father of David** (v. 17), who was the ancestor of Jesus Christ. ✦

INTERACTIVE LEARNING IDEAS

GET THE CLASS INVOLVED
A Love Story Drama

The story of Ruth and Boaz offers a beautiful love story, even if it doesn't follow the pattern of our modern love stories. Invite a few people to read the story in dramatic-reading style, with a narrator and someone reading the dialogue of each of the key characters. It might be fun to have a husband and wife play Ruth and Boaz, although that isn't essential. Have them read today's passage out loud to the class.

When done, take five minutes to talk as a class about what made Ruth and Boaz good "marriage material." If your group is mainly singles, talk about what qualities we should look for in a spouse. Discuss what kind of people we need to be. If your group is mainly married folks, discuss the same qualities and how we can continue to develop them even after marriage. End with a few minutes sharing your own "love stories."

TRY THIS ON YOUR OWN
A Date Like No Other

God wants the best for our marriages, and it's important for couples to encourage and honor godly character in one another. Remember how Boaz told Ruth about the good things he'd heard about her.

Invite your spouse on a date, like you did before you married. Go to dinner and a movie, have a picnic in the park, hike a trail, or walk the beach. But during the date, stop for a moment and share your appreciation for at least three specific godly qualities you see in your spouse. (If your spouse isn't a Christian, just share the qualities you appreciate.) Tell him or her why these characteristics mean so much to you and how those qualities have benefitted your marriage. Then pray for your spouse, thanking God for who that person is.

If you are not married, read through the story of Ruth and Boaz and create a list of godly character qualities you should look for in a spouse. Pray that if God should have you marry, He would be building those qualities in your future spouse. Then ask that He would develop that same character in you. Ask Him to make your focus becoming the person He wants you to be.

TAKING IT TO THE STREET
Worth Far More Than a Dollar

Let the dollar store remind you what matters in a spouse. Gather at a dollar store. Each person should have two dollars. Have everyone split up and purchase two items. One item should represent a godly character quality they appreciate in their spouse. The other should reflect a quality you commit to strengthening for your spouse. It'll be silly, fun, and meaningful. And an easy adaptation for singles is to find one item representing a godly characteristic they should seek in a spouse and one reflecting a Christlike attribute they would like to bring to the relationship.

WITH YOUR FAMILY
And the Award Goes To . . .

Create your own movie of the story of Ruth and Boaz with your family. Only there will be no live people in it. You can use dolls or create puppets out of paper sacks. You can also draw it out on paper. Each sheet is a picture in which the characters move only a slight bit from the last picture. Film each sheet one at a time. Or maybe they hold up posters of the pictures they draw and flip them one at a time. Older kids might enjoy creating a sort of stop-motion animation film with figures made from salt dough or craft clay. Be as creative as you all like.

Help the kids write a script. Then use your video camera (or phone), or borrow one, if you need to. Film your creation. After you watch it together, talk about what made Ruth such a special woman and what made Boaz such a special man. Discuss what made them fall in love with each other. Talk about how God provided for all of them—Ruth, Boaz, and Naomi—and how we can trust Him to care for our needs. ◆

RUTH 3:1–11; 4:12–17

3:1 One day Naomi her mother-in-law said to her, "My daughter, should I not try to find a home for you, where you will be well provided for?

2 Is not Boaz, with whose servant girls you have been, a kinsman of ours? Tonight he will be winnowing barley on the threshing floor.

3 Wash and perfume yourself, and put on your best clothes. Then go down to the threshing floor, but don't let him know you are there until he has finished eating and drinking.

4 When he lies down, note the place where he is lying. Then go and uncover his feet and lie down. He will tell you what to do."

5 "I will do whatever you say," Ruth answered.

6 So she went down to the threshing floor and did everything her mother-in-law told her to do.

7 When Boaz had finished eating and drinking and was in good spirits, he went over to lie down at the far end of the grain pile. Ruth approached quietly, uncovered his feet and lay down.

8 In the middle of the night something startled the man, and he turned and discovered a woman lying at his feet.

9 "Who are you?" he asked. "I am your servant Ruth," she said. "Spread the corner of your garment over me, since you are a kinsman-redeemer."

10 "The LORD bless you, my daughter," he replied. "This kindness is greater than that which you showed earlier: You have not run after the younger men, whether rich or poor.

11 And now, my daughter, don't be afraid. I will do for you all you ask. All my fellow townsmen know that you are a woman of noble character.

4:12 Through the offspring the LORD gives you by this young woman, may your family be like that of Perez, whom Tamar bore to Judah."

13 So Boaz took Ruth and she became his wife. Then he went to her, and the LORD enabled her to conceive, and she gave birth to a son.

14 The women said to Naomi: "Praise be to the LORD, who this day has not left you without a kinsman-redeemer. May he become famous throughout Israel!

15 He will renew your life and sustain you in your old age. For your daughter-in-law, who loves you and who is better to you than seven sons, has given him birth."

16 Then Naomi took the child, laid him in her lap and cared for him.

Do the Right Thing

A God-directed life is its own reward, now and forever.

INTO THE SUBJECT

Nearly everyone enjoys a love story. The story of what happened to Naomi's daughter-in-law Ruth in Bethlehem is an amazing love story. Would you be surprised to learn that God wrote it, and its sequel is eternal?

INTO THE WORD

1. How would you characterize Naomi based on your reading of Ruth 3:1–4?

2. What trait does Ruth reveal in response to Naomi's advice (vv. 5–6)?

3. Do you think Naomi and Ruth had a good mother-in-law/daughter-in-law relationship? Why or why not?

4. How do you know from verses 7–11 that Boaz was a God-fearing, righteous man?

5. If a young Christian woman asked you what kind of man she should marry, what would you tell her?

6. What do you find most uplifting about the "blessings" recorded in Ruth 4:12–5?

7. Compare verse 17 and Matthew 1:1, 5–6. What is the eternal sequel to the love story recorded in the book of Ruth?

INTO THE WORLD

Just as Naomi and Ruth provided support for each other in their times of sorrow and need, so you can provide support for someone who is grieving or struggling in some other way. Be there for that person as an extension of God's love.

17 The women living there said, "Naomi has a son." And they named him Obed. He was the father of Jesse, the father of David.

BOAZ REDEEMS

Write an acronym using the word *kinsman*. Focus your thoughts and writing on the meaning of a kinsman-redeemer, how Boaz fulfilled the role, and the similarities to how Christ is our redeemer. (An acronym is a word formed from initials. Each letter of the word stands for something.) An example for the letter "K" has been provided.

K—Knowing there was a closer realtion to Naomi then he, Boaz sought out the closer kinsman first.

K _____

_____

I _____

_____

N _____

_____

S _____

_____

M _____

_____

A _____

_____

N _____

_____

UNIT 4
REDEEM THE TIME
Connecting with God's Heart

So Many Good Things

Unit 4 Preview

Who doesn't enjoy a church picnic? It seems a church picnic is always well attended, as people anticipate a comfortable summer day outside, good fellowship, and, of course, plenty of good food. It is quite a sight to see picnic tables arranged end to end and covered with such delectable items as fried chicken, hamburgers, hot dogs, casseroles, baked beans, potato salad, coleslaw, corn on the cob, plus a variety of pies and cakes. It's enough to make taste buds dance, children lick their lips, and adults exclaim, "Let's hurry and say grace!"

An Appealing Array of Biblical Topics

This unit's study has arranged a variety of appetizing biblical topics as a veritable spiritual feast. The selection features such topics as the resurrection, honoring our elders, God's plan for our life, God's plan for marriage, kingdom priorities, the Lord's Supper, and faithful stewardship. You can "dig in" every Sunday to feed your soul and strengthen your life. Specifically, you will see how a godly thought life and godly behavior are connected. You will gain a deeper appreciation of God's truth and a stronger commitment to live the truth. You will be inspired to partake of the Lord's Supper with a humble, reverent attitude. Seeing that hypocrisy is offensive to God, you will worship and serve sincerely, with heartfelt love for God. Expect to renew your commitment to be a faithful steward of the resources God has given you. Be challenged to lay worry aside and to trust God to meet all your needs. Gain a better understanding of what it means to be one in Christ, to honor our elders, and to do God's will. Finally, you will see that marriage between a man and a woman was ordained as a holy institution.

Bible Passages Await Your Study

Expect to dig into a variety of Bible passages as you study these topics. You will sample passages from Philippians, Revelation, 2 Peter, 1 Corinthians, Amos, Matthew, Acts, Galatians, Romans, Exodus, John, James, Ephesians, and Genesis.

Pull Up a Chair

This course dispels the notion that Christianity is all about salvation and nothing more. It helps us see that salvation introduces us to so many good things to know and do. So pull a chair up to the picnic table and enjoy the full spread of good things this study offers. ◆

DISCOVERING YOUR PERSONAL HERITAGE

Who are the key people who have personally influenced your beliefs and way of life?

_____

_____

What people from previous generations have shaped your life (whether through their writings, the movement they initiated, or another kind of legacy)?

_____

_____

Who have been your spiritual mentors, whether directly or indirectly?

_____

_____

Who are the people you most admire and would like to emulate their way of life?

_____

_____

What are the key values that you have inherited from the people you have listed above?

_____

_____

What life purpose or mission have you chosen based on the influence of those who have gone before you?

_____

_____

Based on all of the above, what kind of person are you becoming (or do you want to become) in Christ?

_____

_____

Based on all of the above, what kind of mission or goals are you pursuing (or do you want to pursue) in Christ?

_____

_____

LESSON 1

HONORING THE PAST ENLIVENS THE PRESENT
Philippians 4:8–9; Revelation 3:1–6

KEY VERSE

Whatever you have learned or received or heard from me, or seen in me—put it into practice. And the God of peace will be with you.
—Philippians 4:9

BACKGROUND SCRIPTURES

Acts 16:12–40
    Paul's founding of the church at Philippi
2 Corinthians 10:5
    The importance of controlling one's thoughts
Revelation 1:1—3:22
    Introduction to Revelation; description of Jesus; and the complete text of the letters to the seven churches
Revelation 20:15; 21:27
    References to the Book of Life
Matthew 10:32–33
    Jesus' attitude toward those who acknowledge Him or disown Him

DAILY BIBLE READINGS

Monday: Joshua 4:1–7
Tuesday: Jeremiah 6:16–17; Isaiah 30:19–21
Wednesday: Philippians 1:1–11
Thursday: Lamentations 3:19–25
Friday: Proverbs 4:1–9
Saturday: Philippians 4:8–9; Revelation 3:1–6
Sunday: Psalm 41

WHY THIS MATTERS

Church break-ins seem to be on the rise, and some pastors think the crimes may be attributed to the economy. One particularly brazen break-in occurred in DeKalb County, Georgia. Nearly everything inside the targeted church was destroyed. "It looked like a war zone—projectors knocked off the ceiling, offices broken into, all the furnishings turned over, the computers smashed to pieces. Everything was smashed," said the pastor.

Although the church had recently posted a guard, he was missing. Police found his car, keys, and cell phone on the property.

Keeping a vigilant watch of church property is important, but as this lesson points out, it is essential that a church guard the Truth faithfully and stay spiritually alert.

BIBLE COMMENTARY

By Ronald C. McClung

Paul's letter to the Philippians, written while the apostle was imprisoned at Rome, is considered the most joyful and positive of all his letters. Someone has referred to the Philippian congregation as Paul's "sweetheart church." That is perhaps stretching the matter a bit; yet the congregation at Philippi was the first church Paul established in Europe, and that was accomplished at a great personal price. Paul and Silas were beaten severely and thrown into jail at Philippi. Yet the jailer became one of the new converts in this infant church (Acts 16:22–34).

In chapter 4 of Philippians, Paul addressed a serious conflict that threatened to disrupt the peace and unity of the church. He specified two women who were upset with each other, pleading with them "to agree with each other in the Lord" (Phil. 4:2). He admonished them to turn to prayer, praise, and right thinking as the antidote to conflict (vv. 4–9). In this chapter, Paul also thanked the church for its generous gift to him (vv. 10–19).

The Revelation letter to the church at Sardis is one of seven letters in that book addressed to the churches of Asia Minor (see Rev. 2–3). Sardis, standing on a hill about fifteen hundred feet high, had been a great city some seven hundred years before John wrote to these churches. When the population of the city grew too large for the space on top of the hill, another city was formed at the bottom. The most famous king in Sardis's history was Croesus, whose wealth gave rise to the saying, "as rich as Croesus." The city was at its strongest and wealthiest when Croesus reigned.

However, the people of the city became soft and complacent. They felt they were so secure on top of the hill that they often neglected to post a guard. One day an enemy, watching from a distance, saw a soldier inside the city accidentally drop his helmet over the side. Then the enemy watched as the soldier carefully climbed down the steep side of the hill, picked up his helmet, and climbed back to the top. Realizing that there were cracks and crevices in the hillside that made it possible for the soldier to gain a foothold, the enemy led a group of soldiers quietly up the steep hill that night. Arriving at the top, the soldiers discovered that no guards were posted and easily captured the city.

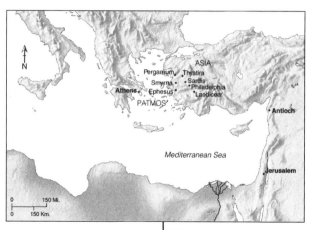

About seventy years before John wrote this letter, a terrible earthquake destroyed the city of Sardis, and the Roman emperor Tiberius subsequently gave a great deal of money to rebuild it. So at the time of this writing, it was once again a wealthy city. But it was also degenerate. The people had become very immoral.

Unfortunately, the Christian church at Sardis had become a great deal like the city. Although it had a history of being spiritually alive, it was now spiritually dead.

What One Thinks about Is Vitally Important (Phil. 4:8–9)

Paul understood that the way out of conflict, and the way to success in any Christian endeavor, is to think properly. The wise man said, "For as he thinks in his heart, so is he" (Prov. 23:7 NKJV).

Therefore, the apostle provided a list of things on which it is appropriate, even desirable, for the Christian to focus. First he challenged his reader to **think about . . . whatever is true** (v. 8). People sometimes refer to "my truth" and "your truth," as if there is no objective truth to which we may appeal. Yet we remember that Satan is himself a liar (John 8:44). He even tried to convince Eve that God had not told her the truth (Gen. 3:1–3). We must set our minds on things that are valid and reliable from the standpoint of God's revealed truth in the Bible.

We must also think about **whatever is noble** (Phil. 4:8). What calls for your reverence and respect? Think about those things, along with what is serious and dignified, avoiding the flippant and cheap. Think about **whatever is right**. Thoughts, words, and behavior that conform to God's standards should claim our attention.

Think about **whatever is pure**. In the first century, as today, Christians were tempted by sexual impurity. Paul called us to lift our thoughts above what William Barclay called the "sordid and shabby and soiled and smutty. We must think about **whatever is lovely**, which refers to what is pleasing, amiable, and beautiful. Set your thoughts on **whatever is admirable**, things that are fit for God to hear, things that are high toned, gracious, and attractive.

Paul further admonished us to consider **anything** that **is excellent or praiseworthy** (v. 8). To strive for excellence is to reject settling for the world's level of mediocrity and to set our sights on what pleases God. To **think about such things** is to fix our mind on these beautiful virtues so they become a part of our character.

THE SEVEN CHURCHES
Revelation 2:1—3:22
The seven churches were located on a major Roman road. A letter carrier would leave the island of Patmos (where John was exiled), arriving first at Ephesus. He would travel north to Smyrna and Pergamum, turn southeast to Thyatira, and continue on to Sardis, Philadelphia, and Laodicea—in the exact order in which the letters were dictated.

WHAT DO YOU THINK?
Suppose you were trying to explain "thinking on things of excellence" to a child. What would you tell the child? How would that be different than how you explained it to an adult?

AHA!
Thinking noble thoughts, or about virtuous things, leads to peace with God.

DID YOU KNOW?
The name "Euodia" means "prosperous journey." The name "Syntyche" means "good fortune."

Paul insisted that his readers take **whatever** they have **learned or received or heard from** him, **or seen in** him, and **put it into practice** (v. 9). One might learn something with the head without receiving it in the heart. We must apply truth to both head and heart. Further, we learn not only from being taught but also by example as we hear and see our teachers. As we apply to our lives what we have learned, both by word and by example, **the God of peace will be with** us, giving us a right relationship both with Him and others.

WHAT DO YOU THINK?
Why is it so important for Christians to remember what they have "received and heard"? What might be the consequences if they didn't?

Jesus' Letter to the Church at Sardis (Rev. 3:1)

The letter to **the church in Sardis**, although written by John, is really from Jesus. He addressed it to **the angel of the church**. The Greek word translated *angel* may also be rendered *messenger*. Some scholars think this referred to the pastor of the church.

Exhortations to Watchfulness	
Be watchful all the time.	1 Corinthians 16:13–14
Be watchful against the schemes of the devil.	1 Peter 5:8
Be watchful against temptation.	Matthew 26:41
Watch against false teaching.	Acts 20:28–29
Watch for the coming of our Lord.	Matthew 24:42

John pictured Jesus as one **who holds the seven spirits of God and the seven stars**. In Revelation 1, the seven spirits were before the throne of God. This reference probably meant the sevenfold Spirit of God about whom we read in Isaiah 11:2. In Scripture, seven is regarded as the perfect, or complete, number. The sevenfold Spirit of God was likely a reference to the Holy Spirit in all His fullness. This expression may also have been a reference to all seven churches (see Rev. 2–3).

Jesus was holding **the seven stars**. These probably represented the pastors of the churches. On the one hand, pastors are comforted to know that Jesus holds them in His hand as they lead one of His churches. On the other hand, if the pastor is leading a church like the one at Sardis—one with **a reputation of being alive**, but actually is **dead**—it would be sobering to think of being held by Jesus. What a heavy responsibility!

AHA!
In the Bible, "white garments" usually represent the purity of those faithful to God.

Instructions for the Church (Rev. 3:2–4)

Christ first instructed the churches to **wake up!** (v. 2). Twice in Sardis's history, the city had been captured. Both times it was because the sentries were not watchful. The church in that city was asleep also. Jesus told the believers there to **strengthen what remains and is about to die**. Although they were asleep, there was a small flickering flame of spiritual life, and He wanted them to fan it into a great fire. Their **deeds** were not **complete in the sight of . . . God** (v. 2). This could mean they did not have enough deeds, but more likely it means that the quality of their work was poor. They did not measure up to God's standard.

DID YOU KNOW?
The reference to "garments" in Revelation 3:4–5 had special significance to the people of Sardis. Sardis was famous for its woolen cloth and garments.

Christ challenged them to **remember** what they had **received and heard** (v. 3). What they had received was the written Word of God, and what they heard was doubtless the teachings of the apostles and other Christian workers who faithfully preached the Word.

Christ also urged them to **repent** (v. 3). The only way to maintain our spiritual life is to turn from our lethargy and run back to Christ, who saved us.

He warned them that if they did **not wake up**, He would **come like a thief** (v. 3). This is not a reference to the second coming, because this coming was tied to their waking up. Christ was saying that some disaster or some great conflict or even death might come to them unexpectedly; and if it did, they would not be ready. Further, they would receive no other warning; they would **not know at what time** the judgment would come.

Verse 4 is the one bright spot in the letter to this church. There were a **few people in Sardis** who had **not soiled their clothes**. In those days, people who went to the pagan temples to worship could not enter the temple if they were wearing dirty clothes. They needed to be outwardly clean. Yet when Jesus referred to the few whose clothes were clean, He was speaking of inner purity, the condition of their hearts. These few had not compromised with the pagan culture around them nor participated in the sins of their neighbors. They were pure in heart.

Encouragement for the Church (Rev. 3:4–6)

Jesus made three promises to those who overcome. First **they will walk with** Him, **dressed in white** garments (v. 4). White robes stood for festivity, which may represent the fact that the faithful will be guests at the banquet of God. White robes also stood for victory. Jesus will give us final victory over the world, the flesh, and the devil. White is the color of purity. Jesus said, "Blessed are the pure in heart, for they shall see God" (Matt. 5:8). White also represents the resurrection. Even though we die, we shall live again and will appear before God dressed in white.

Jesus said **they are worthy** (Rev. 3:4). The only reason any of us is worthy is because the blood of Christ is applied to our hearts.

The second promise is that He **will never blot out** their names **from the book of life** (v. 5). In ancient times, a king kept a record of his citizens' names. When a person committed a crime against the state or when a person died, the king's record keepers would erase that person's name from the register. The people of Sardis would have understood that to have one's name written in the Book of Life means that person is a faithful citizen of the kingdom of God. The Bible tells us that those whose names are not written in the Book of Life will be cast into the lake of fire (Rev. 20:15), and only those who are written in the Lamb's book of life shall enter into heaven (21:27).

The third promise to those who overcome was that Jesus Christ **will acknowledge** their names before His **Father and his angels** (Rev. 3:5). Jesus said, "Whoever acknowledges me before men, I will also acknowledge him before my Father in heaven. But whoever disowns me before men, I will disown him before my Father in heaven" (Matt. 10:32–33). If you are true to Jesus, He will always be true to you.

Finally, as in the other six letters to the churches, Jesus challenged all who have ears to **hear what the Spirit says to the churches** (Rev. 3:6). It was a warning to give vigilant attention to these words of Christ. They will be interpreted by the Spirit as the church and as individuals listen carefully in order to carry out His instructions. ◆

WHAT ABOUT YOU?
How have your thoughts affected your life lately? What things of excellence can fill your thoughts this week in ways that will help you strengthen your life as a disciple of Jesus Christ?

PRAYER
Lord God, help me think thoughts that will lead me to greater peace with You, and to act in true faith in ways that honor You.

INTERACTIVE LEARNING IDEAS

GET THE CLASS INVOLVED
Think on These Things

Toward the beginning of your class, have your students divide into groups of three to five. Instruct the groups to list the movies, books, and TV shows they enjoy. Make sure they list specific items by title. Once they have listed these, instruct them to go item by item and decide if the things they spend their time thinking about or putting into their minds would fall into the categories of true, noble, right, pure, lovely, admirable, excellent, or praiseworthy.

Let the groups discuss:
- Which of your listed items have the qualities listed in Scripture?
- Do your listed items affect you in a positive or negative way? Explain.
- How can trying to follow the guidelines in these verses be a help or a hindrance to your life?
- What actions, if any, do you feel are necessary for you to more closely align with these Scripture verses?

TRY THIS ON YOUR OWN
God, the Original Promise Keeper

God's Word is filled with promises. You probably know many of them by heart. This week consider starting a journal or card file of the promises you know. God's promises make great prayers for ourselves and others.

Start with the three promises from this study. First write down the promise and the Scripture reference. Then underneath, note if there is a condition spelled out in the surrounding verses regarding our responsibility in the promise's fulfillment. Leave room for writing down and cross-referencing similar promises. Last, make a note of the date if this is a promise you would like to claim as your own. Mark the date, then refer to it and note the day God fulfilled the promise in your life.

TAKING IT TO THE STREET
True Religion in Practice

Scripture tells us that true religion that pleases God is the kind that cares for widows and orphans. Who around your church needs that kind of help? Is there an elementary school in your church's neighborhood? Consider adopting that school and becoming a class or church that practices true religion.

Many elementary school families have single parents or children who need practical help. Perhaps they need basics like socks and underwear, food toward the end of the month, or school supplies. By first building a positive relationship with the principal, he or she will be able to let you know of needs in the school. This ministry could grow to the place where you have to open it up to the entire church in order to fulfill the need . . . but isn't that just the kind of church that is "in the hands of Jesus" and making Him happy?

WITH YOUR FAMILY
A New Measurement

Kids will push us as far as we let them. Sometimes it seems easier to just give in: "Aw, let them watch the movie. What can it hurt?" But then we come across a Scripture passage like the one in this study—Philippians 4:8–9—and we have to stop to take stock again of the standards we use to evaluate what we think about.

Try this exercise with your children. On a slip of paper, write each of the words of measurement found in the reference from Philippians. Place them in a bowl or box. Say, "God has given us this list of things that help us measure if something is good for us to think about or even to put in our minds."
- Read the reference with your kids and talk about what it means.
- How do we only think about things that are lovely?
- Why do you think God would put these measurement-words into the Bible?

What about books we read, movies we watch, or TV shows we see—do they "measure up"?

Have each child pick a specific book, movie, song, or TV show. Then have them pick out one of the slips from the bowl. Have them tell why their media pick is or is not like that word they chose. Then ask: How can we learn to love things that measure up to God's measurement?

In the future when someone suggests a media selection, have your family refer to the slips of paper with God's measurements on them. Decide together if that media reflects God's measure for what is good to think about. ◆

PHILIPPIANS 4:8–9; REVELATION 3:1–6

Philippians 4:8 Finally, brothers, whatever is true, whatever is noble, whatever is right, whatever is pure, whatever is lovely, whatever is admirable—if anything is excellent or praiseworthy—think about such things.
9 Whatever you have learned or received or heard from me, or seen in me—put it into practice. And the God of peace will be with you.

Revelation 3:1 "To the angel of the church in Sardis write: These are the words of him who holds the seven spirits of God and the seven stars. I know your deeds; you have a reputation of being alive, but you are dead.
2 Wake up! Strengthen what remains and is about to die, for I have not found your deeds complete in the sight of my God.
3 Remember, therefore, what you have received and heard; obey it, and repent. But if you do not wake up, I will come like a thief, and you will not know at what time I will come to you.
4 Yet you have a few people in Sardis who have not soiled their clothes. They will walk with me, dressed in white, for they are worthy.
5 He who overcomes will, like them, be dressed in white. I will never blot out his name from the book of life, but will acknowledge his name before my Father and his angels.
6 He who has an ear, let him hear what the Spirit says to the churches.

"Blessed is the man who does not walk in the counsel of the wicked or stand in the way of sinners or sit in the seat of mockers. But his delight is in the law of the LORD, and on his law he meditates day and night. He is like a tree planted by streams of water, which yields its fruit in season and whose leaf does not wither. Whatever he does prospers. Not so the wicked! They are like chaff that the wind blows away. Therefore the wicked will not stand in the judgment, nor sinners in the assembly of the righteous. For the LORD watches over the way of the righteous, but the way of the wicked will perish."

—*Psalm 1*

Honoring the Past Enlivens the Present
Remembering our heritage enhances the enjoyment of a full Christian life.

INTO THE SUBJECT
GIGO, a computer term, means "Garbage in, garbage out." What we get out of a computer depends on what has been programmed into it. Similarly, our actions are determined mainly by what we program into our minds. What consumes your thoughts?

INTO THE WORD
1. How well do you suppose your daily thought life conforms to the high standards given in Philippians 4:8?

2. At the time of writing Philippians, how did Paul set a good example for his readers?

3. What kind of influence does each of the following media *mainly* exert on your thinking? Circle each of your responses.
   - TV   negative   positive
   - Secular movies   negative   positive
   - Books and magazines   negative   positive
   - Videos   negative   positive
   - Newspapers   negative   positive

4. How will you curtail the negative influences?

5. Read Psalm 1. How does Philippians 4:8 complement this psalm?

6. What commands you find in Revelation 3:2–6?

7. Why do you agree or disagree that these commands are especially appropriate for the church today?

8. What, if anything, do you think you need to overcome (v. 5)?

INTO THE WORLD
Guard against worldly thinking! Wrong thinking produces wrong behavior, but right thinking produces behavior that glorifies God.

Honor the Past

Remembering the things God has done for you takes intentionality. Read through the list below and select at least one idea to help you appreciate God's work in your life.

Journal

Jot down answers to prayers or insights you gained from sermons, devotionals, or Scripture reading. Even profound moments will fade from memory if not recorded.

Altar

Create a visual reminder of God's work in your life. In Bible times, the people piled stones in a certain location so the next generation would ask about it. Modern-day altars could consist of artwork, poetry, or photographs.

Tradition

Celebrate the anniversary of answered prayers just as you celebrate holidays and birthdays. Call the family together and cook special recipes to remind you of what God has done.

Song

Write lyrics and music to give praise to God for His work in your life.

Scrapbook

Collect newspaper clippings, awards, quotes from loved ones—any reminder of the thing you wish to remember—and lay them out in a scrapbook that can be passed down to the next generation.

We can trust Scripture as truth.

NOTHING BUT THE TRUTH

2 Peter 1:12–21

WHY THIS MATTERS

A good memory is a valuable asset, but it is not a universal asset. A man sought the help of a doctor for his constant forgetfulness. When the doctor asked, "How long has this been going on?" the patient replied, "How long has what been going on?"

Memory doesn't necessarily fade with age, but some elderly people may need help to remember which prescription pills they need to take and when they need to take them. A pill box with compartments labeled with days of the week usually helps.

This lesson emphasizes the need to remember the fundamental truths of the faith. If we forget them, we become vulnerable to false teaching.

BIBLE COMMENTARY

By Wayne Keller

Second Peter 1:1–11 gives a concise summary of the gospel, those truths that are essential for salvation and sanctification or, in Peter's words, for life and godliness.

Looking over what he had already written in this letter, Peter decided he needed to remind believers of things they already knew and refresh their memories so they would remember these fundamental truths (2 Pet. 1:12–15).

Peter wrote of his impending death and his determination to remind his readers of the things recorded in the Scriptures. Because of the limited time Peter had remaining, he was determined to fulfill his calling. His letter served as a reminder to Christians both then and now of the life-transforming truths of the Word of God. Peter spoke plainly of the inspiration and authority of the Scriptures and their importance as God's final revelation.

Peter also reminded us that the one thing that matters most is our relationship to God through Jesus Christ, and that this relationship must be based on the truths of the Word of God, not on cleverly invented stories.

Peter's Eagerness to Remind Readers of the Truth (2 Pet. 1:12–15)

It is clear in verses 12–15 that Peter was focused on reminding his readers. He set out to remind them of what they already knew and accepted as the truth. It is impossible to remind others of what they never knew. Peter wanted these believers to continue to accept the truth, and he reminded them of the things he had already written.

First, we are to remember the reality of salvation and that we have received a precious faith "through the knowledge of God and Jesus our Lord" (2 Pet. 1:1–2). Second, we are to remember that God's "divine power has given us everything we need for life and godliness" (v. 3), that we "participate in the

WHAT DO YOU THINK?
Why do you think believers
are challenged to add the
characteristics listed in
2 Peter 1:5–7 to their faith?

AHA!
God's divine power has
given us everything we
need for life and godliness.

divine nature and escape the corruption in the world" (v. 4). Third, we are called
to remember the responsibility that comes with our salvation to add to our "faith
goodness; and to goodness, knowledge; and to knowledge, self-control; and to
self-control, perseverance; and to perseverance, godliness; and to godliness,
brotherly kindness; and to brotherly kindness, love" (vv. 5–7). The fruit, or the
result, is that these "will keep you from being ineffective and unproductive in
your knowledge of our Lord Jesus Christ" (v. 8).

Peter's concern for remembering these truths was not a passing fancy. He
was committed to **always remind** believers of these things (v. 12). He would
continue to remind them as long as he was able. In fact he would do so with
his dying breath.

Peter knew he would not have much longer to carry on his work, since **our
Lord Jesus Christ** had **made clear** to him that he would **soon put it aside** (v.
14). Peter referred to his **body** as a **tent** (v. 13). He was aware of the transient
nature of life on earth and was determined to be diligent in carrying out his
mission.

Essential Elements of Biblical Interpretation
Consensus. Peter warned that uniqueness in interpretation should be a red flag rather than an attraction. Biblical prophecy has been revealed through a diverse group of individuals over a number of centuries. Peter indicated that these prophets did not even fully understand their own writings (1 Pet. 1:10–12). If God's prophetic word was revealed to many people, then how can its interpretation be the exclusive possession of one person? Biblical prophecy is "hard to understand" (2 Pet. 3:16; 1 Pet. 1:10–12). There are many things over which Bible students disagree. We should be most confident about those matters with which a large number of Christians do agree, not just Christians living in our own time but also those who studied the Scriptures centuries ago.
Divine Guidance. Biblical interpretation can be accomplished only through the ministry of the Holy Spirit. Prophets did not originate prophecy; they were spokespersons for God. Prophecy does not begin with human will but with God's will. Reliance upon the Holy Spirit is the key to accurate interpretation, and the accuracy of this interpretation will be indicated, in part, by the agreement of many interpreters.

As he wrote, Peter seemed to be
aware that he was being used of God
to write Scripture and that his words
would be used as a reminder to
Christians until the Lord Jesus returns.
Peter wrote in order to have an impact
upon believers, both those whom he
knew and others whom he would
never meet.

Reasons Why a Reminder Is Necessary (2 Pet. 1:16–19)

The Christians to whom Peter
wrote had questions about the second
coming. There were false apostles
(see 2 Cor. 11:13) at work who
claimed Christ would not return and
there would be no final judgment (see 2 Pet. 3:3). Peter flatly contradicted
those assertions, saying that these false teachers were telling **cleverly invented
stories** (v. 16). Peter contrasted these stories with the Scriptures God revealed
through His apostles. To explain the certainty of the Scriptures, Peter turned to
the Transfiguration, of which he—along with James and John—was a witness
(see Matt. 17:12).

Like the Old Testament prophets, Peter and the other apostles wrote **about
the power and coming of our Lord Jesus Christ** (v. 16). The apostles' writing was consistent with the writings of the Old Testament prophets, but the witness of the apostles was even more certain, because it was the testimony of
eyewitnesses. The apostles did not write merely of things they had heard but of
things they had seen.

Peter pointed out that he, James, and John did not dream up cleverly
invented stories. They went up on a **sacred mountain** (v. 18) with Jesus to

DID YOU KNOW?
The word translated
"godliness" in 2 Peter 1:6–7
is *eusebeia*. It describes
someone who is in right
relationships with both
God and people.

accompany Him while He prayed. The Lord was transfigured before them. All three apostles heard the **voice** of **God the Father** (v. 17) during the transfiguration scene, recorded in Matthew, Mark, and Luke. That voice was God's, and gave honor to Jesus by identifying Him clearly as **my Son, whom I love; with him I am well pleased**. Consequently, the apostolic witness to Jesus was established by three senses—sight, sound, and touch. The apostles saw the transfigured Lord; they heard the voice of the Father (and the conversation with Moses and Elijah, though Peter did not mention the latter); and the event took place **on the sacred mountain.** This grounded the event in history and removed it from the realm of myth.

Mount Hermon, pictured here, is now believed by many Bible teachers to be the Mount of Transfiguration mentioned in the Gospels and in 2 Peter.

The term **Majestic Glory** (v. 17) refers to the shekinah glory of God (see Ex. 34:29–35). Notice that the transfiguration experience was not the same thing that happened to Moses, whose face shone brightly after his conversation with God during the wilderness experience. Christ's change of appearance resulted from an internal transfiguration that revealed the reality of the glory of His character, permitting, for a moment, that glory to shine through the veil of His flesh. The disciples saw Jesus as He truly is. The transfiguration was a foretaste, not of the resurrection of Jesus, but of his second coming in **honor and glory.** That is why Peter said, **we were eyewitnesses of his majesty** (v. 16).

This is the only time the Greek word here translated *eyewitness* is used in the New Testament. This word was used of spectators to the religious plays put on by the secret-society cults of Peter's day. These plays related the story of a god who suffered, died, and rose again. In these religions, a new worshiper was finally allowed to be present at the play only after a long period of instruction and was offered the experience of becoming one with the dying-and-resurrected god. When a worshiper achieved this stage, he was classified as a privileged "eyewitness" to the experiences of the god. Here Peter was saying that the apostles were not eyewitnesses to a play but eyewitnesses of the true Son of God. The word *majesty* suggests overwhelming glory and beauty that compels the viewer's mind and heart to worship.

Then Peter made the point that **we have the word of the prophets made more certain** (v. 19). Old Testament prophets were chosen by God to be His spokespeople, declaring His message for the present, the future, or both. The prophets were given messages concerning the life, character, ministry, suffering, death, resurrection, ascension, and second coming of Jesus in His glory.

Then Peter gave this warning: **you will do well to pay attention to it, as to a lamp shining in a dark place, until the day dawns and the morning star rises in your hearts**. The **word of the prophets** relating to the second coming of Jesus is a light of hope as we walk through a dark, sinful world. This lamp will keep us from stumbling, and it will burn until the day dawns.

But, Peter said, there is no need for this lamp once the sun comes up, "until the day dawns and the morning star rises." According to Revelation 22:16, Jesus is the Morning Star. When we see the Morning Star, we can put our lamps down. Then the second coming will have been fulfilled. Peter was saying that the prophets foretold Jesus' first coming, and we don't need that particular

WHAT DO YOU THINK?
As you see it, what are some of the important differences between Peter, James, and John being eyewitnesses to Jesus' power and glory and others being trained as eyewitnesses in mystic religions?

AHA!
The events surrounding Jesus on the Mount of Transfiguration make the "word of the prophets" concerning Jesus and His return "more certain."

DID YOU KNOW?
Most conservative Bible scholars place the date of 2 Peter shortly before A.D. 68, at the end of Peter's life.

WHAT ABOUT YOU?
How do you respond when others challenge your faith in Jesus Christ? What could you learn from 2 Peter as you respond?

PRAYER
Lord and King, thank You for the events and the Scriptures that keep me faithful to Your will and ways.

lamp of prophecy anymore because all of those prophecies have already been fulfilled. Now we are to lift up the lamp of prophecy concerning His second coming.

The Christian faith has a unique foundation among world religions. It is based not just on the teachings of its founder, Jesus Christ, but also on events that took place in history and are documented by eyewitnesses.

It has been said that the Bible is not the word of humans about God but is the Word of God to humanity. The Bible claims that both the writers and the writings of Scripture were inspired (2 Pet. 1:19).

The Danger of False Prophecy (2 Pet. 1:20–21)

In verse 20, Peter was not talking about the interpretation of prophecy, but about the fact that when the prophets wrote, their prophecies were not private interpretations or personal opinions. First Peter 1:10–11 indicates that the prophets spoke for God as the Holy Spirit moved them. The prophets did not speak from their own wisdom. Everything came from God.

Peter reminded his readers, including us, that if we are to be instructed about things that are eternally important, that instruction will come from the Scriptures. God has spoken finally and completely through His Son and through the apostles (see Heb. 1:1–3; 2:1–4). We need no additional revelation. What we really need is to understand what God has already said in His Word and to apply these truths to our daily lives. ♦

2 PETER 1:12–21

12 So I will always remind you of these things, even though you know them and are firmly established in the truth you now have.

13 I think it is right to refresh your memory as long as I live in the tent of this body,

14 because I know that I will soon put it aside, as our Lord Jesus Christ has made clear to me.

15 And I will make every effort to see that after my departure you will always be able to remember these things.

16 We did not follow cleverly invented stories when we told you about the power and coming of our Lord Jesus Christ, but we were eyewitnesses of his majesty.

17 For he received honor and glory from God the Father when the voice came to him from the Majestic Glory, saying, "This is my Son, whom I love; with him I am well pleased."

18 We ourselves heard this voice that came from heaven when we were with him on the sacred mountain.

19 And we have the word of the prophets made more certain, and you will do well to pay attention to it, as to a light shining in a dark place, until the day dawns and the morning star rises in your hearts.

20 Above all, you must understand that no prophecy of Scripture came about by the prophet's own interpretation.

21 For prophecy never had its origin in the will of man, but men spoke from God as they were carried along by the Holy Spirit.

"Guide me in your truth and teach me."
—Psalm 25:5

Nothing but the Truth
We can trust Scripture as truth.

INTO THE SUBJECT

A wall plaque reads: "When the memory goes, forget it!" But isn't the memory worth refreshing from time to time?

INTO THE WORD

1. Which truths in 2 Peter 1:1–11 would you place at the top of your list of "Things to Remember"?

2. What clues do you find in verses 13–15 that Peter believed his death was imminent?

3. Why is it important to remember that the human body is a tent (v. 13)?

4. What major differences do you see between false teachings about Jesus and what Peter and the other apostles taught?

5. How could Peter be so sure that Jesus embodied the glory and majesty of God?

6. If someone told you Jesus was just a man, how would you refute the allegation?

7. How do verses 19–21 present a high view of Scripture?

8. How would you respond to a cultist who told you, "I believe the Bible is God's Word, but this other book is God's Word too"?

INTO THE WORLD

We live in an age of relativism. Many people believe there is no absolute truth. As you present the good news, continue to appeal to Scripture as God's unchanging, absolute Truth.

EYEWITNESSES

Unscramble each of the clue words. Copy the letters in the numbered cells to other cells with the same number.

NOSMI REETP
9 16 · 38

DEWNAR
39 12

JEASM OSN FO EEEDBZE
26 6 37

NOHJ
24 11

PIPLIH
2 21 32 25 33

MEOBOLWTRAH
22 34 7 35 20

HOMSAT
28 4

MAETHTW
15 23 29

JAESM NOS FO AESPUAHL
14

DETDHUAS
19

SOINM
5

RYAM TOREMH OF JESSU
27 18 1

MYRA GNMELAEDA
36 8 31

ARMY FO BANHYET
10 30

RAAMHT
13

RUAZASL
17

HOJN HET STTAIBP
3

Solution grid:
1 2 3 4 · 5 6 · 7 8 · 9 10 11 , 12 13 14 15 · 16 · 17 18 19 V ; 20 21 22 23
24 25 26 · 3 · 27 28 · 29 30 31 32 · 33 34 35 36 37 38 39 .

INTERACTIVE LEARNING IDEAS

GET THE CLASS INVOLVED
Remember!

Get a copy of the movie *Star Trek II: The Wrath of Khan*. Cue it to the scene at the end where Spock is dying and performs the "Vulcan mind meld" with Kirk. Start your class by showing this clip. Ask:

- Why was it important for Spock to pass on his information to Kirk?
- Do you think Kirk understood the importance of this action? Why or why not?
- What would have been different if all that Vulcan knowledge had died with Spock?
- What do you have that is as important to pass on to others?

Say: "We have some very important truth hidden in our hearts. God wants us not to hide it there only but to pass it on because it's life-or-death information. Others need to know the truth that we know! Today's study will help us see the importance of that 'mind meld.'"

TRY THIS ON YOUR OWN
Let Me Remind You

We need to remember the basic truths we believe. It's also important to pass those truths on to others. Sometimes a creative or unexpected way of passing truths along allows them to be heard in a new way.

Gather supplies to create some simple note cards. Write basic truths about faith in Christ on the cards. (One item per card is enough.)

Now stop and pray. Ask God to show you at least one person who needs to be reminded of something you put on a card. Write a short note in the card to let the person know you were thinking of him or her and praying for him or her this day. Then send the note to him or her and let God's Spirit do the work of securing that truth in his or her heart.

TAKING IT TO THE STREET
Senior Moment

It can be hard to get old, and not just in the aches-and-pains category. Many of our seniors, even in the body of Christ, feel their usefulness is over. It's important for us to let them know that even though they may not be able to chase kids around at vacation Bible school, they are still loved and treasured for the wisdom and life experience they have.

So host them for dinner. Involve your class. Put your heads together, plan a dinner, and invite the seniors from your church. The meal can be formal or informal. The dinner and decorations can be as fancy or as simple as you choose to make them. The important thing is to honor and bless those seniors. Let them know you remember they are there.

Some things to consider:

- Time of day is a key factor for seniors. Many do not drive at night, so rides may be required if you begin the meal after dark.
- Take food restrictions (salt or sugar, for example) into account. Their ability (or lack thereof) to chew tough meat is also a factor.
- Little things mean a lot. Small decorations and food around a theme can thrill them. Over-the-top and expensive may not impress as much as just seeing that you put some thought into the experience.
- Too many seniors to make this feasible? Break the event down for smaller groups, hosting one group per quarter. Start by asking the oldest or most frail first.

WITH YOUR FAMILY
History Channel

We often know details of our family history, but we don't always know our family's spiritual history. So create one!

Start by creating a basic family tree with your immediate family first. By each person, tell how they came to know the Lord and significant things that have happened in their spiritual life so far. Then send e-mails and make phone calls, or get the kids to write letters to your extended families. Find out things like the following:

- What do you think about God? Why?
- If you are a Christian, how did you make that decision? (Ask the same about other faiths followed by your family members, too.)
- What cool things have you seen God do?
- What is one thing you would like others to know about God?

Compile this information in an album or scrapbook. Let your kids help design each page, with pictures and mementos of the person whose faith journey is being covered. This may be so wonderful you'll have to make copies as Christmas gifts! ◆

The tradition of the Lord's Supper preserves holiness.

LESSON 3

GOD'S GRAND CHANNEL OF GRACE
1 Corinthians 11:23–32

KEY VERSE

For whenever you eat this
bread and drink this cup,
you proclaim the Lord's
death until he comes.
          —1 Corinthians 11:26

BACKGROUND SCRIPTURES

Exodus 12:1–30, 43–50
      The Jewish Passover
      feast
Matthew 26:17–35;
Mark 14:12–26;
Luke 22:7–38
      The Lord's Supper
John 7:30–58
      The Bread of Life
      from heaven
Acts 2:46–47
      Origin of the love feast
1 Corinthians 10:14–22
      Idol feasts and the
      Lord's Supper
2 Peter 2:13
      False teachers at
      love feasts
Jude 12
      False teachers at
      love feasts

DAILY BIBLE READINGS

Monday: Luke 22:17–20,
            29–30
Tuesday: Philippians
            3:7–12
Wednesday: Galatians
            2:20–21; 6:14
Thursday: Mark 10:35–45
Friday: 1 Peter 2:9–10,
            24–25
Saturday: 1 Corinthians
            11:23–32
Sunday: Psalm 43

WHY THIS MATTERS

In 1787 when John Wesley was eighty-four years old, he wrote a tract called "The Duty of Constant Communion." In his tract, he answered those who absented themselves from the Lord's Table because they feared they might be "unworthy." Wesley argued that believers should attend the Lord's Table regularly because they are commanded to do so. He also argued that Jesus called His followers His friends (John 15:15). "Now," wrote Wesley, "if our Lord draws us so intimately into his mind and heart as to call us friends, surely we can't turn down his final request [to observe the Lord's Supper]. What friend turns down his dying friend's final request?"

This lesson inspires us to partake of the Lord's Supper faithfully in holiness.

BIBLE COMMENTARY

By Lee M. Haines

The Corinthian church is often spoken of as Paul's "problem church." In both letters to this church, Paul dealt with many problems that existed there. In 1 Corinthians, a significant portion of the letter was spent in answering questions about which the Corinthians had written to Paul. This section of 1 Corinthians runs from 7:1 through 14:40. In 7:1, Paul said, "Now for the matters you wrote about." Similar phrases carry his discussion forward in 8:1 and 12:1. Our study for today comes in chapter 11, which deals largely with worship. In 11:2, Paul praised the Corinthians for remembering him in everything "and for holding to the teachings just as [he] passed them on." But in 11:17, when he turned to discuss their observance of the Lord's Supper and their love feasts, Paul said, "In the following directions I have no praise for you, for your meetings do more harm than good." This is one of the most severe assessments of a local church in all of the New Testament. How tragic it is when the church's meetings together do more harm than good! What caused Paul to make such a severe statement?

In the New Testament church, the Lord's Supper was observed in conjunction with a common meal, sometimes referred to as a love feast (compare Acts 2:46: "They broke bread in their homes and ate together with glad and sincere hearts"). The passage in 1 Corinthians 11:18–22, 33–34 reveals that at such gatherings, each person or family brought food to contribute for all to eat. It seems probable that these were evening meals. The problem at Corinth was that the richer persons in the congregation, who also brought most of the food and the best food, were arriving early and not waiting for the poor and the slaves, who had to work until later. By the time those who brought less arrived, the richer members had already partaken. They ended up stuffed and even drunk, while the poor and the slaves were deprived of what was probably one of the few adequate meals of their week. What a contradiction of the gospel!

The observance of the Lord's Supper as a part of the love feast continued until about A.D. 150, when the two were separated. The discontinuance of the combination may have resulted from such abuses as Paul rebukes here. References in 2 Peter 2:13 and Jude 12 indicate that false teachers took advantage of the love feasts also.

In dealing with these disorders, Paul set forth the origin, meaning, and purpose of the Lord's Supper. It was instituted by Jesus just before He gave His life for us. It is indeed a visible, physical way of remembering that sacrifice. It was intended to promote and preserve holy living.

The Provision for Holiness (1 Cor. 11:23–26)

Paul indicated in 1 Corinthians 11:23 that he had **received from the Lord** that which he had **passed on** to them. Bible scholars are divided on the meaning of this statement. It might be expected that, since Paul was not a disciple of Jesus while He walked on this world, he would have heard about things Jesus did and said from the persons who were with Him then. Eyewitnesses at the Last Supper would be the ones we would expect had informed Paul. But Paul insisted he had received his gospel not from men but rather directly from the Lord (Gal. 1:11–12). And Paul's statement seems to mean that what he was going to tell them about the Lord's Supper, he had heard directly by divine revelation. Or it might mean he had received his interpretation of the Lord's Supper directly from the Lord. Because 1 Corinthians was probably written before any of the four Gospels, Paul's quotations of Jesus' statements constitute our first known record of anything Jesus said while on earth.

Paul indicated that the Lord's Supper had been instituted by Jesus himself **on the night he was betrayed** (1 Cor. 11:23). As we know from the Gospels, Jesus and His disciples were celebrating the Jewish Passover. It was normal for Jews to begin a meal with thanksgiving. Verse 24 indicates that at the beginning of the meal, Jesus gave thanks and then broke the bread. He then said, **This is my body, which is for you; do this in remembrance of me**. Then Paul indicated that the passing of the cup came **after supper** (v. 25). This would have been at the point in the Jewish Passover when a cup of thanksgiving was shared. **In the same way** can well mean that Jesus again gave thanks and followed by **saying, "This cup is the new covenant in my blood; do this whenever you drink it, in remembrance of me."** The words *new covenant* tie this to Exodus 24:8, which records that Moses instituted the old covenant with the shedding of blood.

WHAT DO YOU THINK?
How would you describe the importance of celebrating the Lord's Supper to someone unfamiliar with the Christian faith?

AHA!
Biblical covenants were often put into effect by the shedding of blood. The shedding of Jesus' blood put the new covenant into effect.

DID YOU KNOW?
The Feast of the Passover, during which Jesus instituted the Lord's Supper, is also a meal of remembrance. It calls to mind God's sparing of Israel's firstborn as Israel prepared to leave Egypt.

Seven Aspects of the Lord's Supper	
1. Commemoration	We commemorate what Christ did at Calvary and the works of grace He has done in our hearts and lives.
2. Thanksgiving	Just as the Jews gave thanks for the Passover deliverance, we are thankful for Christ's deliverance of us from the bondage of sin and for all His blessings to us.
3. Sacrifice	The elements represent the offering at the center of our faith—Christ Jesus himself, expended for our benefit just as the bread and wine are.
4. Communion	Because of Christ's work, we have an open relationship with God. Our communion with Him is especially meaningful at the Lord's Table.
5. Fellowship	In Christ we are equals, totally dependent on God's mercy. Our relationship with fellow believers is most apparent during Communion.
6. Mystery	We marvel at the work of grace that God does in our hearts as the Holy Spirit helps us mature in the faith.
7. Anticipation	We expect the imminent return of our Lord.

WHAT DO YOU THINK?
In one sentence, describe
what it means to take the
Lord's Supper in an
unworthy manner.

AHA!
The Lord's Supper reminds
us of Jesus' sacrificial
death on our behalf.

DID YOU KNOW?
The Greek word translated
"supper" in this passage is
deipnon. It is the main meal
of the day, and indicates an
event where people both eat
together and take time with
each other.

The simple celebration
of the Lord's Supper has
reminded Christians from
all cultures and from all
times of Jesus' sacrifice
for us.

Covenants were often made effective by the shedding of blood. In fact, the common expression for creating a covenant in the Old Testament was to "cut" a covenant. In Genesis 15, the Lord made a covenant with Abraham. Abraham prepared several sacrificial animals and then cut them in half, putting one set of halves on one side and the other set of halves on the other side. A smoking firepot with a blazing torch, representing the presence of the Lord, passed between the pieces. This symbolized that partition and death could be visited upon the parties of the covenant if they failed to keep it. Jesus' reference to a covenant also certainly reflected Jeremiah's prediction of a new covenant that would affect the mind and the heart (Jer. 31:31–34).

Then Paul summed up what the Lord's Supper was all about. Participating in it would **proclaim the Lord's death until he comes** (1 Cor. 11:26). The sacrifice Jesus made on the cross was for us (v. 24), and this is a visual and physical way of reminding ourselves and others of this throughout the church age. The purpose of His death was to provide for our forgiveness, redemption, and transformation. This was to lead to holy living. Jesus indicated this in John 17:19 when He said, "For them I sanctify myself, that they too may be truly sanctified." He set himself apart to death on the cross that we might be set apart to God in holiness. The writer to the Hebrews declared, "And so Jesus also suffered outside the city gate to make the people holy through his own blood" (Heb. 13:12).

The Profanation of Holiness (1 Cor. 11:27, 29)

Against the background of Jesus' instituting of the Lord's Supper and what it means, Paul pointed out how appalling it was that the Corinthians had turned their love feasts into times of arrogance, divisiveness, and broken fellowship. He wrote, **Whoever eats the bread or drinks the cup of the Lord in an unworthy manner will be guilty of sinning against the body and blood of the Lord** (v. 27). He also defined this as not **recognizing the body of the Lord** (v. 29). It should be noted that Paul was not talking about an unworthy *person* partaking of the Supper. For none of us can be worthy of the Lord's goodness—it is all a matter of grace. It was partaking in an unworthy *manner* that drew Paul's criticism. Certainly, the poor relationships in the Corinthian church and the lack of loving concern for one another would qualify as an "unworthy manner." In verse 29, Paul talked about **recognizing the body of the Lord.** This may refer to partakers not thinking about the broken bread as a symbol for the Lord's broken body. But Paul also spoke in 1 Corinthians 12 about the church as the body of Christ (12:27), and the Corinthians' disregard for their brothers and sisters could be also a failure to recognize the church as the body of the Lord. Paul described the conduct in 11:27 as constituting sin **against the body and blood of the Lord,** and the conduct in verse 29 as eating and drinking **judgment** on those who did it. These were serious profanations of what should be considered most sacred and holy.

The Preserving of Holiness (1 Cor. 11:28–32)

Paul used the bad situation at Corinth to instruct his readers as to the proper way to approach the Lord's table. **A man ought to examine himself before he eats of the bread and drinks of the**

cup, Paul wrote (v. 28). A believer must check up on him- or herself to see if some corrections in attitude or relationship need to be made. Otherwise a person **eats and drinks judgment on himself** (v. 29). This judgment had resulted in illness and even death among the Corinthians, perhaps spiritually, or perhaps even physically (v. 30). Guilt before God can affect our bodies. But this judgment is not intended to cut us off from God. For when He judges, **we are being disciplined so that we will not be condemned with the world** (v. 32). God disciplines us to save us, not to damn us. And if we had examined ourselves to begin with, we would have **judged ourselves** and **not come under** God's **judgment** and discipline (v. 31). So we are to use our participation in the Lord's Supper to keep check on ourselves and discipline ourselves. In other words, the Lord's Supper can be a means of grace to preserve the holiness Christ bought for us on Calvary.

In the closing verses of the chapter (vv. 33–34), Paul told the Corinthians that when they came together to eat, they should wait for each other. Those who were overcome with hunger were to satisfy it at home so the meetings would not result in judgment. Paul indicated that there were still other directions he would give in person when he came.

Some traditions in the church are short-lived and local; they come and they go. But there are some that have been constant in all generations from the New Testament until now. Baptism, the Lord's Supper, the reading and expounding of Scripture, prayer, and singing—these have lasted. When we come to the Lord's Table, by means of overlapping generations, we come to partake together with Paul and Peter, with Augustine and Chrysostom, with Luther, Calvin, Wesley, and all the rest. It is an illustrious and enormous fellowship that binds us all together with our Lord. ✦

WHAT ABOUT YOU?
How does the Lord's Supper help you better understand or experience the Christian faith?

PRAYER
Lord God, let me love and understand You better as I remember Jesus' death through the Lord's Supper.

INTERACTIVE LEARNING IDEAS

GET THE CLASS INVOLVED
Communion

Before class, gather grapes and saltine crackers (one grape per person and one cracker for every two people). Check with your pastor to make sure that using grapes as a substitute for grape juice for the Lord's Supper is allowed in your congregation's tradition.

Toward the end of your study today, hold your own scaled-back version of Communion. Ask each person to find a partner. Distribute the crackers, one per pair. Read the passage from today's study regarding the body of Christ. Then instruct the pairs to break their crackers, offer a piece to their partner, and say, "This is Christ's body, broken for you." Each may eat the cracker.

Then distribute the grapes, one per person. Read the passage from the study regarding the cup. Have each person give their grape to their partner and say, "This represents the cup of the new covenant. Remember what Jesus did for you." Each may eat the grape.

Pray and thank God for what you have learned today about Communion and its importance. Close with a Communion song of your choice.

TRY THIS ON YOUR OWN
Digging Deeper

The Lord's Supper is one of the universal aspects of the church. Even so, there are many different traditions of how to observe Communion. Yet if we're honest and look openly at Scripture we may be able to see common ground between traditions.

Take a fresh look at what the Bible says about Communion. Pick at least three of the background Scriptures from page 306 and look them up. If you have different versions of the Bible available to you, compare the passages between versions.

- What things are similar between these Scripture passages?
- How do these verses compare to what you read in the study this week?
- What five things can you say with authority about the Lord's Supper based on these passages and those from the study?
- How do these things change the way you look at Communion? Why?
- If you were planning a Communion service, how would you do it? What would you include? Try to think a bit outside the box of your tradition.

TAKING IT TO THE STREET
Commune

There are many different connotations of the word *commune*. You can commune with nature. We commune with each other when we fellowship together. Some people choose to live in a commune. We join together when we partake of Communion. We have communion with God through Jesus, and so forth.

This week plan an outing with your class to do some communing. Agree on a time to meet at a local park. Instruct the class members to bring grape juice with them. It might be a good idea to have some juice boxes available for those who forget. Assign someone to bring a small loaf of bread.

At the park, hold a short prayer walk and enjoy what God has done in nature. Stop along the way to pray and give thanks for His handiwork.

When you all reach the designated end of your walk, stop and have a simple Communion service using the bread and juice you brought.

Then spend some time playing together, communing with the body of Christ.

WITH YOUR FAMILY
The Lord's Supper behind the Scenes

According to the traditions of your church, see about involving your family in various aspects of a service featuring the Lord's Supper.

Many churches allow a volunteer rotation as Communion servers. Small children will need to be helped, but most can participate even if just by being held and observing.

Another way to be involved is to check into the possibility of baking bread that can then be used as a Communion loaf on a special Sunday. Allow the children to be included in the measuring and stirring, and especially in the kneading of the dough and shaping the loaf.

Some churches also look for volunteer help to fill all the little Communion cups before a Communion Sunday. Other volunteers cut the bread into bite-sized cubes. These are tasks your family might enjoy getting involved in doing together. Involving your children in these tasks takes Communion from something only to be watched to something they are included in, in a new and more intimate way. ◆

1 CORINTHIANS 11:23–32

23 For I received from the Lord what I also passed on to you: The Lord Jesus, on the night he was betrayed, took bread,

24 and when he had given thanks, he broke it and said, "This is my body, which is for you; do this in remembrance of me."

25 In the same way, after supper he took the cup, saying, "This cup is the new covenant in my blood; do this, whenever you drink it, in remembrance of me."

26 For whenever you eat this bread and drink this cup, you proclaim the Lord's death until he comes.

27 Therefore, whoever eats the bread or drinks the cup of the Lord in an unworthy manner will be guilty of sinning against the body and blood of the Lord.

28 A man ought to examine himself before he eats of the bread and drinks of the cup.

29 For anyone who eats and drinks without recognizing the body of the Lord eats and drinks judgment on himself.

30 That is why many among you are weak and sick, and a number of you have fallen asleep.

31 But if we judged ourselves, we would not come under judgment.

32 When we are judged by the Lord, we are being disciplined so that we will not be condemned with the world.

"This is my blood . . .
poured out for many."
—Mark 14:24

God's Grand Channel of Grace

*The tradition of the Lord's Supper
preserves holiness.*

INTO THE SUBJECT

Arlington National Cemetery marks the final resting place of the bodies of more than three hundred thousand of America's war dead. It is somber, quiet place—a place to pause, reflect, remember, and give thanks. How does the Lord's Supper help believers to pause, reflect, remember, and give thanks?

INTO THE WORD

1. How do you think Paul received teaching about the Lord's Supper from the Lord?

2. Why do you agree or disagree that the Passover provided a highly appropriate setting for the Lord's Supper?

3. How do you know from 1 Corinthians 11:24–25 that Jesus knew He would die on the cross as our substitute?

4. How often do you think believers should observe the Lord's Supper? Why?

5. For how long a period did Jesus institute the Lord's Supper?

6. Does the Lord's Supper heighten your anticipation of Jesus' return? If so, how?

7. What do you think it means to fail to recognize the body of the Lord (v. 29)?

8. What do you think a believer should include in his or her personal examination before partaking of the Lord's Supper?

INTO THE WORLD

Your thankfulness for Jesus' sacrifice on the cross should not be confined to the Lord's Supper. This week, let at least one person in the community know you are thankful that Jesus died for you.

THE LAST SUPPER QUIZ

1. What is the Last Supper?
   a. the meal Jesus ate before He ran out of food
   b. the meal that was served to Jesus by Pontius Pilate
   c. the meal held by Christ and His disciples the evening before He was crucified
   d. a book of the Bible

2. According to the Bible, when did the Last Supper take place?
   a. Tuesday
   b. Wednesday
   c. Thursday
   d. Friday

3. Where did the Last Supper take place?
   a. on top of a camel
   b. in an upper room
   c. in a barn on a haystack
   d. in a stable

4. What year did the Last Supper occur?
   a. 7 B.C.
   b. A.D. 33
   c. A.D. 2012
   d. A.D. 0

5. What is the full name of the person who betrayed Jesus?
   a. Pontius Pilate
   b. Simon Peter
   c. Julius Caesar
   d. Judas Iscariot

6. What did Jesus tell His disciples at the Last Supper?
   a. One of you will betray Me.
   b. Judas is stealing money.
   c. Peter will never die.
   d. God helps those who help themselves.

Only the biblical gospel message has the power to bring scriptural salvation to our lives.

THE POWER OF GOD FOR SALVATION

1 Corinthians 15:1–11

WHY THIS MATTERS

A former evangelist said a group of kids had gathered at a corner lot to play baseball. A few had brought bats; some had brought baseball gloves; but no one had brought a baseball. After choosing teams, they realized they didn't have a baseball. "What should we do?" one kid asked. "We don't have a ball."

"Forget it!" yelled another kid. "Let's just get on with the game."

Just as a ball is essential to baseball, so the gospel is essential to the ministry of a church. No church can function as God intends if it thinks it can forget about the gospel and "just get on with the game."

This lesson inspires us to cherish the gospel and proclaim it.

BIBLE COMMENTARY

By Lee M. Haines

Paul discussed many issues in 1 Corinthians. He talked about divisions over leaders in chapters 1–4. He rebuked the Corinthians' casual attitude toward sexual immorality in chapter 5. He dealt with lawsuits between Christians and sexual immorality in chapter 6. He began to answer questions from the Corinthians in 7:1, dealing with marriage in chapter 7, food sacrificed to idols in chapter 8, the rights of an apostle in chapter 9. He dealt with idol worship and believers' freedom in chapter 10, with worship and the Lord's Supper in chapter 11. He answered questions about spiritual gifts in chapters 12–14.

Now, in chapter 15, Paul came to one of the most important issues—the resurrection. Just as 1 Corinthians 13 is the love chapter and Hebrews 11 is the faith chapter, so 1 Corinthians 15 is the resurrection chapter.

The church at Corinth probably included a few converts from Judaism as well as many Gentile converts. The Jews were divided on what happens after death. The Pharisees, of whom Paul had been one, believed in the resurrection of the dead. But the Sadducees did not believe in either the immortality of the soul or the resurrection of the body. However, Corinth was a Greek city. Greeks believed in the immortality of the soul but were appalled at the idea of a resurrection of the body. To them, the body was a burden, something they could get rid of at death and set the soul free. The Stoics, a certain school of Greek philosophy, believed there was a bit of God, a spark of divinity, in each person, which, once freed from the body, would fly back to God and be absorbed in Him once again. So their immortality of the soul carried with it no concept of a continuing personality or individual identity. Gnostic beliefs (a philosophical school of thought that later became a threat to Christianity) were already appearing in rudimentary form among the Gentiles. Gnostics also looked upon the body as evil—along with all matter—and something to be escaped. So when Paul and others preached the resurrection,

KEY VERSE

By this gospel you are saved, if you hold firmly to the word I preached to you. Otherwise, you have believed in vain.
—1 Corinthians 15:2

BACKGROUND SCRIPTURES

Matthew 22:23–33
  Jesus corrected the Sadducees.
John 11:17–44
  Jesus as the resurrection and the life
Acts 2:25–32
  Peter cited Old Testament prophecy of Jesus' resurrection.
Acts 4:2
  Preaching resurrection in Jerusalem
Acts 17:18, 31
  Paul preached resurrection in Athens.
Romans 1:1–4
  Jesus proclaimed Son of God by resurrection
Philippians 3:10
  Paul's goal: the resurrection
1 Peter 1:3
  The resurrection, a living hope

DAILY BIBLE READINGS

Monday: John 3:16–21
Tuesday: Romans 3:19–26
Wednesday: Galatians 1:6–10
Thursday: Hebrews 4:1–7
Friday: 2 Timothy 1:7–14
Saturday: 1 Corinthians 15:1–11
Sunday: Psalm 44

they were greeted with rejection and even ridicule from the Greeks (Acts 17:22–32).

Some Corinthian church members were beginning to question the resurrection of the body. Paul answered their questions in 1 Corinthians 15. It is the fullest and strongest treatment of the subject in the Scriptures. Paul made it clear that this belief is at the heart of the gospel.

The Gospel Saves (1 Cor. 15:1–2)

Paul began the chapter by addressing his readers as **brothers** (v. 1). Paul addressed them this way at least seventeen times in 1 Corinthians, including four times in chapter 15. He also referred to individuals as *brother* and *brothers*. And he used the terms *dear children* (4:14) and *dear friend* (10:14). Since much of the letter was given to attempts to straighten out the Corinthians' thinking or behavior, Paul was trying to keep clear the fact that he considered them part of the family and was concerned only for their best interests.

Paul said he wanted **to remind** them **of the gospel** he had **preached to** them (15:1). He was going to be dealing with a familiar subject. There was perhaps here a gentle hint that this really should not be necessary. It should have been very familiar to them, since it was what they had **received** and **on which** they had **taken** their **stand**. It was what Paul had preached and what they had responded to favorably at the beginning.

In fact, Paul told his readers, **By this gospel you are saved** (v. 2). The term *saved* is used frequently in the New Testament to indicate that Christ has rescued us from spiritual bondage and the eternal penalty for a sinful life. The salvation of the Corinthians was conditional, however. Paul wrote, **You are saved, if you hold firmly to the word I preached to you**. They must not waver back and forth in their belief. The doctrines Paul was about to repeat for them must be held firmly. **Otherwise,** Paul admonished, **you have believed in vain**. Faith must be maintained as long as we are in this life. It was our key response to God's loving invitation, and it is our key response that is necessary for us to be saved at last.

The Gospel: Jesus' Death, Burial, and Resurrection (1 Cor. 15:3–4)

Paul spoke of having **received** the gospel and that he **passed** it **on** to the Corinthians (v. 3). The verbs used were technical terms for passing on traditions, including religious traditions, from one generation to another. This would seem to indicate that Paul had heard these matters from those who were Christians before he was. This need not conflict with Paul's statement in Galatians 1:12 that he had not received the gospel he preached "from any man," but "rather . . . received it by revelation from Jesus Christ." It would still leave room for Paul to have picked up details from fellow believers.

Paul said also that he had **passed** it **on . . . as of first importance** (1 Cor. 15:3). What he was about to discuss was the very heart of the gospel, that on which everything else depended. Then he listed three primary teachings in an almost creedal fashion. **Christ died for our sins . . . was buried . . . was raised on the third day** (vv. 3–4). Throughout Paul's writings there are short bursts of poetry or other literary forms that may have quoted statements familiar to and frequently repeated by early Christians. (Compare Phil. 2:6–11; Col. 1:15–20;

WHAT DO YOU THINK?
Why was it so important for Paul to teach the early church about the resurrection of the body?

AHA!
For Paul, the heart of the gospel was that Christ died for our sins, was buried, and was raised on the third day—all according to the Scriptures.

DID YOU KNOW?
Because Jesus took on a body when He came to earth, many Greeks believed He could not be a deity. They believed God would never come in contact with anything material, especially flesh, which would corrupt His spiritual nature.

1 Tim. 3:16; 2 Tim. 2:11–13; Titus 3:4–7.) First Corinthians 15:3–4 is another repeatable, creedal statement. It may mark the beginning of what we know now as the Apostles' Creed. In both the earlier old Roman form and the present form of the creed, the three matters Paul mentioned are given in form similar to what is here. Twice in this short statement, Paul said the events happened **according to the Scriptures** (1 Cor. 15:3–4). The first was a reference to Christ's death "for our sins." While Paul did not cite specific Scriptures, this could well be a reference to Isaiah 53:5–6, 11. The second was a reference to Jesus being "raised on the third day." This could refer back to Psalm 16:8–11 and Hosea 6:2. Jesus tied the three-day factor to Jonah 1:17 (compare Matt. 12:39–41; Luke 11:29–32). Paul's appeal to the Scriptures would help convince the Jews. The fact that Jesus was buried and was not raised until the third day (1 Cor. 15:4) would be strong evidence to the Gentiles that Jesus did in fact die on the cross.

The Gospel's Witnesses (1 Cor. 15:5–7)

The gospel of the death, burial, and resurrection of Jesus was witnessed by persons who were still living, whom Paul cited as support for his teaching. The first one named was **Peter** (v. 5; compare Luke 24:34). Peter was popular enough at Corinth to have a group that claimed him as their leader (1 Cor. 1:12: *Cephas* was the Aramaic equivalent of the Greek *Peter*). So his testimony would bear considerable weight in the Corinthian church. The second witness was a collective one—**the Twelve** (15:5). Actually, the first appearance of Jesus to this group was to only ten of them; Judas had committed suicide and Thomas was absent (Mark 16:14; Luke 24:36–43; John 20:19–25). The larger number was familiar and was used as meaning Jesus' special disciples. The third witness was even a larger group—**more than five hundred of the brethren at the same time, most of whom** were **still living, though some** had **fallen asleep** (1 Cor. 15:6). There is no mention of an appearance to a group of this size in the Gospels, although some Bible scholars identify this with the appearance recorded in Matthew 28:16–20. That occurred in Galilee, which would have been a safer and more likely site for such a large gathering. The phrase "some have fallen asleep" reflects a common reference to death by early Christians (compare 1 Cor. 15:18, 20; 1 Thess. 4:13). Jesus had used the expression with reference to Jairus's daughter (Mark 5:39) and Lazarus (John 11:11–14).

Witnesses to Jesus' Resurrection from 1 Corinthians 15			
Witness	**Place**	**Time**	**Scripture Reference**
Peter	Jerusalem	Resurrection Sunday	Luke 24:34; 1 Corinthians 15:5
The Twelve (designates any group of the original disciples)	Jerusalem, upper room	Resurrection Sunday	Luke 24:36–43; John 20:19–25; 1 Corinthians 15:5
The Eleven	Jerusalem, upper room	Sunday following Resurrection Sunday	Mark 16:14; John 20:26–31
The Twelve	Sea of Galilee	A later time	John 21:1–23
The Eleven	Galilee, on a mountain	A later time	Matthew 28:16–20; Mark 16:15–18
More than five hundred	Unknown	A later time	1 Corinthians 15:6
James	Unknown	A later time	1 Corinthians 15:7
All the apostles	Mount of Olives (Ascension)	Forty days after the resurrection	Luke 24:44–49; Acts 1:3–8; 1 Corinthians 15:7
Paul	Damascus	Several years later	Acts 9:1–19; 1 Corinthians 15:8

The fourth witness was **James** (1 Cor. 15:7), the brother of Jesus, who by the time of Paul's writing was the leader of the church in Jerusalem. James had been a nonbeliever before the crucifixion (Mark 3:21, 31–32; John 7:5). But between the resurrection of Jesus and Pentecost, he and Jesus' other brothers had joined the believers (Acts 1:14). This appearance is not mentioned in the Gospels. The fact that Jesus appeared after the resurrection individually to Peter, who had denied Him, and James, who had doubted Him, reveals His great heart of love. The fifth appearance was **to all the apostles** (1 Cor. 15:7). This may have been the appearance that included Thomas (John 20:26–28), or it may have been a larger group than just the eleven, as other persons in the New Testament were referred to as apostles; it may have been in conjunction with the Ascension (Luke 24:44–53; Acts 1:3–12).

Paul did not cite all of the appearances mentioned in the Gospels. He did not mention Jesus' appearances to Mary Magdalene (John 20:11–18) and to the other women (Matt. 28:5–10). He did not mention the appearance to Cleopas and his companion on the road to Emmaus (Luke 24:13–32), nor the appearance to the seven disciples who had gone fishing (John 21:1–22), nor the appearance in conjunction with the ascension (Mark 16:19; Luke 24:44–53; Acts 1:3–12).

The Gospel's Chief Proclaimer (1 Cor. 15:8–11)

The sixth witness Paul cited was himself—**last of all he appeared to me also** (v. 8). Paul did not consider his experience on the Damascus road to be a vision but rather an actual appearance of the resurrected Lord. Paul's references to himself were expressions of complete humility. He referred to himself as **one abnormally born**. This did not refer to his being converted after all the rest. Rather, the Greek word referred to an abortion, a miscarriage, or a stillborn infant. Some Bible scholars believe Paul's enemies had actually called him this, belittling his claim to apostleship. For the moment, he acknowledged his unusual beginning, so different from the other apostles. He said he was **the least of the apostles** and did **not even deserve to be called an apostle** because he had **persecuted the church of God** (v. 9). But **the grace of God** (v. 10) had been effective. In fact, he had **worked harder than all of them**. But he quickly added, **yet not I, but the grace of God that was with me**. Paul ended his statement about the gospel by pointing out the unity of those who preach the gospel. He and the others had told the story alike and **this is what we preach, and this is what you believed** (v. 11). ✦

WHAT ABOUT YOU?
What does your understanding of the resurrection (as the body, soul, and spirit alike being raised from the dead) affect your understanding of Jesus' resurrection? Why is the resurrection of the body important to the Christian faith?

PRAYER
Lord of my future, remind me to stand in the hope You give me through the resurrection of Jesus.

1 CORINTHIANS 15:1–11

1 Now, brothers, I want to remind you of the gospel I preached to you, which you received and on which you have taken your stand.
2 By this gospel you are saved, if you hold firmly to the word I preached to you. Otherwise, you have believed in vain.
3 For what I received I passed on to you as of first importance: that Christ died for our sins according to the Scriptures,
4 that he was buried, that he was raised on the third day according to the Scriptures,
5 and that he appeared to Peter, and then to the Twelve.
6 After that, he appeared to more than five hundred of the brothers at the same time, most of whom are still living, though some have fallen asleep.
7 Then he appeared to James, then to all the apostles,
8 and last of all he appeared to me also, as to one abnormally born.
9 For I am the least of the apostles and do not even deserve to be called an apostle, because I persecuted the church of God.
10 But by the grace of God I am what I am, and his grace to me was not without effect. No, I worked harder than all of them—yet not I, but the grace of God that was with me.
11 Whether, then, it was I or they, this is what we preach, and this is what you believed.

"I have set the LORD always before me.
Because he is at my right hand,
I will not be shaken. Therefore my heart
is glad and my tongue rejoices; my
body also will rest secure, because you
will not abandon me to the grave, nor
will you let your Holy One see decay."
—Psalm 16:8–10

The Power of God for Salvation

Only the biblical gospel message has the power to bring scriptural salvation to our lives.

INTO THE SUBJECT

No one in his or her right mind would purchase a car without an engine and expect to drive it home from the dealership. Most prospective buyers look under the hood before deciding to buy. Have you examined the power of Christ's resurrection in a close, personal way?

INTO THE WORD

1. What is significant about Paul's use of the term *brothers* in addressing the dysfunctional Christians at Corinth (v. 1)?

2. How do you define *gospel*?

3. What essential elements of the gospel do you find in verses 3–5?

4. What evidence of Paul's humility do you see in verses 1, 7–11?

5. What measures might a church take to pass the gospel along to future generations of its members?

6. Which Old Testament prophecy about Jesus' death comes to your mind?

7. Read Psalm 16:8–10. How does this passage predict Christ's resurrection?

8. How important is it that Christ's resurrection was not a secret?

INTO THE WORLD

When you share the gospel this week, include the wonderful news that Jesus arose and is alive forever.

APOSTLES' CREED

Memorize this creed so you'll always have an answer for what you believe.

I believe in God the Father Almighty,

maker of heaven and earth;

And in Jesus Christ, His only Son, our Lord:

who was conceived by the Holy Spirit,

born of the Virgin Mary,

suffered under Pontius Pilate,

was crucified, dead, and buried;

He descended into hell.

The third day He rose again from the dead;

He ascended into heaven,

and sits at the right hand of God the Father Almighty;

from there He shall come to judge the living and the dead.

I believe in the Holy Spirit, the holy catholic Church,

the communion of saints, the forgiveness of sins,

the resurrection of the body, and the life everlasting.

Amen.

For a great explanation of this creed, read Keith Drury's *Common Ground: What All Christians Believe and Why It Matters* (Indianapolis, Ind.: Wesleyan Publishing House, 2008).

INTERACTIVE LEARNING IDEAS

GET THE CLASS INVOLVED
Think Fast

You'll need a lightweight ball like a beach ball for this exercise.

Say, "If someone asked you to tell them the most important things about the Christian faith, what would you tell them? Paul was able to come up with many points he thought were pivotal issues in our faith. We'll play a game to see how many you can come up with."

Have your class arrange their chairs in a circle. Give them three minutes to think of several items they think are fundamental to our faith. They cannot make notes; everything must be from memory. Start the game by giving the ball to someone. Ask the person to offer a pivotal point of faith. After the point is given, the person throws the ball to any other person in the circle. That person must catch the ball and say another point. Points may not be repeated. If someone can't come up with a new item, the person is out of the game and must leave the circle. Play continues until people can't come up with new items, or your circle decreases to one person.

TRY THIS ON YOUR OWN
It's a Winner

Think back to the things Paul said were most important when he was writing to the Corinthians. Are there other things you would add to the list? Use a piece of paper to make a list called "The Most Important Things in My Faith." (Make sure you can back these items up with Scripture.)

On another piece of paper, draw a big scale like the kind you'd find at an amusement park where you hit the pad and a ball flies up to ring a bell. On your scale, decide an order of importance for the items you listed. Place the ones of lesser importance toward the bottom of your scale and the more important toward the top. Which item is the most important in your mind? Place it at the top. Ask yourself:

- How can I communicate the need for these items to be a part of my faith life? Of someone else's faith life?
- How can I live to show these things in my life?
- What is one thing I can do this week to show the item at the top of my scale is important to my faith?

TAKING IT TO THE STREET
Serving for Life

What place celebrates new life more often than a crisis pregnancy center? Even when the road ahead looks hard, there are still new lives to rejoice over.

Agree together as a class to volunteer and serve those moms who are connected with a crisis pregnancy center in your town or area. (If such a center is not present in your community, perhaps there are several pregnant women in your church family who could use a hand.) Talk with the staff in charge and suggest ways you would like to serve these women at either location. The following are some ideas to get you started:

- Create several teams of cleaners to go into homes and clean for the women. Bathrooms, floors, cat litter boxes, etc., are things that may need cleaning before the baby comes.
- Help them with basic car maintenance.
- Take them groceries or a hot meal.
- Offer to come and do their laundry for them, or take it and bring it back clean.
- Walk their dogs.
- Provide money so they can get a sitter and go out for an evening or offer to babysit yourself (if they feel comfortable with that).

WITH YOUR FAMILY
R Is for Resurrection

The resurrection is a central theme in our faith. Spend some time talking with your children about the resurrection and all that it means. You can adapt it to all levels as needed.

Then take the family for an alphabet walk. As you stroll, go letter by letter and come up with things for each letter that have something to do with the resurrection. Give extra points if you can tie it in to something you see as you walk. For example, "T is for tree, and Jesus' cross was made from a tree . . . but He didn't stay dead!" The more creative the connections, the more fun your kids will have. ◆

Beware of the danger of form without meaning.

LESSON 5

MORE IMPORTANT MATTERS

Amos 5:21–24; Matthew 23:16–23

KEY VERSE

Woe to you, teachers of the law and Pharisees, you hypocrites! You give a tenth of your spices—mint, dill and cummin. But you have neglected the more important matters of the law—justice, mercy and faithfulness. You should have practiced the latter, without neglecting the former.

—Matthew 23:23

BACKGROUND SCRIPTURES

Genesis 4:5; Leviticus 7:18; 1 Samuel 13:9; Psalm 50:9; Isaiah 1:11; 66:3; Jeremiah 6:20; 14:12; Hosea 8:13; Malachi 1:8
    Unacceptable offerings
Matthew 23:13–15, 23, 25, 27, 29; Mark 12:38; Luke 20:46
    Woes pronounced
    upon hypocrites
Mark 2:24; Luke 6:2; 13:14; John 5:10; Acts 15:5; 16:3; 21:20; Romans 10:2; Galatians 1:14
    Warnings against
    legalism

DAILY BIBLE READINGS

Monday: John 4:21–24
Tuesday: Isaiah 1:11–17
Wednesday: Jeremiah
             7:21–31
Thursday: Ecclesiastes
             5:1–7
Friday: Romans
             7:14—8:1
Saturday: Amos 5:21–24;
             Matthew
             23:16–23
Sunday: Psalm 45

WHY THIS MATTERS

Both in the time of the prophet Amos and in Jesus' day, hypocrisy was rampant. Amos rebuked empty ritualism, and Jesus exposed the religious leaders of His day as hypocrites and blind fools.

In the time of Plato, the word *hypocrite* referred to play-acting. Soon an actor who played various roles was called *hypocrites*. Today, the designation applies to anyone who pretends to be a sincere and devout. The Roman statesman Cicero (106–43 B.C.) opined: "Of all villainy there is none more base than that of the hypocrite, who, at the moment he is most false, takes care to appear most virtuous."

This lesson inspires us to practice genuine faith and devotion.

BIBLE COMMENTARY

By Wayne Keller

The religious feasts of the Israelites had become rituals without meaning. The people were so out of fellowship with the Lord that their worship had become pointless repetition. Their assemblies had become so saturated with tradition that, without realizing it, the people worshiped the tradition instead of the Lord. The pointless traditions of the Israelites had become stumbling blocks to true worship.

There is nothing wrong with continuing a tradition that accurately helps worshipers to revere the Lord. Many traditions are helpful in directing attention to the Lord. The secret is to keep God as the focal point. When a tradition becomes meaningless and destructive, we should have the willingness and good judgment to change it. Because the Israelites' worship did not bring honor to the Lord, He rejected it.

Can our worship and service to the Lord be sabotaged by our attitude to the poor and exploited of our society? In Amos 5:21–24, that question was addressed by one of the most disturbing oracles in the Old Testament.

During the first century, the Pharisees and scribes were experts in the law. They were masters of a system that had become so corrupt that it required continuous explanation to be applied by ordinary people. The Pharisees and scribes attempted to make a distinction between oaths that needed to be honored and those that could broken by legalistic trickery. They paid attention to the finer points of the tithing laws at the same time ignoring the major themes and principles. Jesus sharply confronted this legalistic religion. His compassion caused Him to grieve over the hypocrisy of the Pharisees and scribes, but His Holiness required Him to condemn their sins.

Paying Lip Service with Feasts and Assemblies (Amos 5:21)

The Lord was displeased by the lip service the people paid Him when they observed the **religious feasts** and special **assemblies**. The Bible says He hated and despised it, and that He could **not stand** their **assemblies**.

Amos was not the only one to observe that the religious feast and assemblies were revolting to the Lord. Isaiah wrote, "Stop bringing meaningless offerings! Your incense is detestable to me" (Isa. 1:13).

The term *religious feasts* usually refers to feasts that took place once a year. There were thought to be three annual religious feasts—the Feast of Unleavened Bread, the Feast of Weeks, and the Feast of Tabernacles (2 Chron. 8:13). There were also general, unspecified feasts mentioned in the Old Testament.

The assemblies required a solemnization from the participants that recognized the worship they were about to perform was special. Amos's prophecy made the charge that the uniqueness and reverence of these observances had been lost.

Religious Feasts and Assemblies		
Feast	Old Testament References	New Testament References
Sabbath	Exodus 20:8–11; 31:12–17; Leviticus 23:3; Deuteronomy 5:12–15	Matthew 12:1–14; 28:1; Luke 4:16; John 5:9; Acts 13:42; Colossians 2:16; Hebrews 4:1–11
Sabbath Year	Exodus 23:10–11; Leviticus 25:1–7	
Year of Jubilee	Leviticus 25:8–55; 27:17–24; Numbers 36:4	
Passover	Exodus 12:1–14; Leviticus 23:5; Numbers 9:1–14; 28:16; Deuteronomy 16:1–3, 4–7	Matthew 28:17; Mark 14:12–26; John 2:13; 11:55; 1 Corinthians 5:7; Hebrews 11:28
Unleavened Bread	Exodus 12:15–20; 13:3–10; 23:15; 34:18	Mark 14:1; Acts 12:3; 1 Corinthians 5:6–8
Firstfruits	Leviticus 23:9–14	Romans 8:23; 1 Corinthians 15:20–23
Weeks, Pentecost, Harvest	Exodus 23:16; 34:22	Acts 2:1–4; 20:16; 1 Corinthians 16:8
Trumpets	Leviticus 23:23–25; Numbers 29:1–6	
Day of Atonement	Leviticus 16; 23:26; Numbers 29:7–11	
Tabernacles, Booths, Ingathering	Exodus 23:16; 34:22; Leviticus 23:33–36, 39–43; Numbers 29:12–34; Deuteronomy 16:13–15; Zechariah 14:16–19	John 7:2, 37
Sacred Assembly	Leviticus 23:36; Numbers 29:35–38	
Purim	Esther 9:18–32	

Unacceptable Sacrifices (Amos 5:22)

The acceptance of persons by the Lord was accomplished by sacrificial offerings, stipulated by law as recorded in the first seven chapters of Leviticus. The purpose was to obtain forgiveness for the sins of the Israelites and to restore their relationship with the Lord. Sacrifices were also a means of giving to the Lord freely, without obligation.

Three types of offerings are discussed here: **burnt offerings**, **grain offerings**, and **fellowship offerings**. The Lord showed His displeasure with the Israelites by saying He would **not accept** the first two offerings and would **have no regard for** the third. Even though the Israelites were presumably following the letter of the law in preparing the offerings, they were not acceptable to the Lord because of the way the Israelites were living.

WHAT DO YOU THINK?
How does one's everyday life affect the quality of one's worship?

AHA!
Simply following the forms of worship in services or rituals doesn't please God. What matters is one's heart.

DID YOU KNOW?
Amos was not a court prophet or from a family of temple priests. He tended both sheep and figs for a living.

Gustave Doré's engraving of the prophet Amos captures the shepherd-prophet as he considers the task to which God has called him: to deliver the message of true worship and righteous conduct.

WHAT DO YOU THINK?

What are some specific ways the church today might be like the Pharisees in Matthew 23:16–23?

AHA!

God calls us to live lives overflowing with justice and righteousness.

DID YOU KNOW?

The Pharisees accepted their oral tradition as having the same authority as the Torah.

The burnt offering dealt with the consequences of sin. It was a voluntary act of worship aimed at making the worshiper acceptable before the Lord (Lev. 1:3) and leading to atonement for unintentional sin (Lev. 1:4).

The grain offering was a voluntary act of worship that recognized the Lord's goodness and provisions (Lev. 2; 6:14–23). Because there was no shedding of blood, there was no atonement for sin by means of a grain offering. The sacrifice was made to acknowledge the Lord as sovereign.

The fellowship offering was a voluntary act of worship also, in which atonement was not received (Lev. 3; 7:11–34). This offering was made for three reasons: to show thanksgiving to the Lord (7:12), to make a vow to the Lord (7:16), or to make a freewill offering to the Lord (7:16).

The Need for Righteousness (Amos 5:23–24)

The lack of righteousness on the part of Israelites led to the Lord's condemnation of their worship. By stating He would no longer even listen to Israel's music, the Lord rejected their worship as hypocritical, dishonest, and meaningless. Songs that did not come from the heart were mere **noise** (v. 23) to the Lord.

Words offered to the Lord in song are offensive to Him when the singer cares more about his or her own interests than about the things that concern the Lord. No amount of religious observance can offset sin.

Because the Israelites had removed **justice** and **righteousness** (v. 24) from their society (5:7), they were expected to restore it. The imperative is presented in the form of a contrast.

The Lord's command here isn't that there might be a trickle of justice in a dry valley bed or a shower of righteousness upon a thirsty and dry land. Instead, He's states that **justice** should **roll on like a river**, and **righteousness like a never-failing stream!**

The virtue of justice ensures that good triumphs over evil in society and that the decisions of the law are based on righteousness, not self-interest. Righteousness means doing what is right in the eyes of the Lord in everyday life.

Amos's statements revealed the ethical concern of the Lord. He is a God who demands justice rather than sacrifice, righteousness rather than ritual. The most fashionable worship is an insult to the Lord when offered by those who have no intention of accepting His ethical demands.

Blind Fools Are Intellectually Dishonest (Matt. 23:16–23)

Jesus charged that the scribes and Pharisees were intellectually dishonest and, therefore, were guilty of deliberately misleading the people. These **blind guides** (v. 16) taught that to swear by the **temple . . . means nothing, but** swearing **by the gold of the temple** made the **oath** binding. Claiming to be leaders, they misled even themselves. Jesus challenged such nonsense with simple logic, pointing out that the only thing that **makes the gold sacred** is the fact that it is in the **temple** (v. 17). The same can be said about the **gift on** the

altar (v. 18). Jesus drew the obvious conclusion that the temple makes the gold sacred and the altar makes the sacrifice on it sacred—not the other way around. By doing so, He challenged the religious system that placed great value on small things but ignored weightier matters, such as one's relationship with God.

The scribes and the Pharisees were meticulous in enforcing the regulations of the Jewish Law. For example, they insisted that tithes be paid even on small items such as the cooking herbs **mint, dill, and cumin** (v. 23). But the scribes and Pharisees **neglected** the moral and spiritual parts of the law: **justice, mercy and faithfulness**.

All three of these virtues refer to our relationship with each other. All three result from having a right relationship with God. ◆

INTERACTIVE LEARNING IDEAS

GET THE CLASS INVOLVED
Scrambled Verses

Before class prepare a memory verse scramble for your class to do. You will need the words to Micah 6:8 from the most-used Bible version among your class members. From that translation, write each word of the verse on a separate index card. Prepare enough of these for as many small groups as you wish to make from your class. Some in your class may be familiar with this verse already, but encourage them to participate anyway.

Divide the class into small groups. Do not tell them the verse reference, but tell them that the cards hold a Scripture verse that summarizes most of what Amos and Matthew said in this lesson. Ask the groups to put the words on the cards together to express the central message of the lesson. Instruct the groups to lay out the words and put them together to express what they think needs to be said to summarize the study. (Ask those who may have quickly figured out the verse not to tell the others what it is. This way, the rest of the class can enjoy the fun of going through the exercise.)

After all the groups are done, let each one share their verse. Then read it as it is found in the translation you chose.

TRY THIS ON YOUR OWN
Your Own River

No matter who we are, we each need justice and righteousness to roll over us. The fact that God wants justice and righteousness for us, and provided a way for it to happen, is a big part of the good news. Grace is all about not deserving the good that God gives us—but He lavishes it on us anyway!

That grace is so amazing that we need to share it. So this week, offer some grace to others. At home, do a task that is normally assigned to someone else without that person knowing who did it. At work, be the one who cleans up the break room even if you're cleaning up someone else's mess. When shopping, give up the good place in line to someone who looks like they haven't had a smile in a long time.

The ideas here are endless. Create your own river of justice and righteousness and watch it roll on.

TAKING IT TO THE STREET
Make Lemonade

Invite your class to bring their families to the church on a Saturday and do a lemonade stand—but with a twist. Everyone expects to pay at least a quarter for a drink from a lemonade stand, right? The difference with yours is that the lemonade you serve will be FREE. Advertise it that way! Flag down people driving by and give out glasses of the cold, sweet drink. Don't let them give you money.

When they ask why you are doing this, let them know that God gave us a free gift and you'd like to give one to them. If someone insists on giving money, ask them to give it to the next person they see who might need it. They got free lemonade, and so now they can give a free gift, too. Remember, it's all about grace!

WITH YOUR FAMILY
Lemonade on the Go

Your family can do their own free lemonade stand. But perhaps they can take it a step further.

Work together to come up with a list of elderly people you know. If you don't know many, ask your church to give you some names and addresses. Focus on the elderly who might not have many friends or family members in town; they're probably in need of extra grace every day! Prepare your lemonade, and maybe have the kids make some happy yellow cards with a cheery note inside. Then hop in the car and make your lemonade deliveries. Stop long enough to pour your recipients a glass of lemonade and present them with their card. Then slip out and head to the next senior person's home. Make sure you leave some hugs with the "seasoned" citizens on your list! ◆

AMOS 5:21–24; MATTHEW 23:16–23

Amos 5:21 "I hate, I despise your religious feasts; I cannot stand your assemblies.

22 Even though you bring me burnt offerings and grain offerings, I will not accept them. Though you bring choice fellowship offerings, I will have no regard for them.

23 Away with the noise of your songs! I will not listen to the music of your harps.

24 But let justice roll on like a river, righteousness like a never-failing stream!

Matthew 23:16 "Woe to you, blind guides! You say, 'If anyone swears by the temple, it means nothing; but if anyone swears by the gold of the temple, he is bound by his oath.'

17 You blind fools! Which is greater: the gold, or the temple that makes the gold sacred?

18 You also say, 'If anyone swears by the altar, it means nothing; but if anyone swears by the gift on it, he is bound by his oath.'

19 You blind men! Which is greater: the gift, or the altar that makes the gift sacred?

20 Therefore, he who swears by the altar swears by it and by everything on it.

21 And he who swears by the temple swears by it and by the one who dwells in it.

22 And he who swears by heaven swears by God's throne and by the one who sits on it.

23 "Woe to you, teachers of the law and Pharisees, you hypocrites! You give a tenth of your spices— mint, dill and cummin. But you have neglected the more important matters of the law—justice, mercy and faithfulness. You should have practiced the latter, without neglecting the former.

"Let justice roll on . . ."
—*Amos 5:24*

More Important Matters

*Beware of the danger of form
without meaning.*

INTO THE SUBJECT

Kids like to pretend. They may pretend to have an imaginary friend or pretend they are soldiers or animals. Pretending may be just innocent fun for kids, but isn't it quite a different matter when adults pretend to be what they are not?

INTO THE WORD

1. According to Amos 5:21, how strongly does God dislike hypocritical worship?

2. Does the amount of one's offering matter to the Lord if it is given only to impress others? Explain your answer.

3. How much attention do you think worshipers give to the words of the hymns and choruses they sing? How might a church safeguard praise and worship against hypocrisy?

4. According to Amos 5:24, what two things please the Lord?

5. How can you show justice and righteousness this week?

6. What designations did Jesus apply to Israel's religious leaders? (See Matt. 23:16–23.)

7. How might one's devotion to legalism be hypocritical?

INTO THE WORD

Live in such a way that no one can legitimately call you a hypocrite!

TRUE WORSHIP

God clearly expects His people to live holy lives—which includes tithing, participating in religious rituals, studying His Word, behaving morally; but all of this is meaningless if we don't love others.

What can you do to show justice, mercy, and faithfulness . . .

In your family:

_____

_____

_____

In your neighborhood:

_____

_____

_____

In your church:

_____

_____

_____

In the city nearest to you:

_____

_____

_____

In the world:

_____

_____

_____

Christians are called to serve, not to be served.

AN ILLUSTRATION OF GREATNESS

John 13:1–17

WHY THIS MATTERS

You won't see a touring golf pro carry his golf bag. His caddy does that—and more. A good caddy encourages the golfer he caddies for. He advises him about yardage, pin placement, wind direction, and club selection. He keeps the golfer's clubs and golf balls clean. He rakes a sand trap after the golfer blasts out of it. And a good caddy smiles when his "boss" finishes well. He is pleased to have served to the best of his ability.

Jesus attached an extreme importance to service. Serving others, after all, follows the example Jesus set. He came to earth to serve and to give His life for others.

This lesson inspires us to serve others humbly as Jesus' selfless followers.

BIBLE COMMENTARY

By Patricia J. David

Matthew, Mark, and Luke gave us similar accounts of the night before Jesus' crucifixion. They told how Jesus passed the bread and wine, entreating His disciples to "do this in remembrance of me." But John gave us a more extensive look at what took place between Jesus and His disciples in the upper room in Jerusalem, devoting five chapters to it.

"It was just before the Passover Feast" (13:1) when these events took place. The Passover was the annual reminder of the events surrounding the deliverance of the Jews from bondage in Egypt some fourteen hundred years earlier. In Exodus 12, God commanded each household to slaughter a flawless lamb at midnight on the fourteenth day of Nissan (the first month of their year). The blood of the lamb applied to their doorposts would cause the angel of death to "pass over" their homes on that fateful night when every firstborn in Egypt would die. Every succeeding generation was to celebrate a seven-day annual feast (the Feast of Unleavened Bread) in order to pass down the story of the Passover and the exodus to their children.

The other Gospels tell us the Last Supper took place on the first day of the Feast of Unleavened Bread, when the Passover lamb had to be sacrificed (see Matt. 26:17; Mark 14:12; Luke 22:7). Jesus told His disciples that He eagerly desired to share this Passover meal with them (Matt. 26:18; Mark 14:14; Luke 22:11). So, the events of John 13–17 took place on the fourteenth of Nissan, Thursday night. As the perfect "Lamb of God, who takes away the sin of the world" (John 1:29) and the One who would deliver them from eternal death and bondage to sin, Jesus wanted them to understand the significance of the timing of His death: He was the embodiment of their celebration, the fulfillment of which their annual celebration was merely a shadow.

KEY VERSE

I tell you the truth, no servant is greater than his master, nor is a messenger greater than the one who sent him.
—John 13:16

BACKGROUND SCRIPTURES

Matthew 26:17–35;
Mark 14:12–26;
Luke 22:7–38
    Synoptic accounts of
    the Last Supper
Genesis 18:4; 19:2; 25:32;
43:24; Judges 19:21;
1 Samuel 25:41; 2 Samuel
11:8; 1 Timothy 5:10
    Other references to
    foot washing
Matthew 18:1–4; 20:20–28;
23:11–12; Mark 9:33–37;
Luke 9:46–48; 14:7–11;
18:14; 22:24–30
    Significant passages
    on servanthood or
    humility
Isaiah 53
    Prophecy that the
    Messiah would come
    as the suffering servant

DAILY BIBLE READINGS

Monday: Philippians
               2:5–11
Tuesday: Matthew
               20:25–28
Wednesday: Romans 2:1–8
Thursday: Philippians
               3:7–11
Friday: Colossians
               3:1–4, 15–17
Saturday: John 13:1–17
Sunday: Psalm 46

The day of preparation on which Jesus was crucified as mentioned in John 19:14 and 19:42 must refer to preparation for the Sabbath, not for the Passover. In John 18:28, during Jesus' trial, the Jews didn't want to enter a Gentile court, which would make them ceremonially unclean; "they wanted to be able to eat the Passover." At this time, the entire seven-day Feast of Unleavened Bread was referred to as "Passover," and it would include a number of meals (including the Sabbath day meal), so John wasn't necessarily contradicting the Synoptic Gospels. But the topic and timing are much debated. Many commentators believe the lamb was to be sacrificed the day before Passover, which would have begun on Friday night, since the Jewish day began at sunset. Using that timetable, Jesus' last supper with His disciples took place a full day before the Passover.

Jesus' Illustration (John 13:1–5)

Jesus knew that the time had come for him to leave this world and go to the Father (v. 1). While at other times Jesus stated that His time had not yet come (2:4; 7:6, 8, 30), now it had (12:23, 27). The events that would transpire later in the night and the next day would come as no surprise. Jesus knew His death was imminent. He had already predicted it. He was ready to show His disciples **the full extent of his love**, not simply through the humble foot washing of John 13, but through the full course of events that were beginning to unfold.

There was no turning back. **The devil had already prompted Judas Iscariot . . . to betray Jesus** (13:2). In 6:70–71, Jesus had revealed that one of the Twelve was "a devil," and in 13:27, we learn that Satan entered into Judas (see also Luke 22:3). Let there be no mistake: this was a confrontation between Satan and Jesus. His crucifixion wasn't the result of a disgruntled disciple trying to make some extra cash. It was the consummation of a struggle that had begun at the fall (see Gen. 3:15). Ephesians 6:12 reminds us, "For our struggle is not against flesh and blood, but against the rulers, against the authorities, against the powers of this dark world and against the spiritual forces of evil in the heavenly realms."

The evening meal was being served (John 13:2), but they had probably not yet begun to eat. It was customary for the host to provide a servant to wash the feet of his guests upon their arrival at his home. But, since this was a private meal, no servant was available to perform the menial task. Surely none of the disciples would think to take the task upon himself. After all, they had been arguing about who would be greatest in the kingdom (Luke 22:24). And so Jesus took it upon himself to take the place of the servant. No doubt everyone at the table noticed their need of foot washing. But only Jesus did something about it. He **wrapped a towel around his waist . . . poured water into a basin and began to wash his disciples' feet, drying them with the towel that was wrapped around him** (John 13:4–6). Jesus, the one who "did not come to be served, but to serve, and to give his life as a ransom for many" (Matt. 20:28), took this opportunity to teach them once again the nature of the kingdom and their role in it.

John 13:3 tells us what prompted Jesus to do this: He **knew that the Father had put all things under his power, and that he had come from God and**

WHAT DO YOU THINK?
How would you explain to a teenager leading by serving, as did Jesus in this passage?

AHA!
The Scriptures make it clear that the confrontation in this chapter was not so much between Jesus and Judas, but rather between Jesus and Satan.

DID YOU KNOW?
The gospel of John has the most to say about the Last Supper, but does not say anything about Jesus instituting the Lord's Supper.

was returning to God. Because Jesus understood clearly who He was, where He came from, and where He was going, He was able to take on the role of a servant without feeling it was beneath Him or that it somehow diminished His authority. People who are confident in their calling and position don't feel the need to impress others by snubbing lowly service. Paul exhorted, "Your attitude should be the same as that of Christ Jesus: Who, being in very nature God, did not consider equality with God something to be grasped, but made himself nothing, taking the very nature of a servant, being made in human likeness" (Phil. 2:5–7). Jesus himself said, "**I have set you an example**" (John 13:15).

The image of Jesus washing His disciples' feet is a powerfully simple illustration of what it means to lead by serving.

Peter's Remonstration (John 13:6–11)

Peter's response to Jesus' humble act of servitude was classic: "**Lord, are you going to wash my feet?**" (v. 6). In the Greek, the words *you* and *my* are emphatic. Peter said, "Are *you* going to wash *my* feet?" He objected strongly to having someone who was obviously his superior perform such a lowly task for him. How much easier it would have been for Peter if the roles had been reversed. Then it would have been proper.

Are we any different than Peter? How many times have we refused to be the recipients of someone else's act of kindness, either because we felt undeserving or because it hurt our pride or our self-sufficiency? With Peter, we say, "**No . . . you shall never wash my feet**" (v. 8).

Jesus used this occasion to draw a spiritual application for Peter and the rest of the disciples: **Unless I wash you, you have no part with me**. He was not referring to the physical washing of their feet, but to the washing away of their sins through His coming death (see 1 John 1:7; 1 Cor. 6:11; Titus 3:5–6). Peter, slow to understand but quick to express his devotion to Jesus, exuberantly exclaimed, "**Then, Lord, . . . not just my feet but my hands and my head as well!**" (John 13:9).

Jesus' response is further proof that He was explaining the nature of salvation and forgiveness: **A person who has had a bath needs only to wash his feet; his whole body is clean** (v. 10). It was customary at Passover to bathe twice. But walking the dusty roads in sandals made the traveler's feet unacceptably dirty. What was needed was not another bath but a cleansing of the incidental dirt picked up along the road. So it is with our relationship with the Lord. Once we have been bathed (washed clean through the blood of Christ), there is still a need to have our feet washed—to have our occasional sins, failures, and transgressions forgiven. We don't need to be saved all over again, but the dirt picked up along the way needs to be cleansed. Our relationship with Christ is ongoing. We have a continual need to be in relationship with Him, experiencing His grace upon our lives. This concept is clear in the words and tenses Jesus used. *Wash* in verses 5, 6, 8, and 10 refers to cleaning a part of the body, whereas *bath* in verse 10 involves a complete washing. *Wash* is also used in the Greek aorist tense, referring to a single act, while Jesus used the perfect tense in speaking of taking a bath, implying a present state based on a past act.

Jesus acknowledged that **not every one** (v. 11) of them was clean. Judas, though his physical feet had been washed by the Lord, was not "clean." Jesus knew who was His and who was not. Though outwardly Judas appeared to be clean, it was the inward attitude of the heart that made the difference.

The Disciples' Expectation (John 13:12–17)

Jesus' illustration of servanthood and salvation was not simply for the disciples' enlightenment. He expected them to follow His example.

When He returned to the table, He asked, **"Do you understand what I have done for you?"** (v. 12). Commentator Adam Clarke believed this statement should be imperative (a command): "Understand what I have done for you" (the Greek used here can be translated either way; also, "asked" in the New International Version is actually *said* in the Greek). In verse 7, He had told Peter, "You do not realize now what I am doing, but later you will understand." Has the "later" already arrived? Jesus wanted them to understand now, yet they would not understand fully until after His death and resurrection. Now they were able to comprehend servanthood, but a full understanding of forgiveness and salvation would have to wait until later.

Jesus told them three times what He expected of them: **Now that I, your Lord and Teacher, have washed your feet, you also should wash one another's feet** (v. 14); **You should do as I have done for you** (v. 15); **Now that you know these things, you will be blessed if you do them** (v. 17). He wasn't telling them to begin having foot-washing services when they gathered together. He set for them **an example** (v. 15), literally a pattern. Notice the use of foot washing in 1 Timothy 5:10, where Paul talked about a widow who was "well known for her good deeds, such as bringing up children, showing hospitality, washing the feet of the saints, helping those in trouble and devoting herself to all kinds of good deeds." It is obvious that foot washing was used symbolically of the humble act of serving one another.

Jesus' expectation of His disciples—and of us—is to humbly serve one another. Perhaps Jesus even had forgiveness in view here and how we are to "be kind and compassionate to one another, forgiving each other, just as in Christ God forgave you" (Eph. 4:32). If the King of Kings and Lord of Lords could humble himself to serve and forgive, so can we. For a "student is not above his teacher, nor a servant above his master" (Matt. 10:24). ◆

JOHN 13:1–17

1 It was just before the Passover Feast. Jesus knew that the time had come for him to leave this world and go to the Father. Having loved his own who were in the world, he now showed them the full extent of his love.
2 The evening meal was being served, and the devil had already prompted Judas Iscariot, son of Simon, to betray Jesus.
3 Jesus knew that the Father had put all things under his power, and that he had come from God and was returning to God;
4 so he got up from the meal, took off his outer clothing, and wrapped a towel around his waist.
5 After that, he poured water into a basin and began to wash his disciples' feet, drying them with the towel that was wrapped around him.
6 He came to Simon Peter, who said to him, "Lord, are you going to wash my feet?"
7 Jesus replied, "You do not realize now what I am doing, but later you will understand."
8 "No," said Peter, "you shall never wash my feet." Jesus answered, "Unless I wash you, you have no part with me."
9 "Then, Lord," Simon Peter replied, "not just my feet but my hands and my head as well!"
10 Jesus answered, "A person who has had a bath needs only to wash his feet; his whole body is clean. And you are clean, though not every one of you."
11 For he knew who was going to betray him, and that was why he said not every one was clean.
12 When he had finished washing their feet, he put on his clothes and returned to his place. "Do you understand what I have done for you?" he asked them.
13 "You call me 'Teacher' and 'Lord,' and rightly so, for that is what I am.
14 Now that I, your Lord and Teacher, have washed your feet, you also should wash one another's feet.
15 I have set you an example that you should do as I have done for you.
16 I tell you the truth, no servant is greater than his master, nor is a messenger greater than the one who sent him.
17 Now that you know these things, you will be blessed if you do them.

An Illustration of Greatness

Christians are called to serve,
not to be served.

INTO THE SUBJECT

Undercover Boss, a television reality show, featured a different company CEO each week who secretly worked at various employee jobs. However, none of the bosses became a slave. What would it be like to assume the role of a household slave and wash the feet of all who entered the house?

INTO THE WORD

1. What important Jewish holiday did Jesus observe with His disciples, according to John 13:1?

2. What horrific event did Jesus anticipate?

3. How would Jesus show His disciples the full extent of His love?

4. How did Jesus perform the role of a household slave?

5. What spiritual meaning do you find in verses 8–10?

6. Which disciple was not "clean"?

7. How might you follow Jesus' example of humility on behalf of others?

INTO THE WORLD

Decide one or more ways you can humbly minister to someone this week.

TRUE HUMILITY

It's been said that everybody wants to be called a servant, but nobody wants to be treated as one. To follow Jesus' example of serving others—not for the praise of others, but to truly assist them—your heart must be right.

For each item below, prayerfully assess whether you've done it for personal gain or to bless others. Put a checkmark in the appropriate column. (Sometimes it will be both; our motives are often mixed.)

✓ For personal glory	HUMILITY	✓ To bless others
	Donated money	
	Offered a word of encouragement	
	Served at church	
	Sat next to a difficult person	
	Refused to take credit	
	Picked up the tab	
	Served in the community	
	Listened attentively to a boring person	
	Forgiven someone	

INTERACTIVE LEARNING IDEAS

GET THE CLASS INVOLVED
Wash Up for Dinner

Before class, gather paper towels and wet wipes.

We probably all grew up with our moms telling us, "Wash up before dinner." It was a ritual in some homes. This study gave us a good look at Jesus showing His disciples (and us) the need to "wash up before dinner." Of course, His point was not only to be clean for the meal, but to make sure we are clean inwardly and to carry that mindset with us through life. And as we now know, His example to us was to teach us to serve each other in the same way He served His disciples. It goes far beyond merely washing feet, but that is a good place to start.

Have your class get into pairs. Hand out paper towels and wet wipes to each pair. Let them take turns washing at least one foot of their partner (if time allows, do both feet.)

Close this time by asking each person to pray blessings on the other person.

TRY THIS ON YOUR OWN
God Bless You

The words "God bless you" are often heard when someone sneezes, or as a way to say hello or good-bye. But there can be real power in those words when they are said in a way to get someone thinking.

Jesus showed us clearly how to serve one another. His aim was to teach us how to "be God" to the people around us. Every day we have opportunities to offer this blessing to others.

This week ask God to show you times when you can perform some random acts of kindness to people you know (or not). Then act on them. The main part of this exercise will be to make sure you tell the person, "God bless you." This blessing may be the one time in their day that causes them to think of God, if even for a moment.

TAKING IT TO THE STREET
Progressive Clean Up

Jesus gave us an example to serve one another. There are many creative ways to approach this. It can be a labor of love and a whole lot of fun at the same time.

This exercise allows your class to hold a progressive dinner but also help each other clean up your yards (or other specified tasks). This can be done at any time of year. You can rake leaves, shovel snow, plant flowers, or do a small summer project. This works best if you divide a larger class up into groups of enough families to correspond with each course you will serve in your progressive dinner (usually four or five). This is an all-day event.

Once you have your class divided into dinner groups, have each group get together to decide who will host appetizers, salad, soup, the main course, and dessert. Then have each family decide one yard-work project that can be completed with the help of these friends in about an hour.

On the day of the progressive dinner, make sure everyone has the needed tools with them. Begin the event at the "appetizer home." Your groups can decide if they want to work first or eat first. At each home the group does one project for the hosts, eats, and then travels to the next home. This repeats until all jobs are done (and all the food is eaten, of course).

WITH YOUR FAMILY
Tent Time

Serve the kids in your family with a simple and fun evening. Pick a night this week and gather blankets and chairs. Have your children help you build a big "tent" that you can all get inside. Throw the blankets over the chairs, and then weight them down with books or clip clothespins to hold the blankets in place. Plan a fun snack you all can eat while you are inside the tent. Make sure you have flashlights with good batteries.

Invite everyone to crawl into the tent. Enjoy the snacks while you read out loud to each other. Choose a favorite book, start a new one together, or read a child's version of the Scripture verses you studied in this lesson. Talk and laugh together. Who knew that "washing feet" could be this much fun? ◆

Stewardship is faithfully using what God has entrusted to us.

GOOD STEWARDS, FAITHFUL IN SERVICE

Matthew 25:14–30

His master replied, "Well done, good and faithful servant! You have been faithful with a few things; I will put you in charge of many things. Come and share your master's happiness!"

—Matthew 25:21

Matthew 24
    The Olivet Discourse
Matthew 25:31–46
    Jesus' description of
    the final judgment
Mark 13
    The Little Apocalypse
Acts 1:4–5, 7–8, 11
    Last words of Jesus
    and the ascension
1 Corinthians 12:7–11
    The Holy Spirit's
    distribution of gifts
Galatians 6:7–10
    The law of sowing
    and reaping
Revelation 22:12
    Good words by the
    Master given to the
    faithful

Monday: Luke 12:42–48
Tuesday: 2 Corinthians
            9:6–11
Wednesday: Luke 19:12–26
Thursday: Proverbs 3:1–12
Friday: John 12:41–44
Saturday: Matthew
            25:14–30
Sunday: Psalm 47

WHY THIS MATTERS

Occasionally, a religious leader prognosticates the end of the world. That happened in 2011, when a radio preacher announced categorically that the world would end May 21 of that year. The preacher attracted some followers and plenty of media attention, but the sun rose May 22 and the world continued.

We cannot predict the day or the hour of our Lord's return, but we can invest our time wisely every day. As long as we live, we have work to do for Him. If we are faithful stewards of time, talent, and possessions, He will reward us. If we squander or hoard what He has entrusted to us, we will suffer loss.

This lesson motivates us to be faithful stewards.

BIBLE COMMENTARY

By Wayne Caldwell

It is significant that, when Jesus came near the end of His earthly ministry, the disciples wanted to know some interesting things about the future. They had not understood everything He had told them. They were curious to know what would happen to the temple Herod the Great had started to refurbish forty-six years before (John 2:20). Jesus surely would have known what was to happen at the end of the age. Matthew records Jesus' answer to the disciples' question in what we call the "Olivet Discourse" in chapter 24 (compare Mark 13, known as the Little Apocalypse).

Matthew 23 ends with a description of the destruction of the temple and of the second coming of Christ (23:38–39). Both of these topics are addressed by Jesus in chapter 24 and expanded in chapter 25. To the questions of the disciples— "When will the temple be destroyed?" and "How will we know when the end is near?"—the Master gave several replies. First, they must be careful not to be deceived by false christs. Second, they should not be alarmed at calamities and disasters. Third, they should remain faithful in spite of what happens. Fourth, they should be ready at any time for Christ's return.

Leaders in the church as well as all believers should be reminded today of these same teachings of Christ. Christ may come at any moment; therefore it is imperative that we remain faithful and watchful. The parable of the ten virgins (25:1–13) immediately precedes the lesson text chosen for this study. The general meaning of the parable of the talents (25:14–30) is that a long wait for Christ's return could easily lead to apathy and carelessness. Failure to use what God has bestowed will result in judgment. The antidote to laziness is active service.

This parable of the loaned money is a poignant reminder and example of Christ our Lord, who is like a man traveling into a far country or on an extended journey. One of the last things Jesus told His disciples was that they should "wait for the gift my Father promised . . . [for] in a few days you will be baptized with the Holy Spirit" (Acts 1:4–5).

Jesus told them it was not for them "to know the times or dates the Father has set by his own authority. But you will receive power when the Holy Spirit comes on you" (Acts 1:7–8). At His ascension two men dressed in white told the disciples, "This same Jesus, who has been taken from you into heaven, will come back in the same way you have seen him go into heaven" (Acts 1:11). These words should be key information for all believers today. Empowerment by the Holy Spirit is sorely needed to carry out the Master's directives.

WHAT DO YOU THINK?
If you knew Jesus would return later today, how would you spend your time between now and then?

The Master's Distribution of Talents (Matt. 25:14–18)

It is wise for **a man going on a journey** to entrust **his property** to **his servants** (v. 14). It was a kindness on the master's part to give his servants something with which they could get gain. They did not deserve anything and they had not worked for the money. It was not for them to keep, but for their delight in seeing how much they could help the master. This is exactly what Jesus did when He gave the Great Commission to His disciples (Matt. 28:18–20). In the parable, **five talents**, **two talents**, and **one talent of money** (25:15) were distributed to three different servants. The symbolism is clear when we consider the various gifts of the Spirit that are distributed to believers, just as the Spirit determines (1 Cor. 12:7–11).

The word *talent* was first used as a measure of weight. Then it came to be a sum of money in silver or gold equal to a talent in weight. Other than the references in this parable, the only other use of the word in the original language in the New Testament is in Matthew 18:24. The word *talent* is now often used to designate the abilities or skills we have received or developed.

The distribution was made **according to** each one's **ability** (Matt. 25:15). It was with wisdom and discretion that the master gave to each servant what he thought they had the ability to improve. None of the three could complain that he was overlooked. Noteworthy, too, is the fact that each of the servants **went at once** (v. 16) to do something with the money entrusted to him. The imperative action of the servants shows that every day has its opportunities, and grace is given to those who work in the marketplace. The first two men **put their money to work** and doubled what had been given to them. But the man who had been given **one talent went off, dug a hole in the ground and hid his master's money** (v. 18).

The lesson is clear that if we use what is given to us there will be an increase for our investment of time or material goods. Faithful spiritual investments, more than any other, are promised vast returns (Gal. 6:7–10). It is a matter of observation that those who have limited talents or abilities are apt to do nothing with what they have. As believers in the body of Christ, we must encourage each other to use what we have for God's glory.

AHA!
We must be ready for Jesus' return at any time.

The Master's Accounting (Matt. 25:19–23)

Sooner or later, even **after a long time, the master** will settle **accounts** (v. 19). What a wonderful day it was when the faithful servants came with their gains to give their master and to hear his greeting: **"Well done, good and faithful**

DID YOU KNOW?
In Luke's account of this parable (Luke 19:12–27), Jesus seems to have used the historical example of the Herods as the figure of the master.

For what reasons do you let your talents show?

servant!" (vv. 21, 23). Our Lord will not be in debt to anyone who faithfully uses what has been distributed. We will always be under obligation to Him for His trusted investment in our lives. An accounting day will come at an unappointed time.

The "well done" words that come from our coworkers are heartwarming. But the words from the Master himself that top them all are: **You have been faithful with a few things; I will put you in charge of many things. Come and share your master's happiness** (vv. 21, 23). Those words at the end of life will be given to all believers who are faithful to our Lord (compare Rev. 22:12).

We will not be rewarded on the basis of *how much* work has been done, but on *how well* we have used what we have been given by the Master—quality, not quantity. It must always be remembered that the best preparation for the master's return, however long it may be delayed or however sudden and unexpected it may be, is active service and doing good to those who are in need.

The Master's Disappointment (Matt. 25:24–27)

The third man in the parable had a lame excuse for his master. His sad words were **you are a hard man** (v. 24), followed by **So I was afraid and went out and hid your talent in the ground. See, here is what belongs to you** (v. 25). This man was thinking only of himself and how he could be protected from a **hard man**. He tried to play it safe. If he lost it all, he would have nothing to show his master. But if he dug a hole and hid the money, at least he would have everything he had been given. "No risk, no gain" became "No risk, no loss."

The master's rebuke was quick and sharp: **You wicked, lazy servant! . . . you should have put my money on deposit with the bankers, so that when I returned I would have received it back with interest** (vv. 26–27). The lesson is clear that if anyone ignores, abuses, or squanders what is given, a rebuke will await that person. Jesus made this doubly clear in His description of the final judgment that follows this lesson (Matt. 25:31–46).

The Master's Judgment (Matt. 25:28–30)

It was a keen disappointment that the third man lost all he had. It was not all loss, however, because his money was given to **the one who** had **the ten talents** (v. 28). The law of return is clear at this point: **For everyone who has will be given more, and he will have an abundance** (v. 29). This law is also emphasized in Paul's symbolism of sowing and reaping (Gal. 6:7–10). The law extended in its context shows that there will always be a harvest; it will be more than what was sown, and it will always be of the same kind that is sown.

Not only was what the man had for use **taken from him** (Matt. 25:29), but the master spoke the most devastating words of all: **throw that worthless servant outside, into the darkness, where there will be weeping and gnashing of teeth** (v. 30). The servant was reproached as being wicked and slothful, he was stripped of what he had, and he was punished with an everlasting doom.

To that person who refuses to risk anything for fear of failure, the lesson is clear: Faith is inherently taking a leap into the unknown; but with God, faithfulness results in fruitfulness. Responsibility given with expected accountability keeps us all on the alert for our Master. ✦

WHAT ABOUT YOU?
How are you investing your God-given talents to increase God's kingdom?

PRAYER
Lord and Master, thank You for the gifts and talents You have given me. Show me ways to make the most of them for Your glory.

INTERACTIVE LEARNING IDEAS

GET THE CLASS INVOLVED
Talents Galore

The parable of the talents makes it very clear that God intends us to dive right in and multiply what He has entrusted to us. But sometimes we can be stymied by wondering what talents God has entrusted us with. They aren't always clear cut and easily defined.

Ask your class to begin to name things they like doing. This can be anything from reading to rebuilding old cars. Have someone write down everything on a large piece of paper or whiteboard. Once the class has compiled a good list, have them start thinking how those enjoyable pastimes, or talents, can be used to serve others. For example, someone who loves to read can volunteer at an elementary school to help with the reading program. Try to come up with a way to serve God or people with each item on the list. Multiply those talents!

TRY THIS ON YOUR OWN
Make It Personal

God has poured His Spirit into you and given you talents and abilities that make you unique. There may be others who are better at something you enjoy, but the mix of all the "ingredients" God has used to make you who you are—your life experiences, natural abilities, learned talents—make you uniquely qualified to represent God in a way no one else can. The Master has entrusted you with talents. He expects you to not bury them.

Take some time to think about what you have a real knack for doing. How can these gifts be used to help others? If you spend your whole day working on computers, you may not want to spend your service time doing that. But perhaps a one-time lesson at the church for seniors who are completely overwhelmed by computers would be a good way to serve. Before you stop this exercise, come up with at least three things you can do to use your talents. Ask God which He wants you to do, and then do it!

TAKING IT TO THE STREET
Create a Holiday

Here is a way to work together as a class to be sure you are not burying your talents. Whatever time of year it is, find a holiday from the opposite time of year. Then, as a class, throw a Christmas in July or Fourth of July in January celebration. Invite kids from a local school. Put it on for people at a shelter. Invite military families. Get the creative people in your class to brainstorm activities and games. Have your planners figure out a food budget, logistics, and a timeframe. Have your doers start to pull it together. Use all the talents in your class to work together to bring this idea to life.

WITH YOUR FAMILY
The God Jar

Your kids can learn a lot by serving others. God has already placed in them giftings, talents, and creative energies that He will use to build His kingdom. Help them train their spiritual antennae to recognize opportunities that allow those talents to grow. This exercise will give you a springboard to work together as a family in serving and using those things God has planted in each of you.

Find a large plastic jar (the kind big pretzels come in would work well) to use for your "God Jar." Let your kids decorate a cover to tape onto the jar.

Sit down together and come up with ideas of things your family can do to serve other people. If one child is really artistic, he or she might design some cards to give away or sell to raise money for a charity. Perhaps you all could volunteer at a soup kitchen. Try to get at least one idea for each person's talents/gifts. Write each one on a slip of paper or index card and drop them into your jar. Then at designated times (once a month, or on fifth Saturdays), pull one slip out of the jar and do it together.

As you come up with new ideas, add them to the jar. This jar should never get completely empty. Once a year, take out all the slips left in the jar and decide if you want to leave each one in the jar. Make a rule that for every slip removed, a new idea must be added. ◆

MATTHEW 25:14–30

14 "Again, it will be like a man going on a journey, who called his servants and entrusted his property to them.

15 To one he gave five talents of money, to another two talents, and to another one talent, each according to his ability. Then he went on his journey.

16 The man who had received the five talents went at once and put his money to work and gained five more.

17 So also, the one with the two talents gained two more.

18 But the man who had received the one talent went off, dug a hole in the ground and hid his master's money.

19 "After a long time the master of those servants returned and settled accounts with them.

20 The man who had received the five talents brought the other five. 'Master,' he said, 'you entrusted me with five talents. See, I have gained five more.'

21 "His master replied, 'Well done, good and faithful servant! You have been faithful with a few things; I will put you in charge of many things. Come and share your master's happiness!'

22 "The man with the two talents also came. 'Master,' he said, 'you entrusted me with two talents; see, I have gained two more.'

23 "His master replied, 'Well done, good and faithful servant! You have been faithful with a few things; I will put you in charge of many things. Come and share your master's happiness!'

24 "Then the man who had received the one talent came. 'Master,' he said, 'I knew that you are a hard man, harvesting where you have not sown and gathering where you have not scattered seed.

25 So I was afraid and went out and hid your talent in the ground. See, here is what belongs to you.'

26 "His master replied, 'You wicked, lazy servant! So you knew that I harvest where I have not sown and gather where I have not scattered seed?

27 Well then, you should have put my money on deposit with the bankers, so that when I returned I would have received it back with interest.

28 "'Take the talent from him and give it to the one who has the ten talents.

29 For everyone who has will be given more, and he will have an abundance. Whoever does not have, even what he has will be taken from him.

30 And throw that worthless servant outside, into the darkness, where there will be weeping and gnashing of teeth.'

Good Stewards, Faithful in Service

*Stewardship is faithfully using what
God has entrusted to us.*

INTO THE SUBJECT

Semper Fidelis, often shortened to *Semper Fi*, is the motto of the United States Marine Corps. It is Latin for "Always Faithful." Isn't it also an appropriate motto for all who serve their Commander-in-Chief, Jesus?

INTO THE WORD

1. What do you think "each according to his ability" (Matt. 25:15) means?

2. Would you argue that 10 percent of what the Lord has entrusted to us belongs to Him, but the other 90 percent is ours to use as we wish? Why or why not?

3. Which of the following statements do you agree with more fully, and why: (a) With responsibility comes privilege; (b) With privilege comes responsibility?

4. Why do you agree or disagree that the Lord has given every Christian what he or she needs to honor Him and benefit others?

5. Read 1 Corinthians 12:14–18. Why should a Christian not envy others' spiritual gifts?

6. According to 1 Corinthians 4:2, what does God require of stewards?

7. What might happen if every believer used his or her spiritual gifts faithfully?

8. How faithfully have you been employing your spiritual gifts?

9. How will you employ your spiritual gifts faithfully in the future?

INTO THE WORLD

God has entrusted every Christian with the gospel. How will you invest the gospel in the lives of others this week?

INVENTORY OF GOD'S GIFTS

God has certainly gifted you,
in a small or big way.
Stop now to inventory your riches.

	insufficient	enough	more than enough
material wealth			
supportive family or community			
physical health			
education			
personal freedom			
skills/talents			
food			
lodging			
love			

Now consider whether you are using the wealth God has given you to increase His kingdom.

Stewardship involves making God's kingdom our first priority.

KINGDOM PRIORITIES

Matthew 6:19–34

WHY THIS MATTERS

Birds seem to get along just fine without money, possessions, and bank accounts. If their singing means anything, they appear quite happy. They flit about as though they don't have a care in the world. Quite a contrast to humans! So many of us, even Christians, fret over matters that may never come to pass. We worry about our future finances, health, and employment. Although wise planning is commendable, worry accomplishes nothing. No wonder Jesus told us to "look at the birds of the air" and not worry. He said our heavenly Father places more value on us than on the birds, and will take care of us.

This lesson encourages us to trust God to meet our needs.

BIBLE COMMENTARY

By Gareth Lee Cockerill

This lesson, Matthew 6:19–34, comes from the heart of the Sermon on the Mount, found in Matthew 5:1—7:29. This often-quoted sermon is the longest and best-known record of Jesus' teaching. In these verses, Jesus described life in the kingdom of God. When Jesus came, God's kingly rule or authority came into the world in a new way. Jesus delivered people from sin and bondage to the devil. He called people to submit to God's rule and receive this deliverance. Those who submitted were set free from their sin and brought into a new relationship with God. By God's grace they were able to live a new kind of life.

The Beatitudes (Matt. 5:1–12) introduce the sermon by describing those who enter God's kingdom. Such people realize they are utterly destitute before God. They have nothing within themselves that can enable them to live the life of people in God's kingdom. They mourn (5:4) for their sins and sincerely hunger and thirst (5:6) for the new relationship with God that Christ provides. God blesses the people who come to Him in this way by giving them the new life of the kingdom. This new life enables them to live according to the instructions given in the rest of the Sermon on the Mount.

The people described in the Beatitudes are to live out their discipleship in the world (Matt. 5:13–16). Others will see the new life they live and come to believe in Christ. But what will this new life look like? It will be greater and deeper than life lived by a legalistic keeping of the Mosaic Law (5:17–20). Life in the kingdom is not a life based on rule keeping. It is based on true inner transformation. According to Jesus, this kind of life fulfills the true meaning of the Old Testament law.

Jesus gave a series of contrasts between life based on keeping the letter of the Mosaic Law and on the inner transformation of the kingdom (Matt. 5:21–48). These contrasts describe how this inner transformation affects our relationship to others. In each contrast, Jesus introduced life according to the

KEY VERSE

But seek first his kingdom and his righteousness, and all these things will be given to you as well.
—Matthew 6:33

BACKGROUND SCRIPTURES

1 John 2:15–17
  Don't love the things of the world, because they are temporary.
Romans 12:1–2
  Give yourself to God and allow Him to transform you from within.
Philippians 4:6–7
  Commit your worries to God in prayer and experience His peace.
Ephesians 4:28
  We don't worry, but we work to supply our needs and be generous to others.

DAILY BIBLE READINGS

Monday: John 17:20–26
Tuesday: Matthew 19:23–30
Wednesday: Psalm 37:3–9
Thursday: John 21:15–19
Friday: Deuteronomy 6:4–9
Saturday: Matthew 6:19–34
Sunday: Psalm 48

letter of the law by saying, "You have heard that it was said" or "It was said" (5:21, 27, 31, 33, 38, 43). Life based on inner transformation by God's grace is introduced by the words "But I tell you" (5:22, 28, 32, 34, 39, 44). Jesus is the One who gives the true meaning of the law.

Jesus then showed how the inner transforming power of the kingdom transforms our relationship with God (6:1–34). How does life in the kingdom transform our pursuit of prestige and material wealth and security? The person of the kingdom seeks God's approval, not human acclaim (6:1–18). The person of the kingdom seeks for God's will to be done and His kingdom to be established rather than for the material possessions and pleasures of this life (6:19–34).

We are invited to enter God's kingdom by trusting Him for the things of this world and setting our hearts wholly on doing and promoting His will.

Where Is Your Treasure? (Matt. 6:19–24)

Jesus painted three pictures—stored treasure, the eye of the body, and two masters. The message of these verses is to give yourself fully to God's kingdom rather than the pursuit of material security. The heart and the eye represent who we really are. Who will be the "master" of that true "me"?

The first picture is of stored treasure (vv. 19–21). **Do not store up for yourselves treasures on earth . . . But store up for yourselves treasures in heaven** (vv. 19–20). The first of these commands is clear: Don't spend your life accumulating material goods. We store up treasures in heaven by setting our hearts on and directing our actions toward doing God's will on earth as zealously as others set their attention on material accumulation. We should accept Jesus' invitation because treasure on earth is so unstable! The **moth and rust** (v. 19) of the stock market can **destroy** it in a moment. No amount of insurance will protect it. **Thieves** can swindle us out of it. Treasure in heaven is absolutely secure from all of these things! There is a dual relationship between our **treasure** and our **heart** (v. 21). If our heart is set on the things of earth, we will amass earthly treasure; if on the things of heaven, heavenly treasure. But also, if we have been storing up treasure in heaven, our hearts will be on heaven. We will think about and give our efforts toward the place **where our treasure is**.

The second picture (vv. 22–23) is the picture of the eye and the body. The physical **eye is the lamp of the body** (v. 22). The eye enables the body to perceive light, to see, and thus to direct its life properly. Thus, if a person's **eyes are good** or "healthy" (NRSV), then that person's **whole body will be full of light**. They will be able to see, to understand what is around them, and to live accordingly. On the other hand, if a person's eyes are "unhealthy," that person won't be able to see to conduct his or her life properly. Our eyes in this picture are equivalent to our heart in the treasure picture. Our eyes are our true selves.

WHAT DO YOU THINK?
In your own words, describe how someone stores up treasure in heaven.

AHA!
Treasure in heaven is about doing God's will on earth with as much enthusiasm as others show in the pursuit of money!

DID YOU KNOW?
Earthly riches, in and of themselves, are rarely condemned in the Bible. However, greed, selfishness, and loving possessions more than God are clearly spoken against.

I'll Let God Be My Heavenly Father (Matt. 6:19–34)
I'll Serve Him!
"Seek first his kingdom and his righteousness . . ." (Matt. 6:33) by:
1. Storing up my treasures in heaven (6:19–21).
2. Keeping my eyes fixed on His light (6:22–23).
3. Letting Him be my master (6:24).
I'll Trust Him!
". . . and all these things will be given to you as well" (Matt. 6:33).
1. He feeds the birds; He'll certainly feed me (6:25–27).
2. He clothes the grass; He'll certainly clothe me (6:28–31).
3. I won't be like the people who know no heavenly Father (6:32).

If we have fixed our spiritual gaze on the kingdom of God, then our whole lives are full of light. We can live as God would have us live. But if not, then our whole lives are **full of darkness** (v. 23). Without God's kingdom, **how great is that darkness**!

The final picture in verse 24 brings out the significance of the previous two. No person can **serve** or give total allegiance to **two masters**. The images of **hate** and **love**, **be devoted** and **despise**, express this truth in the strongest way. To serve two masters would be like playing on two opposing football teams or joining two opposing armies. One master will take precedence over the other. A person cannot be devoted both to **God** and to **Money**. The word the NIV translates **Money** can better be translated "wealth" (NRSV, NASB). It refers to all of the material benefits and enjoyments of this world. If our lives are focused on obtaining the things of this world, then we cannot truly serve God.

But how can we allow God to be first in our lives? How can we make His kingdom, His rule on earth, our first priority? After all, we need money to live. We have to have food. We need clothes. The next section of our study answers this question. We can trust the God we serve. He will take care of us.

Your Father Cares for You (Matt. 6:25–34)

Jesus told us the things of this life are not to be our goal. In verse 25, He assured us we don't even have to **worry about** them! Jesus didn't mean we should become lazy. We are to work to provide for our needs. But He commanded us: **do not worry about your life**, **what you will eat** to preserve it; **or about your body, what you will wear** to cover it. God cares for you and will supply! He has already given you life; will He not give you the food to sustain it? He has already given you a body; will He not provide the clothes necessary to cover it?

Jesus gave us two examples of God's care: **the birds of the air** (v. 26) give us a perfect example of how God will provide our food; **the lilies of the field** (v. 28) demonstrate God's provision of clothes.

Birds don't **sow**, **reap**, or **store** food. They don't grow, process, or distribute it; yet God feeds them. Since He is **your heavenly Father**, **you** are much more important to Him than all the birds in the world! We can worry all we want to about getting the things of this life, but all our **worrying** won't **add a single hour to** our lives (v. 27).

Worry about clothes (v. 28)? How ridiculous! Nobody cultivates the **lilies of the field**. They are wildflowers. But look at them! **They do not labor or spin**. They don't grow cotton, make thread, weave cloth, or sew clothes. Yet their blossoms are more beautiful than **even Solomon in all his splendor** (v. 29). Second Chronicles 9:13–28 describes the fantastic wealth and majesty of Solomon's court. His legendary splendor was greater than the splendor of any other Israelite king. Yet his finest clothes could not compare to the glory of a wildflower. God does this for **the grass of the field** (v. 30), which lives only for a moment. In wood-poor Palestine, grass was dried and used for fuel. How much

WHAT ABOUT YOU?

What causes you to worry about tomorrow? How will you let God help you through your worries this week?

PRAYER

Lord God, You are my provider and helper. This week, please help me to remember that I have no need to worry about material wealth, because I am a child of Yours.

more will God care for **you**, His children? Certainly He will **clothe you**! These two examples show both God's ability and care. When we worry about food and clothes and run after them, we don't trust our heavenly Father's care. We deserve to be addressed as **you of little faith**.

Verses 31–33 summarize Jesus' point, with a prohibition (v. 31), followed by the reason for the prohibition (v. 32), then an admonition (v. 33), followed by the reason for the admonition (v. 33).

First, the prohibition: **Do not worry, saying, "What shall we eat? . . . drink? . . . wear?"** (v. 31). Can you see the picture of people scurrying around all their lives seeking food, drink, and clothes? Don't do it! If you do, you are acting like **the pagans** (v. 32). The pagans are the people who don't know God as their loving **heavenly Father**. Certainly the heavenly Father can and will care for His children's earthly needs!

So, **seek first his kingdom and his righteousness** (v. 33). When we know God as our heavenly Father, we give our lives to promoting His kingly rule on earth and to doing His will. Those who love the heavenly Father live to please Him. They live out their love. And when they love the Father, He takes care of them! **All these things will be given to you as well**. What are **all these things**? Why, the food and clothes that others so feverishly seek. Jesus didn't mean that the Father would make all His children wealthy. He will care for our needs and do what is best for us. Ultimately, He will bring us into His eternal kingdom where suffering will be no more. But the important thing now, whether we have little or much, is to trust Him.

Verse 34 is a parting shot at worry. Like verse 27, it shows us the complete futility of being anxious over the future. Don't **worry about tomorrow**, because if you do you are just borrowing trouble. Today has enough to take care of. You don't even know what tomorrow's troubles will be, and you can't do anything about them anyway. Since we can't really deal with the future, how blessed we are to have a heavenly Father who can and will! ◆

MATTHEW 6:19–34

19 "Do not store up for yourselves treasures on earth, where moth and rust destroy, and where thieves break in and steal.

20 But store up for yourselves treasures in heaven, where moth and rust do not destroy, and where thieves do not break in and steal.

21 For where your treasure is, there your heart will be also.

22 "The eye is the lamp of the body. If your eyes are good, your whole body will be full of light.

23 But if your eyes are bad, your whole body will be full of darkness. If then the light within you is darkness, how great is that darkness!

24 "No one can serve two masters. Either he will hate the one and love the other, or he will be devoted to the one and despise the other. You cannot serve both God and Money.

25 "Therefore I tell you, do not worry about your life, what you will eat or drink; or about your body, what you will wear. Is not life more important than food, and the body more important than clothes?

26 Look at the birds of the air; they do not sow or reap or store away in barns, and yet your heavenly Father feeds them. Are you not much more valuable than they?

27 Who of you by worrying can add a single hour to his life?

28 "And why do you worry about clothes? See how the lilies of the field grow. They do not labor or spin.

29 Yet I tell you that not even Solomon in all his splendor was dressed like one of these.

30 If that is how God clothes the grass of the field, which is here today and tomorrow is thrown into the fire, will he not much more clothe you, O you of little faith?

31 So do not worry, saying, 'What shall we eat?' or 'What shall we drink?' or 'What shall we wear?'

32 For the pagans run after all these things, and your heavenly Father knows that you need them.

33 But seek first his kingdom and his righteousness, and all these things will be given to you as well.

34 Therefore do not worry about tomorrow, for tomorrow will worry about itself. Each day has enough trouble of its own.

Kingdom Priorities

Stewardship involves making God's kingdom our first priority.

INTO THE SUBJECT

Some people don't trust banks, so they stash their savings in a mattress or freezer, or they bury it. Others sock it away in a bank, credit union, or brokerage. What is the best place to store treasure?

INTO THE WORD

1. According to Matthew 6:19–20, what choice do you have for storing up treasures?

2. Looking over the past month, where have you stored most of your "assets"?

3. Why do you agree or disagree that it is possible for a poor person to be more materialistic than a rich person?

4. Do you know someone who seems to be money hungry? How would you describe what you believe to be his or her relationship with God?

5. Do you think the phrase "happy as a lark" is well founded, according to Matthew 6:26?

6. How should believers' attitudes about material things differ noticeably from those of pagans (vv. 31–32)?

7. What does it mean to seek first God's kingdom and righteousness?

8. If you were to list what matters most to you, where would you place "God," "family," "money," and "possessions"?

9. Why did you arrange the list as you did?

INTO THE WORLD

Ask someone this week what he or she wants most out of life. Use the response as an opportunity to discuss eternal values.

DON'T WORRY

If you struggle with anxiety, write a couple of the quotes below on sticky notes, and place them where you'll see them often.

If I had my life to live over, I would perhaps have more actual troubles but I'd have fewer imaginary ones.
—Don Herold

Drag your thoughts away from your troubles . . . by the ears, by the heels, or any other way you can manage it.
—Mark Twain

Let us be of good cheer, remembering that the misfortunes hardest to bear are those which will never happen.
—James Russel Lowell

If things go wrong, don't go with them.
—Roger Babson

Troubles are a lot like people—they grow bigger if you nurse them.
—author unknown

If you want to test your memory, try to recall what you were worrying about one year ago today.
—E. Joseph Cossman

You can't wring your hands and roll up your sleeves at the same time.
—Pat Schroeder

The greatest mistake you can make in life is to be continually fearing you will make one.
—Elbert Hubbard

Worrying is like a rocking chair, it gives you something to do, but it gets you nowhere.
—Glenn Turner

People become attached to their burdens sometimes more than the burdens are attached to them.
—George Bernard Shaw

For peace of mind, resign as general manager of the universe.
—author unknown

Worry often gives a small thing a big shadow.
—Swedish Proverb

That the birds of worry and care fly over your head, this you cannot change, but that they build nests in your hair, this you can prevent.
—Chinese Proverb

You can never worry your way to enlightenment.
—Terri Guillemets

Any concern too small to be turned into a prayer is too small to be made into a burden.
—Corrie ten Boom

I am reminded of the advice of my neighbor. "Never worry about your heart till it stops beating."
—E. B. White

There are two days in the week about which and upon which I never worry . . . yesterday and tomorrow.
—Robert Jones Burdette

A day of worry is more exhausting than a day of work.
—John Lubbock

Worry is rust upon the blade.
—Henry Ward Hughes

Heavy thoughts bring on physical maladies; when the soul is oppressed so is the body.
—Martin Luther

INTERACTIVE LEARNING IDEAS

GET THE CLASS INVOLVED
The Lost Art of Letter Writing

Before class, write the name of each class member on a slip of paper. Fold the slips and put them in a bowl or container of some sort. At the start of this exercise allow each person to draw a name from the bowl. Pass out paper and an envelope to each person. Make sure each person has a pen or pencil.

Say, "God's Word is one big love letter. He writes to us in the Scriptures to allow us to get to know Him. He wants us to understand how He cares for us and how to live in response to that love. Today we are going to write a letter based on God's letter to us."

Have some volunteers read the passages from this study aloud to the class. Instruct your class members to write a letter to the person whose name they drew from the bowl. Have them put the ideas and thoughts from the Scripture reading in their own words. If they were telling the things this passage says to this person, how would they say it? If this passage was written only for that person, how would they express it to him or her? When everyone is done, have them seal the letter in the envelope and write the person's name on it. Each person can pick up his or her letter after class is over.

TRY THIS ON YOUR OWN
Treasure Chest

Make a list of all the things you treasure. Include the activities and all the people you treasure. Take some time creating this list. Think about why you treasure these things. What makes them worthy of this distinction? How is this list different than one you could have made ten years ago?

Once you are finished with your list, pray over each entry. Ask God to bless each person, prosper each activity, and help you to have proper attitudes toward each "thing." Ask God to help the things you treasure to line up with what He wants you to treasure, so your heart is where He wants it to be.

TAKING IT TO THE STREET
Storing Up Treasure

Many churches have food pantries that they stock so when a need arises they can immediately respond with help. But how about a twist on that idea? Why not develop a clothing pantry to be able to respond to a different, but just as big, need?

Ask church members to begin to think a little bit bigger when they go to the store to fill basic needs for their families. When the kids need socks or underwear, buy an extra package and donate it to the clothing pantry. When you see flip-flops or snow boots on sale at the end of the year for a fantastic price, buy extra and give it to the clothing pantry. Is the department store closing out those jeans? Buy a couple pairs for the pantry.

Then when someone has a fire, or you hear of a need at your kids' school, you can go to the pantry and meet that need.

WITH YOUR FAMILY
Operation Thinking Ahead

There are some wonderful ministries who give gifts to kids at Christmastime—locally and around the world. It can get expensive, though, if you wait till Christmastime to do all the buying to join in giving gifts for these children.

However, if you buy little things throughout the year, your wallet won't take quite the hit. You'll find you can bless many more children than if you only buy at that busy (and expensive) time of year.

Get the whole family involved in this project. Designate a box to store the items you find over the year. You can even call it your "Treasure Chest." As you shop for school supplies, get extra pencils and sharpeners and put them in the box. If you buy small toys for birthday treats, get a couple extra for the treasure chest. By the time you need to assemble the gifts at Christmas, you'll have more than enough to give. ◆

A spirit of generosity benefits others and builds the kingdom of God.

LESSON 9

GENEROSITY: A MEASURE OF SPIRITUAL HEALTH

Acts 4:32—5:11

KEY VERSE
All the believers were one in heart and mind. No one claimed that any of his possessions was his own, but they shared everything they had.

—Acts 4:32

BACKGROUND SCRIPTURES
Matthew 6:1–4
    Jesus' teaching on
    giving in secret
2 Corinthians 8–9
    Significant passage on
    giving and generosity
Malachi 3:8–12
    God's blessing
    when we tithe

DAILY BIBLE READINGS
Monday: 2 Corinthians
           8:1–7
Tuesday: 2 Corinthians
           8:8–15
Wednesday: 2 Corinthians
           9:12–15
Thursday: Ecclesiastes
           11:1–8
Friday: 1 Timothy
           6:17–19
Saturday: Acts 4:32—5:11
Sunday: Psalm 49

WHY THIS MATTERS

"Mine!" Isn't this often one of the first words a child says? When a child reaches for another child's toy, the possessive child screams, "Mine!"

Sinful human nature tends to be selfish and possessive. But the new nature, produced in believers by the Holy Spirit, enables us to be selfless, loving, and caring. It is not unusual to find these qualities at work in a congregation. Genuine believers open their hearts, purses, and homes to help fellow believers in need. Like the outpouring of mutual love in the church at Jerusalem, the sharing is voluntary, not forced.

This lesson helps us share with those in need what God has given to us. It helps us look at our resources and say "His" not "mine."

BIBLE COMMENTARY

By Patricia J. David

The book of Acts was written around A.D. 63 by Luke, a Gentile historian and doctor who was also a close companion of the apostle Paul. In this second volume of his writings (the gospel of Luke being the first), he recorded for us the first thirty years in the life of the church.

Jesus had been crucified on a Roman cross and buried in a borrowed tomb. But after three days in the grave, He rose triumphantly from the dead. After ministering for another forty days, He ascended into heaven, leaving His disciples to carry on His message and ministry. Before His departure, Jesus instructed His followers to tarry in Jerusalem until they were endued with power from the Holy Spirit (1:8). Acts chapter 2 records the coming of the Holy Spirit on the day of Pentecost and the miraculous conversion of about three thousand souls in response to Peter's preaching. The church was unleashed. And the world would never be the same.

Interspersed among the stories of the early church are summary statements that give the reader a bird's-eye view of what the church was really like. They can be found in Acts 2:42–47; 4:32–35; 5:12–16; and 5:42.

The summary in 4:32–35 also serves as an introduction to the story of Ananias and Sapphira in chapter 5. It is a story the early church might have rather forgotten, or at least not recorded. But it offered an important lesson for succeeding generations: God takes sin seriously.

The Selflessness of the Early Church (Acts 4:32–37)

At this point in the life of the church, **all the believers were one in heart and mind** (v. 32). The phrase "one in heart and mind" was a common expression. It meant they were united spiritually. Their lives had been transformed by the risen Christ, and it was their common love for Him that motivated their actions and attitudes. They had one desire and one purpose: to lift up Christ. They were devoted to one another and to the apostles' teaching (2:42).

No one claimed that any of his possessions was his own, but they shared everything they had (4:32). Contrary to the opinion of some, what was practiced in the early church was not Christian socialism or communism. People did have their own possessions, but their attitude toward them was different from many attitudes today. They recognized that everything they had was given to them by God; they were merely stewards (see David's similar attitude in 1 Chron. 29:14–16). And so they used their possessions in a way that would honor God—to meet the needs of their brothers and sisters in Christ.

Their devotion to the Lord and to one another was a powerful witness to the world around them. No wonder the church was growing by leaps and bounds. Jesus had told them, "By this all men will know that you are my disciples, if you love one another" (John 13:35). And so they testified about the resurrection of Christ **with great power**, and **much grace was upon them all** (Acts 4:33; see also Luke 2:40).

The net result was that **there were no needy persons among them** (Acts 4:34). Within the circle of Christians, needs were taken care of. Luke explained that **from time to time those who owned lands or houses sold them, brought the money from the sales and put it at the apostles' feet, and it was distributed to anyone as he had need** (4:34–35). The sale of property to meet the needs of others was not normative. It was an extraordinary response that only occurred from time to time. So, by no means was such an expression of generosity mandated by the early church. We know that good Christians continued to own homes, because that's where the early church gathered. Later, Paul recognized that some were taking advantage of the generosity of others, so he warned, "If a man will not work, he shall not eat" (1 Thess. 3:10). Christian "welfare" is not being advocated here in Acts. But there is ample indication that because of famine or possibly the loss of family and/or jobs because of conversion, the situation in Jerusalem was dire for many Christians. Where there were legitimate needs, God's people stepped in to help.

Luke offered one example in Acts 4:36–37. Barnabas **sold a field he owned and brought the money and put it at the apostles' feet** (4:37). The repetition of "put it at the apostles' feet" in 4:35, 37, and 5:2 indicates that there was some kind of legal transfer of the property to the apostles for the express purpose of meeting the needs of the poor among them. Barnabas, whose name meant **Son of Encouragement**, is also mentioned in 9:27; 11:22, 25; and 15:37–39. He became Paul's traveling companion and showed encouragement to his cousin John Mark when he seemed to fail in his ministry. Here in Acts 4, Barnabas encouraged the hearts of the needy by selling his field and giving the proceeds for their aid.

Luke tells us that Barnabas, whose Hebrew name was **Joseph**, was **a Levite from Cyprus** (v. 36). Although the Old Testament didn't make provision for the ownership of land in Palestine by Levites (see Num. 18:20; Deut. 10:9), it is apparent that the prohibition was not always followed (for example, Jer. 32:6–15). It's possible that the field Barnabas sold was on Cyprus, an island in the eastern Mediterranean Sea that had been settled by the Jews almost two

God's Spirit doesn't need growing noses to reveal deception.

WHAT DO YOU THINK?
Why do you think it was important for God to show the early church that it could not take sin lightly?

AHA!
Even in the new covenant of grace through Jesus Christ, God takes the issue of sin very seriously.

DID YOU KNOW?
The secular use of the word *ecclesia* referred to a group of people sent into a conquered kingdom to introduce the customs of the nation or king that conquered them.

hundred years earlier, or that he was married and the property belonged to his wife. But Acts 12:12 indicates that John Mark's mother owned a home in Jerusalem, and she, too, would have been a Levite. It's safe to assume that, by Jesus' day, land ownership among Levites was commonplace.

The Selfishness of Ananias and Sapphira (Acts 5:1–11)

The generosity of the early church, typified by Barnabas, stands in sharp contrast to the selfish act of Ananias and Sapphira recounted in 5:1–11. This is one of the most disturbing of all the stories Luke records. Ananias and Sapphira, perhaps inspired by people like Barnabas, **also sold a piece of property** (v. 1). However, unlike Barnabas, they **kept back part of the money . . . but brought the rest and put it at the apostles' feet** (v. 2). The Greek word translated *kept back* is the very same word used in the Septuagint (Greek translation of the Old Testament) in the opening verse of the account of Achan's sin in Joshua 7. Most likely Luke used this word intentionally to remind the reader of this similar account. In Achan's case, he kept back some of the spoils from Jericho in defiance of God's command. In the end, Achan and his entire family were stoned to death. And Ananias and Sapphira met a similar fate: each, in turn, **fell down and died** (5:5, 10).

Most people today have a hard time reconciling this abrupt and merciless judgment with a loving, gracious, and forgiving God. After all, Ananias and Sapphira were being generous; they were giving a portion, if not most, of their proceeds to help others. Even Peter admitted, **Didn't it belong to you before it was sold? And after it was sold, wasn't the money at your disposal?** (v. 4). Their gift was voluntary. But their sin was in lying about what they were giving. They claimed they were giving the full amount, when in reality they kept back part of the money for themselves. Jesus had taught that our giving should be done in secret; we shouldn't let our left hand know what our right hand is doing. He condemned those who made a spectacle out of their giving, wanting only to receive acclaim from people (see Matt. 6:1–4). Ananias and Sapphira wanted others to think they had given everything. They wanted the applause of the Christian community. But they were guilty of deceit. They were thinking only of themselves and what they were to gain; they were not thinking about what consequences their actions might have on the greater church.

Some commentators argue that both Ananias and Sapphira died of shock. Since they were from a superstitious culture, they say, Peter's indictment of Ananias in Acts 5:4 (**You have not lied to men but to God**) and his curse on Sapphira in 5:9 (**The feet of the men who buried your husband are at the door, and they will carry you out also**) caused them to go into shock and die of heart failure. These commentators cannot accept the fact that God would strike down Christians for such a seemingly trivial offense.

But the offense was not trivial. And God has always taken sin seriously. Flip through the Old Testament: Nadab and Abihu were consumed by fire for offering unauthorized fire before the Lord (Lev. 10:2); Achan was stoned for taking some of the spoils of war (Josh. 7:25); Uzzah was killed for simply reaching out to steady the ark of the covenant (2 Sam. 6:7); and one man was sentenced to death for gathering wood on the Sabbath (Num. 15:32–36). Here, at the beginning of the ministry of the church, God's people had to know for certain that His standards were the only acceptable ones for His church. When they lied to those placed in authority over them, they **lied to the Holy Spirit** (Acts 5:3). Peter said, "**You have not lied to men but to God**" (v. 4). Notice here the allusion to the Godhead—the Holy Spirit and God are used interchangeably. If God had simply let this pass, the Christian community, upon learning at some future point of the deception, would have concluded that it was acceptable or, at the very least, not worthy of punishment.

First John 5:16 mentions there is a sin that leads to death, and 1 Corinthians 11:27–30 attributes some sickness and death to taking Communion in an unworthy manner. Even James 5:14–16 seems to indicate that some sickness is caused by sin. Could it be that God still takes sin seriously?

The result of this judgment on Ananias and Sapphira is repeated twice: **great fear seized all who heard what had happened** (Acts 5:5); **great fear seized the whole church and all who heard about these events** (v. 11). The church didn't feel pity. They weren't incredulous. They were afraid. They knew that God was watching. They knew they would be held accountable for their actions and their integrity.

In verse 11, we have the first instance in Acts where Paul used the word *church* (Greek, *ecclesia*) to describe the Christian community. The Jews used two Greek words to translate Old Testament words for the congregation or assembly of God's people: *ecclesia* and *synagogue*. The latter came to signify a place of worship, so the Christian community early took the other word, *ecclesia*, to describe themselves. It was a term used often in the Septuagint, a word with which they were familiar. They saw themselves as the faithful remnant of the people of God. They saw themselves as a continuation of the Old Testament *ecclesia*. And so they learned early on that the God of the Old Testament is also the God of the New. He hadn't tolerated sin in Israel, and so He wouldn't tolerate it in His church. It was a hard lesson to learn, but it was vital to their work and witness in the world. ✦

WHAT ABOUT YOU?
How do you think sin in the church (or in Christians) affects the world's view of us? How might it affect the way we view ourselves?

PRAYER
Holy God, help me to walk a path that has more purity and integrity day by day.

INTERACTIVE LEARNING IDEAS

GET THE CLASS INVOLVED
Compare and Contrast

Many churches today try to be like the first-century church. They desire to give, care for each other, model their worship after, and structure themselves as much like the early church as possible. Yet sometimes it seems we have the tendency to look at the New Testament church through rose-colored glasses. In this study, much of what we read about the early church is incredibly inspiring, but let's face it: when the early church members failed, they often failed in big ways.

Divide the class into small groups. Allow each group to discuss the following questions:

- In what ways is our church similar to this account of the early church?
- In what ways are we different?
- In what ways would you like to be more like the early church? How do you think we can accomplish that to achieve positive outcomes?

Call the groups back together and let them share their answers. Have the class pick one thing from their answers to the last question. Then pray together, asking God to help you to achieve positive results through learning from the first-century church.

TRY THIS ON YOUR OWN
Extra Stuff

Do you have extra stuff lying around, simply taking up space in your home or garage? Consider selling it and giving the proceeds to your church or special mission project.

Take some time to pray, now. Ask the Lord to show you something you have that you really don't need at the moment or for the foreseeable future. Also ask Him where the proceeds of the sale are supposed to be given. It might also be a good idea to ask Him how much to ask for the items you are led to sell. After you have your answers, make arrangements to sell your extra stuff, whether on EBay, Craig's List, or at a garage sale.

Give the proceeds with a full heart, knowing that God was in this action. And enjoy the newfound room you have to walk through your home, tool shed, or garage!

TAKING IT TO THE STREET
Trash into Treasure

As a class, host a church-wide rummage sale. Before you start making preparations for the sale, as a class choose a local charity you'd like to support with the sale proceeds. When you advertise, let the public know that all the proceeds will be going to that specific charity.

Solicit castoff donations from the whole church. Specify a drop-off location and time for people to bring in those donations. Consider asking for baked items as well—small, baked items sell well and will bring in extra cash. You could also sell bottled water or offer free coffee with the purchase of a baked item.

Invite representatives from the charity to join you at the sale. Allow them to hand out information on their mission. Donate any sale items that are left over to a charity's retail thrift shop.

WITH YOUR FAMILY
Ring and Run

It's a lot of fun to be able to help someone you know is in need. It's a great thing to teach your children to do, as well.

Do you know people, perhaps friends of yours or a family from church, who are in need right now? Makes plans together as a family to buy them some groceries. Bring everyone in on what to purchase. Set limits and even a budget, perhaps. Then go together to buy the items.

When you deliver the groceries, do it after dark. Sneak up and put the food by the door. Go back to your car, leaving the fastest runner to ring the bell and run! Your kids will get such a charge out of helping, giving, and keeping the secret behind your "Ring and Run" mission intact. You can decide together if you want to include a note of explanation with the gift, or even a note of disclosure, if you decide you want them to know who gave the gift. ◆

ACTS 4:32—5:11

4:32 All the believers were one in heart and mind. No one claimed that any of his possessions was his own, but they shared everything they had.

33 With great power the apostles continued to testify to the resurrection of the Lord Jesus, and much grace was upon them all.

34 There were no needy persons among them. For from time to time those who owned lands or houses sold them, brought the money from the sales

35 and put it at the apostles' feet, and it was distributed to anyone as he had need.

36 Joseph, a Levite from Cyprus, whom the apostles called Barnabas (which means Son of Encouragement),

37 sold a field he owned and brought the money and put it at the apostles' feet.

5:1 Now a man named Ananias, together with his wife Sapphira, also sold a piece of property.

2 With his wife's full knowledge he kept back part of the money for himself, but brought the rest and put it at the apostles' feet.

3 Then Peter said, "Ananias, how is it that Satan has so filled your heart that you have lied to the Holy Spirit and have kept for yourself some of the money you received for the land?

4 Didn't it belong to you before it was sold? And after it was sold, wasn't the money at your disposal? What made you think of doing such a thing? You have not lied to men but to God."

5 When Ananias heard this, he fell down and died. And great fear seized all who heard what had happened.

6 Then the young men came forward, wrapped up his body, and carried him out and buried him.

7 About three hours later his wife came in, not knowing what had happened.

8 Peter asked her, "Tell me, is this the price you and Ananias got for the land?" "Yes," she said, "that is the price."

9 Peter said to her, "How could you agree to test the Spirit of the Lord? Look! The feet of the men who buried your husband are at the door, and they will carry you out also."

10 At that moment she fell down at his feet and died. Then the young men came in and, finding her dead, carried her out and buried her beside her husband.

11 Great fear seized the whole church and all who heard about these events.

Generosity: A Measure of Spiritual Health

A spirit of generosity benefits others and builds the kingdom of God.

INTO THE SUBJECT

A stingy person might drop a dollar into the offering plate and sing silently, "When we asunder part, it gives me inward pain." Of course, generous giving doesn't earn salvation, but is generosity an indicator of our spiritual health?

INTO THE WORD

1. Read Acts 2:1, 5–11, 38–42. What had contributed to the huge number of believers in the church at Jerusalem?

2. What kinds of economic problems would such a large crowd create?

3. Read Acts 4:32–33. What cause-effect principle do you find in these verses?

4. What tangible expression of generosity do you find in verses 34–35?

5. What vivid contrast do you see in the behavior of Barnabas (vv. 36–37) and Ananias and Sapphira (5:1–2)?

6. What sin had Ananias and Sapphira committed (vv. 3–4)?

7. Why do you think the couple's sin brought such serious consequences (vv. 5–10)?

8. Read verse 11. Why do you agree or disagree that the church today needs a greater fear of God?

9. Why do you agree or disagree that Christians should give generously to (a) their local church, (b) missions, (c) charities, and (d) disaster relief efforts?

INTO THE WORLD

Plan to help a truly needy person or family this week, and carry out your plan.

Freedom to Give

To give generously, you must have something to give, right? And chances are you are heavily in debt or living paycheck to paycheck.

Figure out how much you are spending on interest alone: $_____.
Imagine giving all that money to your church instead of a bank!

Living above your means puts you in debt, making you unable to obey God's command to give generously. It steals your opportunity to make a difference in the lives of others and to experience the joy of financial freedom.

If you are in debt, go online right now to find a financial planning tool or program. Sign up, participate, and apply the principles so you can free up money to bless others.

Being clothed in Christ frees men and women to use their gifts in ministry.

FREE TO SERVE

Galatians 3:26–28; Romans 16:1–7; Acts 18:24–26

WHY THIS MATTERS

A preschool in Sweden called Egalia is trying to establish a gender-free environment for the children who attend. Stories like Cinderella and Snow White have been banned from the school, and so have gender-stereotypical toys. Even the words *him* and *her* have been banned in the classroom. Teachers use the word *friend* and the recently concocted new Swedish gender-neutral pronoun *hen* instead.

This lesson shows how all believers, regardless of gender, are one in Christ, while respecting the gender differences God created. Further, it inspires a high regard for the role of women in the church.

BIBLE COMMENTARY

By Philip Bence

No one disputes the fact that in several New Testament passages, the apostle Paul placed some restrictions on the ministry of first-century women in certain locations (see 1 Cor. 14:34–35; 1 Tim. 2:11–12). Christians ever since have debated the degree to which these apostolic instructions remain in force for female believers of all times and places, or whether Paul intended these words for churches facing unique first-century circumstances.

On what biblical basis do some denominations state that God intended both men and women to serve as His ministers? The Bible study passages for this lesson explore a selection of New Testament references that support the validity of women serving as church leaders.

God Sees All People as Equals (Gal. 3:26–28)

This lesson's first three verses appear in the center of Paul's letter to the Galatians, a treatise on Paul's belief that salvation comes only by the grace of God. This letter is potentially the earliest of the biblical letters Paul wrote, directed to several communities of Christians in what is now central Turkey. In the opening two chapters of this book, Paul recounted a bit of his personal history. By doing this, he showed the divine source and thus the unshakable nature of the gospel he proclaimed. The midsection of this letter highlights the content of this gospel. Galatians 2:15–16 sounds the opening trumpet of Paul's argument: "We . . . know that a [person] is not justified by observing the law, but by faith in Jesus Christ."

In the middle of the letter's central section appear three verses, each of which notes that God offered salvation to all people, whatever their gender, race, or other uniqueness. **You** (believing readers of the letter in "the churches in Galatia") **are all** (note the lack of exceptions) **sons of God** (v. 26). Paul's use of a masculine word *sons* includes both men and women. No believers, no

KEY VERSE

There is neither Jew nor Greek, slave nor free, male nor female, for you are all one in Christ.
—Galatians 3:28

BACKGROUND SCRIPTURES

2 Kings 22:14; Nehemiah 6:14; Luke 2:36; Acts 21:9
    Women as prophetesses
Judges 4:4
    Women as judges
Judges 5:28–29;
2 Samuel 14:2; 20:16
    Women as "the Wise"
2 Kings 11:3
    A woman as a ruler
    of God's people
Matthew 28:8; Mark 16:10;
Luke 24:9; John 20:18
    Women as first
    witnesses to the
    resurrection
Acts 1:14; 2:1–2
    Women as preachers
    on the day of Pentecost
1 Corinthians 11:5
    Women as pray-ers and
    prophetesses in church
    assemblies

DAILY BIBLE READINGS

Monday: Joel 2:28–32
Tuesday: Judges 4:4–9
Wednesday: 2 Kings
                22:11–16
Thursday: Romans
                16:8–16
Friday: John 20:10–18
Saturday: Galatians
                3:26–28;
                Romans 16:1–7;
                Acts 18:24–26
Sunday: Psalm 50

WHAT DO YOU THINK?
Do you think the Bible verses that indicate all people are equal in Christ Jesus apply to who can lead in the church? Why or why not?

matter what their position on the ordination of women, debate that fact. The letter's recipients are children of what parent? Of God himself. God had created both male and female in His own image (Gen. 1:27). Both men and women had, however, through disobedience, lost their perfect relationship with God.

But through His grace, God gladly adopts *all* people who exercise **faith in Christ Jesus** (Gal. 3:26). Earlier in this chapter, Paul had written of Christ, who redeemed us from the curse of the law by dying on the cross for us (3:13). Christ's obedience reversed the consequences of human disobedience. God offered this possibility of restored relationship through His own free grace. To receive this gift, all any person needs to do is reach out to God, believing that He wants to reconcile all people to himself.

Early in the next verse, Paul repeated the key word **all**, meaning **all of you who were baptized into Christ** (v. 27). Why did Paul raise the concept of baptism here? In societies where a person incurs a loss of reputation by swearing allegiance to Jesus Christ (for example, a contemporary Islamic nation or a first-century Galatian community), no one enters baptism lightly. Among Paul's readership, none but sincere, dedicated believers would have requested baptism. For this reason, we can see that, in verse 27, Paul clarified the membership of the group he had addressed in verse 26. All Galatian believers, having been adopted as God's own favored children, had **clothed** themselves **with Christ** (v. 27). Within this analogy, a change in uniform accompanied new believers' change in position. God's Son was as close to them (and as obvious to those around them) as a dramatic change in clothing on their physical bodies.

AHA!
God values women in the same way He does men.

Who could experience this transformation? Or, in other words, people from among what people groups had already experienced this shift? No person was necessarily left out, except by his or her own choice. One's nationality or previous religious affiliation could not exclude a person: **neither Jew nor Greek** (v. 28). With this pairing, Paul divided the world's population into one set of two groups: those who were physical descendents of Abraham and all the others. Paul called the larger group the Greeks, since Greek was the common language spoken by diverse populations around the Mediterranean Sea. One's occupation or economic status did not matter with God: **neither slave nor free**. (With this phrase, Paul offered another way of dividing humanity: first, the majority of the Roman Empire's people who lived in forced service to the minority; and second, that smaller group who lived in freedom. Most relevant to this lesson, God opened the way of salvation to members of both halves of another population grouping: **male** and **female**.

DID YOU KNOW?
Paul's assertion that women were to be considered equals in Christ to men railed against the common Jewish and Roman cultures of his day.

In the twenty-first-century West, where women's rights are guaranteed by law, where discrimination on the basis of race or religion is outlawed, and where slavery (in the traditional use of the word) is fortunately no more than a horrific memory, we do not easily see the revolutionary nature of Paul's assertion in verse 28. Within the first-century Roman culture, few people would ever have questioned what they saw as the obviously lower rank of women and slaves, just as most in North America today unthinkingly accept the premise that human beings have more value than cats. The gospel offers true women's liberation— the good news that God values women in the same way He does men.

Women Serve the Church Faithfully and Fruitfully (Rom. 16:1–7)

During Paul's third missionary journey, the apostle wrote from one urban church to another. From Corinth, a leading city of southern Greece, Paul wrote the church in Rome, the empire's capital. After offering substantive content in both theology and Christian living, Paul signed off by sending a chapter full of personal greetings. In these greetings, he commended many who had served him and the church in one or both locations. Of special interest to us, as part of this lesson, is the fact that Paul's awards ceremony included colleagues of both genders.

I commend to you our sister Phoebe (v. 1). We know nothing of this woman other than what Paul wrote here. Her hometown was **Cenchrea**, a seaside suburb of Corinth. Her immediate role appears to have been traveling from Corinth to Rome, and thus likely carrying this letter from Paul to a church he had not yet personally encountered. Her broader role was a **servant** (the same word is often translated *minister*) **of the church**.

Women in ministry share a heritage extending back to the first-century church.

Paul's instructions to the Romans regarding Phoebe were to **receive her** (v. 2) in the same manner they would receive any **of the saints**, any of God's people. They were to **help** her, to enable her to fulfill her ministry among them, as she had among churches in the neighborhood of Corinth. Paul proudly included **sister Phoebe** (v. 1) among those who had aided him in his own ministry. Do you catch any hint here that Phoebe's service was limited to baking pies and planning wedding receptions? None at all. We cannot ignore the fact that Paul listed Phoebe first in his list of commendations; within his ancient culture, he gave her special honor by this sequencing.

Greet Priscilla and Aquila, my fellow workers in Christ Jesus (v. 3). First-century common usage would have mandated that a writer list a husband before his wife. Paul reversed that common practice, listing Priscilla first. Many interpret this to indicate that Priscilla was the more prominent, more gifted member of this pair. Even ignoring Paul's sequencing, Paul boldly included both wife and husband as fellow workers. (For more information on the nature of this couple's ministry, see comments below on Acts 18:24–26.) Paul's praise continued as he pointed out that both wife and husband had **risked their lives for** (Rom. 16:4) him. Once again, as with his words about Phoebe, with this commendation for Priscilla, a woman, Paul elevated the status of all women.

Greet also the church that meets at their house (v. 5). New Testament Scriptures never speak of any buildings specifically devoted to Christian worship. First-century churches met in people's homes. One such group met not in Aquila's house, but the house managed by both Priscilla and Aquila. Again, Paul refused to subordinate the wife to her husband or the female to any other leader of that particular congregation.

We know little of **Epenetus** (v. 5), the next person to whom Paul sent greetings. Here Paul filled us in a bit. Paul remembered Epenetus as an early **convert** in **Asia** (what is now southwestern Turkey, near the ancient city of Ephesus). Epenetus had at some point emigrated from Ephesus to Rome, taking his Christian faith with him.

Greet Mary, who worked very hard for you (v. 6). These eight words tell us everything we know about this Mary. Her name, then as now, indicates she was

WHAT DO YOU THINK?
Do you think Paul greeted so many women at the end of his letter to the Romans to prove a point about women, or did he simply list those women as being important without thinking about the culture around them? Explain.

AHA!
Luke, the author of Acts, didn't hesitate to tell about the important role Priscilla had as she joined her husband in training Apollos about the complete work of Jesus.

DID YOU KNOW?
Like Paul, Priscilla and Aquila made tents for a living.

female. Paul commended her as a hard worker. We don't know the nature of her work. But we again can't miss the value Paul gave to a woman and her ministry.

Greet Andronicus and Junias (v. 7). Again, this pair receives no other mention in Scripture. But here Paul honored them greatly by describing them as **outstanding among the apostles**. The fact that Paul gave this particular affirmation to ordinary believers is wonderful, but not unique. Other Scripture references extend the word *apostle* beyond the original Twelve (see, for example, Gal. 1:19; Acts 14:4; 1 Thess. 2:6). What is special about this passage is that many translators of the original Greek text name these two Andronicus and Junia. The evidence seems to indicate that Junia was a woman. Paul included a female among the apostles? Yes! The case for women in the ministry is closed. Well, not quite yet.

Further Evidence for Women Taking Leadership in Ministry (Acts 18:24–26)

We have already met Priscilla and Aquila, a powerful wife and husband team. Luke joined Paul in affirming the ministry of this pair. Together Priscilla and Aquila acted as teachers of Scripture and theology.

The context? Acts 18 portrays Paul's ministry in Corinth, the planting of churches in that city and the surrounding area. After Paul left Corinth, he visited Ephesus but did not feel he should stay there for extended ministry. So he did the next best thing, leaving others, including Priscilla and Aquila, who could represent him and minister for Jesus.

In time, a well-intentioned but not fully informed follower of Jesus arrived in Ephesus. This man, **Apollos** (v. 24), knew of and proclaimed **Jesus** (v. 25), but only incompletely.

Around the empire were scattered a few people who had experienced no direct interaction with Jesus or His followers (at least in the latter part of Jesus' ministry, including the time of His death and resurrection), but had either heard the preaching of **John** the Baptist or encountered others who had listened to Jesus' forerunner. These people believed God's Messiah was coming or perhaps even had already arrived, even if they had not yet heard the full story of how Jesus had completed His mission. Apollos was such a person.

What else do we know about Apollos? He came from **Alexandria** (v. 24), an Egyptian city, the second largest center in the Roman Empire. Alexandria's population included a great number of Jews. Alexandria was in fact the site where the Hebrew Scriptures had been translated into Greek. This enabled non-Hebrew-speaking Jews to access their holy book. Apollos **was a learned man** (v. 24). He was a scholar with particular expertise in **the Scriptures**. (At this time, this term would have referred only to the Old Testament.) Although Apollos did not yet know the full gospel, what he did know motivated him to proclamation: **He began to speak boldly in the synagogue** (v. 26).

Priscilla and Aquila likely were glad to have another follower of Jesus join them in ministry to the Jews of Ephesus. But in order to maximize the fruitfulness of Apollos' ministry, they together took him aside to fill out his understanding of Jesus' complete work. Of importance to us is the fact that Luke felt no hesitation in noting how a woman helped in the Christian education of an adult male. ◆

GALATIANS 3:26–28; ROMANS 16:1–7; ACTS 18:24–26

Galatians 3:26 You are all sons of God through faith in Christ Jesus,

27 for all of you who were baptized into Christ have clothed yourselves with Christ.

28 There is neither Jew nor Greek, slave nor free, male nor female, for you are all one in Christ Jesus.

Romans 16:1 I commend to you our sister Phoebe, a servant of the church in Cenchrea.

2 I ask you to receive her in the Lord in a way worthy of the saints and to give her any help she may need from you, for she has been a great help to many people, including me.

3 Greet Priscilla and Aquila, my fellow workers in Christ Jesus.

4 They risked their lives for me. Not only I but all the churches of the Gentiles are grateful to them.

5 Greet also the church that meets at their house. Greet my dear friend Epenetus, who was the first convert to Christ in the province of Asia.

6 Greet Mary, who worked very hard for you.

7 Greet Andronicus and Junias, my relatives who have been in prison with me. They are outstanding among the apostles, and they were in Christ before I was.

Acts 18:24 Meanwhile a Jew named Apollos, a native of Alexandria, came to Ephesus. He was a learned man, with a thorough knowledge of the Scriptures.

25 He had been instructed in the way of the Lord, and he spoke with great fervor and taught about Jesus accurately, though he knew only the baptism of John.

26 He began to speak boldly in the synagogue. When Priscilla and Aquila heard him, they invited him to their home and explained to him the way of God more adequately.

"Do all the good you can, and make as little fuss about it as possible."
—*Charles Dickens*

Free to Serve

Being clothed in Christ frees men and women to use their gifts in ministry.

INTO THE SUBJECT

In some cultures, women are required to cover their bodies, including their faces, when they are in public. Some cultures are so repressive that women are not allowed access to education or a driver's license. How has Christianity affected the role of women?

INTO THE WORD

1. Read Galatians 3:26–28. What condition has led to oneness in Christ?

2. Why do you agree or disagree that Paul's reference to a classless unity in Christ was intended to produce social reform?

3. What prejudice did the apostle James expose in James 2:1–9?

4. Do you believe women should assume leadership roles in church? If so, which leadership roles? If not, why?

5. Find the names of women Paul commended in Romans 16:1–7. What acts of service had they contributed to the cause of Christ?

6. How have Christian women helped you grow spiritually?

7. How did Priscilla and her husband disciple Apollos?

8. Do you believe greater doors of opportunity should open for Christian women who want to serve Christ? Why or why not?

INTO THE WORLD

Make known to non-Christians that there are no gender, social, economic, or racial distinctions in Christ.

WOMEN OF THE BIBLE

```
R W O U Y E A C H K E N O J S
E X N R K A B T M A R T H A E
H N A C A Z E E C W M P O D W
T M Q V U B H R O D L H Y E M
S E V E A R S A E H O S K B H
E F S Z C E H I A B P R H O T
M A I R I M T G U B E H C R U
W L S D E W A U M T H K G A R
E K A P Z R B C O T H S A H S
U W R P R I S C I L L A R H J
T D A U L Y C D R A M A T C H
V S H V L E U E I G C R N Q I
R A R A K J A S K H L I L T C
W S M K L W Y J E R Y O K B S
M B A K I G R L F X R W M U F
```

BATHSHEBA	HAGAR	PHOEBE
DEBORAH	JAEL	PRISCILLA
DORCAS	JUDITH	RACHEL
ELIZABETH	MARTHA	REBEKAH
ESTHER	MARY	RUTH
EVE	MIRIAM	SARAH

INTERACTIVE LEARNING IDEAS

GET THE CLASS INVOLVED
Remember!

Simply put, it is absolutely crucial to hide the Word in our hearts. It can also be hard to do. One of the key passages from today's study is Galatians 3:26–28. These are truly great verses to memorize because they are so rich in truth.

Before class, prepare slips of paper that read "Song," "Poem or Rap," "Memorize," and "Word Scramble." Make at least five of each slip (you will need more if you have a class larger than twenty people.) Put the slips in a container. After everyone is seated, pass the container and have each class member draw a slip. Divide the class into small groups according to the slips they draw.

The small groups will then memorize the Scripture verses by creating a song, poem or rap, just memorizing, or creating a word scramble. (In a word scramble, the group writes each word from the verses on separate slips of paper. Then they "scramble" the slips out of order and try to put the words back in order, using the Bible itself only sparingly. The challenge is to gain familiarity with the verses and then unscramble the words. The more you know the verse, the faster you can unscramble.)

Share the results with the rest of the class. Which way was the easiest to memorize the verses?

TRY THIS ON YOUR OWN
A Rich History

What women have impacted your spiritual life in a positive way? Perhaps they were people who were an intimate part of your life, or perhaps they were people you never met. Maybe they even lived before you were born. Think back over your life and make a quick list of those women and how they made a mark on your life. Were they in formal ministry or part of your life? Were you connected to them through a church or other ministry? Were they family members or neighbors? Were they part of your life for a long time, or was it a shorter, "drive-by" enrichment?

If they are still living, write notes to them to thank them for the roles they played in your spiritual development. Send those notes so they know how God has used them. If they are not living, still write a note to them. Let this be a way to offer thanks to God for their lives and to remember how you saw God through them. Either way, God gets the glory and you get the chance to say thanks.

TAKING IT TO THE STREET
Servants of the Church

In light of the impact of this study, ask your pastor to hold a commissioning service for the women of your class or church. Part of the service could be going back over the points the study brought out. It could include the "laying on of hands" to send these women back into their spheres of influence with a deeper understanding that everything they do is ministry. Take this opportunity to remind them just how important they are in God's eyes, each and every day.

WITH YOUR FAMILY
Train Them Up

If you have daughters, it is important to raise them with a balanced idea of their place in the body of Christ. They need a balanced idea of how God looks at them and what He thinks they are capable of. If you have not done that yet, there is no time like the present to start.

Bring into your conversations examples of the women covered in this study. Tell them about women who have impacted your life and how God used them to draw you to Him. Encourage them that God has a place and a purpose for them, just as He has for all other believers, male or female. As they grow older, consider a blessing party to send them into adulthood, or commission them into their own ministry as it changes and develops through maturity.

No matter how you approach this imparting of God's wisdom regarding women and their place in the kingdom, do it with grace and intention. Giving the girls in your life this gift will potentially place them miles ahead in understanding their true place in the body as compared to many women who lived in previous generations. ◆

God commands His people to respect and care for the elders of society.

LESSON 11

HONORING OUR ELDERS

Exodus 20:12; John 19:25–27; James 1:23–27

KEY VERSE
Honor your father and
your mother, so that you
may live long in the land
the LORD your God is
giving you.
　　　　—Exodus 20:12

BACKGROUND SCRIPTURES
Deuteronomy 6:1–9
　　Parents are to be models
　　for their children.
Matthew 13:55–56; Mark 6:3
　　Jesus' brothers named,
　　sisters not named
Matthew 15:3–9;
Mark 7:9–13
　　Pharisees violated the
　　fifth commandment.
John 7:1–5
　　Jesus' family members
　　were skeptical of Him.
1 Corinthians 15:7
　　Jesus' post-resurrection
　　appearance to His
　　brother James
Ephesians 6:1–2
　　Paul quoted the fifth
　　commandment.

DAILY BIBLE READINGS
Monday:　　Leviticus 19:32;
　　　　　　Proverbs 23:22
Tuesday:　　1 Timothy 5:1–5
Wednesday: 1 John 3:16–20
Thursday:　Ruth 4:14–17
Friday:　　　James 2:14–17
Saturday:　Exodus 20:12;
　　　　　　John 19:25–27;
　　　　　　James 1:23–27
Sunday:　　Psalm 51

WHY THIS MATTERS

Charlotte maligns her parents at every opportunity. Dad was too strict. Mom made her clean house and wash dishes. And they forced her to attend church regularly. So she moved away from home as soon as she could.

Bill will tell you his parents are the best. When he was only five, they led him to Christ, and they gave him a good upbringing. There is nothing he wouldn't do for his mom and dad. Now that they are elderly, he checks in on them every day, runs errands for them, and keeps up their house and property.

This lesson makes it easy to identify which person—Charlotte or Bill—honors Mom and Dad. And it challenges each of us to maintain good parent-child relationships.

BIBLE COMMENTARY
By Wayne E. Caldwell

The Bible passages chosen for this lesson focus on family stewardship. These are only a few of many references that bear upon the topic of our responsibility to our parents and families. The whole of society in every culture has basic mores that direct each generation in its duties. Although these principles may vary slightly, there is a thread of truth that is similar among all peoples.

As an evangelist preaching to new congregations, I often said to families, "Tell me what your family relationships are like at home. Tell me about your spiritual lives at home, and I'll tell you what the family and spiritual life of your church is. The church will rise no higher than what the home lives of its members are." The same is true of the whole community or nation—they will be no better than what the homes are like in those same venues. If children are taught respect and obedience to their parents, to public authorities, and to their elders in the home, they will carry that same attitude into the public schools, the church, and the communities where they live.

Today's study should lead us to remember what God expects of us in our duties to our parents and family.

The Fifth Commandment (Ex. 20:12)

When God led the children of Israel to the Promised Land, He instilled in their minds and hearts the truth that, to live in peace, they would need to respect their leaders and build strong family ties. The primary reason God gave Moses the command **Honor your father and your mother** was that it would honor God, the giver of all life and happiness. "For a considerable time, parents stand as it were in the place of God to their children, and therefore rebellion against their lawful commands has been considered as rebellion against God. This precept therefore prohibits, not only all injurious acts, irreverent and unkind speeches to parents, but enjoins all necessary acts of kindness, filial respect, and obedience. We can scarcely suppose that a man honors his parents who, when they fall weak, blind, or sick, does not exert himself to the uttermost in their support. In such cases God as truly requires the children to provide for their parents as He required the parents to feed, nourish, support, instruct and defend the children when they were in the lowest state of helpless infancy" (*Adam Clarke's Commentary*). The commandment also carried a promise: **so that you may live long in the land the LORD your God is giving you**.

To honor parents means to speak well of them and politely to them. It means to respect and obey them as long as it does not involve disobedience to God. Children are to act in ways that are courteous and generous to their parents. They are to follow the teachings and example set before them, which lay a heavy responsibility on the parents as well (compare Deut. 6:1–9).

The apostle Paul, who was well schooled in Old Testament rabbinic law (compare Acts 5:34; 22:3), wrote to Christians at Ephesus, reminding them of the fifth commandment and its promise. It was quoted as being the first commandment with a promise, which was "that it may go well with you and that you may enjoy long life on the earth" (Eph. 6:1–2). Children are told to obey their parents "in the Lord." They are to obey as long as they are in their parents' care. "Come when they call you, go where they send you, do what they bid you, do not what they forbid you; and this cheerfully and from a principle of love" (*Wesley's Notes on the Bible*, Ex. 20:12).

We conclude that there is a difference between honoring and obeying parents. Adult children do not have to obey or be in subjection to domineering parents. But the responsibility to respect and honor them is for life.

Jesus told the Pharisees that their traditions concerning honor and help for their parents were not according to the teachings of Moses. When they should have helped their parents, they simply said their means were *Corban* (an offering), thus set aside as a gift for God. This was a bold violation of the fifth commandment, and Jesus condemned them for it (compare Matt. 15:3–9; Mark 7:9–13).

Jesus' Care of His Mother (John 19:25–27)

Our Savior was concerned about His mother even while dying on the cross. She was also right where a mother should have been—**near the cross of Jesus stood his mother** (v. 25). She was with Him in the most crucial hours of His life, and He took notice by saying, **Dear woman, here is your son** (v. 26). Likewise to John, **the disciple whom he loved** (v. 26), He said, **Here is your mother** (v. 27).

It is assumed that Joseph was deceased by this time, thus not available to care for Mary. Some Bible readers wonder why Jesus did not ask His half-brothers to care for their mother. There is no evidence that Jesus' half-brothers—James, Joseph, Judas, and Simon (compare Matt. 13:55; Mark 6:3)—were at the cross, though they may have been watching from a distance. It is a matter of record that His family (He also had at least two sisters; compare

---

WHAT DO YOU THINK?
As best you understand it, what is your biblical responsibility to those in your family?

AHA!
Children and adults alike are commanded to honor their parents.

DID YOU KNOW?
The command to honor your parents assumes that the parents are both honoring the covenant with God and teaching their children about Him.

Respect and honor builds families across generations—just as God intended.

WHAT DO YOU THINK?
For what reasons should Christians "keep tight reins" on their tongues?

AHA!
When the church cares for powerless people, such as orphans and widows, we worship in a way that truly pleases God.

DID YOU KNOW?
The prophet Micah was one of many Old Testament prophets who warned that all the right rituals in worship mean nothing if one's life is short of justice, mercy, and humility in action.

Matt. 13:56; Mark 6:3) had a difficult time coming to accept Him as the Messiah (compare John 7:1–5). It may have been only after Jesus' crucifixion and His post-resurrection appearance to His brother (1 Cor. 15:7) that James came to believe in Him.

It is significant that the apostle John was the only one of the Twelve who lived out a natural life, dying in old age perhaps during his exile on the Isle of Patmos. The best extra-biblical information we have is that John stayed with Mary in Jerusalem until her death in A.D. 48. It is also assumed that John had adequate means to care for Mary during this period of fifteen to eighteen years after Jesus' death. Even so, John had some fifty years left to live and minister in other ways, including serving as pastor of the church at Ephesus, prior to his exile.

Listen to What God Says (James 1:23–27)

Listening should not be an end in itself. As important as it is to listen to what God's Word says, it is far more crucial to obey what it commands. **Anyone who listens to the word but does not do what it says is like a man who looks at his face in a mirror and, after looking at himself, goes away and immediately forgets what he looks like** (vv. 23–24). The preaching and hearing of God's Word is a mirror. If believers are "forgetful hearers" (v. 25 KJV), it profits them nothing (compare Heb. 4:2). But if a Christian does not forget **what he has heard . . . he will be blessed in what he does** (James 1:25). The hearing of the gospel gives a new perspective to a Christian's relationship to the law. Release from any enslavement of the law is experienced. It is **the perfect law that gives freedom**.

Jesus warned His hearers when He gave the Sermon on the Mount, making the graphic point about "hearing" his words in His metaphor of the wise and foolish man (Matt. 7:24–27). James, Jesus' half-brother, may have heard one of the disciples relate this truth from the sermon. He learned the meaning well enough to include it here. He continued his essay on listening and doing by stating, **If anyone considers himself religious and yet does not keep a tight rein on his tongue, he deceives himself and his religion is worthless** (James 1:26). A large part of what the mirror of God's Word reveals is that what a person says is of little importance unless it takes others and their needs into account.

Religion that God our Father accepts as pure and faultless is this: to look after orphans and widows in their distress and to keep oneself from being polluted by the world (v. 27). **The perfect law that gives freedom** (v. 25) will never be experienced unless it produces deeds of service, especially on behalf of the most needy. Orphans and widows in the first century as well as in most cultures, had, and still usually have, little means of economic support. When the church cares for these powerless people, it puts God's Word into practice. When there is no hope of receiving something in return, believers enjoy what it means to serve others. Religion that is **pure and faultless** (v. 27) ushers in the relief of the distressed, taking loving care and oversight of their needs.

The application of a rabbinic observation is apropos here: "There are four kinds of men who visit the synagogues: (1) He who enters but does not work; (2) He who works but does not enter; (3) He who enters and works; (4) He who neither enters nor works. The first two are indifferent characters; the third is the righteous man; the fourth is wholly evil" (*Adam Clarke's Commentary*, James 1:25). The believer who obeys the commandment with love, joy, and delight finds true liberty. Parents and the whole family will experience continual blessedness and long life according to God's promise. ✦

WHAT ABOUT YOU?

What are some examples of Christian love in families that inspire you to greater personal action on behalf of your family members? What can you do this week to put that inspiration into action?

PRAYER

Father God, thank You for the family and friends You have given me. Help me to be an example of faith in action to the people You have given me to love.

INTERACTIVE LEARNING IDEAS

GET THE CLASS INVOLVED
Show Me

Divide your class into two groups. Tell the groups they will need to act out situations as you call them out. It's fine to limit their "acting" to dialogue alone and with no movement. One group will act out a positive or healthy response to the situations you call out, and the other will show an unhealthy response. Here are some situation ideas. Feel free to adapt these:

- Small children want something, but the parent is busy.
- Teens are headed out the door, but their homework isn't finished.
- Parents are having a disagreement over money, and their children walk into the room.
- Parents are talking about aging in-laws and their need to have living assistance. The in-laws are not well liked.

Read a situation. Point to one group and say, "Positive." (That makes the other "Negative," of course.) Allow the groups to have a minute to develop their dialogue. Then in turn, ask the groups to perform their dialogues.

Ask: "Do you see your family in any of these scenarios? Positive or negative? If we are honest, we all have room for improvement! Today's study will give us a refresher course on godly family relationships."

TRY THIS ON YOUR OWN
Pray the Scripture

This week start (or continue) the wonderful privilege of praying Scripture over your family. There is power in God's Word. It is alive and active. When you pray Scripture over your family, you'll see God's power come to bear in their lives. It will change them—and you.

The easiest way to get started is to choose one person to pray for each day. Then decide which verses you want to pray for that person. Read the verses with that person in mind. Insert names. Ask God to do the good things mentioned in the verses for that person. Pray the blessings of the Word into his or her life.

Here are some passages to get you started:

- Psalm 127
- Psalm 128
- Ephesians 3:14–21
- Philippians 1:3–11

TAKING IT TO THE STREET
Share the Journey

No matter where we are in life's journey, it's better when we share the ride. You may be just starting out as an adult, or perhaps you are retired. You may have young children at home or be an empty-nester. Maybe you are looking forward to your first child or grandchild. Wherever you find yourself along the way, the body of Christ can be a help to you on the journey.

Agree as a class to try this exercise together. You don't need to keep it just to people within the class, but agree to all try doing this experience.

The important thing about this exercise is to be intentional. Pick someone at a different place in life than you and see if they would like to share the road with you. Perhaps you can offer to watch their children so they can get some much-needed time alone. Maybe they can cut your grass. Perhaps there is someone who could use some cooking lessons, and you could use computer tutoring. Get the idea? After a few months of trying this, most people wonder how they ever got along without people to share their journey.

WITH YOUR FAMILY
Mealtime Fun

Prepare a bunch of brightly colored index cards with various activities to do together at mealtimes. Keep the cards on the dining room table so they will be available whenever you sit down to a meal together. Choose only one card per meal. Involve the kids in coming up with ideas for the cards. Here are some ideas to get you started:

- Items to pray about together.
- Things you want to discuss together—wacky or not.
- Tell a story of a funny thing you or one of the kids did when younger.
- Tell a progressive story where one person starts and then each person adds a sentence or two. Continue around the table, adding whatever comes to mind.
- Tell about your favorite thing that happened today.
- Tell when you saw God working around you or in you today.
- Tell old family stories.
- Answer goofy questions like, "If you were an animal, what would you be?" ◆

EXODUS 20:12; JOHN 19:25–27; JAMES 1:23–27

Exodus 20:12 "Honor your father and your mother, so that you may live long in the land the LORD your God is giving you.

John 19:25 Near the cross of Jesus stood his mother, his mother's sister, Mary the wife of Clopas, and Mary Magdalene.
26 When Jesus saw his mother there, and the disciple whom he loved standing nearby, he said to his mother, "Dear woman, here is your son,"
27 and to the disciple, "Here is your mother." From that time on, this disciple took her into his home.

James 1:23 Anyone who listens to the word but does not do what it says is like a man who looks at his face in a mirror
24 and, after looking at himself, goes away and immediately forgets what he looks like.
25 But the man who looks intently into the perfect law that gives freedom, and continues to do this, not forgetting what he has heard, but doing it—he will be blessed in what he does.
26 If anyone considers himself religious and yet does not keep a tight rein on his tongue, he deceives himself and his religion is worthless.
27 Religion that God our Father accepts as pure and faultless is this: to look after orphans and widows in their distress and to keep oneself from being polluted by the world.

"Look after orphans and widows . . ."
—James 1:27

Honoring Our Elders

God commands His people to respect and care for the elders of society.

INTO THE SUBJECT

As a show of respect for the elderly, the Japanese people celebrate Respect for the Aged Day each September 15. How can we show respect for our elders? Does God honor those who honor their elders?

INTO THE WORD

1. What incentive for honoring one's parents do you find in Exodus 20:12?

2. Do you believe this incentive is an ironclad promise or a general principle? Explain your answer.

3. What do you think it means to honor one's parents?

4. Do you think American culture generally fails to honor its elders? Explain your answer.

5. How did Jesus fulfill the fifth commandment as He was dying on the cross?

6. Do you agree that Jesus paid the apostle John a high compliment by asking him to care for His mother Mary? Why or why not?

7. What responsibility does James 1:27 assign on behalf of widows? How might a church today fulfill this responsibility?

INTO THE WORLD

Do what you can to honor at least one elderly person this week! Perhaps a personal visit to deliver flowers or goodies and to pray would be a good way to honor him or her.

YOUR ELDERS

Write down the names of five people in your life who are over the age of seventy. Include your parents, no matter what their age.

1. _____

_____

_____

2. _____

_____

_____

3. _____

_____

_____

4. _____

_____

_____

5. _____

_____

_____

Consider how you can best honor them. Would they cherish a handwritten letter, a personal visit, a lunch outing? Or maybe they simply want to be heard—to have their opinions matter and their experience respected. Beside their names, jot down what you will do for each of them over the next couple of months to show them respect, and be sure to follow through.

God wants you to discover His love, principles, and purpose.

GOD'S PLAN FOR YOUR LIFE: GROWTH
Ephesians 5:1–20

WHY THIS MATTERS

Seasonal Affective Disorder (SAD) sufferers lack adequate exposure to sunlight. As a result, they usually suffer depression, but other negative health effects may occur. Some medical sources claim SAD may also lead to some forms of cancer, osteoporosis, and even schizophrenia.

Our unsaved contemporaries are engulfed in a different kind of darkness—spiritual darkness—and they suffer dreadful consequences. Their minds and hearts are blind to the truth; they cannot walk uprightly in God's sight; their wills are enslaved to Satan, the Prince of Darkness. They desperately need to be exposed to the light.

This lesson summons believers to walk as children of light, and it explains what it means to do so.

BIBLE COMMENTARY

By Donna E. Brayerton

The letter to the Ephesians outlines our position and responsibility as believers. The book was written by the apostle Paul while he was imprisoned in Rome. Paul had a special bond with the church at Ephesus. He had planted that church on his way home to Jerusalem (Acts 18:19–21) with a promise that he would return to them. One year later, Paul did return and remained with them for three years (Acts 20:31). This church became a strong Christian community under his leadership. Upon his departure, he commended them to the care of the elders of the church (Acts 20:17) and later appointed his beloved son in the faith, Timothy, to minister there (1 Tim. 1:3).

The Ephesian church was situated in a worldly setting. Ephesus was a major seaport as well as a main stop in the land route from Rome to the East. The Christian church's spiritual competition lay with the Temple of Artemis (or Diana), the Romans' fertility goddess. Her temple was considered one of the seven wonders of the ancient world and attracted many tourists. In addition to the temple, Ephesus had an amphitheater that was able to seat twenty-five thousand spectators and a stadium where sporting events were held. The teachings of Christianity posed a major threat to all three of these mainstays of the Ephesian culture. And the worldliness of the city posed a threat to young believers not yet rooted in the teachings of Christ.

The Ephesians lived in a societal structure much like what we experience. Today the spiritual philosophies of Eastern religions and the New Age Movement, as well as the occult, vie for the attention and commitment of people everywhere. Those peddling these new spiritualities present them as contemporary answers to traditional Christianity. They also present Christians as closed-minded and intolerant bigots.

KEY VERSE

For you were once darkness, but now you are light in the Lord. Live as children of light.
—Ephesians 5:8

BACKGROUND SCRIPTURES

Acts 18:19–21
Paul planted the church in Ephesus.

Acts 20:31
Paul remained with the Ephesians for three years.

Acts 20:17
Paul left the Ephesian church in the hands of elders.

1 Timothy 1:3
Timothy was appointed pastor at Ephesus.

Leviticus 7:16
Rules regarding the free-will offering

Leviticus 6:8–13
Mention of offerings as a sweet fragrance

James 3:2–12
Admonition to keep control of one's words

1 Corinthians 15:32
Warning against living licentiously

DAILY BIBLE READINGS

Monday: 1 John 1:5–10
Tuesday: John 8:12; 12:44–46
Wednesday: Philippians 2:14–18
Thursday: Isaiah 9:1–7
Friday: Ephesians 4:17–24
Saturday: Ephesians 5:1–20
Sunday: Psalm 52

As we look at society today, we find that most people are caught up in the trappings of popular culture—vulgar movies, irreverent music, violent sporting events, and so forth. This is really not much different from what life was in Ephesus during the first century.

Paul knew that the trappings of the Ephesian culture could become major hindrances to the young believers in Ephesus, so he set out to remind them of who they were in Christ and how they were to live. The fifth chapter of this letter is in the middle of Paul's instructions on how to practically live out the Christian faith in a world set against everything we believe in.

Live a Life of Love (Eph. 5:1–2)

It is a natural thing for children to want to imitate their parents. We all have certain characteristics and mannerisms that we picked up from our parents. We learn these idiosyncrasies by observing how our parents act and react to life. Because of this, Paul implored believers to **be imitators of God** (v. 1). Since God is our heavenly Father, we should be cultivating a deep and intimate relationship with Him. As we do this, we will begin to emulate all that He is. The better we understand God's ways, the more Christian conduct will become an intrinsic part of who we are rather than something we constantly have to think about.

At the core of God's nature is love. Everything He does comes from love. Therefore, it is not surprising that Paul encouraged us to **live a life of love** (v. 2). Love in the world we live in is much different than God's love. Generally man's love is conditional—"If you do what I want, then I will love you." But God's love is not provisional; it does not depend on us but is solely founded in His nature. Man's love tends to be selfish—"I love you because you meet my needs." God's love is completely unselfish and not dependent on what He receives back from us.

Paul tells us that **Christ loved us and gave himself up for us as a fragrant offering and sacrifice to God** (v. 2). The term *fragrant offering* comes from the Old Testament laws. An offering was a voluntary gift to God just because the bearer wanted to show his appreciation (Lev. 7:16). When the offering was given with a proper attitude, it was spoken of as a "sweet fragrance" or "soothing aroma" to God, meaning that it was an acceptable offering. Likewise, Christ's sacrifice on the cross was a gift freely given and wholly acceptable to God. Truly His life was a fragrant offering because Christ offered himself out of His love for the Father as well as His love for us.

The term *sacrifice* denotes the giving of an animal as an offering of total consecration. The burnt offering was given and then totally burned (Lev. 6:8–13) denoting total submission and commitment of the bearer to God. Christ was our burnt offering or sacrifice. He completely submitted to the Father's will and gave himself as our substitution on the cross.

Keep Yourself Pure (Eph. 5:3–7)

Because of the influence of the Temple of Artemis, Paul reminded the believers to keep themselves pure from **sexual immorality** (v. 3). Activities in this temple were often sexual in nature. In direct opposition to this, the

WHAT DO YOU THINK?
What is the most difficult challenge you face from that part of the culture that stands against Christianity? Why?

AHA!
As Christians, we need to imitate God.

DID YOU KNOW?
Even in the Old Testament, the mere act of sacrifice wasn't enough to make things right with God. The attitude and life of the worshiper had to have integrity, too.

Christians were to keep themselves pure from sexual sin. Although we do not have the Temple of Artemis to contend with, we have the philosophy of the world that condones premarital sex, adultery, and other perverted sexual activities. Pornography is a plague that infects Christians as well as non-Christians. The call for sexual purity must be sounded loudly in this age of sexual promiscuity.

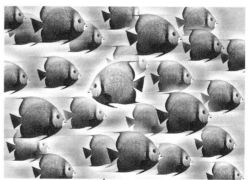

Sometimes living a Christian life in the culture around us feels like swimming upstream!

Not only are we to keep ourselves pure from sexual immorality, but **any kind of impurity**, especially **greed** (v. 3). The lust for money and possessions is running rampant today. Even Christians are getting caught up in the pursuit of money. Every day we are bombarded with get-rich-quick schemes, easy investments, lotteries, and the like. The enticement of owning the newest car, technological gadget, or prestigious home presents itself to us regularly. When we get caught up in this overwhelming need for things, we find ourselves being owned by these items rather than owning them. Our focus becomes how to get more instead of sacrificially living for the Lord.

Language is also an issue for the Christian. We are instructed to remove **obscenity, foolish talk or coarse joking** (v. 4) from our vocabulary. Rather, we are to fill our mouths with **thanksgiving** (v. 4). Perhaps we are not prone to curse or to tell dirty jokes, but how often do we find ourselves involved in foolish talk? The philosophies of the world so easily rub off on us. We find ourselves chiming in with negative talk, anti-Christian ideas, and "me first" attitudes. Keeping control of our tongues is imperative if we are to live in obedience to Christ (James 3:2–12).

WHAT DO YOU THINK?
How would you explain Christian purity to a teenager who asked you about it?

Paul clearly stated that **no immoral, impure or greedy person . . . has any inheritance in the kingdom of Christ and of God** (Eph. 5:5). This refers to those who refuse to repent from evil deeds. Since the unrepentant have no part in the kingdom, it is imperative that we regularly check our hearts to see if we are harboring any impure thoughts, attitudes, or deeds and quickly repent from them. Repenting means much more than just being sorry for our sin. Repentance is literally changing our minds. It is agreeing with God that we have sinned and desiring to stop involving ourselves in these impure thoughts or activities. The Lord has promised to cleanse us from all unrighteousness, if we will confess our sins and genuinely repent of them (1 John 1:9).

AHA!
Christians are called to be *perpetually* filled with the Holy Spirit.

We are given a warning to **let no one deceive** us **with empty words** (Eph. 5:6). The Ephesians were being subjected to those who were protesting that the Christian lifestyle was too demanding and that people should be able to live however they pleased (1 Cor. 15:32). Today we are also being exposed to people who challenge our strict standards of living. Paul warned believers to **not be partners with them** (Eph. 5:7). In other words, we must not allow ourselves to get caught up in anti-Christian philosophies and behavior. We must be careful to keep ourselves pure from all the influences of the world in which we live.

DID YOU KNOW?
As used in the New Testament, truth did not just mean something to be known; it meant something to be done.

Live as Children of Light (Eph. 5:8–16)

Everyone recognizes the dramatic contrast between light and darkness. We are reminded that **now** we **are light in the Lord** (v. 8). As light dispels all darkness, so righteous living dispels the darkness of sin. We are not only to call ourselves Christians, but we are to bear fruit that attests to this fact (v. 9). We are instructed to **find out what pleases the Lord** (v. 10). This means we need to concentrate on learning what the Bible teaches on how we are to live. It means we are to pursue a relationship with the Lord through quiet time and prayer. It means that whatever we learn we are to apply to our lives in order to please God in every respect.

Be very careful, then, how you live—not as unwise but as wise (v. 15). The words *very careful* literally mean "with exactness." We need to strive to live exactly as Christ would have us live. The King James Version says we are to live circumspectly, which means "looking around." We will not fall into the traps placed by our Enemy, the Devil, if we keep our eyes open and continually look around and recognize them. We are to make **the most of every opportunity, because the days are evil** (v. 16). Every day presents itself with opportunities to either obey Christ or deny Him. Moment by moment we are to choose to live as children of light rather than participate in the deeds of darkness.

Be Filled with the Holy Spirit (Eph. 5:17–20)

Finally, we are admonished, **Do not get drunk on wine . . . Instead, be filled with the Spirit** (v. 18). Drinking too much alcohol leads to debauchery and being out of control. The Roman god of wine, Dionysus, demanded drunkenness in order to control his subjects. This often resulted in immoral sexual acts. Rather than giving control to a foreign substance such as alcohol or drugs, we are commanded to yield ourselves to God by being filled with the Holy Spirit, allowing Him full control of our lives.

The grammar here indicates a continual filling with God's Spirit—we are to go on being filled. This is not a once-and-done encounter but something we are to perpetually pursue. Although each one of us must experience a crisis event where we totally submit our lives to Christ, we know the memory of these experiences wanes. We must keep fresh in our hearts our commitment to walk in the Spirit.

The Christian lifestyle we have discussed cannot be consistently lived out without the power of the Holy Spirit. We cannot do this on our own. We need God's power to change us and live through us. If we try to do this without God's empowerment, we find ourselves living in futility. If we cooperate with the Spirit of God, we will have a victorious Christian life.

Living a Spirit-filled life cultivates an everyday attitude of worship. As we are filled with the Holy Spirit, we are to **speak to one another with psalms, hymns and spiritual songs. Sing and make music in your heart to the Lord, always giving thanks to God the Father for everything** (vv. 19–20). As we worship God completely by yielding everything to Him, we will encourage one another and cultivate an ever-deepening appreciation for the Lord of our lives. ◆

WHAT ABOUT YOU?
How can you keep God in full control of your life this week?

PRAYER
Holy God, help me empty myself of the things that draw me away from You; fill me with Your Holy Spirit.

EPHESIANS 5:1–20

1 Be imitators of God, therefore, as dearly loved children

2 and live a life of love, just as Christ loved us and gave himself up for us as a fragrant offering and sacrifice to God.

3 But among you there must not be even a hint of sexual immorality, or of any kind of impurity, or of greed, because these are improper for God's holy people.

4 Nor should there be obscenity, foolish talk or coarse joking, which are out of place, but rather thanksgiving.

5 For of this you can be sure: No immoral, impure or greedy person—such a man is an idolater—has any inheritance in the kingdom of Christ and of God.

6 Let no one deceive you with empty words, for because of such things God's wrath comes on those who are disobedient.

7 Therefore do not be partners with them.

8 For you were once darkness, but now you are light in the Lord. Live as children of light

9 (for the fruit of the light consists in all goodness, righteousness and truth)

10 and find out what pleases the Lord.

11 Have nothing to do with the fruitless deeds of darkness, but rather expose them.

12 For it is shameful even to mention what the disobedient do in secret.

13 But everything exposed by the light becomes visible,

14 for it is light that makes everything visible. This is why it is said: "Wake up, O sleeper, rise from the dead, and Christ will shine on you."

15 Be very careful, then, how you live—not as unwise but as wise,

16 making the most of every opportunity, because the days are evil.

17 Therefore do not be foolish, but understand what the Lord's will is.

18 Do not get drunk on wine, which leads to debauchery. Instead, be filled with the Spirit.

19 Speak to one another with psalms, hymns and spiritual songs. Sing and make music in your heart to the Lord,

20 always giving thanks to God the Father for everything, in the name of our Lord Jesus Christ.

God's Plan for Your Life: Growth

God wants you to discover
His love, principles, and purpose.

INTO THE SUBJECT

Dandelions and other weeds seem to grow without any help from humans; but grass, flowers, and vegetables don't grow well without tender, loving care. Christians, too, need to grow well, but what does that growth involve?

INTO THE WORD

1. What signs of spiritual growth do you see in Ephesians 5:1–11?

2. Does it matter what kind of language Christians use? Why or why not?

3. Why do you agree or disagree that bad language in the media is creeping into Christians' speech patterns?

4. How would you respond to the claim that it's okay to tell a slightly naughty joke?

5. How can you shine your light effectively where you spend most of your daytime hours (at school, work, or home)?

6. What helps you most to know what God's will is?

7. What spiritual exercises flow from the lives of those who are filled with the Spirit?

8. Would you agree that a complaining, negative, ungrateful Christian is not filled with the Spirit? Why?

INTO THE WORLD

Live in such a way that non-Christians will notice that your words and actions are pure. When they ask for a reason, tell them Jesus is the reason.

RENEWING YOUR VOWS

Any living thing that is not growing and thriving is declining. The same is true of your spiritual life. Are you depending on the commitment you made to God many years ago, or are you actively engaging Him so that your relationship with Him will deepen?

_____

_____

_____

_____

Renew your commitment to the Lord today. Write a letter to Him in the space below, telling Him what you love about Him and why you want to be close to Him.

_____

_____

_____

_____

INTERACTIVE LEARNING IDEAS

GET THE CLASS INVOLVED
Let There Be

Before class, gather as many flashlights as you can lay your hands on. You might consider calling some of your class members and asking them to bring all they have as well. The more people who have access to a flashlight for this exercise, the more impact it will have. Make sure you have dark window coverings for this exercise as well.

When your class has arrived, hand out the flashlights. Give instructions that once the lights are out you will turn on your flashlight, and then ask the class to turn theirs on one at a time, going around the room. Before you turn yours on, however, allow the class to sit in the dark for a few seconds. Let the darkness have its effect on them.

When all the flashlights have been turned on, read the Scripture passage from Ephesians, emphasizing the part about being light. Say something like, "This exercise was done to show you the real contrast between light and darkness. We all know it, but sometimes it helps to experience it in a place that is unexpected. In this study, we'll look at what it means to live as if we are not only *in* the light, but we are a part of it."

TRY THIS ON YOUR OWN
One Thing

When we read verses in the Bible about right living, we can become overwhelmed at all the things we must do to be godly. We're called to keep a rein on our tongues, care for widows and orphans, honor our parents, "do" the Word, and so forth. There's a lot in there! The verses from this study alone include many things we are told to do. However, as the Chinese proverb says, "A journey of a thousand miles begins with a single step."

So do you know any widows? Orphans? Are your parents still living so you can honor them? Is there a word you need to cut from your vocabulary to honor your spouse or parent? Pick one thing and do it. Your journey toward holy living starts with one step—doing one thing. Then tomorrow you can do something else. With "a thousand miles" ahead, it's important to keep moving.

TAKING IT TO THE STREET
Pack a Lunch

Most communities have a homeless population. As a class, determine to make the most of the opportunity to serve them in perhaps an unexpected way.

Divide the items needed to pack simple lunches among class members so everyone brings something. Choose a Saturday morning and meet at the church. Put together lunches and bag them up. Have everyone take three or four lunches and then head to the streets. If you know of certain corners where some homeless people hang out, go there and offer them a lunch bag. Or head to a park where they may gather. The point is to give away your lunches. You may even have the chance to pray for some of the people you meet, since you want to "make the most of every opportunity."

Have your class meet back at the church to swap stories from the day. Order pizza—you'll be too busy talking to make lunch!

WITH YOUR FAMILY
Family Chapel

In earlier times, it was very common for homes to have some type of chapel or a space set aside to pray or worship God. We don't see many such rooms anymore. But it might be a wonderful thing to revive that tradition with a modern twist.

Create a prayer garden or an indoor prayer place together as a family. It does not need to be elaborate. Even a space on a bookshelf will do. Let the kids help you gather items for your prayer place such as a candle, Bible, favorite picture with a spiritual connotation, and prayer cards. You could research plants for a prayer garden that have spiritual overtones, such as Bleeding Heart of Jesus or a small dogwood tree. Place a bench or pillows in your garden or by your indoor space so individuals or your whole family can go there to pray.

Have a short ceremony to dedicate your prayer space to the Lord and ask Him to use it to draw your family closer to himself. ◆

LESSON 13

GOD'S PLAN FOR MARRIAGE

Genesis 2:18–25

KEY VERSE

Marriage should be honored by all, and the marriage bed kept pure, for God will judge the adulterer and all the sexually immoral.

—Hebrews 13:4

BACKGROUND SCRIPTURES

Genesis 1:26–31
   The first and more general account of creation
Matthew 19:4–12;
Mark 10:1–12
   Jesus quotes from Genesis 2:24 and teaches on marriage and divorce.

DAILY BIBLE READINGS

Monday: Hebrews 13:1–5
Tuesday: Ecclesiastes 4:9–12
Wednesday: Ephesians 5:22–33
Thursday: Philippians 2:1–5
Friday: Malachi 2:13–16
Saturday: Genesis 2:18–25
Sunday: Psalm 53

WHY THIS MATTERS

No matter how many countries and states legalize homosexual marriage, only a marriage between a man and a woman is valid in God's eyes. After creating the first man, God created Eve—a woman—to be Adam's wife. She would be his helper—his counterpart—to be near his side and heart.

In Christian marriage, a couple dedicated to each other and the Lord presents a clear picture of the love that exists between Christ and His church. The husband relates to his wife with a self-sacrificing love. In turn, the wife honors her husband as the head of their home.

This lesson reflects on history's first marriage and inspires us to perceive marriage as a holy institution.

BIBLE COMMENTARY

By Ronald C. McClung

The story of creation is complete in Genesis 1 in the sense that the writer of Genesis covered all six days of God's creative acts. However, he elaborated on the story of man's creation in chapter 2, giving us considerably more detail. These chapters do not represent two separate accounts of creation, as some have suggested. Instead the writer painted the picture in broad strokes in chapter 1, and then in chapter 2, he filled in the colorful details of God's masterpiece: the creation of man and woman.

As the story expanded into chapter 3, the writer dealt with Adam and Eve's moral problems and their failure to be obedient to God. Their ability to reproduce and the consequent behavior of their offspring come to light in chapter 4.

In the immediate context, the early part of chapter 2, God hallowed the seventh day as a day of rest. The writer then described man's first home, the garden of Eden. It was an ideal place, a perfect environment for the first human family. God gave Adam the responsibility to care for the garden, and then He set some parameters. There were many things Adam could do and one thing he must not: eat from the Tree of Knowledge of Good and Evil. The instructions included a warning—if man ate of the forbidden tree, in that day he would die. Our immediate attention will focus on the specific creation of Adam and Eve and the fact that they were literally "made for each other."

The Loneliness of Man (Gen. 2:18–20)

After creating man, **the LORD God** made a startling statement, unlike any made in Scripture up to this point: **It is not good** (v. 18). Every other aspect of creation up to this point had been declared good. In fact, the ultimate evaluation of all He had made was very good (1:31). However, the fact that **the man** was alone was **not good**. Therefore God announced that He would **make a helper suitable for him** (2:18).

Some Bible teachers have interpreted the word *helper* to mean the woman would be subordinate to man and somehow inferior to him. However, the Hebrew word for *helper* is used twenty-one times in the Old Testament, and fifteen of those usages refer to God helping man in some way. So the term *helper* could not possibly imply inferiority in any sense. It rather refers to a person who would be Adam's counterpart. A helper suitable for Adam would be one who corresponded to him, and would be appropriate to serve alongside him.

The writer emphasized that **the LORD God had formed out of the ground all the beasts . . . and all the birds** (v. 19). They had this in common with Adam, since "the LORD God formed the man from the dust of the ground" (2:7). Yet in an act that would show the keen intelligence of Adam, God **brought** all the animals **to the man to see what he would name them** (3:19). Adam Clarke said one of the reasons God gave Adam this task was "to show him with what comprehensive powers of mind his Maker had endued him." Here is an obvious indication of man's superiority over the animals. God did not ask a chimpanzee, ape, or eagle to name the animals or to decide what to call the man creature. Instead that became Adam's responsibility. We are not told how long this process took and how exhausted Adam was when he finished, but **whatever** he **called each living creature, that was its name**. He doubtless studied each animal, noting its special qualities and features. Then in his superior intelligence, he found an appropriate name for every creature God brought before him.

Yet when it was all done, **for Adam no suitable helper was found** (v. 20). In spite of their common origin in the dust of the earth and in spite of Adam's acquaintance with all the animals, having named each one, he found no creature that was comparable to him. God's stated purpose for Adam was to "be fruitful and increase in number" (1:28). However, he could not "be fruitful and increase," for he had no mate.

It would have been obvious to Adam in the naming process that all the other creatures had mates. So Adam was faced with two problems: (1) he could not reproduce himself without a mate; and (2) seeing himself as different from the animals, he must have had a deep sense of isolation. How lonely he must have felt. He was unique; there was no other creature like him. Perfect in every other way, he must have been nearly overwhelmed by the awareness of how incomplete he was without a mate.

The Creation of Woman (Gen. 2:21–23)

Whether Adam was exhausted after the tremendous task of naming all the animals or God simply wanted him to sleep during the "surgery" required to create Eve, **the LORD God caused the man to fall into a deep sleep** (v. 21).

While Adam **was sleeping**, the Lord **took one of the man's ribs and closed up the place with flesh** (v. 21). With the **rib** He removed from Adam, **the LORD God made a woman** (v. 22). It would appear that in the case of the animals, the male and female of each species were made simultaneously. But this is not the case in the creation of Adam and Eve. They were created separately.

Partners are often helpers who help us get to the next level—especially in marriage.

Wilbur Williams pointed out that some early Jewish rabbis observed that while God "formed" Adam from the dust of the ground, He "built" Eve. When the writer of Genesis said that the LORD **God made a woman** (v. 22), he used the same word for *made* that he used in describing Noah's building of an altar (8:20) and the building of the tower of Babel (11:4). These are only two of the many examples where this same word is rendered *build* or *built*.

Williams also pointed out that there is a similar word in the Hebrew that means "understanding" and "intuition," causing some rabbis to observe that God gave all women, beginning with Eve, greater intuition than men.

When God made Eve, He used a totally different procedure. The animals were "formed out of the ground" (v. 19) and Adam was "formed from the dust of the ground" (2:7), yet Eve was "built" from **one of the man's ribs** (3:21). When Adam awoke and God **brought her to** him (v. 22), he recognized her as "of the same nature, the same identical flesh and blood, and of the same constitution" as himself, Clarke observed.

Some scholars believe that a literal, biological rib is not intended in the creation of the woman from Adam. They say the Hebrew word for *rib* is used throughout the Old Testament to indicate "side." For instance, this is its meaning in the case of the ark of the covenant (Ex. 25:12), where God instructed Moses to "cast four gold rings for it and fasten them to its four feet, with two rings on one side and two rings on the other." When God gave instructions about the building of the tabernacle (Ex. 26:20), He declared, "For the other side, the north side of the tabernacle, make twenty frames." In each case, the word used for *side* is the same as the word for *rib* in Genesis 2:21. Perhaps the writer was saying that God used a "side" or an "aspect" of Adam's personality.

Whether it was an actual rib or an aspect of Adam's personality, God certainly intended for Eve to be alongside Adam. She was his counterpart, one who corresponded to him and was comparable to him.

For those who prefer the literal rib, Matthew Henry's observation is significant: "Not made out of his head to top him, not out of his feet to be trampled upon by him, but out of his side to be equal with him, under his arm to be protected, and near his heart to be beloved."

When God brought the woman to Adam, the man said, **This is now bone of my bones and flesh of my flesh; she shall be called "woman," for she was taken out of man** (3:23). The Hebrew words for man and woman are just as similar to each other as our English words are. Adam recognized that she was not like the animals, but was like him. She was on his level.

Stuart Briscoe observes that the expression **This is now** (v. 23) is an exclamation of great joy. It could be translated, "At last!" Or perhaps, "Wow! Look at that!" Adam was surely delighted that now he had a mate, one similar to himself, yet uniquely and wonderfully different.

The Partnership of Man and Woman (Gen. 2:24–25)

Scholars are not sure who uttered the words in verse 24, whether it was God, Adam, or the writer of Genesis. The significant thing is what the statement emphasizes, which is that **a man will leave his father and mother and be united to his wife, and they will become one flesh** (v. 24). The statement indicates it is **for this reason**, which leads us to ask, "For what reason?" The obvious answer seems to be Adam's observation in verse 23: Eve was "bone of [his] bones and flesh of [his] flesh." They were utterly and inalterably linked to each other. Because of this fact, the man must now give his wife the priority he once gave to his parents. Of course, neither Adam nor Eve had earthly parents so this statement is obviously meant to be a principle established to guide future generations in their family behavior.

They were to **become one flesh** (v. 24), which would certainly refer to sexual intimacy, a physical oneness, but it also implies a spiritual oneness as well. Briscoe points out that those who insist on following this one-flesh relationship, intended only for husband and wife, seem old-fashioned to those who prefer freedom in their sexual expression. He says those who prefer "sexual emancipation" have "high-sounding but low-living ideals." To be sure, those who treat sex casually, even recreationally, are missing God's intention. He meant for sex to unite a man and a woman in an intimate relationship that expresses far more than a physical union.

The husband and wife are to **be united** (v. 24). Stronger words to indicate this bond would be to cleave, cling, or stick to one another. Jesus quoted this verse in Matthew 19:5 and obviously intended to emphasize the permanence of the marriage relationship. As Dr. Lee Haines points out, "The relationship of husband and wife is the strongest, the most indissoluble of all human relationships."

The writer concluded that **the man and his wife were both naked, and they felt no shame** (v. 25). Clarke observed that since sin had not yet entered the world and no part of the human body had ever been used for any improper purpose, there was no reason to be ashamed.

While they were physically without clothes, the statement may also be symbolic in that they were open with each other. They had no secrets, no reservations, nothing to hide. ✦

INTERACTIVE LEARNING IDEAS

GET THE CLASS INVOLVED
Cross Reference

Divide the class into small groups. Referring to the background Scripture, have each group look up a verse. Instruct the groups to read the verses out loud to each other, and then come up with a one-to-three-word summary of the most important point for each verse.

Have the groups share their Scripture and summaries with the rest of the class. If you have time, pursue one or more of these discussion questions:

- What common threads, if any, are there in these Scripture passages?
- How does the word *helper* compare in these passages from the Bible?
- Based on these verses, what do you think God wants us to understand about His view of a helper?
- Who in your life fits the description of "helper" as explained in this lesson?
- What might change in a family if its members applied the role of "helper" to themselves and each other?

TRY THIS ON YOUR OWN
Neighborhood Prayer Walk for Marriages

This week take the time to leave the roof of your home behind, and enjoy a special time of prayer with the Lord under the "roof" He made. Walk through your neighborhood. Pray for the people in each house you pass, whether or not you have any idea of who they are or what their lives are like. You don't have to stop and pray in front of each house or apartment. This exercise is probably better suited for an extended "pray as you go" experience. Here are some things you might pray:

- That the marriage may be strengthened or renewed.
- That they may know real unity in their marriage.
- That they would understand real partnership within the marriage.
- That they would experience a real "wow" moment with each other like Adam did when he met Eve.
- That their children would be blessings and not just burdens to them.
- That their marriage would harbor no secrets and no reservations.
- That their relationship would bring them joy and pass life on to those around them.

TAKING IT TO THE STREET
Marriage Is What Brings Us Here Today

Consider hosting a marriage seminar at your church. This can be a one-day event or a study that continues for several weeks. A marriage seminar can be a great outreach tool, and it can also serve to strengthen the marriages in your church.

There are several good studies available to use. If you prefer, you could bring in a speaker or teacher for the event. You'll want to make sure you provide free child care to make it feasible for parents of young children to attend. Some topics you might want to cover include:

- Personality types
- Money management
- Conflict resolution
- Blended families
- Date nights
- Extended families
- Children
- Having fun together

WITH YOUR FAMILY
Abba's Helper

From a very young age, we have a concept of what it means to be a helper. Being a helper brought us real joy and a sense of accomplishment. Even as children, we understood the importance of being helpers.

Talk with your children about the concepts that were covered in this study. Tell them about God being a helper to us. Ask your children:

- What do you think God wanted Eve to be for Adam?
- Why was it important for Adam to get an "Eve" even after all the animals God made for him?
- How do you think God might want to help you?
- If God is a helper, it must be pretty important to be one. Who can you help?
- In this family, how can we be helpers to each other? ◆

GENESIS 2:18–25

18 The LORD God said, "It is not good for the man to be alone. I will make a helper suitable for him."

19 Now the LORD God had formed out of the ground all the beasts of the field and all the birds of the air. He brought them to the man to see what he would name them; and whatever the man called each living creature, that was its name.

20 So the man gave names to all the livestock, the birds of the air and all the beasts of the field. But for Adam no suitable helper was found.

21 So the LORD God caused the man to fall into a deep sleep; and while he was sleeping, he took one of the man's ribs and closed up the place with flesh.

22 Then the LORD God made a woman from the rib he had taken out of the man, and he brought her to the man.

23 The man said, "This is now bone of my bones and flesh of my flesh; she shall be called 'woman,' for she was taken out of man."

24 For this reason a man will leave his father and mother and be united to his wife, and they will become one flesh.

25 The man and his wife were both naked, and they felt no shame.

"God, when he made the first woman . . . made her not of the head of Adam, for she should not climb to great lordship . . . God made not woman of the foot of Adam, for she should not be holden too low . . . but God made woman of the rib of Adam, for woman should be fellow unto man."

—*Geoffrey Chaucer,* The Persones Tale

God's Plan for Marriage

Marriage is part of God's creation plan to bring completion for humankind.

INTO THE SUBJECT

No one would attempt to build a house without a plan, but some couples try to build a marriage without following God's plan. What is God's plan for marriage?

INTO THE WORD

1. Do you believe the creation of marriage was as miraculous as the creation of the universe? Why or why not?

2. What emotional need did Adam have until God created Eve (v. 18)?

3. Do you agree that God intended marriage to be a partnership? If so, what kind of partnership: 50/50, 75/25, 100/0, or something else? Explain your answer.

4. Do you approve of the Internet as a way for a single person to find a suitable marriage partner? Why or why not?

5. Do you believe a Christian marriage is made in heaven? Why or why not?

6. Do you believe traditional marriage is under attack today? If so, how?

7. According to Ephesians 5:24, how should a wife relate to her husband?

8. According to Ephesians 5:25–28, how should a husband relate to his wife?

9. Which of the following terms best describes the husband's biblical role in a marriage: *dictator, king, leading partner,* or *judge*?

10. How might a married couple retain their independence while showing commendable respect for their parents?

INTO THE WORLD

If you are married, build your marriage according to God's plan. If you are unmarried, do what you can to defend the institution of traditional marriage from every attack.

MARRIAGE

When a man and woman marry, they become one flesh. The needs of one become as important as the needs of the other. Loving the other becomes as important as loving oneself. If you are married, do you treat your spouse with the same care you give yourself? Do you want his or her success and happiness as much as you want your own? Ask your spouse to grade your efforts.

MY SPOUSE . . .

1.	is an equal participant with chores/children.	A	B	C	D	F	NA
2.	shares in decision making.	A	B	C	D	F	NA
3.	communicates emotions and feelings.	A	B	C	D	F	NA
4.	gives feedback in a positive manner.	A	B	C	D	F	NA
5.	keeps commitments and promises.	A	B	C	D	F	NA
6.	remembers and celebrates occasions.	A	B	C	D	F	NA
7.	gives compliments and approval.	A	B	C	D	F	NA
8.	is supportive of my choices and needs.	A	B	C	D	F	NA
9.	spends sufficient time with me.	A	B	C	D	F	NA
10.	encourages my occasional time with friends.	A	B	C	D	F	NA
11.	is a good listener.	A	B	C	D	F	NA
12.	can laugh and take things easy.	A	B	C	D	F	NA
13.	is sexually responsive.	A	B	C	D	F	NA
14.	is physically affectionate.	A	B	C	D	F	NA
15.	is verbally affectionate.	A	B	C	D	F	NA
16.	is polite to my parents/family.	A	B	C	D	F	NA
17.	helps handle problems in my life.	A	B	C	D	F	NA
18.	helps me feel loved.	A	B	C	D	F	NA
19.	puts me (and our family) over work.	A	B	C	D	F	NA
20.	pays attention to grooming and appearance.	A	B	C	D	F	NA
21.	is positive and upbeat.	A	B	C	D	F	NA
22.	doesn't use others to get at me.	A	B	C	D	F	NA
23.	is accepting of my shortcomings.	A	B	C	D	F	NA
24.	treads gently where I am not strong.	A	B	C	D	F	NA
25.	cooperates on parenting strategies.	A	B	C	D	F	NA
26.	responds productively to criticism.	A	B	C	D	F	NA
27.	expresses anger constructively.	A	B	C	D	F	NA
28.	is able to handle worry effectively.	A	B	C	D	F	NA
29.	is good with money.	A	B	C	D	F	NA
30.	is interested in my work.	A	B	C	D	F	NA
31.	is willing to discuss problems.	A	B	C	D	F	NA
32.	is positive with the children.	A	B	C	D	F	NA
33.	is emotionally and physically faithful.	A	B	C	D	F	NA
34.	is able to compromise on issues.	A	B	C	D	F	NA
35.	is happy with his/her life.	A	B	C	D	F	NA
36.	shares many of the same interests.	A	B	C	D	F	NA
37.	is not verbally or physically threatening.	A	B	C	D	F	NA
38.	gets along with his/her family.	A	B	C	D	F	NA
39.	is off the phone when I am around.	A	B	C	D	F	NA
40.	enjoys our (my) children.	A	B	C	D	F	NA
41.	can take a "time out" when fighting.	A	B	C	D	F	NA
42.	accepts me for who I am.	A	B	C	D	F	NA
43.	pays attention to me when we're with others.	A	B	C	D	F	NA
44.	offers to help.	A	B	C	D	F	NA
45.	shows appreciation for what I do.	A	B	C	D	F	NA
46.	creates time to be alone together.	A	B	C	D	F	NA
47.	handles his/her ex in an appropriate manner.	A	B	C	D	F	NA
48.	is compatible on religious issues.	A	B	C	D	F	NA
49.	trusts me.	A	B	C	D	F	NA

NAPKIN THEOLOGY

Jesus the Son

MIKE HILSON

"The virgin will be with child and will give birth to a son, and they will call him Immanuel"— which means "God with us."

—Matthew 1:23

THE CONVERSATION

Sure, Jesus was a great teacher, but was He really God?

Most people have heard of the Christmas story and Jesus' birth. Most have heard of the Easter story and Jesus' death and resurrection. But many have simply taken these in the same light as stories about other great humans who lived and died over the centuries. They miss or ignore the idea that this man was also God. And then when confronted with that reality, they hesitate.

If Jesus is human, how can He be God too? We must begin with the realization that since Jesus is God, He is almost entirely other. But with Jesus, it is different. He is both entirely other and entirely like us. And here is where our conversation gets tough again. I often will share the following statement: Jesus is 100 percent human and 100 percent God; He is the only 200 percent person ever to exist! That statement usually relaxes the tension and allows me to move forward with some of the truth that is shared here. Remember, faith sometimes requires faith. And though the Bible gives us ample evidence for everything that the church teaches about Jesus, there is still the issue of faith.

TEACHABLE QUESTIONS

Is Jesus God?
If Jesus was born and died, how can He be God?
Why does it matter if we see Jesus as human?
Why does it matter if we see Jesus as God?
What good does a 200 percent person do us?
Does the Bible really say Jesus is God?
Does Jesus really claim to be God?

THE NAPKIN

The drawing shows the work of each person of the Trinity in the life of an individual. Here we focus on Jesus, God's Son.

Jesus the Son is beside me.

While, God the Father is entirely other, Jesus is God incarnate. This simply means God in the flesh. Jesus is God with skin.

This truth reminds us that our God understands what we are going through. This truth shows just how much God loves us—so much that He, Jesus the Son, would come personally to teach us and die for us. And this truth assures us that God paid the price for our sin by becoming one of us.

Jesus the Son came and lived, ate, talked, walked, and died with us.

No other god does that. Jesus is beside us.

THE TRUTH

THE CREED OF NICAEA (A.D. 352)

We believe . . . in one Lord Jesus Christ, the Son of God, begotten of the Father . . . of the essence of the Father, God of God, and Light of Light, very God of very God, begotten, not made, being of one substance with the Father; by whom all things were made [in heaven and on earth]; who for us men, and for our salvation, came down and was incarnate and was made man; he suffered, and the third day he rose again, ascended into heaven; from thence he cometh to judge the quick and the dead.[1]

Jesus is human. He was born of a human woman. He ate, slept, cried, tired, bled, and died.

Jesus is God. His birth was announced by angels. He healed the sick, walked on water, fed multitudes with one boy's lunch, brought the dead back to life, and was resurrected from the dead.

Here lies the greatest story of all time. While the two statements—Jesus is human, and Jesus is God— seem contradictory, they are not. Jesus is 100 percent God, and He is 100 percent human. Jesus is God incarnate (God in the flesh). He is, "'Immanuel'— which means 'God with us'" (Matt. 1:23). God's greatest revelation of himself to us is in the person of Jesus, God's Son, the Christ.

Over the centuries, some have argued that Jesus is not fully God and fully man. In fact, the Creed of Nicaea was written at the conclusion of the first Council of Nicaea, which was called to straighten out some false teaching on the person of Jesus. A group led by a man named Arius had decided that Jesus was not fully God. The early church theologians, most notably Athanasius, successfully maintained the historical teaching of the church that Jesus was fully God. Make no mistake, Arius' teaching was not the normal thought of the day. It is clear from Scripture and from the earliest teachings of the church that Jesus was seen as both fully human and fully God. In fact, Jesus himself claimed to be the very image of God among us. Jesus asked, "Don't you know me, Philip, even after I have been among you such a long time? Anyone who has seen me has seen the Father. How can you say, 'Show us the Father'?" (John 14:9).

Furthermore, Jesus laid direct claim to being the Son of God: "They all asked, 'Are you then the Son of God?' He replied, 'You are right in saying I am'" (Luke 22:70).

The Bible is very clear on the divinity and humanity of Jesus the Christ. While some would argue with one side or the other of this issue, the historical tradition of the church has remained firm: Jesus is God. Jesus is human.

Jesus Solves Our Human Problem

Because Jesus was fully human, He could correct the problem that had plagued humanity from the beginning of time: the sin of Adam. The apostle Paul made this clear in his writing to the church at Rome:

"Consequently, just as the result of one trespass was condemnation for all men, so also the result of one act of righteousness was justification that brings life for all men. For just as through the disobedience of the one man [Adam] the many were made sinners, so also through the obedience of the one man [Jesus] the many will be made righteous" (Rom. 5:18–19).

Jesus Provides a Human Example

By being perfectly obedient to the law of the Father, Jesus set an example for us for how to live in this world. The apostle Peter said, "To this you were called, because Christ suffered for you, leaving you an example, that you should follow in his steps" (1 Pet. 2:21). The apostle John said, "Whoever claims to live in him must walk as Jesus did" (1 John 2:6).

Jesus Paid the Ultimate Human Price

By living a perfect life, Jesus also set the stage for the ultimate sacrifice for sins. He paid the price for our sinfulness: "Since the children have flesh and blood, [Jesus] too shared in their humanity so that by his death he might destroy him who holds the power of death—that is, the devil—and free those who all their lives were held in slavery by their fear of death" (Heb. 2:14–15).

Jesus the Divine Creator

Because Jesus was fully God, He held the authority to change our situation. The apostle John was so committed to establishing the life-changing truth of a Savior who was truly God that he began his gospel with these words: "In the beginning was the Word [Jesus], and the Word was with God, and the Word was God. He was with God in the beginning. Through him all things were made; without him nothing was made that has been made. In him was life, and that life was the light of men. The light shines in the darkness, but the darkness has not understood it" (John 1:1–5).

Jesus the Divine Healer

Because Jesus was fully God, He had authority over sickness and demon possession. "Jesus went throughout Galilee, teaching in their synagogues, preaching the good news of the kingdom, and healing every disease and sickness among the people. News about him spread all over Syria, and people brought to him all who were ill with various diseases, those suffering severe pain, the demon-possessed, those having seizures, and the paralyzed, and he healed them" (Matt. 4:23–24).

Jesus the Divine Master of Nature

Because Jesus was fully God, He also exercised power over the forces of nature. "Without warning, a furious storm came up on the lake, so that the waves swept over the boat. But Jesus was sleeping. The disciples went and woke him, saying, 'Lord, save us! We're going to drown!' He replied, 'You of little faith, why are you so afraid?' Then he got up and rebuked the winds and the waves, and it was completely calm. The men were amazed and asked, 'What kind of man is this? Even the winds and the waves obey him!'" (Matt. 8:24–27).

Jesus the Divine Master of Life

Because Jesus was fully God, He exercised authority even over death and the grave. "Soon afterward, Jesus went to a town called Nain, and his disciples and a large crowd went along with him. As he approached the town gate, a dead person was being carried out—the only son of his mother, and she was a widow. And a large crowd from the town was with her. When the Lord saw her, his heart went out to her and he said, 'Don't cry.' Then he went up and touched the coffin, and those carrying it stood still. He said, 'Young man, I say to you, get up!' The dead man sat up and began to talk, and Jesus gave him back to his mother" (Luke 7:11–15).

Jesus the Divine Intercessor

Now, since the example has been set and the price has been paid, Jesus speaks for us to God the Father and is our advocate in heaven. "For there is one God and one mediator between God and men, the man Christ Jesus, who gave himself as a ransom for all men—the testimony given in its proper time" (1 Tim. 2:5–6). ✦

NOTE

1. "The Nicene and Constantinople Creed," Christian Classica Ethereal Library, accessed May 26, 2011, http://www.ccel.org/ccel/schaff/hcc3.iii.xii.xiii.html.

Mike Hilson is pastor of New Life Wesleyan Church in LaPlata, Maryland.

The above article is an excerpt from *Napkin Theology: A Simple Way to Share Sacred Truth.*

FREE AT LAST

Understanding Exodus

STEPHEN J. LENNOX

Freedom. Every human longs for it but, sadly, not all experience it. In Exodus, God freed the Israelites from slavery in Egypt so they could help free humanity from slavery to sin.

OVERVIEW OF EXODUS

God's liberation of Israel came in two stages. First, He freed them in dramatic fashion from the Egyptian pharaoh (Ex. 1–18). But this generation had known only slavery. Before God could use them, He had to liberate them from their self-identity. They were no longer slaves, but a chosen people. One way He accomplished this inner liberation was by giving them the Law (Ex. 19–40).

Liberating the Slaves (Ex. 1–18)

The book opens on a dark note. Egypt, a haven in Joseph's lifetime, was now Israel's prison. In a few centuries, one pharaoh's welcomed guests had become another pharaoh's chain gang, building his cities and working in his fields. He even ordered the death of every Israelite boy as a form of population control (Ex. 1).

One Hebrew mother, desperate to save her infant son, hid him among the reeds along the Nile River, only to have him discovered by the daughter of the pharaoh. The princess felt sorry for the boy and took him home, adopting the boy as her son. She named him Moses, which means "drawn out," because of his rescue from the water (Ex. 2). God would later use Moses to rescue His people from slavery.

The Call. Forty more years of suffering passed. Moses tried to take Israel's well-being into his own hands, but his plan backfired. He became a fugitive, wanted for murder. While wandering in the desert of the Sinai Peninsula, he joined up with a tribe of nomads, married, and became a shepherd. One day while tending the flock near Mount Sinai, he saw a remarkable sight. A bush was on fire but

EXODUS TIMELINE

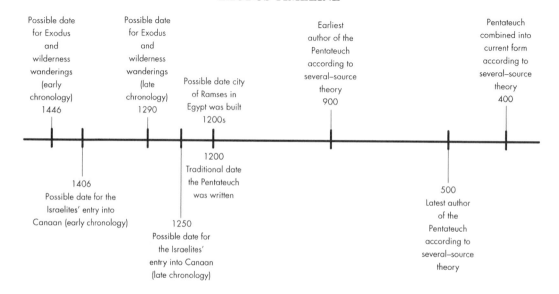

not burning up. The leaves remained green, even in the middle of the flames.

As Moses moved closer to investigate, God spoke to him from the flames. Like the bush, God's people were surviving in the midst of oppression. But the time had come for them to be freed, and Moses was God's man for the job. Needless to say, Moses was reluctant to take on the assignment. After all, he was wanted for murder in Egypt. How could he possibly return and convince Pharaoh to release the Israelites? God heard Moses' hesitation but was insistent: God would free Israel, and He would use Moses to do it (Ex. 3–4).

Moses' first visit to Pharaoh was disastrous. He demanded the king release the Israelites. Angered, Pharaoh made their lives even more miserable. The Israelites were now doubly discouraged and less willing to listen to Moses. All this was exactly what God intended. He was setting up a showdown that would both demonstrate His power to Israel and punish Egypt for oppressing His people (Ex. 5–6).

The Showdown. The showdown came in the form of ten plagues, or judgments, each designed to prove that Israel's God was stronger than the Egyptian gods. The Egyptians worshiped the Nile River as a god, Hopi. When Yahweh turned its waters to blood, He showed that He was greater than Hopi (Ex. 7:14–24). The frog goddess, Heqt, was mocked in the second plague when frogs overran the country (Ex. 8:1–15), as were the bull gods (Apis and Mnevis), the cow god (Hathor), and the ram god (Khnum) with the plague on livestock (Ex. 9:1–7). When God brought darkness in the daytime (Ex. 10:21–29), He demonstrated He was greater than the Egyptian sun god, Ra.

Other plagues ridiculed the Egyptian deities indirectly. The earth god, Geb, could not stop gnats from rising from the ground. Nor could the sky goddess or the air goddess keep the hail, flies, and locusts from passing through the air to harm the Egyptians. None of the Egyptian deities could prevent the plague of boils (Ex. 9:8–12) or the death of the firstborn sons (Ex. 11). By showing himself greater than all other deities, Yahweh gave Israel solid reasons to trust Him.

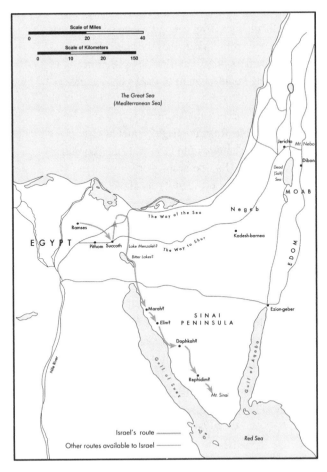

Had Pharaoh given in and released the Israelites, his country would have been spared. But each plague only made him more resolved to say no. When the ten plagues were finished, Egypt was in ruins. Israel not only was permitted to leave; the Egyptians paid them to go. Liberation had begun.

The Journey. There was a quicker route from Egypt to Canaan, but God led His people toward the desert of Sinai first so He could teach them some important lessons. One obstacle in the course God chose was a large body of water called the Red Sea (or Reed Sea). In those days, the Red Sea probably extended much farther north than it does today, making it a barrier to freedom. But with the Egyptian army in hot pursuit, God miraculously parted the waters of the Red Sea to show He would protect the Israelites. He then sent food and water in unusual ways to show He would provide for their needs. By appearing as a huge column of fire and cloud, He showed He would be with them and would guide them (Ex. 12–19). God took them on this longer, more difficult, more frightening route to prepare them for their new role. When they reached the barren, rocky wilderness of Mount Sinai, they were ready to learn what it would mean to be God's chosen nation.

A Deeper Work of Liberation (Ex. 19–40)

Though free from bondage, Israel was not yet free from the centuries-old effects of that bondage. God continued His liberating work by freeing His people from their self-identity as slaves. One way He reshaped their identity was by entering into an agreement with them through the Law He gave on Mount Sinai.

To speak of a law that liberates sounds contradictory at first. But these laws were not just a list of rules; they were part of an agreement between God and the Israelites. Building on the covenant He had made earlier with Abraham (Gen. 12), God entered into a formal relationship with these former slaves. Like the earlier covenant with Abraham (Gen. 17), this was a two-part agreement. God would do His part—caring for them, accompanying them, and protecting them— and they must do their part, keeping the Law.

Living by the Rules. This agreement changed how the Israelites understood themselves. They were no longer slaves, but God's "treasured possession," a "kingdom of priests and a holy nation" (Ex. 19:5–6). God not only freed them from slavery, but He also freed them from their identity as slaves.

Imagine you've adopted a poor, orphaned girl from another country. When she's able to understand, you explain the rules she's expected to follow, not because you want to restrict her freedom, but because she's your daughter. She's no longer an orphan; the rules of your household prove to her that she is a member of your family.

Living among Them. A second way God reshaped His people's identity was to demonstrate again and again that He was present among them as a loving Father. If a famous person moves to your town, it elevates the status of the town. It becomes "the town where so-and-so lives." As the status of your town rises, you and your fellow citizens may see yourselves as more respectable. You realize there must be something special about your town if "so-and-so" chooses to live there.

The Israelites needed to see themselves as God's chosen people. What better way for God to bring about this transformation in self-understanding than by showing He was present among them? That's why He created the pillar of cloud and the pillar of fire (Ex. 13:21–22). God wanted the people to be able to look up at any moment, day or night, and see that He was with them.

That's why He had them build the tabernacle, a portable temple representing God's house, and set it up in the middle of the camp (Ex. 25–40). The tabernacle was another physical reminder that God was with them. As He said in Exodus 25:8, "Have them make a sanctuary for me, and I will dwell among them." They built the sanctuary, and God kept His promise by visibly moving in (Ex. 40:34).

GOD'S GREAT PLAN IN EXODUS

To redeem the world through His people Israel, God formed them into a nation. This began in Genesis when He chose Abraham and eventually led his family to Egypt, where they became a large group of people. Then He liberated them from Egyptian slavery and made a covenant with them at Mount Sinai. Once they were free and could better understand their role as God's people, He proceeded with His plan to reunite the world to himself.

God's liberation not only prepared Israel to carry out His plan of reconciliation, it also showed them what reconciliation with God meant. As the Israelites were slaves to the Egyptians, unable to free themselves, so humanity was enslaved to sin and its effects because of its sin. As God rescued the Israelites, so He would mercifully rescue all humanity. God's ultimate goal has always been to restore people to fellowship with Him; in Exodus He comes to live among the Israelites. In so doing, God not only moved closer to reconciliation, He also illustrated what reconciliation means. Little wonder that Jews and Christians alike would look back to the events of this book as symbolizing God's plan.

WHAT WE LEARN ABOUT GOD FROM EXODUS

Repeatedly in Exodus, God revealed His concern for the Israelites. He heard their cries for help, chose Moses, called him at the burning bush, and granted him success in liberating the Israelites. Over and over, as they traveled toward Mount Sinai, God supplied their need for protection, food, and water, like a shepherd for his sheep. Often He would work miraculously: parting the Red Sea so the Israelites could escape, drowning the Egyptian army to prevent their recapture, sending bread from heaven, providing huge flocks of quail on the wind, and furnishing water from rocks.

By giving the Law, God demonstrated His compassion. He gave these commands for Israel's benefit so their society would be just and fair. They were taught to avoid what would harm them and pursue what would benefit them. Giving the Law also mercifully altered Israel's self-understanding from that of slave to "treasured possession" (Ex. 19:5). He patiently endured their complaints. Even when He judged them, God was compassionate and merciful. Like a father, He punished only as much as necessary to preserve Israel's faithful obedience.

God Is Compassionate

When God wanted to describe himself to Moses and the Israelites, He emphasized His compassion: "The LORD, the LORD, the compassionate and gracious God, slow to anger, abounding in love and faithfulness, maintaining love to thousands, and forgiving wickedness, rebellion and sin (Ex. 34:6–7). After suffering years of slavery, the Israelites needed this reminder of God's compassion. For centuries, they would look back to the exodus as God's most merciful moment.

God Is Powerful

Exodus also emphasizes God's power. The ten plagues revealed how much stronger He was than Pharaoh and all the gods of Egypt. By parting the Red Sea and providing food and water in unusual ways, God displayed His power over the natural world. On Mount Sinai, God's power—evident in the thunder, lightning, fire, cloud, smoke, and trumpet blast—so terrified the people that they trembled with fear.

Why does God flex His mighty muscle so often in this book? Because He needed to. Egypt would not allow the Israelites to leave without a fight. The Hebrews could not walk on water; the sea had to part if they were to escape. The Sinai wilderness

was no breadbasket; finding food for the Israelites required a miracle.

It seems as if God at times deliberately backed himself into a corner so He could demonstrate His power. He could have led Israel out of Egypt years earlier, before Pharaoh began to oppress them. He could have chosen another route and bypassed the Red Sea. He could have taken them through more hospitable territory, where food and water were easier to find.

God created opportunities to show His power because Israel needed to see His power. Just like Abraham, the Israelites needed to learn to walk by faith if they were to accomplish their mission. So God put them in situations where they had to trust Him, and then He came through for them. The exodus was not just about liberation from Egypt. It was also about liberation from doubt. God continued to build their faith all the time they were in the wilderness. The next chapter explores this faith-building process as described in Leviticus, Numbers, and Deuteronomy. ✦

Exodus at a Glance

Authorship: traditionally, Moses

Date of Writing: mid-1400s or late 1200s B.C.

Date of Events: mid-1400s or late 1200s B.C.

Purpose: to describe God's liberation of the Israelites from captivity in Egypt and their establishment as His chosen nation

Form: primarily narrative and Law

Part of God's Plan: God continues to prepare His people to be a source of blessing for all by liberating them and illustrating what redemption means.

Key Elements of God's Character: compassion, power

Stephen J. Lennox is professor of Bible and Theology at Indiana Wesleyan University in Marion, Indiana.

The above article is an excerpt from *God's Story Revealed: A Guide for Understanding the Old Testament.*

LEARNING TO TRUST

STAN TOLER

GOD IS TRUSTWORTHY

Over the years, I have met some people who were hard to trust. Once someone has violated that trust, it makes it hard to trust that person again. I'm sure that you have met some in life who you can't trust.

But there are people who I know I could trust with my life. It wouldn't matter what the situation was, if they gave me their word, I would believe them with no questions asked. They are absolutely reliable.

That's the way God is. He is completely dependable, and you can always trust Him.

Abraham had been following the Lord faithfully ever since God called him out of the land of Ur. We're not sure how many years had passed since God first spoke to Abraham in Genesis 12 until He spoke to him again in Genesis 15, but by that time, Abraham had been learning to trust the Lord for some time. When God spoke to him again, Abraham asked God about the promises He had made to him and his descendants.

Abraham was now an older man, somewhere between seventy-five and eighty-six years old. He knew that his wife Sarah could no longer bear children, and the couple was childless. If I were Abraham, I'd have been wondering, "What is God up to? How in the world can He keep His promise now?" Abraham was beginning to think about who would inherit his property when he died. He identified a servant, Eliezer of Damascus, as the one who stood next in line for his estate (Gen. 15:2). He didn't think that was what God had intended in His promise, so he raised the question.

In other words, Abraham was trying to believe God, but he was having a moment of doubt.

Has that ever happened to you? You really want to trust God, but you're just not sure you can. Maybe that happens when someone you love becomes ill. You want to believe that God is good, but can you really trust Him? Maybe that happens when you find yourself in financial need. You want to believe that God will provide for your every need, but can you trust Him?

God has given us His word that He is faithful. The Bible has many examples of people who experienced God's faithfulness to them. Adam and Eve, Noah, Abraham, Jacob, Joseph, Esther, Joshua, Ruth, and Samuel are a few who found God to be faithful to His word. The psalmist David said, "The LORD is faithful to all his promises and loving toward all he has made" (Ps. 145:13). When we have moments of doubts, we can read about or remember those to whom God has proven himself. We can know that as He proved trustworthy to them, He will also be worthy of our trust. He won't fail us. We have His word on it, and we can trust Him. You can be sure that God keeps His word. Time after time, He has proven that what He has said, He will do.

Are you willing to believe that today—and everyday?

ACTING IN TRUST

It's one thing to know that God is reliable; it's another thing to actually trust Him. That's the difference between faith and action. At some point, you and I will have to take that step of faith, putting our complete confidence in God.

Abraham believed God, but he had trouble trusting Him. As a result, he got himself into some rather trying situations. Once, he and Sarah went to Egypt. Abraham was afraid Pharaoh would kill him so Pharaoh could take Sarah as his wife. So Abraham told Sarah to say he was her brother (Gen. 12:10–20). This was not totally untrue, since they were in fact half brother and sister. But it was deceitful, and they needed the Lord's intervention to get them out of the mess they were in. Oh, and once wasn't enough. They did the same thing later in Gerar (Gen. 20).

That time, too, God straightened out the problem they created.

Perhaps more critical to Abraham's trust in God was Abraham's decision to father a child with Hagar. Sarah suggested it, and Abraham acted on her suggestion (Gen. 16). They had somehow rationalized that this was the way God would keep His promise of children to them. After it was done, God came again to Abraham to renew His promise that Abraham and Sarah would have a son. The Lord said that He would bless the son of Hagar and he'd be the father of twelve tribes, but the unique covenant people would come through Sarah's son (Gen. 17).

God honored His promises to Abraham. He also honored Abraham's faith and helped him grow in his confidence of God. Abraham's faith in God is noted throughout the Bible. Genesis 15:6 says, "Abraham believed the LORD, and he credited it to him as righteousness." This verse is quoted in four other places (Rom. 4:3, 9; Gal. 3:6; James 2:23), and in each instance, Abraham's faith is cited as a model of the kind of faith you and I can have.

Abraham was living in the difficult position between receiving God's promise and having it fulfilled. He understood the promise but was having trouble putting that faith into action.

If you are going to totally trust God, you must come to the point of acting on what you believe. You must not only believe that God provides, you must act as if God is going to take care of you. You must not only believe that there is a heaven, you must live as if heaven is your home.

LEAN YOUR WHOLE WEIGHT UPON HIM

The story is told of missionary John Paton who found a unique way to communicate the necessity of trusting in God:

Three months after arriving on the island of Tanna, Paton's young wife died, followed by their five-week-old son. For three more years, Paton labored alone among the hostile islanders, ignoring their threats, and seeking to make Christ known to them before escaping with his life. Later he returned and spent fifteen years on another island.

Paton was working one day in his home on the translation of John's gospel, puzzling over John's favorite expression . . . "to believe in" or "to trust in" Jesus Christ—a phrase that occurs first in John 1:12. "How can I translate it?" Paton wondered. The islanders were cannibals; nobody trusted anybody else. There was no word for *trust* in their language.

His native servant came in. "What am I doing?" Paton asked him. "Sitting at your desk," the man replied. Paton then raised both feet off the floor and sat back on his chair. "What am I doing now?" In reply, Paton's servant used a verb that means "to lean your whole weight upon." That's the phrase Paton used throughout John's gospel to translate "believe in."[1]

We need to put our whole weight upon God. He can hold us. He wants to hold us. He will hold us if we lean our whole weight on Him in total trust. Because He is trustworthy, we can rely on Him. Do you believe God is trustworthy? Are you willing to lean your whole weight on Him? Will you let Him carry you and all the concerns of life that you have? Isaiah 50:10 calls a person to "trust in the name of the LORD and rely on his God." Are you ready to lay all you are in His hands and rely on Him?

EXERCISE TRUST

Just as Abraham had to make a conscious decision to trust God, we must also choose to trust Him. We'll find that some days it is easier to trust than others, but even when moments of doubt come, we can still choose to trust God.

Here's a gentle way to remind ourselves that trusting in God is fundamental to every aspect of our lives. The story has been told of a woman and her husband who were invited to spend the weekend at the husband's employer's home. She was nervous about the weekend. The boss was wealthy with a fine home on the waterway and cars costing more than her house. The first day and evening went well, and she was delighted to have this rare glimpse into how the very wealthy live.

The husband's employer was quite generous as a host and took them to the finest restaurants. She knew she would never have the opportunity to indulge in this kind of extravagance again and was enjoying herself immensely.

As the three of them were about to enter an exclusive restaurant that evening, the boss was walking slightly ahead of her and her husband. He stopped suddenly, looking down on the pavement for a long, silent moment. The lady wondered if she was supposed to pass him. There was nothing on the ground except a single darkened penny that someone had dropped and a few cigarette butts.

Still silent, the man reached down and picked up the penny. He held it up and smiled, then put it in his pocket as if he had found a great treasure. How absurd! What need did this man have for a single penny? Why would he even take the time to stop and pick it up?

Throughout dinner, the entire scene nagged at her. Finally, she could stand it no longer. She casually mentioned that her daughter once had a coin collection and asked if the penny he had found had been of some value. A smile crept across the man's face as he reached into his pocket for the penny and held it out for her to see. She had seen many pennies before! What was the point of this?

"Look at it," he said. "Read what it says." She read the words "United States of America."

"No, not that; read further."

"One cent?"

"No, keep reading."

"In God we trust?"

"Yes!"

"And?"

"And if I trust in God, the name of God is holy, even on a coin. Whenever I find a coin, I see that inscription. It is written on every single United States coin, but we never seem to notice it. If God drops a message right in front of me telling me to trust Him, who am I to pass it by?

Are you willing to trust God today with everything in your life? With your finances? With your family? With your health? With your career? With your future?

Perhaps today you will want to do an exercise of trust. Imagine yourself in a large room, and you are there with God. All your interests, possessions, family, friends, resources, and things of personal value are around you. Take each person or thing and place it into God's hands. Trust Him with your most prized possessions. Trust Him with your most valued relationships. Give Him everything you have and are. If you find you're having trouble giving Him something, spend some time praying about it. He is trustworthy. You can rely on Him.

I like the way the poet expressed it:

Trust Him when dark doubts assail thee,
Trust Him when thy strength is small,
Trust Him when to simply trust Him
Seems the hardest thing of all.
Trust Him; He is ever faithful;
Trust Him, for his will is best;
Trust Him, for the heart of Jesus
Is the only place of rest.[2] ◆

NOTES

1. "Trials of a Missionary," Bible.org, accessed December 15, 2011, http://bible.org/illustration/trials-missionary.

2. "Trust Him When Thy Wants Are Many," Hymnal.net, accessed January 27, 2012, http://www.hymnal.net/hymn.php/nt/647.

Stan Toler is a general superintendent in the Church of the Nazarene.

The above article is an excerpt from Give to Live: The Freedom of Being Generous with Your Life.

THE ROOTS OF WESLEYANISM IN AMERICA

BOB BLACK AND KEITH DRURY

On May 24, 1738, at a small group meeting on Aldersgate Street in London, John Wesley's life was transformed. "I felt my heart strangely warmed," he wrote in his journal. "I felt I did trust in Christ, Christ alone, for salvation; and an assurance was given me that He had taken away my sins, even mine, and saved me from the law of sin and death." Wesley had found his faith and with it the message he would preach for the next half century.

John Wesley. God used John Wesley in the 1700s to spark a spiritual awakening known as the "Wesleyan Revival" in the British Isles. That revival gave birth to Methodism and eventually to the Methodist family of churches worldwide. Wesleyans look to John Wesley— reformer, evangelist, and lifelong Anglican priest—as their spiritual forefather.

THE WORLD HIS PARISH

The following year he found his method. Reluctantly accepting an invitation from George Whitefield to adopt his practice of preaching in the open air, Wesley was amazed at the result. He began preaching four or five times a day in public squares, in the fields, from the porches of private homes, and once even from his father's tombstone. Over a fifty-year period, he traveled a quarter of a million miles on horseback (or, in old age, in a carriage) to spread the gospel.

What John accomplished through preaching and organization, his brother Charles multiplied through music. He wrote over six thousand hymns during his lifetime, several of them widely acknowledged to be among the greatest ever written. The ministries of the Wesleys complemented each other perfectly, and under the blessing of God, the Wesleyan revival was the result.

As the number of the converted grew, John Wesley organized them into societies, classes, and bands. It was a remarkably effective network of Methodist believers. To provide leadership, he mobilized lay preachers and, true to form, organized them as well; they met with him annually in what he called a conference. Wesley never left the Church of England, and he did not intend for his new Methodist movement to compete with it. Methodism was intended to be a renewal movement within the church.

Still, opposition mounted. When an Anglican bishop ordered him to stop preaching in other priests' parishes, Wesley reminded him that the Oxford credentials he still held allowed him to preach wherever he chose. "The world is my parish," he once wrote. Those were prophetic words.

Wesley faced opposition outside the church too. In the early years of Methodism, he and his lay preachers were pelted with rocks and rotten eggs, harassed by mobs, ridiculed in the press, and, in the case of some of his preachers, even forced into military service on the spot. Despite it all, Methodism continued to grow in size and influence.

"GOD IS WITH US"

As a result, England experienced a revival that changed not only the church, but society as well. Wesley the evangelist was also Wesley the reformer, all in the name of Christ. His passion for reform found expression in many ways:

- He was an early opponent of slavery, calling for its abolition in a day when few seemed concerned.
- He took up the cause of the poor, creating interest-free loans, free medical services, and a jobs program that was far ahead of its time.

- John Howard, the reformer who awakened England's conscience to the abuses in its brutal prison system, credited Wesley as his inspiration.
- In a nation addicted to gin—London had more than 7,000 gin sellers in the 1730s for a population numbering only about 600,000—Wesley led the fight against the distilleries.
- He elevated the role of women. God seemed to be using women in ministry, Wesley once pointed out to a questioner, and who was he to withstand God?

And then there was Wesley the theologian. His contributions to Christian thought are significant. There's his strong defense of free will; his recovery of the message of Christian holiness or perfect love, which he believed to be the truth God had raised up the Methodists to proclaim; and his welcome emphasis on the assurance of our salvation. At the time, most believed that you could only hope that you were saved; Wesley taught that you could know. On his death bed at age eighty-seven, that assurance was his. "The best of all, God is with us," he said. Because of the life and legacy of John Wesley, many others can say the same.

John Wesley was buried behind his City Road Chapel in London on March 9, 1791, in a 5:00 a.m. service. It was an unusual time for a funeral, but it was chosen for the expressed purpose of avoiding the massive crowd that might otherwise be expected, a crowd so large as to be unmanageable. His obituary declared that, apart from the king, he had become the most widely known man in England. Even at that predawn hour, a substantial number stood quietly by his graveside. One of Wesley's lay preachers conducted the service, and when he reached the traditional reference to "the soul of our dear brother," he paused and softly substituted, "our dear father." To his Methodists, he was nothing less.

METHODISM IN AMERICA

For years Methodist emigrants from England had brought their faith with them to the American colonies, and in 1769 Wesley sent two volunteers, Richard Boardman and Joseph Pilmoor, to organize and expand Methodist ministries in America. When Francis Asbury followed two years later, American Methodism found its version of John Wesley.

Asbury was a young man of twenty-six when he arrived in the colonies, and his total dedication to the cause combined with his natural gifts to make him the acknowledged leader of the small but dedicated cadre of Methodists, numbering at the time about six hundred. After the Revolutionary War ended in 1783 and with the blessing of Wesley, Asbury led American Methodism to become the first religious body in the newly independent United States to work out an independent national organization of their own. The Methodist Episcopal Church (*Episcopal* simply meaning it would be governed by bishops) was formed in late December 1784 at a gathering in Baltimore, Maryland, known to history as the "Christmas Conference." It was no longer an extension of British Methodism—an important consideration, given the depth of anti-British feeling associated with the war—but the spiritual ties with Wesley and his Methodists in England remained strong. Asbury believed that the end of the war meant the beginning of Methodist growth in America. He was right. He was also largely responsible for that growth.

Francis Asbury and Thomas Coke became American Methodism's first bishops, a title Wesley argued against because of his negative experiences with bishops in the Church of England. Asbury and Coke had his full support personally, however, and he resigned himself to their choice of labels.

Coke's passion was missions, and his work in America was interrupted by numerous trips abroad to plant Methodist missions in foreign lands. Asbury's travels were just as extensive but all within the boundaries of America. He traveled the Eastern Seaboard again and again, planting churches, shaping new converts and young congregations, and taking Christ into settings as diverse as the streets of Manhattan and the backcountry of the Carolinas. His *Journal* records sixty-three crossings of the Appalachian or Allegheny Mountains.

Asbury's leadership positioned the Methodists to capitalize on the moving of God's Spirit in the national revival known as the Second Great Awakening. Taking a page from the journals of Asbury and Wesley, Methodist circuit riders on horseback crisscrossed the American frontier as ambassadors of Christ in places where civilization was only a rumor—first in the untamed expanses of western Kentucky, Indiana, and Illinois, and eventually across the Mississippi and into the Great Plains. A popular saying was a testament to their dedication: "The weather's so bad that nothing's stirring except mad dogs and Methodist preachers." Year in and year out, in good conditions and bad, "in season and out of season," Methodist circuit riders moved westward with the people and helped to build the country while they built the kingdom.

Another factor in the growth of Methodism was its leading role in the Holiness Revival. In 1835 Phoebe Palmer, wife of a New York City physician and a lay theologian in her own right, joined with her sister Sarah Lankford to make the case for Christian holiness in a series of small group gatherings for women held in the Palmer home. These "Tuesday meetings" proved extremely popular, and by 1839 attendance was opened to men also. The Tuesday meetings led to a periodical, *Guide to Holiness*, which at its peak counted an impressive thirty thousand subscribers.

Phoebe Palmer championed John Wesley's doctrine of holiness—the idea that believers can be sanctified or made holy in this life through a second work of God's grace in their hearts—but many believe that she modified it in one important regard. She linked Paul's words in Romans 12 about offering ourselves as living sacrifices with Jesus' reference in Matthew 23:19 to the altar that sanctifies the gift (KJV). As a result, she proposed a well-defined and easy-to-grasp, three-step path to entire sanctification or Christian perfection: consecration, faith, and testimony. This view, which came to be called "the Shorter Way" in contrast to Wesley's more conservative counsel to wait for the inner witness of the

The Methodist Library Collection at Drew University

Phoebe Palmer. The American holiness movement's forefather is John Wesley, but its mother is Phoebe Palmer. Like Wesley, she combined personal piety with compassionate ministries, but her lasting legacy is theological. She urged seekers after entire sanctification not only to receive the second work of grace by faith but to claim it the same way, making her emphasis more immediate than Wesley's.

Holy Spirit before claiming sanctification, proved popular in Methodist circles and beyond. With this simple formula, holiness seemed more accessible to the man or woman in the street than ever before. Traditional Methodist theologians had reservations, but the message of holiness gained popularity among the common people. So did Methodism.

By 1820 the Methodist Episcopal Church was the largest denomination in the nation. From 15,000 members at the close of the Revolutionary War, the church had grown to almost 250,000 in less than forty years. By 1860 every third church member in America was a Methodist. After the federal government and the political parties, the Methodist Episcopal Church was the largest single national institution.

But with size and status came the desire to protect those gains. The great national debate was on slavery, and the bishops feared its potential to divide the church. If keeping silent on the question of slavery was necessary to prevent regional divisions from slowing Methodist momentum, the bishops were determined to maintain that silence.

They would find some Methodists equally determined to break it. ◆

Bob Black is a member of the religion faculty at Southern Wesleyan University in Central, South Carolina.

Keith Drury is a professor of religion at Indiana Wesleyan University in Marion, Indiana.

The above article is an excerpt from *The Story of the Wesleyan Church.*

WESLEY BIBLE LESSON COMMENTARY SERIES

Are you interested in a particular topic or book of the Bible? Use the chart below to refer to a specific volume of the *Wesley Bible Lesson Commentary* series for more in-depth study.

	UNIT 1	UNIT 2	UNIT 3	UNIT 4
Volume 1 (Available as *Wesley Bible Lesson Commentary 2008–2009*)	Revelation	Minor Prophets	1–2 Peter Jude	Life Issues Holiness Evangelism
Volume 2 (Available as *Wesley Bible Lesson Commentary 2009–2010*)	Jeremiah Lamentations Ezekiel Daniel	Matthew	James	1–2 Samuel 1–2 Kings 1–2 Chronicles
Volume 3 (Available as *Wesley Bible Lesson Commentary 2010–2011*)	Romans	Galatians Ephesians Philippians Colossians Philemon	Leviticus Numbers Deuteronomy	Spiritual Disciplines Wesley's Life Doctrines
Volume 4	John	Ezra Nehemiah Esther	1–2 Thessalonians	1–2 Timothy Titus
Volume 5	Hebrews	Exodus	Joshua Judges Ruth	Spiritual Heritage Stewardship Social Issues
Volume 6 (Available summer 2013)	Mark	Isaiah	1–3 John	Job Psalms Proverbs Ecclesiastes Song of Solomon
Volume 7 (Available summer 2014)	Genesis	Luke	Acts	1–2 Corinthians

Call 1-800-493-7539 or visit www.wesleyan.org/wph to order your copy!

WESLEY ADULT BIBLE STUDIES SCOPE AND SEQUENCE

Use this reference chart to compare *Wesley Bible Lesson Commentary Volume 5*
to connect with your Sunday school curriculum and grow further in the Lord.

UNIT 1
CHRIST ALONE: THE SUPREMACY OF THE GOSPEL

(Same as fall 2012 in Wesley Adult Bible Studies)

Lesson 1	September 2, 2012	The Finality of God's Salvation	Hebrews 1:1–14
Lesson 2	September 9, 2012	Treasure Your Greatest Treasure	Hebrews 2:1–18
Lesson 3	September 16, 2012	Fix Your Eyes on Jesus	Hebrews 3:1–19
Lesson 4	September 23, 2012	Faith—The Key to Entering God's Rest	Hebrews 4:1–16
Lesson 5	September 30, 2012	Jesus Meets the Qualifications	Hebrews 5:1–14
Lesson 6	October 7, 2012	Pursuing Perfection	Hebrews 6:1–20
Lesson 7	October 14, 2012	Do We Need a High Priest?	Hebrews 7:11–17, 25; 8:1–7
Lesson 8	October 21, 2012	The Precious Blood of Christ	Hebrews 9:11–28
Lesson 9	October 28, 2012	Walking Together by Faith	Hebrews 10:19–39
Lesson 10	November 4, 2012	Faith That Moves God	Hebrews 11:1–16
Lesson 11	November 11, 2012	New Life Changes Everything	Hebrews 12:14–29
Lesson 12	November 18, 2012	Thankfulness—The Loving Sacrifice	Hebrews 13:15–16; Acts 2:42–47
Lesson 13	November 25, 2012	Holy Actions Follow Holy Motives	Hebrews 13:1–21

UNIT 2
DELIVER US: GOD REDEEMS HIS PEOPLE

(Same as winter 2012–2013 in Wesley Adult Bible Studies)

Lesson 1	December 2, 2012	God, Unstopping and Unstoppable	Exodus 1:6–22
Lesson 2	December 9, 2012	The Deliverance of a Deliverer	Exodus 2:1–15
Lesson 3	December 16, 2012	Say Yes to God's Call	Exodus 3:1–15
Lesson 4	December 23, 2012	A Savior Is Born	Luke 2:1–20
Lesson 5	December 30, 2012	God Works through Obedient People	Exodus 6:28—7:6, 14–24
Lesson 6	January 6, 2013	God's Provision for Deliverance	Exodus 12:1–14, 29–30
Lesson 7	January 13, 2013	Deliverance When All Seems Lost	Exodus 14:10–31
Lesson 8	January 20, 2013	Receiving God's Covenant	Exodus 19:3–25
Lesson 9	January 27, 2013	God's Life-Sparing Commands	Exodus 20:1–20
Lesson 10	February 3, 2013	God Expects Exclusive Worship	Exodus 32:1–6, 19–24, 30–35
Lesson 11	February 10, 2013	Intimacy with God	Exodus 33:7–23
Lesson 12	February 17, 2013	Enabled to Do What He Commands	Exodus 35:30—36:5
Lesson 13	February 24, 2013	God Dwells among His People	Exodus 40:17–38

UNIT 3
FOLLOW ME: GOD IS FAITHFUL TO HIS PEOPLE

(Same as spring 2013 in Wesley Adult Bible Studies)

Lesson 1	March 3, 2013	God Chooses a Leader	Joshua 1:1–17
Lesson 2	March 10, 2013	Breaking Down Walls	Joshua 2:1–14, 17–21
Lesson 3	March 17, 2013	We Worship and God Works	Joshua 3:5–17; 4:4–7
Lesson 4	March 24, 2013	Sin Infects and Affects	Joshua 7:2–13, 19–26
Lesson 5	March 31, 2013	The Empty Tomb—A Gift for Eternity	Mark 16:1–16
Lesson 6	April 7, 2013	The Secrets of Wholehearted Devotion	Joshua 14:5–15
Lesson 7	April 14, 2013	Renewing Your Covenant with God	Joshua 24:14–27
Lesson 8	April 21, 2013	What about the Next Generation?	Judges 2:6–23
Lesson 9	April 28, 2013	Godly Leadership	Judges 4:4–16
Lesson 10	May 5, 2013	The Battle Belongs to the Lord	Judges 7:1–8, 19–21
Lesson 11	May 12, 2013	Failure Is Not Final	Judges 13:2–5; 16:23–31
Lesson 12	May 19, 2013	Faithfulness Requires Courage	Ruth 1:3–18
Lesson 13	May 26, 2013	Do the Right Thing	Ruth 3:1–11; 4:12–17

UNIT 4
REDEEM THE TIME: CONNECTING WITH GOD'S HEART

(Same as summer 2013 in Wesley Adult Bible Studies)

Lesson 1	June 2, 2013	Honoring the Past Enlivens the Present	Philippians 4:8–9; Revelation 3:1–6
Lesson 2	June 9, 2013	Nothing but the Truth	2 Peter 1:12–21
Lesson 3	June 16, 2013	God's Grand Channel of Grace	1 Corinthians 11:23–32
Lesson 4	June 23, 2013	The Power of God for Salvation	1 Corinthians 15:1–11
Lesson 5	June 30, 2013	More Important Matters	Amos 5:21–24; Matthew 23:16–23
Lesson 6	July 7, 2013	An Illustration of Greatness	John 13:1–17
Lesson 7	July 14, 2013	Good Stewards, Faithful in Service	Matthew 25:14–30
Lesson 8	July 21, 2013	Kingdom Priorities	Matthew 6:19–34
Lesson 9	July 28, 2013	Generosity: A Measure of Spiritual Health	Acts 4:32—5:11
Lesson 10	August 4, 2013	Free to Serve	Galatians 3:26–28; Romans 16:1–7; Acts 18:24–36
Lesson 11	August 11, 2013	Honoring Our Elders	Exodus 20:12; John 19:25–27; James 1:23–27
Lesson 12	August 18, 2013	God's Plan for Your Life: Growth	Ephesians 5:1–20
Lesson 13	August 25, 2013	God's Plan for Marriage	Genesis 2:18–25

ONE-YEAR BIBLE READING PLAN

By reading for about fifteen minutes each day, you can read every chapter of the Bible in one year!
Begin anytime!

JANUARY

- ❑ 1 Gen. 1–3
- ❑ 2 Gen. 4–7
- ❑ 3 Gen. 8–11
- ❑ 4 Gen. 12–16
- ❑ 5 Gen. 17–19
- ❑ 6 Gen. 20–23
- ❑ 7 Gen. 24–25
- ❑ 8 Gen. 26–28
- ❑ 9 Gen. 29–30
- ❑ 10 Gen. 31–33
- ❑ 11 Gen. 34–36
- ❑ 12 Gen. 37–39
- ❑ 13 Gen. 40–42
- ❑ 14 Gen. 43–45
- ❑ 15 Gen. 46–47
- ❑ 16 Gen. 48–50
- ❑ 17 Matt. 1–4
- ❑ 18 Matt. 5–7
- ❑ 19 Matt. 8–9
- ❑ 20 Matt. 10–12
- ❑ 21 Matt. 13–14
- ❑ 22 Matt. 15–17
- ❑ 23 Matt. 18–20
- ❑ 24 Matt. 21–22
- ❑ 25 Matt. 23–24
- ❑ 26 Matt. 25–26
- ❑ 27 Matt. 27–28
- ❑ 28 Ex. 1–4
- ❑ 29 Ex. 5–7
- ❑ 30 Ex. 8–10
- ❑ 31 Ex. 11–13

FEBRUARY

- ❑ 1 Ex. 14–16
- ❑ 2 Ex. 17–20
- ❑ 3 Ex. 21–23
- ❑ 4 Ex. 24–27
- ❑ 5 Ex. 28–30
- ❑ 6 Ex. 31–34
- ❑ 7 Ex. 35–37
- ❑ 8 Ex. 38–40
- ❑ 9 Mark 1–3
- ❑ 10 Mark 4–5
- ❑ 11 Mark 6–7
- ❑ 12 Mark 8–9
- ❑ 13 Mark 10–11
- ❑ 14 Mark 12–13
- ❑ 15 Mark 14–16

- ❑ 16 Lev. 1–4
- ❑ 17 Lev. 5–7
- ❑ 18 Lev. 8–11
- ❑ 19 Lev. 12–14
- ❑ 20 Lev. 15–17
- ❑ 21 Lev. 18–20
- ❑ 22 Lev. 21–23
- ❑ 23 Lev. 24–25
- ❑ 24 Lev. 26–27
- ❑ 25 Luke 1
- ❑ 26 Luke 2–3
- ❑ 27 Luke 4–5
- ❑ 28 Luke 6–7

MARCH

- ❑ 1 Luke 8–9
- ❑ 2 Luke 10–11
- ❑ 3 Luke 12–13
- ❑ 4 Luke 14–16
- ❑ 5 Luke 17–18
- ❑ 6 Luke 19–20
- ❑ 7 Luke 21–22
- ❑ 8 Luke 23–24
- ❑ 9 Num. 1–2
- ❑ 10 Num. 3–4
- ❑ 11 Num. 5–6
- ❑ 12 Num. 7–8
- ❑ 13 Num. 9–11
- ❑ 14 Num. 12–14
- ❑ 15 Num. 15–17
- ❑ 16 Num. 18–20
- ❑ 17 Num. 21–23
- ❑ 18 Num. 24–26
- ❑ 19 Num. 27–30
- ❑ 20 Num. 31–33
- ❑ 21 Num. 34–36

- ❑ 22 John 1–3
- ❑ 23 John 4–5
- ❑ 24 John 6–7
- ❑ 25 John 8–9
- ❑ 26 John 10–11
- ❑ 27 John 12–13
- ❑ 28 John 14–17
- ❑ 29 John 18–19
- ❑ 30 John 20–21
- ❑ 31 Deut. 1–2

APRIL

- ❑ 1 Deut. 3–4
- ❑ 2 Deut. 5–7
- ❑ 3 Deut. 8–11
- ❑ 4 Deut. 12–15
- ❑ 5 Deut. 16–19
- ❑ 6 Deut. 20–23
- ❑ 7 Deut. 24–27
- ❑ 8 Deut. 28–29
- ❑ 9 Deut. 30–31
- ❑ 10 Deut. 32–34
- ❑ 11 Acts 1–3
- ❑ 12 Acts 4–6
- ❑ 13 Acts 7–8
- ❑ 14 Acts 9–10
- ❑ 15 Acts 11–13
- ❑ 16 Acts 14–16
- ❑ 17 Acts 17–19
- ❑ 18 Acts 20–22
- ❑ 19 Acts 23–25
- ❑ 20 Acts 26–28
- ❑ 21 Josh. 1–4
- ❑ 22 Josh. 5–7
- ❑ 23 Josh. 8–10
- ❑ 24 Josh. 11–14

- ❑ 25 Josh. 15–18
- ❑ 26 Josh. 19–21
- ❑ 27 Josh. 22–24
- ❑ 28 Rom. 1–3
- ❑ 29 Rom. 4–7
- ❑ 30 Rom. 8–10

MAY

- ❑ 1 Rom. 11–13
- ❑ 2 Rom. 14–16
- ❑ 3 Judg. 1–3
- ❑ 4 Judg. 4–5
- ❑ 5 Judg. 6–8
- ❑ 6 Judg. 9–11
- ❑ 7 Judg. 12–15
- ❑ 8 Judg. 16–18
- ❑ 9 Judg. 19–21
- ❑ 10 Ruth 1–4
- ❑ 11 1 Cor. 1–4
- ❑ 12 1 Cor. 5–9
- ❑ 13 1 Cor. 10–13
- ❑ 14 1 Cor. 14–16
- ❑ 15 1 Sam. 1–3
- ❑ 16 1 Sam. 4–7
- ❑ 17 1 Sam. 8–10
- ❑ 18 1 Sam. 11–13
- ❑ 19 1 Sam. 14–15
- ❑ 20 1 Sam. 16–17
- ❑ 21 1 Sam. 18–20
- ❑ 22 1 Sam. 21–24
- ❑ 23 1 Sam. 25–27
- ❑ 24 1 Sam. 28–31
- ❑ 25 2 Cor. 1–4
- ❑ 26 2 Cor. 5–8
- ❑ 27 2 Cor. 9–13
- ❑ 28 2 Sam. 1–3
- ❑ 29 2 Sam. 4–7
- ❑ 30 2 Sam. 8–11
- ❑ 31 2 Sam. 12–13

JUNE

- ❑ 1 2 Sam. 14–15
- ❑ 2 2 Sam. 16–18
- ❑ 3 2 Sam. 19–20
- ❑ 4 2 Sam. 21–22
- ❑ 5 2 Sam. 23–24
- ❑ 6 Gal. 1–3
- ❑ 7 Gal. 4–6
- ❑ 8 1 Kings 1–2

❑	9	1 Kings 3–5
❑	10	1 Kings 6–7
❑	11	1 Kings 8–9
❑	12	1 Kings 10–12
❑	13	1 Kings 13–15
❑	14	1 Kings 16–18
❑	15	1 Kings 19–20
❑	16	1 Kings 21–22
❑	17	Eph. 1–3
❑	18	Eph. 4–6
❑	19	2 Kings 1–3
❑	20	2 Kings 4–5
❑	21	2 Kings 6–8
❑	22	2 Kings 9–11
❑	23	2 Kings 12–14
❑	24	2 Kings 15–17
❑	25	2 Kings 18–20
❑	26	2 Kings 21–23
❑	27	2 Kings 24–25
❑	28	Phil. 1–4
❑	29	1 Chron. 1–2
❑	30	1 Chron. 3–5

JULY

❑	1	1 Chron. 6–7
❑	2	1 Chron. 8–10
❑	3	1 Chron. 11–13
❑	4	1 Chron. 14–16
❑	5	1 Chron. 17–20
❑	6	1 Chron. 21–23
❑	7	1 Chron. 24–26
❑	8	1 Chron. 27–29
❑	9	Col. 1–4
❑	10	2 Chron. 1–4
❑	11	2 Chron. 5–7
❑	12	2 Chron. 8–11
❑	13	2 Chron. 12–16
❑	14	2 Chron. 17–19
❑	15	2 Chron. 20–22
❑	16	2 Chron. 23–25
❑	17	2 Chron. 26–29
❑	18	2 Chron. 30–32
❑	19	2 Chron. 33–34
❑	20	2 Chron. 35–36
❑	21	1 Thess. 1–5
❑	22	Ezra 1–4
❑	23	Ezra 5–7
❑	24	Ezra 8–10
❑	25	Neh. 1–4
❑	26	Neh. 5–7
❑	27	Neh. 8–10
❑	28	Neh. 11–13
❑	29	2 Thess. 1–3
❑	30	Est. 1–4
❑	31	Est. 5–10

AUGUST

❑	1	Job 1–4
❑	2	Job 5–8
❑	3	Job 9–12
❑	4	Job 13–17
❑	5	Job 18–21
❑	6	Job 22–26
❑	7	Job 27–30
❑	8	Job 31–34
❑	9	Job 35–38
❑	10	Job 39–42
❑	11	1 Tim. 1–6
❑	12	2 Tim. 1–4
❑	13	Pss. 1–7
❑	14	Pss. 8–14
❑	15	Pss. 15–18
❑	16	Pss. 19–24
❑	17	Pss. 25–30
❑	18	Pss. 31–34
❑	19	Pss. 35–37
❑	20	Pss. 38–42
❑	21	Pss. 43–48
❑	22	Pss. 49–54
❑	23	Pss. 55–60
❑	24	Pss. 61–67
❑	25	Pss. 68–71
❑	26	Pss. 72–75
❑	27	Pss. 76–78
❑	28	Pss. 79–84
❑	29	Pss. 85–89
❑	30	Pss. 90–95
❑	31	Pss. 96–102

SEPTEMBER

❑	1	Pss. 103–105
❑	2	Pss. 106–108
❑	3	Pss. 109–115
❑	4	Pss. 116–119:64
❑	5	Pss. 119:65–176
❑	6	Pss. 120–131
❑	7	Pss. 132–138
❑	8	Pss. 139–144
❑	9	Pss. 145–150
❑	10	Prov. 1–3
❑	11	Prov. 4–7
❑	12	Prov. 8–10
❑	13	Prov. 11–13
❑	14	Prov. 14–16
❑	15	Prov. 17–19
❑	16	Prov. 20–22
❑	17	Prov. 23–25
❑	18	Prov. 26–28
❑	19	Prov. 29–31
❑	20	Titus & Philem.
❑	21	Eccl. 1–4

❑	22	Eccl. 5–8
❑	23	Eccl. 9–12
❑	24	Song 1–4
❑	25	Song 5–8
❑	26	Heb. 1–4
❑	27	Heb. 5–7
❑	28	Heb. 8–10
❑	29	Heb. 11–13
❑	30	Isa. 1–3

OCTOBER

❑	1	Isa. 4–6
❑	2	Isa. 7–9
❑	3	Isa. 10–13
❑	4	Isa. 14–16
❑	5	Isa. 17–21
❑	6	Isa. 22–25
❑	7	Isa. 26–28
❑	8	Isa. 29–31
❑	9	Isa. 32–34
❑	10	Isa. 35–37
❑	11	Isa. 38–40
❑	12	Isa. 41–42
❑	13	Isa. 43–44
❑	14	Isa. 45–47
❑	15	Isa. 48–50
❑	16	Isa. 51–53
❑	17	Isa. 54–57
❑	18	Isa. 58–60
❑	19	Isa. 61–64
❑	20	Isa. 65–66
❑	21	James 1–5
❑	22	Jer. 1–3
❑	23	Jer. 4–5
❑	24	Jer. 6–8
❑	25	Jer. 9–11
❑	26	Jer. 12–14
❑	27	Jer. 15–17
❑	28	Jer. 18–21
❑	29	Jer. 22–23
❑	30	Jer. 24–26
❑	31	Jer. 27–29

NOVEMBER

❑	1	Jer. 30–31
❑	2	Jer. 32–34
❑	3	Jer. 35–37
❑	4	Jer. 38–41
❑	5	Jer. 42–45
❑	6	Jer. 46–48
❑	7	Jer. 49
❑	8	Jer. 50
❑	9	Jer. 51–52
❑	10	Lam. 1–2
❑	11	Lam. 3–5

❑	12	1 Pet. 1–2
❑	13	1 Pet. 3–5
❑	14	Ezek. 1–4
❑	15	Ezek. 5–9
❑	16	Ezek. 10–13
❑	17	Ezek. 14–16
❑	18	Ezek. 17–19
❑	19	Ezek. 20–21
❑	20	Ezek. 22–23
❑	21	Ezek. 24–26
❑	22	Ezek. 27–28
❑	23	Ezek. 29–31
❑	24	Ezek. 32–33
❑	25	Ezek. 34–36
❑	26	Ezek. 37–39
❑	27	Ezek. 40–42
❑	28	Ezek. 43–45
❑	29	Ezek. 46–48
❑	30	2 Pet. 1–3

DECEMBER

❑	1	Dan. 1–2
❑	2	Dan. 3–4
❑	3	Dan. 5–6
❑	4	Dan. 7–9
❑	5	Dan. 10–12
❑	6	Hos. 1–4
❑	7	Hos. 5–9
❑	8	Hos. 10–14
❑	9	Joel 1–3
❑	10	Amos 1–3
❑	11	Amos 4–6
❑	12	Amos 7–9
❑	13	Obad. & Jon.
❑	14	1 John 1–5
❑	15	Mic. 1–4
❑	16	Mic. 5–7
❑	17	Nah. 1–3
❑	18	Hab. 1–3
❑	19	Zeph. 1–3
❑	20	Hag. 1–2
❑	21	2, 3 John & Jude
❑	22	Zech. 1–6
❑	23	Zech. 7–10
❑	24	Zech. 11–14
❑	25	Mal. 1–4
❑	26	Rev. 1–3
❑	27	Rev. 4–7
❑	28	Rev. 8–12
❑	29	Rev. 13–16
❑	30	Rev. 17–19
❑	31	Rev. 20–22